Introduction to Emergency Management

Introduction to Emergency Management

Brenda D. Phillips ◆ David M. Neal ◆ Gary R. Webb

CRC Press
Taylor & Francis Group
Boca Raton London New York

CRC Press is an imprint of the
Taylor & Francis Group, an **informa** business

CRC Press
Taylor & Francis Group
6000 Broken Sound Parkway NW, Suite 300
Boca Raton, FL 33487-2742

© 2012 by Taylor & Francis Group, LLC
CRC Press is an imprint of Taylor & Francis Group, an Informa business

No claim to original U.S. Government works

Printed in the United States of America on acid-free paper
Version Date: 20110831

International Standard Book Number: 978-1-4398-3070-3 (Hardback)

Visit the Taylor & Francis Web site at
http://www.taylorandfrancis.com

and the CRC Press Web site at
http://www.crcpress.com

Dedication

We dedicate this book to our students—past, present, and future—with appreciation for their efforts to make our communities safer places to live.

Contents

Preface

We have written this book for our students: past, present, and future. They leave their academic studies prepared to take on the challenges of an especially rewarding profession: emergency management. Yet working in an emergency management agency, a non-governmental organization, the private sector, or through international humanitarian relief represents only a slice of what they do. They spend hours working diligently to keep us all safe in our homes, communities, businesses, schools, and while traveling. They put together preparedness campaigns to educate us, spend considerable time crafting and exercising response plans, build support for mitigation projects, and face the long challenges of recovery. While most of us go about our daily lives not having to think about the worst of times, they make advance preparations so that we can worry less and emerge from a natural, technological, or terrorist threat with our lives and property intact. We are so very proud of what our students have given to our communities and incorporate some of their experiences into this book to inspire future generations.

We wish to thank colleagues and students who made special contributions to this book: Bill Anderson, DeeDee Bennett, Cody Bruce, Eve Coles, Bob Counsellor, Elizabeth Davis, Michel Dore, Jessica Fernandes-Flack, Dean Findley, Scott Harris, Paul Hewett, Joselin Landry, Roger Hovis, Njoki Mwarumba, Sarah Stuart-Black, Jodi Ouellette, Ann Patton, Jenniffer Santos-Hernandez, Shane Stovall, and Monica Teets Farris.

Our appreciation extends to the entire Taylor & Francis team, especially editor Mark Listewnik, Stephanie Morkert, and Prudence Taylor Board. Your efforts and professionalism have made this task so much easier. We labored for many years without textbooks, and your efforts have improved considerably the experience of teaching in this field. We appreciate the vision that you have had for the CRC Press series of books on emergency management and acknowledge them as a critical step forward in teaching this emerging discipline of emergency management.

Our sincere appreciation also goes to family members who made it possible for us to write and who encouraged our efforts: Frank and Mary Jane Phillips, Robert Neal, Joyce Stanley, Lisa Dalton-Webb, and Spencer Webb. For those who appreciate the pet preparedness sections, we thank Krissy, Scarlet, and Lucy who inspired that content.

We remain mindful of those who taught us what they know about disaster management, especially our own professors and mentors: E.L. Quarantelli, Russell R. Dynes, Joseph B. Perry, Kathleen Tierney, Gary Kreps, and Bill Anderson.

The content of this book was inspired by empirical research and we have labored diligently to include critically important references. Our thanks go out to colleagues who have shared their work with us over the years at conferences, through journals, and in great conversations. We hope that we have honored your work and we have not overlooked anyone unintentionally. In many ways, we have lived the content in the book either vicariously through research or directly through consultancies and volunteer work. In places where references are not indicated, content originates from those experiences because emergency management does require an integration of both research and experience. We offer this textbook based on our cumulative years of experience in teaching in the field. The content has been tested with our students, and we believe it has been successful.

We have attempted to include not only thorough coverage but content that we know appeals to students, usually tried and proven in our own classrooms. We hope that you enjoy the journey you are about to take in this book and that you find a path here to increase your own personal safety—and possibly a career or volunteer opportunity somewhere in the field.

About the Authors

The three authors of this text bring nearly seventy-five collective years of experience in the field to this project including direct classroom experience, successful efforts in developing new emergency management programs at multiple institutions, extensive relevant research backgrounds, volunteer work, and consulting.

Brenda Phillips, PhD, is a professor in the Fire and Emergency Management Program, an affiliated faculty member in the Gender and Women's Studies and the International Studies Programs, and a senior researcher with the Center for the Study of Disasters and Extreme Events at Oklahoma State University. Her work has included assisting with the development of emergency management degree programs in the United States, Canada, Mexico, New Zealand, and Costa Rica. She is the author of *Disaster Recovery* (CRC Press). She recently co-edited *Women and Disasters: From Theory to Practice* with Betty Hearn Morrow and served as the lead editor on *Social Vulnerability to Disasters* with Deborah Thomas, Alice Fothergill, and Lynn Blinn (CRC Press). She is a member of the Gender and Disaster Network and the International Research Committee on Disasters. Professor Phillips has conducted research on disaster recovery since 1982, beginning as a student of E.L. Quarantelli's at The Ohio State University's Disaster Research Center. Her published research can be found in a variety of journals including the *International Journal of Mass Emergencies and Disasters, Disaster Prevention, Disasters, Humanity and Society,* the *Journal of Emergency*

Management, Natural Hazards Review, and *Environmental Hazards.* She has been funded multiple times by the National Science Foundation to study disasters and vulnerable populations and serves as a subject matter expert for several federal agencies. Dr. Phillips has been invited to teach, consult, or lecture in New Zealand, Australia, Germany, India, Costa Rica, Mexico, Canada, and the People's Republic of China. She is a graduate of Bluffton University (Ohio) and The Ohio State University.

Dave Neal, PhD, is a professor with the Fire and Emergency Management Program and Director of the Center for the Study of Disasters and Extreme Events at Oklahoma State University. Since the completion of his thesis on disaster preparedness in 1978, he has been actively engaged in disaster research. Since then, he has studied a wide range of events (e.g., tornadoes, floods, hurricanes, earthquakes) throughout the United States, and also in Sweden and India. Organizations including FEMA, NASA, the National Science Foundation, the American National Red Cross, and others have supported his research. He has published numerous articles on disasters. He taught his first class on disasters in 1979. In 1989 he joined the faculty of the Institute of Emergency Administration and Planning, the first bachelor's degree program in the world in emergency management, and later served as its director. He has also published articles related to developing degree programs in disaster management, virtual teaching environments, and has served as a consultant for universities starting degree programs in disaster management. He received both his bachelor's and master's degrees from Bowling Green State University. He obtained his PhD in sociology from The Ohio State University, where he also served as a research assistant with the Disaster Research Center.

Gary Webb, PhD, has recently been appointed an associate professor of public administration at the University of North Texas. Previously he was a faculty member in the sociology department at Oklahoma State University. He holds a PhD from the University of Delaware, where he worked at the Disaster Research Center. Dr. Webb has conducted extensive research on organizational preparedness for and response to numerous disasters in the United States and abroad. His research has been supported by various agencies, including the U.S. National Science Foundation, and it has appeared in a variety of professional journals, including the *International Journal of Mass Emergencies and Disasters*, *International Journal of Emergency Management*, *Environmental Hazards*, *Natural Hazards Review*, *Rural Sociology*, and *Sociological Focus*. His research has also been featured in national media outlets, including the *Los Angeles Times*, *Newsday*, and *Christian Science Monitor*. He has been invited to teach or present his research to international audiences in Denmark, France, South Korea, The Netherlands, and Turkey.

Chapter **1**

History and Current Status of Emergency Management

1.1 Chapter Objectives

Upon completing this chapter, readers should be able to:

1. Describe the development of emergency management in the United States.
2. Recognize the role of the private sector in disasters.
3. Discern the role of the public sector in disasters.
4. Understand the role of volunteer organizations in disasters.
5. Be familiar with the fundamental elements of international disaster relief.

1.2 Introduction

Noah was the first emergency manager (Dynes 2003), and he faced the same problems and issues that emergency managers face today. Although Noah received news about a major flood from an impeccable source, most people ignored him. People would not change their behavior to mitigate the flood. Few helped Noah build an Ark to prepare for the flood. Today, many ignore disaster warnings and do not or cannot prepare for disasters. Although emergency managers stress efforts to lessen the impacts of disasters, many politicians have different priorities. Emergency management thus represents a challenging field, albeit one in which you can make a difference professionally and personally.

Despite many of these obstacles and barriers to keeping the public safe, the field of emergency management has grown dramatically over the last fifty years. A wide range of events, including floods, hurricanes, tornados, tsunamis, earthquakes, volcanoes, massive explosions, large hazardous waste sites, and terrorist attacks all highlight the importance of understanding how people and organizations behave when confronted by disasters.

This chapter describes how the field of emergency management has grown, especially since World War II. As our primary audience for this text is in the U.S., we concentrate on the historical evolution of the field there (for an example from the United Kingdom, please view Box 1.1). We focus upon the field's roots in civil defense and natural disasters. Next, we discuss the creation and role of the Federal Emergency Management Agency (FEMA) and later the Department of Homeland Security (DHS) in disaster management. Finally, we provide a few brief examples of the different types of organizations involved in disaster issues today, including non-emergency management public agencies, the private sector, and voluntary organizations.

BOX 1.1   EMERGENCY MANAGEMENT IN ENGLAND AND WALES

Eve Coles

Eve Coles is a senior fellow in civil protection at Leeds University Business School where she has responsibility for the academic oversight of qualifications in emergency management and civil protection developed in partnership with the Cabinet Office Emergency Planning College. Her research interests include emergency management policy in the U.K. and resilience management for public sector organizations. Eve is editor of a new U.K. peer-reviewed journal called *Emergency Management Review* and serves as chair of the Emergency Planning Society's Education Standards Group.

Emergency management provision and legislation in England and Wales[*]* evolved from the 1948 Civil Defence Act that enabled a response to hostile situations to the 2004 Civil Contingencies Act that for the first time placed a statutory duty on local responders to plan for emergencies. The proliferation of major incidents and crises in the 1980s (known as the decade of disasters) and the early 1990s led to a fragmented range of ad hoc measures that allowed civil defence funding to be spent on peacetime disasters and introduced the concept of integrated emergency management.

However, it was not until after the chaos of the fuel crisis and severe flooding experienced during 2000 and the foot and mouth disease crisis of 2001 (collectively known as the 3 Fs) that exposed serious weaknesses in the capability to deal with wide area emergencies did things begin to change. The terrorist attacks of September 11, 2001 in the U.S. further emphasised the ad hoc nature of the U.K. system and added impetus to the need to restructure.

Restructuring began in November 2001 when responsibility for emergency management moved from the Home Office to the Cabinet Office; under the auspices of the Civil Contingencies Secretariat (CCS) with the aim "... to improve the UK's resilience to disruptive challenges at every level" (Home Office 2001, p. 1). The resilience agenda sought to:

1. Build a comprehensive capability for anticipating major incidents, where possible prevent them or take action in advance that will mitigate their effects.
2. Ensure that planning for response and recovery is geared to the risk therefore ensuring preparedness.
3. Promote a 'culture of resilience' including business continuity thus helping to reduce the disruptive effects of disaster.

The agenda is supported by a raft of ongoing measures including:

- Capabilities Programme
- Civil Contingencies Act 2004
- Statutory Guidelines: Emergency Preparedness
- Fire and Rescue Services Act (2004)
- Anti-Terrorism Act (2005)
- National Flood Risk Policy
- Information to the public on how to prepare for emergencies
- Increased funding mainly for 'blue light' services
- Non-statutory guidance for emergency response and recovery
- Community Resilience Programme
- Flood and Water Bill (Pitt Review 2008)
- Corporate resilience work stream

---

[*] Local emergency management in Scotland comes under the jurisdiction of the Scottish Government and has separate arrangements. In Northern Ireland for security reasons, it was dealt with by the Northern Ireland Office now the Northern Ireland devolved government.

Arguably, the two foundation building blocks of the agenda are the Capabilities Programme and the Civil Contingencies Act 2004. One of the first measures put in place after the 3 Fs and September 11, 2001 was the Capabilities Programme. It is a cyclical auditing programme that is still ongoing and consists of:

- Three structural work streams dealing with the central (national), regional and local response capabilities
- Five work streams concerned with the maintenance of essential services (food, water, fuel, transport, health, financial services)
- Eleven functional work streams dealing with the assessment of risks and consequences; chemical, biological, radiological, and nuclear (CBRN) resilience; human infectious diseases; animal and plant infectious diseases; mass casualties; mass fatalities; mass evacuations; site clearance; warning and informing the public; flooding; humanitarian assistance; and recovery.

Work on the Civil Contingencies Act began in 2002 but it did not achieve royal assent until November 2004 and passed into law in April 2005. It is an enabling act in two parts that encompassed and repealed civil defence and civil protection legislation and the Emergency Powers Act of the 1920s. Part 1 includes:

- A working definition of an emergency
- Provision for a local resilience forum of Category 1 responders (and Category 2 responders when relevant)
- Provision for identification of risks and the development of a community risk register
- A duty to plan for civil emergencies
- A duty for responders to share information
- A duty for first responders to have business continuity plans in place
- A duty on Local Authorities to provide advice and support to the business community
- A categorization of responders
- A duty to warn and inform the public

Part 2 includes:

- Provision to declare a state of emergency on a regional basis (previously only on a national basis)
- Provision for the appointment of regional coordinators and regional resilience forums
- Provision for the Minister of State to draw a regulatory framework for dealing with emergencies

The act also categorizes responders in to two groups. Category 1 responders consist of:

- Local governments
- Emergency services (police forces; fire and rescue authorities; ambulance services)
- National Health Service and health bodies (primary care trusts, acute trusts [hospitals], foundation trusts, port health authorities, Welsh local health boards, government agencies [Environment Agency and Scottish Environment Agency, Maritime and Coastguard Agency, Health Protection Agency]

Category 2 responders include:

- Utilities (water, sewerage, gas, and electricity)
- Telephone service providers
- Railway operators
- Airport operators
- Harbour authorities
- Highways Agency
- Health and Safety Executive
- Strategic health authorities

The Act is currently going through a review and enhancement process likely to be completed in 2011.

Source: *The CCS: What it Means.* 2001. Home Office, England.

1.3 Evolution of Emergency Management in the United States

Fifty years ago, the profession of emergency management did not exist. Within the federal government in the United States, disaster offices were scattered throughout the bureaucracy. Some local governments had offices of civil defense to help protect the nation against a possible attack from the former Soviet Union. Typically, civil defense positions were part-time, low-paying, and required little if any training or education. The American National Red Cross and Salvation Army were about the only volunteer organizations available to assist disaster victims. Businesses typically did not employ disaster planners. Only a few organizations throughout the world provided international disaster relief. No university offered a major or minor in emergency management, nor was any individual course available.

During the last fifty years, emergency management has become a full-fledged profession. Those in the Federal Emergency Management Agency

(FEMA), as a part of the Department of Homeland Security (DHS), coordinate most of our national disaster efforts. All states and most local governments in the U.S. have disaster coordinators. All major businesses have individuals in charge of disaster planning. In addition to the Red Cross and Salvation Army, a large number of volunteer organizations stand ready to assist both victims and responders. A wide range of organizations throughout the world offer disaster relief across national borders. Many professionals in the field today have college degrees, and about 150 universities in the United States alone offer bachelor's, master's, and even PhD's in emergency management. In short, the field of emergency management has grown dramatically over the last fifty years. This chapter provides an overview of this extraordinary growth, and describes organizations today that play key roles in emergency management.

1.3.1 Civil Defense

The federal government in the U.S. played a large role in matters of protecting the nation from foreign attack through the idea of civil defense. During World War II, civil defense activities gave members of the public a chance to contribute to the war effort. For example, civilians were trained to spot enemy aircraft. Cities practiced evening blackouts, turning out all lights so enemy bombers could not find their targets. Others watched coastal waters for enemy submarines. However, these activities did not really enhance the nation's defense, except for giving civilians a feeling that they were contributing to the war effort.

Civil defense became more prominent starting in the early 1950s with the onset of the Cold War. With both the former Soviet Union and the United States becoming bitter ideological enemies and both having nuclear weapons, potential existed for nuclear war. In the United States, the federal government created various offices of civil defense (i.e., Federal Civil Defense Agency 1953–1958; Office of Civil Defense Mobilization 1958–1961; and the Office of Civil Defense 1968–1979) to lead and coordinate efforts to protect residents from chemical and nuclear attack. Well-known activities supported by civil defense include "duck and cover" and assistance with creating nuclear bomb shelters in homes. In addition, some public buildings were designated as civil defense shelters. In the case of nuclear war, citizens would be directed to seek shelter in these buildings, while also being provided food and water (Sylves 2008; Task Force 2010). Often such buildings as schools or county courthouses served as civil defense shelters. Today, we can often still find civil defense shelter signs on public buildings.

Local civil defense directors were more likely than not part-time employees, located in the county court house basements. Many of those hired had retired from the military. These retirees often received military pensions, so local governments could get by with paying these individuals small salaries. In addition, officials assumed that having a civil defense military background would be useful during the "chaos" following a nuclear attack and hired air raid wardens whose job was ultimately to blow the whistles in case of imminent nuclear attack (Waugh 2000). Although this focus on civil defense—and now on terrorism—has reappeared throughout the history of emergency management, other types of disasters have compelled significant changes in the field. In the U.S., for example, flooding is the most common disaster. Other natural and technological disasters have generated both organizational and policy changes.

1.3.2 Managing Natural and Technological Disasters in the U.S.

Until the 1950s, disaster management had been primarily a matter for local and state governments. Only in case-by-case situations did the federal government, primarily though specific legislation, become involved. For example, the U.S. Congress would provide specific funding to aid or assist a community. Voluntary organizations, such as the American National Red Cross or the Salvation Army, were the main consistent national sources of peacetime relief efforts. In 1950, following severe flooding in the upper Midwest, Congress passed the Disaster Relief Act. This legislation allowed the federal government to become involved in any future disaster relief efforts without additional Congressional approval. Although this act provided only a narrow scope of disaster assistance, it created a foundation for Congress to later expand the role of the federal government in disaster. In addition, it gave the President a means to provide disaster assistance without Congressional approval (Kreps 1990; Sylves 2008).

Through the Disaster Relief Act of 1974 and the Stafford Act of 1988, the federal government could provide aid for communities and later directly to disaster victims. Most importantly, these acts describe how the President declares an event a disaster and outlines the kinds of aid that can be delivered. A presidential declaration releases a wide range of resources to disaster-stricken communities and individuals (Sylves 2008). The process of a presidential declaration and the resources made available will be discussed in Chapter 2. In addition, other large disasters (e.g., Hurricane Camille, 1969; San Fernando Earthquake, 1971; Hurricane Agnes, 1972) further broadened the federal government's role during disaster (Kreps 1990).

Thus, while different programs related to civil defense existed throughout the Department of Defense, the federal government had a whole different set of programs to assist those involved in primarily natural disasters and to a lesser degree technological disasters. Simply, the United States government had set up a dual track of emergency management. One track focused on civil defense, while the other focused on natural disasters (and to a lesser extent, technological disasters). Although this unintended dual track may have made some type of sense at the time, it also created problems. First, some redundancy certainly existed between the civil defense and natural disaster offices. Second, emergency management offices were scattered all over the federal bureaucracies. Since these disaster offices were not centralized, problems of communication and inefficiency existed (National Governors' Association 1979). In addition, in both the civil defense and peace-time focused organizations, occasional re-organization seemed to be the norm. For many, the dual tracks (rather than a single centralized federal agency) and constant reorganization hurt the nation's ability to deal with disasters (Kreps 1990). As we describe in more detail later in this chapter, during the late 1970s President Jimmy Carter centralized most of the nation's disaster efforts under one organization by creating the Federal Emergency Management Agency.

1.3.3 Development of the U.S. Federal Emergency Management Agency (FEMA)

Since 1979, FEMA has been the key federal agency for coordinating disaster activities in the United States. This section discusses the factors leading to the creation of FEMA, key events impacting FEMA during its creation and up to the terrorist attacks of September 11, 2001, and FEMA's role and activities since that pivotal date. Keep in mind that until 1979, the federal government had no true centralized department to deal with emergency management issues.

FEMA is now slightly over thirty years old. Yet, during this short time, it has gone through dramatic changes coupled with varying degrees of public concern. FEMA has been recognized in its short life as both the best federal agency in the nation (during the Clinton administration in the mid and late 1990s) to one of the worst run agencies (e.g., following its responses to Hurricane Andrew in 1992 and Hurricane Katrina in 2005; see The White House 2006 and U.S. Congress 2006). The Clinton administration elevated FEMA to a cabinet level post with its administrator reporting directly to the President. The Bush administration subsequently retracted that position, then subsumed FEMA under a new bureaucracy called the Department of Homeland Security (DHS) in response to the terrorist attacks of September 11, 2001. To explain the dynamic evolution of FEMA, the next section briefly describes FEMA's creation in 1979 and some of its main activities since (for an overview, see Figure 1.1).

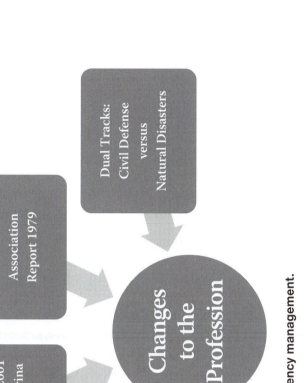

National Governors' Association Report 1979

Major Events September 11, 2001 Hurricane Katrina

Dual Tracks: Civil Defense versus Natural Disasters

Changes to the Profession

Presidential Actions Appointments and Leadership e.g, Carter creates FEMA

FIGURE 1.1   Key factors changing the profession of emergency management.

1.3.3.1 Creation of FEMA

As noted above, a dual track of emergency management organizations existed in the United States. One focused upon civil defense issues, whereas the other focused on natural and technical disasters. Many but not all civil defense programs operated under the U.S. Department of Defense (DOD) while the natural and technological disaster programs were scattered throughout the federal bureaucracy. The dual tracks and lack of a centralized disaster agency created tension and inefficiency within the federal government (NGA 1979; Kreps 1990; Sylves 2008). To improve the overall effectiveness of emergency management in the United States, in 1978 President Carter initiated Reorganization Plan #3 to consolidate almost all emergency management efforts under one federal agency known as FEMA. The list below shows which federal departments became part of FEMA. The organization in parentheses indicates the main department or agency that previously managed them (NGA 1979, p. 3):

- Federal Insurance Administration (Department of Housing and Urban Development)
- National Fire Prevention and Control Administration (Department of Commerce)
- Federal Broadcast System (Executive Office of the President)
- Defense Civil Preparedness Agency (Department of Defense)
- Federal Disaster Assistance Administration (Department of Housing and Urban Development)
- Federal Preparedness Agency (General Services Administration)
- National Weather Service Community Preparedness Program (Department of Commerce)
- Earthquake Hazard Reduction Office (Executive Office of the President)
- Dam Safety Coordination Program (Executive Office of the President)
- Federal Response to Consequences of Terroristic Incidents (no previous assigned agency)
- Coordination of Emergency Warning (no previous assigned agency)

Since FEMA was created in 1979, the agency has experienced a number of changes. Below we describe these changes and their consequences.

1.3.3.2 FEMA as a Stand-Alone Agency

Prior to the development of the Department of Homeland Security, FEMA operated as a stand-alone agency within the federal government. As might be expected from any relatively new bureaucracy, the agency suffered from internal problems, lack of political support, and even public scorn while simultaneously building a capacity to address disasters under guiding legislation. From the Reagan and Bush presidencies (1981–1993) through the Clinton administration (1993–2001), FEMA's reputation ranged from being one of the worst run federal agencies to becoming the best managed. During much of the 1980s, FEMA moved through the process of defining itself and its role in the federal government (Daniels and Clark-Daniels 2000).

During President George H. Bush's administration (1989–1993), criticism over ineffective internal leadership and poor disaster responses led to further questions about FEMA's value. For example, the federal government seemed incapable of providing needed assistance to state and local governments following the "dual disasters" (i.e., Hurricane Hugo and the Loma Prieta Earthquake) during the late summer and early fall of 1989. Politicians, the media, and the public leveled criticisms similar to the 1989 dual disaster response after Hurricane Andrew in 1992 (Daniels and Clark-Daniels 2000).

Following the dual disasters in 1989, concerns grew over the nation's capabilities to manage large scale disasters and catastrophes. To address this gap in federal planning, FEMA coordinated a major effort among federal agencies and the Red Cross to create the Federal Response Plan (FRP). The FRP detailed how a large scale disaster response should be managed, including jurisdictional issues, and which federal agency should coordinate specific tasks (FEMA 1992; Neal 1993). The backbone of the FRP was a structure that outlined key emergency support functions (ESFs). The original FRP listed twelve functions or tasks required to enhance disaster response. These tasks included (FEMA 1992, p. 14):

- ESF #1 Transportation
- ESF #2 Communications
- ESF #3 Public Works and Engineering
- ESF #4 Firefighting
- ESF #5 Information and (Disaster) Planning
- ESF #6 Mass Care
- ESF #7 Resource Support
- ESF #8 Health and Medical Services
- ESF #9 Urban Search and Rescue
- ESF #10 Hazardous Materials
- ESF #11 Food
- ESF #12 Energy

At the time of the FRP's creation, each ESF was coordinated by a federal agency (except ESF #6, Mass Care, which was headed by the Red Cross). The logic behind the ESF format was simple. A federal agency related to a specific function would coordinate the overall efforts with other federal agencies to mobilize key resources toward an overall response. Let's take the 1992 version of ESF #8, Health and Medical Services, as a brief example. The primary agency coordinating the ESF #8 efforts would be the Department of Human Services (specifically through the U.S. Public Health Service). Examples of tasks coordinated by the Department of Human Services in ESF #8 would include (FEMA 1992, pp. 8-1 to 8-2):

- Assessment of health and medical needs
- Health surveillance
- Medical care personnel
- Health/medical equipment and supplies
- Patient evacuation
- In-hospital care
- Food, drug, and medical device safety
- Worker health/safety
- Radiological, chemical, and biological hazards
- Mental health
- Water issues
- Victim identification and mortuary services

Certainly, the Department of Human Services does not have all the resources or capabilities to accomplish all these tasks alone. To do so, it would draw upon support agencies to assist. Examples of support agencies for ESF #8 included the Department of Agriculture, Department of Defense, Department of Justice, Department of Transportation, and Department of Veterans' Affairs among many others (FEMA 1992).

Soon after the federal government completed the final version of the FRP, during late August 1992, Hurricane Andrew struck the East Coast of Florida, moving in to impact the Dade County and Miami, Florida area. Although final data vary, losses were large. Recent data suggests that Hurricane Andrew damaged or destroyed about 125,000 residences, killed at least 61 people, and caused $27 billion (or $40 billion in 2007 dollars) in economic losses (NOAA 2011). Since the hurricane was considered close to catastrophic, government officials quickly shipped hundreds of copies of the FRP to provide help and direction with the overall clean-up (Neal 1993). Observers generally graded the overall response as an abysmal failure. Federal assistance arrived slowly to disaster areas, in some cases taking over 10 days, primarily due to poor initial reconnaissance and damage assessment. Congressional hearings following Hurricane Andrew questioned why FEMA directors and those in top management possessed little if any background in disaster management (NAPA 1993, pp. 1–3; Neal 1993). Senator Barbara Mikulski of Maryland, in a letter to the Comptroller General of the United States, stated that the response to Hurricane Andrew was "pathetically sluggish and ill-planned" (NAPA 1993, p. 1).

Through the years, the name of the FRP has changed (i.e., from the Federal Response Plan to the current National Response Framework). Some general

FIGURE 1.2   James Lee Witt (center), former FEMA administrator, speaks with homeowners affected by a Georgia tornado in 2000. (*Source:* FEMA News Photo/ Liz Roll.)

management issues have changed through the years, but the main idea and format of the ESF structure remain today. In addition, over the last two decades, local emergency coordinators have written their disaster plans based upon the ESF format with some local emergency operating center designs relying upon the ESF framework as well. In short, the ESF format as outlined in the original FRP in 1992 has become an important component of disaster planning and response. We will have more current information about the National Response Framework and the ESF system in Chapter 7 (Planning).

After winning the 1992 election, President Bill Clinton appointed James Lee Witt as the new FEMA director (Figure 1.2). Clinton's appointment set the stage for a number of improvements that FEMA would experience during an eight-year period. For the first time in FEMA's history, a person with actual disaster management experience held the post of director. As a county judge in Arkansas, Witt had also served as the county emergency manager. Later, Witt became the state's director of emergency management when Clinton was elected governor. Witt arrived at FEMA well-grounded in disaster terminology and issues while also understanding the roles of the local, state, and federal governments during disasters. In addition, other appointed FEMA officials at the federal and regional offices brought extensive emergency management experience (Daniels and Clark-Daniels 2000; FEMA 2010a). Clinton also made FEMA a cabinet-level post, ensuring that disaster handling became a top priority in his administration and that the FEMA director would have straight access to the president (Daniels and Clark-Daniels 2000).

During his tenure as FEMA director, Witt emphasized mitigation— defined as effort to reduce the effects of future disasters. Seeing the millions of dollars spent on response and recovery, Witt realized that steps taken to minimize the impact of a disaster could ultimately save millions of dollars. He initiated a number of programs designed to reduce physical, human, and financial impacts of disasters. One key initial program was Project Impact, a citizen-based, community-wide effort involving individuals, communities, and business leaders (Witt and Morgan 2002, pp. 4–7). By 1999, nearly 200 communities and more than 1,000 business partners nationwide became involved in Project Impact. For example, residents in the City of Chesapeake, Virginia, initiated projects to install storm shutters on their homes. Local governments in the area invested in public buildings and other government facilities to make buildings stronger against high hurricane winds. Regardless of the size or scope of the initiative, building disaster-resistant communities saves lives and prevents damage. In the process, it saves money as well. Current statistics show that for every dollar spent on prevention, at least two dollars are saved on disaster repairs (FEMA 1999). Through its four-pronged program, Project Impact built safer communities after individuals, businesses, and community leaders took the following steps (FEMA 1999, p. 1):

- Identify and recruit Project Impact partners in the community such as local government leaders, civic and volunteer groups, businesses, and individual citizens.
- Determine community risk for falling victim to natural disasters.
- Set priorities and target resources to reduce impact of future disasters.
- Keep the entire community informed and focused on Project Impact's ability to reduce damage and costs of future disasters.

General mitigation efforts and Project Impact did not stand in a vacuum. As Witt (Witt and Morgan 2002, pp. 4–7) described, for too long FEMA and emergency management had become reactive, focusing primarily on response. Rather, Witt transformed FEMA into a proactive agency through the efforts of mitigation. By decreasing the impacts of disaster through mitigation, responding to and recovering from disasters became more manageable and less expensive.

Witt's actions went beyond mitigation and even the four phases of emergency management. As a manager, he held informal discussions with his employees, noting that many FEMA staff members never met the director. He searched for new ways to solve old problems. He and his colleagues found ways to streamline the bureaucratic process such as the development and use of a national Tele-Registration Center located in Denton, Texas to quickly and effectively provide aid. Also, for the first time, FEMA developed a strategic plan that gave the organization a better sense of direction and purpose (Witt and Morgan 2002).

1.3.3.3 FEMA, Terrorism, and the Department of Homeland Security (DHS)

Upon his inauguration in 2001, President George W. Bush named one of his top political aides, Joe Allbaugh, as the new FEMA director. Although Allbaugh clearly had strong political connections similar to most previous FEMA directors, he lacked background in emergency management. Soon after Bush's election and much to dismay across the emergency management community, he eliminated Project Impact (Holderman 2005, p. A17). Ironically, the same day of the announcement regarding Project Impact, a magnitude 6.8 earthquake rattled the Seattle area (USGS 2004). Local emergency managers firmly believed that various Project Impact initiatives in the area such as retrofitting homes and schools to absorb shaking more than showed their value. Thus, it appeared to some in the profession, that emergency management was not then a top priority of the Bush administration (Holderman 2005, p. A17).

The terrorist attacks of September 11, 2001 moved emergency management back to a top priority. An analysis following the attacks showed that the federal government had developed many problems related to disaster preparedness and response, along with security issues, all of which led to the attack. In addition, various government agencies failed to share information that could have been useful for stopping a terrorist attack (9/11 Commission Report 2004). After much public debate and a number of steps, President George W. Bush and the U.S. Congress authorized and financed the Department of Homeland Security (DHS). DHS became a formal part of the government on January 24, 2003, with Tom Ridge serving as its first director (DHS 2008a). To protect the homeland in a unified fashion, DHS would focus on four major tasks (DHS 2002, p. 3):

- Border and transportation security
- Emergency preparedness, and response
- Chemical, biological, radiological, and nuclear countermeasures
- Information analysis and infrastructure protection

To pursue these tasks, the new department would integrate twenty-two federal agencies. FEMA no longer had cabinet level status under the DHS organization. In short, DHS would coordinate activities among government organizations to improve the security of the United States.

Although the creation of DHS was intended to improve FEMA, Hurricane Katrina proved otherwise (Waugh 2006). Striking the U.S. Gulf Coast on August 29, 2005, Katrina damaged levees in New Orleans and sent a massive storm surge six to twelve miles inland across Mississippi. The storm killed more than 1,200 people and injured thousands more, while causing some of the largest economic and infrastructural damage in U.S. disaster history. For example, areas around New Orleans and the Mississippi coast sustained about $75 billion worth of damage (NOAA, n.d.). Critics again pointed fingers, charging FEMA, DHS, and state and local governments with slow responses that claimed lives. FEMA's director, Michael Brown, was relieved of his duties. In subsequent investigations by the U.S. Congress and the White House, concerns generated a context for change. As noted in a U.S. Congressional investigation report titled *A Failure of Initiative* (2006, p. 1):

The Select Committee identified failures at all levels of government that significantly undermined and detracted from the heroic efforts of first responders, private individuals and organizations, faith-based groups, and others. The institutional and individual failures we have identified became all the more clear when compared to the heroic efforts of those who acted decisively. Those who didn't flinch, who took matters into their own hands when bureaucratic inertia was causing death, injury, and suffering. Those whose exceptional initiative saved time and money and lives.

However, the massive hurricane generated numerous changes in FEMA besides changes of personnel. New attention focused on those at highest risk including people with disabilities, medical conditions, and lacking transportation to evacuate. States commenced extensive efforts to revise evacuation and shelter plans. Drills and exercises increased to build stronger relationships among involved agencies, particularly across state lines. These efforts paid off in 2008 when Hurricane Ike slammed into Texas. Well in advance, a massive transportation effort took thousands of people to safety. Public shelters opened to serve nursing homes and medically fragile patients. Even pets and livestock were accommodated in special shelters and locations. Hurricane Gustav also prompted evacuation away from New Orleans and into the neighboring states of Mississippi and Alabama. Ready to help, the host states absorbed tens of thousands of evacuees. At the federal level, extensive revisions of the National Response Framework began along with efforts to design new state and local planning guides (for more, see Chapter 7).

After his inauguration, President Barack Obama named Craig Fugate as the new director of FEMA (Figure 1.3). With extensive experience as a fire fighter and paramedic, later becoming a county emergency manager and director of the Florida Division of Emergency Management, Fugate quelled concerns about lack of experience in the agency leadership. In speaking to the FEMA Higher Education Conference in 2009, Fugate supported the value of social science research and encouraged those at the conference to

FIGURE 1.3 FEMA Director Craig Fugate (right) and DHS Secretary Napolitano answer questions at a press briefing. (*Source:* FEMA News Photo/Bill Koplitz.)

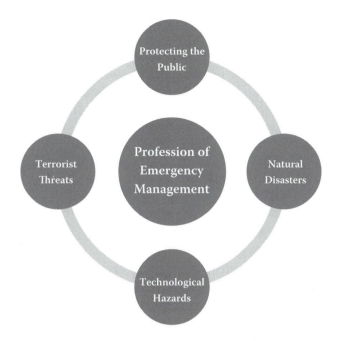

FIGURE 1.4   Emergency management professionals fill critical roles in protecting the public from an array of hazards.

listen to the social scientists and their findings. Many efforts that emerged after Katrina, particularly planning initiatives, gained additional momentum. A National Disaster Housing Strategy developed along with new guidelines to make emergency shelters accessible to people with disabilities (visit http://www.fema.gov/emergency/disasterhousing/).

Currently, FEMA has about 3,700 full-time employees with another 4,000 in reserve, ready to help respond when disaster strikes to meet a variety of threats that affect the public (see Figure 1.4). FEMA's offices include its main location in Washington, D.C., ten regional offices throughout the United States, the Mount Weather Emergency Operations Center, and its training center in Emmitsburg, Maryland. Because coordination of activities is a key task of the agency, FEMA works with twenty-seven different federal agencies and the Red Cross along with many state governments and local jurisdictions throughout the country (FEMA 2010b).

1.4 Native American Tribes

Native American tribes represent an important population regarding disasters in the public sector. Tribes have their own designated political jurisdictions and as a result, fill a wide range of public safety (fire, police, emergency management) related responsibilities. They typically coordinate their activities with surrounding local governments. However, by law, tribes can bypass state governments and work directly with the federal government on disaster issues. FEMA has made working with Native American tribes a top priority in recent years. For example, in 1998 it declared (FEMA 2010c):

> In the spirit of community, FEMA commits itself to building a strong and lasting partnership with American Indians and Alaska Natives to assist them in preparing for the hazards they face, reducing their disaster vulnerabilities, responding quickly and effectively when disasters strike, and recovering in their aftermath. (FEMA Tribal Policy 2010c, p. 2).

In addition, soon after taking office as FEMA director, Craig Fugate contacted all 564 federally recognized tribes to ask for feedback on current existing policy on tribal matters and emergency management (FEMA 2010d).

FEMA has also been working with Native American tribes on historical preservation issues. A wide range of disasters can do great damage to sacred areas. To assist with this issue, FEMA published specific recommendations on how to mitigate sacred or historical site disasters. Simply stated, the federal, state, and local governments should not and legally cannot take Native American lands in an effort to "help" mitigate historical sites from disasters. Rather, FEMA recommends a series of steps that enable all parties to work together. For example, some historical or sacred sites (e.g., archeological areas) demand varying degrees of secrecy and workers must consider the sensitivity of a situation (FEMA 2005).

Any attempts to mitigate for a disaster or recover from a disaster on tribal lands must minimize dramatic changes to the landscape. In areas open to the public, simple plaques or relatively unobtrusive markers should be used. Pathways to historical areas or within floodplains, for example, must blend well with the local surroundings. In addition, ceremonies can be used to mark sacred or important events such as disasters. Tribal members and other local residents can play key roles in commemorating such events (FEMA 2005).

Additionally, mitigation or recovery efforts pertaining to tribal lands require cooperation to operate in good faith among many people. Saving or protecting archeological or burial sites from disaster, for example, involves many people and regulations. Before work begins, good faith efforts must be made by all parties to include all relevant groups for their inputs and perspectives. Involving tribal leaders, local, state and federal agencies, along with historians, archeologists, and others related to a mitigation project is always a good starting point. Finally, tribal representatives and others must continue to work together on tasks such as updating disaster plans and related agreements (FEMA 2005). Sensitivity to cultural contexts underlies FEMA efforts to address tribal concerns. The diversity among the tribes represents a particular challenge in that each tribe has values, norms and customs specific to its ancestry and beliefs. By understanding that diversity and working within a culturally appropriate framework, emergency managers can be more effective in safeguarding the public.

1.5 Other Public Sector Involvement in Emergency Management

Emergency management certainly involves more than the federal government, and even within the federal government, other agencies play key roles supporting FEMA's and DHS's current emergency management and homeland security tasks. Therefore, we first discuss the roles of local and state government in emergency management issues. Next we provide examples of other public agencies that also assist with disaster-related issues. These other organizations include the U.S. Army Corps of Engineers, the Environmental Protection Agency, and the Centers for Disease Control.

1.5.1 Local and State Governments

Drawing upon former Speaker of the House Tip O'Neill's comment that all politics are local, experts in emergency management also stress that all disasters are local. Put slightly differently, the first line of defense against disasters begins in villages and cities with their residents and government workers. State government often works as a conduit between the federal and local governments on emergency management issues. In the post-disaster recovery period and to secure mitigation funding, state offices of emergency management assist local governments with grant writing and project management. They also coordinate with the federal government to provide the necessary training for emergency management personnel and issues related to designing, holding, and evaluating exercises.

Since the creation of FEMA, most states have implemented one office related to emergency management. In some cases, these offices were parts of a larger state bureaucracy (e.g., public safety, adjunct general) or reported directly to the governor. Following the September 11, 2001 terrorist attacks and the creation of DHS, some states followed the federal government's lead and also created a single agency to deal with terror and security issues and maintained the earlier agency to handle other types of disasters. We provide further information on state and local government roles in subsequent chapters.

1.5.2 Public Agencies

Whether preparing for, responding to, recovering from, or mitigating disasters, effective response requires more than emergency management offices. In actuality, as we see below, dealing with disasters includes partnerships with other agencies in the public, private, and volunteer sectors, and in some cases the international relief sector. The section below shows how these other agencies play important roles in disaster management and should alert you to career possibilities as well.

Whether at the local, state, or federal level, people often think strictly of disaster management (e.g., local emergency management agency, state emergency management agency, DHS, and FEMA) or emergency response organizations (fire, police, emergency medical services) as responsible to prepare for, respond to, recover from, and mitigate disasters. Yet, these public sector agencies are only a few that act during disasters. In this section, we highlight a few to give you an idea how such organizations are likely to be involved. For further depth, visit the websites associated with the primary and support agencies listed in Chapter 7 on Planning. The NRF integrates numerous federal agencies to accomplish specific tasks. This section reviews three of those agencies. We will provide more detail how public agencies work together and how they coordinate their activities with the private sector in Chapter 11.

1.5.2.1 U.S. Army Corps of Engineers

Generally, the U.S. Army Corps of Engineers performs multiple tasks related to building projects for the DOD or civilian use. These tasks may occur during war (e.g., construction of airfields or bridges) or peace (building and maintaining dams and levees, flood control, creation of hydroelectricity, managing water recreation areas). During the last century, the Army Corps of Engineers became a key federal agency for dealing with flood issues (U.S. Army Corps of Engineers 2007).

The NRF stresses that various federal agencies must plan, respond, and recover in a coordinated fashion. For example, in the case of public works (roads, bridges), the U.S. Army Corps of Engineers would coordinate ESF #3: Public Works and Engineering. Other federal organizations assisting the U.S. Army Corps of Engineers include the DOD, DHS, and FEMA. Up to seventeen additional organizations, mostly federal agencies, also may provide assistance. In addition to working with other federal agencies, the Army Corps of Engineers coordinates with state and local public works departments to determine needs and obtain resources to rebuild the infrastructures of local communities. Thus, within the framework of the NRF during and after disasters, the Army Corps of Engineers assists with flooding issues and a broader set of reconstruction and recovery activities. It also works with representatives from local, state, and federal governments and members of the private sector (DHS 2008b).

In May, 2011, the U. S. Army Corps of Engineers (USACE) carefully monitored flooding along the Mississippi River. By opening the Morganza Spillway, the USACE reduced flooding in Baton Rouge and New Orleans, although rural, small town, and agricultural areas sustained flooding. The USCACE opened spillway gates slowly over several days to allow wildlife to leave the area, including endangered species.

1.5.2.2 *U.S. Environmental Protection Agency*

As another example, consider the amounts of hazardous materials and waste often generated by disasters. The Environmental Protection Agency (EPA) coordinates federal efforts for ESF # 10: Oil and Hazardous Response Materials. Representatives from DHS and the U.S. Coast Guard provide major assistance with this response. In addition, up to fourteen other federal agencies and departments would assist. EPA also works with state and local environmental offices and monitors debris removal for its potential impact on landfills and through incineration. As we will learn in Chapter 8 (Response), EPA monitoring after the attacks of September 11, 2001 needed to improve to safeguard the health of first responders. EPA's role before, during, and after a disaster is critical to public health and safety including aid to those exposed to potential contaminants (DHS 2008b).

To illustrate, the EPA played a central role in monitoring the sand, air, and water following the BP Deep Water Horizon oil spill (an explosion and massive oil leak in the Gulf of Mexico during the summer of 2010). Not only was it involved with many of the response issues (monitoring the environment, training volunteers for clean-up efforts along the Gulf) after the explosion, but it is now helping with the recovery. For example EPA scientists are assisting other experts in determining how safe the Gulf waters are and analyzing and determining potential impacts to fish and wildlife. These analyses have important implications for the livelihoods and economics for the residents, businesses and communities along the Gulf Coast (EPA 2011).

1.5.2.3 *Centers for Disease Control*

The Centers for Disease Control (CDC) researches health-related issues and gathers data to provide recommendations on a wide range of medical issues. Specifically, CDC provides disaster-related medical information on such topics as bioterrorism, chemical emergencies, radiation emergencies, mass casualties, natural disasters, and recent health issues. State and local public health offices work with CDC to prepare for and respond to potential small and large scale medical crises. In the event of a pandemic, the CDC would play a critical role in monitoring the spread of the disease, recommending protocols to limit transmission, and safeguard public health (CDC 2006).

The CDC and other public health agencies have dealt with disaster-related incidents for decades. However, over the last ten years, local, state, and federal agencies involved with public health have become more active in disaster-related services. First, concerns have grown over the spread of mass illnesses (pandemics) similar to the Influenza Outbreak of 1918 that killed about fifty million people worldwide. Readers may remember the efforts coordinated by local, state, and federal public health agencies to mitigate the H1N1 (swine flu) virus. In addition to vaccination programs, public health agencies provided information on avoiding the virus, preventing its spread, and steps to take if you caught the virus (CDC 2006).

Nationally, CDC plays a central role by working with state and local governments on health issues. In the aftermath of the 2010 Haiti earthquake, the CDC monitored a cholera outbreak and provided advice regarding travel to the area. In addition, public health agencies focus on responding to pandemics created through terrorist attacks. Plans, vaccines, and medications are ready if terrorists use anthrax or other deadly viruses. Furthermore, public health agencies would play a crucial role in the case of a mass casualty event caused by a massive earthquake or terrorism event. Following the anthrax attacks in 2006, the CDC reported (2006, p. 1) it was engaged in:

- Developing plans and procedures to respond to an attack using anthrax.
- Training and equipping emergency response teams to help state and local governments control infection, gather samples, and perform tests. Educating health-care providers, media, and the general public about what to do in the event of an attack.
- Working closely with health departments, veterinarians, and laboratories to watch for suspected cases of anthrax. Developing a national electronic database to track potential cases of anthrax.
- Ensuring that there are enough safe laboratories for quick testing of suspected anthrax cases.
- Working with hospitals, laboratories, emergency response teams, and health-care providers to make sure they have the supplies they need in case of an attack.

Keep in mind that federal, state, and local public health agencies do not work in isolation. They are in constant contact with emergency management organizations nationwide, volunteer organizations, businesses, and other resources.

Overall, emergency management in the public sector involves more than emergency management officials. It includes coordinating the efforts of local government (emergency services organizations, public works departments, public health facilities, elected officials), state governments (offices of emergency management and homeland security, public health facilities, national guard groups, elected officials), the federal government (DHS, FEMA, CDC, and most other federal agencies, elected officials), and tribal governments. In addition, these agencies often work with businesses and volunteer organizations.

1.6 Private Sector Activities

Until rather recently, businesses often ignored the importance of disasters. Many business executives viewed investing in disaster preparedness and response as a waste of resources—until their enterprises were faced with disasters. Typically, we may think about the destruction of a business from a flood, tornado, earthquake, hurricane, or even explosion, but businesses have many other vulnerabilities. The destruction of a facility represents only a small part of a larger issue. Businesses rely upon all kinds of data, today generally stored in computers. Do they have a backup plan for such data? Without accounting receipts, inventory numbers, payroll information, customer lists, and other sets of information, a business cannot survive. Also, consider workers. Does every employer have a procedure to follow during a tornado or hurricane warning? What if workers have to "shelter in place," or stay at work facilities during a crisis while their family members are at home? A disaster may not physically impact a business, but may still affect it. Consider massive evacuations for a hurricane that may or may not hit a community but will affect business. Think about a hazardous materials incident miles away that could disrupt power for or traffic to a business. More generally, FEMA lists general reasons why businesses should be ready to respond to and recover from disasters (FEMA 2010e):

- Companies have a moral duty to protect their employees, area, and environment.
- Companies need to follow existing local, state, and federal laws related to safety.
- Companies can return to business much more quickly, which not only helps the business, but the community and regions.
- Companies diminish their chance of being sued.
- Companies obtain a positive image from good disaster and crisis planning.
- Companies often have their insurance costs reduced.

Today, both businesses and FEMA recognize the importance of disaster preparedness for the private sector. FEMA has taken a lead in assisting the private sector with disaster issues. The second section of Chapter 11 will provide more detail on the role of the private sector in disasters.

1.7 Voluntary Sector Activities

As noted above, at the start of the Cold War, the Red Cross and Salvation Army served as the main voluntary organizations in the U.S. to assist disaster victims and responders. Since then, a large number of voluntary organizations, many faith-based, have entered the scene. For example, The National Voluntary Organizations Active in Disaster (NVOAD) coordinates more than fifty members to provide disaster assistance. NVOAD was created following the aftermath of Hurricane Camille in 1969 to mitigate the challenges that surfaced among volunteer organizations (NVOAD 2011).

Without a doubt, voluntary organizations play an integral role in disasters. From working many events together, most experienced disaster volunteer organizations have determined their own specific sets of tasks. As a result, they can decrease duplication of tasks and maximize resources. Furthermore, different volunteer organizations often work together on specific tasks to ensure more efficient use of resources. For example, in many disasters the Red Cross and the Southern Baptist Men collaborate in providing food for victims. The Baptist group does much of the food preparation and cooking and the Red Cross then delivers the food to the victims. Specific organizations are also well known for specialized responses to disasters. The Medical Reserve Corps, for example, coordinates volunteers with medical experience in times of crisis. Volunteers assist with evacuation and relocation of nursing home residents, conduct triage to evaluate medical conditions, provide first aid support in public shelters, and offer mobile health care in damage zones. In the event of a pandemic, such as mentioned in the CDC section above, the Medical Reserve Corps would play a critical role with responding to the outbreak (for more, visit http://www.medical-reservecorps.gov/HomePage). During recovery phases, Mennonite Disaster Service is well known for repairing or replacing roofs and assisting with other housing repairs and reconstruction. Catholic Charities often funds specific needs such as for people with disabilities. The United Methodist Committee on Relief specializes in recovery and has trained case managers to assist survivors through the confusing morass of relief and rebuilding.

Although exceptions certainly exist, for the most part volunteer organizations focus on "people" needs. Their actions alleviate survivor stress by providing such items as food, shelter, housing, and mental health services. Many of these needs come under the heading of ESF #6 in the National Response Framework so it is not unusual to see many voluntary agencies working from a FEMA joint field office. Also, where necessary, they may also provide similar resources to the many paid and volunteer emergency responders who arrive at a disaster site to help with response and recovery.

An important service for both victims and responders pertains to mental health needs. Disasters can create short term stress. The Red Cross and the American Psychological Association provide certified disaster mental health workers to help those in need. Lutheran Disaster Response offers trained chaplains to assist those bereaved or struggling with trauma. The Church of the Brethren trains child care workers to assist impacted children. In summary, volunteer organizations play important roles in disasters. Rather than focusing on fixing infrastructure (roads, electricity, water, and sewer), they reach out to help people. Volunteer organizations also represent an area for gaining experience needed for a career in emergency management. Even if you do not enter this profession, your service orientation is needed when

BOX 1.2   VOLUNTARY ORGANIZATIONS ACTIVE IN DISASTERS

ACTS World Relief (Foundation of Hope)
Adventist Community Services
American Baptist Men
American Radio Relay League, Inc.
American Red Cross
Billy Graham Rapid Response Team
Brethren Disaster Ministries
Buddhist Tzu Chi Foundation
Catholic Charities USA
Church World Service
Episcopal Relief and Development
Feeding America
Habitat for Humanity International
Operation Hope
Humane Society of the United States
Jewish Federations of North America
Latter Day Saints Charities
Lutheran Disaster Response
Mennonite Disaster Service
Mercy Medical Airlift
National Association of Jewish Chaplains
National Baptist Convention USA
National Organization for Victim Assistance
Nazarene Disaster Response
Noah's Wish
Presbyterian Disaster Assistance
Southern Baptist Convention
Salvation Army
United Church of Christ
United Methodist Committee on Relief
United Way Worldwide
World Vision

Source: NVOAD, http://www.nvoad.org/index.php/member/national-members.html

disaster strikes. Box 1.2 lists faith-based and other volunteer organizations. Volunteer organizations play a key role before, during, and after disasters.

1.8 International Humanitarian Sector

As with local and state governments facing major disasters, many nations also lack sufficient resources to handle disasters. As a result, many nations, especially poor ones, rely on international disaster relief organizations to provide food, water, shelter, equipment, personnel, and other resources to prepare for, respond to, recover from, and mitigate disasters.

Non-governmental organizations (NGOs) deliver crucial assistance in many international settings. For example, NGOs played a crucial role with the initial response and recovery activities after the Indian Ocean tsunami struck thirteen nations. More than 400 NGOs in the area of Naggapattinam, India helped impoverished fisher people with survival needs such as food, shelter, and health care. Local NGOs worked with other organizations to assist the responders and survivors including more than 1,000 new orphans. NGOs obtained materials to bury more than 8,000 dead, helped mobilize potable drinking water, provided immunizations to stop the spread of diseases such as cholera, and provided new fishing boats to help jump-start the local economy (Phillips et al. 2008). International funders rebuilt a local hospital that was nearly destroyed by the water and constructed an entire merchant sector in the coastal community of Velankanni.

Response and recovery capabilities vary dramatically from nation to nation. Developing nations with minimal resources must attend to everyday needs such as food and shelter for their citizens. Disasters may present harsher challenges in providing food security and protection from the elements. It is important to realize that developing nations experience a wider range of disasters than what we may experience in the U.S. Famines, epidemics, and droughts are far more common, prompting people to try to reach refugee camps where humanitarian relief can be secured. Wars, genocide, and other conflicts also drive people into desperate conditions, causing tremendous suffering. In Chapter 2 we will learn about the differences between disasters of conflict and disasters of consensus—people in developing nations suffer greatly from both.

People living in developed nations tend to fare far better when disaster strikes because of the availability of resources, trained personnel, and volunteers. However, as we will learn in this text, great disparities also exist. Even a nation as powerful as the U.S. was unable to save some people with disabilities, senior citizens, and single parents lacking transportation when Hurricane Katrina surged into the U.S. Gulf Coast. Disasters are not equal opportunity events for people in developing nations or those living in economically marginalized conditions. This text is intended to address such conditions and report on ways to relieve suffering, build stronger and more disaster-resilient communities, and inspire you to become a positive part of that process.

1.9 Summary

The field of emergency management has come a long way since the end of World War II and the start of the Cold War when no central U.S. agency existed to coordinate disaster relief activities. Local emergency management offices were located and isolated in the basements of many county courthouses. Civil defense director positions were often filled by military veterans because they could be paid less, help provide "command and control" leadership, and manage the local residents during a chemical or nuclear attack. Today, professionals in local, state, and federal governments work with partners in the private and volunteer sectors to prepare for, respond to, recover from, and mitigate disasters. Career and volunteer opportunities in emergency management abound and we invite you to consider options as you read the remainder of this text. Our hope for you, our reader, is also that you will take the content to heart and help make your home, your workplace, and your community safer places for you, your family, and your neighbors.

Discussion Questions

1. What are the main origins and roots of emergency management?

2. What historical factors helped lay the foundation for the profession of emergency management?

3. Explain the dual tracks of emergency management that became established during the 1950s and 1960s.

4. Why did President Jimmy Carter establish FEMA?

5. What are some of the major successes and failures of FEMA since 1979; what factors led to these successes or failures?

6. What are the key factors in getting the public sector to work together?

7. Why are many parts of the private sector slow to implement or not interested in disaster mitigation or preparedness?

8. What role do volunteers play before or after disaster strikes?

9. Why have volunteers become such important resources for disaster response?

10. What factors must we consider when becoming involved in international disaster situations?

References

Centers for Disease Control (CDC). 2006. "Anthrax: What You Need to Know." Available at http://emergency.cdc.gov/agent/anthrax/needtoknow.asp, last accessed January 7, 2011.

Daniels, Steven R., Carolyn L. Clark-Daniels. 2000. *Transforming Government: The Renewal and Revitalization of the Federal Emergency Management Agency.* 2000 Presidential Transition Series, Birmingham, Alabama: University of Alabama, Birmingham.

Department of Homeland Security (DHS). 2002. The Department of Homeland Security. Available at http://www.dhs.gov/xlibrary/assets/book.pdf, last accessed February 15, 2011.

Department of Homeland Security (DHS). 2008a. *Brief Documentary History of the Department of Homeland Security: 2001-2008.* Available at http://www.dhs.gov/xlibrary/assets/brief_documentary_history_of_dhs_2001_2008.pdf, last accessed February 15, 2011.

Department of Homeland Security (DHS). 2008b. Federal Response Framework. Available at http://www.fema.gov/pdf/emergency/nrf/nrf-core.pdf, last accessed February 22, 2011.

Dynes, Russell R. 2003. "Noah and Disaster Planning." *Journal of Contingencies and Crisis Management* 11/4: 170-177.

Environmental Protection Agency (EPA). 2011. "EPA Response to the BP Spill." Available at http://www.epa.gov/bpspill/ and http://www.restorethegulf.gov/, last accessed February 24, 2011.

Federal Emergency Management Agency (FEMA). 1992. *Federal Response Plan.* Washington, D.C.: U.S. Government Printing Office.

Federal Emergency Management Agency (FEMA). 1999. "Project Impact: Building a Disaster Resistant Community." Available at http://www.fema.gov/news/newsrelease.fema?id=8895, last accessed Dec 11, 2010.

Federal Emergency Management Agency (FEMA). 2005. *Historic Properties and Cultural Resources.* Available at http://www.fema.gov/pdf/fima/386-6_Phase_4.pdf, last accessed February 23, 2011.

Federal Emergency Management Agency (FEMA). 2010a. "FEMA History." Available at http://www.fema.gov/about/history.shtm , last accessed February 15, 20110.

Federal Emergency Management Agency (FEMA). 2010b. "About FEMA." Available at http://www.fema.gov/about/index.shtm, last accessed January 7, 2011.

Federal Emergency Management Agency (FEMA). 2010c. "FEMA Tribal Policy." Available at http://www.fema.gov/government/tribal/natamerpolcy.shtm, last accessed January 7, 2011.

Federal Emergency Management Agency (FEMA). 2010d. "Tribal Information." Available at http://www.fema.gov/government/tribal/index.shtm, last accessed February 23, 2011.

Federal Emergency Management Agency (FEMA). 2010e. "Emergency Management Guide for Business and Industry." Available at *http://www.fema.gov/business/guide/index.shtm*, last accessed on February 24, 2011.

Holderman, Eric. 2005. "Destroying FEMA." The Washington Post. Available at http://www.radixonline.org/resources/destroying_fema.doc, last accessed February 15, 2011.

Kreps, Gary. 1990. "The Federal Emergency Management System in the United States: Past and Present." *International Journal of Mass Emergencies and Disasters* 8/3: 275-300.

National Academy of Public Administration (NAPA). 1993. *Coping with Catastrophe: Building an Emergency Management System to Meet People's Needs in Natural and Manmade Disasters.* Washington, D.C.: National Academy of Public Administration.

National Governors Association (NGA). 1979. *1978 Emergency Preparedness Project: Final Report.* Washington, D.C.: Defense Civil Preparedness Agency.

National Voluntary Organizations Active in Disaster (NVOAD). 2011. "What is National VOAD?" Available at http://www.nvoad.org/index.php/about-us-/what-is-national-voad.html, last accessed February 24, 2011.

National Response Framework (NRF). 2011. Available at http://www.fema.gov/pdf/emergency/nrf/nrf-core.pdf, last accessed February 24, 2011.

NOAA. n.d. "Hurricane History." Available at http://www.nhc.noaa.gov/HAW2/english/history.shtml, last accessed February 15, 2011.

NOAA Economics. 2011. "Extreme Events: Hurricane and Tropical Storm." Available at http://www.economics.noaa.gov/?goal=weather&file=events/hurricane&view=costs, last accessed February 9, 2011.

Neal, David M., 1993."Emergency Response Philosophy of the Federal Response Plan: Implications in the Case of a Catastrophic Disaster." *Proceedings of the 1993 National Earthquake Conference*: 511–518.

Phillips, Brenda, Dave Neal, Tom Wikle, Aswin Subanthore, and Shireen Hyrapiet. 2008. "Mass Fatality Management after the Indian Ocean Tsunami." *Disaster Prevention and Management* 17/5: 681–697.

Sylves, Richard. 2008. *Disaster Policy and Politics: Emergency Management and Homeland Security*. Washington, D.C.: CQ Press.

Task Force. 2010. *Perspective on Preparedness: Taking Stock since 9/11*. Available at http://www.fema.gov/pdf/preparednesstaskforce/perspective_on_preparedness.pdf, last accessed February 9, 2011.

Waugh, William. 2000. *Living with Hazards, Dealing with Disasters: Introduction to Emergency Management*. Armonk, NY: M.E. Sharpe.

Waugh, William. 2006. *Shelter from the Storm: Repairing the National Emergency Management System after Katrina*. The ANNALS of the American Academy of Political and Social Science Series.

United States Army Corps of Engineers. 2007a. *The U.S. Army Corps of Engineers: A Brief History*. Available at http://www.usace.army.mil/History/Documents/Brief/index.html, last accessed February 23, 2011.

United States Congress. 2006. *A Failure of Initiative*. Washington, D.C.: U.S. Congress. Available at http://www.gpoaccess.gov/serialset/creports/katrina.html, last accessed January 7, 2011.

United States Geological Survey (USGS). 2004. "Magnitude 6.8 Washington." Available at http://neic.usgs.gov/neis/eq_depot/2001/eq_010228/, last accessed February 15, 2011.

White House, The. 2006. *The Federal Response to Hurricane Katrina: Lessons Learned*. Washington, D.C.: The White House. Available at http://georgewbush-whitehouse.archives.gov/reports/katrina-lessons-learned/letter.html, last accessed January 7, 2011.

Witt, James Lee and James Morgan. 2002. *Stronger in the Broken Places*. New York: Times Books.

Resources

A number of websites provide good general information on the topics discussed in this chapter.

- To obtain additional information on the history and role of the Federal Emergency Management Agency and the Department of Homeland Security in emergency management, go to www.fema.gov and www.dhs.gov
- For further information on the role of volunteer organizations, see www.nvoad.org. Also, check out the websites of two of the better known and most active volunteer organizations in disaster: the Red

Cross's www.redcross.org and Salvation Army www.salvationarmy-usa.org

- The International Association of Emergency Managers is a key organization for professionals in the field. If you are interested in what emergency managers do and what issues impact the field today, go to www.iaem.com
- With those interested in general information and also job opportunities in the private sector, the *Disaster Recovery Journal's* website www.drj.com is a good starting place with extensive information.

Chapter 2

Key Concepts, Definitions, and Perspectives

2.1 Chapter Objectives

Upon completing this chapter, readers should be able to:

1. Define the concepts of *disaster* and grasp the similarities and differences among them.
2. Understand and distinguish the traditions of hazards, disasters, and risks.
3. Explain the importance of comprehensive emergency management.
4. Know key theoretical perspectives for understanding disaster behavior.
5. Describe current political and social definitions of *disaster*.
6. Explain the emergence and importance of a multidisciplinary approach to emergency management.

2.2 Introduction

In this chapter, we introduce you to a wide range of concepts and ideas that will help you understand the world of emergency management throughout the rest of this text. Decades ago, Quarantelli and Dynes (1970) observed that *disaster* was a sponge concept because the word absorbed many different meanings through the years. For example, some of you may use the word *disaster* if you oversleep and miss an exam. For others, a *disaster* may be losing a sporting event. A *disaster* may range from a speeding ticket to a broken leg. In short, the word in everyday language often means that something bad happened.

More broadly, when people hear the word *disaster*, they may think of an event (a disaster agent such as a tornado, flood, explosion, hurricane, wildfire), the damage caused by an event (destroyed buildings, demolished streets, roads, bridges, electrical and water systems), the number of people injured or killed, the amount of social disruption (massive evacuations, people made homeless, number of people without electricity, water, or food), or the need to provide resources. As a result, when people hear a specific event described as a *disaster,* they may assign different meanings and images to the word. As scientists and emergency managers, those of us who study and manage disasters must have a common or systematic meaning to conduct rigorous research, communicate effectively, and safeguard the public.

2.3 Defining Disaster

Based on the material above and further evidence presented below, we will see that people attach a number of different meanings to the word *disaster*. Even those of us who study disaster have different meanings and views on the topic. However, for the purposes of this text, we will draw on a definition that has guided most researchers, then explain why we want you to think about disasters on a continuum ranging from emergency (or crisis) to disaster to catastrophe. We will deal with some of the other meanings of the word later in this chapter. Noted scholar Charles Fritz (1961, p. 655) defined disasters as:

> …actual or threatened accidental or uncontrollable events that are concentrated in time and space, in which a society, or a relatively self-sufficient subdivision of society undergoes severe danger, and incurs such losses to its members and physical appurtenances that the social structure is disrupted and the fulfillment of all or some of the essential functions of the society, or its subdivision, is prevented.

Notice the key components of this definition. First, disasters are social events—unless an event impacts people, it is not a disaster. For example, if a tidal wave totally covered an island not inhabited by people, the event could not be considered a disaster. The second component is that a situation must cause social disruption for a specific group of people. For example, if a tornado destroys part of a town of 50,000, life will change for many of the town's residents. Most, if not all actions, will focus on responding to and recovering from the disaster. Businesses and government offices may be closed as a result of the destruction.

A third component is the need for the area and people impacted to obtain outside help, for example. External help may include the arrival of search-and-rescue teams, to find and treat victims, companies dispatching staff with bulldozers and chain saws to assist with clearing debris, and utility specialists to fix power lines. Volunteers and volunteer organizations also bring in food and water from other areas to feed both victims and those assisting with search and rescue, debris removal, and other necessary actions to help the community. Another important consideration within Fritz's definition is that a *situation* may not be an actual physical event, but rather the perception that an event will take place. For example, thousands of people may evacuate when a hurricane warning is issued. The warning disrupts the lives of the residents, local, and state government officials, businesses, and volunteer organizations. All their lives change to varying degrees even if the hurricane does not strike, but they eventually resume their day-to-day lives. In short, Fritz's definition (1961) suggests that life as we know it dramatically changes when disaster strikes.

Next, let's look at the differences among emergencies, disasters, and catastrophes.

2.3.1 A Continuum of Disaster

People may think of an event in simple terms—an event is or is not a disaster. A car wreck is not a disaster. A tornado is a disaster. A house fire is not a disaster. A large chemical accident is a disaster. Determining whether an event is a disaster is not a black and white situation (Fischer 2003). We like to think that such events occur along a continuum: some events are day-to-day emergencies; others are disasters (some larger than others); and on rare occasions some events are catastrophes (see Figure 2.1). We now distinguish between emergencies, disasters, and catastrophes.

Emergency Routine	Disaster	Catastrophe
Predictable	Community disruption	Regional impact
Handled locally	Local capacity overwhelmed	Infrastructure compromised
	Outside help needed	Aid slow to arrive

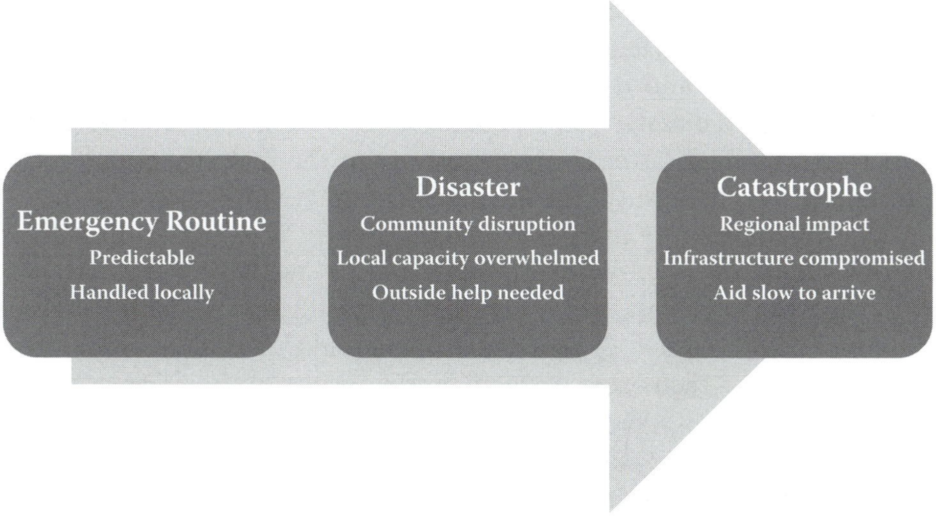

FIGURE 2.1   Continuum of disaster.

2.3.1.1 Emergency

Emergencies are part of everyday life in a community. As a result, local emergency response organizations have the resources and people to respond to them. Emergency response situations may include heart attacks, house fires, and car accidents. Emergency response organizations can generally anticipate their emergency response needs on a yearly basis. For example, in the United States, Independence Day (July 4) and New Year's Day are the busiest days of the year for firefighters. The annual July 4 peak in fire activity results from fireworks and to a lesser degree outside grilling. Outdoor fires around New Year's also reflect the use of firecrackers and disposal of flammable Christmas trees (U.S. Fire Administration 2004). Anyone who works in the medical field knows that weekends generally are busier than weekdays for emergency response organizations. Since these emergency response patterns are predictable, governments can plan accordingly and manage them. For anyone not directly involved in such emergencies, life goes on.

Situations do occasionally require outside help. For example, a fire department may enact a memorandum of understanding (MOU) with nearby fire departments to ensure assistance if a major event such as a large apartment building fire occurs. In such a case, the neighboring fire departments will arrive to help fight the large fire or provide backup if another fire occurs within the city. Thus, although resources may be stretched, local communities can carry on business as usual when an emergency occurs.

2.3.1.2 Disaster

Drawing upon Fritz's definition (1961), a disaster breaks a local community's ability to respond to an event even when outside help is drawn upon. For example, key response organizations such as fire and police may not be able to respond to all immediate needs or may not be able to respond at all. The number of immediate victims may outnumber the availability of emergency responders. Debris and damage may inhibit emergency responders from quickly entering a disaster site. In addition, the emergency responders may be victims also. A disaster is much more than the inability of emergency responders to do their duty. The infrastructure may suffer major damage.

Most of a community may lose electrical power. Water (including drinking water and sewage treatment) may not be available. Highways and bridges may be impassable from excessive debris (from a tornado), inaccessible (flooded), damaged, or destroyed (earthquake). Family members may be separated from each other, have no food or water, or their homes may be destroyed. Businesses, schools, and other organizations will be closed due to damage or destruction; customers, employees, and students will be unable to travel to such locations. In short, everyday life as we know it ceases during a disaster. Priorities change to focus on the event at hand. An affected community cannot fend for itself and needs extensive outside help.

2.3.1.3 Catastrophe

Catastrophes are much more than large disasters. After Hurricane Katrina, Quarantelli (2006) noted that the storm's social impact and aftermath demonstrated the basic characteristics that distinguish a catastrophe from a disaster. First, the disaster agent impacts or destroys most of an area's buildings and infrastructure. As a result of Katrina, more than 80% of New Orleans was flooded and much of the area along the Mississippi coast experienced extensive storm surge damage. The floodwaters and wind directly or indirectly made most of the infrastructure (e.g., electricity, drinking water, sewage, and transportation) inoperable. Police, fire, and other local and even regional emergency response organizations were generally unable to operate because the hurricane's aftermath impacted their buildings and staff. Furthermore, outside assistance (federal, state, and volunteer organizations) had difficulty providing help. Cell phones did not work for most carriers for nearly a week. Transportation was difficult if not impossible. When help did arrive, few facilities were available for use. The sheer magnitude of the event made it difficult to know where to begin.

Many local officials could not tend to their jobs even in the initial recovery period. In many cases, these individuals had no place to go to work, lost their homes, were injured, and even died in the event. The inability of officials to work also became evident after the Indian Ocean tsunami in 2004 and the Haitian Earthquake in 2010. With thousands dead, including key government officials in some places, response activities became difficult if not impossible to coordinate (Quarantelli 2006).

During and after a disaster, help generally arrives quickly. In fact, one problem following a disaster may be that too much help (e.g., workers, food, supplies) arrives—a situation known as *convergence*. We will discuss convergence in more detail in Chapter 8. However, the massive nature of a catastrophe means help is slow to arrive. Large cities cannot help nearby smaller cities and nearby smaller cities cannot help larger cities because they are all impacted. People, food, and other needed supplies initially have no place to go to provide assistance (Quarantelli 2006).

Most daily routines of individuals, families, organizations, governments, businesses, and other facilities are totally disrupted. Consider the case of Hurricane Katrina. With little if any functioning infrastructure, destroyed buildings, and victims in shelters or evacuated elsewhere, the routine of life along the Gulf Coast came to a halt (Quarantelli 2006). Reflect also on the Haitian earthquake, where in addition to massive destruction of buildings and infrastructure, approximately 300,000 people died—many of whom carried out important tasks in government, businesses, and households (Quarantelli 2006).

Finally, the role of politics emerges as a crucial aspect in managing an event. During a disaster, local and state governments serve as the key responders, with the federal government providing some financial aid and resources. In fact, the role of the federal government becomes as much symbolic as functional. However, during a catastrophe, its role moves to center since it has the resources to provide direct assistance to impacted regions. In addition, catastrophes such as Hurricane Katrina cross local, county (parish in this case), and state jurisdictions. Thus the federal government's role becomes even more important in coordinating response and recovery activities (Quarantelli 2006). After the earthquake in Haiti, issues about who was in charge surfaced quickly. The deaths of some politicians and lack of leadership in other areas created a major political vacuum.

In short, catastrophes are very different from disasters. The disaster agent of a catastrophe destroys most if not all of a region's buildings and infrastructure. The lives of individuals and routines of whole communities are totally disrupted. Outside help has difficulty in arriving and even setting up operations. Local, state, and federal government must all become involved to deal with the massive problems generated by a catastrophe.

Now that we have a general understanding of the concept of continuum from emergency to disaster to catastrophe, we will discuss key concepts used by both professionals and researchers to demonstrate how emergency managers organize their daily activities to manage disasters.

2.4 National Governors' Association Report

During the 1970s, the United States struggled with disasters but had no clear or central vision on how to handle them. Two important events that occurred then that continue to impact emergency management today. The first, noted in Chapter 1, is that President Carter established FEMA to centralize and streamline the emergency management process. In 1979, the National Governors' Association (NGA) issued a major report on how to improve emergency management. More than thirty years after the report was published, its key ideas continue to drive and define emergency management. These key concepts not only influenced the emergency management profession, but have also served as important tools for disaster researchers. These concepts, outlined below, are embedded within the idea of comprehensive emergency management (CEM) characterized by an all-hazards approach to disaster across four phases of activities.

CEM encourages a broad holistic approach to managing disasters. First advocated by the NGA report on emergency management, CEM is defined as "a state's responsibility and capability for managing all types of emergencies and disasters by coordinating the actions of numerous agencies. The 'comprehensive' aspect of CEM includes all four phases of disaster or emergency activity: mitigation, preparedness, response, and recovery. It applies to all risks: attack, man-made, and natural, in a federal–state–local partnership" (NGA 1979, p. 11). The four phases and all-hazards approach to disasters continue to serve as foundations for emergency managers and important concepts for disaster researchers. We review these concepts below.

2.4.1 Disaster Life Cycle

Through the years, researchers and professionals have tried to break the disaster process down into specific categories. Some suggested seven phases. Others used terms such as pre-impact, impact, and post-impact. The NGA report (1979) offered four specific disaster phases that those in the field continue to use with some variations. In New Zealand, the phases are known as the Four Rs: readiness, response, recovery, and reduction. Regardless of the organization or nation that faces emergency management tasks, four general phases usually cover what typical emergency managers do (see Figure 2.2). The four phases of emergency management are defined as follows:

Mitigation—This phase includes "any activities that actually eliminate or reduce the probability of occurrence of a disaster … arms build-up, land-use management, establishing CEM (i.e., comprehensive emergency management programs) programs, building safety codes" (NGA 1979, p. 13).

FIGURE 2.2   Four phases in the disaster life cycle.

Preparedness—This encompasses activities "necessary to the extent that mitigation measures have not, or cannot, prevent disasters … developing plans, mounting training exercises, installing warning systems, stockpiling food and medical supplies, mobilizing emergency personnel" (NGA 1979, p. 13).

Response—These "activities follow an emergency or disaster. Generally, they are designed to provide emergency assistance for casualties … seek to reduce the probability of secondary damage … and to speed recovery operations" (NGA 1979, pp. 13–14).

Recovery—Activities of recovery "continue until all systems return to normal or better … . Short-term recovery activities return vital life-support systems to minimum operating standards. Long-term recovery activities … return life to normal or improved levels" (NGA 1979, p. 14).

Both professional emergency managers and researchers have found these categories useful for their work. For professionals, the phases allow them to divide their tasks and focus on their work as described further in Chapter 5. For example, in many state emergency management agencies and in large cities, offices often have specific sections or jobs related to the four phases. Historically, FEMA organized its divisions around the phases. FEMA's current organization chart shows a division dedicated to "Response and Recovery" and another to "Federal Insurance and Mitigation." A major thrust of FEMA's preparedness activities, including its Project Ready, is clearly featured on its website (FEMA 2010a). FEMA also provides grants related to these categories. As a result, states and local communities can secure funds for preparedness, response, recovery, and mitigation activities.

Researchers also use these concepts to categorize their studies. For example, overviews of research (Drabek, Mileti, and Haas 1975; Drabek 1986) show that response is the most popular category to study and far less work has focused on recovery (Mileti 1999). Academic degree programs and textbooks (including this one) for studying disasters draw upon the four phases of emergency management as organizational tools (Neal 2000).

However, we must realize that the four phases were intended as tools to help us deal with disasters. Most importantly, we have to understand that these categories overlap and can influence each other. Let's look first at the overlap issue. For example, the removal of debris from roads to allow emergency response vehicles access to disaster-stricken areas (response) may continue while affected individuals are settling back into their homes (recovery). After a flood, people may be rebuilding their homes (recovery) while government officials are working on levees to lessen the impacts of further floods (mitigation). In addition certain activities may be hard to categorize. For example, public education programs covering disaster warnings educate people about what to do if they hear a disaster warning (preparedness), but the same public education program could be considered mitigation since it can lessen the impact of a disaster by lowering the loss of life and injury (Neal 1997).

To show the connections of the different phases, the NGA report and FEMA depicted the CEM process in a circular fashion (see Figure 2.2). In short, mitigation efforts may help move preparedness activities along. Improved preparedness (and mitigation) lessen physical damage and social needs when disaster strikes. Finally, an effective response should make recovery easier. Any recovery effort should integrate mitigation projects. However, we have also discovered that rather than operating in a circular cycle, the different phases exert broader impacts. For example, enacting stricter building codes in anticipation of earthquakes (mitigation) means generally that less damage will occur during an earthquake and less time and money will be needed to repair buildings and infrastructure (recovery). In short, all the phases clearly impact the other phases (Neal 1997). We will expand on the phase activities undertaken by emergency managers in Chapter 5 and provide substantial detail by phase in subsequent chapters.

2.4.2 All-Hazards Approach

A second idea central to emergency management, formerly called the all-risks approach, is known today as the all-hazards approach. In essence, the NGA report showed that regardless of the event, certain key governmental activities remain the same across events. Two important points are made, however, with the all-hazards approach. First, hazards must be approached across the four phases of emergency management. Too often, the report notes, people focused only on planning and ignored the other phases. All phases, the report stresses, must be considered (NGA 1979). As noted elsewhere, the management process for hazards, risks, and disasters is generally the same. These events must be managed across all four phases and involve coordination among local, state, and federal governments, the public and private sectors, volunteer organizations, and others (IAEM 2007).

Researchers also described an all-hazards approach to disasters as "agent generic." Although specific hazards may create specific problems or issues, overall the same set of issues arises across disasters. For example, the process of educating the public on preparing for a disaster is basically the same. How emergency management officials effectively warn the public about an oncoming disaster follows the same process. During disasters, communication and coordination problems always arise. Those more vulnerable to disasters (the poor, minorities, elderly and some people with disabilities, and others) are more likely to be affected and require more assistance. In short, the overall similarities are much greater than the differences (Dynes 1970; Quarantelli 1982).

2.5 Hazards, Disasters, and Risk

As noted above, people use the word *disaster* broadly. In the profession of emergency management, we often draw upon different perspectives to understand views of hazards, disasters, and risk. Each word represents certain components of emergency management but also reflects important research traditions. When combined and used properly, these words provide a powerful way to view the emergency management world. We review the differences next.

2.5.1 Hazard Tradition

In simple form, hazards are disasters waiting to happen. People may live, work, and play in the paths of floods, tornadoes, hurricanes, and chemical accidents. Hazards occur when people, nature, and technology interact (Cutter 2001). Hazards exist, but only because people live in locations where they may confront earthquakes or tornadoes. When people move to a hazardous area, they place themselves at risk of experiencing a disaster. Mitigation serves as the key activity of an emergency manager to reduce the potential effects of hazards.

Geographer Gilbert White is considered by many to be the father of hazard mitigation (see further detail in Chapter 10). During his long and distinguished career, he focused on the value of structural mitigation projects such as levees and dams to decrease flooding along rivers. Structural mitigation projects reduce the chance that a hazard will become a disaster; they may also provide a sense of false security (Natural Hazards Center n.d.). For example, despite considerable engineering, the Mississippi River flooded multiple states, communities, and homes in 1993 and again in 2011. The Galveston Island (Texas) seawall provides a degree of protection from storm surges but when Hurricane Ike rolled ashore in 2008, the storm devastated the island. In short, hazards exist and people attempt to use technological solutions to manage them. People feel safe and move to ideal locations along beautiful rivers and seashores. Others work in businesses and industries that support the shoreline populations. Then, when a natural event overtaxes technological solutions such as levees and dams, a much worse disaster is created such as the aftermath of Hurricane Katrina.

Under White's leadership, the Natural Hazards Research and Application Information Center (also known as the Natural Hazards Center) formed at the University of Colorado in Boulder in the mid 1970s. White and his colleagues further defined the hazards perspective. Until recently, geographers were key but not sole advocates of this perspective. Due to White's efforts and work of the center, hazards research evolved into a multidisciplinary approach. Geographers, psychologists, sociologists, economists, engineers, and geologists now work together on hazards research and applications. The Natural Hazards Center also has a large resource facility and hosts an annual hazards workshop for professionals, researchers, and others (Myers 1993).

From a more applied perspective, current disaster planning includes hazard analysis. Emergency managers typically determine the fifteen most likely events that could impact their communities. These efforts then assist them in writing disaster plans and identifying (hazard) mitigation projects. Researchers can try to find out why people are willing to make hazard adjustments such as installing safe rooms or preparing evacuation plans. The area of hazard research and analysis today serves the broader public by identifying, explaining, and trying to improve the interactions of people and technology with hazards. We will learn more about hazard identification and analysis in Chapter 6.

2.5.2 Disaster Tradition

The disaster tradition is grounded in preparedness and response activities. Much of this resulted from civil defense activities initiated at the start of the Cold War between the U.S. and the former Soviet Union in the late 1940s until the fall of the Berlin Wall in November 1989. Both countries prepared to respond to massive nuclear strikes. At the start of the Cold War, the U.S. military provided research funding to the University of Chicago in an effort to see how soldiers and civilians would respond to nuclear war and chemical weapons.

The National Opinion Research Center (NORC) at the University of Chicago, led by Charles Fritz, initiated much of the research. Obviously, researchers could not expose cities and people to nuclear bombs or chemical weapons and thus elected to study events similar to wars: disasters. They traveled to disaster sites soon after impacts and studied how people and organizations responded. Contrary to popular belief, researchers found that disasters did not cause such behaviors as mass panic, looting, and hysteria. Rather, disasters brought out the best behavior—altruism abounded (Quarantelli 1987, 1994). Chapter 3 covers the quick response research experience and more on behavioral response can be found in Chapter 8.

Drawing on the quick response research of the NORC studies, sociologists Henry Quarantelli, Russell Dynes, and Eugene Haas at The Ohio State University formed the Disaster Research Center (DRC) in 1963. Dynes and Haas both specialized in organizational behavior; Quarantelli was a graduate student at the University of Chicago during the 1950s and served as a research assistant with NORC during the disaster studies. Like NORC, much of DRC's initial funding came from the Department of Defense and focused on the social aspects of disaster response. DRC's earliest research focused on organizational response to disaster.

Today, DRC (now at the University of Delaware) continues to be a leading international research center studying a wide range of events and topics. Since its creation in 1963, it has studied over 600 events throughout the world (the 1964 Alaska earthquake, 1974 outbreak of tornadoes, the 1989 Loma Prieta earthquake, the 2001 terrorist attacks, and the 2004 Indian Ocean tsunami). In addition to more traditional issues related to disaster research, DRC has focused on innovative research topics including the rituals of handling the dead, sheltering and housing after disasters, mental health delivery systems, assistance before and after disasters by emergent citizen groups, organizational improvisation, hospitals and medical delivery, and crowds and rioting. Another major DRC contribution has arisen from training large numbers of graduate students who have gone on to help define quick response research, provide a clearer understanding of disaster response, and contribute to disaster research. DRC alumni have also helped to design and develop academic programs in disaster management. More broadly, DRC established a model about fifty years ago that similar disaster and hazard centers use throughout the world. DRC also has the world's most comprehensive disaster library collection and scholars from many countries travel to use the collection and meet with center staff (DRC 2011). Two of your authors worked at DRC when it was at The Ohio State University (Phillips and Neal) and the third joined the center after it moved to the University of Delaware (Webb).

The disaster management tradition continues today, from the DRC and from many disaster researchers throughout the U.S. and elsewhere (Dynes, Tierney and Fritz 1994). From a practical view, the disaster research tradition has provided emergency managers with knowledge on how to plan and prepare for disasters and developed more effective ways to respond when disasters occur. New major federal planning documents, such as the *Comprehensive Planning Guide 101* (see Chapter 7), explicitly draw on disaster research to ground its preparedness and response suggestions.

2.5.3 Perspectives in Risk and Risk Perception

Another perspective for enhancing understanding of hazards and disasters arises from risk and risk perception. Originally coming from a social psychological perspective, researchers attempt to understand how individuals view and behave when facing risk. Risk analysis originated from questions of safety related to the use of nuclear power. These issues and concerns intensified after the Three Mile Island nuclear accident in the U.S. in 1979 and the Chernobyl (in the former Soviet Union) nuclear power plant explosion in 1986. Today, the concept of risk goes beyond issues of nuclear power.

For example, a risk perspective may focus on why people perceive some activities as more risky than others (e.g., flying via a commercial airliner versus driving a car). It may also concern environmental issues, such as how much of a hazardous substance should be allowed into rivers and waste sites. Risk can also deal with the trade-offs between having off shore oil wells and their potential damage to the environment from a major oil spill. Not all activities dealing with the risk perspective may deal with hazards and disasters. "Risky activities" include smoking, skydiving, and situations such as possible exposure to cancer from environmental threats. The risk perspective provides insights into all types of hazard and disaster behaviors (Slovic 1987).

Risk is also defined as the probability that an event will occur. We filter risk through various levels of perception and understanding. The "cone of uncertainty" used to describe a projected hurricane path can be very challenging to understand. Public response depends on understanding the way in which the hurricane may move. The cone projects a wide path that changes daily and sometimes hourly. Because we cannot know with a high degree of certainty where a hurricane will strike until twenty-four to thirty-six hours before landfall, it is hard to inform the public, some of whom will have to evacuate, where the impact will occur within forty-eight hours. People may simply take their chances based on an assumption that "it won't happen to me" or their previous experiences with hurricanes. Most people exhibit a low degree of concern about disasters (Tierney, Lindell, and Perry 2001). As a result, it may be very difficult to convince the public that it faces an impending risk. Think, for example, how likely it is that a hazard may generate a major disaster in your area, then consider how many preparations you must take to be ready. Did you pay attention to risk information and see its relevance to your personal safety?

Understanding how people perceive and behave toward risk is another important dimension in dealing with disasters. The issues of risk and risk perception help us understand why people choose to evacuate or not during a hurricane or chemical explosion or why they are willing to live near a potentially hazardous site such as a chemical plant or nuclear power facility. Understanding the public perception of risk makes us more capable of helping the public by designing effective preparedness campaigns and organizing evacuations.

Overall, the study of emergency management draws upon three different traditions: disasters, hazards, and risk. Each perspective grew from different academic areas and different questions to answer. Although these traditions originated from different fields, over the decades their works have complemented each other in helping us understand disasters. As suggested above, by combining these traditions covering the four phases of disaster, we gain a wider and more comprehensive view of the disaster process. A combination of the hazards, disasters, and risk traditions also develops the types of research necessary for students of emergency management.

2.6 Broader Perspectives

To study disasters, we rely on different perspectives of human behavior. No single perspective is right or wrong. They all provide insights into the different types of questions we want to ask and solve. We now provide a brief review of the main perspectives for studying and understanding the social dimension of disaster. No single theoretical perspective has emanated from the emerging discipline of emergency management. Rather, we borrow from other disciplines to generate research, critique planning, and other efforts and move forward the field as a discipline. Without concepts, theories, and methods, a field cannot be defined as a discipline (McEntire 2005; Phillips 2005; Blanchard 2005). Toward that end, we offer common theoretical perspectives from the research community and point out their values to practitioners. These perspectives include emergent norm, systems, and sociopolitical ecology theories.

2.6.1 Emergent Norm Theory

Early disaster researchers drew on studies of collective behavior—studying new types of behavior developed during unusual or new circumstances. Rapidly moving and fluid events (crowds, social protests, riots, and disaster behavior) fall under this definition. Early disaster researchers found that collective behavior theory helped capture the dynamic, changing characteristics of human behavior during disasters. One specific way to study collective behavior events came from the emergent norm theory that allows researchers to capture the spontaneous aspects of disaster behavior, especially during the response phase, by focusing on processes that generate new norms or social structures. Norms are accepted ways of behavior. Social structure reflects how we organize ourselves (knowing who is in charge and who should perform specific tasks). Emergent norm theory is a popular and successful approach to understanding disaster behavior (Turner and Killian 1987; Dynes and Tierney 1994).

Let us provide a few examples in which the emergent norm perspective helped explain disaster behavior. Research from fifty years ago through the present shows that altruism or significant helping behavior develops after a disaster. Neighbor helps neighbor just as emergency responders and volunteers travel from surrounding communities to help those in need. Crime rates drop significantly after disaster despite popular media accounts of looting (Fritz and Mathewson 1957; Fischer 2008). As a current example, consider the outpouring of help, donations, and money following the Haitian Earthquake in January 2010, particularly among international partners who never worked together previously. In short, new norms develop during and following a disaster.

Researchers also found that disasters can dramatically change the structures of organizations. Some organizations must expand to handle an influx of new volunteers. Volunteer organizations such as the Red Cross and Salvation Army change and adapt to manage changes in their routine operations when they respond to disasters. In other cases, organizations must change the tasks they do. Often following a disaster, construction companies cease their day-to-day operations to remove debris from roads and properties. New groups and organizations form to assist with disaster response. Right after a tornado, neighbors often spontaneously form search-and-rescue groups and comb neighborhoods to assist others (Dynes 1970). On a broader level, city governments may dramatically change their structures by putting new people in charge of disaster-related activities and also plugging other organizations temporarily into city government operations (Neal 1985). We will discuss in more detail these events, known as emergent groups and organizations, in Chapter 8. In summary, the findings noted above came from researchers drawing upon collective behavior and emergent norm theory.

2.6.2 Systems Theory

Systems theory in emergency management relates to the interactions of the built environment, the physical environment, and human beings (see Figure 2.3). When all the parts fit well, they work together with minimal problems. However, when one part does not work well, the other parts are affected, and a disaster may result. Next, we define some of the key terms of systems theory and provide an example of how the theory works in emergency management.

The built environment encompasses buildings, the infrastructure including utilities (electricity, gas, water), and transportation (roads, bridges, rail lines, ports), The physical environment includes natural factors such as water (snow, rain, ice), wind (tornadoes, hurricanes), and the earth (earthquakes,

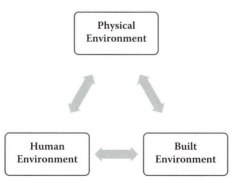

FIGURE 2.3   Systems theory of emergency management. (Based on Mileti 1999.)

landslides). Finally, the human system refers to where and how people live. All these systems interact with each other. Now let's see what can create a hazard leading to a disaster (Mileti 1999).

For thousands of years, people have enjoyed settling next to rivers (physical environment). The waterways provided water, food, and transportation. In short, such locations allowed people to live, develop organized cultures, and create meaningful social relationships (human systems). By putting down roots in such areas, people built highways and bridges, developed water and waste systems, and constructed homes and businesses (built environment). However, heavy rains over a short time (physical environment) can impact the built environment. Roads may flood and prevent transportation; fast moving flood waters can destroy bridges. Flooding can also contaminate water systems and destroy electrical and communication systems. Homes and businesses may be flooding, thus totally disrupting people's lives (human system). People may drown or become injured. Others may have to be evacuated. Businesses may be lost forever.

After such events, local residents, politicians, and the business community (human system) may look at ways to lessen impacts through mitigation. They may not allow homes or businesses to build or rebuild (restore the built environment) in floodplains (physical environment). Authorities may build levees or dikes (built environment) to lessen the impacts of future flooding (physical environment). In summary, the systems approach allows us to see how the human, built, and physical environments interact and tell us how certain actions (living in "Tornado Alley") can impact the residents of an area. In turn, such knowledge can help us mitigate, prepare for, respond to, and recover from events such as earthquakes. It can also allow us to help those more likely to be victims. For example, the poor are more likely to live in inexpensive housing such as mobile homes; when a tornado hits a community, much more damage will occur to mobile homes than to well-built homes. As a result, the poor experience greater vulnerability to disasters than those with more economic resources (Phillips, Thomas, Fothergill, and Pike 2010; Mileti 1999).

2.6.3 Sociopolitical Ecology Theory

Another popular and effective approach to understanding how disasters impact people is sociopolitical ecology theory. It focuses on the human system noted above, but provides a more detailed look. Specifically it suggests we consider competition among various social groups to see who may become victims and who may recover more quickly than others after a disaster (Peacock and Ragsdale 1997); see Figure 2.4. Sociopolitical ecology theory suggests that competition occurs over scarce resources needed for

FIGURE 2.4   FEMA's Marcie Roth, Disability Issues Senior Advisor, testifies on the importance of supporting vulnerable populations during disasters with Jonathan M. Young, chairman of the National Council of Disability; Dr. Carmen J. Spencer, Deputy Assistant Secretary of the Army–Elimination of Chemical Weapons, U. S. Army; and, on the right, Jim Kish, director of the Technological Hazards Division FEMA. (*Source*: FEMA/Bill Koplitz)

mitigation, preparedness, response, and recovery. There will be winners and losers in the process of securing those resources.

Single mothers for example, of whom about one-third live below the poverty line, will simply not be able to afford hurricane shutters or tornado safe rooms. Their families will bear disproportionate risk when hazards evolve into disasters. Similarly the earthquakes that struck in the U.S. compared to the one that devastated Haiti in 2010 demonstrate the battle to secure safe dwellings and workplaces. The Northridge, California, earthquake of 1994 claimed over 60 lives, injured more than 5,000 and left about 25,000 victims homeless (FEMA 2010b). The 2010 Haiti earthquake saw hundreds of thousands killed. Even the cost of developing a preparedness kit, as described in Chapter 6, may be impossible for low-income households, senior citizens, and students. Should a winter storm confine you to your apartment or dormitory, how will you survive? Recovery is even more difficult. Because lower income households can live only in the most affordable units, they tend to dwell in manufactured housing, apartments near floodplains, and buildings that are not seismic resistant. Loss of life from disaster is more common in such locations. Furthermore, the losses of personal possessions, clothing, work resources, and transportation make disaster recovery impossible. Disparities exist even in the business community. Smaller businesses (Chapter 11) fare less well than larger operations with far more assets.

FIGURE 2.5 Hurricane Katrina evacuation, New Orleans, 2005. Older citizens, residents with disabilities, and pets had the greatest needs for evacuation before Hurricane Katrina. Rescuers assist those who could not evacuate a week after the levees broke. (*Source:* FEMA News Photo/Liz Roll.)

Competition for scarce resources is likely to generate conflict. After Katrina, government officials made difficult decisions to destroy public housing units. Local protestors claimed that the buildings remained livable and decried reconstruction choices that reduced the number of affordable units. See Figure 2.5. Five years after Katrina, uneven rebuilding has occurred across New Orleans. Areas historically populated by racial and ethnic minorities were destroyed by high water levels. Elderly African American men died in numbers far higher than their percentage of the city's population would have predicted (Sharkey 2007). Only 24% of the predominantly African American population has returned to live in the Lower Ninth Ward (GNOCDC 2010). Sociopolitical ecology theory directs researchers and emergency managers to determine those in their communities who may face the highest risk for disaster impact and design measures that reduce disproportionate numbers of deaths, injuries, and property losses.

2.7 Current Issues

As noted earlier in this chapter, defining disaster is not a simple task. Scholars continue to debate the issue. We presented some basic ideas that we will use throughout this text. However, we also think it is important to discuss other perspectives and developing issues in the field today. These include political definitions of disaster, slow versus fast moving disasters, non-traditional events seen as disasters, and multidisciplinary perspectives on disaster.

2.7.1 Political Definitions

Politics certainly play a role in whether an event is defined a disaster. Political definitions are important in the U.S. because the amounts and types of aid available during and after events are contingent on how events are defined (e.g., hurricane, flood, landslide) and whether or not the president declares them disasters.

Over the past few decades FEMA established a process and general criteria for a presidential declaration of disaster. Authority for such declarations comes from a number of related sources. In a general sense, Article 2 and Section 3 of the U.S. Constitution implicitly gave the president the power to take emergency action to ensure that all laws are followed and to command the use of the military (as commander in chief). The Disaster Relief Act of 1950 and the Disaster Relief Act of 1974 gave the president further power to provide relief and assistance to disaster victims. Finally, the Robert T. Stafford Disaster Relief and Emergency Assistance Act (the Stafford Act, passed in 1988 and later amended) gave the president further power to declare a disaster more quickly (such as in the case of a terrorist attack), to provide immediate aid, to assist responders and victims. Today, via a presidential declaration, the federal government through the executive (presidential) branch can provide immediate funds for disaster response and recovery. Over the years, Congress has amended the Stafford Act, including the process and general criteria for the declaration of a disaster (Sylves 2008; FEMA 2010c).

FEMA does not have a set of numerical factors for determining whether an event is a disaster. For example, an event could be declared a disaster even if no deaths occur, or an event could not be declared a disaster even if 150 people died. To illustrate, a slow moving flood may not kill anyone, but may be declared a disaster. And, cases certainly exist where a plane crash kills over 100 people, but the president does not declare a disaster. For an event to qualify for a disaster declaration, FEMA focuses on such factors as the severity, magnitude, and impact of the event. To understand the severity, magnitude and impact, FEMA uses the criteria listed below as guidelines for a state governor to use in requesting a federal disaster declaration (FEMA 2010c):

- Amount and type of damage (number of homes destroyed or with major damage)
- Impact on the infrastructure of affected areas or critical facilities
- Imminent threats to public health and safety
- Impacts to essential government services and functions
- Unique capability of the federal government
- Dispersion or concentration of damage
- Level of insurance coverage in place for homeowners and public facilities
- Assistance available from other sources (federal, state, local, voluntary organizations)
- State and local resource commitments from previous, undeclared events
- Frequency of disaster events over a recent time period

The Stafford Act also spells out the specific process local and state governments must follow to apply for a disaster declaration and receive federal resources and aid. Based on the criteria above, local and state officials furnish the state governor with a damage assessment. The governor then submits a formal request to the appropriate FEMA regional office. This request should demonstrate that state and local governments do not have the resources to manage and recover from the event. Both the regional and national FEMA offices will assess the report and then make a recommendation to the president who will accept or reject the recommendation. In short, the president has the final say on whether a request is approved as a declared disaster (FEMA 2010c). Keep in mind that the process and criteria of a presidentially declared disaster can and do change. A look at FEMA's website (www.fema.gov) can help you determine what if any changes have been made since the time of this writing.

Politics can affect the presidentially declared disaster process. We have seen that the number of disasters and the amount of money spent on federally declared disasters have increased over the decades. We can certainly argue that we have seen more disasters over the last few decades (Quarantelli 1986; Mileti 1999). In a specific analysis of presidential disaster declarations from May 1953 through January 2007, a distinct pattern emerged (Sylves 2008). During that period, 1,674 major disaster declarations were issued. This represents an average of 31 declarations a year or close to 2.5 declarations a month. However, if we look at the period from January 1993 through September 2005, we see a dramatic rise in the number of declarations. The average increases to 48.2 per year or 4 per month. Thus, in addition to facing more disasters and declarations, the nation also experienced changes in:

- The public's attitudes about disasters and the federal government's role in providing aid
- Politicians' views and use of federalism (how the state and federal governments interact)
- Presidents' willingness to declare disasters
- Laws providing more aid to disaster-hit communities and victims (Sylves 2008, p. 84).

In short, the examples cited above show that both politics and disaster events have influenced the increased number of major disaster declarations in the U.S. Yet, partisanship does not seem to be part of the political process of major disaster declarations. For example, a request by a republican governor to a democratic president will not diminish the chance of having an event declared a disaster. Conversely, a request by a republican governor to a republican president will not enhance the chance of obtaining a declaration. In a forty-five-year period, researchers found that democratic presidents accepted a higher proportion of declaration requests than republican presidents and a president is more likely to approve a governor's request in response to a natural event rather than a technological event (Sylves and Buzas 2007).

2.7.2 Slow versus Fast Moving Views of Disaster

Generally we think of disasters as events that strike quickly: explosions, floods, earthquakes, and tornadoes. The perspective of looking at sudden or quickly moving events is in part based on the research and professional roots. Remember that dealing with nuclear and chemical warfare at the start of the Cold War drove much of the U.S. view of emergency management. To study human behavior in this context, researchers looked at behavior during sudden or quickly occurring disasters such as explosions and tornadoes. Even today, much of our knowledge of disaster behavior, especially in developed nations such as the U.S., Canada, Japan, and Western Europe focuses on sudden, quick events.

However, not all events occur quickly, suddenly, or without warning. They develop slowly. For example, long-term, slowly changing weather patterns can also create disasters. Meteorologists can often predict long-term patterns of drought in Central Africa. Drought causes crop failures, leading to famine in these countries. In turn, famine often forces large numbers of people to migrate to other areas and even other countries to survive. Mass migrations may lead to civil wars or wars between nations and those who flee devastated lands are subjected to human rights violations. These patterns are predictable and to a degree can be mitigated (Hoffman and Oliver-Smith 2002).

Environmental disasters can also be slow moving. For example, the Love Canal neighborhood in Niagara Falls, New York became contaminated by hazardous waste buried there by Hooker Chemical Company. Love Canal served as a city dump when Hooker acquired the property in 1942 and started dumping chemical waste. During the early and mid 1950s, the property was sold to a developer to build homes and a school was built. By the mid to late 1970s, in addition to odd odors, residents started to notice a pattern of health problems such as higher rates of miscarriages, mental problems, and illnesses. A local newspaper tested the water in the area and found very high contents of hazardous materials. As a result, the local residents formed a protest group to provide help with medical issues, selling homes, and eventually closing the neighborhood. As part of an Environmental Protection Agency program, over 800 families left the neighborhood and most of the homes were demolished (Blum 2008; Levine 1982).

The real issue for Love Canal was—when did the disaster start? For some, it started with the first improper disposal of hazardous waste. For others, it began when the property was sold for development. Perhaps for the residents, the event became defined as a disaster when people started to get sick or when residents and others claimed that the hazardous materials caused the illnesses. By the late 1970s and early 1980s, the federal and state government recognized the event as a disaster. We cannot pinpoint the exact moment when the threshold for calling the event a disaster was met. The disaster was the ongoing process of contaminating people (Blum 2008; Levine 1982). Federal assistance and the Environmental Protection Agency became involved as people moved to safer locations.

Several types of disasters (droughts, famines, hazardous chemical exposures) do not become immediate disasters. Rather, their impacts, consequences, and even public definitions as disasters may take years and even decades to occur. As a result, emergency managers and others cannot state an exact time when such an event becomes a disaster. These types of events slowly creep upon us, until the attributes of a disaster suddenly appear and it may already be too late to mitigate, prepare, or even respond properly.

2.7.3 Non-Traditional Events

Traditionally, emergency managers deal with tornadoes, floods, hurricanes, explosions, and similar events. However, over the last decade or two, those in emergency management have played central roles in planning for or actually helping to coordinate responses to events that we may not consider disasters. For example, city officials may open an Emergency Operating Center (EOC) to observe or coordinate activities involving large crowds such as athletic contests, spontaneous outbursts, social protests, and even riots. An EOC is an ideal place to gather information, house key decision makers, and coordinate activities. These events and their outcomes will involve all facets of local government—police, fire fighters, paramedics, and public works. Local governments must organize their activities with businesses, volunteer organizations, and perhaps with components of state and local governments.

When the space shuttle Columbia disintegrated upon reentry on February 1, 2003, emergency management offices played a central role by handling a number of tasks. Experts determined that an area 240 miles long and 10 miles wide had to be searched thoroughly to find debris and remains. The search was complicated because the intent was to find a wide range of objects including human remains, hazardous materials, and debris. FEMA coordinated the activities of many organizations. Along with FEMA, NASA, the U.S. Forest Service, and the Environmental Protection Agency (EPA) supervised key search activities. As the search needs expanded and hazardous materials became a main concern, the U.S. Coast Guard, the Gulf Strike Team, and a private contracting firm tested for contaminants in the water and atmosphere (none was found). Also included in the recovery process were the FBI, the National Guard, search-and-rescue organizations, and the Texas Department of Public Safety. By February 4, other organizations from Texas, Louisiana, Oklahoma, and New Mexico became involved (FEMA 2003). Thus, FEMA and state and local emergency management offices played key roles in coordinating the following activities:

- Collecting about 82,500 pieces of the shuttle
- Searching over 2.28 million acres
- Testing more than twenty-three square miles of water for contamination
- Coordinating the efforts of 16,500 people involved in the search
- Reimbursing states for search and rescue costs estimated at $10 million
- Managing 130 federal, state, and local agencies
- Coordinating the 270 organizations assisting with the response and recovery

In summary, emergency managers can play integral roles in different or extraordinary events. One primary role is developing connections among people and organizations that may be useful for all types of disasters. Whether they deal with an occasional event like a major crowd of 40,000 to 100,000 people or a rare event such as a space shuttle accident, emergency managers should have the resources and the social connections to help coordinate materials and communications among the relevant key players. In Chapter 4, we discuss increasing disaster events and their different aspects and how professional disaster managers play bigger roles in such situations.

2.7.4 Multidisciplinary Views of Disaster

As noted earlier, hazards, disasters, and risk are important terms for emergency management. Initially, geography helped establish the hazards perspective, sociology provided the foundation for dealing with disasters, and psychology informed risk assessment. The hazards perspective first developed a more multidisciplinary approach, drawing also upon sociology and social psychology. Then scholars from other social sciences (psychology, political science, public administration, anthropology) became involved. Over the past decade, social scientists learned that a combination of social science perspectives can give us better insight into disaster behavior.

Of course, meteorologists, physicists, geologists, engineers, and other professionals made many contributions by studying hazard agents and how they impact build environments. If these scientists are to design better buildings and stronger bridges or invent improved warning technologies, they must consider the human factor. By the early 1980s meteorologists had devised sophisticated equipment to detect, show, and predict the strengths and paths of tornadoes. Despite this advance, the number of annual deaths due to tornadoes and severe storms did not decline. The reason was simple— the meteorologists ignored the human factor in disaster warnings. They and others believed that sophisticated new equipment ensured that people would hear the warnings and take proper action. However, people are more complex. Research showed that people must be made aware of a hazard, be educated about warning systems and how they work, and be told what to do if they hear warnings. Studies also suggested that warning messages must also be repeated and the geographical region must be specified to make an event "real" in the perceptions of the people receiving the message. After meteorologists worked with social scientists to devise a social science-based tornado warning system coupled with the sophisticated equipment, deaths from tornadoes and severe storms decreased (Quarantelli 1994). Recently, the Office of the Federal Coordinator of Meteorology established a working group to further integrate social science findings into partnerships with those who detect, predict, and deliver meteorological information. The goal is to reduce deaths among those most vulnerable to weather, particularly senior citizens, the poor, people with disabilities, and the traveling public that may be unaware of risks (for more, see the Resources section).

Sylves (2008) punctuates the importance of a multidisciplinary approach toward disasters for policy making in governmental settings. Whether at local, state, or national level, those involved in disaster policy must have a wide range of knowledge. For example, a policy on earthquake preparedness should include geologists (who understand fault lines in an area), planners and geographers (land use) and architects (creating building codes), and sociologists (public education and risk communication programs). In short, as the research field grew and the profession developed, academics and professionals realized that the four phases of emergency management required a multidisciplinary perspective.

2.8 Summary

Disaster takes on many meanings. For purposes of this text, we focus on how disasters impact people. Within the profession of emergency management and among researchers, three different traditions related to disasters exist. The hazard tradition, initiated by geographers, seeks to understand interactions among people and the built and physical environments. From this interaction, researchers see how people try to mitigate and prepare for disasters. Sociologists initially focused on preparation for and response to disaster, particularly fast moving disasters such as earthquakes, explosions, and tornadoes. Understanding how people perceive and respond to various types of risks was the task of social psychologists. Although these perspectives came from different origins and developed different ways of understanding how people behave, professionals and researchers now realize that all of these views offer critical insights of value to emergency management settings and activities. To put these different approaches in perspective, researchers use various theories (emergent norm theory, systems theory, sociopolitical ecology theory) to describe and explain disaster events.

Disasters also have political definitions that influence how people see events and, more importantly, how much federal money can be obtained by state and local governments for responding to and rebuilding after an event. Emergency managers also assist with events that are not disasters since they have the skills to coordinate people from local, state, and federal jurisdictions and manage resources from the private, public, and volunteer sectors. Situations such as managing large crowd events and response and recovery efforts related to the space shuttle Challenger illustrate the important roles of emergency managers in non-disaster situations.

Discussion Questions

1. Why does *disasters* have many meanings and how can the various meanings lead to confusion in dealing with disasters?

2. Explain and distinguish the traditions of hazards, disasters, and risks.

3. Why after more than thirty years of use is comprehensive emergency management still important today for emergency managers and disaster researchers?

4. How do the emergent norm perspective, systems theory, and the sociopolitical ecology theory all give us different views of the same event?

Which theory may help us describe and explain certain types of situations that occur during a disaster?

5. Do you think the field will ever have one view or perspective of disaster or will it continue to have multiple definitions? What are the pros and cons of each side?

6. Why does emergency management integrate a number of the social sciences along with other sciences and engineering? What are some examples where different (social) sciences work together to make our world safer?

References

Blanchard, B. Wayne. 2005. "Top Ten Competencies for Professional Emergency Management." Available at training.fema.gov/EMIWeb/edu/docs/Blanchard%20 -%20Competencies%20EM%20HiEd.doc-2006-02-13, last accessed February 25, 2011.

Blum, Elizabeth D. 2008. *Love Canal Revisited*. Kansas: University of Kansas Press.

Cutter, Susan L. 2001. "The Changing Nature of Risks and Hazards." Pp. 1–12 in *American Hazardscapes* (Susan L. Cutter, ed.). Washington D. C.: Joseph Henry Press.

Disaster Research Center (DRC). 2011. "About DRC." Available at http://www.udel.edu/ DRC/aboutus/index.html, last accessed February 25, 2011.

Dynes, Russell R. and Kathleen J. Tierney. 1994. *Disasters, Collective Behavior, and Social Organization*. Newark: University of Delaware Press.

Dynes, Russell, Kathleen J. Tierney and Charles E. Fritz. 1994. "Forward: The Emergence and Importance of Social Organization: The Contributions of E. L. Quarantelli." Pp. 9–17 in *Disasters, Collective Behavior, and Social Organization* (Russell R. Dynes and Kathleen J. Tierney, eds.). Newark: University of Delaware Press.

Federal Emergency Management Agency. 2010. Earthquakes in the United States. Available at http://www.fema.gov/hazard/earthquake/usquakes.shtm, last accessed February 23, 2011).

Federal Emergency Management Agency. 2010a. http://www.fema.gov/pdf/about/org_ chart.pdf (accessed January 6, 2011).

Federal Emergency Management Agency. 2010b. *Declaration Process Fact Sheet*. http://www.fema.gov/media/fact_sheets/declaration_process.shtm

Federal Emergency Management Agency. 2003. "Recap of the Search for Columbia Shuttle Material." Available at http://www.fema.gov/news/newsrelease.fema?id=2808, last accessed December 23, 2008.

Fischer, Henry W. 2003. "The Sociology of Disaster: Definitions, Research Questions and Measurements," *International Journal of Mass Emergencies and Disasters* 21/19: 91–108.

Fischer, Henry. 2008. *Response to Disaster: Fact Versus Fiction and Its Perpetuation: The Sociology of Disaster, 3rd Edition*. New York: University Press of America.

Fritz, Charles E. 1961. "Disaster." Pp. 651–694 in *Contemporary Social Problems* (Robert K. Merton and Robert A. Nisbet, eds). New York: Harcourt Brace Jovanovich.

Fritz, Charles E. and J. H. Mathewson. 1957. *Convergence Behavior in Disasters: A Problem in Social Control*. Washington: D.C.: National Academy of Sciences, National Research Council.

GNOCDC/Greater New Orleans Community Data Center. 2010. *Neighborhood Recovery Rates*. Retrieved January 18, 2011 http://www.gnocdc.org/RecoveryByNeighborhood/ index.html).

Hoffman, Susanna M. and Anthony Oliver-Smith. 2002. *Catastrophe and Culture: The Anthropology of Disaster*. Sante Fe: School of American Research Press.

International Association of Emergency Managers. 2007. *Principles of Emergency Management Supplement*. http://www.iaem.com/publications/documents/ PrinciplesofEmergencyManagement.pdf, assessed January 3, 2011.

Levine, Adeline Gordon. 1982. *Love Canal: Science, Politics and People*. New York: D. C. Heath and Company.

McEntire, David M. 2005. "Emergency Management Theory: Issues, Barriers and Recommendations for Improvement." *Journal of Emergency Management* 3/3: 44–54.

Mileti, Dennis. 1999. *Disasters by Design*. Washington, D.C.: Joseph Henry Press.

Myers, Mary Fran. 1993. "Bridging the Gap between Research and Practice: The Natural Hazards Research and Applications Information Center." *International Journal of Mass Emergencies and Disasters* 11/1: 41–54.

National Governors Association (NGS). 1979. *1978 Emergency Preparedness Project: Final Report*. Washington, D.C.: Defense Civil Preparedness Agency.

Neal, David M. 1985. *A Cross Societal Comparison of Emergent Group Behavior in Disaster: A Look at Sweden and the United States*. Dissertation, Department of Sociology, The Ohio State University, Columbus, Ohio.

Neal, David M., 2000. "Developing Degree Programs in Disaster Management: Some Reflections and Observations." *International Journal of Mass Emergencies and Disasters* 18/3: 417–437.

Neal, David M., 1997. "Reconsidering the Phases of Disaster." *International Journal of Mass Emergencies and Disasters* 15/2: 239–264.

Natural Hazards Center. n.d. "Gilbert White." Available at http://www.colorado.edu/ hazards/gfw/, last accessed February 23, 2011.

Peacock, W., and A. K. Ragsdale. 1997. "Social Systems, Ecological Networks, and Disasters: Toward a Socio-political Ecology of Disasters." Pp. 20–35 in *Hurricane Andrew: Ethnicity, Gender and the Sociology of Disasters*, (W. G. Peacock, B. H. Morrow, and H. Gladwin, eds.). London: Routledge.

Phillips, Brenda. 2005. "Disasters as a Discipline: the Status of EmergencyManagement Education in the U.S." *International Journal of Mass Emergencies and Disasters* 23/1: 85–110.

Phillips, Brenda, Deborah Thomas, Alice Fothergill, Lynn Pike, eds. 2010. *Social Vulnerability to Disaster*. Boca Raton, FL: CRC Press.

Quarantelli, E. L. 1986. *Organizational Behavior in Disasters and Implications for Disaster Planning*. Monograph Series 1/2. Emmitsburg, MD: National Emergency Training Center.

Quarantelli E. L. 1982. "What is a Disaster?: An Agent Specific or an All Disaster Spectrum Approach to Socio-behavioral Aspects of Earthquakes." Pp. 453–478 in *Social and Economic Aspects of Earthquakes*, (B. Jones and M. Tomazevic, eds.). NY: Cornell University, Program in Urban and Regional Studies.

Quarantelli, E. L. 1987. "Disaster Studies: An Analysis of the Social Historical Factors Affecting the Development of Research in the Area." *International Journal of Mass Emergencies and Disasters* 5/3: 285–310.

Quarantelli, E. L. 1994. "Disaster Studies: The Consequences of the Historical Use of a Sociological Approach in the Development of Research." *International Journal of Mass Emergencies and Disasters*. 12/1: 5–23.

Quarantelli, E. L. 2006. "Understanding Katrina: Catastrophes Are Different from Disasters." *Perspectives from the Social Sciences*, http://understandingkatrina.ssrc.org/Quarantelli/, accessed January 3, 2011.

Quarantelli, E. L., and Russell R. Dynes. 1970. "Property Norms and Looting: Their Patterns in Community Crises." *Phylon* 31: 168–182.

Slovic, Paul. 1987. "Perception of Risk." *Science 236/4799*: 280–285.

Sylves, Richard. 2008. *Disaster Policy and Politics: Emergency Management and Homeland Security*. Washington, D.C.: CQ Press.

Sylves, Richard, and Zoltan Buzas. 2007. "Presidential Disaster Declaration Decisions, 1953–2003: What Influences Odds of Approval?" *State and Local Government Review* 39/1: 3–15.

Tierney, Kathleen, Michael Lindell and Ron W. Perry. 2001. *Facing the Unexpected*. Washington, D.C.: Joseph Henry Press.

Sharkey, P. 2007. "Survival and Death in New Orleans." *Journal of Black Studies* 37/4: 482–501.

Turner, Ralph and Killian. 1987. *Collective Behavior*, third edition. Englewood, NJ: Prentice Hall.

U. S. Fire Administration, 2004. *The Seasonal Incidents of Fire in 2000*. Topical Fire Research Series Issue 6 Volume 3. Washington, D. C.: FEMA.

Resources

- The development of the Disaster Research Center, now at the University of Delaware, and the Natural Hazards Center at the University of Colorado at Boulder are central to the development of research and defining the field. Their websites provide extensive information about their origins, current projects, and trends in the field. The link to the Disaster Research Center is http://www.udel.edu/DRC/ and the link to the Natural Hazards Center is http://www.colorado.edu/hazards/

- This chapter provided a brief overview of how the president declares an event a disaster. To appreciate fully the legal nature of the process and other rules and regulations, here is the link to the complete, current version of the Robert T. Stafford Relief and Assistance Act (Public Law 93-288) as amended: http://www.fema.gov/about/stafact.shtm

- To learn more about the continuing bridge between the social science and meteorological communities, review the presentations from a pivotal exploratory mini-workshop titled Framing the Questions, Addressing the Needs: Moving to Incorporate Social Science Results into Meteorological Operations and Services sponsored by the Office of the Federal Coordinator of Meteorology. http://www.ofcm.gov/wg-ssr/workshop05-2010/index.htm

Research Methods and the Practice of Emergency Management

3.1 Chapter Objectives

Upon completing this chapter, readers should be able to:

1. Discuss the relevance of disaster research to the practice of emergency management and the benefits of having a basic understanding of research methods and findings.
2. Outline the historical origins of disaster research and identify some of the key research centers active in the field today.
3. Understand the value of studying disasters from a multidisciplinary perspective and provide examples of contributions made by researchers in various fields.
4. Explain the various methods used to gather data on disasters and provide examples of how they have been used to study the four phases of disaster.
5. Describe ethical guidelines for studying human subjects and identify challenges involved in conducting disaster research.

3.2 Introduction

Disasters interest people for many reasons. Novelists and filmmakers craft compelling storylines celebrating selfless acts of heroism or, more commonly, images of chaos and pandemonium in the wake of catastrophe. Members of the mass media flock to the scenes of disasters, often conveying those same images of civil disorder and social breakdown to their viewers, readers, and listeners. In contrast to those who exploit disasters for sales and ratings, emergency managers, first responders, public officials, and volunteers have a professional interest in disasters and a strong desire to alleviate the suffering of those impacted by them.

Researchers also have a professional interest in disasters, and they share a common vision of reducing the human and financial costs of disasters. Ultimately, the goal of scholarly research is to generate insights and contribute to a safer, more sustainable future. While you may not see them on the front line throwing sandbags or delivering meals, engineers, geologists, and social scientists work hard at testing building construction practices, mapping hazardous areas, observing organizational responses to disasters, evaluating disaster-related policies and programs, and identifying vulnerable populations who are most susceptible to the devastating impacts of disasters. The results of their work may not always produce immediate benefits, but over the long term the findings of disaster research can contribute significantly to a more resilient society.

3.2.1 Benefits of Understanding Research

As a future emergency manager, you will benefit from having a basic understanding of disaster research in several ways. First, you will develop transferrable skills. The ability to gather information, analyze data, and communicate the results of your analysis to others is a skill that is recognized and valued in virtually all professional settings. As an emergency manager, for example, you may be asked to conduct a hazard analysis, assess the degree to which your community is prepared for a disaster, or identify populations with special needs in the event of a disaster. By having some familiarity with the methods of data collection described in this chapter, you will be much better equipped to perform those kinds of tasks.

Second, having research-based knowledge of how people and organizations actually behave in disasters will enhance your effectiveness as an emergency manager. As will be discussed in Chapter 8, there are many myths about human response to disaster, all of which assume that society breaks down under extreme stress. In reality, however, rather than having to control a helpless mob of panic-stricken victims, emergency managers must instead devise strategies for coordinating the efforts of the enormous numbers of survivors and volunteers who invariably want to help.

Finally, your introduction to the tradition and practice of disaster research will benefit you by exposing you to valuable lessons learned from systematic studies of past disasters. As will be discussed later in this chapter, researchers have studied disasters in part because they have sought answers to interesting scientific questions, but they have also been driven to answer highly practical questions about how best to respond to, prepare for, or recover from large-scale disasters.

3.2.2 Sources of Knowledge for Emergency Managers

As a professional emergency manager, you will continue to learn throughout your career, and the knowledge you acquire will come from various sources, including (1) formal education, (2) field experience, and (3) disaster research. It is very likely that as your career advances the relative impacts of these three sources of knowledge on how you do your job will shift from time to time. For example, you may be assigned a new task about which you know very little and find yourself combing through your old class notes looking for guidance. Or, a colleague may come to you about a challenge he or she is facing in his or her community, and you will be able to share your own experiences in dealing with the same problem. Finally, you may encounter something so unique and perplexing that you decide to seek out research on the issue to see what others have learned about it.

3.2.2.1 Education-Based Knowledge

In most undergraduate degree programs, including emergency management, students are required to take classes in a wide range of disciplines including the natural sciences, social sciences, and humanities. Students often feel that their classes are disjointed and haphazard, and they do not always see the value in taking so many disparate courses. But there is a good reason for exposing you to so many different topics. In addition to preparing you for careers in particular fields, a college education is also aimed at equipping you with broader skills for life in general. These include critical thinking, creative problem solving, and strong communication skills. Thus, it is possible that some of your least favorite classes may pay dividends much later in life. It is also possible that certain topics covered in some of your favorite classes that may not capture your interest at the time—such as research methods in emergency management—may be vitally important to you later in your career.

3.2.2.2 Experience-Based Knowledge

Another valuable source of information about the profession will come from real-world experiences. Within your professional networks, for example, you will hear plenty of "war stories" as colleagues share their experiences from the field with you. Over time, you will also gain valuable experiences of your own that will surely serve you well. Those experiences will be critical to your development as a professional emergency manager, and they are all steps in becoming a seasoned veteran. Early in your career, it is very likely that you will feel overwhelmed, exhausted, and emotionally drained during your first encounters with large-scale disasters. Over time, however, based largely on previous experiences, you will develop much more sustainable work routines, more effective coping strategies, and more efficient solutions to the common problems you will face.

3.2.2.3 Research-Based Knowledge

It is our hope that in addition to these education- and experience-based ways of knowing, you will continue to expand your research-based knowledge throughout your career. Experience certainly matters, and the knowledge you acquire from your years of service will be invaluable. However, scientific research is also important and from it we can learn a great deal about the world around us, as described in Box 3.1. For the professional emergency manager, research findings from disaster studies can be valuable sources of knowledge for three primary reasons.

First, researchers rely on *systematic observations* in which they thoroughly document what they see and hear in the field. In contrast, experience-based knowledge is often based on selective observations and anecdotal accounts of what happened in a disaster. Second, researchers gather *empirical evidence* to support their findings. Rather than relying on rampant rumors or media sensationalism and speculation, researchers report what actually happened and systematically amass evidence to substantiate their findings. Finally, disaster studies are valuable sources of knowledge to emergency managers because researchers collect *perishable information* that is critical to understanding post-disaster events fully. By deploying as rapidly as possible to the scene of a disaster, researchers can paint an accurate picture of the response effort—a task that becomes much more difficult as time passes, memories fade, response teams leave, and ad hoc ways of working are replaced by normal routines. Researchers bring a neutral stance to observing events and thus generate more objective, measurable results that can steadily improve emergency management practice.

3.3 Brief History of Disaster Research

Many students are surprised when they learn that there is an established field of research devoted to the study of disasters. They also tend to be surprised when they learn when and why the field emerged in the first place. While a few early isolated studies were pursued, systematic efforts of social scientists to examine the human dimensions of disasters began in earnest in the early 1950s.

BOX 3.1   VALUE OF RESEARCH FOR EMERGENCY MANAGEMENT

William Anderson

Dr. William Anderson, a graduate of The Ohio State University and an alumnus of the Disaster Research Center, writes here about the value of research for emergency managers. Dr. Anderson, who first studied the 1964 Alaska earthquake, went on to a distinguished career at the U.S. National Science Foundation and the National Academy of Sciences.

Emergency managers can access and apply findings and principles from decades of disaster research when undertaking such actions as communicating risk information to the public, developing disaster preparedness plans, and undertaking crucial disaster response and recovery activities. Disaster researchers continue to produce new knowledge on such subjects. Thus emergency managers need to periodically update their understanding of advances in the disaster research field as they pursue the goal of making their communities more disaster resilient. Staying abreast of new insights from disaster research can be rather challenging, but it should be a lifetime commitment for career emergency managers.

Many senior emergency managers have set a good example for the next generation by successfully bridging the gap between the emergency management and disaster research communities throughout their careers. Thus the emerging generation of emergency managers can gain much in the way of their own continued growth by emulating them. There are several ways in which emergency managers have been able to access disaster research information on a career-long basis, enabling them to apply it strategically in their professional work.

Interpersonal Connections

Experience has shown that emergency managers can learn much from disaster researchers through personal contact with them. Many emergency managers have established important long-term ties with disaster researchers at their local universities or those in the immediate region for the purpose of gaining knowledge useful for their decision making. Emergency managers discover that most disaster researchers are quite eager to discuss and share their expert knowledge with them and also point them toward valuable resources such as publications, courses, workshops, and other learning opportunities. The message here is that making friends with approachable disaster scholars should be a top priority for young emergency management practitioners.

Continuing Education

Many emergency managers understand the importance of continuing education for those in their profession. Thus many obtain additional education after they have completed college and launched their careers. To help meet the needs of today's emergency management practitioners, there is quite a variety of learning experiences to choose from that are offered by disaster scholars at local universities as well as those made available online by experts at distant universities, including degree and non-degree courses, full- and short-term courses, and seminars.

Conferences and Workshops

As disasters have drawn more attention in the past several years, there has been a surge in the number of conferences and workshops that bring together disaster scholars, emergency management practitioners, and disaster reduction policy makers to exchange ideas and experiences through discussions and presentations. The workshops organized by the Disasters Roundtable at the National Academy of Sciences in Washington, D.C. and the Annual Hazards Workshop organized by the Natural Hazards Center at the University of Colorado in Boulder are two examples of such activities that involve the active participation of emergency managers, providing them with the opportunity to learn about discoveries in disaster research directly from researchers. Of course, disaster researchers also learn much from emergency managers during such exchanges.

Publications

The above learning strategies involve social interaction, mostly the critical face-to-face variety, between emergency managers and researchers. This is crucial because most emergency managers are seldom inclined to spend much time reading through the technical terminology and explanations of scientific research methodology found in leading scholarly research publications. However, there are publications geared to making disaster research more understandable to emergency management practitioners and these do attract a sizable number of them, including the two editions of *Emergency Management: Principles and Practice for Local Government* (Drabek and Hoetmer 1991; Waugh and Tierney 2007) published by ICMA, a leading professional association for local government managers. Newsletters like the *Natural Hazards Observer* and the online publication *Disaster Research*, both published by the Natural Hazards Center, are other sources of written information about developments in the disaster field that are reader friendly to emergency managers.

New Media

In this information technology age, emergency managers can now turn to new media sources for information on disaster research, and many are doing so. This is an area where young emergency managers may eclipse their elders in the field. Important information on disaster research can be accessed through Google searches and some disaster scholars make information available on their blogs. Also, the emergence of web-based social media, such as Facebook, Twitter and YouTube, offers unparalleled access to disaster research information of value to emergency managers.

In conclusion, acquiring relevant insights from the disaster research field throughout their careers in ways noted here, and effectively applying them, will help make the next generation of emergency managers the leaders their communities need to combat natural, technological, and human-induced disasters.

3.3.1 Military Influences

Interestingly, the impetus for establishing a field of study devoted specifically to social aspects of disasters came from the United States military. During World War II, the U.S. military conducted extensive studies of its bombing campaigns against Germany and Japan (Fritz 1961). Those studies revealed that the bombings did not have severely debilitating effects. Both Germany and Japan demonstrated strong resilience and an impressive capacity to rebound in the wake of such massive destruction. Based on these observations, the central question for the military became, what would happen if a major U.S. city was unexpectedly attacked by an enemy? Would civil society remain intact or would social order break down into chaos?

3.3.2 Early Disaster Studies

Recognizing that an experimental design would be impossible, the military sought an alternative approach to answer these profound questions. Specifically, they issued research grants to social scientists to study how people respond to disasters. Initially, studies were conducted by social scientists at the University of Chicago's National Opinion Research Center (NORC), the University of Oklahoma, and the University of Texas. Subsequent studies were conducted by researchers affiliated with the National Academy of Sciences Disaster Research Group. These early researchers studied human responses to tornadoes, airplane crashes, and chemical plant explosions (Quarantelli 1987). For their purposes, the type of event was not important, as long as it happened quickly and unexpectedly. In other words, the researchers were tasked with studying events that resembled bombing attacks. As Charles Fritz (1961, p. 653), one of the pioneers of disaster research, wrote:

> The impetus for systematic studies of human behavior in disaster developed primarily from two interrelated practical needs: first, to secure more adequate protection of the nation from the destructive and disruptive consequences of potential atomic, biological, and chemical attack; and second, to produce the maximal amount of disruption to the enemy in the event of a war.

For the most part, these early studies that focused on the impacts of disasters on individuals and families reached the same conclusion as the military's investigations during World War II. They generally concluded that survivors of natural and technological disasters in the U.S. exhibited the same kind of resilience and recuperative capacity as residents of the cities bombed in Germany and Japan.

3.3.3 Establishment of the Disaster Research Center

In the early 1960s, the focus of disaster studies shifted in an important way that would significantly shape the field's development and enhance its future relevance to the profession of emergency management. Specifically, the Disaster Research Center (DRC) was established at The Ohio State University in 1963. Rather than focusing on the impacts of disasters on individuals and families, DRC researchers devoted their attention to the organizational level of analysis. They studied a diverse array of community organizations (police and fire departments), voluntary associations (Red Cross), and other groups that responded to disasters. As described in Chapter 8, studies conducted by the DRC led to the development of a typology of organized responses to disasters that remains relevant today, particularly for emergency managers who must coordinate the activities of various community organizations both before and after disaster strikes.

3.3.4 Contemporary Research Centers

Today, several major centers devoted to the study of disasters continue to make significant contributions to the field of disaster research and the practice of emergency management (see Box 3.2). The oldest is the DRC, now located at the University of Delaware. The DRC plays a vital role in the disaster research and emergency management communities both by continuing its studies of organizational and community responses to disasters and by housing a sizable and ever-expanding resource collection for researchers and practitioners. The Natural Hazards Center at the University of Colorado also plays a significant role in the hazards and disasters arena. The center conducts a wide variety of studies, provides small grants to other researchers outside the center to conduct quick-response studies after disasters, and also maintains a resource collection. It also hosts an annual conference that brings together researchers, emergency management professionals, representatives from federal agencies, and policy makers.

Another well established facility is the Hazard Reduction and Recovery Center at Texas A&M University, where researchers devote much of their attention to land use planning and coastal issues. In recent years, numerous

---

BOX 3.2   RESEARCH CENTERS WORLDWIDE

Research centers have played a pivotal role in the development of disaster research in the United States and around the world. These centers that typically rely on funding from various governmental agencies, non-profit foundations, and in some cases corporations engage in cutting-edge research that has real-life applications for emergency managers. While some centers may devote more attention to a particular type of hazard (e.g., floods) or a specific disaster phase (e.g., response), most embrace the all-hazards view embodied in comprehensive and integrated emergency management.

Because most research centers are based at universities, they also serve as fertile training grounds for students at both undergraduate and graduate levels interested in the study of disasters and the practice of emergency management. In many cases, student researchers receive valuable benefits including financial stipends, tuition waivers, and course credits. By exposing students to the research process from beginning to end—from formulating a research question, to gathering data, to conducting analyses and writing the results—research centers actively groom the next generation of scholars.

In addition to training and mentoring students, research centers also provide valuable services to society at large. Researchers from these centers, for example, sometimes provide expert testimony to state and federal legislative bodies seeking to pass hazards- and disaster-related laws and policies. They also sometimes serve as consultants to governmental agencies conducting, for example, evaluation studies of new policies or programs. Researchers also regularly deliver presentations at conferences and workshops attended by emergency management professionals that serve as effective strategies for breaking the barrier that often exists between the two communities. Finally, in addition to publishing the results of their studies in academic journals, including those listed in Box 3.3, some research centers maintain specialized libraries and resource collections to further facilitate knowledge transfer. The most established research centers in the U.S. are:

- Disaster Research Center at the University of Delaware (www. udel.edu/DRC).
- Natural Hazards Center at the University of Colorado (www. colorado.edu/hazards).
- Hazard Reduction and Recovery Center at Texas A&M University (http://archone.tamu.edu.hrrc/).

In recent years, numerous university-based research centers have been established in various countries. A few examples include the:

- Flood Research Centre at Middlesex University (http://www. mdx.ac.uk/research/areas/geography/flood-hazard/index. aspx.).
- Centre for Risk and Community Safety at the Royal Melbourne Institute of Technology in Australia (http://www.rmit.edu.au/ browse;ID=6ccvow449s3t).
- Crisis Research Center at Leiden University in the Netherlands (http://www.socialsciences.leiden.edu/publicadministration/ research/crisis-research-center.html).
- Risk and Crisis Research Center at Mid Sweden University (http://www.miun.se/en/Research/Our-Research/ Centers-and-Institutes/RCR/).

other centers and institutes have made significant contributions to the field and broadened its horizons. Some examples are the Center for the Study of Disasters and Extreme Events at Oklahoma State University, the Hazards and Vulnerability Research Institute at the University of South Carolina, the Center for Disaster and Risk Analysis at Colorado State University, the Center for Disaster Research and Education at Millersville University, and the Stephenson Disaster Management Institute at Louisiana State University.

3.3.5 Disaster Research in an International Context

In recent years, the field of disaster research has grown into a global community of scholars, with researchers from all over the world studying the impacts of disasters on human societies. Although the field was born in the U.S., it has a much farther reach now than ever before. The globalization of disaster research has benefitted the field in several important ways.

First, researchers outside the U.S. have conducted studies of the impacts of disasters on some of the least developed countries in the world. For example, they have studied cyclones in Bangladesh, flooding and landslides in Honduras, earthquakes in India and Pakistan, and the tsunami of 2004 that devastated several Asian countries. These kinds of studies are invaluable because disasters in developing countries are much more catastrophic than those experienced in the U.S. Although events like the attacks on the World Trade Center and Hurricane Katrina are certainly tragic, they produce relatively low death tolls and constitute relatively low-impact events relative to the remaining financial resources, social capital, and physical infrastructure. Disasters in the least developed countries of the world, on the other hand, often produce death tolls in the tens or hundreds of thousands, completely devastate entire towns and villages, and severely disrupt community life for months or years. Fortunately, with the growth of disaster research around the world, we are beginning to learn much more about these kinds of catastrophic events.

Second, the increased involvement of scholars around the world has broadened horizons in disaster research. As explained above, the field has its origins in the U.S. military's concerns about how well American cities would survive in the event of an enemy attack. To address those concerns, researchers went into the field and studied events that resembled such attacks, that is, events that were unexpected, developed rapidly, and produced heavy but geographically concentrated impacts.

In contrast, researchers from various European countries including Sweden, Netherlands, and France, take a much broader view of disasters. In fact, researchers in those countries are much more likely to use the term *crisis* instead of *disaster* because it connotes a broader range of threats to society including creeping threats. Creeping threats are crises that develop over a period of months or years, and despite their obvious potential, they often go unforeseen until it is too late. European researchers also devote considerable attention to the cascading effects of crises and disasters, particularly when the threats cross international boundaries, which is increasingly common in today's world. Cascading effects are often unpredictable and unanticipated impacts on technical systems, critical infrastructure, and social institutions, such as power failures that cross state or national lines and threaten transportation, medical care and communications. Thus, in addition to studying conventional types of disasters, European researchers, with their interests in creeping threats and cascading effects, have also studied financial crises, food contamination outbreaks, and transportation system failures.

Finally, as the field of disaster research has grown to include scholars from many countries outside the U.S., researchers have increased efforts to reach, expand, and strengthen the sense of community among those working in the field. Perhaps the strongest contribution to that effort was the creation of the International Research Committee on Disasters (IRCD) in the 1980s. Although the IRCD is a research committee within the International Sociological Association (ISA), its membership includes scholars from a range of scientific disciplines and practitioners of emergency management. Its membership also includes scholars from the Americas (North, South, and Central), Europe, Asia, Russia and Australia. In addition to convening meetings every four years in conjunction with the ISA World Congress of Sociology, the IRCD publishes the *International Journal of Mass Emergencies and Disasters* (IJMED). The journal is published three times per year and serves as the flagship journal of the disaster research community. The journal contains scholarly research articles from various disciplines, book reviews, and special comments from researchers in the field. As seen in Box 3.3, in addition to *IJMED*, numerous journals now publish disaster research findings and represent valuable resources as you launch your career in emergency management.

3.4 Disaster Research as a Multidisciplinary Field

An important point to remember, which has been alluded to in the above sections, is that the field of disaster research is inherently multidisciplinary in nature. While some disciplines such as sociology and geography have older, more established, and more extensive traditions of research, numerous other disciplines have made important contributions to our understanding of disasters and how best to manage them. As described in Chapter 4, disasters are complex events that involve interactions of the natural environment,

BOX 3.3 ACADEMIC JOURNALS IN EMERGENCY MANAGEMENT

Australian Journal of Emergency Management
Disaster Management and Response
Disaster Prevention and Management
Disasters
Emergency Management Review
Environmental Hazards
International Journal of Emergency Management
International Journal of Mass Emergencies and Disasters
Journal of Contingencies and Crisis Management
Journal of Emergency Management
Journal of Homeland Security and Emergency Management
Natural Hazards Review
Prehospital and Disaster Medicine

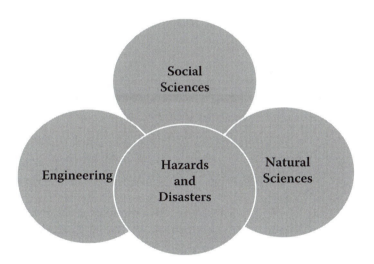

FIGURE 3.1   **Interactions of scientific disciplines.**

the built environment, technology, and human societies (Mileti 1999). Thus, as depicted in Figure 3.1, a comprehensive understanding of disasters requires insights and inputs from multiple scientific disciplines.

3.4.1 Natural Sciences

Because many of the disasters we face are weather-induced or result from the earth's processes, the role of the natural sciences in the study of disasters is obvious. For example, some geologists specialize in the study of earthquakes, volcanoes, landslides, and other hazards. With increased concern around the world about the problem of climate change and global warming, more people are aware of the work of climatologists and meteorologists who study short- and long-term variations in weather conditions and patterns. Similarly, the threats of nuclear, chemical, and biological terrorism and recent talk about expanding the use of nuclear power have enhanced the prominence and relevance of research conducted by chemists, physicists, and biologists.

3.4.2 Engineering

Of course, natural processes and events alone do not constitute disasters. Rather, such events are recognizable as disasters by the extensive physical damage they cause to the built environment. As a result, the discipline of engineering is central to our understanding of disasters and our efforts to ameliorate their effects. Some structural engineers, for example, specialize in earthquake engineering. These specialists study the wide array of building practices used around the world and attempt to assess the functionality, appropriateness, and resilience of different kinds of structures. They also devise strategies for retrofitting or strengthening older structures that are deemed more vulnerable to damage or collapse than newer buildings.

Through their studies, earthquake engineers have identified risky construction practices that led to catastrophic damages and massive death tolls following seismic events in places like Turkey, China, and Haiti. Conversely, they have studied events like the Northridge earthquake that struck near Los Angeles in 1994 in which the shaking intensity was relatively high but the death toll was significantly lower because many buildings were able to withstand the shaking.

Civil engineers specialize in critical infrastructures such as transportation systems and utility lifelines, including electricity, telecommunications, and water distribution. In addition to conducting field studies to assess the performance of these systems in actual disasters, civil engineers also use advanced computer software applications to model the performance of infrastructure systems in simulated events and devise ways for improving them. Importantly, because the performance of technical systems hinges on the actions of people using them, civil engineers often collaborate with social scientists to ensure that their computer models and simulations are based on realistic assumptions about human behavior in disaster.

Following the 1999 Marmara earthquake in Turkey, for example, the Multidisciplinary Center for Earthquake Engineering Research (MCEER) dispatched a team of engineers and social scientists to the impacted region to gather various kinds of data. Engineers on the team assessed the impacts of the earthquake on roads and bridges, gas and electric utilities, water systems, and industrial facilities. Social scientists studied the emergency responses to the event including sheltering and housing, delivery of emergency medical services, search-and-rescue activities, and the role of nongovernmental organizations (Scawthorn 2000).

3.4.3 Social Sciences

As described previously, social scientists were among the first to initiate systematic studies of disasters. With funding from the military, they conducted the first field studies in the early 1950s. In addition to answering the applied question posed by the military as to how U.S. communities would fare in the aftermath of a bombing attack, social scientists had their own theoretical and intellectual reasons for studying disasters. As Fritz (1961, p. 654) noted:

> Social scientists conducting field studies of disaster quickly discovered, however, that disasters also provide exceptionally valuable opportunities to study basic and enduring scientific problems about the nature of human nature and group life. Disasters provide realistic laboratories for testing the integration, stamina, and recuperative powers of large-scale social systems. They are the sociological equivalents of engineering experiments that test the capacity of machines to withstand extreme physical stresses.

The above statement certainly makes a compelling case for sociological studies of disasters, but it should be noted that numerous other social science disciplines have compelling reasons of their own for studying disasters. Indeed, sociologists, geographers, anthropologists, political scientists, psychologists, and economists have all made significant contributions to our understanding of disasters.

3.4.3.1 Sociology

Because sociologists were among the first to conduct the military-funded field studies in the 1950s, they developed a strong and well-established tradition of disaster research within their discipline (Quarantelli 1994). The pioneers of disaster research in sociology include Charles Fritz, who viewed disasters as laboratories, and E.L. Quarantelli and Russell R. Dynes who, along with J. Eugene Haas, co-founded the Disaster Research Center. As described earlier, the DRC continues to play a prominent role in the field today. The early work of these pioneers documented the resilience and adaptive capacity of social systems under stress and laid the foundation for future generations of sociologists interested in disasters.

As a discipline, sociology is fundamentally concerned with questions about social order and social change. Under ordinary circumstances, societies remain relatively stable, but periodically they experience major disruptions that produce widespread social changes. Indeed, the founders of sociology were primarily interested in understanding how powerful social transformations—political upheavals, industrialization, and urbanization—would impact society's ability to function and the quality of life for its members.

Although disasters may not produce those kinds of sweeping and far-reaching transformations, they are nonetheless catalytic events that dramatically impact social systems (Kreps 1995). The role of the sociologist, therefore, is to document how a social system responds to such environmental jolts. It is important to note here that sociologists are concerned with the reactions not of individuals but of collectivities (families and households, organizations, and communities). As stated earlier, sociologists who have conducted studies of those reactions can provide invaluable information to emergency managers who need realistic information on community responses to disaster. It should also be noted that although the view of disasters as jolts or disruptions has led sociologists to focus largely on the response phase, they also study the other phases: mitigation, preparedness, and recovery.

3.4.3.2 Geography

The discipline of geography also has a long and well-established tradition of hazard and disaster research. Its pioneering researcher was Gilbert F. White (see Box 10.1 in Chapter 10) who specialized in floodplain management and spent his entire career advocating sustainable adaptations to flood hazards. He also founded the Natural Hazards Research and Applications Information Center (NHRAIC, commonly called the Natural Hazards Center). As noted earlier, the center is one of the primary facilities still in existence and devoted to studying hazards and disasters. Like the pioneers in sociology, White (Hinshaw 2006) laid a strong foundation for future generations of geographers interested in hazards and disasters and his legacy of work continues to exert a profound influence on the field today.

As a discipline, geography is primarily concerned with describing the physical properties of the natural environment and explaining the relationships of human societies and their environments. Because of its dual focus, the discipline is often described as having two separate but related branches: physical geography and cultural geography. Physical geographers map land masses, elevations, and bodies of water, and their work is essential to emergency managers in terms of identifying natural hazards in their communities (Figure 3.2)

Cultural geographers, on the other hand, seek to understand the relationships human societies have to their natural environments. For example, geographers interested in the issue of social vulnerability, which will be discussed throughout this text, map the proximities of certain segments of

FIGURE 3.2 Thomas Wikle (Oklahoma State University) and Mazen Jouaneh (Infograph) set up a temporary GPS base station on a rooftop in Amman, Jordan in support of GPS data field collection. (*Source:* Photo courtesy of Thomas Wikle. With permission.)

the population, such as the poor, the elderly, and racial and ethnic minorities, to natural and technological hazards (Phillips et al. 2010; Heinz Center 2002). Cultural geographers have also studied the ways in which human societies develop attachments to places because of their scenic beauty, resource abundance, or long-standing traditions even when those places are hazardous (Cutter 2001). This line of research is highly relevant to the practice of emergency management. In recent years, community relocation has been discussed as a way of adjusting to hazards and reducing disaster impacts. In theory it sounds simple and logical to just move people out of harm's way. However, as both geographers and sociologists who have conducted research on these issues have found, in practice it is very complicated and often controversial, largely because even in hazardous areas people form deep attachments to places and strong feelings of collective identity and community solidarity (Handmer 1985).

3.4.3.3 Anthropology

Like geography, anthropology is also divided into two branches: physical and cultural. Physical anthropologists are basically interested in tracing the historical roots of human life and studying human evolution. They use fossils, skeletal remains, and other data to better understand the distribution and movements of human populations throughout history. Cultural anthropologists are interested in studying the numerous and varied cultures around the world and throughout human history. They attempt to understand what different societies value most and the different norms and taboos that regulate mate selection, family and kinship patterns, and other critical aspects of human social life. Cultural anthropologists also seek to understand how societies build cultural protections to cope with hazards in their environments and how cultural beliefs and practices change after disasters (see Hoffman and Oliver-Smith 2002; Oliver-Smith and Hoffman 1999).

The work of these anthropologists is very similar to and compatible with that of sociologists and cultural geographers, particularly those who study human attachments to places, and it too is highly relevant to the field of emergency management. Perhaps the most important insight emergency managers can gain from anthropology is the need to respect and understand the diversity of cultures in our communities and the different ways in which people think about and cope with risks, hazards, and disasters.

3.4.3.4 Political Science

Although the discipline of political science is broad and diverse, one of its central aims is to describe and better understand the law and related policy-making processes. Political scientists conduct research on the agenda setting process, whereby competing interest groups attempt to frame policy debates in particular ways and mobilize support for their causes. They also study the process by which proposals are debated and modified and the impacts of lobbying and political compromises. Finally, an important area of political science is devoted to studying the policy implementation process and identifying barriers to effective implementation. Related to this last point, the field of public administration, which at some colleges and universities is a complete department and at others is housed within political science departments, examines the role of public sector bureaucracies in translating laws and policies into practice and identifies structures and processes of bureaucracies that facilitate or impede their effective and efficient functioning.

In the area of hazard and disaster research, several scholars from political science and public administration have made significant contributions to our knowledge of the politics of disasters and how to manage them more effectively (Birkland 2007; Sylves 2008; Olson 2000; Platt 1999). William Waugh (2000) has written extensively about the all-hazards approach to emergency management and the relevance of the four phases of disaster to understanding and managing natural disasters and terrorist events. However, he has also suggested that structural changes at the federal level after the attacks of September 11, 2001—namely, the creation of the Department of Homeland Security and the placement of FEMA under its umbrella resulted in a narrow focus on terrorism that undermined the all-hazards approach and weakened our nation's capacity to respond to other threats (Waugh 2006).

Thomas Birkland has described disasters as focusing events that can thrust hazard mitigation issues onto the public policy agenda and open a window of opportunity for proponents of such policies to mobilize broad-based support among lawmakers and the public at large for their proposals (Birkland 1997).

3.4.3.5 Psychology

As a discipline, psychology is primarily concerned with understanding the thoughts and actions of individuals. Psychology is similar to sociology in that it recognizes that groups can influence how individuals think, act, and feel, but ultimately the individual per se is the primary focus of psychological research. Perhaps the best way to contrast the two disciplines is to say that psychology is a *micro-level* perspective that prioritizes the individual and sociology is a *macro-level* approach that emphasizes collectivities of people. Psychology is a very broad discipline including topics such as developing personality inventories, creating scales and indices to assess psychiatric and behavioral disorders, examining peer influence on behavior, studying the link between violent media and aggressive behavior, and many others.

In the field of disaster research, psychologists have made important contributions. For example, they have studied the ways individuals perceive risks and make decisions about accepting, avoiding, or mitigating them (Norris et al. 2002a; 2002b). They also have conducted extensive research on post-traumatic stress disorder (PTSD) among children, emergency workers, and others in the contexts of natural disasters and terrorist attacks (North et al. 2002; Pfefferbaum, Call, and Sconzo 1999; Jenkins 1998). As with the other social sciences, emergency managers can benefit immensely from research conducted by psychologists. For example, risk perception research can offer guidance on how to craft more effective disaster warning messages that will have the greatest impacts on individuals and motivate them to take protective actions. PTSD research can sensitize emergency managers to the special needs of children and even first responders and provide guidance on how best to address those needs.

3.4.3.6 Economics

Economics aims to describe the various ways societies around the world produce, distribute, and consume goods and services. The discipline is divided into micro and macro branches. Micro-economics focuses largely on consumer behavior, including identifying factors that affect consumer confidence and willingness to spend or invest. Macro-economics focuses on larger issues of resource availability, the viability and well-being of different sectors of the economy (manufacturing, financial services, retail, etc.), and global economic issues (trade surpluses and deficits, monetary exchange rates, etc.).

Related to hazards and disasters, economists have conducted extensive research on the financial costs of natural disasters (Dacy and Kunreuther

1969). Interestingly, just as sociologists have found social systems to be resilient in the face of disaster, researchers have found that economies are also largely capable of absorbing the financial impacts of disasters (Wright et al. 1979). Although the economic consequences of disasters may appear devastating at the local level, their impacts are far less severe at the regional, national, and international levels. Furthermore, as discussed in Chapter 11, some businesses, such as construction firms, benefit from the boom that often follows a disaster as a community rebuilds and starts the recovery process. As discussed in Chapter 9, this kind of knowledge can be very beneficial to you as an emergency manager in terms of developing an effective recovery plan that identifies and prioritizes economic needs and strategically targets aid and relief programs.

3.5 Types of Research

Having discussed the importance and relevance of disaster research to emergency management, its historical origins, and its multidisciplinary nature, we now turn to a more in-depth discussion of how research is actually conducted. This discussion will be beneficial to you by providing guidance on how to conduct your own research and also give you a basis upon which to evaluate the quality and usefulness of research conducted by others. Before describing the specific methods typically used to gather data on disasters, we will discuss the different types of research.

3.5.1 Basic and Applied Research

On a general level, research can be characterized as basic or applied. *Basic research* is conducted to satisfy intellectual curiosity, explore previously uninvestigated topics, or address core theoretical debates in a discipline. While the results of basic research may not have immediate applicability to solving social or technical problems faced by society, it is possible that over time this kind of research will change the way scientists think about an issue, stimulate new lines of inquiry, and ultimately produce results that can be translated into practical solutions to problems. *Applied research*, on the other hand, begins with a specific problem identified by a user community and seeks to provide practical, data-based guidance for solving the problem. For example, evaluation studies are often conducted in various settings to assess the effectiveness of new policies, programs, or technologies (see Ritchie and MacDonald 2010).

Both types of research are common in the field of disaster research. As Fritz (1961) pointed out (cited earlier in this chapter), since its inception the field has sought to answer both basic and applied questions. Basic disaster research seeks to better understand how social systems respond to disruptions and refine theories about how society works. A good example of such research is Gary Kreps' work to develop a theory of organizations (Kreps 1989). Like Fritz, he views disasters as strategic sites for answering basic questions about society and sees organizations as central elements of the social structure. He has attempted to conceptually isolate the core properties of organizations and empirically document the timing and sequencing of those properties. Kreps' work may sound highly theoretical and abstract at first, but it has important implications for maximizing the efficiency and effectiveness of organizations responding to disasters.

Disaster researchers are perhaps best known for their applied research, which in some form or fashion, seeks to improve some aspect of society's readiness for, response to, or recovery from disasters. For example, they have conducted extensive research on preparedness levels, warning systems, evacuation behavior, inter-governmental coordination, and many other topics. They have also performed evaluation studies of disaster-related programs such as FEMA's Project Impact, a community-based mitigation program designed to enhance disaster resilience in the U.S. (Wachtendorf 2001; Wachtendorf and Kompanik 2000).

3.5.2 Primary and Secondary Research

Whether you are conducting a study of your own or reading research done by someone else, you will find two main sources of data: primary and secondary. *Primary research* involves the collection of original data obtained through surveys, interviews, or observations to answer a basic or applied research question. As discussed in the next section, there are various ways in which those data can be collected, but the important point is that primary research is based on new data. *Secondary research* is based on data that already exist and were gathered by someone else. As an emergency manager, you will find numerous sources of secondary data useful. For example, the U.S. Census Bureau maintains massive amounts of data that you can use to study the demographics of your community. The data cover age distribution, racial composition, income and education levels, home ownership rates, and many other characteristics. As will be seen in Chapter 6, these factors play a significant role in determining how prepared households and communities are for disasters.

3.5.3 Cross-Sectional and Longitudinal Research

Another issue to consider in conducting or reading research is the time frame over which information used in the study was or will be collected. *Cross-sectional research* is based on data gathered at one point in time and is often described as offering a snapshot of reality at a particular time. In cross-sectional research, the goal is to present a picture of how things look at the time of data collection, not predict how they might look in the future. *Longitudinal research*, on the other hand, involves prolonged data collection over time.

The goal of this kind of research is to track changes over time. As an emergency manager, you will find both approaches useful. For example, if you need a benchmark of how prepared your community currently is for a disaster, a cross-sectional study would be fine. However, if your community has recently been struck by a disaster and you want to monitor its recovery over time to see whether conditions are improving or getting worse, a longitudinal approach would be more appropriate.

3.5.4 Individual and Aggregate Research

When gathering data on disasters or any topic for that matter, you must decide the level at which you need information. Are you seeking to understand something about individuals or larger social groupings such as households or organizations? *Individual-level research* seeks to describe and explain the attitudes and behaviors of individuals. For example, if you are interested in risk perception levels of people living near a nuclear power plant, you must determine how likely they think an accident is.

If you want to know whether people in your community are suffering negative psychological consequences from a recent disaster or other community emergency, you must ask them about their feelings and experiences with the event. If, on the other hand, you want to know how well the police and fire departments communicated while responding to a recent emergency in your community, you will need *aggregate-level research* to describe and explain characteristics of collectivities, including households, organizations, communities, or entire societies.

Since disasters are large-scale events that are recognizable primarily by their impacts on collectivities, much of the research you conduct or read will be based on aggregate-level data. It is important to note, however, that even if we are studying a larger social grouping, such as a fire department, we often must collect information from individuals in the department. As a result, there is an important distinction to be made between respondents and informants in our studies. *Respondents* are people from whom we gather specific information to understand their thoughts, feelings, or behaviors. *Informants*, on the other hand, provide general information about a larger group to which they belong, whether a family or household, neighborhood association, informal search-and-rescue crew, police department, or other collectivity.

The distinction between respondents and informants is vitally important. For example, you may be involved in conducting an after-action study to assess how local governmental agencies performed while responding to an event in your community. In doing so, you would likely collect information from directors of the various departments and divisions. When it comes time to analyze the data, you will need to know whether department heads provided information on their own activities or the actions carried out by the unit as a whole.

3.5.5 Quantitative and Qualitative Research

Another important distinction you will encounter in conducting your own studies or reading works by others is between quantitative and qualitative research. At the most basic level, *quantitative research* is the application of mathematical principles and statistical analyses to the study of social life. Stated another way, quantitative studies seek to describe and explain variation in the numeric properties of some aspect of social life. For example, researchers have developed elaborate scales and indices to precisely measure and quantify levels of risk perception and disaster preparedness. They also employ sophisticated statistical techniques to identify factors that contribute to higher or lower levels of these phenomena (Bourque, Shoaf and Nguyen 2002).

Qualitative research, on the other hand, seeks to describe and explain the processes involved in some aspect of social life. Whereas quantitative research largely assumes that social life is patterned and predictable, qualitative research assumes that reality is variable, fluid, and less predictable.

While both quantitative and qualitative studies are common in disaster research, qualitative methods are particularly useful in the early aftermath of a disaster. During that period, there is a great deal of ambiguity and a tremendous amount of activity, much of which is unplanned and improvised, as survivors, first responders, governmental agencies, and voluntary organizations converge on a scene and initiate a response. As Phillips (2002) points out, because qualitative methods focus on social processes and afford the researcher flexibility, they are well suited for the post-disaster environment. Indeed, there is a long tradition of quick-response field studies in disaster research in which researchers are dispatched to the site of a disaster as quickly as possible after impact to gather valuable data that might otherwise perish (Quarantelli 2002; Michaels 2003).

3.6 Research Methods and the Phases of Disaster

There are numerous ways in which researchers have gathered data on disasters, and knowledge of those methods may help you as an emergency manager to measure preparedness levels in your community, monitor the performance of local agencies and departments in responding to a disaster, gauge short- and long-term recovery after a disaster, and assess community support for a proposed mitigation program or policy. Each of the following methods is appropriate for gathering data on all four phases of a disaster, but, as described below, some approaches have been used more than others in particular phases.

In collecting information about disasters, the most important consideration is to select a methodology that will appropriately and adequately provide data on the question or questions you pose. Researchers, analysts, and other professionals certainly develop clear preferences for methods of gathering data. For example, some people are quantitatively inclined and feel best if they can see statistics on the magnitude of a problem. Others are more visually inclined and prefer to see maps and other spatial or visual representations of an issue. Still others are more qualitatively oriented and want to gain in-depth understandings of disasters from the perspective of those experiencing them. Fortunately, researchers, emergency managers, and others interested in gathering disaster data have a broad and diverse range of tools available for such purposes. Indeed, probably the best way of gathering data on any social phenomenon is through *triangulation*—the use of multiple methodologies.

3.6.1 Surveys

If you are interested in learning about a relatively large population of people, the survey is an appropriate choice. Surveys involve the administration of a standardized questionnaire to a sample of people to better understand perceptions, attitudes, opinions, preferences, and behaviors prevalent in a larger population. The most common approaches to administering surveys are by telephone, mail, face-to-face meetings, and increasingly via the Internet. Questions on surveys are usually closed-ended; respondents are forced to select one response option for each question. These kinds of questions are preferred in survey research because they are easier to quantify and subject to statistical analyses.

In designing a survey questionnaire, it is important to develop questions that are reliable and valid. *Reliability* is best described as a measure of consistency. In other words, reliable questions should elicit common responses in repeated administrations of a survey instrument. In reality, of course, a survey is administered only once to respondents, so it is important to spend a lot of time and effort crafting good questions. Pilot testing of surveys usually results in clear wording that respondents can understand and thus select responses that best fit their perceptions.

Validity is best described as a measure of accuracy. Valid questions should elicit accurate information on the phenomena they seek to address. If you are interested, for example, in understanding people's perceptions of the likelihood of a terrorist attack in their community, you do not want to ask questions that instead measure their fear of terrorism. The two concepts may be similar, but they are not the same. Indeed, to illustrate how they are actually two separate (albeit related) concepts, consider the hypothesis that those with higher levels of fear of terrorism will also perceive a greater likelihood of an attack.

Importantly, surveys typically involve *random sampling* techniques, whereby every person in the study population has an equal chance of being asked to participate. This ensures *representativeness* of a sample: the demographic, attitudinal, and behavioral characteristics of the people who complete the questionnaire should closely resemble those of others in the population who were not selected for participation. Thus, findings from properly conducted surveys are *generalizable*: statistics generated from the sample of study participants can be used to estimate and make projections about the attitudes and behaviors of others in the larger population. For example, national political polls that project how tens of millions of people will likely vote in an election are typically based on samples of approximately 1,000 respondents. That is the strength and power of applying mathematical principles and theorems to the study of social life.

Surveys have been used extensively in disaster research to study a wide variety of topics. In terms of *preparedness*, for example, researchers have conducted surveys to assess the degree to which households and organizations have undertaken various precautionary measures (Chapter 6) and identify factors such as household income or organizational size that contribute to higher or lower levels of preparedness. Researchers have also used surveys to study the *response* phase, looking at such issues as the timing of decisions to evacuate and factors such as family size and previous disaster experience that affect those decisions. Surveys have also been used to study the short- and long-term *recovery* of households and businesses. Respondents to these surveys are typically asked to compare their current circumstances to the period just before a disaster struck. They may also be asked to indicate types of recovery assistance they have used and rate the usefulness of the assistance. Finally, in terms of *mitigation*, researchers have used surveys to assess willingness to pay for community safety measures and gauge public support for the siting of hazardous or controversial facilities.

3.6.2 Interviews

In some cases you may be less interested in making generalizations about a very large population and more interested in the experiences of a smaller, more select group of people or organizations. In those cases, you may find interviewing a more appropriate technique for gathering information than surveys. *Interviews* are focused conversations conducted to gain in-depth understanding of the views and experiences of respondents (Rubin and Rubin 2005). Although interviews are similar to surveys in that they seek to obtain respondent answers to particular questions, they are different in several important ways.

First, while surveys ask standardized questions of all respondents, interviews are typically conducted with the assistance of an interview guide. Interview guides provide researchers with a list of topics to cover and some topical questions to ask but allow flexibility in the order in which they are covered. In contrast to the closed-ended questions common in surveys, interviews typically rely on open-ended questions designed to elicit thoughtful, detailed, and in-depth responses from interview subjects. For example, you might ask the head of a local agency or department, "What are the most important challenges your agency has faced in the days since the disaster?" In depth interviewing allows you to follow the thread of a conversation that may lead in a fruitful direction as interview subjects add depth and breadth to the topic you are studying. You may also uncover unexpected insights that yield greater understanding. These emergent pieces of data often generate productive lines of inquiry for a current study and future direction.

Second, instead of random sampling techniques, interview studies typically employ a more purposive approach. *Purposive sampling* involves selecting respondents to participate based on the relevance of their knowledge and experiences to the objectives of the study. For example, if you are interested in understanding how a recent disaster impacted those with special needs in your community, a large-scale survey may not be necessary. Instead, you might conduct interviews at nursing homes, local shelters, or other appropriate places. In addition to beginning with a purposive approach, interview studies often proceed through the use of snowball sampling. *Snowball sampling* is an approach to recruiting additional participants to a study by getting recommendations from past respondents. For example, you might interview the director of public works about that department's role in responding to a recent disaster and he or she may recommend that you talk to specific people in the department to gain more detail. For disaster researchers, it may also be necessary to interview people in specific spatial zones such as the immediate impact area, outer areas, and non-affected areas. Imagine, for example, being able to track the flow of resources into an area from the outside to the inside as a way to study donations management. Time sampling also matters with disasters: the first twenty minutes after impact certainly differ from the next twenty hours or twenty days (Killian 2002). Fatality management studies, for example, benefit from time sampling to determine how various disasters impact the ability to conduct search and rescue operations over time.

Finally, while a major objective of survey research is to generalize findings from a sample of respondents to a much larger population, interview studies and qualitative approaches to research generally follow a different approach (Lincoln and Guba 1985). Qualitative research assumes that social reality, rather than being patterned and predictable, is fluid and dynamic, and while different social settings may be similar, they will always exhibit important differences. Instead of generalizability, which assumes that patterns identified among a relatively small sample of people can be inferred to exist in a much larger population, qualitative researchers focus instead upon transferability. *Transferability* is the degree to which insights gained from studying one social setting or group of people are applicable to others. In emergency management, transferability is a very useful concept. While disasters may create unique challenges for communities impacted by them, they also produce many of the same problems. Thus, by studying how one community dealt with those problems, we can learn valuable lessons that may not be directly generalizable to another community but are certainly transferable.

Like surveys, interviewing is a versatile and widely used tool for gathering data on disasters in all four phases. In terms of *preparedness*, interviews can help us gain a more holistic understanding of the degree to which communities as a whole are ready for disasters. Surveys and the preparedness checklists they typically contain give us a good look at how prepared households and organizations are for disasters, but they do not necessarily capture interactions—or the lack thereof—between various organizations in the community and the degree to which they coordinate their planning and preparedness efforts. Interviews with key officials in a community are much more effective at tapping into those dynamics.

Interviews have proven to be particularly useful in both the *response* and *recovery* phases. Qualitative research can capture social processes as they unfold, and, because of that emphasis, interviews are well suited for gaining a deeper understanding of response and recovery dynamics. Through in-depth interviews with those affected by disasters, we can learn a great deal about their activities in responding to a disaster and the challenges they faced in recovering.

Finally, interviews can also be useful for gathering information about *mitigation*. For example, in their systematic evaluation of FEMA's Project Impact, researchers at the DRC conducted focus group interviews with key participants from select communities across the country to assess the challenges involved in building effective public-private partnerships to mitigate against disasters (Wachtendorf 2001).

3.6.3 Observations

Observational research involves the systematic identification of patterns and trends in a social setting. It is an invaluable tool for disaster researchers because it offers a holistic view of activities in a post-disaster environment. While researchers often use observations in conjunction with interviews to gain a more comprehensive understanding of disasters, in some cases they must rely heavily on observations because respondents may not be readily available for interviews or a language barrier may exist. There are several important issues to consider when conducting observational research. First, of course, is deciding what to observe. Every social setting involves a tremendous amount of activity, even when it appears that nothing meaningful is happening. After a disaster, when researchers may feel overwhelmed and bombarded with information, they must make critical decisions about focusing their observations (Spradley 1980).

Second, you must devise an effective strategy for recording observations. With so much activity over a relatively wide area, it is not realistic to think after a disaster that you will be able to carry your laptop computer everywhere and enter observations directly. More often researchers make notes of their observations throughout the day and enter them into a computer in more elaborate form later. *Visual methods* such as photographs and video recordings can supplement observations or serve as stand-alone techniques. In one unique study, researchers gave cameras to shelter residents to record their personal experiences, thus uncovering valuable lessons for shelter managers (Pike, Phillips and Reeves 2006).

Finally, researchers must make decisions about their degree of involvement in a social setting. *Participant observation* involves researchers becoming active members, at least to a degree, of the setting or group studied. *Participatory action research* involves researchers and people in the setting who work together to improve some aspect of social life. For example, in a classic disaster study, Taylor, Zurcher, and Key (1970) worked alongside others in a community struck by a tornado, all the while making observations about the group's activities, and later wrote a book about the experience. *Non-participant observation* involves maintaining a distance from the activities observed to minimize the researcher's role in and impact on a group or setting studied. In this approach, the researcher attempts to act as a "fly on the wall" by quietly observing the group or setting. In most cases, researchers find themselves playing a role between full-fledged participant and non-participant observer.

As with interviewing, observational research is a useful tool for capturing dynamic social processes as they unfold. Thus, observational methods are most often used for gathering data during the *response* and *recovery* periods. During those phases, things happen very quickly. If events are not thoroughly documented "on the spot," valuable information will perish. By conducting systematic observations and recording them in notes, photographs, or videos, we can more accurately reconstruct what happened during the response phase and chart the progress of recovery.

In the immediate aftermath of a disaster, with so much happening in a relatively short and condensed time frame, the challenge for those interested in gathering systematic information is often deciding what exactly to observe. It is impossible, of course, to observe everything, so you have to determine the focus of your observations on particular topics or issues. For example, if you are seeking to improve and strengthen communications among various city departments during emergencies and disasters, you might observe and document interactions of departmental representatives at the emergency operations center when it is activated. In most cases, you will have multiple reasons for making observations, so a checklist of topics or issues upon which to focus may be helpful. In addition to the response and recovery phases, observation can also be a useful tool for gathering information about *preparedness*. Observations are often used, for example, in disaster drills and exercises to document what works and does not work and identify areas for improvement in the event of an actual disaster.

3.6.4 Archives

Archival information is another valuable source of data for those wanting to learn more about the impacts of disasters on communities (Wenger 1989). *Archives* are documents that attest to or provide an account of historical happenings. As society has grown in complexity and developed new technologies for producing, recording, and storing information, the amount of archival information available has vastly expanded. Indeed, the documents of life, as Plummer (2001) refers to archives, abound and are literally all around us.

Archival sources of data include newspapers, organizational memos, after-action reports, minutes of meetings, transcripts of congressional testimony, and other useful information. The major advantages of using these kinds of data are that they are plentiful, often easily accessible, and usually inexpensive to obtain. Disadvantages are that archival collections may be scattered or disorganized, data storage and retrieval systems become outdated, documents are sometimes illegible, and, in some cases, items may have been destroyed intentionally.

Many studies in the field of disaster research are based on archival data. For example, Kreps and his colleagues conducted extensive research on archives maintained by the DRC to study organizational dynamics in the aftermaths of disasters (Kreps 1989). Similarly, Mendonça and his colleagues (2007) used archival data from the 1995 bombing of the Murrah Federal Building in Oklahoma City and the 2001 attacks on the World Trade Center to study improvisation among first responders to disasters, a topic that will be discussed in depth in Chapter 8.

Archival research may require considerable detective work as the effort may require you to move from public archives into those maintained privately by individuals and organizations. Documents present some challenges such as selective deposit by their creators (Webb et al. 1999), but they also generate useful insights, supplement other techniques, and allow a comparison of events on paper with realities, for example, the differences between a written response plan and an actual response effort.

Archives can provide useful information about the various phases of a disaster. Indeed, in launching a comprehensive study of a community and its experience with a disaster, the best place to start is often the local library. In terms of *preparedness*, published reports of special investigative commissions like those formed after September 11, 2001 and Hurricane Katrina can be valuable sources of information for understanding the degree to which various organizations were aware of potential threats and whether or not they took the threats seriously. A good example of the usefulness of these kinds of documents is a classic study by Barry Turner (1976) in which he argued that organizations often suffer from a "failure of foresight" by failing to think creatively and prepare for exigencies that in hindsight should have been foreseeable.

Although many *response* activities are unplanned, unscripted, and even undocumented, organizations nevertheless produce plenty of reports, memos, agendas, meeting minutes, and other documents that can be very useful. Archival data such as newspaper articles are well suited for studying *recovery* processes, particularly over the long term. Newspaper articles and other archives can also be helpful for gathering information about *mitigation*. Some researchers have examined challenges such as inter-group conflicts associated with community relocation—a strategy sometimes used in cases of severe environmental contamination (Shriver and Kennedy 2005). While these studies typically involve interviews and observations, they also tend to rely heavily on archival sources.

3.6.5 Spatial Tools

Recent advances in technology have dramatically expanded and enhanced our ability to gather massive amounts of data on all kinds of topics including disaster and emergency management. Laptop computers and other portable devices, for example, make it much easier for researchers to process information including observation notes and interview transcripts from the field. Digital voice recorders are much smaller and less obtrusive than old tape recorders and reel-to-reel machines that researchers carried into the field. Improved statistical software packages allow massive amounts of data such as those gathered from surveys to be analyzed rapidly and in increasingly sophisticated ways. All these advances have made the research enterprise much more efficient and far less daunting than it used to be.

In disaster research, perhaps the most important technological developments with the greatest potential for advancing the field are those designed to enhance spatial data collection and analysis. Geographical information systems (GISs) are probably the most common and widely used spatial applications in the hazards and disaster area (Dash 2002; Thomas, Ertuğay, and Kemeç 2006). These programs allow researchers to attach spatial coordinates to various sources of data, all of which can then be visually depicted on maps. With appropriate GIS software, users can overlay all kinds of information on top of their geo-coded data to show roads and bridges, waterways, and environmental hazards. In addition to GIS, researchers now have access to satellite imaging and remote sensing technologies that can be very useful after a disaster.

Spatial tools are becoming much more prevalent in the field of disaster research and as technologies continue to improve, it is likely that these tools will become even more common in the future. For researchers and emergency managers, these tools have many possible applications during the four phases of a disaster. To ensure *preparedness*, for example, maps locating hospitals, schools, nursing homes, hazardous facilities, and other sites can be produced and distributed. Additionally, survey data on levels of household preparedness could be geo-coded and mapped to provide emergency managers with snapshots of preparedness levels in their communities.

Researchers have also used GIS to identify and visually depict vulnerable populations in communities across the U.S.—those with high concentrations of poverty and high percentages of minority residents and those in close proximity to natural and technological hazards (Cutter 2001). GIS and remote sensing tools have also proven useful in the *response* phase, allowing researchers to rapidly, efficiently, and accurately conduct damage assessments based on visual displays of areas with high concentrations of damage. These tools can be valuable resources for emergency managers who need to prioritize response activities (Eguchi et al. 2000).

Spatial data collected during the response phase can serve as baseline data for assessing short- and long-term *recovery* in a community. As new maps and images are produced, they can be juxtaposed with earlier ones, allowing users to visually track recovery over time. Imagine, for example, the ability to spatially depict volunteer activities after a catastrophic event to allow better preparation for the next event (Greiner and Wikle 2008). As for *mitigation*, the maps used in the preparedness phase to identify hazardous places and vulnerable populations can and ideally would be used by city commissions, planning and zoning departments, and other public officials to make informed land use decisions that minimize future risks to their communities.

3.7 Ethics and Challenges of Disaster Research

An important consideration in all fields of research is ethics. For disaster researchers, ethical concerns are perhaps more salient than in other fields because they deal with events and circumstances that entail enormous human suffering. To some, Fritz's (1961) early characterization of disasters as "laboratories" for studying basic human social processes may seem callous and exploitative. Yet, if we want to enhance the safety of society, it is imperative that we study these tragic events to learn lessons from them that can be applied to the future. In other words, we hope that our research will produce tangible benefits to society in general and those who participate in our research in particular.

3.7.1 Research Ethics

While there are no definitive, universal standards of ethics against which to judge science and research, the U.S. government has provided helpful guidelines (Babbie 2011). The primary goal of these guidelines is to provide adequate protections to human subjects of research to minimize the risk of adverse effects—psychological, emotional, financial, or social—from their participation.

The first ethical guideline is *respect for persons.* To show appropriate respect for persons, researchers must demonstrate that subjects voluntarily consented to participate, that is, they were not tricked, misled, or coerced. Subjects must be informed of their right to withdraw their participation at any time without consequence; and researchers must take adequate measures to protect the confidentiality of information provided by subjects.

Benefits and risks constitute the second ethical guideline cited in federal policies governing research. Researchers must demonstrate that the benefits of the research to subjects, society, or the scientific community outweigh the potential risks to subjects. While the risks to subjects from social science research are far less consequential than the risks from research on new medicines or experimental treatment regimes, we need to be mindful of and sensitive to the experiences of those who participate in our research.

The final ethical consideration is *justice.* This essentially means that both the risks and benefits of research should be distributed fairly in society. For example, it would be considered unjust if the only people who participated in test studies of new medicines were prison inmates or poor people in public hospitals. Similarly, it would be unjust if the new medicines that came from those studies were not made widely available but instead were reserved for a select group of fortunate or prominent people.

It is important to note that not all research involves the participation of human subjects. For example, as described in the previous section, archival and spatial data can be gathered without interactions with people. In many cases, however, we are required to interact with people to gather the information we need. For researchers at universities, like many of those whose work is cited throughout this book, that means getting approval for a study before going into the field. That approval comes from an institutional review board (IRB). IRBs are committees that exist at all universities that receive federal support for research. The job of an IRB is to review research proposals submitted by faculty researchers to ensure that they have provided adequate protections to their subjects based on the ethical guidelines described previously.

3.7.2 Research Challenges

In addition to providing adequate human subject protection, disaster researchers face other challenges in conducting studies. Of course, all research can be difficult, but the challenges of disaster research seem particularly pronounced. For example, disaster researchers face basic *logistical challenges* not present in other types of research. They must travel to disaster-stricken communities on very short notice, gain IRB approval for the research before they leave, find available and affordable lodging, and navigate debris-filled, barricaded communities upon arrival.

Researchers in all fields must find study participants and figure out ways to deal with those who decline participation. For disaster researchers, the problem of *respondent availability and accessibility* can be particularly pronounced. In studies aimed at understanding the impacts of disasters on ordinary citizens, researchers may have to travel to surrounding communities to track down survivors or visit with them in shelters or temporary "tent cities." Similarly, when researchers want to study public officials and their activities after a disaster (a common focus of research) they may find access very difficult for several reasons. First, it is possible or even likely that instead of working from their normal offices, the relevant public officials will work from an alternative temporary location such as an EOC or somewhere else in the community. Second, even when we locate such officials, it may be difficult for them to stop what they are doing and find time to talk with researchers. It is important, therefore, for researchers to be flexible and accommodating in the field.

In recent years a new phenomenon has made it more difficult for researchers to access potential respondents. Indeed, the events of September 11, 2001 led to a noticeable change in post-disaster environments. Specifically, in the era of concern about homeland security, disaster sites are increasingly treated like crime scenes. As a result, law enforcement agencies have ramped up their efforts to restrict access to disaster-stricken communities and public officials appear less willing to talk to researchers, reporters, and the public at large about their activities. This is a disturbing trend because, as stated previously, a major goal of research is to learn lessons from past disasters to prevent mistakes in the future. If officials are unwilling to talk publicly about their activities including their mistakes, the prospects for uncovering lessons learned are severely diminished.

Another prominent challenge in disaster research is dealing with *emotions and human suffering*. Disasters are tragic events. Although as researchers we approach them with a certain degree of scientific objectivity and emotional distance, the devastation caused by disasters cannot be totally ignored. Researchers in the field see the physical damage, social disruption, and human suffering caused by disasters. They also hear stories, both heroic and tragic, from respondents about what happened and can experience feelings of sadness, sympathy, and strong desires to help those suffering. One way of managing those feelings is to recognize the value of their own work. As stated previously, their studies may not produce immediate, tangible benefits to the community, but over time studies of disasters will contribute to a safer future.

3.8 Summary

The term *emergency management* conjures up many images, but for most people scientific research is probably not what comes to mind when thinking about the profession. Yet, as we have seen in this chapter, the profession of emergency management and the field of disaster research have much in common, including a desire to improve society's ability prepare for, respond to, recover from, and mitigate against future disasters. As a future emergency manager, you will benefit from understanding the research methods described in this chapter and the research-based findings discussed throughout this book.

Whether you are interested in conducting a study of your own or finding out what others have already learned about a topic, this chapter provides a strong foundation to help you move forward. You are now familiar with the various methodological tools available for answering all kinds of disaster- and emergency management-related questions: How prepared are households and businesses in my community for a future disaster? What kinds of problems did agencies and departments in my community confront in responding to a past disaster? What is the status of my community's recovery from a past disaster as a whole, for businesses, and for certain groups in the population? And, finally, how supportive are people in my community of a newly proposed mitigation measure?

Throughout your career, you will gain valuable knowledge through first-hand encounters with disasters. That kind of hands-on experience is essential to your professional development and will serve as a tremendous confidence builder. As we discussed in this chapter, there are many other sources of knowledge including research on which you can and should draw. Regardless of profession, whether practicing medicine or managing emergencies, experience matters, but it also important to keep up with research and stay abreast of the latest developments in the field.

Discussion Questions

1. Why is scientific research valuable to the practice of emergency management? What are some of the benefits to understanding science and research? How does a research-based perspective on disasters differ from the way disasters are often characterized on television news?

2. Imagine your community has launched a new educational campaign to promote increased levels of preparedness among citizens. How would you evaluate the effectiveness of the campaign? What kinds of research tools would you use?

3. Locate and read a research article on a topic of interest to you published in one of the academic journals listed in Box 3.3. What was the primary research question? How did the researcher(s) gather data to answer the question? Do you agree with the findings? How could the research have been improved?

4. Why did the U.S. military begin funding researchers to study disasters in the 1950s? What kinds of questions did the military want answered? What answers have researchers provided over the years?

5. What are the primary ethical guidelines for conducting research involving human subjects? Are there any special considerations for studying people impacted by disasters? How can we best protect the rights of human subjects?

References

Babbie, Earl. 2011. *The Basics of Social Research*. Belmont, CA:Thomson Wadsworth.

Birkland, Thomas A. 1997. *After Disaster: Agenda Setting, Public Policy and Focusing Events*. Washington, D.C.: Georgetown University Press.

Birkland, Thomas A. 2007. *Lessons of Disaster: Policy Change after Catastrophic Disasters*. Washington, D.C.: Georgetown.

Bourque, Linda B., Kimberley I. Shoaf, and Loc H. Nguyen. 2002. "Survey Research." Pp. 157–193 in *Methods of Disaster Research*, (Robert A. Stallings, ed.). Philadelphia, PA: Xlibris/International Research Committee on Disasters.

Cutter, Susan L. 2001. ed. *American Hazardscapes: The Regionalization of Hazards and Disasters*. Washington, D.C.: Joseph Henry Press.

Dacy, Douglas C. and Howard Kunreuther. 1969. *The Economics of Natural Disasters*. New York: The Free Press.

Dash, Nicole. 2002. "The Use of Geographic Information Systems in Disaster Research." Pp. 320–333 in *Methods of Disaster Research*, (Robert A. Stallings, ed.). Philadelphia, PA: XLibris/International Research Committee on Disasters.

Eguchi, Ronald, Charles Huyck, Bijan Houshmand, Babak Mansouri, Masanobu Shinozuka, Fumio Yamazaki, Masashi Matsuoka, and Suha Ülgen. 2000. "The Marmara Earthquake: A View from Space." Pp. 151–169 in *The Marmara, Turkey Earthquake of August 17, 1999: Reconnaissance Report*, ed. Charles Scawthorn. Buffalo, NY: Multidisciplinary Center for Earthquake Engineering Research.

Fritz, Charles E. 1961. "Disaster." Pp. 651–694 in *Contemporary Social Problems*, (Robert K. Merton and Robert A. Nisbet, eds.). New York: Harcourt, Brace and World, Inc.

Greiner, Alyson L. and Wikle, Thomas A. 2008. "Episodic Volunteerism after Hurricane Katrina: Insights from Pass Christian, Mississippi." *International Journal of Volunteer Administration*, Volume 25/3: pp 14–25.

Handmer, J. 1985. "Local Reaction to Acquisition: An Australian study." Working Paper #53, Centre for Resource and Environmental Studies, Australian National University.

Heinz Center. 2002. *Human Links to Coastal Disasters*. Washington, D.C., The Heinz Center. Available at http://www.heinzctr.org/publications/PDF/Full_report_human_links.pdf, last accessed January 6, 2011.

Hinshaw, Robert. E. 2006. *Living with Nature's Extremes: The Life of Gilbert Fowler White*. Boulder, CO: Natural Hazards Center.

Hoffman, Susanna and Anthony Oliver-Smith, editors. 2002. *Catastrophe and Culture: The Anthropology of Disaster*. Santa Fe: School of American Research Press.

Jenkins, Sharon. 1998. "Emergency Workers' Mass Shooting Incident Stress and Psychological Reactions." *International Journal of Mass Emergencies and Disasters* 16/2: 181–195.

Kreps, Gary A., editor. 1989. *Social Structure and Disaster*. Newark, DE: University of Delaware Press.

Kreps, Gary A. 1995. "Disaster as Systemic Event and Social Catalyst: A Clarification of the Subject Matter." *International Journal of Mass Emergencies and Disasters* 13/3: 255–284.

Killian, Lewis. 2002. "An Introduction to Methodological Problems of Field Studies in Disasters." Pp. 49–93 in *Methods of Disaster Research*, (Robert A. Stallings, ed.). Philadelphia, PA: Xlibris/International Research Committee on Disasters.

Lincoln, Yvonna S. and Egon G. Guba. 1985. *Naturalistic Inquiry*. Newbury Park, CA: Sage.

Mendonça, David, Carter Butts, and Gary Webb. 2007. "Learning from the Response to Two Extreme Events." *Contingency Today*: June 4.

Michaels, Sarah. 2003. "Perishable Information, Enduring Insights? Understanding Quick Response Research." Pp. 15–48 in *Beyond September 11th: An Account of Post-Disaster Research*, (Jacquelyn L. Monday, ed.). Boulder, CO: Natural Hazards Research and Applications Information Center.

Mileti, Dennis. 1999. *Disasters by Design: A Reassessment of Natural Hazards in the United States*. Washington, D.C.: Joseph Henry Press.

Norris, Fran H., M. J. Friedman, and P. J. Watson. 2002a. "60,000 Disaster Victims Speak: Part II. Summary and Implications of the Disaster Mental Health Research." *Psychiatry* 65/3: 240–260.

Norris, Fran. H., M. J. Friedman, P. J. Watson, C. M. Byrne, E. Diaz, and K. Kaniasty. 2002b. 60,000 Disaster Victims Speak: Part I. An Empirical Review of the Empirical Literature, 1981–2001." *Psychiatry* 65/3: 207–239.

North, Carol. S., L. Tivis, J. C. McMillen, B. Pfefferbaum, J. Cox, E. L. Spitznagel, K. Bunch, J. Schorr, and E. M. Smith. 2002. "Coping, Functioning, and Adjustment of Rescue Workers after the Oklahoma City Bombing." *Journal of Traumatic Stress* 15/3: 171–175.

Oliver-Smith, Anthony and Susanna Hoffman. 1999. *The Angry Earth: Disaster in Anthropological Perspective*. NY: Routledge.

Olson, Richard Stuart. 2000. "Toward a Politics of Disaster: Losses, Values, Agendas, and Blame." *International Journal of Mass Emergencies and Disasters* 18: 265–287.

Pfefferbaum, B., J. A. Call, and G. M. Sconzo. 1999. "Mental Health Services for Children in the First Two Years after the 1995 Oklahoma City Terrorist Bombing." *Psychiatric Services* 50/7: 956–958.

Phillips, Brenda D. 2002. "Qualitative Methods of Disaster Research." Pp.194–211 in *Methods of Disaster Research*, (Robert A. Stallings, ed.). Philadelphia, PA: Xlibris/ International Research Committee on Disasters.

Phillips, Brenda D., Deborah S.K. Thomas, Alice Fothergill and Lynn Pike, eds. 2010. *Social Vulnerability to Disaster*. Boca Raton, FL: CRC Press.

Pike, Lynn, Brenda D. Phillips and Patsilu Reeves. 2006. "Shelter Life after Katrina: A Visual Analysis of Evacuee Perspectives." *International Journal of Mass Emergencies and Disasters* 24/3: 303–330.

Platt, Rutherford H. 1999. *Disasters and Democracy: The Politics of Extreme Natural Events*. Washington, D.C.: Island Press.

Plummer, Kenneth. 2001. *Documents of Life 2*. Thousand Oaks, CA; Sage.

Quarantelli, E.L. 1987. "Disaster Studies: An Analysis of the Social and Historical Factors Affecting the Development of Research in the Area." *International Journal of Mass Emergencies and Disasters* 5: 285–310.

Quarantelli, E.L. 1994. "Disaster Studies: The Consequences of the Historical Use of a Sociological Approach in the Development of Research." *International Journal of Mass Emergencies and Disasters* 12: 25–49.

Quarantelli, E.L. 2002. "The Disaster Research Center (DRC) Field Studies of Organized Behavior in the Crisis Time Period of Disasters." Pp. 94–126 in *Methods of Disaster Research*, (Robert A. Stallings, ed.). Philadelphia, PA: Xlibris/International Research Committee on Disasters.

Ritchie, Liesel Ashley and Wayne MacDonald, eds. 2010. "Enhancing Disaster and Emergency Preparedness, Response and Recovery through Evaluation." *New Directions for Evaluation*, Number 126.

Rubin, Herbert J. and Irene S. Rubin. 2005. *Qualitative Interviewing: The Art of Hearing Data*. Newbury Park, CA: Sage.

Scawthorn, Charles, ed. 2000. *The Marmara, Turkey Earthquake of August 17, 1999: Reconnaissance Report*. Buffalo, NY: Multidisciplinary Center for Earthquake Engineering Research.

Shriver, Thomas E. and Dennis Kennedy. 2005. "Contested Environmental Hazards and Community Conflict over Relocation." *Rural Sociology* 70/4: 491–513.

Spradley, James P. 1980. *Participant Observation*. Fort Worth, TX: Harcourt, Brace, Jovanovich College Publishers.

Sylves, Richard. 2008. *Disaster Policy and Politics: Emergency Management and Homeland Security*. Washington, D.C.: CQ Press.

Taylor, James B., Louis A. Zurcher and William H. Key. 1970. *Tornado: A Community Responds to Disaster*. Seattle, WA: University of Washington Press.

Thomas, Deborah S.K., Kivanç Ertuğay, and Serkan Kemeç. 2006. "The Role of Geographic Information Systems/Remote Sensing in Disaster Management. Pp. 83–96 in *Handbook of Disaster Research*, eds. Havidán Rogríguez, E.L. Quarantelli and Russell R. Dynes. New York: Springer.

Turner, Barry A. 1976. "The Organizational and Inter-Organizational Development of Disasters." *Administrative Science Quarterly* 21: 378–397.

Wachtendorf, Tricia. 2001. "Building Community Partnerships Toward a National Mitigation Effort: Inter-Organizational Collaboration in the Project Impact Initiative." Invited paper presented at the annual workshop for the Comparative Study on Urban Earthquake Disaster Management, Kobe, Japan, January 18.

Wachtendorf, Tricia, and Kristy Kompanik. 2000. "An Ongoing Assessment of the Project Impact Implementation Process: Recommendations and Lessons Learned." Poster presented at the Annual Project Impact Summit. Washington, D.C., November 13.

Waugh, William. 2000. *Living with Hazards, Dealing with Disasters: Introduction to Emergency Management*. Armonk, NY: M.E. Sharpe.

Waugh, William. 2006. "Shelter from the Storm: Repairing the National Emergency Management System after Katrina." *The ANNALS of the American Academy of Political and Social Science* 604: 288–332.

Webb, Eugene, Donald T. Campbell, Richard D. Schwartz, and Lee Sechrest. 1999. *Unobtrusive Measures*, second edition. Thousand Oaks, CA: Sage.

Wenger, Dennis E. 1989. "The Role of Archives for Comparative Studies of Social Structure and Disaster." Pp. 238–250 in *Social Structure and Disaster*, (Gary A. Kreps, ed.). Newark, DE: University of Delaware Press.

Wright, James D., Peter H. Rossi, Sonia R. Wright, and Eleanor Weber-Burdin. 1979. *After the Clean-Up: Long-Range Effects of Natural Disasters*. Beverly Hills, CA: Sage.

Resources

- The U.S. Census Bureau regularly collects and disseminates data on communities and households throughout the country and much of the data is relevant to emergency managers. To learn more, visit the official website at www.census.gov

- The Disaster Research Center at the University of Delaware houses the E.L. Quarantelli Resource Collection, the world's most complete collection on the social and behavioral science aspects of disasters. To learn more about the collection that now contains more than 55,000 items visit www.udel.edu/DRC

- The Natural Hazards Center at the University of Colorado also maintains one of the world's most unique collections of social science literature related to hazards and disasters. To learn more about the Natural Hazards Center Library, visit www.colorado.edu/hazards/library

Chapter **4**

New and Emerging Disasters and Hazards

4.1 Chapter Objectives

Upon completing this chapter, readers should be able to:

1. Realize that we will have more, worse, and new types of disasters.
2. Comprehend the rationale behind this trend of disasters.
3. Make clear the different scales, measures, and types of natural disasters.
4. Explain how humans influence disaster types and trends.
5. Understand terrorists' tools for creating disasters.
6. Point out new disasters that could happen and are causing emergency management agencies to take action now.

4.2 Introduction

In the 1980s, Quarantelli (1996, 2001) predicted more disasters, worse disasters, new types of disasters, and an increase of catastrophic events. He also believed that the number of deaths and injuries would increase and that economic impacts from disasters would continue to worsen. He based his predictions upon two conditions. First, increasing industrialization in both developing and developed countries would put more people at risk. For example, a rise in the number of hazardous materials plants would simply expand the potential for accidents. Any such events would likely result in environmental contamination and degradation. The chemical accident in Bhopal, India (see below) certainly punctuates his point.

The second condition, demographic trends (increased population, more residents living in hazardous areas), puts more people at risk. People like to live in beautiful areas and those who can afford to do so hire and rely on others to provide services. Increased needs for a range of housing leads or led to higher population densities and consequently more people living in less safe areas. Larger populations in riskier places result in greater property damage and more injuries and even deaths. Making these demographic trends worse in some communities is the fact that new residents may not be well educated about the hazards, for example, in hurricane-prone locations. Some population trends, such as the "snowbirds" who move to the Florida coast may put the elderly at higher risk. Notice how industrialization and population factors can interact to make a bad situation worse (Quarantelli 1996, 2001).

Recent research has shown Quarantelli to be correct. Mileti (1999) points out that from 1974 to 1994, dollar losses from disasters continued to increase, and that seven of the top ten most costly disasters occurred during this timeframe. Mileti explains these increasing disaster trends as an ever-changing physical environment (e.g., dramatic climate changes), more people living in known hazardous areas (e.g., along fault lines and coastal areas subject to hurricanes), and the destruction of some ecosystem components (e.g., building on hillsides, draining of swamps). In short, Mileti confirms Quarantelli's assessment.

Since Mileti published his book in 1999, we have seen his concerns play out. Major events including the Indian Ocean tsunami, Hurricane Katrina and the Haiti earthquake claimed hundreds of thousands of lives and billions of dollars in economic and infrastructure damages. Terrorism has become a worldwide concern and the *weapons of mass destruction* phrase is an addition to our risk management vocabulary. Threats such as H1N1 (swine flu) require coordination and collaboration across national boundaries. In fact, the Center for Research on the Epidemiology of Disasters reports that 2010 was the deadliest year in decades. Disasters killed more than 300,000 people and affected another 208,000,000—due in great extent to the catastrophic Haitian earthquake and Russian heat wave. The costs of the 373 natural disasters in 2010 were estimated at $110 billion (Leggiere 2011).

As a result of more and different disasters, the role of the disaster coordinator in the private, public, or volunteer sector is becoming more complex. To help sort through these issues, this chapter looks at current and emerging trends related to natural hazards, technological hazards, and terrorism. In addition, we provide examples of possible disasters that emergency coordinators must consider. Clearly, the role of a disaster coordinator, whether employed by government or the private or volunteer sector, becomes more complex with each passing decade.

4.3 Natural Hazards

As we noted in Chapter 2, people enjoy living near hazards. We settle along coastlines (hurricanes), next to rivers (floods), in cold weather areas (blizzards), nestle in mountains (earthquakes, volcanoes), in extreme climate locales (heat waves and droughts), and in areas subject to sudden and extreme weather changes (tornadoes and hail). In short, we do not and probably cannot avoid disasters. But we need to be wise about living and interacting with the natural environment.

To understand the destructive nature of disasters and their social impacts, scientists have developed measures for specific natural hazards that we believe are worth reviewing in this chapter. You may already be familiar with the measures developed for tornadoes, hurricanes, and earthquakes. Next, we discuss the most common disaster in the United States: floods. Finally, we provide a brief overview of other natural disasters.

4.3.1 Tornadoes

Tornadoes represent common hazards in the United States, with an average of 1,200 per year—a figure that has increased annually since the early 1990s. To demonstrate the impacts of tornadoes, geographer T. Theodore Fujita devised the F-Scale in the early 1970s to reflect the wind intensity, wind speed, and damage caused by a tornado. The F-Scale became a valuable tool for understanding the impacts of tornadoes after the "Super Outbreak" on April 3 and 4, 1974. Over an eighteen-hour period, a total of 148 tornadoes killed 335 people and left more than 6,000 injured across ten U.S. states. About thirty of the tornadoes were ranked at F-4 or F-5 levels. Some tornadoes traveled on the ground for more than ninety miles. As a result, the F-Scale became the standard for describing tornadoes (NOAA 2009a; Corfidi, Levit and Weiss, n.d.) and scientists continue to look for ways to improve event measurements.

After the Jarrell, Texas, tornado in 1997 and the Oklahoma tornado outbreak in 1999, scientists determined that the F-Scale wind estimates and damage may have been too high. As a result, the Enhanced F-Scale (EF-Scale) was devised (see Figure 4.1). In principle, the new EF-Scale was designed to allow strong comparisons of tornadoes based on the original F-Scale (NOAA 2009) and ascertain tornado levels based on the types of structures impacted. For example, think about the potential impact of an EF-1 tornado approaching your area. If your dwelling is a brick house with a basement shelter, you will be much safer than if you live in a mobile home.

Fujita Scale			Derived EF Scale		Operational EF Scale	
F Number	Fastest 1/4-mile (mph)	3 Second Gust (mph)	EF Number	3 Second Gust (mph)	EF Number	3 Second Gust (mph)
0	40–72	45–78	0	65–85	0	65–85
1	73–112	79–117	1	86–109	1	86–110
2	113–157	118–161	2	110–137	2	111–135
3	158–207	162–209	3	138–167	3	136–165
4	208–260	210–261	4	168–199	4	166–200
5	261–318	262–317	5	200–234	5	Over 200

FIGURE 4.1   Enhanced Fujita (EF) Scale. (*Source*: National Oceanic and Atmospheric Administration. 2007. http://www.spc.noaa.gov/faq/tornado/ef-scale.html)

4.3.2 Hurricanes

Unlike many other hazards, hurricanes reflect a somewhat cyclical pattern of occurrence. At the time of this writing, the average number of major storms and hurricanes spawned in the Atlantic Ocean over the last fifteen years appears to be in an upswing (see Figure 4.2). For example, between 1995 and 2005, the average number of hurricanes increased five per year. Furthermore, 2005 emerged as the most active year since formal recording began in 1944.

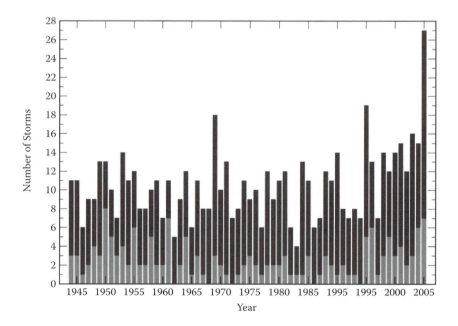

FIGURE 4.2   Annual numbers of named storms and major hurricanes. Black = number of storms. Gray = number of major hurricanes. (*Source*: National Oceanic and Atmospheric Administration. 2005a. www.ncdc.noaa.gov/img/climate/research/2005/ann/namedstorms-majorhurr.gif)

Hurricane experts determined that twenty-seven major storms developed in 2005 and fourteen became hurricanes. In addition, meteorologists found that since the early 1970s, hurricanes have become more destructive. An increase of average water temperature in the Atlantic and air temperatures over land makes them much more powerful (NOAA 2005a).

During the early 1970s, wind engineer Herb Saffir and meteorologist Bob Simpson devised a scale to measure the general strength of a hurricane based on sustained wind speed (Figure 4.3). The primary audience for this scale was the general public. The scale allowed the public to understand the power of a hurricane before (i.e., during a warning) it arrived or afterward. No disaster scale, especially one designed with the public in mind, captures all the important nuances of a weather event. For example, such factors as how quickly a hurricane moves over land, the amount and intensity of rainfall, subsequent floods, tornadoes and storm surge are not integrated into the scale.

Category	Wind (mph)	Effects
1	74–95	No real damage to building structures. Damage primarily to unanchored mobile homes, shrubbery, and trees. Also, some coastal road flooding and minor pier damage.
2	96–110	Some roofing material, door, and window damage to buildings. Considerable damage to vegetation, mobile homes, and piers. Coastal and low-lying escape routes flood 2–4 hours before arrival of center. Small craft in unprotected anchorages break moorings.
3	111–130	Some structural damage to small residences and utility buildings with a minor amount of curtain wall failures. Mobile homes destroyed. Flooding near the coast destroys smaller structures with larger structures damaged by floating debris. Terrain continuously lower than 5 feet ASL may be flooded inland 8 miles or more.
4	131–155	More extensive curtain wall failures with some complete roof structure failure on small residences. Major erosion of beach. Major damage to lower floors of structures near shore. Terrain continuously lower than 10 feet ASL may be flooded requiring massive evacuation of residential areas inland as far as 6 miles.
5	>155	Complete roof failure on many residences and industrial buildings. Some complete building failures with small utility buildings blown over or away. Major damage to lower floors of all structures located less than 15 feet ASL and within 500 yards of shoreline. Massive evacuation of residential areas on low ground within 5 to 10 miles of the shoreline may be required.

FIGURE 4.3   Saffir-Simpson Hurricane Scale. (*Source*: National Oceanic and Atmospheric Administration. n.d.a. http://www.aoml.noaa.gov/general/lib/laescae.html)

The Saffir-Simpson, the Enhanced F-Scale, and the Mercalli Earthquake Scale (see below) do not consider factors such as the types, qualities, and ages of buildings in the path of a natural disaster. Despite that shortcoming, the Saffir-Simpson Wind Scale provides the public, disaster planners, and others a means to assess the strength of a hurricane and potential risk. As Figure 4.3 indicates, the Saffir-Simpson is based on a 1 (weakest) to 5 (strongest) scale (Schott et al. 2010). Although all levels of hurricanes can damage buildings and infrastructure and kill people, as shown in Figure 4.3, levels 3, 4, and 5 cause the most concern. Below, we discuss the impact of Category 3 (Katrina) and Category 5 (Andrew) hurricanes.

Hurricane Katrina struck Southern Florida and then scoured a path affecting Louisiana, Mississippi, and Alabama, killed more than 1,300 people, and caused massive economic and infrastructural damage. Although Katrina made landfall as a Category 3 storm, a surge resulting from its Category 5 strength at sea pushed flooding inland and through waterways. Bridges disappeared and roads moved. The coastal fishing industry and the ports along the rivers suffered extensive losses. In comparison to Hurricane Camille that struck the same area in 1969 as a Category 5, Katrina caused far more damage because of the storm surge. Hurricane impacts on land vary—a fact not revealed by the categories of the Saffir-Simpson scale. Hurricane Andrew that initially struck the coast of Florida and later Louisiana in late August 1992 reflects the destructiveness of a Category 5 hurricane. It produced a storm surge of seventeen feet in some places in Florida and killed twenty-three people in the United States. However, its greatest impact was from wind; it caused more than $26.5 billion in damage in the U.S. and $25.5 billion in Florida (NOAA n.d.b).

4.3.3 Earthquakes

Unlike many disasters, earthquakes cannot be predicted with a high degree of accuracy or specificity. Let's take the San Andreas Fault line in California as an example. The fault was responsible for the massive 7.8 Richter Scale San Francisco earthquake in 1906 and the 6.9 Richter Scale Loma Prieta earthquake in the San Francisco Bay Area in 1989. The differences among tornado, hurricane, and earthquake scales are clear. Tornado strengths are measured after an event even though we can see them coming. Hurricanes can be estimated days in advance. Earthquakes are not so easily measured or observed for emergency management warning and response purposes. No one can say, "Simply, on November 10, 2013, we will have an M 7.0 earthquake along the San Andreas fault." Any prediction claims such as watching the behavior of catfish, birds, and other animals are purely fiction. Rather, we hear broad projections couched in probabilities over 50- or 100-year periods. For example, our best prediction is that "the probability of a large earthquake on the San Andreas Fault in the next thirty years is about 21%, or about 1 out of 5" (USGS 2008).

In 1935, Charles Richter of the California Institute of Technology developed a scale to measure moderate level earthquakes in Southern California. Richter's work effort emerged worldwide as a standardized way to measure and compare the intensity and magnitude of earthquakes. However, his original approach did not reflect the energy released by events exceeding 7.0 on the scale that result in catastrophic damage and losses over wide areas of the planet. As a result, scientists adjusted their methods of measuring earthquake intensity and magnitude. Although the media today still refer to the Richter Scale, scientists prefer to use *Magnitude* as a descriptor and categorize earthquakes as M 3.5 or M 7.1 (USGS n.d.).

The Richter Scale captures the intensity of the earth's shaking and the power released. By comparison, the Modified Mercalli Scale (see Box 4.1) attempts to combine the intensity of the earth's shaking along with human behavior and damage to buildings. In short, it considers the social dimension of earthquakes. For example, depending on how well a community may have taken mitigation measures and prepared for an earthquake, the social consequences of a 5.0 Richter Scale event may vary greatly. In communities with strong mitigation and preparedness programs, the social impacts may be minimal (level III or IV). In areas that lack effective mitigation and preparedness programs, the Modified Mercalli Scale level may be VIII or IX. Although the media generally report only the Richter Scale level after an earthquake, the Modified Mercalli Scale better gauges the social impacts and consequences (USGS 2009).

Earthquakes have caused some of the most devastating losses of life in the world's history. Five of the ten most fatal earthquakes have occurred in the past thirty-five years. For example, the 1976 Tangshan, China earthquake of M 7.1 killed 255,000 people. The Haitian earthquake measuring M 7.0 killed at least 222,570 (and possibly almost 300,000) people and injured another 300,000 in 2010. In Sumatra in 2004, an M 9.1 earthquake killed at least 227,898 people. An M 7.9 event in Chihi, China, claimed 87,587 lives and injured more than 374,000 in 2008. An earthquake of M 7.6 in Pakistan in 2005 took the lives of 86,000 people (USGS 2010a). Despite scientific differences over measurement, we can use the Richter and Mercalli Scales both to understand the damage and devastation from previous events and to help design realistic scenarios for earthquake response exercises. Knowing the magnitude, social impact, and physical location of an event lays a foundation for establishing long-term recovery planning as well.

BOX 4.1   MODIFIED MERCALLI EARTHQUAKE SCALE

   I. Not felt except by a very few under especially favorable conditions.
   II. Felt only by a few persons at rest, especially on upper floors of buildings.
   III. Felt quite noticeably by persons indoors, especially on upper floors of buildings. Many people do not recognize it as an earthquake. Standing motor cars may rock slightly. Vibrations similar to the passing of a truck. Duration estimated.
   IV. Felt indoors by many, outdoors by few during the day. At night, some awakened. Dishes, windows, doors disturbed; walls make cracking sound. Sensation like heavy truck striking building. Standing motor cars rocked noticeably.
   V. Felt by nearly everyone; many awakened. Some dishes, windows broken. Unstable objects overturned. Pendulum clocks may stop.
   VI. Felt by all, many frightened. Some heavy furniture moved; a few instances of fallen plaster. Damage slight.
   VII. Damage negligible in buildings of good design and construction; slight to moderate in well-built ordinary structures; considerable damage in poorly built or badly designed structures; some chimneys broken.
   VIII. Damage slight in specially designed structures; considerable damage in ordinary substantial buildings with partial collapse. Damage great in poorly built structures. Fall of chimneys, factory stacks, columns, monuments, walls. Heavy furniture overturned.
   IX. Damage considerable in specially designed structures; well-designed frame structures thrown out of plumb. Damage great in substantial buildings, with partial collapse. Buildings shifted off foundations.
   X. Some well-built wooden structures destroyed; most masonry and frame structures destroyed with foundations. Rails bent.
   XI. Few, if any (masonry) structures remain standing. Bridges destroyed. Rails bent greatly.
   XII. Damage total. Lines of sight and level are distorted. Objects thrown into the air.

Source: U.S. Geological Survey, 2009. http://earthquake.usgs.gov/learn/topics/mercalli.php

4.3.4 Floods

On an annual basis, floods represent the most lethal natural hazards and cause the most economic damage in the U.S. Experts estimate that flooding kills an average of 127 people and creates $5 billion in damage annually in the U.S. Over the past ten years, at least 50% of all flood deaths occurred when people were trapped in vehicles (NOAA 2009b; NOAA 2009c). Flooding is also a major problem worldwide. On average, flooding impacts about 520 million people and claims about 25,000 lives every year. In addition to the impact on human lives, flooding undermines the world's economy by $50 billion to $60 billion annually. Although flooding is a worldwide hazard, Asia bears the greatest risk (United Nations 2007). As we finished this book in early 2011, floodwaters inundated dozens of communities, states along the Mississippi River, and large areas of Queensland, Australia (Reuters 2011). Brazil experienced massive rains and mudslides that killed more than 400 people (Bell 2011). New disasters occur almost weekly.

In simple terms, flooding occurs when water covers land that is normally dry. However, flooding takes on many different shapes and forms. We may typically think that flooding happens when a river overflows its banks. However, other types of flooding put people and property at risk. Hurricanes and tropical storms along coastlines drop excessive rain or cause storm surges that push inland. In 1900, a hurricane pushed a storm surge across Galveston Island and caused at least 8,000 people to lose their lives. Most of the estimated 1,500 deaths from Hurricane Katrina in 2005 were drownings. Major storms also drop large amounts of rain in a short time and create inland flooding along rivers or low-lying areas. Dam and levee failures cause water to rush into inhabited areas (NOAA, 2009d).

Flash floods are another dangerous and deadly type. A flash flood occurs when water rises rapidly over a short time in low-lying urban areas or along rivers, streams, or canyons. Flash floods may result from heavy rainfall over a short period caused by hurricanes, tropical storms, thunderstorms, or similar events. Dam and levee breaks, the fracturing of an ice jam in a river, or heavy mountain rains can also cause flash floods. Since flash floods typically occur with little or no warning, those living next to rivers, streams, or arroyos face great danger. People often underestimate the power of flash floods. Such events can involve walls of water up to thirty feet high and are powerful enough to move large boulders, cars, and even bridges. Mudslides can also result from flash floods (NOAA 2009d). Floods cause many deaths worldwide every year. If you live in an area subject to heavy rains or prone to flooding, it is best to follow the advice of the National Weather Service: turn around, don't drown.

4.3.5 Wildfires

Wildfires can occur naturally (lightning strike) or from human actions (tossing a lighted cigarette out a car window). Regardless of cause, the number of wildfires, especially in the western U.S., has increased dramatically (see Figure 4.4). Since 1987, we have seen four times as many wildfires covering six times the area. These trends, scientists argue, result in part from overall warming trends (Biello 2006). Seven of the ten most expensive wildfires in the U.S. occurred since 1999 (Nazzaro 2009).

Historically Significant Wildland Fires

Date	Name	Location	Acres	Significance
1987	Siege of '87	California	640,000	Valuable timber lost in Klamath and Stanislaus National Forests
1988	Yellowstone	Montana and Idaho	1,585,000	Large amount of acreage burned
September 1988	Canyon Creek	Montana	250,000	Large amount of acreage burned
June 1990	Painted Cave	California	4,900	641 structures destroyed
June 1990	Dude Fire	Arizona	24,174	6 lives lost; 63 homes destroyed
October 1991	Oakland Hills	California	1,500	25 lives lost; 2,900 structures destroyed
August 1992	Foothills Fire	Idaho	257,000	1 life lost
1993	Laguna Hills	California	17,000	366 structures destroyed in 6 hours
July 1994	South Canyon Fire	Colorado	1,856	14 lives lost
July 1994	Idaho City Complex	Idaho	154,000	1 life lost
August 1995	Sunrise	Long Island	5,000	Alerted public that the East can have fires similar to the West
August 1996	Cox Wells	Idaho	219,000	Largest fire of year
June 1996	Millers Reach	Alaska	37,336	344 structures destroyed
July 1997	Inowak	Alaska	610,000	Threatened 3 villages
1998	Volusia Complex	Florida	111,130	Thousands of people evacuated from several counties
1998	Flagler/ St. John	Florida	94,656	Forced evacuation of thousands of residents
August 1999	Dunn Glen Complex	Nevada	288,220	Largest fire of year
August–November 1999	Big Bar Complex	California	140,947	Series of fires causing several evacuations over 3½ months
September–November 1999	Kirk Complex	California	86,700	Hundreds of people evacuated by series of fires spanning almost 3 months

FIGURE 4.4 Wildfires in the United States. (*Source*: National Integration Fire Center. 2007. http://www.nifc.gov/fire_info/historical_stats.htm)

Date	Name	Location	Acres	Significance
May 2000	Cerro Grande	New Mexico	47,650	Originally a prescribed fire; 235 structures destroyed; Los Alamos National Laboratory damaged
July 2001	Thirty Mile	Washington	9,300	14 fire shelters were deployed; 4 lives lost
June 2002	Hayman	Colorado	136,000	600 structures destroyed
June 2002	Rodeo-Chediski	Arizona	462,000	426 structures destroyed
July 2003	Cramer	Idaho	13,845	2 lives lost
October 2003	Cedar	California	275,000	2,400 structures destroyed; 15 lives lost
2004	Taylor Complex	Alaska	1,305,592	Fires burned over 6.38 million acres throughout state
June 2005	Cave Creek Complex	Arizona	248,310	11 structures destroyed; largest fire ever recorded in Sonoran Desert
March 2006	East Amarillo Complex	Texas	907,245	80 structures destroyed; 12 lives lost; largest fire of 2006 season
April 2007	Big Turnaround Complex	Georgia	388,017	Largest fire outside Alaska for U.S. Fish & Wildlife Service
July 2007	Murphy Complex	Idaho	652,016	One of the largest fires in Idaho

FIGURE 4.4 Continued.

Other factors make wildfires worse. For years, we prevented the natural burning of forests; this practice created additional "fuel" for fires. Controlled burns now represent one means of reducing wildfire fuel. In addition people who choose to live in or near wooded areas put their own homes at risk of fire by failing to maintain cleared distances around their homes (Nazzaro 2009). The invasion of non-native plants also generates fuel that may spread a budding fire rapidly. As Figure 4.4 shows, increasing wildfires in the U.S. cause losses of lives and property and managing these events costs millions of dollars.

Wildfires exist worldwide. Australia has a long history of severe wildfires. In 2009, hot weather conditions (113°F), drought, and high winds created a firestorm that killed about 200 people, destroyed more than 750 homes, and burned more than 815,000 acres of land. Similar to patterns in the U.S., Australian wildfires in the last thirty years have worsened (Lite 2009). Anthropologist Susanna Hoffman survived the Oakland Hills (CA) fire of

1991 and wrote about her experience in several books. Within four hours, the wildfire killed twenty-five people, burned more than 3,800 residences, and left about 6,000 victims homeless. Although the event undermined valued social relationships, the help of families and women-dominated networks fostered a slow recovery (Hoffman 1998).

4.3.6 Other Natural Hazards

The hazards noted above produced huge impacts worldwide. However, other types of natural hazards kill and injure people, disrupt lives, create millions of dollars in economic losses and thus deserve mention.

Although they create little long-term physical damage, blizzards and heat waves kill people and exert major impacts on local economies. Volcanoes, for example, sit silent for thousands of years and then suddenly erupt. The eruption of Mt. St. Helens in 1980 in the state of Washington only hinted at the damages such events incur. The volcano caused more than a billion dollars in damage, stranded about 10,000, isolated communities, and stopped all forms of transportation. About 900 million tons of white ash from the explosion caused much of the damage and social disruption (USGS 2005). The recent eruptions of a volcano in Iceland disrupted international air travel between Europe and North America for days, causing enormous economic losses to individuals and businesses. Slowly developing hazards such as droughts kill people, devastate local economics, and may also lead to civil war in some nations.

The issue of global warming has engendered much political debate. Many meteorologists suggest that global warming may increase the number and power of hurricanes, floods, blizzards, heat waves, and other meteorological events (NOAA 2008a). Research indicates that average temperatures worldwide have risen 0.74°C (1.3°F) over the past 100 years, mostly in the northern hemisphere. The eight warmest years on record spanned 2001 through 2008 and temperatures over the past decade have probably been the warmest in at least 1,000 years. Sea levels have also risen over the past 100 years (NOAA 2008a). The cause of global warming is the more contentious issue. Evidence suggests that pollutants such as carbon dioxide are creating a greenhouse effect. More broadly, many scientists suggest that human activities are raising the overall temperature of the planet. Also, solar activity (e.g., sunspots) and the position of the earth can create long-term effects on temperature. Scientists continue to research the causes of the increased temperatures. Regardless of cause, data clearly show that global temperatures are on the rise (NOAA 2008a and 2009e). A further concern is that the temperature increase may increase coastal flooding.

4.4 Human-Made Hazards

Human-made hazards represent growing concerns to the public as well as local, state, and federal governments. Some hazards such as massive explosions and large leaks of lethal material appear quickly. Others such as toxic material infiltration of ground water, air, and soil develop more slowly. Some events such as the recent BP Deep Water Horizon oil platform explosion in the Gulf of Mexico produce both immediate and long-term impacts. The initial explosion killed eleven workers, then destroyed aquatic, avian, and plant life. Scientists continue to analyze the long-term impacts such as contamination of fishing areas, coastlines, and wildlife.

In this section, we review some the typical technological hazards that emergency managers must face. To approach the topic systematically, we will use a common term devised by disaster planners: chemical, biological, radiological, and nuclear (CBRN) events. Although useful for considering community hazards, the term is also appropriate in relation to terrorist threats worldwide (CIA 2007). In this section, we provide examples of these hazards in non-terrorist settings; the threats and impacts of terrorism will be covered in the following section

4.4.1 Chemical Hazards

Chemical disasters have occurred worldwide throughout history. Some see such events as part of the price we pay for industrialization and modernization (Quarantelli 1996). However, two events within months of each other, one in India and the other in the U.S., forced the U.S. government to improve and standardize emergency management practices for hazardous materials. In December 1985, a pesticide plant in Bhopal, India spewed at least forty tons of lethal methyl isocyanate gas into the environment.

Experts estimated that the chemical leak quickly killed at least 2,000 people (others suggest that the initial death toll was at least 3,800 lives) and immediately injured another 170,000 victims. However, methyl isocyanate also creates long-term lethal and chronic impacts. Experts estimate that at least 10,000 people died soon after the release and another 15,000 to 20,000 died from exposure over a twenty-year period. Indian courts awarded cash settlements to more than 500,000 people injured in the accident. Bhopal was the worst industrial and chemical accident in history (Broughton 2005; EPA 2000), and the tragedy struck a chord worldwide. Tragically, a few months later, another methyl isocyanate leak occurred at a chemical plant operated by the same company in Institute, West Virginia. Although the accident did not take lives, the leak injured more than 100 residents (EPA 2000).

The Bhopal and Institute incidents, along with other chemical disasters, forced the U. S. Congress to pass legislation requiring planning for and responding to chemical hazards. In 1986, Congress passed the Emergency Planning and Community Right to Know Act (EPCRA) that improved local emergency planning for a wide range of hazardous materials events. Communities formed local emergency planning committees (LEPCs) to enhance communication among organizations (private industry, local and state governments, emergency management, volunteer organizations, hospitals, the media) involved in a hazardous materials response. In addition, EPA regulations forced businesses and other organizations that stored hazardous chemicals to keep records and inform local emergency management offices about the types and amounts of chemicals on site. Thus, if an event occurred, local emergency management could provide information to first responders (fire, police) to assist in handling situations (EPA 2000). Despite all the federal, state, and local legislation, chemical accidents including explosions still occur. In summary, when city planning and zoning authorities allow residents to live near hazardous facilities, when companies fail to follow safety regulations, or terrorism is looming, chemical disasters will occur.

4.4.2 Biological Hazards

Throughout history, we find examples of biological hazards that produced mass deaths and massive demographic changes. Some of these hazards developed naturally, then spread quickly through human populations. Examples include the bubonic plague in Europe, North Africa, and the Near East; the potato blight in Ireland; pandemics in the New World; the influenza pandemic during World War I; and even biological risks from space travel.

The bubonic plague or "black death" struck Europe beginning in the mid-1300s, killing 25 to 33% of Europe's population. Parts of Northern Africa and the Near East had similar death rates. Bubonic plague occurs naturally, and rats are the disease carriers. However, historical evidence indicates that the dead bodies of plague victims were then used as a form of biological warfare to spread the disease in Italy. The black death outbreak became one of the deadliest "attacks" in history and less severe outbreaks afflicted Europe periodically for the next 500 years (Wheelis 2002).

Biological hazards need not strike people directly, as illustrated by the Irish potato blight and famine in the 1840s. The inexpensive and easy-to-grow potato as a source of food played a role in increasing the Irish population from 3,000,000 in 1780 to about 8,000,000 by the 1840s. However, a potato blight struck much of the 1845 crop and the 1846 crop failed. People died of starvation, a circumstance that fomented political violence. By the end of that decade, about 1.5 million people died of starvation and another million immigrated primarily to the U.S. Irish immigration to other countries continued for decades as a result of the potato blight and famine (Barton 1970).

Disease epidemics also spread through North and South America between the 1500s and 1700s. European explorers brought with them measles, mumps, smallpox, and other diseases. The native populations that lacked immunity against these diseases often died after exposure. Outbreaks in islands in the Caribbean and in Mexico killed at least a third of the local populations (Wilson 1995).

At the end of World War I (1917–1919), a vicious strain of influenza spread throughout the world. Experts estimate that the virus infected a third of the world's population, killing least 50 million people. Others estimate the total number of deaths closer to 100 million. The virus was an H1N1 type, similar to the H1N1 that emerged in 2009 (Taubenberger and Morens 2006). In short, natural biological hazards can impact humans. Today, many of us are vaccinated against the measles, influenza, and other diseases. Such vaccinations can be a form of mitigation, but an unknown or new strain of a disease such as the 1918 influenza may kill thousands if not millions of people.

Science fiction authors recognized the possibility of massive deaths caused by "alien" viruses. H. G. Wells' famous *War of the Worlds* novel had us defeat the invading Martians because they had no immunity against human disease. Michael Crichton's *The Andromeda Strain* portrayed a government spacecraft that captured microorganisms high in our atmosphere for use in biological warfare. The satellite crashed upon return to the earth, exposing humans to horrible deaths. However, possible attack by cosmic viruses or bacteria now extends to reality. When the first moon landing missions returned to Earth, scuba divers scrubbed clean the Apollo spacecraft and the astronauts were kept in quarantine for two weeks to ensure that they had contracted no diseases. When future missions from Mars return to earth, scientists will utilize similar quarantines (NASA 2002).

4.4.3 Radiological and Nuclear Hazards

Of all technological hazards, perhaps those involving nuclear or radiological threats present the greatest fear factor. Perhaps the images and figures from the devastating impacts of the bombs dropped over Hiroshima and Nagasaki at the end of World War II remain fresh in the world's mind. Of course, two major nuclear reactor accidents caught the world's attention in 1979 and 1986. The Three Mile Island nuclear accident in Pennsylvania, although not causing any deaths, demonstrated the potential of a nuclear power plant accident.

That potential became reality in 1986 with the meltdown and explosion of the Chernobyl nuclear power plant in the Ukraine. Due to the type and location of the accident, the exact death toll is hard to determine, but hundreds of thousands of people were exposed to radiation including 350,000 residents and 200,000 emergency workers. An eighteen-mile radius around the facility remains closed. Airborne radiation from the explosion traveled to Scandinavia and other parts of Europe (U.S. NRC 2009a). The long-term effects of radiation (with the half lives of some nuclear materials ranging from 24,000 years,[e.g., plutonium 239], to 80,000,00 years, and the longest being plutonium 244; U.S. NRC 2009b) also frighten people. Certainly the possibility of a radiological or nuclear blast remains a key terrorist threat. The 2011 Japanese tsunami that damaged the Fukushima nuclear plant represents another hazard of concern.

4.5 Terrorism

For many of you reading this text, terrorism entered your consciousness on September 11, 2001. However, acts of terror occurred before that one, and several have followed it since in both the U.S. and elsewhere. Between 1983 (beginning with a suicide car bombing in Beirut) and 2000, twenty-one terrorist attacks have killed Americans at home and overseas (Terrorism Project 2009). Although terrorism is not new, activity worldwide appears to be on the increase. However, as we show below, terrorism is not new. Acts of terrorism have occurred for thousands of years, and definitions of terrorism differ. We find Waugh's (2007, p. 393) four elements of terrorism most useful in identifying key components:

- Credible threat of extraordinary violence
- Purpose or goal
- Choice of targets for their symbolic nature
- Intent to influence a broader audience than the immediate victims

Although we in the U.S. may see terrorism as mainly a U.S. concern, it is a problem that plagues countries around the world. Figure 4.5 provides a summary of terrorist attacks and their outcomes worldwide from 2005 through 2009. For example, in 2009, nearly 11,000 terrorist attacks killed about 15,000 people and injured 34,000 more. As the data indicate, the numbers of attacks, deaths, and injuries have decreased to a degree since 2005. In addition, although not shown in the table, about two-thirds of the terror attacks during this period occurred in Asia (U.S. Department of State 2010).

Terrorists make their political statements through death and destruction. The goal may not be as much winning the battle as it is to challenge or change a secure way of life. Preventing and battling terror domestically and worldwide is not a simple task. Facile approaches may increase the terror threats rather than decrease or eliminate them. Terrorism, however, is now a threat most people must consider daily.

Experts use the CBRN designation (see above) to distinguish the different ways terrorists may inflict harm (CIA 2007). We briefly address the use of

	2005	2006	2007	2008	2009
Attacks worldwide	11,023	14,443	14,435	11,725	10,999
Attacks resulting in at least 1 death, injury, or kidnapping	7,963	11,278	11,097	8.411	7,875
Attacks resulting in death of at least 1 individual	5,083	7,412	7,235	5,045	4,764
Attacks resulting in no deaths	5,940	7,031	7,200	6,680	6,235
Attacks resulting in death of only 1 individual	2,853	4,127	3,984	2,870	2,694
Attacks resulting in deaths of at least 10 individuals	226	295	353	234	234
Attacks resulting in injury of at least 1 individual	3,805	5,774	6,243	4,869	4,536
Attacks resulting in kidnapping of at least 1 individual	1,156	1,343	1,156	961	877
People killed, injured or kidnapped as result of terrorism	74,327	74,616	71,856	54,653	58,142
People worldwide killed as result of terrorism	14,482	20,515	22,736	15,727	14,971
People worldwide injured as result of terrorism	24,795	38,314	44,139	34,057	34,057
People worldwide kidnapped as result of terrorism	35,050	15,787	4,981	4,869	4,869

FIGURE 4.5   Worldwide terrorism incidents 2005–2009. (*Source*: U.S. Department of State. 2010. http://www.state.gov/s/ct/rls/crt/2009/140902.htm)

CBRN materials for terrorist use. Generally, the chemical explosion appears to be the preferred method. Chemicals for explosives are relatively easy to obtain both legally and via the black market. Information for making bombs is available on the Internet and common household materials can be used to construct many types of bombs. Chemical weapons are occasionally weapons of choice but they are difficult to obtain and transport to a selected location. In a 1995 subway attack in Japan, domestic terrorists used sarin, a colorless, odorless chemical that attacks the nervous system.

Biological attacks such as those caused by using anthrax are initially hard to detect. However, manufacturing and transporting biological agents can be difficult. After the September 11, 2001 events, an unknown person sent anthrax through the mail. Eleven people were directly exposed and five of them died. Eleven others were indirectly exposed, required medical treatment, and survived. As shown in Box 4.2, biological attacks have been used successfully throughout history (DHS 2009).

A radiological attack would require insertion of radiological material into a large bomb. The explosion would be intended not to kill people by

BOX 4.2 HISTORICAL PERSPECTIVE ON BIOLOGICAL ATTACK

- In 2001, anthrax attacks through the U.S. mail infected 11 people with inhalational anthrax, of whom 5 died. An additional 11 people were infected with cutaneous (skin) anthrax, of which there were no fatalities.
- In the 1990s, the cult Aum Shinrikyo failed in its attempts to release anthrax and botulinum toxin in Tokyo but did succeed in a chemical attack with sarin nerve agent.
- In 1984, the cult followers of Baghwan Shree Rajneesh sickened 751 people in Oregon by placing Salmonella bacteria in salad bars in 10 restaurants to keep people from voting in an election.
- In World War II, Unit 731 in Japanese-occupied Manchuria dropped plague-infected fleas in China, allegedly resulting in more than 50,000 deaths.
- In World War I, German agents successfully infected Allied livestock with anthrax and glanders.
- In the 1340s, Europeans threw plague-infected cadavers over city walls to infect those within.

Source: U.S. Department of Homeland Security. http://www.dhs.gov/files/publications/gc_1245183510280.shtm

the blast, but to spread radiation and contaminate both people and property (National Academy of Sciences 2004). The most destructive form of attack would be detonation of a nuclear bomb in a major city such as New York. The initial blast could kill hundreds of thousands and contaminate the ground in the area of the blast. Fallout (debris made radioactive by the explosion and falling to the ground) would contaminate more area and poison and probably kill more people (National Academy of Sciences 2005). However, the steps involved in obtaining the needed material, manufacturing a bomb, and transporting it to a proper location would be difficult though not impossible.

4.6 New and Emerging Hazards

As Quarantelli predicted in the early 1980s, we face new and emerging types of hazards and disasters. We now briefly review some of these threats. Examples of new and emerging hazards include natechs—combinations of natural disasters with technological events such as computer failures, cyberterrorism, pandemics, bioterrorism attacks, and hazards from outer space. This list by no means covers all possibilities nor do we offer a complete discussion of them because these hazards are both new and emerging. However, these examples illustrate the types of problems and issues emergency managers will encounter in the future.

4.6.1 Natechs

Typically, when we consider a hazard or disaster, we think of one type of disaster agent or event. A hurricane floods large areas and high winds and water destroy buildings and infrastructure. Massive wildfires destroy homes, cause evacuations, and burn large swaths of land. Natech events go one step further: a natural disaster (hurricane or flood) creates a technological disaster (e.g., hazardous materials release or explosion). The *natech* term combines the first two letters of *natural* and the first four letters of *technological* to describe a single event involving both types of disasters (Cruz et al. 2004). Below, we discuss specific examples.

Natechs do impact the U.S. Hurricane Georges (1998) and Hurricane Floyd (1999) caused hazardous materials to pollute water, and such spills occurred again during Hurricane Katrina (2005). The Northridge earthquake (1994) led to 134 documented hazardous materials releases and the Loma Prieta earthquake caused many hazardous materials spills in laboratories and hospitals. A lightning strike at a Louisiana oil refinery in 2001 created a large fire that required the evacuation of a nearby community (Cruz et al. 2004).

The Tokachi-oke earthquake in Japan in 2003 is another example as is the 2011 tsunami. The M 8.0 earthquake killed 2 people, injured more than 840, and created $187 million in economic damages. It also damaged 45 of 105 tanks at an oil refinery, causing two major fires. The fires and aftermath created further damage, fouled the air, and closed the port of Tokakomai for days (Cruz et al. 2004).

The 7.4 Kocaeli earthquake in Turkey in 1999 killed more than 17,000 and injured at least 40,000. In addition to the response problems generated by the earthquake, at least twenty-one major hazardous materials releases occurred. Large amounts of crude oil spilled into Izmir Bay. Other chemicals were released into the atmosphere and contaminated the ground. Power failures made communications for responders extremely complicated (Cruz et al. 2004). In summary, natechs will continue to occur worldwide. Emergency managers may encounter difficulties mitigating or preparing for natechs because the effects of a natural disaster that trigger a technological disaster are not always known.

4.6.2 Compounding Natural Disasters

The idea of compounding natural disaster is somewhat similar to a natech and Perrow's "normal accident" concept (1984). In this case, one natural disaster helps set the stage to create another event and the problem is compounded when people decide to live in at-risk areas. Consider Southern California. The areas around Los Angeles often face droughts and the mountains become very dry. Through a natural cause (lightning) or a human activity, a fire begins and burns hundreds of acres of mountain lands. The fire undermines vegetation that holds the soil. Hard, heavy rains then cause massive mudslides of soil from the mountains. An earthquake can also cause landslides. Rivers freeze during the winter. As spring approaches and parts of the river thaw, the ice breaks and creates a dam, stopping the flow of the water. Flooding occurs behind the ice jam. As with natechs, disaster planners must be aware of possible compounding natural disasters.

4.6.3 Computer Failures and Cyberterrorism

Computers manage much of our lives today. Computer failures literally shut down activities we take for granted: electrical power, commercial aviation, phone service, and Internet communications.

Computer failures can be accidental or intentional (through terrorism). Consider the fears of the predicted Y2K computer failures at the turn of the millennium. To save computer memory, early programmers designated years by their last two numbers (e.g., 1976 would be 76). As a result, computer experts and government and business leaders feared that computers would read 2000 as 1900 or worse, could not determine the year and would shut down progressively as the year 2000 moved across the planet. Although many experts expressed concern, the public generally did not see the importance of the issue. Fortunately, the world avoided a major computer disaster because businesses, governments, and individuals made appropriate fixes (Powell, Bodon, and Hickson 2001). However, unknown programming errors, cascading losses of electrical power, and computer viruses continue to present future threats.

Recent media reports suggest that cyberterrorism is reality, for example, Iran's recent attempt to build nuclear weapons utilized sabotaged software that run centrifuges and produce nuclear fuel. During the recent Wikileaks exposé of international secrets, its website came under attack and was shut down by unknown sources. The U.S. government established a Computer Readiness Team that operates on a twenty-four-hour basis to detect and fight cyberterror attacks on government facilities (DHS 2008). The concern is real: more than 100 foreign intelligence offices continuously attempt to infiltrate military computer installations, and the number of attempts over the past ten years has increased exponentially (Garamone 2010; Figure 4.6).

4.6.4 Pandemics and Bioterrorism

A wide range of pathogens and diseases exist that can accidentally or intentionally kill or injure thousands if not millions. Pandemics spread worldwide (Kilbourne 2006). Many factors make biological agents dangerous.

FIGURE 4.6   FEMA staff testify before the House Homeland Security Hearing, Subcommittee on Emerging Threats, Cybersecurity, and Science and Technology. (*Source:* FEMA News Photo/Bill Koplitz.)

They occur naturally so differentiating a natural event from a terrorist attack is difficult. Pathogens can spread through air, water, or food. Since they are difficult to detect quickly, effective response is difficult. Also, appropriate vaccines and drugs may not be available or may be delivered too late. A disease agent may mutate, making known drugs ineffective.

Note how new and different types of disasters may overlap. Major computer shutdowns caused by poor programming or terror attack could cause cascading electrical blackouts. A natech event could interact with a biological hazard, creating an emergency management nightmare. Many U.S. planners have considered scenarios in which terrorists wait for a catastrophic event such as a Hurricane Katrina-type event, then unleash their weapons of mass destruction.

In summary, when emergency managers perform hazard analyses, they must think beyond the events normally expected in their geographical areas. West coast managers must think beyond earthquakes and wildfires. Those in the Midwest should expand their thinking outside the contexts of tornadoes and floods. Managers in coastal areas need to consider events other than hurricanes, high winds, and floods. Emergency managers must consider the possible interactions of two known hazards; one may cause another or a series of circumstances may lead to a cascade of events. They need to think about the likelihood that a terrorist attack 500 or 1,000 miles away coupled with another event could impact their communities. They must be ready for a wide range of unknowns in our uncertain world (see Box 4.3).

4.6.5 Hazards from Outer Space

Space presents hazards that could create catastrophes if they impact the Earth. We are all aware that the impact of an asteroid hitting the earth sixty-five million years ago killed the dinosaurs by dramatically changing the climate. Scientists continue to discover and track asteroids and other

BOX 4.3 PANDEMICS AND IMPACTS ON SOCIETY AND GOVERNMENT

Roger Hovis

Roger Hovis is the Director of Public Health Preparedness for Region 3, South Carolina Department of Health and Environmental Control. Previously a research scientist for the Battelle Memorial Institute, he integrated civilian emergency and security practices into National Security and Department of Defense policy for the Departments of the Army and Navy. Roger is also an adjunct instructor of emergency management and homeland security for Virginia Commonwealth University and the University of Richmond.

> Everybody knows that pestilences have a way of recurring in the world; yet somehow we find it hard to believe in ones that crash down on our heads from a blue sky.
>
> Albert Camus—*The Plague*

Managing the consequences of a deadly pandemic will be enormous and requires the cooperation of all planning partners in your emergency management community. Pandemic influenza (PI) planning began nationally in grant year 2005–2006 with the release of federal funds from the U.S. Department of Health and Human Services. Approximately $576 million went to state and local public health preparedness programs to hire planners, draft plans, design and carry out exercises, and capture the results with an evaluation of the processes. For the next several years, PI funding was given to states and locals in various amounts but by 2008 the funds were no longer available to many programs. As a result, the planners hired in 2006 went away or were shuffled elsewhere within the health agencies where they worked. During the 2009–2010 H1N1 pandemic, my office was able to re-engage some of these "pan flu" workers and bring them back into the fight. This rare moment in government work was a godsend for us. We had a pandemic, and we had experienced planners who had thought through the process of setting up mass vaccination clinics.

My team worked extensively with emergency management partners, health care providers, and most importantly the K–12 public and private school system in South Carolina. We engaged our partners at the University of South Carolina and shared ideas on vaccinations and the epidemiology (tracking) of H1N1's progression. Partnerships created early on were the keys to success. In one of our school districts, over 11,050 kids and staff were immunized in thirteen days using school nurses from the district and our team for support. I had read of other jurisdictions struggling to find enough nursing help to just start the process of giving shots. I guess we will never know how many lives were saved, although I believe many were.

As stated previously, cooperation is key for emergency managers. Your plan (EOP or other document) should have a health and medical section, typically titled ESF-8 under federal guidelines. Obviously this part of the plan describes the general actions taken by health and medical stakeholders associated with your plan. Hospital processes, EMS processes, shelter processes, mass causality and fatality planning may all be rolled up under this section as annexes to the basic plan. Planning considerations for PI may include:

1. The potential risks of a pandemic. These risks may be measured as extensive life-threatening illness, extreme loss of life, economic losses, the struggle to continue life as we know it—maintaining government, schools, and businesses.

2. What you do to mitigate such events. Duct tape and plastic won't work here. Mass clinics will be staged in large venue locations. The U.S. Postal Service may deliver medical countermeasures to your home or office. As we witnessed in 2009–2010, even private sector pharmacies (drug stores) dispensed medical countermeasures free of charge. This process took place through a federal plan from the CDC's Strategic National Stockpile (SNS) and state and local health agencies.

3. Ethically, how will we deal with life and death situations when our health and medical systems are so overwhelmed that normal triage and treatment protocols become ineffective? We know there are only so many respiratory ventilators available so who will make the call as to who gets one and who does not? The decision most likely means someone will not receive life saving measures. PI ethics committees have been established at federal, state, and local

levels to study this emotional issue. How might an emergency manager contribute to an ethics committee?

4. Public Information: as with an earthquake or hurricane, our information systems during a PI will need to be out in front of the disease spread. In other words, messages describing preventive measures must be broadcast in a timely and coordinated method by emergency management and/or public health preparedness officials.

A pandemic, whether influenza or some other infectious disease, is one of those events we know will occur. Our nation has been tested in the recent past. Were we ready? Perhaps, but the H1N1 pandemic was not the killer event we have been planning for. We stumbled, we endured. We faced an unsure public, but we learned many valuable lessons to advance our emergency management planning and preparedness.

near-earth objects via a new satellite called the wide field infrared survey explorer (WISE) and other means. Data are sent to the Minor Planet Center in Cambridge, Massachusetts to determine whether objects present dangers to the Earth (NASA 2011a).

Another threat comes from the sun. Massive solar flares occasionally shoot out toward Earth; they can damage and destroy satellites. Think how much of our life today is based on the use of satellites including geographical positioning systems (GPS), television, voice and data communications, and weather data. Interference with satellites would affect commercial aviation, television transmission, and accuracy of weather predictions. Our national security would be compromised if our spy and other satellites did not function (Murtagh 2010). Solar flares are genuine threats. NASA dispatched a warning about a major solar flare that occurred on February 14, 2011. Fortunately, no damage resulted (NASA 2011b; Box 4.4).

Some flares may be strong enough to penetrate the Earth's atmosphere. As a result, most of our electronics could be damaged or destroyed. Think how dramatically our lives would change without electronics. The effects would be far more serious than not being able to watch TV, use cell phones, or operate iPods. Scientists have found these flares dangerous enough to require scales similar to the EF Scale for tornadoes and the Mercalli Scale for earthquakes (Box 4.1; NOAA 2005b; Murtaugh 2010). A flare event would alter how we eat, travel, work, and live. Before the twentieth century, solar flares did not represent threats to the Earth and its inhabitants. Most people did not rely on electricity. In the U.S. today, only a few groups such as the Amish (who for religious reasons do not use modern conveniences including electricity and cars) would avoid disaster.

Concerns related to events that occur outside our atmosphere (called space weather) are very real. Meteorologists, emergency managers, and

BOX 4.4   NOAA SPACE WEATHER SCALE FOR GEOMAGNETIC STORMS

Category		Effect	Physical measure	Average Frequency (1 cycle = 11 years)
Scale	Descriptor	Duration of event will influence severity of effects		
			Kp values* determined every 3 hours	Number of storm events when Kp level was met; (number of storm days)
		Geomagnetic Storms		
G 5	Extreme	Power systems: widespread voltage control problems and protective system problems can occur, some grid systems may experience complete collapse or blackouts. Transformers may experience damage.	Kp = 9	4 per cycle (4 days per cycle)
		Spacecraft operations: may experience extensive surface charging, problems with orientation, uplink/downlink and tracking satellites.		
		Other systems: pipeline currents can reach hundreds of amps, HF (high frequency) radio propagation may be impossible in many areas for one to two days, satellite navigation may be degraded for days, low-frequency radio navigation can be out for hours, and aurora has been seen as low as Florida and southern Texas (typically 40° geomagnetic lat.)**.		

Category		Effect	Physical measure	Average Frequency (1 cycle = 11 years)
Scale	Descriptor	Duration of event will influence severity of effects		
		Geomagnetic Storms	Kp values* determined every 3 hours	Number of storm events when Kp level was met; (number of storm days)
G 4	Severe	Power systems: possible widespread voltage control problems and some protective systems will mistakenly trip out key assets from the grid.	Kp = 8, including a 9	100 per cycle (60 days per cycle)
		Spacecraft operations: may experience surface charging and tracking problems, corrections may be needed for orientation problems.		
		Other systems: induced pipeline currents affect preventive measures, HF radio propagation sporadic, satellite navigation degraded for hours, low-frequency radio navigation disrupted, and aurora has been seen as low as Alabama and northern California (typically 45° geomagnetic lat.)**.		
G 3	Strong	Power systems: voltage corrections may be required, false alarms triggered on some protection devices.	Kp = 7	200 per cycle (130 days per cycle)

	Category		Effect	Physical measure	Average Frequency (1 cycle = 11 years)
Scale	Descriptor		Duration of event will influence severity of effects		
		Geomagnetic Storms		Kp values* determined every 3 hours	Number of storm events when Kp level was met; (number of storm days)
			Spacecraft operations: surface charging may occur on satellite components, drag may increase on low Earth-orbit satellites, and corrections may be needed for orientation problems.		
			Other systems: intermittent satellite navigation and low-frequency radio navigation problems may occur, HF radio may be intermittent, and aurora has been seen as low as Illinois and Oregon (typically 50° geomagnetic lat.)**.		
G 2	Moderate		Power systems: high-latitude power systems may experience voltage alarms, long-duration storms may cause transformer damage.	Kp = 6	600 per cycle (360 days per cycle)
			Spacecraft operations: corrective actions to orientation may be required by ground control; possible changes in drag affect orbit predictions.		

Category		Effect	Physical measure	Average Frequency (1 cycle = 11 years)
Scale	Descriptor	Duration of event will influence severity of effects		
		Geomagnetic Storms	Kp values* determined every 3 hours	Number of storm events when Kp level was met; (number of storm days)
		Other systems: HF radio propagation can fade at higher latitudes, and aurora has been seen as low as New York and Idaho (typically 55° geomagnetic lat.)**.		
G 1	Minor	Power systems: weak power grid fluctuations can occur.	Kp = 5	1700 per cycle (900 days per cycle)
		Spacecraft operations: minor impact on satellite operations possible.		
		Other systems: migratory animals are affected at this and higher levels; aurora is commonly visible at high latitudes (northern Michigan and Maine)**.		

* The K-indexes used to generate these messages are derived in real-time from the Boulder NOAA Magnetometer. The Boulder K-index, in most cases, approximates the Planetary Kp-index referenced in the NOAA Space Weather Scales. The Planetary Kp-index is not available in real-time. ** For specific locations around the globe, use geomagnetic latitude to determine likely sightings (Tips on Viewing the Aurora)

NOAA SPACE WEATHER SCALE FOR SOLAR RADIATION STORMS

Category		Effect	Physical measure	Average Frequency (1 cycle = 11 years)
Scale	Descriptor	Duration of event will influence severity of effects		
		Solar Radiation Storms	Flux level of >= 10 MeV particles (ions)*	Number of events when flux level was met (number of storm days**)
S 5	Extreme	Biological: unavoidable high radiation hazard to astronauts on EVA (extra-vehicular activity); passengers and crew in high-flying aircraft at high latitudes may be exposed to radiation risk.***	10^5	Fewer than 1 per cycle
		Satellite operations: satellites may be rendered useless, memory impacts can cause loss of control, may cause serious noise in image data, star-trackers may be unable to locate sources; permanent damage to solar panels possible.		
		Other systems: complete blackout of HF (high frequency) communications possible through the polar regions, and position errors make navigation operations extremely difficult.		
S 4	Severe	Biological: unavoidable radiation hazard to astronauts on EVA; passengers and crew in high-flying aircraft at high latitudes may be exposed to radiation risk.***	10^4	3 per cycle

Category		Effect	Physical measure	Average Frequency (1 cycle = 11 years)
Scale	Descriptor	Duration of event will influence severity of effects		
		Solar Radiation Storms	Flux level of >= 10 MeV particles (ions)*	Number of events when flux level was met (number of storm days**)
		Satellite operations: may experience memory device problems and noise on imaging systems; star-tracker problems may cause orientation problems, and solar panel efficiency can be degraded.		
		Other systems: blackout of HF radio communications through the polar regions and increased navigation errors over several days are likely.		
S 3	Strong	Biological: radiation hazard avoidance recommended for astronauts on EVA; passengers and crew in high-flying aircraft at high latitudes may be exposed to radiation risk.***	10^3	10 per cycle
		Satellite operations: single-event upsets, noise in imaging systems, and slight reduction of efficiency in solar panel is likely.		

Scale	Category Descriptor	Effect Duration of event will influence severity of effects Solar Radiation Storms	Physical measure Flux level of >= 10 MeV particles (ions)*	Average Frequency (1 cycle = 11 years) Number of events when flux level was met (number of storm days**)
		Other systems: degraded HF radio propagation through the polar regions and navigation position errors likely.		
S 2	Moderate	Biological: passengers and crew in high-flying aircraft at high latitudes may be exposed to elevated radiation risk.***	10^2	25 per cycle
		Satellite operations: infrequent single-event upsets possible.		
		Other systems: small effects on HF propagation through the polar regions and navigation at polar cap locations possibly affected.		
S 1	Minor	Biological: none. Satellite operations: none. Other systems: minor impacts on HF radio in the polar regions.	10	50 per cycle

* Flux levels are 5 minute averages. Flux in particles·s⁻¹·ster⁻¹·cm⁻². Based on this measure, but other physical measures are also considered.

** These events can last more than one day.

*** High energy particle measurements (>100 MeV) are a better indicator of radiation risk to passenger and crews. Pregnant women are particularly susceptible.

Source: National Oceanic and Atmospheric Administration. http://www.swpc.noaa.gov/NOAAscales/NOAAscales.pdf

academics are currently investigating the best ways to deliver information to the public that clearly describe the potential hazards and appropriate responses. Transforming an unfamiliar hazard into an event that requires individual planning and response represents a particular challenge that will take all our collective ideas and energies to address. Imagine, for example, asteroid alerts or solar flare warnings. How would you react? Are you aware that we expect a solar flare surge as early as 2013? Public officials, with the support of the Office of the Federal Coordinator of Meteorology (2010) are currently working on ways to inform the public because such events could cause significant disruptions to the power grid. Based on our dependence on power, the event could be catastrophic. Stay alert for public education efforts on this emerging hazard.

Ironically, the wide use of social media before, during, and after disasters is becoming a norm. Emergency managers, responders, potential victims, the news media, and others increasingly rely on the Internet, cell phones, and other similar devices to deal with disasters. Box 4.5 describes the emerging role of social media during disasters. Except for solar flares and nuclear explosions, emergency managers, the media, and the public rely on social media for information about disasters, especially during the warning and response periods.

BOX 4.5 SOCIAL MEDIA AND EMERGENCY MANAGEMENT

DeeDee Bennett and Njoki Mwarumba

DeeDee Bennett earned a BS in electrical engineering and an MS in public policy at the Georgia Institute of Technology. Published in the *International Journal of Emergency Management*, she is interested in social vulnerabilities and communications as they relate to emergency management. She is currently pursuing a doctorate in emergency management at Oklahoma State University.

Njoki Mwarumba earned a BA in communications and community development in Kenya. She is currently pursuing doctorate studies in emergency management at Oklahoma State University. She is also consulting on a USAID grant (PREPARE) focusing on multisectoral pandemic preparedness in developing countries in Africa and Asia.

Social media have proven useful resources across the life cycle of mitigation, preparedness, response, and recovery. Social media differ from other media outlets in that they provide a dynamic and interactive means for communication. The information is read, created, shared, and edited by the public. Subsequently, emergency managers can use this information to disseminate information and capture intelligence. While there are many social media sites, Facebook, Twitter, and Wikipedia represent the most widely used forums (Palen 2009).

Through the use of Twitter and Facebook, FEMA, EPA, and CDC are able to warn the general public of disasters. Craig Fugate, FEMA administrator, wants to harness the power of the digital world to help the U.S. government, private sector, and citizens respond to disasters (Zurer 2011). Using the geographic information systems (GISs) associated with social media, emergency management agencies can predict impending tornado and hurricane paths and other natural disasters for specific areas. GIS applications integrate software and data capture to manage, analyze, and display geographical information (Anon 2011). These applications include crowdmapping and crowdsourcing and can allow you to view crisis information on maps and timelines from multiple sources.

Social Media Usage

During the 2007 Virginia Tech shooting, victims used social media to disseminate information in real time. Researchers found that users uploaded information to social media sites well before traditional news outlets began reporting. Interestingly, researchers found that users generated over 500 Facebook groups and one Wikipedia page with accurate and timely content (Palen et al. 2007). Also in 2007, use of social media during the southern California wildfires was studied. Researchers found that social media was used for "back-channel" communications as well as by media outlets (Sutton et al. 2008).

In 2010, those immediately affected by the Haiti earthquake used Twitter to provide images and information as events unfolded. By following the tweets (Twitter messages limited to 140 character or fewer), response and recovery organizations could identify what and where resources were most needed. Despite the failure of traditional communications in Haiti, CNN received 218 reports of needs, missing loved ones, and locations of damages. Clearly, social media offers emergency management officials potential benefits for enhancing their work (Frank 2010).

In 2010, during the Hawaii tsunami warning, social media were used to aid evacuation. The Honolulu emergency management department reported to news reporters that "Tweets and other forms of social networking helped create a relatively smooth evacuation of as many as 50,000 people on Oahu as a tsunami raced toward Hawaii" (AP 2011).

The same activity was seen during the Australian floods in 2011. Both Twitter and Facebook were used by emergency services. Axel Bruns, Queensland University of Technology professor noted, "Twitter was more effective at spreading items of information widely and rapidly, but Facebook proved more useful in providing detail and coordinating activities" (IANS 2011).

At the ESRI Federal User Conference in 2011, the current FEMA administrator, Craig Fugate, mentioned uses for social media and related applications during emergencies. He specifically mentioned the use of GIS applications. "GIS applications can be useful during response and recovery, by getting search and rescue to specific locations quickly and efficiently. Social media efforts can also be used to determine the status of store inventories in affected areas" (Fugate 2011).

During the Haiti earthquake, media reports were derived almost entirely from social media. Notable news sources such as CNN and BBC used Twitter to gain the latest information. Noticing the uses for social media for useful information, in 2006, CNN launched iReports, a user generated section of the news. While iReports constitutes a news-inspired social medium, CNN also takes the time to fact check some of the articles.

In the figure below, social media is explained in terms of the four phases of disasters. It presents a brief explanation and example of social media use for each phase. Although the phases overlap, the figure is meant to highlight the usefulness of social media as tools in emergency management.

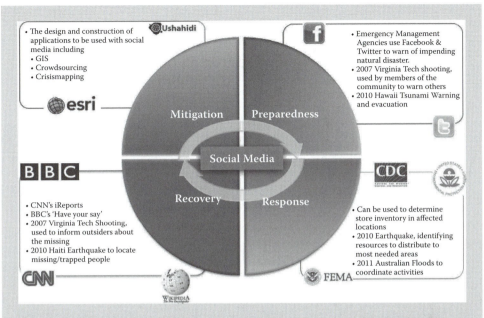

- The design and construction of applications to be used with social media including
  - GIS
  - Crowdsourcing
  - Crisismapping

Ushahidi

esri

Mitigation

Preparedness

Social Media

- Emergency Management Agencies use Facebook & Twitter to warn of impending natural disaster.
- 2007 Virginia Tech shooting, used by members of the community to warn others
- 2010 Hawaii Tsunami Warning and evacuation

BBC

- CNN's iReports
- BBC's 'Have your say'
- 2007 Virginia Tech Shooting, used to inform outsiders about the missing
- 2010 Haiti Earthquake to locate missing/trapped people

CNN

Recovery

Response

WIKIPEDIA

CDC

- Can be used to determine store inventory in affected locations
- 2010 Earthquake, identifying resources to distribute to most needed areas
- 2011 Australian Floods to coordinate activities

FEMA

Overview of social media and how they relate to the phases of disasters.

Inaccurate Information

There has been looming concern about possible inaccuracies arising from use of social media. Ideally, social media present awareness of an issue and should be used in conjunction with other sources. It is important to note that because social media are dynamic outlets, incorrect information is corrected by others almost instantly. Furthermore, information provided via social media that includes pictures, geographic locations, and GIS data can be viewed as more credible and easier to validate.

Best Use

For emergency management and disaster response, Twitter is best used in the following ways:

- For citizen first responders, to disseminate pertinent information emergency managers can gather to better respond to victims during recovery efforts.
- For back-channel informal inter- and intra-agency communication; emergency management officials, organizations, and corporations can informally express needs for help from each other.
- For facilitation of volunteers; social media can be used to direct the flow of, assess needs for, and determine the most important uses of volunteer traffic.

Sources

Anon. 2011. About GIS. www.GIS.com

Associated Press. 2010 Social Media Helped with Hawaii Tsunami Evacuation. ABC News, March 1. http://abcnews.go.com/US/wireStory?id=9981620

FEMA. 2011. FEMA Blog. http://blog.fema.gov/2011/01/social-media-emergency-management.html

Frank, Thomas. 2010. Social Media Play Part in Haiti's Recovery Efforts. *USA Today*, February 10. http://www.usatoday.com/tech/news/2010-02-01-haiti-monitor-social-media_N.htm

Fugate, Craig. 2011. Keynote address, ESRI Federal User Conference, Washington, D.C., January 19–21.

IANS. 2011. Twitter, Facebook Saviour during Australia Floods, *Times of India*, January 20. http://timesofindia.indiatimes.com/tech/social-media/Twitter-Facebook-saviour-during-Australia-floods/articleshow/7327761.cms#ixzz1CAJjUC7z

Palen, L. and A. L. Hughes. 2009. Twitter Adoption and Use in Mass Convergence and Emergency Events. Sixth International ISCRAM Conference, Gothenburg, Sweden.

Palen, Leysia, S. Vieweg, J. Sutton et al. 2007. Crisis Informatics: Studying Crisis in a Networked World. Third International Conference on e-Social Science, Ann Arbor, MI.

Sutton, Jeannette and L. Palen. 2008. Backchannels on the Front Lines: Emergent Uses of Social Media in the 2007 Southern California Wildfires. Fifth International ISCRAM Conference, Washington, D.C.

Zurer, Rachel. 2011 Storyboard: FEMA Chief says Social Media Aid Disaster Response. *Wired Magazine*, January 20. http://www.wired.com/magazine/2011/01/storyboard-fema-craig-fugate/

In summary, emergency managers performing hazard analysis must think beyond the expected types of events that may occur in their areas—earthquakes and wildfires on the West Coast; tornadoes and floods in the Midwest; hurricanes, high winds, and floods in coastal areas. Emergency managers must consider how two known hazards may interact or lead to a cascading series of events. In addition to local terrorist attacks, they must consider possible impacts from an attack 500 or 1,000 miles away, perhaps coupled with another event. They must be ready for a wide range of unknowns in today's uncertain world.

4.7 Summary

As this chapter points out, we face many types of hazards and challenges. People face daily risks arising from chemical, biological, nuclear, and radiological hazards that we have created and such hazards can lead to accidents, some of which could have been prevented. When they happen, great amounts of damage occur and many people sustain injuries or die. Terrorists use CBRN technologies to spread fear. We have seen over the past twenty years a focus on chemical use by terrorists (primarily through explosions or releases of toxic elements) and infrequent use of biological weapons (anthrax). For many, the greatest worries are biological, radiological, and nuclear weapons. Although they are not common now, they may become so in the future and will certainly produce the most destructive impacts.

Clearly, the numbers and types of "typical" disasters we face continue to rise. Increased industrialization (creating more technological hazards) and changes in demographic trends (e.g., more people living in hazardous areas) have contributed to the increasing frequency of disasters. Box 4.6 details the catastrophic Japan earthquake of March 2011. We are seeing Quarantelli's 1996 prediction come true: we face new, worse, and more catastrophic events.

BOX 4.6   JAPAN CATASTROPHE

Much of this chapter focused on the idea that we now face increasing disasters and catastrophes, resulting in more injuries, deaths, and economic losses worldwide. We also are vulnerable to new and more dangerous types of events. For example, one disaster may lead to another disaster, creating cascading natural (earthquake leading to a tsunami) or natech (natural event creating a technological breakdown) disasters. Such combinations would in turn create catastrophic events. We thought we provided good examples to make our key points in this chapter. And then the Japanese catastrophe struck.

On the afternoon of March 11, 2011, an M 9.0 earthquake violently shook northern and central Japan. The earthquake damaged and destroyed buildings, along with key components of the infrastructure (roads, bridges, electrical power). This event alone would be difficult to manage. Since the earthquake occurred just off the northern Japanese coast, government officials issued tsunami warnings along the east coast, telling people to go to higher ground. About thirty to forty minutes after the earthquake and declaration of a tsunami warming, a massive wall of water impacted the northern coast. In some cases, the tsunami wave height reached thirty feet and in some places crashed almost six miles inland. More deaths and additional massive destruction followed. Thus, in under an hour, Japan experienced two catastrophic events but the nation's problems were by no means over (*New York Times* 2011).

The tsunami crippled electrical power and back-up systems to the Fukushima Daiichi nuclear power plant. During the first ten days of the crisis, power plant representatives dealt with explosions, major and minor radiation leaks, and the potential for complete meltdowns of up to six reactors and nuclear fuel storage areas (*New York Times* 2011). The Japanese government first suggested that residents living within six miles of the reactors evacuate. As events became more unpredictable, they widened the evacuation zone to a twelve-mile radius and suggested that residents twelve to nineteen miles away shelter in place. Soon, the U.S. government urged its own residents living within fifty miles from the plants to evacuate, creating confusion about the severity of the situation (Tracy and Favole 2011, p. A13). At least 200,000 people evacuated from the twelve-mile zone (*New York*

Times 2011). As we send this brief section to the publisher, reports indicate that low level radiation has infiltrated milk supplies, some crops (e.g., spinach), and even drinking water located near the nuclear reactors (CNN 2011). Trace amounts of radiation from the Japanese reactors reached the U.S. west coast by March 18, 2011 (DOE 2011).

Other problems plagued the initial response to this catastrophe. More than two dozen constant aftershocks over M 6.0 kept people on edge (USGS 2011). A volcano erupted in Southern Japan (Hennessy-Fiske 2011). A dam shaken by the earthquake broke a few days later (Water Power and Dam Construction 2011). Snow and severe cold in Northern Japan about five days after the initial earthquake and tsunami hampered rescue operations. Since much of Northern Japan had no electricity, shelters and other locations had no way of keeping 700,000 homeless people warm (Fackler 2011). Due to power shortages caused by the earthquake and damage to the nuclear power plants, rolling blackouts were expected to continue over much of the country through April 2011 and perhaps longer (Fukase 2011, p. A11).

Data on the losses from these events are still hard to obtain—and they are only early indicators and estimates. Ten days after the event, Japanese government officials said that more than 8,000 people died and at least 13,000 more remain missing. The World Bank estimates that damages exceed $235 billion (Nakamura and Achenbach 2011). The media noted that the elderly are much more likely to die than other groups (Stringer and Gelineau 2011). Because much of the media coverage focuses on the nuclear power plant crises, we have no clear picture of the social impacts created by the earthquake and tsunami. Anyone who doubts the scenarios and possibilities presented earlier in this chapter should consider the results of the Japanese catastrophe.

References

CNN. 2011. WHO: No Short-term Risk with Contaminated Food. http://www.cnn.com/2011/WORLD/asiapcf/03/21/japan.nuclear.food/index.html?hpt=T2

Department of Energy. 2011. Situation in Japan. http://blog.energy.gov/content/situation-japan

Fackler, Martin. 2011. Misery and Uncertainty Fill Shelters. http://www.nytimes.com/2011/03/17/world/asia/17cope.html

Fukase, Atsuko. 2011. Electricity Outages Amplify the Anger. *Wall Street Journal* Vol. 257, No. 60, Tuesday, March 15.

Hennessy-Fiske, Molly. 2011. Volcano in Southern Japan Erupts. http://www.latimes.com/news/nationworld/world/la-fgw-japan-quake-volcano-20110314,0,2486939.story

Nakamura, David and Joel Achenbach. 2011. Death Toll from Japan's Disasters over 8,000; More than 13,000 Still Missing. *Washington Post*. http://www.washingtonpost.com/world/death-toll-from-japans-disasters-over-8000-more-than-12000-missing-/2011/03/20/ABF4yV0_story.html

New York Times. 2011. Japan: Earthquake, Tsunami, and Nuclear Crisis. http://topics.nytimes.com/top/news/international/countriesandterritories/japan/index.html

Stringer, David and Kristen Gelineau. 2011. Hope Fades for Missing Japanese Elderly. *Time*. http://www.time.com/time/world/article/0,8599,2059577-2,00.html

Tracy, Tennille and Jared Favole. 2011. U.S., Japan Split on Zone of Evacuation. *Wall Street Journal*, Vol. 257, No. 62,Thursday, March 17.
USGS.2011.StrongAftershocksContinuetoAffectJapan.http://www.usgs.gov/blogs/features/2011/03/11/preliminary-magnitude-8-9-near-the-east-coast-of-japan/
Water Power and Dam Construction. 2011. http://www.waterpowermagazine.com/story.asp?sc=2059132

Discussion Questions

1. Think about your own community. Have any changes made it a more hazardous place to live over the last twenty to thirty years? If so, what are the changes? Do any of these changes fit with Quarantelli's reasons for expecting more and worse disasters?

2. Explain why these worsening disaster trends hold true worldwide.

3. What is (or are) the general purpose(s) of the disaster scales presented in this chapter? How are they used? For whom are these scales useful?

4. What factors may explain why the number of natural disasters continues to increase? Are there simply more disasters, are other factors involved, or are both numbers and factors responsible?

4. What are natech events and how might they impact your community? Is there any way to identify, prepare for, or mitigate natechs?

5. Name some examples of natural or technological disasters that could also be used as tools by terrorists.

6. How do terrorists use CBRN to create disasters?

7. How does modernization make us more vulnerable not only to common disasters, but also to new and emerging hazards? What can we do to prepare for or mitigate new and emerging hazards?

References

Barton, Allen. 1970. *Communities in Disaster*. New York: Anchor Books.
Bell, Melissa. 2011. "Brazil Mudslides Kill Hundreds." Available at http://voices.washingtonpost.com/blog-post/2011/01/brazil_mudslides_kill_hundreds.html, last accessed March 1, 2011.
Biello, David. 2006. "Warming Climate May Increase Western Wildfire Woes," Scientific American. Available at http://www.scientificamerican.com/article.cfm?id=warming-climate-may-incre, last accessed February 4, 2011.
Broughton, Edward. 2005. "The Bhopal Disaster and Its Aftermath: A Review." *Environmental Health: A Global Access Science Journal* 4/6. Available at http://www.ehjournal.net/content/pdf/1476-069X-4-6.pdf, last accessed February 27, 2011.

CIA. 2007. Terrorist CBRN: Materials and Effects. Available at https://www.cia.gov/library/reports/general-reports-1/terrorist_cbrn/terrorist_CBRN.htm, last accessed January 25, 2011.

Cruz, Ana Maria, Laura J. Steinbert, Anna Lisa Vetere Arellano, Jean-Pierre Nordvik, and Francesco Pisano. 2004. *State of the Art in Natech Risk Management*. Italy: European Union.

DHS. 2008. "Cyber Security Awareness Month," *Leadership Journal Archive*. Available at http://www.dhs.gov/journal/leadership/2008/10/cyber-security-awareness-month.html, last accessed January 30, 2011.

DHS. 2009. "Biological Attack: the Danger." Available at http://www.dhs.gov/files/publications/gc_1245183510280.shtm, last accessed January 31, 2011.

Environmental Protection Agency (EPA). 2000. Guidance for the Implementation of the General Duty Clause Clean Air Act Section 112(r)(1). Available at http://www.epa.gov/compliance/resources/policies/civil/caa/gdc/gendutyclause-rpt.pdf, last accessed January 31, 2011.

Corfidi, Stephen F., Jason J. Levi, and Steven J. Weiss. No date. "The Super Outbreak." Available at http://www.spc.noaa.gov/publications/corfidi/3apr74.pdf, last accessed January 26, 2011.

Garamone, Jim. 2010. "Lynn Changes Approach to Changes in Warfare," U.S., Department of Defense. Available at http://www.defense.gov/news/newsarticle.aspx?id=58930, last accessed January 30, 2011.

Hoffman, Susanna M. 1998. "Eve and Adam among the Embers: Gender Patterns after the Berkeley Firestorm." In *The Gendered Terrain of Disaster*, eds. Elaine Enarson and Betty Hearn Morrow. Westport, Conn: Praeger.

Kilbourne ED. 2006. "Influenza Pandemics of the 20th Century." *Emergent Infectious Diseases*. Available at http://www.cdc.gov/ncidod/EID/vol12no01/05-1254.htm, last accessed January 30, 2010.

Leggiere, Phil. 2011. "2010 Disasters: Deadliest in Decades." Homeland Security News, Insight & Analysis." Available at http://www.hstoday.us/single-article/2010-disasters-deadliest-in-decades/fb168a0fadc9cc02aa717ab66751ecf3.html, last accessed January 31, 2011.

Lite, Jordan. 2009. "Death Toll Climbs in Aussie Wildfires." *Scientific American*. Available at http://www.scientificamerican.com/blog/post.cfm?id=death-toll-climbs-in-aussie-wildfir-2009-02-09, last accessed February 4, 2011.

Mileti, Dennis D. 1999. *Disasters by Design*. Washington, D.C.: Joseph Henry Press.

Murtagh, Bill. 2010. "Space Weather Storms: Responding to Global Concerns." Paper Presented to FEMA, Atlanta, Georgia, November 18.

NASA. 2002. "The Lunar Quarantine Program." Available at http://lsda.jsc.nasa.gov/books/apollo/s5ch1.htm, last accessed February 27, 2011.

NASA. 2011a. "Near Earth Object Program." Available at http://neo.jpl.nasa.gov/neo/, last accessed February 27. 2011.

NASA. 2011b. "Valentine's Day Solar Flare." Available at http://www.nasa.gov/mission_pages/sunearth/news/News021411-xclass.html, last accessed February 27, 2011.

National Academy of Sciences. 2004. "Radiological Attack: Dirty Bombs and Other Devices." Available at http://www.dhs.gov/xlibrary/assets/prep_radiological_fact_sheet.pdf, last accessed January 31, 2011.

National Academy of Sciences. 2005. "Nuclear Attack." Available at http://www.dhs.gov/xlibrary/assets/prep_nuclear_fact_sheet.pdf, last accessed January 31, 2011.

National Integrated Fire Agency. 2007. "Fire Information—Wildland Fire Statistics." Available at http://www.nifc.gov/fire_info/fire_stats.htm, last accessed February 6, 2011.

NOAA. No date a. "Saffir-Simpson Hurricane Scale." Available at http://www.aoml.noaa.gov/general/lib/laescae.html, last accessed January 25, 2011.

NOAA. No date b. "Hurricane History." Available at http://www.nhc.noaa.gov/HAW2/english/history.shtml, last accessed January 26, 2011.

NOAA. 2005a. "State of the Climate: Hurricane & Tropical Storms." Available at http://www.ncdc.noaa.gov/img/climate/research/2005/ann/namedstorms-majorhurr.gif, last accessed January 25, 2011.

NOAA. 2005b. "Space Weather Scales." Available at http://www.spc.noaa.gov/faq/tornado/ef-scale.html, last accessed February 27, 2011.

NOAA, 2007. "The Enhanced Fujita Scale." Available at http://www.spc.noaa.gov/faq/tornado/ef-scale.html, last accessed January 25, 2011.

NOAA, 2008a. "Global Warming." Available at http://www.ncdc.noaa.gov/oa/climate/globalwarming.html#q8, last accessed January 30, 2011.

NOAA. 2008b. "Global and Hemispheric Annual Combined Land–Surface Air Temperature and SST Anomilies." Available at http://www.ncdc.noaa.gov/img/climate/globalwarming/ar4-fig-3-6.gif, last accessed January 30, 2011.

NOAA. 2009a. "The Enhanced Fujita Scale." Available at http://www.spc.noaa.gov/efscale/, last accessed January 25, 2011.

NOAA. 2009b. "Flood Safety." Available at http://www.weather.gov/floodsafety/floodsafe.shtml, last accessed January 27th, 2011).

NOAA. 2009c. "Flood Fatalities." Available at http://www.nws.noaa.gov/oh/hic/flood_stats/recent_individual_deaths.shtml, last accessed January 27th, 2011.

NOAA. 2009d. "Flood Basics." http://www.nssl.noaa.gov/primer/flood/fld_basics.html (accessed January 27th, 2011).

NOAA. 2009e. "A Paleo Perspective on Global Warming." Available at http://www.ncdc.noaa.gov/paleo/globalwarming/end.html, last accessed January 30, 2011.

Office of the Federal Coordinator of Meteorology. 2010. "2010 Space Weather Enterprise Forum Summary Report." Available at http://www.ofcm.gov/swef/2010/SWEF_2010_Summary_Report_%28Final%29.pdf, last accessed March 1, 2011.

Perrow, Charles. 1984. *Normal Accidents.* New York: Basic Books.

Powell, Larry, Jean Bodon, and Mark Hickson III. 2001. "Rejection of Crisis Information: Public Apathy and the Crisis of Y2K." *Communication Research Reports* 18/1: 84–92.

Quarantelli, E. L. 1996. "The Future is Not the Past Repeated: Projecting Disasters in the 21st Century from Current Trends." *Journal of Contingencies and Crisis Management* 4/4: 228–240.

Quarantelli, E. L. 2001. "Another Selective Look at Future Social Crises: Some Aspects of Which We Can already See in the Present." *Journal of Contingencies and Crisis Management* 9/4: 233–237.

Reuters. 2011. "Australian Flood Clean-up Starts." Available at http://www.reuters.com/article/2011/01/13/us-australia-floods-idUSTRE6BU09620110113, last accessed February 28, 2011.

Schott, Timothy et al. 2010. "Saffir-Simpson Hurricane Wind Scale." NOAA, National Weather Service. Available at http://www.nhc.noaa.gov/sshws.shtml, last accessed January 25, 2011.

Taubenberger, Jeffery K. and David M. Morens. 2006. "1918 Influenza: The Mother of All Pandemics." *Emerging Infectious Diseases*, http://www.cdc.gov/ncidod/eid/vol12no01/05-0979.htm, last accessed February 6, 2011.

Terrorism Project. 2009. "Chronology of Major Terrorist Attacks against the United States." Available at http://www.cdi.org/terrorism/chronology.html, last accessed January 30, 2011.

United Nations. 2007. "International Flood Imitative." Available at http://unesdoc.unesco.org/images/0015/001512/151208e.pdf, last accessed January 27, 2011.

USGS. No date. "Measuring Earthquakes." Available at http://earthquake.usgs.gov/learn/faq/?faqID=24, last accessed January 25, 2011.

USGS. 2005. "Description: Economic Impacts of the May18, 1980 Eruption." Available at http://pubs.usgs.gov/fs/fs027-00/fs027-00.pdf, last accessed February 27, 2011.

USGS. 2008. "2008 Bay Area Earthquake Probabilities." Available at http://earthquake.usgs.gov/regional/nca/ucerf/, last accessed January 25, 2011.

USGS. 2009. "The Modified Mercalli Scale." Available at http://earthquake.usgs.gov/learn/topics/mercalli.php, last accessed January 25, 2011.

USGS. 2010a. "Earthquakes with 50,000 or More Deaths." Available at http://earthquake.usgs.gov/earthquakes/world/most_destructive.php, last accessed January 26, 2011.

USGS. 2010b. "USGS Earthquake Magnitude Policy." Available at http://earthquake.usgs.gov/aboutus/docs/020204mag_policy.php, last accessed January 26, 2011.

United States Department of State. 2010. "Developing Statistical Information." Available at http://www.state.gov/s/ct/rls/crt/2009/140902.htm, last accessed January 29, 2011.

United States Nuclear Regulatory Commission (U.S. NRC). 2009a. "Backgrounder on Chernobyl Nuclear Power Plant Accident." Available at, http://www.nrc.gov/reading-rm/doc-collections/fact-sheets/chernobyl-bg.html, last accessed February 27, 2011.

United States Nuclear Regulatory Commission (U.S. NRC). 2009b. "Fact Sheet on Plutonium." Available at http://www.nrc.gov/reading-rm/doc-collections/fact-sheets/plutonium.html, last accessed February 27, 2011.

Waugh, William L, Jr. 2006. "Terrorism as Disaster." Pp. 388–404 in *Handbook of Disaster Research*, (H. Rodriguez, E. L. Quarantelli, and Russell R. Dynes, eds.). New York: Springer.

Wheelis, Mark. 2002. "Biological Warfare at the 1386 Siege of Caffa." *Historical Review* 8/9: 971–975.

Wilson, Mary E. 1995. "Travel and the Emergence of Infectious Diseases." EID 1/2. Available at http://www.cdc.gov/ncidod/eid/vol1no2/wilson.htm, last accessed February 27, 2011.

Resources

Many federal agencies provide additional, extensive, and much more technological information about the hazards discussed in this chapter. Further information about these types of hazards can be found on the following government websites.

- Tornadoes, hurricanes, floods, and other weather related events: www.noaa.gov
- Earthquakes: www.usgs.gov
- Wildfires: www.nifc.gov
- Terrorism: www.dhs.gov
- Chemical and hazardous materials incidents: www.epa.gov

- Biological diseases and terror attacks: www.cdc.gov
- Nuclear and radiological events: www.doe.gov
- Space weather and asteroid strikes: www.nasa.gov, www.ofcm.gov

Although too numerous to list here, many state offices of emergency management and offices of homeland security have specific information about natural and technological hazards and dealing with terrorism.

The 9/11 Commission Report provides an even-handed detail of the events leading to and following the September 11, 2001 terrorist attacks. These documents offer a good starting point for a more in-depth look at terrorism and related issues. A complete copy of the report and extensive supporting documents can be found at: http://www.9-11commission.gov

Chapter **5**

Becoming an Emergency Management Professional

5.1 Chapter Objectives

Upon completing this chapter, readers should be able to:

1. Understand the relevance of recommended core competencies for emergency management practice.
2. Compare and contrast professional competency standards and professional qualities for a practitioner of emergency management.
3. Explain ethical practice standards and behavioral expectations for the practice of emergency management.
4. Identify and provide an overview of organizations involved in the field of emergency management.
5. Illustrate the traditional activities of the emergency manager during routine days and during times of disaster.
6. Discuss why certification is considered an important step in developing a professional identity as an emergency manager.

5.2 Introduction

In this chapter, we explore the profession of emergency management so that those of you interested in a career will understand what is expected of you. We also hope to entice those with an interest in the topic to consider a career or volunteer for disaster service. For those taking the course as an elective, we hope that you learn about the field in general so that you will be able to use the content as a homeowner, parent, or neighbor, or as a working professional in fields like social service, journalism, engineering, and meteorology, to name a few. We start by introducing you to the core competencies an emergency management professional should possess.

Dr. Wayne Blanchard (2005), the first director of the FEMA Higher Education Project in the U.S., compiled a list of core competencies from a wide set of academics and practitioners who attended dozens of workshops and conferences in the past fifteen years. Blanchard lists these core areas as competencies that emergency managers should possess (see Box 5.1 for core competencies in the United Kingdom):

1. *Comprehensive emergency management framework or philosophy*— A comprehensive approach means that emergency managers must embrace an all-hazards perspective (for a definition, see Chapter 2). Doing so means that an emergency manager does not and cannot focus on one single, overriding hazard. By addressing the range of risks that may face his or her community, the emergency manager seeks to reduce risk widely. The all-hazards approach means that emergency managers economize their activities across hazards. To illustrate, writing an emergency operations plan for every possible hazard would require considerable time, training, and exercising. By emphasizing a more functional approach to planning, it is possible to organize response for any hazard into specific areas such as transportation, communication, mass care of the public, and other functions. Elements of hazards that require unique attention such as hazardous materials releases or terrorism can then be planned for specifically. Indeed, the functional approach has been adopted by the U.S. in its National Response Framework (see Chapter 7). As discussed in Chapter 2, the National Governors' Association (1979) first organized emergency management activities into four phases: preparedness, response, recovery, and mitigation. Activities within these phases will be discussed further in this chapter as they lay an important foundation for organizing the daily life of a local emergency manager and the organizational structure for national-level ministries and agencies in many nations. An all-hazards approach applies across these four phases.

2. *Leadership and team building*—Working together in a collaborative manner helps emergency managers meet the demands that disasters place on those who prepare the public and respond to their needs. Leadership of that team is also critical. It is important to note,

BOX 5.1   CORE COMPETENCES IN THE U.K.

Eve Coles

Eve Coles, the editor of *Emergency Management Review* and noted scholar in emergency management education, returns again in this chapter to address core competencies in the United Kingdom. Please revisit Chapter 1 for Dr. Coles' information on the rise of the profession in the U.K.

The drive to professionalize emergency management in the United Kingdom (U.K.) arose from the need to restructure the U.K. system following the events of 2000 and 2001 (flooding, fuel crisis, and the foot and mouth outbreak). The need to professionalize emergency management was recognised by commentators in the past and in particular the Association of Civil Defence and Emergency Planning Officers (a forerunner of the Emergency Planning Society [EPS] in 1990 when they noted that emergency planning was "one of the few professions within local government for which no formal academic qualifications were required"—a situation that remained until the new millennium.

The initial development of competences in the U.K. began in 2006 and was a two-stage approach supported financially by the Cabinet Office Civil Contingencies Secretariat (CCS). Two projects, the National Occupational Standards (NOS) in Civil Contingencies and the EPS Core Competences Framework, were undertaken in partnership; both projects share the research and development process, thus ensuring that a coherent framework was developed.

The NOS for Civil Contingencies are essentially technical and are built around knowledge and understanding, performance criteria, and skills. The eight core competence areas closely follow the duties under the Civil Contingencies Act 2004 and are underpinned by the concept of multi-agency integrated emergency management:

- Co-operate with other organizations.
- Work in co-operation with other organizations.
- Share information with other organizations.
- Anticipate and assess the risk of emergencies.
- Plan for emergencies.
- Develop, maintain, and evaluate emergency plans and arrangements.
- Plan for business continuity.
- Develop, maintain, and evaluate business continuity plans and arrangements.
- Promote business continuity management.
- Validate emergency or business continuity plans.
- Create exercises to practice or validate emergency or business continuity plans or arrangements.

- Direct and facilitate exercises to practice or validate emergency or business continuity arrangements.
- Develop training to support emergency or business continuity arrangements.
- Communicate with the community to enhance resilience.
- Raise awareness of risks, potential impacts, and arrangements in place for emergencies.
- Warn, inform, and advise the community in the events of emergencies.
- Manage responses to emergencies.
- Respond to emergencies at the strategic (gold) level.
- Respond to emergencies at the tactical (silver) level.
- Respond to emergencies at the operational (bronze) level.
- Address the needs of individuals during the initial responses to emergencies.
- Manage volunteers during initial responses to emergencies.
- Manage recovery from emergencies.
- Provide ongoing support to meet the needs of individuals affected by emergencies.
- Manage community recovery from emergencies.
- Manage volunteers during recovery from emergencies.

The EPS Core Competences Framework has been designed to include areas considered essential to the practice of emergency management and at its heart is the vision of the 'competent practitioner.' The framework utilizes the eight technical areas of the NOS to form the foundation of the framework and extends them to include four further areas of competence:

- *Theories and concepts in emergency management*—The aim is to equip the aspiring practitioner with the fundamental knowledge and understanding to be able to effectively participate in emergency management activities.
- *Acting effectively across your organisation*—This ensures the organisation recognises its responsibilities and is ready to deliver its functions in response to emergencies.
- *Debriefing after an emergency, exercise or other activity*—Organising and conducting debriefs following an emergency, exercise, or other activity enables organisations both individually and as multiagency groups to identify lessons to be learned from such events.
- *Managing computer-generated data to support decision making*—This requires management of information and knowledge generated by computer-based information systems such as Geographical Information Systems (GIS) and Management Information Systems (MIS) and its effective use to support decision making in emergency management both in day-to-day activities and during emergencies.

Three additional elements of competence (behaviour, attitudes, and professional outcomes) were also added to those included in the NOS. Each of the competence areas is discrete and may be used individually to form the basis of the development of an area of expertise or collectively as a guide to developing a generic foundation for those entering the profession

It is intended that the framework will help the emergency management profession in the U.K. define its purpose more clearly, identify the standards it wishes to require of those who wish to join it, and increase its public standing. It is also hoped that the framework will assist government in achieving consistency of performance in specific areas across numerous organisations, localities, and jurisdictions.

though, that such leadership does not imply a command and control approach. Rather, "leadership is needed—not just an ability to provide a command presence, but the demonstration of vision, compassion, flexibility, imagination, resolve, and courage" (Blanchard 2010). Flexibility may be the most important quality of all, as disasters do not know the plan and tend to require improvisation.

3. *Management*—Blanchard notes that management is different from leadership. Managers take on tasks and direct activities to accomplish a particular job or mission. Someone who manages preparedness, for example, would be tasked with facilitating planning as well as public education. Managers facilitate and also ensure implementation of the efforts. Before disaster, it is necessary to design a warning system that reaches all the public. Good managers ensure that the best warning system been identified and purchased, implemented, tested, and explained fully to the public that needs to know how to respond when the emergency managers issue warnings. Leaders provide inspiration and direction; managers ensure that teams get things done.

4. *Networking and coordination*—Networking is really about relationships. In emergency management, you will interact with a wide array of partners as described in an upcoming section. You may work or volunteer across city government or within the vertical and horizontal levels of another type of organization. Should a disaster affect your community beyond available resources, it will be necessary to contact other partners, organizations, and levels of government. Such collaboration requires advance work to get to know which organizations can do what. You must know which organizations will step up and which personnel can be counted on in the worst of times. Significant levels of effort to coordinate those partners must be undertaken well in advance of an event. Because of considerable turnover in some partners, particularly elected officials, it is necessary to view this competency as an ongoing and never-ending

activity. Emergency managers are always working with and educating their partners on procedures and plans. You cannot be an educator when a tornado is bearing down on your community.

5. *Integrated emergency management*—During a disaster, you may be surprised at how many organizations and agencies become involved—not just the emergency management agency and first responders. For example, transportation agencies support evacuation of those without cars. Prior to Hurricane Gustav in 2008, Louisiana used buses to send thousands of residents to safety in Mississippi and Alabama. In Texas, a massive effort coordinated across most of the state (second largest in the U.S.) moved hundreds of thousands of people to safety from Hurricane Ike. Moving people required advanced medical support for seriously ill people and those in nursing homes and the integration of public health agencies, medical volunteers, air ambulances, the military, and animal care providers. As another example, the Department of Public works will set up barricades in flooded areas and help with debris removal after tornadoes. Even the local public health office will help in shelters by ensuring hygienic conditions and offering immunizations in long-term shelter situations to reduce the spread of influenza and other respiratory diseases. In short, integrated emergency management requires planning and coordination with a variety of offices and agencies to address the potential damage and destruction a disaster can bring.

6. *Key emergency management functions*—A later section in this chapter will explain functional activities tied to the phases of emergency management. Blanchard's (2005) compilation identifies these core functional areas:

   - *Risk Assessment.* A first critical function of any emergency management agency is to identify the local hazards and to assess the potential impact on an area's population, infrastructure (highways, bridges, roads) and lifelines like electricity, water, and wastewater systems.

   - *Planning.* Emergency managers spend considerable time planning strategies and operational procedures for response and also for recovery and mitigation. The mitigation activity is the key to reducing response and recovery expenses and impacts.

   - *Training and Exercising.* Training means that people learn the plan, particularly their roles and responsibilities. Agencies, organizations, and individuals likely to be active in a response period must learn the division of labor, the tasks to be undertaken, and the ways in which the tasks can be safely carried out. After learning plans and procedures, an exercise can be undertaken as a table-top event in which people explain what they would do or a full-scale event allowing people to take on roles and respond to a given scenario. As you will discover in Chapter 7, planning does not mean rigid adherence to a strict set of procedures. Rather, as indicated in these core competencies, adaptability to crisis is required. The motto of the Florida Division of Emergency Management echoes this principle: *Semper Gumby* or always flexible.

- *Emergency Operations Center (EOC) Functions.* An EOC serves as a location where emergency management agencies can coordinate and communicate during a crisis. Prior to a disaster, EOCs must be designed, organized, and resourced to cover the functional areas set out in the agency's plan. An EOC can be set up as a fixed or mobile location with specially designed vehicles or even as an ad hoc setting near a disaster site. An EOC can even be handled virtually though special software that allows for communication and recording of critical information. EOCs vary considerably in design and structure, something you will learn about further in Chapter 8.

- *Establishing Interoperable Communications.* Interoperability emerged as a critical problem after numerous disasters, defined as the inability to communicate (interoperate) across the communication technologies used by various responders and emergency management agencies. As part of rebuilding a response system after the September 11, 2001 attacks, efforts to fix the problem accelerated. Simply put, interoperability means the capacity to communicate across organizations. One example concerns radio communications. When different organizations use different frequencies or equipment, they may not be able to talk to each other. Interoperability also involves communication within and across organizational cultures. By now, you have probably realized that many acronyms are used in this profession. Learning acronyms is part of your task this semester, as it is part of the language of the culture of emergency management. Because emergency management emanates from multiple disciplines, learning to speak across disciplinary jargons is necessary too. Be sure to pay attention to acronyms in your general education curriculum courses as they will enhance your abilities to communicate.

- *Applying Lessons Learned and Research Findings.* It is common after a disaster to look for what was missed, did not work, or needs improvement. By looking for those lessons to be learned, an emergency manager can increase effectiveness in future events and in working with the partnerships that will participate. As you will discover in the content of this book, though, existing research exists to inform emergency managers. In short, learning your lessons begins here by acquiring the knowledge that informs best practices in the field of emergency management.

7. *Political, bureaucratic, and social contexts*—Context specifies time, place, and circumstances. The contexts in which emergency managers practice their profession differ considerably. The New Zealand context, for example, requires an understanding of the diverse populations and cultures on the islands and the country's geographic risks: earthquakes, volcanoes, and tsunamis. New Zealand organizes its emergency management responsibilities in a national-level Ministry of Civil Defence and Emergency Management. By having a system of civil defense emergency management groups in place, many search and rescue activities after the February 2011 earthquake were carried out by civilians. In India, an emerging emergency response framework tapped administrative professionals within the State of Tamil Nadu government to manage tsunami response. They handled debris removal, established temporary shelters, provided food and water, and dealt with over 10,000 fatalities. The 2010 earthquake in Haiti destroyed critical emergency response facilities and killed both responders and officials. Assisting the badly damaged capital city of Port-au-Prince required extensive, multinational collaboration for search and rescue, mass care (shelter, food, water), emergency surgeries, continuing health care, rebuilding, and debris removal. As these examples demonstrate, context influences where emergency management functions are, the resources available to manage events, and the hazards and impacts that result. An emergency management agency may vary from minimally organized to overly bureaucratic to the point of inflexibility. Political contexts may generate additional challenges, particularly since public officials often bear responsibility for issuing evacuation orders and approving expenses for preparedness through recovery and prioritizing mitigation projects. Without political support and well informed government officials, emergency management capabilities suffer. Being politically savvy and able to work within a specific context can make a considerable difference to emergency management success.

8. *Technical systems and standards*—Technology presents both challenges and resources. In a damaged environment, technology (computer systems, cell phones, power) may not be available. With a supportive infrastructure, technology can expedite communications, transmit critical information, and record data for useful analysis. Practitioners of emergency management would be well advised to learn about emergency communication systems, warning

technologies, and software packages such as geographic information systems (GISs) and WebEOC, a virtual platform that can record critical event data in real time. It has become increasingly important to know how to use social media and related tools to educate, prepare, and warn a widespread online society. Because technologies can fail and because some people may not access social media, backup and redundant systems are critical.

9. *Social vulnerability reduction approach*—Technologies may not be the panaceas that solve all problems in a disaster in part because emergency managers may lack expertise or not use technologies to ensure that information reaches everyone. National Weather Service meteorologists Woods and Weisman (2003) warn us of a "hole in the weather warning system," meaning that people who are deaf or hard of hearing often do not receive warnings or alerts. This occurs because emergency warning systems have not adapted their procedures and technologies to the lives of real people in their communities. The sheer diversity of any community means that someone may not get a warning or be able to respond as desired without warning systems designed to reach them. The failure of many people to evacuate for Hurricane Katrina may be explained by a social vulnerability approach. The elderly, people with disabilities, and caregivers for these populations lacked the means to evacuate including accessible transportation vehicles (National Council on Disability 2009). The urban population of New Orleans also lacked cars—a problem that could affect Miami, New York, Chicago, and San Francisco where people use mass transit systems. Today's emergency manager must look at vulnerable individuals; in the past we failed to understand people's life circumstances and establish emergency procedures to ensure their safety. Telling people to evacuate, and making that happen for a community with dozens of nursing homes, recent immigrants who may not speak the language, and tourists takes sensitivity to its diversity (Phillips et al. 2010).

10. *Experience*—Without "boots on the ground" experience and realistic exposures to a disaster context, an emergency manager cannot be effective. Understanding an event and experiencing it are completely different. While understanding can inform principles and practices for approaching a disaster, effective management requires being "in the trenches" to get a real feel for the challenges and to learn how to apply the knowledge gained in educational programs. New York City, for example, was well prepared for emergencies. Yet, the September 11, 2001 attack on and collapse of the Twin Towers destroyed a state-of-the-art emergency operations center. Emergency managers rebuilt a new EOC in a nearby warehouse within 48 hours

and led the city through relief efforts and trauma. Doing so in the context of losing fellow citizens and the damage to the infrastructure surrounding Ground Zero took experience, strong interorganizational relationships, good leaders, and effective managers—all the core competencies contained in this list.

5.3 Practice Standards and Ethics

Emergency management, despite its important role in safeguarding communities, is a fairly new profession. Professional standards for the practice of emergency management vary around the nation and the world, but increasingly we are seeing more common sets of expectations. In this section, we review two of the more influential pieces that embrace concepts written about earlier in this volume.

5.3.1 NFPA 1600 Standards

Emergency management professionals around the world have begun to outline what they consider the elements required for an emergency management program to succeed. In the U.S., the National Fire Protection Association (NFPA) has a well established legacy of forming committees to establish such standards. In 1991, the NFPA convened a Disaster Management Committee that produced the NFPA 1600 Standard on Disaster, Emergency Management, and Business Continuity Programs by 1995. Several editions followed in 2000, 2004, and most recently 2007. The 1600 standard embraces the four phases of preparedness—response, recovery, and mitigation. Prevention was added in 2007 (NFPA 2007).

To set out common program elements, NFPA's committee members established criteria for developing and assessing emergency management programs. These elements address the activities that an emergency management agency should address and accomplish. The starting point is typically a *risk analysis* that rests on identification of local hazards (see Chapter 6) and allows a local agency to review the history of past hazards and the possibility that they will happen again—and who and what they will impact. Understanding the local hazards forms a base for *preventing incidents* through *mitigation* (see Chapter 10). As defined later, mitigation efforts target local hazards and try to reduce their impacts, for example, constructing a dam in an area prone to flooding.

Responding to incidents requires effective *resource management and logistical coordination* of facilities, services, equipment, and personnel (see Chapter 8). By understanding local hazards and amassing the assets necessary to respond, an agency can determine its capabilities. When needed, an emergency manager will turn to *mutual aid agreements* with local partners. This requires careful *planning* across all of the phases of a disaster and must involve the key stakeholders and the public at large in carrying out the plan (see Chapter 7). During the response and recovery phases, *incident management* serves as the focus (see Chapters 8 and 9). Such management requires attention to inter- and intraorganizational *communication, crisis communication, warning dissemination*, and *informing the public. Operational procedures* must cover standard operations to ensure life safety, situational analyses of events as they unfold, and damage assessments in the aftermaths. *Facilities*, as mentioned in the core competencies above, must accommodate the development, maintenance, and operation of the EOC. Carrying out all these tasks means involving critical personnel in *training, education*, and *exercises*. Finally, because most emergency managers report to a public, corporate or non-governmental structure, an agency must show *financial accountability.*

5.3.2 Ethical Behavior

The International Association of Emergency Managers (IAEM) established a Code of Ethics to guide the work and to enhance professionalism of those working in the field. With 5,000 members across fifty-eight nations, IAEM serves as a lead organization for networking. IAEM also provides certification standards for working professionals that lead to the Certified Emergency Manager designation described later in this chapter. Following the principles of respect, commitment, and professionalism, IAEM (2010) members hold to certain ethical standards:[*]

- Respect for supervising officials, colleagues, associates, and most importantly, for the people we serve is the standard for IAEM members. We comply with all laws and regulations applicable to our purpose and position, and responsibly and impartially apply them to all concerned. We respect fiscal resources by evaluating organizational decisions to provide the best service or product at a minimal cost without sacrificing quality.
- IAEM members commit themselves to promoting decisions that engender trust and those we serve. We commit to continuous improvement by fairly administering the affairs of our positions, by fostering honest and trustworthy relationships, and by striving for impeccable accuracy and clarity in what we say or write. We commit to enhancing stewardship of resources and the caliber of service we deliver while striving to improve the quality of life in the community we serve.

---

[*] *Source*: http://www.iaem.com/about/IAEMCodeofEthics.htm

- IAEM is an organization that actively promotes professionalism to ensure public confidence in emergency management. Our reputations are built on the faithful discharge of our duties. Our professionalism is founded on education, safety, and protection of life and property.

Behaving in an ethical manner yields enormous benefits. People are more willing to work with each other and to serve as partners. Elected officials feel they can trust you—and you can trust them. The public supports those who safeguard not only their lives but the resources that they pay through taxes or donations. Loss of confidence in the ethical behavior of an emergency manager or public official charged with public safety means that people are less likely to listen to future messages or to heed warnings, to support necessary mitigation projects, or to vote for increased taxes, levies or the like. Emergency managers must generate a strong connection to the public and others they work with if they want to be effective.

5.4 Emergency Management Organizations and Agencies

The field of emergency management presents a number of work locations and career opportunities for you to consider (Edwards and Daniel 2007). In this section, we discuss a number of key governmental, non-governmental, and professional organizations. The intent of this section is to illustrate the range of agencies active in emergency management and cite some domestic and international examples. Throughout the remaining chapters, readers will be introduced to dozens of additional governmental and non-governmental organizations.

5.4.1 Governmental Agencies

Government agencies operate at local, state, regional, national, and also at international levels. To be effective in a disaster, they must coordinate, communicate, and collaborate despite political, social, and developmental differences. Lives are on the line, not just during an emergency response, but also throughout a lingering recovery. Each level of government brings different insights, resources, and aid that must be understood and managed (Figure 5.1).

5.4.1.1 Local Level

As noted in previous chapters, disasters are best viewed as local events. A tornado may impact a neighborhood or a community—most disasters tend

FIGURE 5.1 **State Representatives discuss damage from Tennessee flooding with FEMA Administrator Craig Fugate and FEMA Federal Coordinating Officer.** (*Source:* **FEMA News Photo/David Fine.**)

to affect fairly localized settings. Exceptions are catastrophic or near-catastrophic events such as the 2010 earthquake in Haiti and Hurricane Katrina that struck the Gulf Coast in 2005. Because disasters are usually experienced locally, the local emergency management agency (LEMA; Lindell 1994) takes responsibility for organizing preparedness, response, recovery, and mitigation activities. A LEMA may be a small office in the basement of a city hall staffed mostly by volunteers or a major urban operation with staffs to handle specialized areas. LEMAs may also function at city, county, and parish levels (EMAs).

EMAs may differ structurally (Labadie 1984). Probably the two most common forms are the departmental and embedded structures. In the departmental structure, an emergency manager serves as the head of a department much like a department of public works or a department of parks and recreation. He or she serves under the city manager or elected official responsible for the department. Such a model implies competition with other departments for personnel, budget, and resources. This intraorganizational department structure may not work effectively during a disaster when rapidly changing conditions require immediate, adaptable management rather than a standardized, bureaucratic response (Neal and Phillips 1995).

Another EMA organizational matter to consider is the number of personnel that should be hired. In 2007, one published set of guidelines in the U.S. suggested that a local EMA should have at least one professional emergency manager for every 100,000 persons in the population. Most countries including the U.S. do not meet that benchmark although emergency management operations continue to hire new people while other professions are downsizing.

5.4.1.2 State or Provincial Level

In many areas, the next level of emergency management is the state or provincial level. In the U.S., for example, all 50 states host emergency management agencies with staffs and emergency operations centers (EOCs). Because the sizes and resources of states vary, staff numbers and facilities also vary. The Florida Division of Emergency Management, for example, faces annual hurricane threats and must bring considerable resources to bear on preparing for and managing this significant risk (see Box 5.2). Similarly, along the eastern coast of Australia, Emergency Management Queensland (EMQ) dedicates local and regional time to prepare for cyclone, bushfire, and flooding threats (massive flooding there inundated hundreds of towns in early 2011). As a state level agency, EMQ includes both first responder units like helicopter rescue and disaster management services that link local and district levels to critical resources:

> Due to the high incidence of natural disasters experienced in Queensland, it is imperative that we have a well developed and effective system that ensures coordinated capabilities at all levels of government. The Queensland Disaster Management System is a multi-tiered system of committees and coordination centres at State, Disaster District and at Local level that, in partnership, ensure a coordinated and effective capability to help prevent, prepare for, respond to and recover from disasters in Queensland.[*]

In most circumstances, the state acts as a provider of resources and as a liaison between locally affected communities and national-level resources. Funds may flow through the state to the local level and the state may advocate with regional or national partners to secure additional assistance. In the U.S., a presidential disaster declaration cannot be issued to cover a local area unless a request passes through the state-level agency and the governor of the state. Without a declaration, resources may not be made available under the Stafford Act.

---

[*] *Source*: http://www.disaster.qld.gov.au/about

BOX 5.2   STATE AND PROVINCIAL LEVEL EMERGENCY MANAGEMENT AGENCIES

Florida Division of Emergency Management

The Division of Emergency Management plans for and responds to both natural and man-made disasters. These range from floods and hurricanes to incidents involving hazardous materials or nuclear power. The division prepares and implements a statewide Comprehensive Emergency Management Plan, and routinely conducts extensive exercises to test state and county emergency response capabilities.

The division is the state's liaison with federal and local agencies on emergencies of all kinds. Division staff members provide technical assistance to local governments as they prepare emergency plans and procedures. They also conduct emergency operations training for state and local governmental agencies.

After a disaster, the division conducts damage assessment surveys and advises the Governor on whether or not to declare an emergency and seek federal relief funds. The division maintains a primary Emergency Operations Center (EOC) in Tallahassee. The EOC serves as the communications and command center for reporting emergencies and coordinating state response activities. The division also operates the State Warning Point, a state emergency communications center staffed twenty-four hours each day. The center maintains statewide communications with county emergency officials. (http://floridadisaster.org/about_the_division.htm)

Emergency Management Queensland, Australia

EMQ contributes to safer, more resilient, and sustainable communities by delivering services through:

- Leading and coordinating activities undertaken before, during and after a disaster or emergency to minimise adverse community impacts
- Disaster awareness including community safety and education programs, and the Emergency Services Cadets
- Response and recovery services including State Emergency Service (SES) volunteers, Emergency Service Units, EMQ Helicopter Rescue and state disaster response management
- Supporting volunteer marine rescue organisations as well as contract and community helicopter providers
- Actively engaging with local government to promote disaster management and volunteer management priorities (http://www.emergency.qld.gov.au/emq/)

5.4.1.3 Interstate Support

Disasters cross jurisdictional boundaries routinely. The 2005 Indian Ocean tsunami affected thirteen nations. Within India alone, it damaged over 1,200 kilometers of coastline, spanning several states. In 2010, hurricane warnings were implemented for most of the eastern coastline of the U.S. as Category 4 Hurricane Earl neared. In such circumstances, it is necessary to cooperate across state and even national lines to prepare for, respond to, and recover from an event. In the U.S., the Emergency Management Association Compact (EMAC) facilitates partnerships across state lines. EMAC is designed to work as an interstate network of resources. Congress approved EMAC in 1996 as Public Law 104-321—the first such law since the Civil Defense Act of 1950 (Kapucu, Augustin, and Garayev 2009).

EMAC functions as a mutual aid agreement by which processes are designed and approved by state legislatures. EMAC spells out standard operating procedures for reimbursement, equipment, personnel, liability, and related matters. All fifty states, the District of Columbia, Puerto Rico, and the U.S. Virgin Islands now participate in EMAC. How useful can an interstate network be? For Hurricane Katrina, forty-eight of the fifty states sent equipment and 66,000 workers at a cost of $830 million—an impressive level of assistance.

5.4.1.4 National Level

On a national level, abilities to prepare for and manage disasters vary considerably. In 2010, for example, extensive flooding covered both rural and urban areas of Pakistan. The flooding became so extensive that it threatened to cut off food reserves and supplies to the major city of Karachi (population over eighteen million). Across the nation, infrastructure including roads and bridges failed, making it difficult for rescuers to reach and help survivors. Pakistan's abilities to respond have always been challenging due to its development status. By August, 1,600 people perished, and 1,237,343 homes were lost (USAID 2010a). Five years earlier a report published, for the United Nations World Conference on Disasters (2005) indicated that Pakistan joined a regional effort for flood mitigation. Because monsoonal rains cross national borders, efforts to reduce risks would require involvement of regional partners including Bhutan, China, India, Nepal, Bangladesh, and Pakistan.

New Zealand established the Ministry of Civil Defence and Emergency Management (MCDEM) to manage risks such as earthquakes, flooding, tsunamis, and wildfires. MCDEM recognizes the importance of connections to local emergency managers and NGOs and designed guidance materials to encourage and foster the development of localized civil defence emergency management groups (CDEMs). New Zealand urges local capacity building across government, private, and community agencies and the integration of utilities, infrastructure managers, health care systems, and more to stand ready should disaster occur. The efforts paid off when a major earthquake severely damaged Christchurch in February 2011.

In the U.S., national-level efforts transformed after the terrorist attacks of September 11, 2001. In an attempt to leverage the knowledge, capabilities, and resources of twenty-two federal agencies (Figure 5.2), President Bush created the Department of Homeland Security (DHS). Now organized into directorates (see Box 5.3), DHS manages functional areas through federal agencies responsible for transportation security, immigration, border control, law enforcement, and disasters.

FEMA, a stand-alone agency with a cabinet-level director under President Clinton, became subsumed under the DHS after September 11, 2001. FEMA is organized into sections that deal with response, recovery, logistics management, mission support, mitigation, and fire (Figure 5.3; FEMA n.d.).

Specific offices offer support for faith-based initiatives and neighborhood partnerships, disability coordination, external affairs, policy and programs analysis, and other activities. Across the U.S., ten regional offices support several states and collaborate on major events. Region I, for example, includes Connecticut, Maine, Massachusetts, New Hampshire, Rhode Island, and Vermont. Careers are possible in any of these locations or areas.

Although many citizens assume that FEMA is designed to respond to a disaster, FEMA is actually not a first-responder. Its mission is to "support our citizens and first responders to ensure that as a nation we work together to build, sustain, and improve our capability to prepare for, protect against, respond to, recover from, and mitigate all hazards." Its activities are bounded by the Stafford Act. An agency governed by legislation is limited in what it can and cannot do—a true challenge since the public expects the government to respond in times of crisis. In reality, you should expect to be on your own for up to seventy-two hours after a disaster before outside assistance arrives and commences to help in an organized manner.

To summarize, emergency management truly begins at the local level. When disasters overwhelm local capacity, the state or regional level provides assistance. If a state is overwhelmed, at least in the U.S., federal assistance can be requested through the state governor, but exceptions apply. If a major event such as a strong hurricane is expected, federal assets can be staged through pre-designated sites. As a hurricane moves toward land and officials become more certain where it will strike, the assets can be moved where they will be needed. Most pre-staging current occurs in a hurricane context or a slow-moving flood similar to the Mississippi River flooding in May 2011. Federal assistance in other disasters is designed to arrive within one to three days after an event, usually in the form of advisors and funding. Depending on the event, securing federal assistance can take even longer as the application and approval process unfolds.

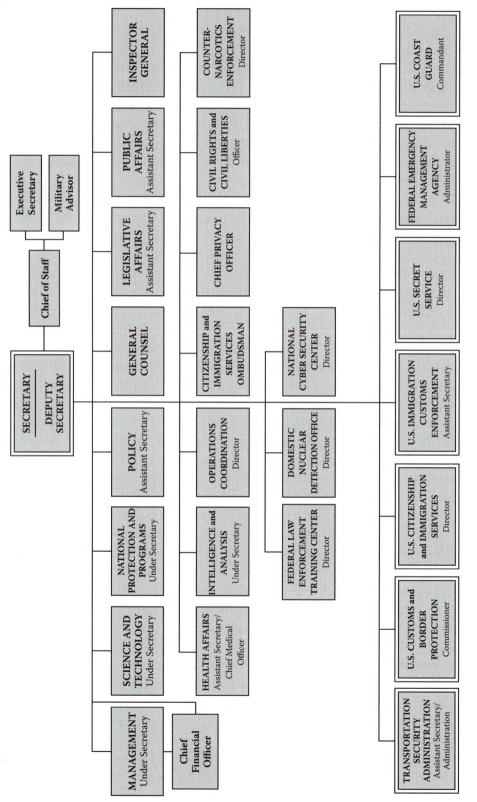

FIGURE 5.2 Federal agencies involved in disaster management. *Source:* Department of Homeland Security.

BOX 5.3 U.S. DEPARTMENT OF HOMELAND SECURITY DIRECTORATES

The Directorate for National Protection and Programs works to advance the Department's risk-reduction mission. Reducing risk requires an integrated approach that encompasses both physical and virtual threats and their associated human elements.

The Directorate for Science and Technology is the primary research and development arm of the Department. It provides federal, state, and local officials with the technology and capabilities to protect the homeland.

The Directorate for Management is responsible for Department budgets and appropriations, expenditure of funds, accounting and finance, procurement, human resources, information technology systems, facilities and equipment, and the identification and tracking of performance measurements.

The Office of Policy is the primary policy formulation and coordination component for the Department of Homeland Security. It provides a centralized, coordinated focus to the development of Department-wide, long-range planning to protect the United States.

The Office of Health Affairs coordinates all medical activities of the Department of Homeland Security to ensure appropriate preparation for and response to incidents having medical significance.

The Office of Intelligence and Analysis is responsible for using information and intelligence from multiple sources to identify and assess current and future threats to the United States.

The Office of Operations Coordination and Planning is responsible for monitoring the security of the United States on a daily basis and coordinating activities within the Department and with governors, Homeland Security Advisors, law enforcement partners, and critical infrastructure operators in all fifty states and more than fifty major urban areas nationwide.

The Federal Law Enforcement Training Center provides career-long training to law enforcement professionals to help them fulfill their responsibilities safely and proficiently.

The Domestic Nuclear Detection Office works to enhance the nuclear detection efforts of federal, state, territorial, tribal, and local governments, and the private sector and to ensure a coordinated response to such threats.

The Transportation Security Administration (TSA) protects the nation's transportation systems to ensure freedom of movement for people and commerce.

United States Customs and Border Protection (CBP) is responsible for protecting our nation's borders in order to prevent terrorists and terrorist weapons from entering the United States, while facilitating the flow of legitimate trade and travel.

United States Citizenship and Immigration Services is responsible for the administration of immigration and naturalization adjudication functions and establishing immigration services, policies, and priorities.

United States Immigration and Customs Enforcement (ICE), the largest investigative arm of the Department of Homeland Security, is responsible for identifying and shutting down vulnerabilities in the nation's border, economic, transportation, and infrastructure security.

The United States Coast Guard protects the public, the environment, and U.S. economic interests in the nation's ports and waterways, along the coast, on international waters, or in any maritime region as required to support national security."

The Federal Emergency Management Agency (FEMA) prepares the nation for hazards, manages federal response and recovery efforts following any national incident, and administers the National Flood Insurance Program.

The United States Secret Service protects the President and other high-level officials and investigates counterfeiting and other financial crimes, including financial institution fraud, identity theft, computer fraud, and computer-based attacks on our nation's financial, banking, and telecommunications infrastructure.

Source: U.S. Department of Homeland Security

5.4.2 Non-Governmental Organizations

Depending on location, non-governmental organizations (NGOs) may play support roles or serve as first responders, emergency managers, and recovery agencies. After the Haiti earthquake, NGOs worked closely with Haitian and outside government agencies. The January 2010 earthquake claimed close to 300,000 lives—one of the worst disasters in history. Three million people experienced the event and 1.6 million lingered in temporary shelters six months after the event. NGOs played a pivotal relief and recovery role that will continue for years to come. Brief examples of initial donations (USAID 2010b) include:

- $3.4 million for health and nutritional support from the Pan American Health Organization
- $4.7 million in market assistance from the Seventh Day Adventists
- $4.8 million in economic recovery from the International Rescue Committee
- $323,150 in translation services from the U.S. Peace Corps
- $4.4 million in shelter services from the American Red Cross
- $11.5 million in emergency food and related support from UNICEF

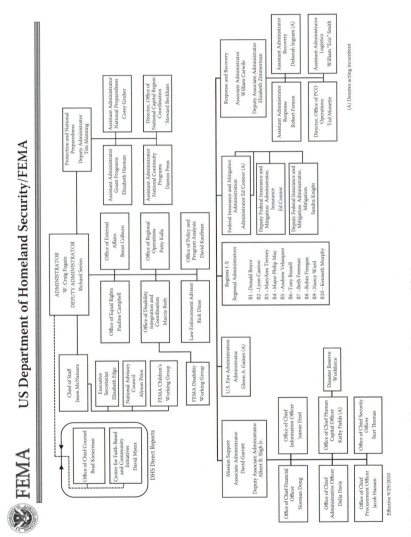

FIGURE 5.3   The U.S. Federal Emergency Management Agency, 2011.

Exceptions to such cooperation occurs, of course. When a massive cyclone struck Myanmar (formerly Burma), the military government refused entry to humanitarian organizations. It is widely believed that the reason was fear that the ruling junta would be destabilized. Amid worldwide outcry and accusations of misappropriation of resources, the Myanmar military attempted to deliver assistance while millions suffered. An estimated 100,000 people are believed to have died in the catastrophe.

NGOs in the U.S. play an important support role during disasters. In a major event such as Hurricane Katrina, NGOs may work in clearly defined support roles under FEMA's National Response Framework. Emergency Support Function #6 (mass care and shelters) names the American Red Cross as a primary shelter provider. Other NGOs may become involved in a variety of capacities from managing donations to offering mobile medical and dental services and child care. Recovery for many citizens, particularly those at low incomes, would be impossible without contributions of such faith-based, voluntary and community organizations (Phillips and Jenkins 2009).

Fifty national organizations in the U.S. are affiliated with the National Voluntary Organizations Active in Disaster (NVOAD), an umbrella organization under which NGOs collaborate on and coordinate their efforts. More information on NVOAD can be found in Chapter 12. At this point, you should know that NVOAD has been critical for facilitating the coordination and collaboration of NGOs since the 1960s when NVOAD organizations observed the challenges of unsolicited donations and overlapping efforts. Based on these observations and extensive discussions, networking, and problem solving, NVOAD-affiliated organizations handle specialized areas. The Church of the Brethren offers highly qualified and credentialed disaster child care workers (Peek, Sutton, and Gump 2008). The Seventh Day Adventists specialize in warehouse management for unsolicited donations. Mennonite Disaster Service concentrates on clean-up, repairs, and reconstruction.

Regional organizations also offer support through NGOs. In Latin America and the Caribbean, the Pan American Health Organization (PAHO) provides training, publications, guidance, and relief funds. After the Haitian earthquake, PAHO assisted with health issues including disposal of medical and related hazardous wastes. PAHO promotes health through disaster prevention activities and education. When disaster strikes, PAHO helps mobilize regional health disaster response teams, supports decision making in emergency operations centers, and ensures delivery of humanitarian supplies (see www.paho.org/disaster). PAHO is only one of dozens of humanitarian organizations worldwide that seek to address human vulnerability by meeting critical needs both before and after disaster strikes (for more information, see Chapter 12).

5.4.3 Community Support

Many communities have created ways to involve their citizens in preparedness, response, recovery, and mitigation activities. Ideally, they will be well trained so they can provide proper support without coming to harm or interfering with emergency operations.

Several grassroots-based disaster response capacities have been built in the U.S. Most of them support preparedness efforts or response operations. The Citizen Corps may include community emergency response teams (CERTs), volunteers in police service (VIPS), fire corps, Neighborhood Watch groups, and medical reserve corps among others. Citizen Corps emerged after September 11, 2001 with a mission to "harness the power of every individual through education, training, and volunteer service to make communities safer, stronger, and better prepared to respond to the threats of terrorism, crime, public health issues, and disasters of all kinds" (www.citizencorps.gov). As a grass roots effort, Citizen Corps is the type of group that students, community residents and future emergency management professionals could and should join to learn basic skills that can support a community in an emergency.

Citizen Corps also serves as a model for collaboration between professionals and potential disaster victims. These programs can make a difference because most communities must be prepared to take care of their own for up to seventy-two hours before federal assistance arrives. By involving volunteers in community preparedness and response, Citizen Corps activities can leverage the social capital in a community and ensure a better prepared citizenry and more rapid response. As will be discussed in Chapter 8, the first search and rescue effort usually involves family, friends, and neighbors who search the rubble. By learning how to do such rescue work through certified training, you can protect yourself and those you assist. You need to know what you can do and where you can go without harming yourself or others.

In New Zealand, an integrated approach to emergency management was launched as a result of the Civil Defence Emergency Management Act of 2002. This act links government, emergency services, lifeline utilities, and the public at large in risk reduction. The main principle is partnership at the community level that promotes a culture of prevention. By training, planning, and exercising the plan, communities can better "undertake risk management, build operational capabilities for response, and recover from emergencies." In Hawke's Bay, where a massive earthquake and fire destroyed Napier in 1931, a high level of motivation exists to prevent repeat events. Hawke's Bay Civil Defence and Emergency Management is currently conducting outreach to encourage public preparedness because, "Impact is always felt at the community level although it may hit one or several communities at once. These communities constitute what are referred to as 'disaster fronts.' Being at the forefronts, communities need to have capacity to respond to threats themselves. It is for this reason that communities should be involved in managing the risks that may threaten their well-being (http://www.cdemhawkesbay.govt.nz). For this hazardous location along the eastern side of New Zealand's north island, public involvement is designed to save lives, reduce financial costs, and enhance government abilities to respond to disasters.

Well-credentialed groups support emergency management from the volunteer side although some may also receive remuneration for their time. Such groups may involve medical professionals on disaster medical assistance teams (DMATs) within the National Disaster Medical System in the U.S. Various states, cities, and regions host DMATs and the teams are prepared to deploy as needed. They may perform triage for injured survivors, help with evacuation, provide medical care in shelters, or offer first aid. DMATs can help fill the seventy-two-hour gap until federal assets arrive and are usually sponsored by state and federal funding. Specialized DMATs may furnish more critical care. Careful training, screening, and credentialing are required to join a DMAT (www.dmat.org and http://www.phe.gov/Preparedness/responders/ndms/teams/Pages/dmat.aspx).

Similarly, a veterinary medical assistance team (VMAT) can provide rapid responses for injured livestock and pets. VMATS are associated with the American Veterinary Medical Association (AVMA). They send professional veterinarians, veterinary medical students, and animal technicians to locations in need of support. After Hurricane Katrina, VMATs helped at large pet shelters, participated in pet rescues, and worked at critical care facilities established by local university veterinary schools. Because animals are easily injured in disasters, advance preparedness is key—as is the capacity to provide help with evacuation and shelter. Animal evacuation also spurs human evacuation. Since Katrina, some states have made animal evacuations mandatory. In Texas, the Houston Society for the Prevention of Cruelty to Animals* for example, implemented plans after Hurricane Ike devastated Galveston Island in 2008:

> Houston SPCA rescue teams are in a race against time to save innocent storm victims like these who were left behind on the Island to fend for themselves. Thousands of dogs, cats, horses, puppies and kittens, birds and other pets have found a safe haven at the Houston SPCA. On Saturday, we sheltered 233 animals from Galveston, took in another 149 at the temporary shelter on the Island and conducted 141 rescues. Overall, nearly 600 animals have arrived from our Island's temporary shelter and our teams in the field have conducted over 600 rescues. In addition, hundreds of Houstonians responded to

---

* http://www.houstonspca.org/

our 'Operation Save-a-Life' plea and have opened their hearts and homes to foster Galveston pets for 10 days.

No matter what your passion or interest, there is probably an organization interested in your time and talents. For those seeking careers in emergency management, such inexpensive training coupled with experience can help a résumé rise from the bottom toward the top of the application pool.

5.4.4 Private Sector

The private sector includes businesses that need emergency managers and consultant companies that work for and with federal, state, and local agencies. The Deep Water Horizon oil spill from a British Petroleum (BP) platform in the U.S. Gulf of Mexico in 2010 represents just such a need. In the aftermath of the spill, BP administration and the company's contingency planners had to work with local, state, and federal emergency managers from several agencies and also with elected officials, the military, and private citizens affected by the spill. In addition to existing staff, BP paid significant amounts of money to hire, supervise, and deploy workers in airborne and waterborne response units along beaches, in the marshes, and in the Gulf. Other industries and commercial operations including department stores, public malls, banks, and insurance providers also hire emergency management professionals.

The private sector also includes consultant groups that usually compete for contracts and grants from government agencies and private groups. These consultants may work on specific tasks such as planning or provide guidance for a recovery process or insight on specific needs such as handling disability issues during an evacuation. After finishing this book, you should be able to discern a qualified consultant from one who is not. Many seek contracts, grants, and funding but lack the requisite experience and knowledge to be of real help.

5.5 Seasonal Life of the Emergency Manager

Seasons connote a regular sense of rhythm or activity, often in tune with nature. Some disasters arrive with seasons. In Oklahoma, Texas, Arkansas, Alabama, and Kansas, tornado season commences on March 1 when storm activity increases. The tornado season serves a public education purpose by alerting citizens to risks and preparations. Hurricane season, from June 1 through November 30, alerts coastal residents in the Americas and Caribbean to develop or review evacuation plans and set aside resources to do so. Cyclone season spans November 1 through April 30 in the South Pacific. Californians are urged to reduce wildfire fuel from May through November while Australia prepares for the onset of fire events in August. Depending on where you live, ice storms, blizzards, and spring rains that generate river and flash flooding can be anticipated.

Other disasters do not offer advance warnings. Earthquakes can happen at any time although locations of seismic risk and possible magnitude can be discerned. Earthquake-prone areas such as the Hayward fault in northern California and shifts along the Indian subcontinent that cause shaking in Pakistan, India, and Afghanistan carry significantly higher threats than areas farther away. Offshore earthquakes can generate significant tsunami waves such as the Indian Ocean tsunami that affected thirteen nations on December 26, 2004 and the waves that washed across American Samoa in October 2009 and Japan in 2011.

Terrorist attacks occur without warning although recent events indicate such disasters can be and are being anticipated. Improvised explosive devices lie in wait for Israeli buses and ambulances. Transportation Security Administration personnel scan baggage at all U.S. airports and some facilities conduct full body scans using electromagnetic technology to reveal non-metallic threats such as plastics and chemicals.

Discerning seasonal patterns and anticipating threats are parts of the emergency manager's job. Using that knowledge is key to conducting effective pre-disaster work that will reduce the effects such as injuries and deaths along with economic, environmental, and psychological harm. Much of the work of an emergency manager is daily and fairly routine. Time must be spent to develop working relationships with key personnel and across organizations and plan for disaster response including short- and long-term recovery. A lot of the work occurs behind the scenes, even during the response phase.

5.6 Working in Emergency Management

By this time you should have a feel for the career paths and exciting fields that may be opening up for you as well as volunteer opportunities. Hopefully you are interested in working in the emergency management field and also want to make your home and community safer. In this section, we will explore multiple paths that lead to career and volunteer opportunities. We will cover entry into the field of emergency management during and after graduation from a college or university program.

Emergency management offices routinely need assistance; they are often overworked and understaffed. By securing a student internship and completing duties assigned, you can add experience to your résumé, obtain academic credit, and secure a letter of recommendation for a job well done. An internship may lead to paid employment in the agency or through referral by a supervisor. Internships can reveal exciting opportunities. FEMA offers up to fifteen student internships in directorates like response, recovery, mitigation, and even congressional affairs. The Natural Hazards Program of the Organization of American States invites internship applications for "economic, engineering, environmental, geographical, meteorological, or political aspects of natural hazard mitigation" (www.oas.org/nhp/internships.html).

Consider asking your professors about opportunities to work on their projects. Research universities expect faculty to produce new knowledge that contributes to their disciplines. Faculty members in emergency management, sociology, geography, psychology, business, veterinary medicine, and other disciplines routinely offer paid employment to students. At Oklahoma State University, for example, students have received fellowships from DHS to learn about topics such as preparedness, response, and disabilities. Faculty across the U.S. have earned Research Experiences for Undergraduate (REU) grants from the National Science Foundation. The grants enable students to learn how to conduct research in their fields. At the University of Delaware's Disaster Research Center, students participate in learning about disaster studies and gathering and analyzing data to present at professional conferences (www.udel.edu/DRC).

Most first jobs are entry-level positions. With experience, you should be able to find and move into an interesting career that presents increasing responsibility. Box 5.4 lists jobs posted in 2010. Entry level positions may open quickly when a disaster strikes. The ability to immediately deploy to a disaster site can get your "boots on the ground" and add practical experience to your résumé. Individuals who tend to come and go as jobs related to disasters open and close are described as "disaster gypsies." FEMA maintains a list of about 4,000 disaster reservists for deployment in an emergency. In major disasters, it is not unusual to start in such a position and then move into a better job.

After you secure some experience and scientific knowledge of the field, it is time to search for a career in the public, private, non-governmental, and international sectors. At present, most graduates from degree programs head to the public sector. They may work as emergency management professionals in public government or as city personnel tasked with administrative work that includes disaster management. Careers may also involve work for the military, fire and emergency medical services, law enforcement, hazardous materials, occupational health and safety, and environmental sciences (Huseman and Buchanan 2005).

BOX 5.4 EMPLOYMENT OPPORTUNITIES IN EMERGENCY MANAGEMENT

- *U.S. FEMA, Emergency Management Program Specialist-GS-0301-12.* You will perform the following duties under the general guidance of the Operations Integration Branch Chief and employ the policies, concepts, and doctrines provided by FEMA. You will be responsible for developing detailed emergency plans and procedures at the Regional Federal level, to provide emergency assistance to save lives and protect property, execute logistics requirements, and address public health and safety issues during significant emergencies.
- *U.S. FEMA, Regional Disability Integration Specialist GS-0301-12.* The primary purpose of this position is to prepare individuals and families and in strengthening communities before, during and after a disaster by providing guidance, tools, methods, and strategies to integrate and coordinate emergency management efforts to meet the needs of all citizens, including children and adults with disabilities and others with access and functional needs.
- *Haiti, Catholic Relief Services Program Manager II/Field Office Director* (Listed August 2010). Competencies required included abilities to communicate under pressure, an ability to manage stress and complexity, to promote safety and security and to manage high-quality emergency programs. The position required a master's degree in international development or non-profit management along with experience in managing complex emergencies. Proficiency in French or Creole was indicated too (*Source*: https://sh.webhire.com/servlet/av/jd?ai=495&ji=2440823&sn=I).
- *New Zealand Christchurch City Council, Emergency Management Advisor.* Legislation requires local authorities to coordinate planning, programmes, and activities related to civil defence emergency management across the areas of reduction, readiness, response, and recovery. The Emergency Management Advisor plays a pivotal role in meeting this requirement by engaging with various organisations within Christchurch City. To be successful in this role, the Emergency Management Advisor will be required to undertake planning and preparation for emergencies and for response and recovery in the event of an emergency; be experienced in the development of emergency management plans, standard operating procedures and process improvement; and have experience in telecommunications and information systems. Having a Diploma in Emergency Management accompanied with several years experience in emergency management would be an advantage. (*Source*: http://www.civildefence.govt.nz/memwebsite.nsf/wpg_URL/About-the-Ministry-Vacancies-Index?OpenDocument)

The private sector lures graduates who may work in insurance, business continuity, oil and gas industries, banking, department stores, emergency management consulting, and other corporate settings. Industries need people who can plan for untoward events, build effective emergency management teams, and communicate well in a crisis context. NGOs also hire graduates of emergency management programs. Working for a Red Cross chapter or a non-profit relief organization can be meaningful and fulfilling. Faith-based organizations also hire staff to manage large-scale reconstruction projects and participate in internal management. Those interested in careers that feature travel should consider the international sector for humanitarian relief work. Such work may not focus exclusively on disasters; it may involve educating people to people for and mitigate against the impacts of disasters such as earthquakes, floods, droughts, epidemics, and famines. No matter what your interest, some field of emergency management will be applicable. Many communities in risky locations need the expertise you will acquire in an introductory course such as the one you are taking now.

Regardless of the path you choose, continuing your education and training is crucial. Emergency management changes continually. Large-scale events tend to trigger changes in policies and practices. Only ten years ago, little attention was given to social vulnerability issues such as disaster preparation and evacuating senior citizens and people with disabilities who require assistance. In 2009, the U.S. Federal Highway Administration issued guidance on evacuating higher risk populations. In 2010, FEMA listed ten new regional level disability coordinator positions. By remaining connected to educational and training opportunities, attending workshops and seminars, and continuing your education in a graduate program, you can enhance your potential to experience an upwardly mobile career. Your career options will be wide open if you couple education with experience acquired in the field.

5.7 Practicing Emergency Management

The National Governors' Association (1979; see Chapter 2) first organized the activities of emergency managers into four phases known as preparedness, response, recovery, and mitigation. Most nations use a similar rubric. In New Zealand, emergency managers organize their work into the Four Rs: readiness, response, recovery, and reduction. Regardless of the terminology, the four phases constitute an organizing framework for the activities of an emergency manager. Although the phases are not neatly encapsulated and tend to overlap, as when response bleeds into recovery, understanding the phases allows you to consider a specialty area. In this section, we expand on the concepts of the four phases described in Chapter 2 and list related activities. Subsequent chapters expand upon all the phases with increasing detail.

Although many people enter the field because they want to help during times of crisis, the reality is that most work occurs outside the response phase. *Preparedness* includes efforts to educate the public, plan with responding partners, and instill a degree of readiness across communities likely to be affected by disaster. Emergency managers may be involved in writing plans to detail responses of their organizations and their inter-organizational partners in a crisis. More importantly, during the preparedness phase, emergency managers must involve their staffs and partners in learning, drilling, and testing plans. Conducting exercises reveals areas that need improvement. Emergency managers use preparedness periods to assess their assets and determine further needs. They design warning systems to alert the public and test the systems to ensure that they work effectively—those at risk receive the message and respond accordingly. Preparedness requires education of the public. Sadly, much of the public at large does not pay attention until disasters loom and they must take action—then learn they do not know the best course of action or were unprepared for the event. We will learn more about this in Chapters 6 and 7.

The response phase of a disaster involves a wide range of partners participating in organized efforts to activate warning systems, support evacuation or shelter in place, conduct search and rescue operations, and engage in actions to limit further damage, injuries, and deaths. Public works and police may erect and staff barricades to prevent entry into a hazardous area. Firefighters, emergency medical services, and airborne and water-based rescue teams may try to help those who did not or could not adhere to warning and protective action recommendations. Initial debris removal is required before emergency response vehicles can be deployed where help is needed. Voluntary organizations and medical teams set up shelters before or after disasters to serve those dislocated from their homes. Local and state officials work to assess damages and request needed outside help. Experienced voluntary organizations may begin moving into an area to help with clean-up and initial repairs. If damages warrant, outside aid will arrive from both governments and NGOs to provide immediate relief and longer-term reconstruction efforts. We will expand on response further in Chapter 8.

The line between response and recovery may be blurred, but after the roads are cleared and injured people are stabilized, the transition usually begins. Recovery requires many partners to collaborate to conduct needs assessments and determine how to meet those needs. In many countries, experienced organizations work together to identify needs that they can address collaboratively. Organizations are often mission-specific. OXFAM, for example, provided tent shelters and guidelines for safeguarding women and children living in tent cities. Faith-based organizations like Presbyterian Disaster

Assistance offer clean-up, repair, and other assistance. The American Red Cross may offer mental health services for those whose lives are disrupted by traumatic events. Governments may deploy agencies and organizations to erect temporary housing sites, repair bridges and roads, and aid private utilities in restoring communications, power, and other services. The role of an emergency manager can vary considerably during recovery when much of the work is handled by others. Wise emergency managers have written pre-disaster recovery plans with their partners and are poised to implement them. More on recovery is outlined in Chapter 9.

Ideally, an emergency management agency will have conducted mitigation planning before a disaster and put into place mitigation measures to reduce the impact and costs of response and recovery. The first step of mitigation is identifying areas of risk in a community that require directed actions that may be classified as structural or non-structural measures. A structural or built mitigation measure may be a seawall, dam, levee, or a building retrofitted to withstand earthquakes or terrorist attacks. Non-structural mitigation measures include intangibles like buying insurance to offset the expenses of rebuilding, zoning that sets aside floodplains as non-building areas, creating codes that require hurricane clamps on roofs, and preserving coastal wetlands, barrier islands, and beach dunes that break storm surges. Mitigation is covered in more detail in Chapter 10.

5.8 Emergency Manager Certification

By the early 1990s, members of The National Coordinating Council for Emergency Management (NCCEM) became concerned about the perception of emergency managers and their profession. Overall, they felt that some local, state, and federal government groups did not take the profession of emergency management seriously. Furthermore, NCCEM members wanted to increase their salaries because some incomes were among the lowest paid positions in local governments. As a result, NCCEM established a committee to advance emergency management toward a true profession. The main goal was to establish a foundation to offer qualified individuals the title of Certified Emergency Manager (CEM). Committee members believed that CEM designation would increase status and pay while raising standards and increasing respect from colleagues.

To assist with the creation of the CEM program, NCCEM surveyed local emergency managers to understand the people in the profession. A key finding was that half of those surveyed had high school educations or less. Education is one of the three ways to measure socioeconomic status (the others are occupation and income). The three measures often interact: low education yields low pay. People with lower pay typically experience lower socioeconomic status and less respect from peers.

The emergency management profession also lacked diversity. Many local coordinators were white males over fifty years of age and many had military backgrounds. The diversity of the nation and the very real threats of disaster vulnerability among women, racial and ethnic minorities, and people with disabilities indicated that professionalization would attract a more heterogeneous set of emergency managers that reflected the demographics of the larger population.

To enhance the potential for emergency management to be viewed as a profession, the CEM committee debated requirements for prospective candidates. Discussion centered on requiring a minimum of five years in the field along with 100 hours of training and a bachelor's degree. Candidates would take an exam, and retake it again in a few years to renew their CEM credentials. The requirements for CEM designation were no different from those for other professions. Most on the committee had little problem with a minimum number of years experience in the field and 100 hours of training courses, but the education requirement generated considerable debate. Some committee members did not see the value of a bachelor's degree vis-á-vis experience. Some saw little use in "book learning" and felt that books had little to do with reality. Fortunately, committee members and NCCEM past presidents Ellis Stanley (emergency coordinator of Fulton County and Atlanta, Georgia) and John Picket (emergency coordinator for Dallas, Texas) argued for the college requirement. Eventually, the committee agreed to a five-year window during which applicants who met all the criteria but the college degree could become CEMs.

Another aspect of professionalization concerned a name change from NCCEM to the International Association of Emergency Managers (IAEM). This change reflected the move toward professionalization and also captured the international dimension of the profession. IAEM wanted to invite those in the public and volunteer sectors to consider the CEM credential. In 2007, IAEM developed further criteria for professional emergency managers (IAEM 2007, p. 9). Generally emergency managers should ... value a science and knowledge-based approach based on training, education, experience, ethical practice, public stewardship, and continuous improvement along with a:

- Code of ethics
- Membership to key professional emergency management organizations
- Board certification for CEM designation
- Body of knowledge (history of disasters, academic knowledge, emergency management standards, practices, and guidelines)
- Standards and best practices

Today, the following *general* requirements apply for CEM recognition:

- Three years of experience
- Bachelor's degree
- Contributions to the field (leadership role in the profession, attending professional meetings, writing article for a professional magazine)

To acknowledge that not everyone can pursue a four-year degree, IAEM also offers an associate emergency manager (AEM) designation. The requirements include:

- 200 training hours over ten years (100 hours in emergency management and 100 in general management)
- Writing a management essay
- Three reference letters
- Attaining a score of at least 75% on a 100-item multiple choice test

The path to professional status in emergency management has been slow and marked by struggles about educational levels. However, the work of IAEM over the past two decades is starting to show benefits. IAEM members now testify before Congress and lobby for legislation to help the profession. Salaries have improved and increasing numbers of job postings require college education (sometimes specifically in emergency management) or CEM status.

5.9 Summary

In this chapter we learned about requirements to become an emergency management professional. A critical starting point stems from what academics and professionals call the core competencies. It is worth noting that, rather than specific skills, these core competencies reflect professional characteristics, demeanors, and behaviors that enable success. Critical to that success is an understanding of what the profession demands in terms of daily and seasonal activities. By understanding the range of activities subsumed in the disaster life cycle, an emergency manager can organize activities, develop partnerships, and accomplish the challenging work of keeping the public safe.

Emergency managers work in a range of locations—all levels of government from local through national, NGOs, in the private sector, and with international humanitarian relief agencies. You may also seek to volunteer in these areas as an emergency management professional or as a journalist, public health employee, or engineer involved in disaster work. Emergency management affects everyone's life sooner or later when large and small disasters strike directly at home or into your heart as you view destroyed lives unfold on television. The remaining chapters cover what to do to help and how to do it in an ethical manner. Thank you for taking this class and reading this book. You are taking an important step in making the world a safer and healthier place for all.

Study Questions

1. What are the implications when a disaster is considered a local event? What can you expect to happen during most disasters considering the contexts in which they occur?

2. What kinds of variations may occur across a nation's developmental status or from local through national levels of response?

3. Research a recent disaster in your community, state, or region. Which governmental and non-governmental organizations responded? What were their roles? How long were they active? Did they contribute to the long-term recovery beyond the response period?

4. Collect, compare, and contrast job levels, education requirements, and salaries in government, non-governmental, international, and private sector organizations. What differences do you note? What kinds of intangibles (e.g., job satisfaction) exist in these jobs? For example, do you see yourself as a civil servant working in the interests of the broader public? Is your heart with those most at risk of impact from a disaster and often served by NGOs? Do you find international travel exciting enough to offset the challenges of working in remote locations?

5. Consider the life cycle of emergency management. If you are a local emergency manager, you will need to know and work in all phases, often simultaneously. If you work in a large organization or at the state, national, or international level you may be able to specialize. Which phase interests you the most as a possible career path?

6. Visit the FEMA website and review the list of free online independent study courses at http://training.fema.gov/IS/crslist.asp. You can earn certificates in these courses, which would serve as a first step toward becoming a professional emergency manager.

References

Blanchard, B. Wayne. 2005. "Top Ten Competencies for Professional Emergency Management." Available at http://training.fema.gov/EMIWeb/edu/EMCompetencies.asp, last accessed August 31, 2010.

Edwards, Frances. L., & Goodrich, Daniel. C. 2007. "Organizing for Emergency Management." Pp. 39–56 *Emergency management: Principles and practices,* second edition, (William Waugh and Kathleen Tierney, eds.). Washington, D.C.: International City/County Management Association.

Federal Emergency Management Agency. No date. IS-1 Emergency Manager: An Orientation to the Position. Emmittsburg, MD: FEMA. Available at http://training. fema.gov/EMIWeb/IS/is1.asp, last accessed January 23, 2011.

Huseman, Kim and Monika Buchanan. 2005. "Emergency Management and Related Labor Market Data Statistics." Report prepared for the FEMA Higher Education Project, available at www.fema.gov, last accessed January 23, 2011.

International Association of Emergency Managers. 2010. *Principles of Emergency Management Supplement*. Available at http://www.iaem.com/publications/documents/ PrinciplesofEmergencyManagement.pdf, last accessed January 23, 2011.

Kapucu, Naim, Maria Elana Augustin, and Vener Garayev. 2009. "Interstate Partnerships in Emergency Management: Emergency Management Assistance Compact in Response to Catastrophic Disasters." *Public Administration Review* 69: 297–310.

Labadie, John. R. 1984. "Problems in Local Emergency Management." *Environmental Management* 8(6): 489–494.

Lindell, Michael. 1994. "Are Local Emergency Management Agencies Effective in Developing Community Preparedness?" *International Journal of Mass Emergencies and Disasters* 12/2: 159–182.

National Council on Disability. 2009. *Effective Emergency Management: Making Improvements for Communities and People with Disabilities*. Washington, D.C.: National Council on Disability.

National Fire Protection Association. 2007. *NFPA 1600 Standard on Disaster/Emergency Management and Business Continuity Programs*. Batterymarch Park, Quincy, MA: National Fire Protection Association.

National Governors Association. 1979. *Comprehensive Emergency Management*. Washington, D.C.: National Governor's Association.

Neal, David M. and Brenda D. Phillips. 1995. "Effective Emergency Management: Reconsidering the Bureaucratic Approach." *Disasters* 19: 327–337.

Phillips, Brenda D. and Pam Jenkins. 2009. "The Roles of Faith-based Organizations after Hurricane Katrina." Pp. 215–238 in *Meeting the needs of children, families, and communities post-disaster: Lessons learned from Hurricane Katrina and its aftermath* (Ryan P. Kilmer, et al., eds.). Washington, D.C.: American Psychological Association.

Phillips, Brenda D., Deborah S.K. Thomas, Alice Fothergill and Lynn Pike, editors. 2010. *Social Vulnerability to Disasters*. Boca Raton, FL: CRC Press.

Peek, Lori, Jeannette Sutton, and Judy Gump. 2008. "Caring for Children in the Aftermath of Disaster: the Church of the Brethren Children's Disaster Services Program." *Children, Youth and Environments* 18/1: 408–421.

United Nations World Conference on Disasters. 2005. *A Review of Disaster Management Policies and Systems in Pakistan*. Available at http://www.unisdr.org/eng/country-inform/reports/Pakistan-report.pdf, last accessed August 25, 2010.

U.S. Agency for International Development. 2010a. *Pakistan Floods, Fact Sheet #8*. Available at http://www.usaid.gov/our_work/humanitarian_assistance/disaster_assistance/ countries/pakistan/template/fs_sr/fy2010/pakistan_fl_fs08_08-25-2010.pdf,Xlast accessed August 25, 2010.

U.S. Agency for International Development. 2010b. *Haiti Earthquake, Fact Sheet #63*, July 16, 2010. Available at http://www.usaid.gov/our_work/humanitarian_assistance/ disaster_assistance/countries/haiti/template/fs_sr/fy2010/haiti_eq_fs63_07-16-2010.pdf, last accessed August 25, 2010.

Waugh, William L. and Gregory Streib. 2006. "Collaboration and Leadership for Effective Emergency Management." *Public Administration Review* 66: 131–140.

Wood, V. T., and R. A. Weisman. 2003. "A Hole in the Weather Warning System: Improving Access to Hazardous Weather Information for Deaf and Hard of Hearing People." *Bulletin of the American Meteorological. Society* 84: 187–194.

Resources

A wide array of websites shows what agencies and organizations provide career and volunteer opportunities in emergency management:

- American Red Cross, www.redcross.org
- Citizen Corps, www.citizencorps.gov
- International Association of Emergency Managers, www.iaem.com
- National Voluntary Organizations Active in Disaster, www.nvoad. org
- New Zealand Ministry of Civil Defence and Emergency Management, http://www.civildefence.govt.nz/
- NFPA 1600, http://www.nfpa.org/assets/files/PDF/NFPA1600.pdf
- U.S. Federal Emergency Management Agency, www.fema.gov
- U.S. Department of Homeland Security, www.dhs.gov
- Videos on FEMA careers, http://www.fema.gov/medialibrary/ collections/1084

Chapter **6**

Preparedness

6.1 Chapter Objectives

Upon completing this chapter, readers should be able to:

1. Define preparedness and understand its relationship to the broader life cycle of emergency management.
2. Identify various types of preparedness activities that can be undertaken at the individual, household, organizational, and community levels.
3. Describe levels of disaster preparedness among individuals and households, organizations, and communities, and identify factors that influence preparedness levels.
4. Identify particular groups that remain at risk due to lack of preparedness and list suggestions for enhancing their readiness.
5. Provide examples of preparedness initiatives at the state, national, and international levels.
6. Outline steps in conducting a hazard identification and risk analysis as the first critical step in preparedness and planning efforts.
7. Identify potential places to work and volunteer in the field of preparedness.

6.2 Introduction

In this chapter, we learn about preparedness, which serves as the most important phase prior to the onset of disasters. We also learn that preparedness levels fall far short of what needs to be done. It is the work of the emergency manager and the public to ensure that they are both ready for disaster. To understand this problem, the first half of this chapter defines preparedness and outlines types of preparedness activities. The full range of preparedness activities includes educating the public for individual preparedness followed by the emergency management agencies conducting training, drills, and exercises to ensure readiness. We also learn about the startlingly low levels of preparedness for households, communities, and nations as well as the factors that influence preparedness. This chapter lays an important foundation for the chapter that follows on planning, often considered a subset of preparedness activities.

6.2.1 Defining Preparedness

Preparedness is a central concept in the fields of disaster research and emergency management, and numerous definitions have been suggested over the years (Drabek 1986; Gillespie and Streeter 1987; Mileti 1999; Tierney, Lindell, and Perry 2001; Kirschenbaum 2002). *Preparedness* commonly refers to activities undertaken prior to the onset of a disaster to enhance the response capacities of individuals and households, organizations, communities, states, and nations. But what does it really mean to "enhance response capacities?"

At the most general level, *enhanced response capacity* refers to the ability of social units to accurately assess a hazard, realistically anticipate likely problems in the event of an actual disaster, and appropriately take precautionary measures to reduce impacts and ensure an efficient and effective response. We will discuss specific types of preparedness activities in the next section, but for now the general point is that we can dramatically improve our ability to respond to disasters by taking appropriate actions before they ever strike.

By defining preparedness in a way that emphasizes improving response capacities, we make an important assumption about disasters. Despite the best efforts of societies to mitigate natural and technological hazards, we are assuming in this chapter that *disasters will occur*. That is not to say that some disasters cannot be prevented or that mitigation efforts should be abandoned. Rather, by assuming that disasters will occur, we are simply acknowledging the reality of modern living and encouraging appropriate protective actions. As discussed in Chapters 2 and 4, disasters come in various forms and seem to be increasing in frequency, scale, and complexity. As a result, households, organizations, and communities must continue to devise effective means for protecting themselves against those threats.

In discussing and thinking about preparedness, several important points should be kept in mind. First, preparedness can be viewed and measured at different *levels of analysis*. At one extreme, for example, individuals and households can take protective measures such as storing first aid kits to ensure their personal safety in the event of a disaster. At the other extreme, nations of the world can enter into agreements to provide disaster relief when a disaster strikes an impoverished country such as Honduras. Between these two extremes, we can also think about preparedness at the organizational, community, and state levels of analysis.

Second, we should keep in mind the varying *degrees of preparedness*. Disaster readiness is not a simple either–or proposition dictating that a household, organization, or community is *either* prepared *or* not prepared. Preparedness is a matter of degree, ranging from low to high, with some social units engaging in few or no preparedness activities and others undertaking as many precautionary measures as possible. Of course, most households, organizations, and communities fall somewhere between the two extremes and unfortunately, many lean toward the lower end of the continuum. We also know that levels of preparedness vary over time and across locations, and, as we will see later in this chapter, several important factors influence the number and type of preparedness activities undertaken by various social units.

Third, we lack a *standardized measure of disaster preparedness* at the community, state, national, and international levels of analysis. At the household and organizational levels of analysis, researchers typically use checklists to measure disaster preparedness, asking respondents to indicate which activities they have undertaken, many of which are described in the next section (Tierney et al. 2001). Using such checklists, we have learned a great deal about preparedness levels among households and organizations, including businesses, and identified numerous factors that influence preparedness levels. Preparedness is much more difficult to measure, however, at higher levels of analysis, including communities, states, and nations. At these higher levels of analysis, it is not simply a matter of how many items on a checklist have been performed. Rather, we must consider issues such as the strength and legitimacy of political institutions, intergovernmental relationships, locations and priorities of emergency management functions, social and financial capital, and other factors. In light of these measurement challenges, it is difficult to meaningfully compare communities, states, and nations in terms of disaster readiness (Simpson 2008).

Fourth, we must consider disaster preparedness in a *cultural context*. Culture is a central feature of every society that exerts a powerful influence over individual behavior. In talking about culture, sociologists and anthropologists typically distinguish material from non-material elements. *Material culture* includes the clothes we wear, the houses we live in, the tools we use, the stories we write, the monuments we build, and other physical objects produced by societies. *Non-material culture* covers shared values, our moral beliefs about right and wrong, the norms and rules governing our behavior, traditions, and the sense of collective identity that binds us together. Of course, the two elements of culture are closely interrelated. In the U.S., for example, think about how values of individualism, competition, and material achievement are reflected by and embodied in the kinds of cars people drive, the houses they live in, and the places (often hazardous) where some choose to build them.

Just as culture influences decisions about buying cars and houses, it also profoundly shapes thinking about hazards and disasters (Webb, Wachtendorf, and Eyre 2000; Webb 2006). At the most general level, for individuals or social groups to attempt to mitigate or prepare for a future disaster, they must first believe that they can do something about the threat. However, this sense of self- and collective efficacy is not a cultural universal. In other words, not all societies believe they control their own destinies and can prevent disasters and other events from happening. Indeed, in many parts of the world, disasters such as earthquakes, floods, and tsunamis, are commonly viewed as "acts of God" (Schmuck 2000; Ghafory-Ashtiany 2009). As a result, local populations often develop fatalistic attitudes about disasters, attributing the widespread human suffering and loss of life to a kind of divine punishment and assuming that nothing can be done to prevent or prepare for future catastrophes.

It should be noted, however, that fatalism and apathy in the face of hazards and disasters are not limited to traditional, isolated, or impoverished regions. Even in the wealthiest and most developed countries, preparedness levels are generally low, risks may be ignored or underestimated, and dangerous decisions are made, laying the groundwork for future disasters. In the interest of promoting economic growth and development, for example, local planning commissions and city councils allow contractors to build neighborhoods in hazardous places such as flood-prone areas (Mileti 1999). State and national governments approve high-risk ventures such as deepwater oil drilling without first considering and fully understanding the possibilities and consequences of catastrophic failures (Clarke 2005). In weighing decisions about vehicle design, U.S. automobile manufacturers have a long history of placing profit ahead of safety and strongly resisting government regulation of the industry (Mashaw and Harfst 1990).

As these examples clearly demonstrate, culture has a major impact on disaster preparedness. In some societies, traditional religious beliefs prevent people from taking proactive precautionary measures and in others the pervasiveness of the profit motive impedes safety. It may be tempting to conclude that the key to increasing disaster preparedness is changing the way people think. Cultural beliefs, however, are firmly entrenched, slow to change, and strongly resistant to outside influence. In the context of disaster preparedness, we must respect cultural diversity and work hard to inform people about the hazards and risks they face, educate them about appropriate mitigation and preparedness measures, and motivate them to take action.

Finally, another issue to keep in mind when thinking about preparedness is the value of the *all-hazards approach* to emergency management. As discussed throughout this book, communities face a wide range of hazards, risks, and disasters whose impacts are very similar. Thus, the typical preparedness activities discussed in the next section apply to all kinds of natural and technological disasters. Certainly some hazard-specific strategies such as installing shutters in hurricane-prone areas, purchasing an in-ground shelter in tornado-prone places, and storing a gas mask when living near a chemical weapons incinerator may be pursued. But for the most part the preparedness activities described in the next section are generic, that is, they apply to multiple hazard contexts. Rather than preparing for each threat separately—which is unrealistic—households, organizations, and communities can maximize the effectiveness of their preparedness efforts and make the most of limited resources by embracing the all-hazards approach. Basic provisions such as non-perishable food items, water, radios, flashlights, and batteries, are needed after any natural or technological disaster. The value of the all-hazards approach to planning and preparing for disasters is discussed in detail in Chapter 7.

6.2.2 Types of Preparedness Activities

Preparedness can involve a range of activities, whether you are an individual, a member of a household unit, or responsible in some way for a larger organization or the broader community. While each of us must accept some degree of responsibility for personal preparedness, as we will learn later, doing so may require support and assistance. Participating in neighborhood and community preparedness activities helps our neighbors and also allows them to help us if a disaster strikes. Furthermore, such efforts reduce the burdens of emergency responders, emergency managers, and community officials.

6.2.2.1 Individual and Household Preparedness Activities

As discussed in the previous section, individual and household preparedness activities are often measured using checklists of actions people take prior to a disaster such as (Tierney et al. 2001, p. 34):

- Obtaining disaster-related information.
- Attending meetings to learn about disaster preparedness.

- Purchasing food and water.
- Storing a flashlight, radio, batteries and a first aid kit.
- Learning first aid.
- Developing and practicing a family emergency plan.
- Bracing furniture (in earthquake-prone areas).
- Installing shutters (in hurricane-prone areas) or a safe room or storm cellar (in tornado-prone areas).
- Purchasing hazard-specific insurance.

As you can see from this list, individuals and households can take many steps to prepare for disasters. In light of all these possibilities, some people may become confused as to what exactly they should do to prepare. To simplify and clarify disaster preparation for the general public, the Federal Emergency Management Agency (FEMA) advises them to (1) get a disaster kit, (2) make a plan, and (3) be informed (www.ready.gov). As you can see in Box 6.1, FEMA recommends stocking disaster kits with three days' worth of basic provisions and other items, many of which appear on the above list. Figure 6.1 depicts why it is important for households to prepare. As shown by Figure 6.2, people should also think about preparation for their neighborhoods.

BOX 6.1   PREPAREDNESS RECOMMENDATIONS

When preparing for a possible emergency situation, think first about the basics of survival: fresh water, food, clean air, and warmth.

Recommended Items to Include in Basic Emergency Supply Kit

- Water (1 gallon per person per day for at least three days) for drinking and sanitation
- Non-perishable food (at least three-day supply)
- Battery-powered or hand-crank radio and a NOAA Weather Radio with tone alert and extra batteries for both
- Flashlight and extra batteries
- First aid kit
- Whistle to signal for help
- Dust mask to help filter contaminated air, plastic sheeting, and duct tape to shelter in place
- Moist towelettes, garbage bags, and plastic ties for personal sanitation
- Wrench or pliers to turn off utilities
- Can opener (if kit contains canned food)
- Local maps
- Cell phone with chargers

Source: www.ready.gov

Additional Items to Consider Adding to Emergency Supply Kit

- Prescription medications and glasses
- Infant formula and diapers
- Pet food and extra water for pet
- Important family documents such as copies of insurance policies, identification, and bank account records in a waterproof, portable container
- Cash or travelers' checks and change
- Emergency reference material such as a first aid book or information from www.ready.gov
- Sleeping bag or warm blanket for each person; additional bedding if you live in a cold-weather climate
- Complete change of clothing including a long sleeved shirt, long pants, and sturdy shoes; additional clothing if you live in a cold-weather climate
- Household chlorine bleach and medicine dropper (When diluted 9 parts water to 1 part bleach, bleach can be used as a disinfectant; in an emergency, you can use it to treat water by adding 16 drops of household liquid bleach to a gallon of water. Do not use scented or color-safe bleaches or those containing other cleaners.)
- Fire extinguisher
- Matches in waterproof container
- Feminine supplies and personal hygiene items
- Mess kits, paper cups, plates and plastic utensils, paper towels
- Paper and pencil
- Books, games, puzzles, and other activities for children

Source: www.ready.gov

6.2.2.2 Organizational Preparedness Activities

For organizations including the public (government) and private (business) sectors, typical preparedness checklists include many of the same activities that apply to households and some additional measures such as (Webb, Tierney, and Dahlhamer 2000, p. 84):

- Talking to employees about disaster preparedness.
- Conducting drills and exercises.
- Receiving specialized training.
- Developing relocation plans.
- Obtaining an emergency generator.
- Purchasing business interruption insurance.

In Figure 6.3, FEMA describes organizational readiness efforts as a preparedness cycle of five key elements: planning, organizing and equipping,

FIGURE 6.1   Home in New Orleans suburb sustains substantial damage from Hurricane Katrina. (*Source:* Gary Webb.)

FIGURE 6.2   New Orleans neighborhood struggles to clean up several weeks after Hurricane Katrina. (*Source:* Gary Webb.)

FIGURE 6.3   FEMA preparedness cycle for organizations. (*Source:* www.ready.gov)

> **BOX 6.2   RECOMMENDATIONS FOR PREPARING EMPLOYEES**
>
> One of the best methods of assuring your company's recovery is to provide for your co-workers' well-being. Communicate regularly with employees before, during, and after an incident.
>
> - Involve co-workers from all levels in emergency planning.
> - Use newsletters, intranets, staff meetings, and other internal communication tools to communicate emergency plans and procedures.
> - Set up procedures to warn employees. Plan how you will communicate with people who are hearing impaired or have other disabilities or do not speak English.
> - Consider setting up a telephone call tree, password-protected page on the company website, email alert, or call-in voice recording to communicate with employees in an emergency.
> - Designate an out-of-town phone number where employees can leave "I'm okay" messages in a catastrophic situation. Minimize your calls and keep them short so others can get through.
> - Encourage employees to have alternate means and routes for getting to and from work in case their normal modes of transportation are interrupted.
> - Keep a record of employee emergency contact information with other important documents in your emergency kit and at an off-site location.
> - If you rent, lease, or share space with other businesses, it is important to communicate, share, and coordinate evacuation procedures and other emergency plans.
>
> *Source*: www.ready.gov/business

training, exercising, and evaluating and improving by applying lessons learned. Box 6.2 lists specific steps business owners can take to ready their employees for a disaster.

6.2.2.3 Community Preparedness Activities

Finally, at the community level of analysis, typical preparedness actions include many of the same organizational level activities and some additional ones including (Tierney et al. 2001, p. 27):

- Testing sirens, emergency alert, and other warning systems.
- Conducting educational programs and distributing disaster-related information.
- Conducting multi-organizational drills and exercises.
- Establishing mutual aid agreements with surrounding communities.
- Maintaining an emergency operations center.
- Conducting a hazard identification and risk analysis.

As you can see from the lists of activities for organizations and communities, drills and exercises are fairly common. However, as with developing disaster plans (discussed in detail in Chapter 7), simply participating in a drill or exercise does not guarantee success when a disaster strikes. Disaster drills and exercises are most effective as preparedness tools when they are based on:

- Realistic scenarios, including accurate assumptions about disaster-induced demands, resource shortages, and communication difficulties
- Accurate assumptions about how people and organizations respond to disasters, rather than myths of disaster (see Chapter 8)
- Meaningful involvement rather than ritualistic, symbolic, or mandated participation
- Integration of multiple organizations and levels of government with citizen participants
- Recognition that disasters do not always follow plans and often require participants to think creatively and improvise to solve unanticipated problems

6.2.3 Dimensions of Preparedness

The lists above clearly show that preparedness includes a wide range of possible activities. It may be useful, therefore, to review the lists and identify some important *dimensions of preparedness*. First, these activities can be grouped in terms of their *primary objectives*. Certain activities such as learning first aid and stockpiling food and water focus on ensuring life safety. Installing shutters and bracing furniture emphasize protecting property. Some activities such as obtaining disaster information and conducting a community educational program are geared toward knowledge acquisition and dissemination. Purchasing hazard insurance and developing relocation plans aim to contain losses and ensure continuity of operations.

Second, preparedness activities vary in terms of their *degree of coordination*. Conducting a tornado drill at an elementary school is a fairly simple task and can be done in relative isolation. Other steps such as conducting a community-wide drill involving multiple organizations (police and fire departments, hospitals, schools, hazardous materials teams and others) are much more complex and require extensive coordination. Indeed, as we will see later in this chapter, the tendency to prepare in isolation from others is a major impediment to effective disaster preparedness at the organizational and community levels.

Finally, preparedness activities obviously vary based on *financial cost*. Of course, any consideration of costs must be sensitive to vast inequalities of wealth and recognize that what some may consider inexpensive seems an exorbitant burden to others. While it is relatively inexpensive to store food and water, installing a safe room or underground storm cellar may be extremely costly. As a result, preparedness levels remain uneven in our society and leave some segments of the population at much greater risk when a disaster strikes. In recent years, disaster researchers and emergency managers have devoted far more attention to identifying vulnerable populations and better integrating them into the four phases of emergency management.

6.2.4 Preparedness and the Life Cycle of Emergency Management

It is probably clear by now that preparedness is closely related to the response phase of disaster management. As noted in this chapter, the primary objective of preparedness is to improve our ability to respond more effectively. Gillespie and Streeter (1987, p. 157) suggest that "disaster preparedness entails planning, establishing resources, developing warning systems, skills in training and practicing, and almost any pre-disaster action which is assumed to improve the safety or effectiveness of disaster response."

Similarly, Tierney et al. (2001, p. 27) write, "Broadly speaking, the objective of emergency preparedness is to enhance the ability of social units to respond when a disaster occurs." Furthermore, the primary goal of preparedness is "… to develop appropriate strategies for responding … ensuring that resources necessary to carrying out an effective response are in place prior to the onset of a disaster or that they can be obtained promptly when needed." Finally, according to Mileti (1999, p. 215), "The purpose of preparedness is to anticipate problems in disasters so that ways can be devised to address the problems effectively and so that resources needed for an effective response are in place beforehand."

While its relationship to response is obvious, preparedness is also closely related to the mitigation and recovery phases. Drabek (1986, p. 21) states that preparedness and mitigation are very similar, and describes the line between as "blurry." He defines mitigation as "purposive acts designed toward the elimination of, reduction in probability of, or reduction of the effects of potential disasters." Preparedness activities, on the other hand, "are predicated on the assumption that disasters of various forms will occur, but that their negative consequences may be reduced—mitigated, if you will, but in this special sense." Thus the combined goals of mitigation and preparedness are (1) preventing disasters from occurring in the first place via measures such as stricter building codes and land-use ordinances banning development in flood-prone areas and (2) reducing the impacts of disasters, primarily by adequately preparing for them ahead of time.

Preparedness is also relevant to the recovery phase. As discussed in Chapter 7, planning is an important element of preparedness, and emergency managers are increasingly encouraged to devote efforts to developing short- and long-term recovery plans. Much of the new emphasis on recovery planning in the U.S. resulted from Hurricane Katrina. The hurricane displaced thousands of people from their homes and scattered them throughout the region and across the country. Several years later, many of them still have not returned to New Orleans and other places. We learned from Katrina that our nation lacks effective plans for dealing with a massive displacement of people from their homes for a prolonged period. Hopefully, with greater foresight and dedicated preparedness and planning efforts, we will be better equipped to deal with the next major disaster.

6.3 Levels of Preparedness

In the previous sections, we defined preparedness, described the types of activities that can be undertaken at various levels, and discussed the relevance of preparedness to response, recovery, and mitigation. We covered a lot of ground, but a critical question remains. How prepared are we for disasters? The simple answer is: not very or not enough, but in reality the answer is more complicated. Some individuals and households are more prepared than others; some organizations have more experience with disasters and are thus better equipped to respond; some communities devote greater resources to emergency management and disaster preparedness than others. For states and nations, the picture is even more complex and involves vast disparities in preparedness levels across countries and around the globe.

6.3.1 Individual and Household

Over the past several decades, individual and household preparedness for disasters in the U.S. has been studied extensively. As noted in Chapter 3, researchers typically conduct surveys in person or via mail or telephone and ask respondents to indicate their preparedness activities on a checklist similar to the ones described earlier in this chapter. What do these studies tell us about individual and household preparedness? First, overall levels of preparedness are alarmingly low; second, various factors contribute to higher or lower levels of preparedness.

In a comprehensive review of preparedness studies conducted after the 1970s, Tierney et al. (2001) found that most respondents in survey after survey reported that they had not undertaken a single preparedness measure. Moreover, even individuals and households engaging in some type of preparedness tended to do very little. When presented with checklists like the ones described previously, it was highly unusual for respondents to check off more than a few items. Most respondents typically undertook one or two activities, usually those focused on protecting life. Very few achieved half of the checklist items and fewer still indicated completion of all of them. In summary, individual and household preparedness levels in the U.S. are historically low.

Perhaps what is most surprising about these low levels of preparedness is that most studies reviewed by Tierney et al. (2001) involved surveys of people in earthquake-prone (high seismic activity) areas. In a later study of households in Florida, Kapucu (2008) found a similar pattern of under-preparedness. Despite the obvious hurricane threats, he found that half the survey respondents had hurricane evacuation plans in place and only a fourth practiced executing the plans with family members. More startling, however, was his finding that only 8% of respondents said they had disaster supply kits stocked with enough basic provisions to shelter in place for three days (the FEMA recommendation)

While overall preparedness levels are low, there is some variation among households. As illustrated in Figure 6.4, higher socioeconomic status and levels of education, the presence of children, and home ownership all con-tribute to higher levels of readiness. Conversely, the poor, racial and ethnic minorities, and those who do not own their homes tend to be far less pre-pared (Mileti 1999; Tierney et al. 2001). As cited earlier, some preparedness activities are very costly and even those that are relatively affordable to some may be cost-prohibitive to others. Thus, a major challenge for emergency managers is devising strategies to increase the preparedness levels of all the households in their communities. Our discussion of populations at risk later in this chapter will provide some insights along those lines.

In addition to individual and household characteristics, preparedness levels are also affected by previous disaster experience and risk perception. For the most part, preparedness levels tend to be higher among those who

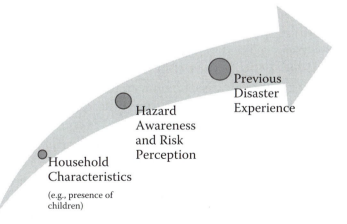

Previous Disaster Experience

Hazard Awareness and Risk Perception

Household Characteristics

(e.g., presence of children)

FIGURE 6.4   Factors affecting household level preparedness.

experienced previous disasters, but, as we will see, experience can also lead to complacency and reduced disaster readiness. Preparedness also tends to be higher among those who are knowledgeable about hazards and perceive the risk of a disaster as relatively high in the short term. Later in this chapter we will discuss risk perception and its relationship to preparedness in detail and identify characteristics of effective risk communication strategies that promote preparedness.

6.3.2 Organizations

As with households, organizations also vary tremendously in the degrees to which they are prepared for disasters. The huge variations arise in part because there are so many different types of organizations in the public and private sectors. Public sector organizations include governmental agencies and departments, schools, police and fire departments, and some hospitals. Private sector organizations consist primarily of local businesses, franchises, and large corporations. Preparedness levels vary between and within the two sectors.

For the most part, public organizations are better prepared for disasters than their private sector counterparts. However, even within the public sector, preparedness levels show variations. Local emergency management agencies, for example, have explicit disaster responsibilities, and their levels of preparedness have improved significantly (Wenger, Quarantelli, and Dynes 1986). As Mileti (1999) notes, these agencies are most effective when their activities are integrated into the day-to-day operations of local government, they coordinate their preparedness efforts with other community organizations, and engage in realistic disaster planning (Chapter 7) based on how organizations and people actually respond to disasters (Chapter 8).

In addition to local emergency management agencies, police and fire departments and emergency medical service (EMS) units have explicit disaster-related responsibilities in the public sector. Although they play vital roles in virtually every disaster, research has revealed problems in their approaches to preparedness (Quarantelli 1983; Wenger, Quarantelli, and Dynes 1989; Mileti 1999; Tierney et al. 2001). Many of these organizations tend to plan and prepare for disasters internally and in isolation from other community organizations. In some communities, open hostilities between police and fire personnel further impede effective coordination in the event of a disaster. These organizations sometimes fail to appreciate the significant difference between everyday emergencies and disasters as described in Chapter 2. As a result, they often assume that disasters can be handled by simply expanding normal emergency procedures and fail to prepare at an appropriate scale. In their research on Hurricane Katrina, for example, Neal and Webb (2006) found that some firefighters questioned whether the incident command system (ICS) that serves as a useful strategy for managing routine emergencies was the most appropriate management framework for responding to such a large-scale catastrophe.

Most of what we know about organizational preparedness is based on public sector organizations, particularly those with disaster-related responsibilities. In recent years we have learned much more about the private sector (Webb et al. 2000). Unfortunately, what we have learned about private sector businesses is similar to what we already knew about households: they are woefully under-prepared for disasters.

Based on large-scale mail surveys of business owners in Tennessee, Iowa, California, and Florida, Webb et al. (2000) report that when faced with a variety of hazards such as floods, hurricanes, and earthquakes, business owners do very little preparation. In response to a checklist of fifteen possible preparedness activities, business owners on average reported engaging in only four and the most common was obtaining first aid supplies. While such safety steps are certainly important, they do little to ensure operational continuity, continued profitability, and long-term recovery and survival. As we will see in Chapters 9 (Recovery) and 11 (Public and Private Partnerships), businesses can play a vital role in a community's response to and recovery from a disaster.

6.3.3 Community

We now know much more about the nature and extent of household and organizational preparedness than we do about community efforts. To illustrate this point, David Simpson (2008, p. 646), a researcher at the University of Louisville, posed a simple question in an article he wrote about community disaster preparedness: Which city is more prepared for a disaster: Detroit, Michigan or San Antonio, Texas? He also stated the answer: We don't know.

After decades of research on disasters and in light of recent catastrophes like Hurricane Katrina, is it really possible that we do not know how prepared U.S. cities are? It would certainly be helpful to know this information. It would allow us to compare cities across the country and perhaps divert necessary resources to those that are under-prepared for the threats they face. As an emergency manager, you would benefit by knowing how prepared your community is compared to surrounding cities and towns and comparable communities in other parts of the country. Indeed, if you found your community lagged behind, you could use that information to motivate local decision makers, agency department heads and directors, and citizens to do more. In making decisions about spending on police and fire, parks and recreation, and other important functions, local communities often compare themselves to others to see how they measure up. In the realm of disaster preparedness, such comparisons are much more difficult.

As Simpson (2008) notes, some hazard-related tools can be used to make community comparisons. The Insurance Services Office (ISO) rates communities based on their fire response capabilities and the effectiveness of their building codes through the Code Enforcement Grading System (CEGS). The National Flood Insurance Program (NFIP) uses a Community Rating System (CRS) that offers policy credits where mitigation measures have been taken. Finally, FEMA's State Capability Assessment for Readiness (CAR) program asks state governments to rank their abilities to perform various emergency management functions.

As Simpson (2008) discovered, these approaches carry important limitations. For example, the ISO and NFIP rating systems are hazard-specific, focusing exclusively on fires, hurricanes, or floods. The FEMA CAR program aims to measure preparedness at the state rather than the community level. Additionally, because of its self-reporting design, it is subject to inaccuracies. On the one hand, for example, states may want to demonstrate a need for federal dollars to support terrorism readiness efforts and thus underestimate their preparedness levels. Conversely, states may want to highlight their accomplishments and over-estimate their levels of preparedness.

Importantly, these community and state rating systems were never intended to assess and allow comparisons of overall disaster preparedness levels. To fill that need and give communities a tool that will allow such comparisons, Simpson (2008) proposed and tested a *comprehensive community disaster preparedness index* for scoring communities based on several factors:

- Fire protection
- Emergency medical services
- Public safety and police
- Planning and zoning
- Emergency management office
- Other emergency functions (local emergency planning committees)
- Additional community measures (voluntary organizations)
- Hazard exposure
- Evacuation plans and warning systems
- Community resiliency and recovery potential (financial resources)

To test this new measure, Simpson (2008) compared two Midwest communities' overall preparedness levels: Sikeston, Missouri and Carbondale, Illinois. Which one was more prepared? According to Simpson's measure, Carbondale was 33% more prepared than Sikeston.

As you can see, measuring disaster preparedness at the community level is somewhat tricky. Nevertheless, efforts are underway to improve our understanding of preparedness beyond household and organization levels. Refining community measures is a crucial step in that direction. Meaningful measures of community preparedness benefit citizens who may use the information in deciding where to live; the insurance industry can use the information to calculate premium rates; and emergency managers can use it to promote greater preparedness in their communities. Although measuring preparedness at higher levels of analysis is challenging, later in this chapter we will discuss specific examples of preparedness initiatives at the state, national, and international levels.

6.4 Factors Influencing Levels of Preparedness

In this section, we will find that preparedness is more than an issue of personal responsibility. We will uncover multiple factors that influence how much and how effectively people prepare for disasters. Before reading this section, you might refer to back to Box 6.1 to see how well you have prepared for a disaster. How would you grade yourself in terms of personal preparedness? Next, consider each factor explained vis-á-vis your own level of preparedness. Do any of them ring true?

6.4.1 Previous Disaster Experience

Survivors of a previous disaster are far more likely to prepare for another even if the first one affected them only indirectly. Watching the tragedy of Hurricane Katrina unfold prompted a massive evacuation when Hurricane Rita threatened Texas a few weeks later. For individuals and households, the positive effect of a recent experience with disaster on future preparedness is firmly established in the research literature (Tierney et al. 2001). Evidence also indicates that past disaster experience stimulates preparedness at the organizational level, including in the private sector (Dahlhamer and D'Souza 1997). At the community level, repeated threats generate "local wisdom" that enhances the capacity to respond when disasters strike (Drabek 2010, p. 66).

Previous disaster experience tends to increase preparedness levels for several reasons. First, by witnessing a disaster, people and organizations develop *heightened hazard awareness and risk perception* that is positively associated with preparedness. Second, on the basis of past experience, people and organizations develop a more realistic understanding of what happens in a disaster and are thus more likely to take proactive measures to prevent or minimize potential problems from future disasters. Finally, at the community level, previous disaster experiences can contribute to the formation of what is called a *disaster subculture* of people and organizations that are extremely familiar with a threat and know what to do in a disaster (Drabek 2010). Think about "tornado alley," earthquake threats in California, and hurricane season in Florida.

While disaster subcultures often exhibit resilience in the aftermath of a disaster, they can also lead to *complacency and inaction*. As Drabek (2010, p. 67) suggests, certain "elements of the subculture … neutralize adaptive responses." He mentions hurricane parties at which people gather to "ride out" a storm despite evacuation warnings of public officials. Why do people who know better choose to stay? One reason may be that their experiences with a previous disaster were less traumatic and difficult than expected or possibly even positive. They may develop a *false sense of confidence* toward future disasters. Additionally, with the threat of a disaster always lingering in the background but usually not materializing, people tend to *normalize risk* and assume a disaster will not occur. As we will see in the next section, risk perception is an important influence on preparedness levels.

6.4.2 Risk Perception

Anyone who has watched driver education films and then ignored speed limits or traffic signs understands immediately that risk is not always respected. "It won't happen here … or to me" is a common response of people questioned about their own risks. With so many risks associated with modern living, we constantly judge what is safe and what is not. In making those judgments, we almost never calculate the statistical probabilities of illness, injury, or death. Instead, we draw on past experiences, pay vague attention to the warnings of experts, and sometimes consciously decide to take our chances. Think about the number of people who still smoke cigarettes despite their proven deleterious health effects and drivers who refuse to buckle up even when confronted with the prospects of traffic tickets, property damage, injury, or death in an accident.

Smoking and driving without a seat belt are examples of risky behaviors that present reasonably high chances of causing negative impacts. How do we act toward risks that have much lower chances of happening? Consider disasters, commonly called *low-probability/high-consequence events*. They are not nearly as common as other types of threats but have the potential to produce devastating effects. Thus, a major challenge for emergency managers is convincing a skeptical public, budget-strapped leaders, and over-extended division heads and directors in local government to spend time and money to prepare for something that may not ever happen. People and organizations are much more likely to prepare when they perceive a risk as highly likely in the short-term (Tierney et al. 2001).

Fortunately, research suggests that emergency managers can influence risk perceptions and promote greater levels of preparedness in their communities via effective risk communication (Faupel, Kelley, and Petee 1992; Mileti 1999; Tierney et al. 2001). Risk communication is intended to educate people and organizations about the hazards they face, inform them about risks and likelihoods that the hazards will produce disasters, and persuade them to take appropriate measures to protect themselves and better meet the challenges resulting from disasters. Risk communication, including educational campaigns to raise hazard awareness, is most effective when it is delivered through multiple channels, consistent across the channels, details the nature of threats and their possible impacts, specific about what people and organizations can do to protect themselves, and perceived as coming from credible sources (Mileti and Fitzpatrick 1993). As we will see in Chapter 8, issuing disaster warnings is a specific risk communication used when a disaster is imminent or has already begun. In this chapter, we are referring to ongoing risk communication utilized during normal times.

6.4.3 Populations at Risk

A persistent theme throughout this text is that disasters are not equal opportunity events. Some groups bear disproportionate risk, especially when they already face exacerbating factors such as poverty. People in less developed nations bear the highest risks, as evidenced when over 300,000 died in the Indian Ocean tsunami of 2004 and about that same number perished in the Haiti earthquake of 2010.

6.4.3.1 Race and Ethnicity

Even in developed nations, some groups are more vulnerable to risks. Hurricane Katrina caused disproportionate deaths among African Americans (Sharkey 2007). Was race the only factor? No. The answer lies in preparedness and planning at all levels. People living in urban areas lack private transportation and when plans are not in place to evacuate those at risk, they cannot leave. Urban areas such as New Orleans have higher percentages of African American residents. If those at risk and those who prepare do not coordinate efforts in advance and deploy transportation assets, these residents cannot leave. Older residents, for example, awaited social security and disability checks so that they could travel and buy gas, food, and medicines. Because Katrina hit at the end of the month, they lacked the financial resources to evacuate—and would have been hard-pressed to do so even if their entitlement checks arrived.

Historic patterns of segregation tied to lingering effects of prejudice and stereotypes increase preparedness challenges for some racial and ethnic minority groups (Heinz Center 2002). Hazardous materials sites, for example, tend to be closer to minority populations than to locations where dominant groups reside (Bullard 1990). Such sites expose minority populations to higher risk. Recent research suggests that Native Americans are also disproportionately exposed to technological hazards such as oil refineries and other petroleum-based operations (Shriver and Webb 2009).

Those involved in preparedness and planning also fail to understand the cultural processes important to minority groups. Some researchers have found that minority groups delay evacuation until they gather their family members (Perry and Mushkatel 1986; Lindell and Perry 2004). In some racial and ethnic groups, multiple generations living in multiple locations may have to be located and coordinated. Longer warnings specific to the populations likely to be affected are needed.

Lingering effects of prejudice also mean that minorities, especially older residents, are more likely to live in weak structures that fail when disasters occur (Dash 2010). Exposure, damage, and injury also lead to higher rates of psychological trauma for racial and ethnic minorities (Norris et al. 2002a and b). For racial and ethnic minorities with low incomes, the challenges to prepare for and respond to disasters increase. In short, building the capacities of those at risk by actively targeting and involving them in readiness efforts is crucial. Doing so in culturally appropriate ways is even more important.

6.4.3.2 Senior Citizens

Senior citizens represent particular concerns although research about their disaster experiences remains scattered and uneven (Peek 2010; Bolin and Klenow 1988; Kilijanek and Drabek 1979; Poulshock and Cohen 1975; Friedsam 1962). Older residents of many nations often live at low income levels. Their resources simply do not cover the costs of preparedness items. People are told to have food, water, and medications on hand, but it may not be possible to do so. Many seniors stretch minimal budgets to cover living costs and this impedes their abilities to prepare for future events. Government plans and personal funds may not allow seniors to purchase adequate medications for future use so having them on hand for an evacuation may not be possible. Chronic medical conditions may decrease willingness to evacuate or move to a shelter and seniors often assume that the comfort of home with familiar resources is a better choice.

Other conditions exacerbate the challenges facing some senior citizens. Older residents, particularly men, may be socially isolated (Klinenberg 2002). For preparedness and warning response purposes, links to others through social networks increase the chances that people will get information and be able to respond with adequate support (Peek 2010). It is critical that community organizations, the faith-based sector, neighbors, family members, and friends reach out to widows, people who live alone, and other older residents when disaster threatens. The combination of gender-based isolation with age and/or poverty may explain why so many older African American men died during Hurricane Katrina (Sharkey 2007).

It is not enough to simply assume that seniors are at risk; it is vital to understand the combinations of factors that increase potential impacts. Consider, for example, an older woman who may be fully independent, enjoy rich networks, and have sufficient resources. The prevalence of osteoporosis is higher among women and increases with age. The medical condition of our example in combination with her gender and age increases her potential for fracture. Blizzards increase slip and fall injuries, tornadoes launch projectiles, and earthquakes topple bookcases. However, because average incomes of women typically fall below those of men, a woman is more likely to experience considerable financial challenges. She may not qualify for federal loans; available grants may not be sufficient to help her recover (Childers 2008). Frail elderly need particular attention due to the risks they may experience from a disaster event (Fernandez et al. 2002; Eldar 1992).

By targeting vulnerable populations in preparedness efforts, particularly public education tied to action initiatives, we can lessen disaster impact. In Florida and Alabama, senior centers have partnered with state agencies and local communities. They created the safe center–safe senior concept and constructed or used existing senior centers for disaster locations. With clearly visible blue roofs, the centers normally host typical senior center events and activities. But they also distribute preparedness information and convert to evacuation destinations, public shelters, and recovery centers as needed. Because the centers are familiar and people know the locations will be ready for their needs, they are more likely to use them in a disaster. The centers involve familiar and trusted social networks to prepare and respond to senior citizens facing threats and are thus far more likely to be effective.

6.4.3.3 People with Disabilities

Similar challenges exist for people with disabilities who tend to have lower incomes and until recently have not been targeted for preparedness activities. After Hurricane Katrina, the Louisiana Department of Rehabilitation had to work for nearly a year to locate the mobility devices of people with disabilities. In the massive evacuation of New Orleans after the flooding, many of those devices remained abandoned in the airport. People were hurriedly flown to safety without their wheelchairs and other critical resources. In public shelters, workers struggled to provide sign language interpretation, adequate nutrition, and assistive tools. People with disabilities remained longer in public shelters than others due to a lack of accessible temporary homes.

Conditions in the U.S. changed after Hurricane Katrina. The National Organization on Disability, FEMA, and the National Council on Disability led important preparedness efforts ranging from developing evacuation protocols to training first responders to move people with disabilities. A particularly important step has been involving people with disability organizations and their advocates in preparedness and planning efforts. Most recently, FEMA called on each state to include disability concerns in designing post-disaster housing (National Organization on Disability 2005; Government Accountability Office 2006; National Council on Disability 2009; Phillips 2009; Clive et al. 2010; Phillips et al. 2010; FEMA 2010).

To prepare people with disabilities and the communities and agencies that support them, the starting point is to assume such people are and can be independent, make decisions, and take care of their own needs. Preparedness efforts and planners often assume that disability equates to inability when this is simply not true. The current term in use is to prepare and plan around *functional needs* that typically include ensuring that evacuation personnel, shelters, and others are prepared to support people with varying communication (language, speaking ability, comprehension); supervisory (dementia); transportation (accessible evacuation vehicles); and medical needs (Kailes and Enders 2007). Medical needs require considerable preparedness and planning. It is essential that individuals are ready to be transported or to evacuate with their medications, assistive devices, and service animals. Those providing transportation and shelter must be adequately prepared to host and support individuals with medical needs (Klein and Nagel 2007). This is particularly important for congregate populations whose medical needs vary and who may require advanced medical support in a functional needs shelter. Providing continuity of care is critical for those undergoing dialysis, cancer treatment, and similar continuing medical needs. Health care offices and staff can assist by conducting business continuity planning and coordinating with those involved in disaster preparedness and planning to support their patients (Phillips 2009).

6.4.3.4 Children

Children constitute another group that should be covered by preparedness efforts. Schools conduct fire drills and may hold tornado or earthquake drills, but children may not know how to respond when a disaster occurs. Box 6.3 lists school-related preparedness activities. However, children may not be at school where responsible adults can guide them when a disaster occurs. Children home alone, for example, may not know that a hazardous material has spilled nearby or where to go when a major earthquake knocks down furniture (Phillips and Hewett 2005). Research indicates that places such as day care centers and recreational facilities where children gather are not adequately prepared (Peek 2010).

Children can learn about area hazards and even become actively involved in their own preparedness. The Red Cross offers courses and online materials

BOX 6.3   SCHOOL PREPAREDNESS CHECKLIST

Essential Items

- Crisis team response roster and contact information
- Student attendance rosters
- Student disposition forms and emergency data cards
- Student photos
- Functional needs data
- Staff roster
- Keys to your classroom and the building

Teacher Bags

- Current class roster
- Copy of emergency procedures
- First aid supplies
- Flashlight and extra batteries
- Activities for students
- Paper and pens
- Clipboard
- Cell phone and charger and alternative communication device

Source: U.S. Department of Education. http://www.ed.gov/admins/lead/safety/emergencyplan/index.html

as do other national agencies and NGOs. Working with children to prepare them for what they may face alone or with adults will make them more resilient and more likely to survive and recover from the psychological trauma associated with disaster.

Psychological trauma is not the only issue that schools and similar facilities must manage when disaster occurs. After the September 11, 2001 attacks, FEMA assisted New York City schools with:

- Air monitoring and cleaning
- Lost instructional time
- Transportation costs
- Loss of perishable food
- Textbooks
- Student relocation
- Supplies and equipment
- Structural and safety inspections
- Crisis counseling

Families, child care centers, and schools bear responsibilities for preparing children to face disasters. Schools frequently conduct tornado and fire drills and require personnel to have first aid skills. It is important to move beyond those basic steps because disaster can strike without notice. Having trained people who have prepared and drilled for a variety of scenarios on hand will result in quicker action that will save lives.

The age of a child makes a difference too. Younger children require frequent training with rewards for mastering behaviors. Older children also benefit from training and drills and can also learn from materials included in their school curricula. To prepare children, break tasks to be learned into steps. Ask first responders, emergency managers, and other disaster professionals to confirm that your training is complete and you have not forgotten an important item.

Many parents, for example, teach their children to drop and roll if clothing catches on fire. What they often miss is telling their children to "keep rolling." In training children, model the behavior you want and train them individually. Do not assume they will do what you want them to do and do not believe them when they say they know how to do it. Train and reward, and then train and reward again. Reward children positively to reinforce the behavior, and praise them for correctly following the steps.

6.4.3.5 Gender

Parents serve as critical links to children affected by disaster and some parents have a harder time preparing. This is particularly so for low-income and single parents. Female-headed families represent the largest group of single parents and a third of them live below the poverty line.

Gender, often coupled with income, matters. It influences preparedness in several ways. Historically, women have been excluded from emergency preparedness and planning efforts in what has largely been a male-dominated field (Enarson 2008; Enarson and Phillips 2008). Does representation matter? Absolutely, because presence at the preparedness and planning table surfaces concerns that others may not recognize. When Hurricane Andrew struck Florida, researchers learned how single mothers struggled to protect their homes without adequate resources. The storm severely damaged their homes, and they faced difficult battles securing recovery resources while they worked and cared for their children (Morrow and Enarson 1996). After a flood in Grand Forks, North Dakota, women who owned businesses lost their inventories and assets (Enarson 2001). Smaller businesses, many of which are owned by women, are less likely to have prepared and are thus more likely to fail (see Chapter 11).

The World Health Organization (WHO; 2005, see Resources section) offers a gender-sensitive disaster assessment tool. WHO encourages us to think through how gender influences people in disaster situations. Preparedness campaign information is typically distributed via brochures and various outreach efforts. WHO asks us to consider those who have less access to that information because they lack mobility, Internet access, and literacy or may be subject to social isolation or restrictions formed by culture, religion, or patriarchy.

In short, we need to make women and girls visible in disasters so that they experience appropriate advance preparedness measures that decrease suffering and lead to quicker recovery (Fordham 1998). Preparedness thus means ensuring that those who provide relief do so in a gender-sensitive manner. Organizations involved in setting up shelters after the Indian Ocean tsunami realized too late they failed to consider health, hygiene, and privacy for girls and women, have resources on hand for pregnant and lactating mothers, and prevent personal violence (Phillips, Jenkins and Enarson, 2010). Concern also erupted over the potential for exploiting women and girls through human trafficking.

Again, the lesson is to involve the population at risk in preparedness and planning and address areas where personal resources fall short. Actively involving women's organizations such as shelters for battered women, lactation support organizations, and faith-based organizations that focus on elderly women is an important first step. WHO recommends basic principles to guide those involved in preparedness and response efforts:

- Involve women in decision making at all levels: individual, household, community.
- Collect data on disaster impacts on women and girls; then prepare and plan accordingly.
- Identify and prepare for sex-specific needs.
- Focus on socially excluded women such as widows, heads of households, and women with disabilities.

6.4.3.6 Language

Language is another facet of culture that must be considered in preparedness and planning efforts. Language is the foundation of culture and the means by which people share information and connect. Accents, word choices, and language matter when designing brochures and outreach efforts and issuing warnings. Those at risk are more likely to listen when the person reaching out to them sounds like them and speaks their language. Using the language of a culture increases the credibility and trustworthiness of the speaker or author, especially with people who were previously excluded or harmed.

Language makes a difference in educating people about risks they face. Speaking the most common language in an area does not guarantee that all people will receive preparedness information. People who are hard of hearing (including senior citizens) or deaf will not get spoken messages. Presenting information from the view of a literate person excludes people with lower literacy levels from those who cannot read well or at all to those who do not know the language well, including tourists, recent immigrants, and family members from other countries (Morrow 2010).

Language makes a difference because people grasp content more effectively when it is presented in a familiar voice, using understood words or symbols—someone who sounds like they do (Mitchell 2007). The level at which information is presented matters too. Literacy levels for preparedness information should be pre-tested with a given population. A number of tools exist to test the reading levels of documents. One is the Flesch-Kincaid method. Such tools help ensure that preparedness information is readily understood. If you have ever tried to read the statistics section of a scholarly journal, perhaps you understand. Think also about grandparents or children who have different reading levels and people working on your campus who may have low literacy levels. Not everyone can read well, but they all face the same disaster threats.

6.4.3.7 Pre-Disaster Homeless

Another group that should be considered is people who are homeless before a disaster occurs (Phillips 1996). There are several categories of homeless people. First are the people we see on the street who are homeless every day. Second are people who are marginally housed and live doubled or tripled up with family or friends and join the first group as circumstances require. When Hurricane Mitch struck Honduras in 1998, an estimated 10,000 street children died. In many countries including the U.S., families with children constitute the most rapidly growing group of homeless people. Recent concern focuses on homeless returning war veterans with disabilities.

Clearly, people who are homeless are not there by choice, but from circumstances often beyond their control. Organizations that reach out to and connect with the homeless via soup kitchens, mobile health care units, social workers, and faith-based activities represent the links most likely to be able to prepare these extremely vulnerable people for disasters.

6.4.3.8 Pets

Many of you probably have pets you consider important members of your family. Have you thought through how to prepare them for a disaster (Figure 6.5)? You have a personal responsibility to get them ready for a disaster because they are critically vulnerable to weather, fire, flying debris, and more. The American Society for the Prevention of Cruelty to Animals (ASPCA) recommends that you start with a few basic steps. First, put a rescue alert sticker on your home. Second, take animal training classes to increase your ability to bond with and help your pet during an emergency. Third, arrange for a safe haven for your pet that might be another family

FIGURE 6.5 Animals must be prepared for evacuation to safe locations too. (*Source:* FEMA News Photo/Patsy Lynch.)

member or friend who can take in your dog, cat, bird, or other beloved pet or a pet shelter. Fourth, develop a pet preparedness kit (Federal Highway Administration). At a minimum it should contain:

- Proof of vaccination and veterinary records
- Licenses, rabies, and identification tags
- Two weeks of food, water, and medications
- Bedding and toys.
- Litter box, litter, and a scoop
- Food and water bowls
- Information on medication and feeding schedules
- Newspapers, pee pads, cleaning supplies
- Collars, leashes, muzzles, harnesses
- First aid kit
- Manual can opener and spoons
- Stakes and a break-proof rope or tie down

Who will evacuate with their pets? The best predictor is the level of attachment to their pets (Heath et al. 2001). Without us, pets remain at risk for their lives. In recent years, a number of states and emergency management agencies have partnered with other organizations to establish best practices for pet preparedness and response. Formalized planning has taken place and many efforts have been integrated into local, state, and national planning initiatives, usually through Emergency Support Function 11 which falls under the U.S. Department of Agriculture. The American Veterinary Medical Association (AVMA) established protocols for the care of animals and both community and professional veterinarian groups have collaborated to prepare and care for animals in pet and livestock shelters. The protocol at present, particularly in hurricane areas, is to evacuate animals with their owners. The AVMA and others have provided financial resources to some states in high risk areas for the purchases of appropriate pet transportation vehicles.

Ideally, pets and their human caregivers enjoy co-located shelters—they are sheltered next to (but not with) each other. Livestock are harder to accommodate but increasingly county fairgrounds are used to shelter

FIGURE 6.6 **Livestock represent a particularly challenging population to prepare for disasters. (*Source:* FEMA News Photo/Andrea Booher.)**

animals outside impact areas (Figure 6.6). Owners retain responsibility to care for their animals with the support of local animal care organizations and veterinarians. A veterinary medical assistance team (VMAT) may provide additional care and veterinarian schools have provided emergency care during past disasters. Pet preparedness not only saves the lives of our beloved animals, but also serves a human function. Sheltering animals with owners spurs evacuation and reduces the chances that people will return to damaged and dangerous area to rescue their pets (Heath et al. 2000).

6.5 Preparedness Initiatives at State, National, and International Levels

Earlier in this chapter we discussed levels of preparedness at the household, organizational, and community levels, and we pointed out that preparedness levels tend to be low but with variations. We also identified various factors including risk perception, previous disaster experience, and others that influence preparedness levels. In discussing community preparedness, however, we noted that because of the lack of a standardized measure of preparedness, it is difficult, if not impossible, to make meaningful comparisons across communities. To do so at the state, national, and international levels is even more problematic. Nevertheless, in this section we discuss specific examples of preparedness initiatives at these higher levels of analysis. Our goal is not to measure how much various states, and nations are doing but instead to gain a sense of what can be and is being done to prepare for disasters at every level.

6.5.1 Examples of State Level Preparedness Initiatives

Preparedness initiatives at the state and national levels typically involve educational campaigns, large-scale drills and exercises, and the development of disaster warning systems. A good example of a state-level educational campaign is the *Red Dirt Ready* campaign administered by the Oklahoma Office of Homeland Security (http://www.ok.gov/reddirtready). Through a series of radio and television commercials, a website, and printed materials, Red Dirt Ready urges individuals and households, organizations, neighborhoods, and businesses to prepare for all kinds of disasters. The activities it recommends are similar to those described in the checklists earlier in this chapter and consistent with the recommendations of FEMA's *Ready.gov* campaign mentioned earlier and described below in more detail. Importantly, specific information is provided for the elderly, those with disabilities, pet owners, and businesses. In other words, this campaign addresses the issues raised in this chapter about populations at risk.

Another example of a state-level preparedness initiative is the *Great California Shakeout* (http://www.shakeout.org/). This is a state-wide earthquake drill that aims to educate the public about earthquakes and how to prepare for them. As part of the drill, people are instructed to "drop, cover, and hold on," and practice how they would protect themselves in a real earthquake. In 2008, a shakeout drill was conducted in Southern California and the program was expanded in 2009 to include all fifty-eight counties in California. That year, 6.9 million people participated in the drill, and in 2010, there were 7.9 million participants. Organizers hope to see even greater involvement in future drills.

6.5.2 Examples of National Level Preparedness Initiatives

In many instances, national preparedness initiatives are prompted by major disasters (Mileti 1999). For example, as discussed in more detail in Chapter 8, in the months following the September 11, 2001 terrorist attacks, the U.S. Department of Homeland Security (DHS) developed the *Homeland Security Alert System* (HSAS), a color-coded alert system to inform the public and governmental organizations about the risk of a future terrorist attack. That system drew substantial criticism, and in January 2011, DHS announced that it will be replaced by a new warning system (www.dhs.gov).

Other preparedness initiatives at the national level include FEMA's Ready.gov and its *National Exercise Program* (NEP). Ready.gov is an educational campaign for encouraging individuals, households, organizations, and communities to prepare for disasters. The campaign provides vast amounts of information on its website, including specific information for children, the elderly, the disabled, military families, pet owners, and businesses. Like the Red Dirt Ready campaign in Oklahoma, the national Ready.gov campaign recognizes the need to address the special needs of populations at risk.

Since 2000, FEMA has conducted annual exercises to assess response capabilities and identify problems of inter-governmental coordination in catastrophic scenarios. In 2007, these Tier I national level exercises (NLEs), formerly known as TOPOFF due to the involvement of top officials from various federal agencies, became part of the NEP. The primary purpose of the NEP is to coordinate federal, state, and regional exercise activities. In the past, NLEs have been based on simulated large-scale terrorist attacks. The 2011 scenario was a catastrophic earthquake along the New Madrid fault in the central U.S. States involved in the exercise included Alabama, Arkansas, Kentucky, Illinois, Indiana, Mississippi, Missouri, and Tennessee. You can find more information at http://www.fema.gov/emergency/nrf/nationalexerciseprogram.htm.

6.5.3 Examples of International Preparedness Initiatives

Although we tend to think primarily about disasters that impact our own local communities, recent events, including the earthquake in Haiti and the tsunami in Japan, have dramatically underscored the need to think about disasters on a global scale. As discussed in Chapter 8, the most impoverished and least developed nations in the world suffer the harshest impacts of disasters, including exorbitant financial costs, widespread physical damage, and massive death tolls. Given their extreme poverty under ordinary circumstances, these same nations face the greatest challenges in responding to disasters when they occur and desperately need help from the international community.

As Wachtendorf (2000) suggests, we also need to think about disasters in international terms because they sometimes defy national boundaries. For example, the 2004 tsunami impacted several countries in the region, recent floods impacted multiple countries in Western Europe, and cities in both the U.S. and Canada have been simultaneously inundated by floods. In these events, cooperation and coordination between governments is critical and may be facilitated through pre-disaster preparedness efforts.

Recognizing the uneven impacts of disasters across the globe and the possibility of trans-national events, the United Nations launched the *International Strategy for Disaster Reduction* (UN ISDR) in 2000. Its primary aim is to reduce disaster losses and build resilient nations (http://unisdr.org), and it involves "numerous organizations, states, intergovernmental and non-governmental organizations, financial institutions, technical bodies, and civil society, which work together and share information to reduce disaster risk." Its activities include coordinating international disaster relief efforts, advocating for greater investment in disaster reduction activities, conducting educational campaigns about disasters and risk reduction measures, organizing global conferences, and publishing reports on disasters across the globe.

6.6 Hazard Identification and Risk Analysis

As you will read throughout this text, emergency management is a process. The definition of a process is to engage in and move through a series of steps and stages toward an end point. The first step important to any kind of preparedness, response, recovery, or mitigation initiative is a hazard identification and a subsequent analysis of the risk it poses to people and places. To identify hazards, you must research the history of the area so that you can determine the kinds of events that occurred in the past. Talking with residents, researching newspaper and library archives, and poring over websites on hazards are good starting points. It is always important to verify information as sources can be wrong. Because human lives, pets, livestock, and property depend on your assessment, get it right. After reading Chapter 4, you know that looking at the past is not enough. To really understand disasters, you must assess new and emerging threats to ascertain their potential impacts on your community. Looking at natural, technological, and terrorist threats is not enough now that pandemics have emerged as concerns and cyberthreats can disrupt area businesses.

A next step is to map the hazards. Many existing tools such as floodplain maps and other resources from government agencies can help you with this. As a start, visit pages for the U.S. Geological Survey (www.usgs.gov), the National Hurricane Center (http://www.nhc.noaa.gov/), and the Office of the Federal Coordinator of Meteorology (www.ofcm.gov). Hazard-specific pages may also provide information such as the Tornado Project (http://tornadoproject.com/). Ideally you will then create mapped overlays that juxtapose the hazards alongside human elements including populations and buildings.

Certain populations may merit increased attention, for example, the locations of nursing homes and elementary schools. High-rise buildings also pose concern as they host larger concentrations of people at certain times of day. Knowing where such facilities are and who will be in them is part of analyzing the risk. Census data (www.census.gov) will provide basic overviews of who lives in your community, the number of poor and elderly, local languages, and the ages of area housing. Census data are not always complete, however, and may mask the existence of some populations including new arrivals, immigrants, tourists, pre-disaster homeless, and even student populations.

By knowing your community, which means involving area agencies and leaders in the effort, your risk analysis will be more robust. A particularly useful (and free) tool for estimating losses from hurricanes, earthquakes, and floods is *Hazus-MH*. FEMA provides this software to assess economic,

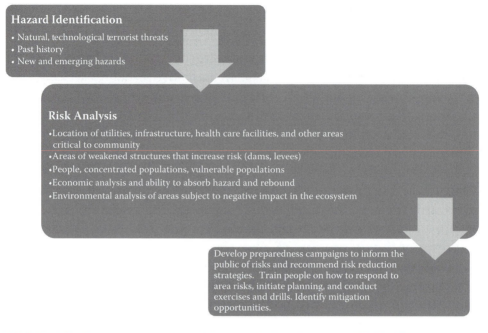

Hazard Identification
• Natural, technological terrorist threats
• Past history
• New and emerging hazards

Risk Analysis
• Location of utilities, infrastructure, health care facilities, and other areas critical to community
• Areas of weakened structures that increase risk (dams, levees)
• People, concentrated populations, vulnerable populations
• Economic analysis and ability to absorb hazard and rebound
• Environmental analysis of areas subject to negative impact in the ecosystem

Develop preparedness campaigns to inform the public of risks and recommend risk reduction strategies. Train people on how to respond to area risks, initiate planning, and conduct exercises and drills. Identify mitigation opportunities.

FIGURE 6.7 Community vulnerability analysis. (*Sources*: FEMA, Thomas et al. 2010.)

societal, and physical impacts from its website (http://www.fema.gov/plan/prevent/hazus/). The Hazus-MH software illustrates risk graphically and spatially to enable assessments leading to preparedness campaigns, planning initiatives, response operations, and mitigation projects

Additional steps move you into a more organized community vulnerability analysis or CVA (Thomas et al. 2010; Figure 6.7). Other sectors of the community require assessment too. For example, how strong is the business sector? Is it sufficiently robust economically to survive a disaster financially and physically (see Chapter 11)? How strong is the tax base? It is not enough to consider only major employers. Agriculture operations, food producers, small and home-based businesses, and temporary labor must also be included. Another element often overlooked is the environment. All communities include ecologically sensitive areas and animal life that should be considered for disaster impacts, particularly from hazardous materials. By knowing where such areas exist, a task as simple as alternative transportation routing of dangerous chemicals may safeguard both people and places.

To summarize, hazards identification walks an emergency manager or preparedness team through understanding the potential impacts of disasters. Astute preparedness efforts account for both past and present disasters. Along with a risk analysis, a hazard identification takes on a new life as it demonstrates how disasters have the potential to hurt people, property, and animals. Reducing that risk is the work of the emergency management professional and volunteers.

6.7 Working and Volunteering in Preparedness

In reality, we all need to work and volunteer to achieve preparedness. It is not sufficient to be the local emergency manager who focuses on preparedness. That individual needs to be a leader who motivates others to work in the area. The emergency manager, for example, must reach out to and involve the media in crafting and disseminating preparedness messages. Other agencies also bear responsibilities for preparedness.

If a blizzard threatens an area, transportation agencies must inform the public of routes likely to close so that lives can be saved. Physicians and health care providers should ask their patients how prepared they are and distribute information to them. They can even use preparedness checklists as part of annual physical examinations. Teachers need to prepare their students for untoward events so that they respond as directed when situations warrant. Elected officials must inform themselves so that they can reach out to their constituents and encourage proper advance preparation; they bear a special responsibility for the most vulnerable among us who need protection.

Health care centers also employ preparedness experts. In 2011, a hospital in Oregon advertised the position of emergency preparedness coordinator and expected the successful applicant to work in collaboration across the hospital and the community, design exercises and events, conduct training, and ensure continuity of operations for the hospital and its patients. The hospital accepted applications from individuals with degrees in nursing, biology, public health, environmental health, or emergency management and sought three years of experience in emergency preparedness and planning.

Students often ask us how to get those three years of experience. Several routes open that door. One is internship experience in an agency that works on emergency preparedness. Another route is working at an entry-level job to gain experience and earn "boots on the ground" experience with preparedness, planning, training, and exercising. A final route emerges through volunteer efforts. In the U.S., the Citizen Corps offers a chance to participate in preparedness and response activities. The corps brings volunteers into several different kinds of organizations. The most common assignments since September 11, 2001 have been community emergency response teams (CERTs). Others are volunteers in police service, fire corps, medical reserve corps, and Neighborhood Watch. A webinar library at www.citizencorps.gov covers topics such as collaborative planning and partnerships, youth preparedness, business continuity planning, and more.

You do not have to join a group to become more involved in preparedness. Start with your own family and neighborhood (Andrews 2001). Host a neighborhood meeting or picnic and invite the fire department and emergency management agency to visit and distribute preparedness materials.

Since the most trusted information comes from social networks, use yours to prepare those around you. Canvass your community and assess what is needed. Invite professionals to create safety programs for your neighborhood. Use your school club to launch a preparedness effort directed at elderly residents with disabilities or purchase resources for local schools. Gaining experience in preparedness can be as easy as knocking on your neighbor's door with a checklist from this textbook. Preparedness starts at home.

6.8 Summary

In this chapter, we discussed both the good news and the bad news about disaster preparedness. The bad news, of course, is that disaster preparedness levels are alarmingly low for individuals and households, organizations, communities, states, and nations. Moreover, preparedness levels vary in large part because some people, households, and even nations simply do not have the resources to adequately prepare themselves. As a result, when disasters occur they impact some groups much more harshly than others, as evidenced by the recent earthquake in Haiti, Hurricane Katrina in the U.S., and the tsunami in Asia.

The good news about preparedness is that steps can be taken to enhance readiness for disasters. Many of the activities described in this chapter are simple and relatively inexpensive. We can greatly increase the number of people taking those actions through effective educational campaigns like the ones described in this chapter, by reaching out to populations at risk, and by providing assistance when necessary. While disaster preparedness is in some sense a personal responsibility, it is also a shared, collective responsibility. By increasing readiness at all levels, from individuals and households to entire nations, we can greatly improve public safety and dramatically enhance the resilience of our communities to disasters.

Discussion Questions

1. How prepared is your community for a disaster? What are some factors that you would consider in answering that question? Is your town or city more or less prepared than surrounding communities?

2. Identify a hazard in your community and devise a risk communication strategy for the public. What would you tell people about the hazard? What should they do to prepare themselves? How would you disseminate this information?

3. What groups in your community are most at risk in a disaster? How prepared are they? What could you do as an emergency manager to assist them in preparing?

4. Consider the location where you, a family member or a friend works. To what degree is the business ready for a disaster to strike? Have you and your fellow employees ever practiced what to do?

5. Think about recent international disasters like the 2010 Haiti earthquake and the 2004 Indian Ocean tsunami. What can be done to increase preparedness at the international level? How can we reduce the devastating impacts of such disasters?

References

Andrews, Jill. H. 2001. "Safe in the 'Hood: Earthquake Preparedness in Midcity Los Angeles." *Natural Hazards Review* 2/1: 2–11.

Bolin, Robert and Daniel J. Klenow. 1988. "Older People in Disaster: A Comparison of Black and White Victims." *International Journal of Aging and Human Development* 26/1: 29–43.

Bullard, Robert D. 1990. *Dumping in Dixie: Race, Class, and Environmental Quality*. Boulder, CO: Westview Press.

Childers, Cheryl. 2008. "Elderly Female-Headed Households in the Disaster Loan Process." Pp. 182–193 in *Women and Disasters: from theory to practice*, (Brenda Phillips and Betty Morrow, eds.). Philadelphia: International Research Committee on Disasters.

Clarke, Lee. 2005. *Worst Cases: Terror and Catastrophe in the Popular Imagination*. Chicago: University of Chicago Press.

Clive, Alan, Elizabeth Davis, Rebecca Hansen and Jennifer Mincin. 2010. "Disability." Pp. 187–216 in 256 in *Social Vulnerability to Disaster*, (Brenda Phillips, Deborah Thomas, Alice Fothergill and Lynn Pike, eds.). Boca Raton, FL: CRC Press.

Dahlhamer, James M. and Melvin J. D'Souza. 1997. "Determinants of Business Disaster Preparedness in Two U.S. Metropolitan Areas." *International Journal of Mass Emergencies and Disasters* 15: 265–281.

Dash. Nicole. 2010. "Race and Ethnicity." Pp. 101–121 in *Social Vulnerability to Disasters*, (Brenda Phillips, Deborah Thomas, Alice Fothergill, and Lynn Blinn-Pike, eds.). Boca Raton, FL: Taylor and Francis/CRC Press.

Drabek, Thomas. 1986. *Human System Responses To Disaster: An Inventory of Sociological Findings*. NY: Springer-Verlag.

Drabek, Thomas E. 2010. *The Human Side of Disaster*. Boca Raton, FL: CRC Press.

Eldar, R. 1992. "The Needs of Elderly Persons in Natural Disasters." *Disasters* 16/4: 355–58.

Enarson, Elaine. 2001. "What Women Do: Gendered Labor in the Red River Valley Flood." *Environmental Hazards* 3/1: 1–18.

Enarson, Elaine. 2008. "Gender Mainstreaming in Emergency Management." Paper prepared for the Public Health Agency of Canada. Available at http://www.gdnonline.org/, last accessed February 7, 2011.

Enarson, Elaine and Brenda D. Phillips. 2008. "Invitation to a New Feminist Disaster Sociology." Pp. 41–74 in *Women in Disaster*, (Brenda D. Phillips and Betty Morrow, eds.). Philadelphia, PA: Xlibris/International Research Committee on Disaster.

Faupel, Charles E., Susan P. Kelley, and Thomas Petee. 1992. "The Impact of Disaster Education on Household Preparedness for Hurricane Hugo." *International Journal of Mass Emergencies and Disasters* 10/1: 5–24.

Federal Emergency Management Agency. 2010. *National Disaster Housing Strategy*. Washington, D.C.: FEMA.

Fernandez, Lauren, Deana Byard, Chien-Chih Lin, Samuel Benson, and Joseph A. Barbera. 2002. "Frail Elderly as Disaster Victims: Emergency Management Strategies." *Prehospital and Disaster Medicine* 17/2: 67–74.

Fordham, Maureen. 1998. "Making Women Visible in Disasters." *Disasters* 22/2: 236–143.

Ghafory-Ashtiany, Mohsen. 2009. "View of Islam on Earthquakes, Human Vitality, and Disaster." *Disaster Prevention and Management* 18/3: 218–232.

Government Accountability Organization. 2006. *Transportation-Disadvantaged Populations: Actions Needed to Clarify Responsibilities and Increase Preparedness for Evacuations.* Washington, D.C.: GAO Report GAO-07-44.

Gillespie, David F. and Calvin L. Streeter. 1987. "Conceptualizing and Measuring Disaster Preparedness." *International Journal of Mass Emergencies and Disasters* 5: 155–176.

Heath, S. E., S. K. Voeks, and L. T. Glickman. 2000. "A Study of Pet Rescue in Two Disasters." *International Journal of Mass Emergencies and Disasters* 18/3: 361–81.

Heath, Sebastian E., Alan Beck, Philip H.Kass, Larry Glickman. 2001. "Risk Factors for Pet Evacuation Failure after a Slow Onset Disaster." *Journal of the American Veterinary Medical Association* 218/12: 1905–1910.

Heinz Center, The. 2002. *Human Links to Coastal Disasters*. Washington, D.C.: The Heinz Center Foundation.

Kailes, June and Alexandra Enders. 2007. "Moving Beyond Special Needs." *Journal of Disability Policy Studies* 17/4: 230–237.

Kapucu, Naim. 2008. "Culture of Preparedness: Household Disaster Preparedness." *Disaster Prevention and Management* 17/4: 526–535.

Kirschenbaum, Alan. 2002. "Disaster Preparedness: A Conceptual and Empirical Reevaluation." *International Journal of Mass Emergencies and Disasters* 20/1: 5–28.

Klein, Kelly R. and Nanci E. Nagel. 2007. "Mass Medical Evacuation: Hurricane Katrina and Nursing Experiences at the New Orleans Airport." *Disaster Management and Response* 5/2: 56–61.

Klinenberg, Eric. 2002. *Heat Wave: A Social Autopsy of Disaster in Chicago*. Chicago: University of Chicago Press.

Lindell, Michael K. and Ronald W. Perry. 2004. *Communicating Risk in Multi-Ethnic Communities*. Thousand Oaks, CA: Sage.

Mashaw, Jerry L. and David L. Harfst. 1990. *The Struggle for Auto Safety*. Cambridge, MA: Harvard University Press.

Mileti, Dennis. 1999. *Disasters by Design*. Washington, D.C.: Joseph Henry Press.

Mileti, Dennis and Colleen Fitzpatrick. 1993. *The Great Earthquake Experiment: Risk Communication and Public Action*. Boulder, CO: Westview Press.

Mitchell, Louise. 2007. *Guidelines for Emergency Managers Working With Culturally and Linguistically Diverse Communities*. Emergency Management Australia. Available at: www.ema.gov.au/agd/EMA/emaInternet.nsf/Page/Communities_Research_Research, last accessed March 15, 2011.

Morrow, Betty. 2010. "Language and Literacy." Pp. 243–256 in *Social Vulnerability to Disaster*, (Brenda D. Phillips, Deborah Thomas, Alice Fothergill and Lynn Pike, eds.). Boca Raton, FL: CRC Press.

Morrow, Betty and Elaine Enarson. 1996. "Hurricane Andrew Through Women's Eyes." *International Journal of Mass Emergencies and Disasters* 14/1: 1–22.

National Organization on Disability. 2005. "Special Needs Assessment of Katrina Evacuees." Washington, D.C.: National Organization on Disability.

Neal, David M. and Gary R. Webb. 2006. "Structural Barriers to Implementing the National Incident Management System." Pp. 263–282 in *Learning from Catastrophe: Quick Response Research in the Wake of Hurricane Katrina*, (Christine Bvec, ed.). Boulder, CO: Natural Hazards Center–University of Colorado.

Norris, Fran. H., M. J. Friedman, and P. J. Watson. 2002a. "60,000 Disaster Victims Speak: Part II. Summary and Implications of the Disaster Mental Health Research." *Psychiatry* 65/3: 240–260.

Norris, Fran. H., M. J. Friedman, P. J. Watson, C. M. Byrne, E. Diaz, and K. Kaniasty. 2002b. "60,000 Disaster Victims Speak: Part I. An Empirical Review of the Empirical Literature, 1981–2001." *Psychiatry* 65/3: 207–239.

Peek, Lori. 2010. "Age." Pp. 155–186 in *Social Vulnerability to Disasters*, (Brenda D. Phillips, Deborah Thomas, Alice Fothergill, and Lynn Pike, eds.). Boca Raton, FL: Taylor and Francis CRC Press.

Perry Ronald W. and Alvin H. Mushkatel. 1986. *Minority Citizens in Disasters*. Athens, GA: University of Georgia Press.

Phillips, Brenda D. 2009. "Special Needs Populations." Pp. 113–132 in *Disaster Medicine: Comprehensive Principles and Practices*. (Kristi Koenig and Carl Schutz, eds.). Cambridge University Press.

Phillips, Brenda D. 1996. "Homelessness and the Social Construction of Places: The Loma Prieta Earthquake." *Humanity and Society* 19/4: 94–101.

Phillips, Brenda D., Elizabeth Harris, Elizabeth A. Davis, Rebecca Hansen, Kelly Rouba, Jessica Love. 2011/Forthcoming. "Delivery of Behavioral Health Services in General and Functional Needs Shelters." In *Behavioral Health Response to Disasters*, (Martin Teasley, ed.). Boca Raton, FL: CRC Press.

Phillips, Brenda and Paul Hewett. 2005. "Home Alone: Disasters, Mass Emergencies and Children in Self-Care." *Journal of Emergency Management* 3/2: 31–35.

Poulshock, S. and E. Cohen. 1975. "The Elderly in the Aftermath of Disaster." *The Gerontologist* 15/4: 357–61.

Quarantelli, E.L. 1983. *Delivery of Emergency Medical Services in Disasters: Assumptions and Realities*. New York: Irvington Publishers.

Schmuck, Hannah. 2000. "'An Act of Allah': Religious Explanations for Floods in Bangladesh as Survival Strategy." *International Journal of Mass Emergencies and Disasters* 18: 85–96.

Sharkey, Patrick. 2007. "Survival and Death in New Orleans." *Journal of Black Studies* 37/4: 482–501.

Shriver, Thomas E. and Gary R. Webb. 2009. "Rethinking the Scope of Environmental Justice: Perceptions of Health Hazards in a Rural Native American Community Exposed to Carbon Black." *Rural Sociology* 74/2: 270–292.

Simpson, David M. 2008. "Disaster Preparedness Measures: A Test Case Development and Application." *Disaster Prevention and Management* 17/5: 645–661.

Thomas, Deborah, Pamela K. Stephens and Jennifer Goldsmith. 2010. "Measuring and Conveying Vulnerability Analysis." Pp. 323–344 in *Social Vulnerability to Disasters*, (Brenda D. Phillips, Deborah Thomas, Alice Fothergill, and Lynn Pike, eds.). Boca Raton, FL: CRC Press.

Tierney, Kathleen J., Michael K. Lindell and Ronald W. Perry. 2001. *Facing the Unexpected*. Washington, D.C.: Joseph Henry Press.

Wachtendorf, Tricia. 2000. "When Disasters Defy Borders: What We Can Learn from the Red River Flood about Transnational Disasters." *Australian Journal of Emergency Management* 15/3: 36–41.

Webb, Gary R. 2006. "The Popular Culture of Disaster: Exploring a New Dimension of Disaster Research." Pp. 430–440 in *Handbook of Disaster Research*, (Havidan Rodriguez, E.L. Quarantelli, and Russell R. Dynes, eds.). New York: Springer.

Webb, Gary R., Kathleen J. Tierney, and James M. Dahlhamer. 2000. "Businesses and Disasters: Empirical Patterns and Unanswered Questions." *Natural Hazards Review* 1/2: 83–90.

Webb, Gary R., Tricia Wachtendorf, and Anne Eyre. 2000. "Bringing Culture Back In: Exploring the Cultural Dimensions of Disaster." *International Journal of Mass Emergencies and Disasters* 18/1: 5–19.

Wenger, Dennis E., E.L. Quarantelli, and Russell R. Dynes. 1986. *Disaster Analysis: Local Emergency Management Offices and Arrangements*. Newark, DE: University of Delaware, Disaster Research Center. Final Project Report No. 34.

Wenger, Dennis E., E.L. Quarantelli, and Russell R. Dynes. 1989. *Disaster Analysis: Police and Fire Departments*. Newark, DE: University of Delaware, Disaster Research Center. Final Project Report No. 37.

Resources

- A starting point for personal preparedness in the U.S. is www.ready.gov.
- Free preparedness and educational materials for children can be found at www.fema.gov/kids.
- The U.S. Department of Education offers numerous resources on disaster planning at http://www.ed.gov/admins/lead/safety/emergencyplan/index.html#planning
- Gender-inclusive preparedness information from the Gender and Disaster Network can be found at www.gdnonline.org and through the World Health Organization at http://www.who.int/gender/other_health/en/gwhdisasterassessment.pdf
- The Federal Highway Administration offers guidance on functional needs evacuation and on pets. http://ops.fhwa.dot.gov/publications/fhwahop09022/index.htm
- The U.S. Small Business Administration offers advice for preparing businesses for disasters and describes sources of assistance for business owners at http://www.sba.gov/content/disaster-preparedness and http://www.sba.gov/content/disaster-assistance

Chapter **7**

Planning

7.1 Chapter Objectives

Upon completing this chapter, readers should be able to:

1. Understand that disaster planning serves as a central means to enhance all levels of preparedness.
2. Explain why disaster planning is a process, not just completing a piece of paper.
3. Outline critical steps involved in family and household disaster planning.
4. Describe fundamental steps involved in organizational and community disaster planning.
5. Identify career paths in disaster planning as well as volunteer opportunities.

7.2 Introduction

Disaster planning is a key part of overall disaster preparedness. Without proper planning, the other preparedness activities noted in Chapter 6 will not be as effective. Proper planning allows for better drills, exercises, hazard and risk analyses, response, and even recovery. In Chapter 7, we look first at what factors influence individual, family, and household planning

215

for disasters. We then consider various types of planning followed by recommendations for planning at the community, national, and cross-national levels for a variety of disasters.

Most people give little thought to the household level of disaster planning. Time, resources, and individual priorities all conspire against families planning for events that seem far off and often unlikely. In most cases, disaster planning may even occur well after authorities issue a warning for an event. For example, severe blizzards occur occasionally in Northwestern Ohio. Since blizzards do not occur every year, people do not always plan for them. Often, materials people already have on hand (candles, extra batteries, even food) will get most of them through a severe snowstorm. As a result, planning for a blizzard is not a top priority in the region. For example, on January 25, 1976, authorities issued a blizzard warning across much of Ohio—one that two of our authors personally experienced.

Many people who heard and believed the warning bought extra supplies (Neal et al. 1982) but that appeared to be the extent of their planning. At the campuses we were on, everything came to a halt. Students on one campus operated the food service without supervision for five days. We managed without power or heat for several days and worried about families we could not contact by telephone. But together, using the resources we had, we emerged from the event smarter and eventually warmer and less hungry!

We often see the same minimal preparation for hurricanes. People wait until a hurricane appears to be headed toward their area before thinking about planning their responses. Those with the economic resources may take some time to plan and purchase supplies for specific hazards. Mothers in single parent households may also exert a little more time and energy in planning to protect their children but also lack resources to do so (Morrow 2000; Pike 2010). Some families may discuss how they will evacuate or take protective action, establish potential meeting points if they are separated, or develop alternative communication plans when a disaster strikes. Overall, people appear to be too busy, lack the economic resources, or have other priorities that preclude disaster planning (Tierney, Lindell, and Perry 2001).

Household preparedness is similar throughout the world. In most modern, wealthy nations, low perceptions of risk and other priorities may explain why planning does not occur. In poorer nations, most residents do not have the funds and have much greater priorities (finding the next day's food and water) than concerning themselves over a flood, earthquake, or other possible event. One exception exists: Israel. Since Israel became a nation in 1948, it has faced constant threats of war and has been attacked numerous times. For the civilian population, planning for conventional and nuclear bombing and chemical weapons has become a way life (Kirschenbaum 1992).

7.3 Planning as a Process

Researchers have uncovered a great deal on how communities and organizations can best approach disaster planning. Drawing upon extensive research, these guidelines for creating disaster plans have been summarized best by Quarantelli (1988; 1994; 1997).

Disasters are different from day-to-day accidents and emergencies. The magnitude, scope, and impact of a disaster require that a fuller set of partners join in the response and recovery efforts. Where accidents and emergencies require first responders and medical professionals, disasters roll out additional partners including public works, psychologists, the faith-based community, engineering assessment teams, environmental protection specialists, animal rescue teams, shelter providers, housing reconstruction teams, and more. A disaster plan of any kind must take into consideration all the people that are needed for the particular focus of the plan and consider both a range of hazards and the impact they may have. Then, a community can initiate planning among all the partners likely to be part of the disaster event.

A plan is not the final outcome of disaster planning because planning never stops. Plans must be living, actively revised documents. As found in Chapter 4, new disasters present themselves all the time. Pandemics, terrorism, and cyberwarfare represent recent threats around which planning has occurred. Partners also change, people leave their positions, new technology becomes available, and offices move. The dynamic nature of our professional and personal lives thus compels us to revisit planning documents to ascertain their relevance and accuracy. As one example, call-down lists used to alert emergency response partners change frequently and require continual updating. The dynamic nature of population movement also means that new groups, such as evacuees, immigrants, and newly disabled veterans arrive in communities. To ensure that plans take their needs into consideration requires an active planning approach.

Creating a plan means assuming an agent-generic approach toward planning, not creating a plan for each specific type of hazard. Any community may be faced with a range of threats. Planning for each type of event requires time that most agencies cannot devote to such a widespread effort. Many agencies lack the personnel and expertise to do so. Further, certain functional needs such as communication, coordination, and decision making authority occur across disasters. By focusing on the common areas, a planner can achieve broad-based planning for a range of hazards. The U.S. National Response Framework (NRF) uses this approach. Within the NRF, emergency support functions (ESFs) address specific areas that allow a national response to be issued. ESF #6, for example, centers on mass care (sheltering, housing, feeding)—a common need regardless of the type of event. Specific annexes then address concerns such as terrorism.

FIGURE 7.1 Emergency operations planning requires extensive planning and integration of volunteer efforts as seen here in Fargo, North Dakota. Volunteers and officials stockpiled 300,000 sand bags in a day to protect homes and businesses from Red River Valley flooding. (*Source:* FEMA News Photo/Andrea Booher.)

Plans must assume that unpredictable events, improvisation, and group emergence will occur. When disasters strike, emergent groups and organizations form to fulfill unmet needs (search and rescue, debris removal, massive sandbagging efforts to prevent flooding) during the response. Often, friends and people who know each other through existing social networks form the bases for emergent groups and organizations. During a disaster, relationships that developed during the planning process may help an emergent group form that may in turn assist more rapidly and effectively with the disaster response (Figure 7.1).

Plans must focus on coordination and flexibility, not on maintaining a rigid command and control bureaucracy. As we discuss in Chapter 8, rigid bureaucracies do not perform well under most disaster circumstances. Disasters disrupt established routines and present new challenges. Consider, for example, when an F3 tornado tore through Fort Worth, Texas in 2000. An FBI building lost its windows along with critical case files. Police facilities experienced the same damages in New Orleans after Hurricane Katrina. Retrieving and replacing evidence presented a new challenge, one that is typically not addressed in a plan. As another example, the attack on the World Trade Center resulted in the destruction of state-of-the-art emergency management facilities. To respond, surviving employees had to reconstruct a makeshift emergency operations center a few blocks from the site (Kendra and Wachtendorf 2003).

The planning process should create a set of general guidelines or principles for a disaster response. Disaster planners should not adhere to a rigid set of standard operating procedures. While certain procedures such as stages for opening an emergency operations center can be anticipated, technical aspects for a hazardous materials event and keeping a log of event-general guidelines and principles can be more effectively applied to a broad set of disaster threats. In 2011, planners worked diligently to protect the public from a terrorist attack at the Super Bowl. However, a winter blizzard, icy conditions, unusually low wind chill factors, and rolling blackouts caused unexpected disruption. If planners create guidelines for communications, emergency transportation, and utility restoration, EOC staff can implement them regardless of the type of event.

Disaster plans must avoid integrating the myths of such events as mass hysteria, panic, looting, and other incorrect assumptions of general antisocial behavior by victims. Disasters generally bring out the best in people. If a planner anticipates that the first responders will be neighbors and friends, he or she can train neighborhood teams how to conduct basic search and rescue safely and render first aid until help arrives. If a planner assumes that looting is more likely than pro-social behavior, critical assets like National Guard troops may not be deployed to locations for search and rescue purposes. When disaster threatens, knowing that people usually do not panic should prompt early warnings to inspire evacuation. If these behaviors surprise you, look forward to learning more about them in Chapter 8 on response.

The planning process must stress people working on the plan within and across organizations. Planning should never be conducted within a "silo." Organizations that will function together in a crisis event must plan together during non-crisis times and involve a range of partners within and across organizations. Janitors, typically at the bottom of an organizational hierarchy, know a great deal about buildings and where resources are stored so janitors are critical in an emergency. Similarly, chief executive officers must be involved because they may have to make decisions that determine the fate of a business or agency. Because agencies work across their silos in a disaster, they must sit at the planning table together. As an example, consider how a university might plan for a terrorist attack on a football stadium. Planning requires involvement of university leaders as well as the temporary day labor used to route people into and out of the location. Police, paramedics, firefighters, and traffic control people are parts of the operational team as are the university communications personnel and public relations officer among others.

The planning process and plans must be guided by the science of disaster behavior. "There I was …" stories produce biased, unrealistic assumptions about disaster behavior. Surgery requires specific expertise, knowing what works and does not work for a procedure. Disaster planning and operations should follow the same route. Ensuring community safety demands knowledge of the best that science can offer. Operating on the basis of what you think would work or what worked earlier may not work this time. To illustrate, consider that the U.S. government did not offer planning guidance to protect people with disabilities until well after Hurricane Katrina. Many people could not evacuate without assistance and hundreds had to be rescued after the levees broke. Planners must consider the full range of the population including realities that may exist outside their own frames of reference. Scientific research alerts us to those broader realities and can enhance planning (see Chapter 3).

Although disaster planning is part of the preparedness phase, planning should also integrate mitigation, response, and recovery. As noted earlier, a community may engage in a range of planning activities. Planners increasingly recognize the linkages of various kinds of plans and are moving forward accordingly. Designing a recovery plan with mitigation initiatives improves disaster resilience for future events and reduces the burden placed on emergency management.

In addition to the points covered above, two key principles emphasize the main elements of community or organizational disaster planning: (1) planning is a process, not a piece of paper; (2) networks, networks, and more networks. In short, planning produces many benefits. First, those involved with the planning process will learn the plan. They will not have to find the plan, locate the correct page number, and follow a script. They will know where and how to step into their roles through training, drills, and exercises. In fact, when disasters strike, disaster managers become too busy to even consult written plans. You need to know the plan, not find it and read it when a disaster threatens.

Second, the planning process helps create connections or networks among key decision makers. The mayor gets to know the fire chief better, the head of public works learns how to work with the police chief better, the city manager increases trust in the emergency manager, the head of the Red Cross works more closely with the director of the local hospital, and a committee representing faith-based groups establishes ties with community organizations. Creating plans may force people from different jurisdictions to work together.

County government representatives may have to coordinate their plans with local or municipal governments. County sheriffs may have to synchronize efforts with local police departments. In addition to learning the disaster plan through the planning process, key individuals in an organization get to know the people they will work with during a disaster. Furthermore, during planning, people learn whom they can trust, whom they can count on, how planning participants communicate, and who may talk rather than provide supportive action. Such knowledge can be important when emergency managers must make quick decisions to save lives and properties.

7.4 Types of Planning

Several kinds of planning exist, and timing is a factor. Most planning occurs before disaster strikes, particularly in the preparedness and mitigation phases. However, despite recommendations from researchers and experts in the field to plan early, some mitigation and recovery planning occurs only after a disaster has struck. In this section, we review the kinds of planning typically conducted by emergency managers. Additional planning content can be found in the chapters on recovery (Chapter 9), mitigation (Chapter 10), and private and public sector partnerships (Chapter 11).

7.4.1 Planning across the Emergency Management Life Cycle

A range of planning activities awaits those involved in managing disasters. Many think that the response phase represents the timeframe most important for planning. However, the full life cycle of emergency management needs to be considered. Response activities influence how recovery unfolds. Recovery plans should incorporate mitigation measures to reduce future disaster impacts. Even preparedness requires planning to conduct exercises and drills, roll out public education campaigns, and offer training.

Response plans are usually referred to as emergency operations plans (EOPs). They can vary in focus, length, and format but most center on coordinating activities from warning the public through search and rescue and rapid restoration of key services such as utilities. It is probably true that the most time spent on planning occurs around the response phase because that is when life-saving activities take place. As members of a human society, our shared value for human life compels us to concentrate on this critical planning phase.

Around the world, response plans vary considerably based on available resources and expertise. Most plans in the U.S. mimic the National Response Framework and its Emergency Support Functions (discussed in an upcoming section). An impoverished nation lacks the resources to conduct even basic firefighting operations and cannot afford rescue assets such as highly skilled rescue teams, air and ground ambulances, and critical care facilities. The earthquake that struck Haiti in January 2010 required external assistance yet 300,000 lives were lost. Ten months later, a cholera outbreak claimed another 1,000 lives. In economically privileged nations like Israel and the U.S., the extent of response planning varies from rural locations with minimal resources to urban areas with significant levels of planning and response capabilities. Events like September 11, 2001 heightened response planning and asset accumulation even further.

Recovery, the phase that follows response, lacks planning worldwide. Few jurisdictions expend time or resources to think about planning a recovery effort. Failure to do so, however, wastes valuable time in the aftermath of an event. The recovery period—when sleep is sorely needed to drive efforts, visioning, and projects—demands an organized plan. Two types of recovery

FIGURE 7.2 **Citizens impacted by Hurricanes Katrina and Rita work on long-term recovery issues 6 months after landfall severely damaged areas in Texas, Louisiana, Mississippi and Alabama. (*Source:* FEMA News Photo/Robert Kaufmann.)**

planning are typical. *Pre-event recovery planning* rarely occurs but for jurisdictions such as Los Angeles that are able to implement such planning, efforts to restore normalcy are expedited. *Post-event recovery planning* is more typical and unfortunately takes longer to conduct and implement (Figure 7.2). Sitting amidst the debris is not the place (or time) to plan but most communities conduct recovery planning this way.

Common elements of a recovery plan address housing, roads and bridges, environmental resources, historic and cultural preservation, businesses, utilities, and more. Communities with the energy, time, and funding to do so may opt to reconsider their environment and redesign to enhance traffic flow, increase green space, reinvigorate a business sector, and mitigate future risks. Increasingly, communities seek to rebuild in environmentally friendly ways, as Greensburg, Kansas did after a tornado destroyed the entire town. More on recovery planning can be found in Chapter 9.

Mitigation planning is conducted to identify local hazards, assess the probabilities of where and how they will harm people and places, and select feasible ways to reduce their potential impact. Mitigation planning involves stakeholders such as the business, education, utility, and health care sectors with the public in identifying and prioritizing areas for risk reduction. Mitigation measures can include structural projects such as the construction of levees along rivers that flood or installing rebar inside homes to resist earthquake shaking. Non-structural efforts are not built measures. Insurance is one example, because purchasing a policy can afford you the means to recover. Building codes serve as another example. In hurricane areas, for example, a city may require that builders install hurricane clamps on roofs to prevent roofs from blowing off during high winds. Locations that face wildfire threats may disallow wood shingles on roofs. Both kinds of mitigation measures are ways of reducing disaster impacts. Additional ideas for mitigation planning can be found in Chapter 10.

7.4.2 Business Continuity Planning

Business-related planning is specialized but also reflects the four disaster phases. For example, businesses must consider how they will respond to various kinds of disruptions or destruction (see Chapter 11). Floods may not directly impact a business but can cut off customers or deliveries. Planning must cover both direct and indirect impacts. Businesses may experience downtimes when they cannot open to provide goods and services or may be displaced temporarily or permanently. Each day that a business is not open represents a potential threat to its survival. Businesses must plan to safeguard inventory as well as buildings, employees, records, and even customers. Unfortunately, the most common form of business planning is spotty accumulation of first aid kits and conducting minimal training (Meszaros and Fiegener 2004).

As we will learn in Chapter 11, certain factors account for the lack of planning in the business sector. Size matters. Larger firms have more resources to hire contingency planners and write plans. Companies with multiple locations can draw from those resources to recover. Smaller firms struggle more with contingency planning and consequently are more likely to fail when disaster strikes. Previous experience also influences whether and how businesses plan. Those that have faced prior threats are more likely to plan, set aside resources, and be ready to regroup.

To plan for disaster requires that businesses be ready financially as well as physically and emotionally. Training people really does help. The World Trade Center in New York City was attacked twice. The first bombing in 1993 resulted in an evacuation that while effective was relatively slow. Getting thousands of people out of two massive buildings takes time. In 2001, additional training, planning, and practice resulted in a more rapid evacuation that ultimately saved many lives. "At the organizational level, evacuation was affected by worksite preparedness planning, including the training and education of building occupants, and risk communication" (Gershon et al. 2007). It is also true that people in their place of employment will step up. When a supper club caught on fire near Cincinnati, Ohio, waiters and other kitchen staff led customers to safety. Although 165 people died, the employees of the supper club saved lives through their knowledge of the facility and where to escape the deadly smoke (Johnson 1988). Are you ready where you work?

7.5 Planning Guidance

In this section we review planning guidance and relevant critiques. The considerable body of guidance in existence does not always follow the admonitions listed above to incorporate research, conduct planning as a process, and build networks (see Box 7.1). Perhaps most importantly, planning

BOX 7.1 NEW ZEALAND MINISTRY OF CIVIL DEFENCE AND EMERGENCY MANAGEMENT

Sarah Stuart-Black

Sarah Stuart-Black serves as a manager, CDEM Specialist Services, in the Ministry of Civil Defence and Emergency Management in New Zealand. She is experienced in public health, emergency management, and vulnerability studies. As a practitioner and a published author, she offers insights here on how New Zealand incorporates research with planning activities.

In New Zealand, research and a strong evidence basis for practice are fundamental to the way we approach Civil Defence Emergency Management. New Zealand's wild and diverse landscape, our relatively isolated geographic location, and our economic reliance on primary production such as agriculture and forestry mean that we are and will continue to be at risk from a broad range of hazards. The North Island of New Zealand, for example, straddles the Pacific and Australasian tectonic plates, has several active volcanoes, and has a number of areas prone to severe flooding—all within only 43,911 square miles. Many communities and much industry and infrastructure are located in areas that are likely to be affected by hazards.

New Zealand's vision is to build a resilient and safer New Zealand with communities understanding and managing their hazards and risks. Realising this vision relies on everyone participating from the government, local authorities, individual departments, businesses, and volunteer organisations, right down to individual families.

Scientific research into the New Zealand hazardscape continues to identify new hazards and often points to a greater risk from our known hazards than was previously understood.

So while on the one hand, empirical research helps us to understand what is occurring and has occurred around us, it also helps us to consider what sorts of new and potentially unknown hazards and risks may be around the corner, and therefore need to be planned for. This is especially important in the development of legislation and policy, where decisions are made that will affect people's lives and their ability to recover after a disaster. These decisions must always be grounded in solid evidence, and this evidence is arrived at through research. Research becomes most useful when it is actually applied to the way we practice emergency management in New Zealand.

The Ministry of Civil Defence and Emergency Management and the range of stakeholders we work with recognise the critical role that science, research, and expert advice has for informing continuous improvement and supporting strategic and operational emergency management. Due to the Ministry's limited size and resourcing, its main influence on national research priorities is through advocacy and advice to funding and provider agencies. The Ministry is involved in the generation, consumption, and transfer of research as funder, user, advocate, and facilitator and works directly with research and science providers to develop arrangements for coordination across agencies and disciplines, at both the strategic and operational levels.

The importance of research in supporting and underpinning emergency management was reinforced recently during the response to and ongoing recovery from the 7.1 M Darfield earthquake that significantly impacted the Canterbury region of New Zealand on 4 September 2010 but with no loss of life. The research undertaken before the Darfield earthquake to understand the hazards and risks in New Zealand and formulate the approach for response and ongoing recovery from this emergency also underpins legislation (such as the New Zealand Building Act 2004), policies, and practice.

A long history of research has contributed to building codes and standards for New Zealand that resulted in relatively low levels of damage and low casualties in Canterbury. The earthquake has opened new research opportunities, including exploring this area where no active faults had previously been mapped and no large historical earthquakes are known to have occurred. There is research being undertaken to look at the impacts of school closures on children and their families. The New Zealand Society for Earthquake Engineering published a comprehensive bulletin in December 2010 to capture the range of research that was undertaken between 4 September and December 2010. The research that has been and continues to be undertaken since the Darfield Earthquake will enhance our knowledge and understanding of what happened and whether enhancements to current arrangements are required, and importantly, it will provide opportunities to share new knowledge with stakeholders outside of New Zealand.

Emergency management-related research in New Zealand is diverse and spans multiple disciplines across physical and social sciences. The value and importance of research have been proven and reinforced with each new emergency. New Zealand's continued commitment to research and an evidenced-based approach to the development of legislation, policy, and practice in emergency management enhance our ability to reduce the risks from hazards, to plan and prepare better, and to respond and recover from future emergencies.

should not be a cookie-cutter approach where a cut-and-paste effort results in a plan. The BP oil spill along the U.S. Gulf Coast revealed this variance from recommended best practices when media alerted the public that the BP plan covered efforts to rescue walruses—an aquatic species not native to the area. Apparently, a West Coast oil spill plan served as the basis for handling a Gulf oil spill and produced considerable criticism of several oil producers including BP and Exxon/Mobil by the U.S. Congress.

7.5.1 Personal and Household Level Planning

Many websites and organizations tell you to be ready for disaster and to "make a plan." What does making a plan mean at the individual and household level? At this point you should have some good ideas about general preparedness after reading Chapter 6 and understand that you bear responsibility for your personal safety. To the greatest extent possible, you should develop a series of steps to take if a hazard occurs in your area. Have you walked your family or roommates through steps that need to be planned out for various scenarios such as fire, severe weather, and an extended period of isolation from a blizzard or pandemic?

It is not enough to be familiar with conditions where you live. You should consider your other environments such as school, work, and other places you may visit. Imagine, for example, going on vacation in another state and realizing that a tornado outbreak is expected. You look at the weather map but have no idea where you are in relation to the threat. If you are outside and hail is falling and you need to seek immediate shelter, where do you go? You may be in a hotel when the fire alarm goes off. Did you read the emergency information the hotel provides in a folio or on the back of the door before the alarm sounded? Did you count the number of doors to the closest exit so that you can crawl under the smoke to safety?

Planning at the personal level starts with familiarizing yourself with area hazards and the risks they pose to you. Many Internet sites and local libraries offer information that can help you understand the disaster history of an area. The emergency management agency probably offers information on websites and may even have a preparedness and planning campaign with downloadable materials. At the national level, FEMA provides an online family emergency plan tool that walks you through planning and generates a printable plan with wallet-sized note cards for family members (www.ready.gov). Why not put the book down for fifteen minutes and start that process?

Several first steps should launch your plan. The first is what to do in case a disaster bears down as an immediate threat. You must plan to shelter in place or evacuate. Sheltering in place requires that you know the safest place to protect you from the expected hazard. Should disaster destroy your home when you are separated from family and friends, you should have a place to meet near the neighborhood. You should plan one site within walking distance and an out-of-town location. Alternatively, you may be able to evacuate in advance of a threat so knowing safe nearby locations and how to get there serves as part of the planning process.

Deciding how, when, and where to evacuate beyond your home requires considerably more planning effort. You must determine where you can go and how you will get there. Personal transportation may or may not be an option so knowing people who can assist you to travel and public transportation options is critical. Local agencies may have a registry of people who need transportation although most communities do not. If your community has such a registry, always update your information when your location or contact information changes (Metz et al. 2002).

Family and household members with functional or medical needs should participate actively in the planning process. Individuals with disabilities know best what works for them and can inform co-planners of their specific needs. At a minimum, planning should include ways to secure and evacuate (as needed) with medications, medical records, assistive devices and other technologies, and service animals. Caregivers must be active in planning so that they remain with an individual at risk during a disaster. This is particularly important during an evacuation, so plan to keep families and households together with caregivers.

Members with special needs include pets and livestock. Ensure that you have planned for your pets by recording medical information and taking it along with food, water, leashes, and comfort items should an evacuation warrant. As part of your plan, be sure that someone remains alert to changing weather conditions so that pets can be brought indoors to safety when heat, cold, and dangerous weather threaten. Livestock can be protected from the elements by farm buildings and shelters or evacuated to shelters in areas outside the immediate threat. For more on assisting your animals, see the resources section of this chapter and Chapter 6 on preparedness.

Finally, do not forget to develop a communications plan. Assume that you will lose your cell phone and/or its charger and that callers will overwhelm cellular capacities after a disaster. What is your next strategy to let people know where you are and what you need? Planning alternative means to communicate is critical. Land lines, email, text messaging, and social media all serve as possible alternatives. You should also designate certain people to serve as central communication points so that you can contact them and they can pass on information about what you may need. By planning, you can decrease the impact on your personal safety and that of your loved ones. Most planning can take place over a couple of family or household dinners. The time and effort certainly seem worthwhile given the alternative.

7.5.2 Community-Based Planning

As Quarantelli (1994) stressed, planning is a process, not a piece of paper. Whether planning involves a family in one household or a large community with thousands, people must work together to devise plans. As we note throughout the text, disasters are not equal opportunity events. Certain groups of people, such as the poor, the elderly, racial and ethnic minorities, and people with disabilities are more likely to be exposed to disaster impacts. By involving the full community in the planning process, we can identify and anticipate those at higher risk, plan more effectively for their survival, and empower a broader range of citizens to be proactive. By leveraging the social capital that they bring to the planning table, we ultimately strengthen the disaster resilience of historically disadvantaged populations and reduce the impacts on emergency managers.

The World Health Organization (WHO) serves as a center for pandemic planning which will be discussed shortly. WHO (2005, p. vii) encourages widespread community participation in planning:

> A multisectoral approach means the involvement of many levels of government, and people with various specialties including policy development, legislative review and drafting, animal health, public health, patient care, laboratory diagnosis, laboratory test development, communication expertise and disaster management. Community involvement means making optimal use of local knowledge, expertise, resources and networks. It is a powerful way to engage people and to build the commitment needed for policy decisions.

A main principle for any kind of emergency planning is to involve the public to the best degree possible. Response planning requires certain levels of expertise from firefighters who know how to enter burning buildings and conduct extractions and emergency managers who coordinate activities behind the scenes. Public involvement is also useful. For many years, communities failed to involve people with disabilities in response planning. In recent situations, people with disabilities have educated first responders about how they should be moved, why their assistive devices must be retrieved, and how to help their service animals. It is also true that families, friends, and neighbors are usually the first to respond to a scene. Connecting them to the response effort ensures that they do so safely.

Recovery planning efforts should involve community representatives and inform the community about what the recovery planning team is considering. Stakeholders must come from a broad range of the public including businesses, residents, utility companies, environmental experts, and those concerned with historic and cultural preservation. Each brings a valuable perspective to the recovery planning process and can make suggestions that help restore quality of life. Community-based planning must also consider the needs of various groups when reconstruction is launched. Age matters, for example. Seniors may benefit from new codes that upgrade homes using universal design features (helpful to all of us) such as levers that open doors more easily than knobs. Children's needs may include additional park space or safe bike routes from home to school. If a community moves structures out of floodplains, parklands can be created. The community must be consulted about preferences ranging from establishing a nature preserve to creating soccer fields or a dog park. Community investment in any planning process means that people are more likely to return to a disaster site and rebuild in a way that gives meaningful social interaction to their lives.

Community involvement can be conducted in several ways. A typical form is to create a planning team consisting of representatives from various sectors. Those individuals must stay in touch with the broader constituencies and consult them for preferences. Communities can also hold public forums to present options and secure input. Electronic means to do so have become increasingly common, especially when residents experience displacement to other cities. Electronic surveys, websites, social media, and other sources can tap into public opinion. Radio and television shows can afford chances for the public to air their thoughts (see Box 7.2). Community involvement can also be as simple as having people gather for public meetings in the local bayous, city halls, or university auditoriums.

Community participation empowers those often left with nothing to move forward individually and collectively. Their ideas and energy can be harnessed to generate new insights and pathways for a community. What they know from the standpoint of their own lives can positively influence all kinds of planning. By finding ways to reach out we can further empower public input. Public outreach should reflect the community by offering information in various formats for those who cannot see or hear, for those with low literacy levels, and for those who may not speak the local language. Planning should never become an exercise in exclusion. Inadequate planning costs lives.

BOX 7.2 STRATEGIES TO INVOLVE THE PUBLIC IN PLANNING

How can we encourage the public to participate in and reflect on planning initiatives? While you will learn more in Chapter 9 on Recovery and Chapter 10 on Mitigation, here are some typical strategies for reaching out to and involving citizens:

Electronic Tools

- *Social Media*. Increasingly, social media are used to solicit responses. Facebook pages, for example, collect comments on a range of topics dedicated to emergency management. FEMA has a Facebook page as do many state and local offices of emergency management. Voluntary organizations also host pages where people can offer comments on impending actions.
- *Websites*. Another electronic means to gather information comes from the Internet. Organizations may use their websites to gather information by soliciting comments on various documents. To illustrate, FEMA has engaged stakeholders by requesting electronic feedback on new versions of the National Response Framework, the National Recovery Plan, and more.
- *Online Surveys*. Data can also be gathered electronically through online surveys that capture individual perspectives at a specific point (see Chapter 3). Online tools collect information immediately and allow users to analyze the feedback for planning purposes.
- *Electronic Town Halls*. The availability of streaming technologies has increased the ability of people to participate in planning initiatives across distance. These tools were used, for example, after Hurricane Katrina. Because people evacuated from the Gulf Coast states to dozens of states across the U.S., planners convened stakeholders via televised, satellite, and Internet-based tools.

Face- to-Face Tools

- *Planning Charettes*. A charette brings people together to focus on a specific concern such as recovery planning. A facilitator typically establishes a set schedule and moves participants through a feedback process that results in a consensus-based understanding of what the plan should represent. Information should be captured carefully so that it can be used for future purposes.
- *Workshops*. A workshop differs from a planning charette in that it is typically less structured. Workshops focus people on a theme and encourage them to discuss their thoughts and reflections. Workshops may generate subcommittees to address emerging issues.
- *Public Meetings*. These events range from formal presentations by experts to open forums allowing questions and answers and

give-and-take discussions. Public meetings are more likely to take the form of information given than information solicited, depending on how they are structured.

- *Field Trips.* The purpose is for people to observe a planning issue first-hand. Participants may become more visibly engaged by conducting a field trip as they must confront the various dimensions of planning issues. After disasters, for example, it is not unusual for governmental officials to meet with affected residents of damaged areas to visualize where they need to go from here.

Source: Natural Hazards Center and Public Entity Risk Institute. 2006. *Holistic Disaster Recovery*. Boulder, CO: Natural Hazards Research and Applications Information Center and PERI.

7.5.3 State Planning Guidance

The federal government generally provides disaster planning guidance for state (and even local) governments. The state's role generally is three-fold. First, a state will follow federal guidance and create training opportunities for state and local governments. For example, and as we detail below, following the September 11, 2001 terrorist attacks, the federal government required that all federal, state, and local officials involved in emergency management become trained in use of the National Incident Management System (NIMS).

Second, the states were to model their planning processes upon the federal recommendations. This approach shows federalism at work in emergency management. Specifically, although the U.S. has national policies, states can relate the federal politics to their own political and disaster climates. Considering the diverse politics and hazards throughout the country, a federalist approach to emergency management makes sense (McEntire and Dawson 2007). Detailed in Box 7.3, the new *Comprehensive Planning Guide (CPG) 101* takes such an approach. CPG-101 provides guidance—not requirements—for disaster planning. Rather than forcing each state of the union to take a specific approach to disaster planning, it provides suggestions for different ways states can approach planning to fit their own unique needs.

Finally, the governor of a state may submit a request to the president through FEMA to secure a presidential disaster declaration. Requests must be routed from a local community through a state unable to supply sufficient resources to meet disaster-generated needs and then to the federal government. The governor and state will then likely serve as a pass-through and partner for funds provided by FEMA and other federal agencies. The state will also be responsible for providing a matching portion of funds; in many cases, FEMA will provide 75% of the cost for a disaster project matched by a 25% cost-share from state and local government. Leadership from the state may constitute the top elected official (Figure 7.3) and directors and staffs of state agencies.

BOX 7.3 FEMA'S COMPREHENSIVE PREPAREDNESS GUIDE (CPG) 101: INTEGRATING RESEARCH INTO PLANNING

Paul Hewett

Paul Hewett is the deputy director of the Center for Integrated Emergency Preparedness, Decision and Information Sciences Division, Argonne National Laboratory. He is responsible for developing programs, conducting research, and developing and implementing innovative approaches to resolving a wide spectrum of emergency preparedness issues. His research interests include planning modernization, exercise evaluation methodologies, and vulnerable population assistance. He is the author or co-author of numerous journal articles and reports on emergency planning, evaluations systems, and lessons-learned processes.

Comprehensive Preparedness Guide (CPG) 101, *Developing and Maintaining Emergency Operations Plans*, provides the Federal Emergency Management Agency's (FEMA) emergency planning doctrine and guidance on developing emergency operations plans. Work on CPG 101 began in October 2006, with FEMA establishing a multidisciplinary working group with membership drawn from professional associations, state and local governments, universities, and other research organizations, and interested citizens.

The motivations for producing CPG 101 were many; however, the primary cause was the overwhelming evidence from post-Hurricane Katrina studies suggesting that plans and planning systems needed strengthening.* Additionally, the nationwide plan review conducted by FEMA in 2006 indicated that outmoded planning processes, products, and tools contribute to inadequate emergency planning across the nation.[†]

Planning guidance existed before the work on CPG 101 started. In 1996, FEMA published its State and Local Guide (SLG) 101, *Guide for All-Hazard Emergency Operations Planning*. A series of Civil Preparedness Guides published between 1977 and 1991 also were available to the planning community. However, none of that guidance reflected the lessons learned from the World Trade Center and Pentagon attacks of September 11, 2001, the SARS outbreak in 2003, the Indonesian tsunami of 2004, and Hurricanes Katrina and Rita in 2005. Nor did it consider changes in law (e.g., Disaster Mitigation Act of 2000, Homeland Security Act of 2002, and Post-Katrina Emergency Management Reform Act of 2006) and policy (e.g., the series of homeland security presidential directives, the National Response Framework, and the National Incident Management System) that made much of that guidance obsolete.

The CPG working group designed CPG 101 to be both a doctrinal document and a job aid for emergency planners. Therefore, the group had to find a balance between presenting planning theory and providing practical planning guidance and also present a single planning process that could be used at all levels of government. To achieve these sometimes conflicting goals, the working group designed a two-part document. The main document provides details for planners who want depth and have time for in-depth reading. An appendix summarizes the planning process outlined in the main document and presents a guide for the potential content of an emergency plan.

The main theme of CPG 101 is building relationships and establishing linkages of individuals and organizations involved in emergency operations through planning. It recommends that locations use a planning team concept to avoid having clusters of planners who have little contact with each other. The goal is to ensure that each group understands its role and the roles of other groups in a disaster operation. Additionally, CPG 101 places a special emphasis on community-based planning—planning for the whole community that involves the whole community. Therefore, it strongly suggests that a location's planning team include citizen membership and actively seek representatives from disability groups and ethnic communities.

---

* The Federal Response to Hurricane Katrina: Lessons Learned (The White House, February 2006); A Failure of Initiative (United States House of Representatives, February 2006); Hurricane Katrina: A Nation Still Unprepared (United States Senate, May 2006); Hurricane Katrina: GAO's Preliminary Observations Regarding Preparedness, Response, and Recovery (GAO-06-442T, March 2006); A Performance Review of FEMA's Disaster Management Activities in Response to Hurricane Katrina (DHS Office of Inspections and Special Reviews, OIG-06-32, March 2006).
† Nationwide Plan Review Phase 2 Report, Department of Homeland Security, June 2006.

CPG 101 also provides an explanation of the planning environment, detailing the relationship between federal-level response concept plans and state and local emergency operations plans. It identifies two perspectives that drive the national planning structure. The national-level planning perspective looks at how and when the federal government adds its resources to a community's response efforts. Its planning efforts tend to focus more on supporting hazard-specific disasters and catastrophes. The state and local planning perspective involves trying to determine how to work with response organizations, obtain additional resources, and work with the general public. The state and local focus is on all hazards and events that range from simple emergencies through disasters. CPG 101 clearly identifies the FEMA regional offices and multi-state regional consortiums as the points of intersection for these two perspectives.

CPG 101 is not the only planning guidance that the working group is developing. They are working on a series of complementary CPGs that will provide specific planning considerations for a variety of hazards and emergency functions. The intent is to provide a library of planning resources that an emergency planning team can use as it solves the response problems posed by the hazards its community faces.

FIGURE 7.3   Governor Togiola Tulafono (left) and FEMA Federal Coordinating Officer Kenneth R. Tingman (right) conduct a planning meeting after earthquake, tsunami, and flood damage in American Samoa, 2009. (*Source:* FEMA News Photo/ Richard O'Reilly.)

7.5.4 National Planning Guidance

National planning guidance is a cumbersome term because its application is so broadly based. National-level planning assumes a central governmental structure that assumes responsibility for citizens under its governance. The structure may vary considerably from ruthless dictatorships to full democracies. Governments, regardless of structure, may shoulder different levels of responsibility for planning and planning may emanate from administrative components, legislation, or legal decisions.

A ruling political party may lead planning or may direct the effort to a specific agency. The ruling party may activate a plan when appropriate or may stall the decision to proceed. Those in leadership by voter choice or military might can thwart others from implementing plans to aid in a response. Furthermore, a centralized government may also stall response capabilities if lower level staff remains reluctant to take action (Britton 2006). Thus, the notion of national planning needs to be understood in a widely varying set of contexts and circumstances.

National planning guidance may also emerge within a nation or from outside events as we will see in the example of pandemic planning. In the U.S., a combination of choices, events, and circumstances has driven national-level planning. The president, for example, can issue an executive order (EO) to drive forward an area of planning. Perhaps the most influential EO of the last decade occurred on October 8, 2001 when President George W. Bush established the U.S. Department of Homeland Security. A portion of that EO reads, "The Office of Homeland Security shall coordinate national efforts to prepare for and mitigate the consequences of terrorist threats or attacks within the United States. In performing this function, the Office shall work with Federal, State, and local agencies, and private entities, as appropriate, to: (i) review and assess the adequacy of the portions of all Federal emergency response plans that pertain to terrorist threats or attacks within the United States." A series of homeland security presidential directives mandated the development of strategies, policies, and plans to increase public safety against the threats of terrorism and other hazards (for a full list, visit http://www.dhs.gov/xabout/laws/editorial_0607.shtm).

Events have revealed the failings and limitations of plans and the results of not implementing plans. In the aftermath of Hurricane Katrina, both the White House and the U.S. Congress issued reports on failed systems and called for enhanced planning efforts. As a consequence, extensive review took place and led to reinvigorated plans and integrated planning across agencies. Certainly, lawsuits have generated additional planning and programs. For example, *Brou v. FEMA* resulted in new efforts to increase accessible, temporary disaster housing for people with disabilities and gave momentum to a new national disaster housing strategy. In summary, several avenues influence national planning guidance.

Britton (2006, p. 365) compared national planning in Japan, New Zealand, and the Philippines. He determined that carrying out planning responsibilities tends to "reflect cultural values and assumptions, including previous disaster experiences." Japan, for example, invested 5 to 8% of its annual national budget to disaster reduction and most of the investment focused on mitigation initiatives. Based on the significant risks Japan faces from earthquake threats in particular, the effort is understandable. The Great Hanshin earthquake in Kobe in 1995 killed over 6,000 citizens. A plethora of laws led efforts to increase Japan's capabilities and readiness. The 1998 Comprehensive National Development Act for example required that the government make the nation "a safe and comfortable place to live." Nonetheless, criticism has centered on a lack of coordinated policies and the public officials' view that disaster programs are "nuisances that interfere in routine administrative tasks" (Britton 2006, p. 357), a belief that may change further after the tsunami in 2011. In New Zealand, a task force found "unrealistically high public expectations" because citizens assumed capabilities beyond what the government could provide. In response (and as found in this text; see Box 7.1), the government led initiatives to establish local civil defence and emergency management groups. Integration of scientific and empirical work drove much of their work to situate emergency management in a local context and empower citizen involvement.

Returning to the U.S., FEMA and DHS led efforts to revise national-level planning and create a National Response Framework. Evolution over time reflects the natural progression of planning at the national level. As Chapter 4 told us, new disasters will emerge and the impacts are expected to worsen. The national level "is the only sector that has a commission to develop nationwide strategies with power to bind, power to commit public resources and influence private resources" (Britton 2006, p. 366).

As briefly noted above, NIMS is another important planning document that in theory should improve overall disaster coordination and response. Following the September 11, 2001 terrorist attacks, many agreed that the overall emergency response to the events, especially in New York City, could have been much better (see *The 9/11 Commission Report* 2004). Set in the context of other poor responses to major disasters, President Bush asked the director of Homeland Security to devise a means to improve disaster response. As a result, on March 1, 2004, NIMS became the standard means to respond to disaster. The idea behind NIMS is to provide a management structure that is flexible yet standard, enabling people to communicate and coordinate more effectively, in a format that any person or agency can learn to use (FEMA 2004).

NIMS is based upon the Incident Command System (ICS) designed and used by firefighters since the early 1970s. Reduced to its basic structure, ICS

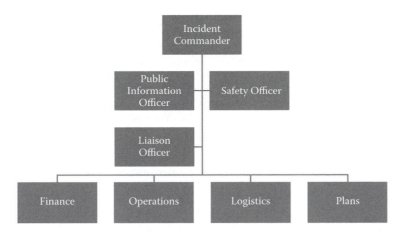

FIGURE 7.4   Incident Command System (ICS) structure.

has five key functions. The incident commander (IC) oversees and coordinates activities during an event. Individuals in charge of finance, logistics, operations, and planning report to the IC to share their information so the IC can make well informed decisions. The finance function tracks the budget and funds spent. Logistics pertains to obtaining and delivering resources to the disaster site. Finally, planning gathers information to determine what resources (people, equipment) are needed to perform vital tasks (debris removal). In theory, ICS has a simple organizational structure (Figure 7.4) that can expand or contract as driven by a situation.

Firefighters can use this basic structure to fight fires; local, state, and federal governments can use the same type of structure, but with thousands of people, to respond to larger events (FEMA 2008). However, others have raised serious issues about the effective of the NIMS in a disaster and questioned such factors as flexibility, use in large-scale events, and training. In addition, officials made NIMS a federal policy with no set of studies demonstrating its effectiveness. In the limited studies available on ICS, variation occurred across agencies and individuals who used it, with equally varying levels of understanding of how it functions (Neal and Webb 2004; Jensen 2010).

The federal government is firmly committed to NIMS. In fact, federal, state, and local governments must train their employees fully in NIMS to obtain any type of federal funding or reimbursements following a disaster. To meet these needs, FEMA devised a five-year plan to make the nation "NIMS compliant." In short, training emergency responders and emergency managers at all levels of government is central to disaster planning in the U.S. (FEMA 2008).

7.5.5 Cross-National Guidance

Disasters do not respect national boundaries. Flooding crosses borders, blizzards and volcanic ash shut down international airports, and terrorism affects people and structures. Nations must work together to plan for various threats, and that is certainly a challenging task given political differences, resource bases, and how various hazards present risks disproportionately to various populations. In this section, we look at cross-national planning by considering a hazard that certainly affects our readers: influenza pandemics.

No one wants to get the flu, and in today's society with rapid transportation of people across national borders, the potential for a major outbreak is everywhere. We need to take the threat of influenza seriously. In 1918–1919 the "Spanish" flu killed twenty million to fifty million people. The flu strain took its heaviest toll on young people. Later pandemics in 1957 (Asian flu) and 1969 (Hong Kong Flu) took a lesser toll worldwide, but senior citizens and those with chronic medical conditions fared the worst (Cox, Tamblyn, and Tam 2003).

Along with losses of lives, pandemics cause considerable social disruption when schools and child care centers close, hospitals and medical facilities experience massive influxes of patients, and businesses lose customers. The economic impact can be significant (Cox et al. 2003). Because we cannot eliminate influenza viruses, we must plan for their impact. The effort to do so also benefits other planning efforts because "pandemic preparedness planning can be usefully linked to response planning for other public health emergencies, including bioterrorism threats" (Cox et al. 2003, p. 1801).

How seriously are nations taking the pandemic threat? The World Health Organization (2005) estimates that a major influenza pandemic could result in 233 million outpatient visits, 5.2 million in-patient admissions, and 7.4 million deaths within a relatively short time. Imagine the social and economic disruptions that would result along with the grief that would affect so many households. To determine appropriate action steps, nations with pandemic plans rely on activation phases and levels with recommended action steps. The European Union, for example, coordinates most of its activation levels across twenty-seven nations using WHO criteria:

Interpandemic Period
    Phase 1. No new strain in humans; may be present in animals
    Phase 2. Virus circulating in animals
Pandemic Alert Period
    Phase 3. Human illnesses develop but not transmitted to other humans
    Phase 4. Illness transmitted in small, localized clusters
    Phase 5. Larger clusters but still localized; pandemic possible
Pandemic Period
    Phase 6. Rapid transmission across populations and locations
Post-Pandemic Period
    Return to normal

1 • Prepare for the Emergency
  • Convene a community-based planning team to conduct risk assessment, plan communications, and consider legal and ethical issues. Develop a response plan based on pandemic phase.

2 • Surveillance
  • Gather information on the pandemic breakout and increase surveillance as events warrant.

3 • Case Investigation and Treatment
  • Initiate diagnosis using appropriate laboratories, investigate epidemiologically, and manage clinics.

4 • Preventing the Spread of the Disease in the Community
  • Initiate public health measures including social distancing and quarantine; vaccinate, use anti-virals.

5 • Maintain Essential Services
  • Ensure health services can be offered. Respond to patient surge with additional personnel and resources.

6 • Research and Evaluation
  • Investigate to determine the full implications of the outbreak and identify recommendations for future events.

7 • Implementation, Testing and Revision of the Plan
  • Plans should always be revised based on the previous event for empirically verified lessons learned.

FIGURE 7.5   World Health Organization pandemic planning recommendations.

The World Health Organization (WHO 2005) recommends a series of steps for nations conducting pandemic planning (Figure 7.5). A first step sets planners on creating a task force or planning team. Planning elements for pandemics include conducting a risk assessment to determine who would be most likely to be affected. Certainly, some populations suffer more than others as indicated by influenza history. Those living in impoverished or socially disadvantaged locations are "among those least likely to receive effective medical counter-measures or to benefit from nonmedical public health interventions, and they will be among those most likely to die as a result of infection" (Usher-Pines et al. 2007, p. 32). Some estimates indicate that 96% of deaths would occur in developing nations but in more advantaged nations the economically and socially disadvantaged would likely suffer more. In 2006, a group of experts recommended that planners (Usher-Pines et al. 2007):

• Identify historically disadvantaged populations as among those most likely to be affected by a pandemic. Depending on location, these groups may include the poor and political minorities. In recent outbreaks, poultry farmers whose livestock was destroyed suffered both influenza and economic losses. Another disadvantaged group may be people without health care insurance.

- Involve these populations in planning for a potential pandemic. They will know their life circumstances best and can identify effective means for communicating influenza information within their communities—a key component of pandemic planning.
- List and design solutions for special needs within the population. Special needs might include disseminating information in appropriate languages, offering social services, counseling, and special housing. People who remain home-bound may need outreach, food, and medications delivered directly to them.

Initial steps also involve crafting public education information. Messaging must target those particularly at risk and should be diverse enough to reach across various populations and the information media they access. The recent outbreak of H1N1 virus illustrates the concerns of planners clearly: those most at risk were pregnant women. Delivering recommended protocols to them and their health care providers emerged as a critical action.

Public health officials must next monitor an outbreak, carefully documenting and verifying symptoms as the illness spreads. By investigating the dissemination of the illness, epidemiologists can determine those at the highest risk and geographic locations of concern. You would probably not be surprised to learn that most universities and colleges have pandemic plans in place for shutdown or quarantine. Some have taken a second step to transition classes into online platforms so that students can continue to make progress toward their degrees. The traveling public may also face restrictions or health checks in passport control to reduce the spread of the disease.

Final steps address the needs of the health community as it responds to illness phases. Even they are not immune to becoming sick, and staff numbers and facilities may be compromised by an outbreak. Ensuring that sufficient numbers of health care personnel can step in supports the health care system's capacity to respond. An expected patient surge in the U.S. is to be met by a cadre of health care professionals including the "National Disaster Medical System (NDMS), the Commissioned Corps of the U.S. Public Health Service (USPHS), the Strategic National Stockpile (SNS), and federal volunteers and temporary employees" (Department of Health and Human Services; see Resources). The U.S. bases its planning on several assumptions (see Box 7.4) that suggest how important it is to mitigate your own risks (see Chapter 10).

As with any good planning effort, activation of a plan during an event requires careful evaluation. Often called "hot washes" or debriefings, planners and those involved in activating the plan conduct a review. It is critical that those present at a review honestly and thoroughly critique the plan's implementation and effectiveness. This is not a time to say "job well done." It is an opportunity to identify plan weaknesses and revise accordingly.

BOX 7.4   U.S. NATIONAL PANDEMIC PLANNING

The U.S. Department of Health and Human Services developed an influenza pandemic plan (http://www.hhs.gov/pandemicflu/implementationplan/pdf/introduction.pdf) based on these assumptions:

- An influenza pandemic will most likely originate overseas and not in the U.S.
- Susceptibility to the pandemic influenza virus will be nearly universal.
- Efficient and sustained person-to-person transmission will signal an imminent pandemic.
- The clinical disease attack rate will likely be 30% or higher. Illness rates will be highest among school-aged children (about 40%) and decline with age. Among working adults, an average of 20% will become ill during a community outbreak.
- Some persons will become infected, but not develop clinically significant symptoms. Asymptomatic or minimally symptomatic individuals can transmit infection and develop immunity to subsequent infection.
- The typical incubation period (interval between infection and onset of symptoms) for influenza will be approximately two days.
- Persons who become infected will shed virus and may transmit infection as much as a day before the onset of illness. Persons will transmit infection for at least two days after the onset of symptoms. Children will shed the greatest amount of virus and are likely to pose the greatest risks for disease transmission.
- On average, each infected person will transmit infection to approximately two other people.
- Fifty percent of those who become ill will seek outpatient medical care. With the availability of effective antiviral drugs for treatment, this proportion could be higher.
- The number of hospitalizations and deaths will depend on the virulence of the pandemic virus. Two scenarios are presented based on extrapolation of past pandemic experience. HHS planning utilizes the more severe scenario.
- Risk groups for severe and fatal infection cannot be predicted with certainty, but will likely include infants, the elderly, pregnant women, and persons with chronic medical conditions.
- Rates of absenteeism in workplaces will depend on the severity of the pandemic. In a severe pandemic, absenteeism will reach 40% during the peak weeks of a community outbreak, with lower rates of absenteeism during the weeks before and after the peak.
- Certain public health measures (closing schools, quarantining household contacts of infected individuals, sheltering in place ["snow days"]) will increase rates of absenteeism in workplaces.
- In an affected community, a pandemic outbreak will last about six to eight weeks.

Multiple waves (periods during which community outbreaks occur across the country) of illness will occur, and each wave could last two–three months. Historically, the largest waves occurred in the fall and winter, but the seasonality of a pandemic cannot be predicted with certainty.

7.6 Working and Volunteering in Planning

Jobs in disaster planning may be stand-alone opportunities or embedded within a more general position. Note, for example, the Centers for Disease Control listings below. Components of these positions include planning elements and developing guidance materials and organizing training, drills, and exercises to test the plans for general emergency responses and for public health measures including handling of potential pandemics (www.cdc.gov, search Employment):

- Emergency response specialists serve as integral members of a team responsible for coordinating emergency preparedness and responses to natural and man-made hazards and disasters. They may provide all-hazards public health watch support; incident emergency alert, notification and escalation; and support for emergency incident drills, exercises, and actual emergencies. The specialists coordinate health consultation services; develop guidance material for response personnel; and manage and direct demonstration and training programs for state and local health personnel involved in emergency preparedness and response.

- Public health advisors (overseas) perform as public health project officers of grants and cooperative agreements with emphasis on financial accountability, internal controls, strategic planning, and policy. They frequently manage an extensive staff and the logistics and personnel issues that arise in a large office. They may provide guidance and assistance to host country Ministry of Health officials, other USG agencies and international organizations to plan, implement, and evaluate activities for specific public health programs. Program areas that employ public health advisors (Management and Operations) include infectious diseases, zoonotic and emerging infectious diseases, chronic diseases, environmental health, and injury control.

Other positions exist as well. In January 2011, FEMA announced a supervisory program specialist (planning) position in Virginia with a salary ranging from $89,033 to $115,742. The successful applicant would perform a range of duties including training, exercises, response planning, and work in an all-hazard, ICS-compliant planning section. The applicant would need "experience applying the concepts, principles, theories, and practices of the Incident Command System (ICS) planning process in planning, directing, managing, and supervising an emergency management operation in developing strategic, operational and tactical response plans, developing deliberate and incident plans to support emergency management operations, and integrating initiatives into policy documents."

Volunteering opportunities exist also in the area of planning, particularly for the phases of mitigation and post-disaster recovery. Because mitigation planning (see Chapter 10) rolls out more slowly and in a step-wise fashion, it is easier to volunteer as part of a community-based group working to lessen area hazards. After a disaster occurs, communities also convene planning committees and usually offer the public various means to participate such as open forums, housing fairs, and planning charettes (refer to Box 7.2). To become more involved in other phases, volunteer for organizations designing preparedness campaigns and help distribute and explain information to people. Encourage personal and household planning in your own home and across your neighborhood. Form efforts with emergency management officials to support seniors and others with household planning. Response planning typically involves the emergency management and first responder communities. Depending on the size of the communities and their commitments to public involvement, you may be able to participate in the planning process as part of a formal response group dedicated to serving during emergencies. Even if you are not part of the planning process, your participation may be useful during exercises and drills to test plans. Remain alert for opportunities to observe these events as well because they can provide insights and instruction leading to a career path.

7.7 Summary

In this chapter we learned that planning before disaster strikes is a central activity of emergency managers and agency personnel. As part of the preparedness phase, planning brings people together across departments, agencies, disciplines, levels of government, and NGOs. During the planning process, participants develop connections that increase trust, build relationships, and facilitate communications. Planning is more than writing a document that goes on a shelf. Planning involves and integrates stakeholders in building a consensual framework that can be implemented when crises occur. Planning spans the entire life cycle of emergency management beyond preparedness.

Response planning involves at a minimum the development of an emergency operations plan (EOP) for use by an emergency operations center (EOC; see Chapter 8). Additional elements of response planning usually partner emergency managers in organizing efforts with first responders, NGOs and others in search and rescue, evacuation, and shelter management planning. Recovery planning should occur in the pre-disaster stage but often occurs after disaster strikes (see Chapter 9). Mitigation planning should be accomplished long before a threat bears down on a community, but may also occur after disaster strikes when public interest increases (see Chapter 10). Businesses must construct continuity plans to minimize economic losses and protect their employees and customers (see Chapter 11). At a personal level, you bear responsibility for planning at the individual and household level. Ensure that your family is prepared by developing relevant plans and resources before disaster hits home.

Discussion Questions

1. Why is planning best thought of as a process? What do you see as the critical steps to take in forming a planning team?

2. What variations in planning do you see across the four phases of disaster?

3. Why is pre-disaster planning recommended? Why do people, communities, and organizations often fail to plan before a disaster? What kinds of challenges affect planning after an event?

4. Have you and your household undertaken any type of disaster planning? If so, what kind? What remains to be done?

5. What strategies to involve the public represent the ones that would work best in your community? How about for yourself and your friends? What about others who may live in your community such as senior citizens, children, people with disabilities, tribes, and newcomers? How would you integrate them into planning initiatives?

6. What do you see as the three most critical principles for disaster planning?

7. Can you see yourself as a disaster planner? What type of planning seems to be the most interesting to you? What kinds of professional qualities should you develop to be an effective planner?

References

Britton, Neil R. 2006. "National Planning and Response: National Systems." Pp. 347–367 in *Handbook of Disaster Research*, (H. Rodriguez, E.L. Quarantelli & R. Dynes, eds.). NY: Springer.

Brou vs. FEMA. Judgment available at http://www.fema.gov/txt/library/brou_fema.txt. last accessed May 23, 2011.

Cox, Nancy J., Susan E. Tamblyn, and Theresa Tam. 2003. "Influenza Pandemic Planning." *Vaccine* 21: 1801–1803.

Federal Emergency Management Agency (FEMA). 2004. "NIMS and the Incident Command System." Available at http://www.fema.gov/txt/nims/nims_ics_position_paper.txt, last accessed February 26, 2011.

Federal Emergency Management Agency (FEMA). 2008. *National Incident Management System (NIMS): Five Year Training Plan*. Available at http://www.fema.gov/emergency/nims/NIMSTrainingCourses.shtm#item5, last accessed February 26, 2011.

Federal Emergency Management Agency (FEMA). 2010. *Developing and Maintaining Emergency Operating Plans: Comprehensive Planning Guide (CPG) 101, Version 2.0*. Available at http://www.fema.gov/pdf/about/divisions/npd/CPG_101_V2.pdf, last accessed February 26, 2011.

Jensen, Jessica Anne. 2010. *Emergency Management Policy: Predicting National Incident Management System (NIMS) Implementation Behavior*. Dissertation, Department of Sociology, Anthropology and Emergency Management. Fargo, ND: North Dakota State University.

Johnson, Norris. 1988. "Fire in a Crowded Theater." *International Journal of Mass Emergencies and Disasters* 6/1: 7–26.

Kendra, James M., and Tricia Wachtendorf. 2003. "Creativity in Emergency Response after the World Trade Center Attack." Pp. 121–146 in *Beyond September 11th: An Account of Post-Disaster Research*, (Jacquelyn L. Monday, ed.). Special Publication #39 Natural Hazards Research and Applications Information Center, University of Colorado: Boulder, CO.

Kirschenbaum, Alan. 1992. "Warning and Evacuation during a Mass Disaster: A Multivariate Decision Making Model." *International Journal of Mass Emergencies and Disasters*. 10/1: 91–114.

McEntire, David A., and Gregg Dawson. 2007. "The Intergovernmental Context." Pp. 57–70 in *Emergency Management: Principles and Practice for Local Government*, 2nd Edition, (William L. Waugh, Jr. and Kathleen J. Tierney, eds.). Washington, D.C.: ICMA Press.

Meszaros, Jacqueline and Mark Fiegener. 2004. "Predicting Earthquake Preparation." Available at http://www.iitk.ac.in/nicee/wcee/article/13_571.pdf, last accessed January 31, 2011.

Metz, William, Paul Hewett, Edward Tanzman, and Julie Muzzarelli. 2002. "Identifying Special-Needs Households that Need Assistance for Emergency Planning." *International Journal of Mass Emergencies and Disasters* 20/2: 255–281.

Morrow, Betty. 2000. "Stretching the Bonds: The Families of Andrew." Pp. 141–170 in *Hurricane Andrew*, (W. Peacock, B. Morrow, and H. Gladwin, eds.). Miami, FL: International Hurricane Center.

National Commission on Terrorist Attacks upon the United States. 2004. *The 9/11 Commission Report*. Washington, D.C.: Government Printing Office.

Neal, David M., Joseph B. Perry, Jr., and Randolph Hawkins, 1982. "Getting Ready for Blizzards," *Sociological Focus* 15/1: 67–76.

Neal, David M., and Gary R. Webb. 2006. "Structural Barriers to Implementing the National Incident Management System." Pp. 263–282 in *Learning from Catastrophe: Quick Response Research in the Wake of Hurricane Katrina*, (Christine Bvec, ed.). Boulder, CO: Natural Hazards Center–University of Colorado.

Pike, Lynn. 2010. "Households and Families." Pp. 257–278 in *Social Vulnerability to Disasters*, (Brenda D. Phillips, Deborah Thomas, Alice Fothergill, and Lynn Pike, eds.). Boca Raton, FL: CRC Press.

Quarantelli, E.L. 1994. "Research-based Criteria for Evaluating Disaster Planning and Managing." Available at http://www.nifv.nl/upload/179144_668_1168610952796-quarantelli-1998.pdf, last accessed February 1, 2001.

Quarantelli, E.L. 1997. "Ten Criteria for Evaluating the Management of Community Disasters." *Disasters* 21: 39–56.

Quarantellil, E.L. 1988. "Assessing Disaster Preparedness Planning." *Regional Development Dialogue* 9: 48–69.

Tierney, Kathleen, Michael Lindell, and Ron Perry. 2001. *Facing the Unexpected*. Washington, D.C.: Joseph Henry Press.

Usher-Pines, Lori, Patrick S. Duggan, Joshua P. Garron, Ruth A. Karron, Ruth R. Faden. 2007. "Planning for an Influence Pandemic: Social Justice and Disadvantaged Groups." *The Hastings Center Report* 37/4: 32–39.

World Health Organization. 2005. *WHO Checklist for Influenza Pandemic Preparedness Planning*. Available at http://www.who.int/csr/resources/publications/influenza/FluCheck6web.pdf, last accessed February 2, 2011.

Resources

- To create your own emergency plan that can be printed for multiple family members and includes information for emergencies, pets, and family members with any medical or functional needs, visit http://ready.adcouncil.org/fep/
- The American Planning Association, in concert with FEMA, published guidance on recovery planning titled *Post-Disaster Recovery and Reconstruction*. A portion of the book can be downloaded at www.fema.gov (search by title).
- *Holistic Disaster Recovery* includes ideas for planning that work for the recovery phase and also for other phases in the life cycle of a disaster. A copy can be viewed at http://www.colorado.edu/hazards/publications/holistic/holistic2006.html
- The U.S. Government offers a one-stop website for flu information: http://www.pandemicflu.gov/ and a full version of the Department of Health and Human Services Pandemic Plan can be read at http://www.hhs.gov/pandemicflu/implementationplan/
- The European Union pandemic planning documents can be reviewed at http://www.euroflu.org/html/pandemic_europe.html
- Executive orders pertaining to disabilities and emergency management can be viewed at http://disabilitynotes.org/ExecutiveOrders.htm
- Incident Command System resources and links to NIMS can be found at http://training.fema.gov/EMIWeb/IS/ICSResource/index.htm
- National Response Framework Resource Center, http://www.fema.gov/emergency/nrf/
- CPG 101, available at http://www.fema.gov/pdf/about/divisions/npd/CPG_101_V2.pdf

Chapter **8**

Response

8.1 Chapter Objectives

Upon completing this chapter, readers should be able to:

1. Understand the response phase in the context of comprehensive emergency management, and describe inaccuracies in the "command post" image of emergency managers.
2. Define the response phase of disasters and identify some of the major activities typically undertaken during that period.
3. Describe the process of issuing disaster warnings and identify the characteristics of effective disaster warnings that lead people to take appropriate protective actions.
4. Discuss various myths about how individuals, organizations, and communities respond to disasters, and identify sources of those myths.
5. Contrast myths with research-based findings on how individuals, organizations, and communities actually respond to disasters, and identify various sources and limitations of community resilience.
6. Situate the response phase in an international context, and identify relevant issues to consider in applying research findings to developing countries.
7. Identify the most common problems that arise during the response phase and discuss effective principles of emergency management to overcome those challenges.

8.2 Introduction

It is very likely that when you hear or think about *emergency management* you immediately think about the response phase of disaster. You might envision yourself working in an ultra-modern, high-tech emergency operations center (EOC), simultaneously monitoring network news coverage on multiple flat-panel televisions, keeping a close eye on your computer screen as response activities are logged and updated at near real-time speed into an advanced decision support software program, and handling non-stop telephone calls from colleagues out in the field and media seeking a good quote. Indeed, the image of a strong leader asserting command and control over a chaotic situation is one that many people have of the emergency manager. We will refer to this as the "command post" image of the emergency manager.

Despite the pervasiveness, and the appeal even, of this imagery, it is not entirely accurate. In fact, if your idea of an emergency manager is a person whose days are action-packed and spent in the EOC making split-second, life and death decisions, then you will likely be disappointed by the profession. There will be some of that, to be sure, but most of your time will not be spent in the trenches. Rather, you will spend time working to make the trench time effective, efficient, and smooth (see Box 8.1).

As a point of reference, consider the law enforcement profession. When we think of the police, we tend to imagine trained professionals who spend their days chasing criminal suspects, collecting highly sensitive evidence at crime scenes, and solving cold cases. Yet, if you talk to a recently hired police officer about his or her work, you will likely sense at least some disillusionment over how much idle time they have and, even more likely, how much time they spend writing reports.

This is not to say that you will spend all of your time as an emergency manager at a desk, writing and reviewing disaster plans. Indeed, like a police officer called to the scene of a major crime, you will sometimes be sprung into action by a disaster. It is important, however, to realize that responding to actual disasters is only one, albeit a very important, component of an emergency manager's job. Our purpose here is not to shatter your hopes and dreams of saving lives during a disaster but instead to give you a more realistic view of the profession. The command post view of emergency management is inaccurate because it largely ignores the other phases of disaster and their relationship to the response period, it envisions widespread chaos, and it assumes that an effective response is characterized by strong command and control over a situation.

8.2.1 Ignoring Other Phases of Disaster

As we discussed in Chapter 2, the life cycle of disasters includes preparedness, response, recovery, and mitigation. Because you will spread your

BOX 8.1   FIRST RESPONDERS AND EMERGENCY MANAGERS: KEY DIFFERENCES

Dean Findley

Dean Findley joined the Oklahoma City Fire Department in October 1988, promoted through the ranks to major. Major Findley spent the first twenty years of his career responding to emergencies including the bombing of the Alfred P. Murrah building in 1995. In 2008, he accepted a position as the fire department's liaison to the Oklahoma City Office of Emergency Management. Since then, the city has experienced multiple record breaking events, reinforcing the concept of comprehensive emergency management.

Perhaps the best way to contrast the roles of first responders, specifically firefighters, and emergency management is through an illustration. To that end, let's examine how these two professions respond to a tornado striking their community.

Emergency management enters the response phase well in advance of a storm impact. Their work begins as the atmospheric conditions show signs of potential for tornadic activity. After reviewing weather forecasts, emergency management sends a threat assessment to local officials and other response partners alerting them to the potential ahead. The emergency operations center (EOC) ramps up its operations to the next level, which often signals the addition of volunteers to the mix as the approaching storm intensifies. Storm spotters begin staging in key areas to act as the eyes for emergency management.

Meanwhile, first responders monitor the weather and hope that the storm weakens, goes around the area, or only causes minor damage. These public servants have already confirmed that the equipment is ready, a typical activity every day on the job. They have repeatedly trained for this day, hoping these skills are never needed. They are ready but wait patiently for the lights to click on, signaling their entry into the response phase of this event.

The tornado touches down! Storm spotters and local media report structural damage with potentially trapped victims. Calls begin pouring in to 911 operators. The first responders spring into action, not knowing what awaits their arrival on the scene. Based on these damage reports, emergency management bumps the EOC operation level up one more notch. Staffing at the EOC increases to ensure the boots on the ground have what they need to overcome the storm's wrath.

The first responders arrive at the scene and begin pulling people from damaged homes, administering first aid, extinguishing fires, and turning off utilities to damaged structures. They work quickly and efficiently to ensure that all are accounted for and the potential for further damage is averted.

Emergency management is busy contacting various partners, both public and private, whose help may be needed during this disaster. These partnerships are the results of countless hours of relationship building through meetings and planning sessions. Forging these partnerships and speaking face-to-face with these individuals and groups during the down time between disasters makes these calls for help much easier. Provisions for those displaced by the storm are coordinated through the American Red Cross, United Way, Salvation Army, and other non-profit organizations.

The first responders complete their tasks and return to the station to clean up and refuel in preparation for the next storm. Their response to the storm has ended.

After the storm passes, the EOC's level of activation returns to normal. However, emergency management is still responding to the needs of the citizens. Damage assessments begin at first light. Emergency management and volunteers survey the damage and tally the numbers to submit to state and federal officials for use in a declaration request if warranted. Emergency management verifies that all displaced citizens have been take care of and thanks the assisting agencies for their help.

This response phase ends. However, much work lies ahead for emergency management and the community. The emergency management office transitions into the recovery phase of this event to deal with short- and long-term issues such as infrastructure repair, housing, and long-term planning. In addition, emergency management continues to work on various projects in the preparedness and mitigation phases while continuing previous recovery projects and remaining ready for the next storm.

time across all four phases, because actual disaster events are relatively rare, and because emergency managers have numerous job responsibilities (Chapter 5), it is simply inaccurate to assume that most of your time will be spent managing response efforts. However, it is accurate to assume that you will spend a great deal of time *thinking* about response activities. As we discussed in Chapter 6, the time you spend on preparedness-related activities including educating the public about the hazards and risks in your community, talking with organizations such as schools and businesses, and conducting drills and exercises will pay tremendous dividends when it comes to responding to an actual disaster.

Similarly, if your community takes effective, proactive steps to mitigate possible threats, it is likely that disaster impacts will be less severe and enable more manageable responses. While response is the most prevalent phase in the common view of the emergency manager's work, the concept of comprehensive emergency management discussed in Chapter 2 assumes that the other phases are equally important.

8.2.2 Envisioning Chaos

Another reason the command post view of the emergency manager comes to mind so readily is the common notion that disasters create chaos and social disorganization. In the midst of all that confusion, it is assumed by many that we need a calm, level-headed leader to make the right decisions and keep everyone else in line. As we briefly discussed in Chapter 3 and will discuss in much greater detail in this chapter, the concept that disasters create chaos and massive social breakdown is a myth. Instead, as we will see, individuals, organizations, and communities typically show remarkable resilience in the face of disasters.

As Dynes (2003) points out, we continually find "order in disorder" in the immediate aftermaths of large-scale disasters like the terrorist attacks of September 11, 2001. Similarly, Drabek (2010) characterizes the post-disaster environment as "organized-disorganization." However, for reasons we will discuss in this chapter, many people, including some emergency management professionals, continue to believe that chaos prevails in disasters. As a result, the command post image of the emergency manager persists in the minds of many.

8.2.3 Assuming Need for Command and Control

Because it envisions a chaotic scene after a disaster, the command post image also assumes that the best way to effectively manage a disaster is to assert strong command and control over the situation. According to Dynes (1994), this command-and-control model of emergency management is based on numerous false assumptions and inappropriate analogies. Generally, it assumes that civil society is fragile, and the post-disaster environment is analogous to a war-time scenario. In the absence of strong and assertive leadership, the expectation is that lawlessness and anarchy will spread. From this perspective, based largely on a military model of leadership, the emergency manager is essentially a commander, establishing firm control over a situation and unilaterally issuing orders to others. As we will see in this chapter, however, emergency managers are much more effective when they emphasize coordination and communication instead of command and control.

The post-disaster environment is fluid, dynamic, and constantly changing. Decisions must be made quickly, often based on very limited information. In those circumstances, a rigid, hierarchical, and centralized approach is likely to fail. Instead, a decentralized, flexible, problem-solving approach is much better suited to the complexities of the response phase of a disaster (Dynes 1994; Neal and Phillips 1995). Therefore, in sharp contrast to the command post image, it is much more accurate to view emergency management professionals as managers and coordinators, not as commanders.

8.3 Getting Started: Definitions and Activities

Now that you understand that response is only one aspect of an emergency manager's job duties and have been cautioned against embracing a command post view of the profession, the remainder of this chapter will provide an in-depth look at the response period. In this section, we will consider various definitions of response and identify disaster-related activities typically performed during the response phase. In subsequent sections, we will discuss the process of issuing disaster warnings and identify factors that enhance their effectiveness; describe various myths about how people, organizations, and communities respond to disasters; debunk the disaster myths and describe actual responses, including typical patterns and common problems; and discuss the most effective principles of emergency management during the response phase including the all-hazards model, coordination, and flexibility. Despite decades of research on the response phase, misunderstandings about reactions to disasters are still widespread. After reading this chapter, you will have a much better sense of what really happens during disasters and obtain clear guidance on managing responses effectively.

8.3.1 Defining Response

As you will recall from Chapter 2, the response phase is defined as activities "… designed to provide emergency assistance for casualties … seek to reduce the probability of secondary damage … and to speed recovery operations" (National Governors' Report 1979, p. 13). More recently, Tierney, Lindell, and Perry (2001, p. 81) define disaster response activities as "… actions taken at the time a disaster strikes that are intended to reduce threats to life safety, to

care for victims, and to contain secondary hazards and comm
They further explain that during the response phase emergen
must address two sets of demands: those generated from the
those arising from the response effort.

Disaster-induced demands are fairly obvious and arise from
to care for victims and deal with physical damage and soci ._.ɪ up-
tion caused by the event. *Response-induced demands* are far less obvious
but equally important and challenging for emergency managers. They
include the need to coordinate the activities of the multitude of individuals and organizations involved in the response. As we will see later in this
chapter, response-induced demands are plentiful in the wake of a disaster because so many different types of actors and organizations—some
without clearly delineated disaster responsibilities—become involved in
response efforts.

8.3.2 Typical Response Activities

In light of the involvement of so many different individuals, groups, and
agencies and the pressing needs brought on by disasters, the response period
is typically packed with activity. Common components of the response
effort include activating the EOC, warning the public, notifying appropriate authorities, mobilizing personnel and resources, initiating evacuation,
opening shelters, providing medical services, search and rescue operations,
and many others. In an effort to more accurately describe response activities,
Drabek (1986) separates them into pre-impact mobilization and post-impact
emergency action sub-phases. *Pre-impact mobilization* involves warning the
public, initiating evacuation, and establishing shelters. *Post-impact emergency actions* include searching for survivors and providing medical care to
the injured. Tierney et al. (2001, p. 75) categorize response activities in even
greater detail, identifying four related areas of activity:

- Emergency assessment
- Expedient hazard mitigation
- Protective response
- Incident management

Emergency assessment includes monitoring hazards (natural, technological, and human-induced) in your community and assessing damages and
other impacts when a disaster occurs (see Box 8.2). *Expedient hazard mitigation* refers to activities undertaken just prior to or shortly after the onset
of a disaster—sandbagging in a flood and boarding windows in a hurricane—aimed at protecting lives and containing damage. *Protective response*
involves all the activities we typically think about in relation to disasters,

BOX 8.2 PRELIMINARY DAMAGE ASSESSMENT

One of the main tasks of an emergency manager after a disaster is to conduct an emergency assessment. Doing so in the U.S. initiates the process of applying for a presidential disaster declaration that releases federal disaster funding. Called a preliminary damage assessment (PDA), the process sends capable investigators into the field to determine how bad things are after a tornado, flood, or earthquake has struck. They may experience considerable challenges getting to the stricken area due to downed power lines, blown-out bridges, and buckled roads. Arrival may also be compromised by debris or floodwaters that do not allow safe passage.

Several methods offer means to conduct the PDA to be followed by more thorough investigations once the area is accessible. In many locations, a windshield survey may occur; the emergency management team drives through the area and identifies quickly the number of houses, businesses, and infrastructure components compromised. To do so, they generally designate three levels: destroyed, major damage, and minor damage and tally a straightforward account of the apparent damage. Obviously, a drive-by does not allow a good look inside a structure. Even when houses look fine from the exterior, flood waters may have destroyed the interior and all the furnishings. Earthquakes may have undermined the structural integrity of a building and the damage is not easily seen. After the 1989 Loma Prieta earthquake, for example, the exterior of an historic structure in Santa Cruz, California looked to be in good shape, but inside the floors had "pancaked" and the structure could not be saved. Later, those who loved the building as the first location of early government cried when the wrecking balls took it down.

Other means to assess damages include aerial reconnaissance and satellite imagery. The same problems exist with these high-tech solutions as with the windshield survey; the visual images just cannot reach inside a building. In short, the PDA is followed by careful assessments made by qualified engineers. Their determination will result in formal designation of a building. While no one wants to see a red tag on the front door, the tag means that professionals have determined that the building is not safe to re-enter and will be torn down. The PDA system thus serves to safeguard the public, determine the amount of damage to qualify for outside aid, and set up parameters by which voluntary organizations will determine the extent of their assistance. The PDA is, in short, the key step that bridges response into recovery (see more in Chapter 9).

including search and rescue, emergency medical services, sheltering, and others. *Incident management* requires establishing an EOC, inter-agency and inter-governmental coordination, media communications and public information activities, documentation, and administrative and logistic support.

As an emergency manager, it is highly unlikely that you would ever be directly involved in all these response activities. However, it is important that you understand what happens and will happen in your community after a disaster. It is even more important that you understand how best to facilitate *coordination* of all those activities, foster *communication* among all the responding entities, and recognize the value of *flexibility* in maximizing the effectiveness of your community's response to a disaster. These core principles of effective emergency management discussed in Chapter 5 are particularly important in the response phase, as will be evident throughout this chapter.

8.4 Disaster Warnings

Warning the public of an impending threat is a critical first step in responding to disasters. Of course, as discussed in Chapter 2, disasters vary significantly in predictability and length of forewarning. At one extreme, for example, hurricanes can be spotted and tracked well in advance, giving emergency managers and other public officials hours or possibly even days to establish an EOC, mobilize necessary resources, and urge the public to take appropriate protective actions. At the other extreme, an earthquake or chemical plant explosion offers virtually no advance warning. Between these extremes, tornadoes can be located and tracked fairly accurately, giving local officials some time, even if only minutes, to alert the public. Because of the great variability in forewarnings of disasters, it is critical in the preparedness phase for emergency managers to educate the public about the hazards in their communities, test their disaster warning systems, and provide clear guidelines for people and organizations to follow in the event of a disaster when every second counts.

In some sense, therefore, warnings can considered both a preparedness and response activity. In the interests of simplicity and clarity of presentation, we will focus in this chapter only on actual disaster warnings and treat them accordingly as response activities. You should recognize, however, that while disaster warnings fall under response activities, other types of risk communication cut across the phases of disaster and focus on preparedness, recovery, and mitigation. Public education campaigns that seek to inform the public about common causes of wildfires and house fires or about the value of flood insurance are intended to prevent disasters from occurring in the first place or persuading people to take preventive measures that will assist them to respond to or recover from a disaster. In weather forecasting, a distinction is made between watches and warnings. Watches indicate that conditions are favorable for the emergence of a tornado, blizzard, hurricane, or ice storm. A warning indicates that a storm has been spotted. If these efforts are effective, people will pay attention to emergency warnings and respond appropriately, lessening the burdens on emergency management agencies and first responders.

In this section, our primary objective is to gain a better understanding of the disaster warning process and the factors that enhance the effectiveness of warnings. An effective disaster warning persuades people and organizations to take appropriate protective actions. Disaster warnings have been studied extensively for more than forty years and we have learned a great deal (Sorensen 2000; Sorenson and Vogt-Sorensen 2006). Nevertheless, as we will discuss later in this section, public officials continue to develop ineffective warning systems, largely ignoring the recommendations of researchers.

8.4.1 Warning Process

In the wake of Hurricane Katrina, some observers were surprised that so many people did not evacuate New Orleans at the urging of the city's mayor. Many observers attributed much of the suffering and human tragedy that ensued to the failures of some individuals to make the right decisions and leave the area. Inherent in that view, however, are the assumptions that everyone in the impacted area received warning messages, that the messages were clear and interpreted in the same way by all who received them, and that the residents had a level playing field in terms of ability to evacuate.

In reality, people do not always receive and interpret warning messages in the same manner; messages are not always effectively worded and delivered; and social factors such as socioeconomic status, disability, and others impact the ability of people to heed warnings and take protective actions. At first glance, the warning process seems simple and straightforward: public officials issue a warning and people comply with the instructions in the warning. Research, however, suggests that warnings are far more complex. Warning is a social process that involves several steps (Mileti 1999, p. 191; Sorensen and Vogt-Sorensen 2006, p. 191; National Research Council 2010, p. 11):

- Receiving a warning
- Understanding a warning
- Believing a warning is credible
- Confirming the threat
- Personalizing the threat
- Determining whether protective action is needed and feasible
- Taking protective action

As you can see from this list, there is a long way to go from public officials issuing a warning to the point where people and organizations take protective action. Every step presents uncertainties and intervening factors that can negatively impact the process.

8.4.2 Taking Protective Action

By issuing disaster warnings, emergency managers and other public officials hope to enhance life safety by urging citizens and organizations within their communities to take appropriate protective actions. Of course, the nature of a hazard determines what protective actions are appropriate. In the case of a tornado, for example, people are typically urged to get below ground or go to the centers of their houses so that the walls protect against outside threats. On the other hand, in the days before a hurricane makes landfall, people may be asked to leave the area. At times, the primary purpose of a message is simply to urge people to stay tuned for more information and direct them to appropriate sources for additional information. During the winter months when inclement weather is expected, for example, public schools and universities often issue press releases and post announcements on their websites telling people to tune in to certain radio and television stations for important information about opening delays or cancellations.

For community-wide disasters, the primary protective actions are temporary sheltering and evacuation. Over the years, researchers have learned a tremendous amount about these measures and the insights they gained are extremely relevant to the practice of emergency management. If you are involved in setting up temporary shelters during a disaster, you may be surprised when very few people use them. Similarly, if you are involved in issuing an evacuation warning in your community, you may feel frustrated when many people stay put and ignore the warning. Researchers have consistently uncovered these patterns of behavior in their studies of numerous disasters, so we should not be surprised when people do not evacuate or utilize public shelters. In fact, by familiarizing themselves with research findings on sheltering and evacuation, public officials may dramatically improve their ability to persuade the public to take protective actions.

8.4.2.1 Evacuation and Temporary Sheltering

Sheltering and housing activities cut across the phases of disasters, beginning in the response phase and sometimes continuing through much of the recovery. In this section, we consider only temporary or emergency sheltering that falls into two broad types: public shelters and sheltering in place. *Sheltering in place* is a very common response to some hazards such as tornadoes. It involves urging people to stay where they are and giving them specific instructions on how best to protect themselves. For example, advice in a tornado is to seek shelter in a basement, storm cellar, or interior room of a house or building. A chemical or hazardous materials release may require that people remain indoors with windows closed and air conditioning systems turned off. *Public sheltering*, on the other hand, involves urging people to evacuate their homes and go to designated locations for safety. These locations often include school gymnasiums, common areas in churches, and large arenas, stadiums, or convention centers. In the U.S. we are starting to see communities in areas of high risk building congregate shelters to host hundreds of people at risk in a hardened facility (see Chapter 10).

In reviewing the major research findings on sheltering, we will limit discussion to public sheltering, which follows an official recommendation for people to evacuate a hazardous area. As mentioned previously, emergency managers may be puzzled when so few people actually show up at community shelters during and immediately after a disaster. Researchers have known about this pattern for a very long time. For example, in his comprehensive review of several decades of research on the topics of evacuation and sheltering, Drabek (1986) conclusively determined that most people in disaster-impacted communities do not go to public shelters.

Where do people go after a disaster, if not to public shelters? In every disaster, of course, a number of people will simply stay put. During the 1980 eruption of Mt. St. Helens in the state of Washington, a local resident named Harry Truman stubbornly refused to evacuate despite several warnings, and he is presumed to have died and been buried under several feet of ash from the volcano. According to Drabek (1986; 2010), most people who evacuate during a disaster will go to the homes of friends or relatives. While it is impossible for you to know ahead of time exactly how many people in your community will refuse to evacuate, how many will seek refuge with friends or family, and how many will use public shelters, you do not want, as many emergency managers do, to over-estimate the amount of shelter use.

8.4.2.2 Factors Affecting Evacuation and Public Shelter Usage

In addition to relying largely on friends and family for safety, research has shown that several other factors affect the warning process and whether people take protective actions. These factors, described in this section, are summarized in various other publications (Drabek 1986; Mileti 1999; Tierney et al. 2001; Drabek 2010). While some of the social factors impacting people's ability and willingness to take protective actions may make perfect sense to you, others may be surprising. In both cases, you will benefit throughout your career by having a better understanding of these factors.

In their research on evacuation planning, Perry, Lindell, and Greene (1981, p. 160) identify various *community-level factors* that influence shelter usage among evacuees and suggest that "the use of public shelter increases when community preparedness is high, when the entire community must be evacuated, and when the evacuees anticipate that the necessary period of absence will be long." They go on to say that "even under these conditions, public shelters seem to attract only about one fourth of the evacuees at a given site." While Perry et al. recognize that shelter usage is typically low during disasters, they suggest that usage can be increased somewhat through enhanced community preparedness.

Researchers have also identified numerous *individual- and household-level factors* affecting warning responses and protective actions (Mileti 1999). These factors include gender, race, socioeconomic status, education level, knowledge and risk perception, and presence of children. While some of these factors positively impact the warning process, others decrease the likelihood that people will take protective action. Based on past research, it appears that protective actions are more likely to be engaged in by women, households with children, and those with higher socioeconomic status. Additionally, warning messages have more positive impacts on people with higher levels of education, greater knowledge about and heightened perception of risk, and those with more community involvement. On the other hand, racial and ethnic minorities, people of lower socioeconomic status, and those with less education are less positively impacted by official warnings and less likely to take protective actions. Social class significantly shapes exposure to hazards and the ability to escape them, as was dramatically revealed in Hurricane Katrina when many people simply did not have the necessary resources including cars to get out of the city.

Another factor stems from credibility of the person issuing the warning. A person issuing a warning should be as similar as possible to the population the warning should reach. Imagine, for example, someone with a New Jersey accent trying to convince someone in the Deep South to evacuate. A familiar voice will appear credible and thus motivate higher compliance.

Another impediment to public sheltering emerges when people believe that a shelter may not be ready for them. People with disabilities, for example, fear that shelters may not be able to accommodate their needs or perhaps a previous experience was unpleasant (van Willigen et al. 2002). We may also erroneously assume that everyone is warned. National Weather Service meteorologists noted a "hole" in the weather warning system: many systems bypass people with hearing disabilities (Wood and Weisman 2003). Senior citizens may prefer to remain in the comfort of their homes where they have medications, assistive devices, neighbors or family to help them, and pets to comfort them. Both groups experience lower incomes than the general public and have difficulties affording travel to, at, and from a shelter. Hurricane Katrina, for example, occurred at month end when many people waited for government entitlement checks to buy food, gasoline, and medicines.

Other factors you may not have considered are far less intuitive. After Hurricane Katrina and other events, we learned that one major impediment to people seeking safety in public shelters was care of pets and service animals (Heath et al. 2001). Public shelters typically do not allow pets even though owners, particularly the elderly, consider pets essential members of their families and are reluctant to leave them behind. Moreover, service animals provide necessary assistance to the vision impaired. Although public shelters are mandated to accept service animals (U.S. Department of Justice n.d.), not every shelter provider understands this (National Organization on Disability 2005). We talked about vulnerable populations throughout the writing of this book. Social need is an area where emergency management practice can be greatly improved, and lives can be saved by gaining a better understanding of the research literature and the needs of disaster survivors.

Another less obvious impediment to evacuating and seeking refuge in public shelters is the fear of looting (Drabek 2010). As we will see later in this chapter, the idea that looting and stealing are rampant after a disaster is a major myth to which many people subscribe. Although these crimes are rare, people nevertheless make decisions about what protective actions they take on the basis of the looting myth. They fear that looters will target their property and steal their belongings if they leave their homes.

As all of this suggests, several impediments prevent people from taking protective action, in particular going to a public shelter after a warning is issued. Nevertheless, public officials and emergency managers often overestimate how much shelter space will be needed. Envisioning shelters overrun by thousands of frightened evacuees, they sometimes prepare for a massive onslaught that never occurs. As Fischer (2008) notes, it is important for emergency managers to recognize these factors and the actual behavioral patterns during disasters and open shelters accordingly. He suggests opening shelters "as needed," opening new shelters only after existing ones begin to fill.

Finally, we would be remiss if we did not also consider disaster warnings themselves as potential impediments to protective actions. Public officials sometimes wait too long to issue a warning; issue a warning that is too vague about who will be impacted by the impending threat and what actions should be taken; or convey contradictory messages to the public as events unfold. Because it is important for you to understand how to craft warning messages that are timely and accurate and effectively persuade as many people as possible to get out of harm's way, the next section discusses the research-based characteristics of effective warning systems.

8.4.3 Characteristics of Effective Disaster Warnings

Effective warning messages persuade those who receive them to take appropriate protective actions. Several established warning systems have been in operation for many years and new technologies promise to expand the reach and enhance the effectiveness of disaster warnings. Established warning systems include outdoor sirens used to warn of tornadoes and other weather events, the Emergency Alert System that scrolls messages across television screens, weather radio, and others. Newer technologies include cell phones, short message service (SMS) and text alerts, and social media websites including Facebook and Twitter (NRC 2010). In the wake of the tragic shootings at Virginia Tech University in 2007, for example, many universities across the U.S. implemented text alert systems for informing students, faculty, and staff about emergencies on campus and providing brief instructions on what to do.

While researchers and emergency management professionals are hopeful that the new technologies can fill crucial gaps left by the older warning systems, we actually know very little about how and the extent to which people use new technologies during disasters. One thing we do know about various advanced technologies is that they often improve the lives and safety of some but not all, that is, there is often a technological divide between those who have access to the technology and those who do not. Thus, in the realm of emergency management and disaster warnings, we would be wise to acknowledge that reality and recognize the limits of technology for keeping the public safe. Past research suggests that several factors can enhance the effectiveness of disaster warnings (Mileti 1999; Aguirre 1988; National Science and Technology Council 2000; NRC 2010). All of these studies suggest that disaster warnings are most effective when they are:

- Broadcast frequently across multiple media
- Consistent in content and tone over time and across media outlets
- Crafted to reach diverse audiences
- Specific and accurate about where the hazard is and to whom the message applies
- Clear (no technical jargon), containing specific instructions on what actions to take, when, and why
- Truthful and authoritative and delivered by an identifiable and credible source

Drabek (2010, p. 105) offers additional advice for improving the effectiveness of disaster warnings. He suggests that community evacuation can be enhanced when emergency managers and other public officials:

- Encourage family planning for evacuation
- Promote media consistency
- Utilize forceful but not mandatory evacuation policies
- Allay public fears of looting
- Facilitate transportation
- Establish family message centers

Although research is fairly clear on what constitutes an effective disaster warning, warning systems that largely ignore the guidelines continue to be devised. For example, consider DHS's Homeland Security Advisory System (HSAS) put into place by Homeland Security Presidential Directive #3 and unveiled by the newly created DHS in the months following the attacks of September 11, 2001. Its purpose was to educate the public about the threat of terrorism, inform them about changes in risk levels, and encourage them to take precautionary measures.

To achieve those objectives, a color-coded scheme was implemented in which green indicated a low risk of terrorist attacks, blue indicated a general risk, yellow indicated a significant risk, orange indicated a high risk, and red indicated a severe risk. However, based on the characteristics of effective disaster warnings described in this section, the HSAS had major shortcomings. As Aguirre (2004) aptly demonstrated, the terrorism alert system offered only a vague description of the hazard, was non-specific in terms of to whom or even what region it applied, and failed to provide explicit instructions as to what people should do to protect themselves.

Additionally, the HSAS potentially suffered from what has been termed "warning fatigue" whereby the impact of a warning system on behavior is diminished when the public is continually warned about a hazard that does not materialize into a disaster (Sorensen and Vogt-Sorensen, 2006). Because of these and other potential problems, the Secretary of Homeland Security, Janet Napolitano, ordered a review of the system. In September 2009, the Homeland Security Advisory Council submitted its written report, *Homeland Security Advisory System: Task Force Report and Recommendations*, concluding, "The system's ability to communicate useful information in a credible manner to the public is poor. Significant rethinking of how to communicate to this audience is warranted" (p. 1). As a result, in January 2011, Secretary Napolitano announced that the HSAS would be replaced by a new warning system.

To better understand what constitutes an effective disaster warning system, consider news network coverage of severe weather in "tornado alley." If you live in or visit Texas, Oklahoma, or Kansas in the spring, you will undoubtedly experience severe weather and television coverage of it. During a typical broadcast, after a tornado has been spotted, meteorologists and weather forecasters inform viewers of its precise path including its future trajectory and time estimates. Importantly, they tell viewers exactly what to do when the storm reaches their area. For example, viewers are typically told to go to a basement, storm cellar, or the center of the house away from windows. If you find yourself responsible for writing a disaster warning message in the future, think about the contrast between a detailed, highly specific tornado warning and the vague, ambiguous terrorism warning. To maximize the effectiveness of your warning message, model it more after the tornado warning than the terrorism alert.

8.5 Disaster Response: Myths and Realities

Despite what we have learned over the years about effective disaster warnings, some emergency managers and other public officials are still sometimes hesitant or reluctant to issue warnings to the public. Like the individual who refuses to go to a shelter out of fear of his or her home being looted, some officials fear that a premature warning will spark widespread panic in their communities. Indeed, fears about looting and panic in the aftermaths of disasters are fairly widespread among the public, and alarmingly, even among emergency managers. Looting and other anti-social behaviors are exceedingly rare in disasters and commonly called myths by researchers (Fischer 2008). In this section, we will explore these and other response myths in much greater detail, identify some of the sources of these myths, and contrast them with a more realistic, research-based view of the response phase.

At the most basic level, comparing the myth-based view and the research-based views differ in terms of what they assume about social order in disasters. The *myth-based view* assumes that society is fragile, and disasters cause a breakdown in social order, which leads to lawlessness, conflict, and chaos. On the other hand, the *research-based view* recognizes that society is resilient, and disasters typically result in increased helping behavior, consensus, and enhanced social solidarity during the response phase. In fact, since the early 1950s, researchers have continually attempted to debunk the myths of disaster and instead document the recuperative and resilient capacities of societies (Quarantelli 1960; Fritz 1961; Quarantelli and Dynes 1977; Fischer 2008).

In this section, the myth-based view and research-based view are contrasted in terms of how they characterize disaster response at the individual, organizational, and community levels. The myth-based view assumes that individuals will suffer from reduced coping capacity, organizations will lack personnel, and communities will be torn apart. Conversely, the research-based view recognizes that individuals will actively contribute to the response effort, organizations will adapt and change to meet heightened demands, and communities will exhibit significant resilience. The primary purpose of our discussion is to introduce you to the research-based view and demonstrate its relevance to the effective practice of emergency management.

8.5.1 Myth-Based View of Disaster Response

When most people think of disasters, the myth-based view often comes immediately to mind. They envision massive piles of rubble, burning fires, blaring sirens, and traumatized victims milling around a devastated town.

Under those tragic circumstances, it is difficult for many people to imagine anything but chaos and disorder. Associated with this imagery is the notion that the best way of dealing with the aftermath of a disaster is for authorities to swoop in and establish strong command and control over the highly disorganized scene.

At the *individual level*, the myth-based view assumes that panic and psychological breakdown will impede the ability of people to respond in an orderly, rational, and productive manner. In the simplest sense of the term, *panic* refers to highly individualistic, non-rational, flight behavior accompanied by a complete disregard for social rules and attachments (Quarantelli 1954). Thus, the epitome of a panic-stricken person would be a mother who abandons her own child to escape an impending threat or a man who pushes, shoves, and tramples others to escape a burning building. The myth-based view assumes that because panic is a common response to disaster, emergency officials should postpone warning the public of a hazard until absolutely necessary. It also assumes that a major part of the official response will involve controlling and containing all the panicked people in the community.

Another core assumption of the myth-based view about individuals is that disasters will cause severe psychological *shock and dependency*. Because of their psychological impairments, it is assumed that individuals will become immobilized and dependent on response agencies for basic needs. As with the panic myth, the assumption here is that individuals will not be available to participate actively in or contribute to the response. Rather, it is assumed that much of the official response effort must be devoted to addressing the pervasive and widespread psychological trauma brought on by the disaster. As Quarantelli (1960, p. 72) states, "the picture is one of docile and impotent individuals, waiting childlike for someone to take care of them."

At the *organizational level*, the myth-based view assumes that organizations will suffer personnel shortages and be largely ineffective. This assumption has two major components. First, it is often assumed that the only organizations that will respond will be those with clearly delineated disaster responsibilities such as police and fire departments and hospitals. Second, in light of the centrality of these organizations to the response effort, there is concern about the problem of role abandonment. *Role abandonment* is the failure of emergency workers to report to work and instead tend to their own personal or family needs. Because the myth-based view assumes that emergency-relevant organizations will not receive much help from other agencies and individuals in the community, the fear is that the effects of a disaster will be exacerbated if emergency workers do not report to work.

Finally, at the *community level*, the myth-based view assumes widespread social disorganization. It is commonly assumed, for example, that crime rates will dramatically rise after a disaster. If you have watched any network news coverage of a recent disaster, the first thing you will notice is a focus on looting. Indeed, after Hurricane Katrina, the media devoted considerable attention to looting, playing a continuous loop of video footage of people removing merchandise from department stores and conveying reports of organized gangs terrorizing people in public shelters at the Superdome and New Orleans Convention Center. In addition to looting, the myth-based view emphasizes the breakdown of social order more broadly, for example, price gouging by greedy vendors who capitalize on the suffering of others and the emergence and spread of conflict and strife throughout a community.

If panic, looting, and social breakdown are myths, why do so many people including the public, government officials, and even some emergency managers believe them? As discussed in the next section, these myths persist despite several decades of debunking research. We can identify at least three primary reasons for the persistence of disaster myths. First, the *mass media* certainly plays a role in perpetuating disaster myths (Fischer 2008). In an effort to capture the attention of readers, listeners, and viewers (and thus satisfy advertisers), media outlets typically sensationalize disasters, focusing primarily on rare and isolated cases of anti-social behavior and presenting them as the norms rather than the exceptions. Second, as Tierney (2003) points out, various *institutional interests* benefit from depicting disasters as chaotic and lawless, including private security firms, advanced technology companies, and those seeking to establish an increased role for the military in civilian disaster response operations. Finally, Quarantelli (2002) suggests that the myth of panic and social breakdown may serve a useful function for *society at large*. Drawing insights from a classical sociologist named Emile Durkheim who argued that images of crime and criminals are functional for society because they reaffirm the importance of social rules, Quarantelli similarly suggests that perhaps images of panic, chaos, and social breakdown remind us all of the need to conform to cultural norms, maintain social relationships, and preserve social order, even during disasters.

8.5.2 Research-Based View of Disaster Response

The research-based view of disaster response contrasts sharply with the myth-based view. Its central premise is that individuals, organizations, and communities exhibit resilience in the face of disaster. In this context, *resilience* refers to the ability of individuals and social units to absorb and rebound from the impacts of a disaster. As will be discussed in more detail later in this section, certain vulnerable populations are at greater risk and some individuals, organizations, and communities rebound more easily and quickly than others, but the overall pattern of resilience is well established in the research literature (Dynes 2003).

At the *individual level*, the research-based view recognizes that disaster survivors will participate actively in the response effort. In virtually every disaster, survivors are typically the first responders on a scene, initiating search and rescue activities and providing preliminary care to the injured. Rather than having to control panic-stricken people as they flee en masse, emergency managers instead find themselves struggling to manage and coordinate all the people and donations that quickly arrive at disaster scenes.

This mass influx of people and supplies at the scene of a disaster is known as *convergence behavior*. In the first systematic study of the issue, Fritz and Mathewson (1957) identified several types of people who converge on a disaster site: returning survivors, curious spectators, volunteers, and those who seek to exploit the situation for economic gain. In addition to this kind of *personal convergence*, these researchers also discussed *informational convergence*, which in today's world would certainly include the mass media and its round-the-clock coverage of disasters, and *material convergence*—heavy equipment, other relief supplies, and donated items. In a much later study of convergence behavior, Neal (1994; 1995) documented the problems emergency managers faced in South Florida following Hurricane Andrew in 1992 when they were bombarded with unrequested donations including winter coats and mismatched shoes (see Box 8.3).

As far as the panic myth is concerned, extensive research suggests that it is rare or non-existent (Quarantelli 1954; 1957; Johnson 1987; 1988; Clarke and Chess 2008). Norris Johnson (1987), a leading authority, studied victim behavior in a major nightclub fire in which 160 people perished and a crowd surge at a rock concert where 11 people died. On the basis of extensive research, he concluded that in both instances social norms and attachments continued to regulate behavior. For example, in the crowd surge he found that people upheld norms of civility as evidenced by the fact that helping behavior became widespread. Moreover, helping behavior appeared to have been guided by prevailing gender role expectations. Specifically, he found that most women reported receiving help while men were twice as likely to report giving than receiving help. In terms of social attachments, he found in the nightclub fire that the overwhelming tendency was for patrons to attempt to evacuate in the same social groupings—friends and family members—with whom they arrived, a very common phenomenon in building fires.

Many observers point to the attacks on the World Trade Center and remember the images of people leaping to their demise from the upper floors of the burning towers. Even in those desperate circumstances, we heard numerous reports of people first attempting to place phone calls and connect with loved ones before they perished. Indeed, the persistence of social norms and relationships in even the most extreme environments has led scholars in emergency management to question whether the concept of panic serves any useful purposes (Quarantelli 2002). Perhaps Johnson (1987, p. 181-182) has addressed the matter most succinctly: "throughout the analysis I was struck not by the breakdown of social order but by its strength and

BOX 8.3   DONATIONS MANAGEMENT:
CHALLENGES AND SOLUTIONS

"Stop the stuff!" Surprisingly, this is a commonly heard phrase after disasters occur. Media attention draws the concern and compassion of well-intentioned donors who raid their closets and cupboards, load the donations in the car and drop them off at what appears the perfect location. At the location, volunteers expend valuable time sorting through what is and is not needed, organizing it into useful piles, determining where to send it, and transporting it. Surprised? Most people are. Emergency managers and voluntary organizations experienced in disaster management know that the "second disaster" results from donations—the unexpected arrivals that no one can seem to stop (Neal 1994).

Why shouldn't you step up and help out when people seem to be in need? Because unsolicited donations clog aid delivery systems. The most commonly donated item is used clothing, most of which is never needed. Why? Because people need clean, sanitary clothing in the right sizes for the climate where they live and the kind of work they do. If you have the perfect work boots for a shrimper or fisher along a coastal area then maybe that would work, but how do you know they are the right size? Too often, people simply donate what they can spare regardless of whether it will work or not. People who have lost everything need the right things at the right time in the right place, and your help in serving them *effectively* is needed.

Instead of holding a clothing or food drive, contact an experienced disaster organization and see what it needs. You may be surprised and even upset when the answer is money. Why money? Because it allows the organization to buy exactly what is needed. If you do not have a spare set of hearing aids that are perfectly set up for an individual's specific hearing needs, donate cash. If you can't spare a wheelchair customized for a paraplegic's mobility challenges, donate cash. If you no longer have a specific infant formula, donate cash. An experienced, reputable disaster organization can move the money quickly and electronically where it is needed. At a site, case managers and social workers can assess needs and distribute vouchers to ensure that the money is spent for exactly what is needed. A second suggestion is to raise money. Hold a garage sale, pass a bucket, or donate online. Third, send money. Get the picture?

Donations management generally falls to the voluntary sector to coordinate. In big disasters, outside organizations help inventory, organize, and distribute goods or funds donated. In most disasters, the Seventh Day Adventists (a faith-based organization) set up a warehouse. They may get help from Americorps, the military, and other volunteers. From an online inventory, voluntary organizations can then log in to see what is available, then pick up the items or set up a distribution site where survivors can come and apply for what is available. Leftover items may be stored or offered to Goodwill or other store operators for use elsewhere. Used clothing is often sold to businesses that convert them into rags or other recyclable items and the voluntary organization then receives funds from the sale. Do not be part of the problem. Be part of the solution and do the right thing.

Donations taken out for distribution after Hurricane Katrina in the Baton Rouge Area. (*Source:* Photo courtesy of Brenda Phillips.)

Unused surplus of water donated by the public after Hurricane Katrina. (*Source:* Photo courtesy of Brenda Phillips.)

persistence; not by the irrational, individual behavior of popular myth, but by the socially structured, socially responsible, and adaptive actions of those affected." He goes on to conclude that "ruthless competition did not occur, and it did not occur because a functioning social order prevented it."

The issue of psychological stress and impairment has also been the subject of extensive research (for an excellent summary see Edwards 1998). The basic conclusion is that disasters are capable of producing *both* negative and positive mental health effects. While the myth-based view focuses only on the negative effects and the debilitating impacts on individuals, the research-based view also calls attention to the possible positive effects. As Fritz (1961, p. 657) states,

"The traditional emphasis on pathological 'problems' has focused only on the destructive and disintegrative effects of disaster; it has wholly neglected the observable reconstructive and regenerative human responses." Thus, although we should certainly be sensitive to the mental health needs of disaster survivors, we also need to recognize that survivors often experience heightened feelings of solidarity with others around them and a sense of empowerment as they contribute actively to a response effort. This is not to say that there is no need for psychological services after disasters, but just as they do with public sheltering decisions, emergency managers and other public officials sometimes dramatically over-estimate demands for mental health services.

At the *organizational level*, the research-based view suggests that organizations are adaptive and resilient in the face of disasters. Rather than having to deal with personnel shortages from role abandonment, as assumed by the myth-based view, research suggests that organizations, especially those with disaster-related responsibilities will instead be confronted with a massive onslaught of workers and volunteers. Consider the search-and-rescue and clean-up efforts at Ground Zero following the attacks on the World Trade Center. Firefighters, police officers, construction workers, and volunteers from all parts of the country toiled in the rubble for months, working exceedingly long hours and stopping only periodically to recuperate or attend funerals. Far from abandoning their roles, these workers overextended themselves, even placing their own health and safety at risk. Box 8.4

BOX 8.4   PROTECTING FIRST RESPONDERS AND OTHERS AT RISK

In January 2011, the U.S. Congress faced an extended challenge from the attacks of September 11, 2001: workers' compensation for injuries sustained from working at Ground Zero and other locations. House Resolution 847, also known as the James Zadroga 9/11 Health and Compensation Act, addresses lingering and lethal consequences of mass exposure to contaminants resulting from incineration and hazardous materials at the sites of the attack. Some of the firefighters, police officers, and other first responders who stayed to search for the injured, retrieve the deceased, and bring their fallen brothers and sisters home for burial sustained serious health conditions.

The legislation tasks the Department of Health and Human Services to create a World Trade Center Program for emergency responders, recovery, and clean-up workers. The program includes long-term monitoring of those exposed to potential toxins including carcinogens. Workers can also receive health evaluations to screen for medical care. Research records are to be kept as well.

The potential damage to the health of the workers is significant. Respiratory diseases resulting from exposure include asthma, persistent coughs, hoarseness, sore throats, headaches, and cancers (Lin et al. 2005; Landrigan et al. 2004; CDC 2002; Szema et al. 2004; Trout et al. 2002). Concern has also arisen about clean-up workers who did not benefit from protective equipment. Many were Hispanic workers who did not speak English or possess insurance, and they face limited abilities to safeguard their health now and in the future (Malievskaya, Rosenberg, and Markowitz 2002). Some studies, while controversial, also suggest lower birth weights of babies and shorter term pregnancies among pregnant women exposed to airborne contaminants (Landrigan et al. 2004; GAO 2007).

Source: FEMA News Photo/Andrea Booher.

References

General Accountability Office (GAO). 2007. *World Trade Center: EPA's Most Recent Test and Clean Program Raises Concerns That Need to Be Addressed to Better Prepare for Indoor Contamination Following Disasters.* GAO-07-1091. Washington.

House Resolution 847. http://www.gpo.gov/fdsys/pkg/BILLS-111hr847enr/pdf/BILLS-111hr847enr.pdf

Landrigan, P. et al. 2004. Health and environmental consequences of the World Trade Center disaster. *Environmental Health Perspectives,* 112: 731–739.

Lin, S. et al. 2005. Respiratory symptoms and other health effects among residents living near the World Trade Center. *American Journal of Epidemiology,* 162: 499–507.

Malievskaya, E. et al. 2002. Assessing the health of immigrant workers near Ground Zero. *American Journal of Industrial Medicine,* 42: 548–549.

Szema, A. et al. 2004. Clinical deterioration in pediatric asthmatic patients after September 11, 2001. *Journal of Allergy and Clinical Immunology,* 113: 420–426.

Trout, D. et al. 2002. Health effects and occupational exposure among office workers near the World Trade Center disaster. *Journal of Occupational and Environmental Medicine,* 44: 601–605.

	Regular Tasks	Nonregular Tasks
Existing Structure	Established, Type I	Extending, Type III
New Structure	Expanding, Type II	Emergent, Type IV

FIGURE 8.1   Organization types and structures. *Source*: **Dynes (1970–1974).**

describes the health-related problems they faced as a result of their efforts and the federal legislation that was recently passed to address their needs.

The research-based view recognizes that numerous and diverse organizations are typically involved in responding to disasters. While police and fire departments and hospitals may be the operations that come to mind first, many other organizations step up after disasters. In an effort to more accurately describe the range of organizations involved in responding to disasters, the Disaster Research Center (DRC) developed what is now commonly known as the *DRC Typology* (Dynes 1970).

As you can see in Figure 8.1, organizations are classified in terms of their structures and the tasks they perform. Type I, or *established organizations*, such as police and fire departments, perform their regular tasks in a disaster and in so doing rely on existing structures. Type II, or *expanding organizations*, such as the Red Cross or Salvation Army, also perform regular tasks, but they rely on new structures—that is, they grow or expand from a small cadre of full-time professionals to large-scale operations of tens or hundreds of volunteers. Type III, or *extending organizations* have established structures, but take on new tasks in the aftermath of a disaster—for example, a construction crew working on a project in town may lend its personnel and equipment to the clean-up effort. Finally, Type IV, or *emergent organizations*, such as informal search-and-rescue groups, do not exist prior to a disaster, form only after impact, and thus rely on new structures and perform nonregular tasks. The involvement of so many different organizations, as we will see later in this chapter, can create problems in terms of coordination and communication, but these are very different from the problems of role abandonment and organizational ineffectiveness envisioned by the myth-based view of disasters.

At the *community level*, the research-based view emphasizes resilience and social organization, rather than lawlessness and social breakdown. Instead of stealing from and fighting with each other, disaster survivors are much more likely to assist family members, friends, and neighbors. This increase in helping behavior after disasters led early researchers in the field to characterize the post-disaster environment as therapeutic in some respects for disaster-stricken communities. For example, Fritz (1961, p. 694) argued, "Contrary to the traditional pictures of man and society in the process of disintegration, disaster studies show that human societies have enormous resilience and recuperative power."

8.5.2.1 *Sources and Limitations of Community Resilience*

Researchers have identified various sources of community resilience in the face of disasters. First, although they are certainly tragic when they occur and disruptive to those they impact, many disasters are relatively low-impact events in relation to remaining community and societal resources, which allows societies to largely absorb the effects (Wright et al. 1979). Second, disasters are collectively shared experiences that often produce a unifying effect whereby people feel heightened attachment to and responsibility for others, and social distinctions and inequalities are temporarily suspended (Fritz 1961). Third, during a disaster, an emergency consensus typically arises, whereby community priorities that are ordinarily are subject to competition and debate are simplified and oriented toward life safety activities (Dynes 1970). Finally, social capital including cultural values, social norms and obligations, social relationships, and cultural traditions, ensures community survival and provides guidance and resources for responding to disasters (Dynes 2003).

Researchers also recognize, however, that disasters can and do produce negative effects. Indeed, Tierney (2007) cautions researchers against overstating or exaggerating what she refers to as the "good news" paradigm in disaster research. Researchers have begun to identify various limitations of community resilience. First, for example, catastrophic events may severely limit the ability of a community or society to effectively rebound. As discussed in Chapter 2, the scope and magnitude of impact of a catastrophe are so wide and devastating that even the capacity of surrounding communities to offer assistance is diminished. It is important to note, however, that even in catastrophes people remain capable of and typically do exhibit pro-social, helping behavior, as demonstrated in Hurricane Katrina (Rodriguez, Trainor, and Quarantelli 2006). Second, as discussed throughout the text, vulnerable populations including the elderly, racial and ethnic minorities, the poor, and others often suffer much greater impacts from disasters and steeper challenges responding to and recovering from them. Third, problematic pre-disaster conditions such as high crime rates and widespread political corruption may also limit the ability of a community to respond in a productive, pro-social manner, as these same dynamics will likely play out during the disaster (Fischer 2008). Finally, a growing body of research in the field of environmental sociology suggests that technological disasters such as oil spills, rather than producing the therapeutic effects commonly observed in natural disasters, may instead create corrosive communities characterized by heightened psychological stress, intensified conflict over who is to blame, and, in some cases prolonged litigation (Picou, Marshall, and Gill 2004).

8.6 Disaster Response in an International Context

The myths and realities of human response to disaster discussed in this chapter are based largely on research conducted on events in the U.S. In light of that fact, it is reasonable to question whether the same kinds of response patterns would be present in another country. Do people in other countries respond to natural disasters in the same pro-social manner described above? Do they rely as heavily on informal social networks including family and friends? Does the outpouring of support occur in response to international disasters? The simplest answer to these questions is that there are some basic similarities in disaster responses across countries but there are also important differences.

As described in Chapter 3, some research focuses on disasters outside the U.S., and a sizable international network of scholars from many countries conducts it. At the most basic level, international research suggests that societies across the globe exhibit varying degrees of resilience in responding to disasters. In the wealthiest, most developed countries of the world such as the U.S., Canada, Australia, Japan, European Union nations, and others, disaster impacts are typically absorbed relatively effectively, and the general response pattern resembles the research-based view of response described in this chapter. While the financial impacts of disasters in those nations can be very high, loss of human life is typically relatively low. Indeed, on virtually any indicator including financial loss, damage to the built environment, and death toll, the ratio of disaster impacts to remaining societal resources is usually relatively low in the most developed nations.

However, disaster impacts on all of these dimensions are typically very high in developing nations and in the least developed countries of the world. But the initial social response to disaster in those countries is often very similar to the pattern observed in developed nations, including survivors actively engaging in search and rescue and other activities; friends, family members, and neighbors helping each other; and volunteers, supplies, and resources converging on the scene. In other words, *social capital* such as interpersonal relationships, community ties, cultural traditions, and other factors serves as a source of survival and resilience in all societies, from the most impoverished and least powerful to the wealthiest and most powerful.

Disasters in the developing world, however, typically produce much greater devastation and much more complex and difficult response challenges than those in developed nations. Developing nations include Brazil, Guatemala, Honduras, Mexico, Haiti, Honduras, the Dominican Republic, India,

Indonesia, Pakistan, Turkey, Thailand, Sri Lanka, and many others. There are many reasons for the *heightened disaster vulnerability* of these countries.

First, substantial portions of their populations live in *extreme poverty*. As a result, in daily life and certainly when disaster strikes, people have far fewer resources to draw upon than those living in wealthier nations. Second, these societies typically have *vulnerable physical infrastructures*. Because of that vulnerability, the physical impacts of disasters on their built environments are often far more extensive than what we see in the U.S. and other developed countries. Third, stemming from the vulnerable built environment, disasters in developing countries often produce *sizable death tolls*. The January, 2010 earthquake in Haiti and the 2004 Asian tsunami, for example, each resulted in approximately 300,000 deaths. With such widespread loss of human life, disasters in the developing world cause much greater losses in social capital—a primary source of resilience—than they typically do in developed countries.

Fourth, developing countries often have *weak or ineffective political institutions*. Countries like Turkey, for example are known to have reasonable building codes governing development but lack enforcement mechanisms, leading to questionable building practices and massive damage and loss of life when earthquakes occur. In 1999, for example, approximately 20,000 people died in an earthquake in Turkey, largely from building collapses. Fifth, in many cases developing countries are more vulnerable to disasters due to a *lack of effective warning systems*. The death toll in the Asian tsunami in 2004, for example, was so high in large part because the Indian Ocean, unlike the Pacific, was not protected by an advanced tsunami warning system. Finally, developing nations face increased technological hazards. As the wealthiest and most developed countries shift their manufacturing operations to the developing world in search of cheaper labor power and weaker environmental regulations, they are exposing people in those nations to new technological risks. In 1984, for example, thousands of residents of Bhopal, India died from a toxic release at a chemical plant owned by Union Carbide, a U.S. company.

8.7 Disaster Response and Principles of Effective Emergency Management

Based on the topics covered in this chapter, it should be clear that disasters, even in an international context, generally do not produce the kind of chaos and social breakdown envisioned by the myth-based view. Problems arise, to be sure, particularly in developing nations, but they typically do not center on the need to control hordes of unruly people. Instead, the greatest challenge in effectively responding to disasters is organizing and focusing the activities of the numerous individuals, informal groups, voluntary organizations, and public agencies that invariably arrive at the scene of a disaster.

Indeed, probably the two most common problems identified in after-action reports about disasters are the lack of coordination among responding organizations and breakdowns in communication. Throughout your career you can do your part in overcoming those challenges by remembering the principles of effective emergency management introduced in this book. In particular, the most effective strategies to embrace during the response phase are comprehensive emergency management, integrated emergency management, and flexibility.

8.7.1 Comprehensive Emergency Management

As discussed in Chapters 2 and 4, many hazards and disasters confront modern society. These threats vary, of course, in terms of the length of forewarning they afford and the scope, magnitude, and duration of their potential impacts. Each disaster agent is unique. Responding to a chemical, biological, or nuclear attack, for example, would certainly require the involvement of highly trained specialists and the use of specialized equipment not typically needed for natural disasters. *Comprehensive emergency management*, however, recognizes that various types of hazards share a great deal in common. For example, they are all capable of producing extensive physical damage, causing major injuries and deaths, and, importantly, creating major social disruption. Indeed, as presented in Chapter 2, an event is only recognized as a disaster when it impacts human societies.

As social events, then, disasters of all types create some common social responses that have been described in this chapter, and produce common management problems. Convergence behavior, or rushing to the scene of a disaster, is very likely to occur, regardless of the hazardous agent. Additionally, as predicted by the DRC Typology, numerous organizations, both formal and informal and official and unofficial, will invariably become involved in responding to disasters of all types. As a result, regardless of the type of disaster involved, emergency managers will always have to organize and focus the activities of multiple response organizations. By embracing the *all-hazards view*, emergency managers maximize their ability to respond effectively to the broadest range of threats.

8.7.2 Integrated Emergency Management

As described in Chapter 5, integrated emergency management recognizes that all kinds of organizations are involved in responding to disasters. From this perspective, a major challenge for the emergency manager is coordinating, organizing, and focusing the activities of so many different response agencies. Coordination is a vital and far-reaching task. Emergency managers must facilitate coordination of multiple levels of government, coordination of government and NGOs, coordination within single organizations and across multiple organizations, and interactions among official and unofficial response groups and organizations. They must also manage the flow of information throughout the community and through the media and direct the movement of equipment, supplies, and donations.

Based on such a tall order and complex and important tasks, it may be helpful to consider some strategies for improving coordination. Keep in mind that none of these strategies is guaranteed and each has limitations. First, for example, emergency managers can improve coordination through *enhanced emergency operations center (EOC) design*, setting a center up in a way that maximizes communication among responding organizations (Neal 2003; 2005). An EOC is best viewed as a communication hub, not as a command post. Unfortunately, many modern EOCs are so oriented toward advanced technology that they actually impede communication because representatives from agencies sit staring at computer screens rather than interacting with others (see Box 8.5).

Second, *incident management frameworks*, such as the National Incident Management System (NIMS), predicated largely on the Incident Command System (ICS) developed by the fire services, can be useful for improving coordination. These systems are aimed at providing common terminology and organizing response activities into standard, recognizable areas (finance, logistics, operations, and planning). However, in their study of the use of ICS in Hurricane Katrina, Neal and Webb (2006) visited the EOC in New Orleans and the Joint Field Office in Baton Rouge and found wide variation in organizational training in and use of ICS.

Finally, numerous *advanced technologies* can assist emergency managers in coordinating response activities. Geographic information systems (GISs) and global positioning systems (GPSs) can be used to locate and track response teams or map areas of heavy damage. Remote sensing technologies can produce aerial images for damage assessment, and decision support software can be used to log, track, and prioritize response activities. Advanced technologies, however, should be approached with some caution. One reason for caution is that not all jurisdictions have access to the most advanced technologies, creating somewhat of a technological divide in community readiness for disasters. Further, satellites cannot see inside a building to assess damage and may require ground truthing (Eguchi et al. 2003). Another reason is that technological glitches invariably arise, including data compatibility problems and lack of system interoperability. Finally,

BOX 8.5 EMERGENCY OPERATIONS CENTERS

Much of the action phase of emergency management work takes place during response. Coordination, communication, and collaboration require a working environment that facilitates exchanges among people working on a common goal. Emergency operations centers (EOCs) serve that function.

EOCs allow emergency management professionals to identify needs, trouble shoot problems, and address emergency response needs. The sizes, resources, and personnel in EOCs can vary. EOCs can range from small locations with minimal communications equipment and staff to large, state-of-the-art facilities capable of withstanding some of the worst that nature or human-made disasters can bring to bear.

EOCs also may be fixed or mobile locations. Most EOCs are contained within or near the emergency management agency so that personnel can easily activate and use the site. Ideally, the EOC is a relatively self-contained facility where people can work safely and for long shifts. Some EOCs even feature sleeping pods so that staff can benefit from well-deserved rest during stressful events. Mobile locations can also vary from vehicles converted to include basic communications equipment to large units that allow for meeting areas, work stations, and extensive equipment. EOCs usually can be found in local emergency management agencies as well as state, regional and national locations. They may also emerge as needed such as when local, state, and federal officials utilized a makeshift tent EOC after Hurricane Rita damaged the Lake Charles, Louisiana area. Destruction of an EOC located in the World Trade Center required a rapid restoration in a warehouse down the street.

A recent trend in EOCs has been movement toward virtual sites. By connecting over the Internet, it is possible to conduct video exchanges, hold live chats, track and record critical information, and integrate real-time data. The WebEOC program is one example in current use. The Virginia Department of Emergency Management uses the system to link into geographic information systems and the Homeland Security Information Network.

EOCs move through various levels of activation. Typically, EOCs are not activated for routine emergencies as described in Chapter 2. As an emergency looms or spreads to disrupt a community, the impending disaster necessitates a higher level of activation. For events that can be anticipated, an EOC may open to a higher level with limited staff such as during a hurricane or flood watch. Increasing levels of activation result when a disaster worsens and requires additional personnel, the involvement of public officials to make decisions, and collaboration across agencies.

EOCs can vary in structure and design (Neal 2005; 2003). Several critical design features enable or thwart EOC effectiveness. Because EOCs can involve many personnel using different kinds of equipment, the noise levels may be considerable. The ability to communicate (which includes hearing) is key to effective response. Similarly, the ways in which work stations or pods are arranged matters. In addition to working without distraction, people must be able to exchange information. The photos attached to this box illustrate how people relate to each other in the space available.

EOCs serve to monitor, manage, and share information so that officials can make proper decisions. Should a full-scale disaster unfold, the emergency support functions described in this text may be set up to meet emerging or anticipated needs. The EOC will manage information so that chemical spills, wind direction and speed, and potential impact on a population can be assessed. Critical decisions about evacuation versus shelter in place will be made to safeguard the public. Careful records will be kept (sometimes as time allows) so that lessons can be gleaned. Daily or even hourly situation reports (sit reps) will be issued and information—including addressing rumors—will be distributed by a public information officer.

March 11, 2011, FEMA personnel open the National Response Coordination Center after the 9.0 magnitude earthquake and tsunami that struck Japan. (*Source:* FEMA News Photo/Aaron Skolnik.)

Federal officials coordinate in the emergency operations center of the state of Nevada due to a severe storm, canal break, and related flooding. (***Source:*** FEMA News Photo/George Armstrong.)

Federal and local officials conduct a meeting with local officials in Cameron, Louisiana after Hurricane Rita struck the area in 2005. (***Source:*** FEMA News Photo/Marvin Nauman.)

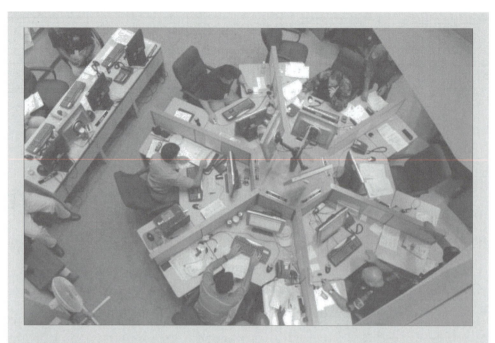

Officials in the emergency operations center of the state of Alabama monitor Hurricane Katrina in 2005. (*Source*: FEMA News Photo/Mark Wolfe.)

Sources

To see how an emergency management agency uses WebEOC, visit the Virginia Department of Emergency Management, http://www.interoperability.virginia.gov/CommunicationSystems/WebEOC.cfm

For an example of a situation report from the state of Minnesota, visit http://www.hsem.state.mn.us/eoc/2010Flood/sitreps/Sit_Rep8_f2010.pdf

Neal, David M. 2003. Design characteristics of emergency operating centers. *Journal of Emergency Management*, 1: 35–38.

Neal, David M. 2005. Case studies of four emergency operating centers. *Journal of Emergency Management*, 3: 29–32.

technology should be viewed with caution to the extent that it may foster over-dependence and constrain the flexibility and creativity of users.

8.7.3 Flexibility in Emergency Management

In addition to embracing comprehensive and integrated emergency management, emergency managers can enhance their ability to overcome response challenges by recognizing the value of flexibility. As discussed in Chapters 6 and 7, preparedness and planning are critical aspects of emergency management. If done successfully, these activities can greatly reduce the amount of damage and disruption caused by a disaster, lessen the number of physical injuries and deaths, and dramatically improve a community's ability to respond. During the response phase, however, emergency managers and other public officials will invariably encounter new problems and unforeseen challenges for which they may not have been trained or to which they may not have given much consideration. When that happens, responders need to think creatively and be flexible about possible solutions.

There are two broad categories of flexibility in responding to disasters. *Individual-level* flexibility refers to improvisations enacted by individual responders and can take various forms. For example, a responder may have to perform a task without his or her usual equipment and rely instead on makeshift provisions. In the aftermath of the bombing of the Murrah Federal Building in Oklahoma City in 1995, for example, first responders used blown-out doors in the fallen debris as stretchers for carrying victims of the blast. As one contributor to the final report on the bombing observed, "Probably the greatest tool of all was the rescue workers' ingenuity. In the early stages of the incident, I saw many circumstances in which rescue workers adapted standard tools to complete tasks for which the tools were not originally designed." The report concludes, "This expedited the rescues of dozens of people in the early stages of the incident" (*Final Report: Alfred P. Murrah Federal Building Bombing, April 19, 1995*, 1996, p. 154).

Organizational-level flexibility involves adaptations on the part of organizations. Similar to individual improvising, organizational adaptations can take several forms and usually result from resource shortages, unforeseen contingencies, or unmet needs and demands. For example, in the aftermath of the September 11, 2001 attacks, New York City's EOC had to be relocated when the building housing it was destroyed (Kendra and Wachtendorf 2003). Also in that event, thousands of people were evacuated from lower Manhattan in an unplanned water rescue operation (Kendra, Wachtendorf, and Quarantelli 2003). At both the individual and organizational levels, flexibility is often necessary to fill gaps left by the planning process and meet heightened demands of a disaster.

Certainly there will be times in your career when you will need to think creatively and exhibit this kind of flexibility. In fact, in all professions, not just emergency management, a premium should be placed on creativity and flexibility because it typically produces positive results. Of course, improvisations occasionally fail or backfire and create undesirable outcomes. In other words, at times doing things "by the book" is the best way to go and at other times it is necessary to "think outside the box." Like the football quarterback who must decide in a split second whether to run a play as called by the coaches or make a quick change at the line of scrimmage, the most effective leaders in any context decide, based on past experience or intuition, which path to follow. As you gain experience in the field of emergency management, your skills in this area will sharpen over time.

Some organizations, however, develop *important limitations on flexibility*. As Webb and Chevreau (2006) suggest, several *internal organizational characteristics* limit flexibility. For example, many organizations actually stifle flexibility and creativity due to their strict adherence to written rules and procedures, extensive specialization of tasks with accompanying diffusion of responsibility, and over-reliance on technology to solve basic problems. Rather than producing innovators and problem solvers, these organizations instead create conformists and ritualists who define their jobs in very narrow terms and rely exclusively on protocol and standard operating procedures to perform tasks. There are also important *external constraints* on organizational and individual flexibility. Drabek (2010) calls attention to the climate of litigation so prevalent in modern society and the possibility that individuals and organizations may be legally liable for damages possibly resulting from failures to follow proper protocol. Additionally, we could consider the broader bureaucratic context under which emergency management falls as a possible external constraint on flexibility. With the creation of DHS, for example, many observers feared that FEMA would lose its autonomy and flexibility to respond to natural disasters when it was placed under the umbrella of homeland security. Those concerns were validated by the federal government's initially slow and ineffective response to Hurricane Katrina (Waugh 2005).

8.8 Working and Volunteering in Response

As described in Box 8.1, considerable differences exist between first responders and emergency managers. Working in the response phase is only one of the activities of the emergency manager and is a role that involves coordination, communication, and collaboration across multiple agencies. In a small town, the emergency manager will likely play the role of EOC facilitator. In larger areas, emergency management professionals play more specific roles during the response period such as specializing in mass care (food and shelter), coordinating debris removal, handling massive unsolicited donations, assessing infrastructure damage and repair needs, re-establishing communications, and working with the media.

To be effective, an emergency manager must pursue education, training, and experience. Anyone who works in an EOC during a response period must be a highly trained professional capable of managing significant amounts of stress, working across agencies, and moving the community through crisis stage by stage. Although you are at the first stages in moving toward working in the response period, you can start by acquiring some knowledge beyond this chapter through the FEMA independent study courses. These free, online courses offer insights into incident command, the National Incident Management System, voluntary organizations and more.

Volunteering during the response period also requires training. You can start with basic first aid and cardio-pulmonary resuscitation (CPR) courses. Many disaster organizations like the Red Cross also offer shelter manager training and integrate volunteers well in advance into disaster action teams. After September 11, 2001, the U.S. also established the Citizen Corps (www.citizencorps.gov). Within your state, community, or possibly your university, you may be able to train for a community emergency response team (CERT) and be activated for crisis events or help with crowd management at a major sporting event. Access http://citizencorps.gov/cert/videos/ for CERT informational videos.

Perhaps you have other kinds of interests. The Medical Reserve Corps integrates medical professionals into volunteer service. When coastal hurricanes threaten nursing home populations, for example, many residents are evacuated inland or to other host states. The Medical Reserve Corps receives, assesses, and cares for arriving evacuees. A fairly new program, called Map Your Neighborhood, in the states of Washington and Oklahoma involves neighbors in identifying people who may need assistance and where neighborhood resources can be located for rescue purposes. If you volunteer for response, do not just show up and hope to help. Known as spontaneous unaffiliated volunteers (SUVs), such convergences of people create more problems than help. Enter a damaged area through an established organization for your own safety as well as that of those you seek to help.

8.9 Summary

This chapter has addressed several important aspects of the response phase of disaster. Having read this chapter, you should now have a much better understanding what actually happens during the response phase and how to maximize the effectiveness of response efforts. For example, we identified the major characteristics of effective disaster warnings: consistency, specificity, and credibility. Additionally, we discussed the myth-based view of disaster that envisions chaos and pervades the popular imagination and contrasted it with the research-based view emphasizing resilience and adaptability.

While the public response to disasters is often productive, adaptive, and pro-social, we have also identified the most common response problems including communication and coordination. We also discussed strategies for overcoming these challenges including enhanced EOC design, appropriate incident management frameworks, and reasonable use of advanced technologies. For international disasters, we identified specific vulnerabilities of developing countries such as extreme poverty, vulnerable infrastructure, weak and ineffective political institutions, and other factors. Finally, we suggested that the key to effectively managing the response phase of disasters is to embrace core principles discussed throughout this book including comprehensive emergency management, integrated emergency management, and flexibility.

Discussion Questions

1. What is your image of the modern emergency manager? How has your impression of the response phase influenced that perception? In what ways has that image changed?

2. How should the response phase be defined and what are some of the likely activities you will undertake as an emergency manager during that phase?

3. Craft a warning message for a likely hazard in your area using the parameters for an effective warning message. Include messages about protective actions. Next, consider how to deliver that message so that all sectors of your local population receive, interpret, and respond to the message as desired.

4. Which of the myths of disaster response surprised you the most and why? Which myths remain hard to dispel?

5. Now that you know how people actually respond in disasters, what assumptions could you make about behavioral responses in a future event affecting your community? Can you count on your fellow citizens or not?

6. How does an international context influence response? What are some critical considerations before initiating a response to assist another nation?

7. What do you see as the three most important principles for an effective emergency management response? What should you keep in mind as you manage an EOC?

References

Aguirre, Benigno E. 1988. "The Lack of Warnings Before the Saragosa Tornado." *The International Journal of Mass Emergencies and Disasters*. 6/1: 65–74.

Aguirre, Benigno E. 2004. "Homeland Security Warnings: Lessons Learned and Unlearned." *International Journal of Mass Emergencies and Disasters* 22/2: 103–115.

Clarke, Lee and Caron Chess. 2008. "Elites and Panic: More to Fear than Fear Itself." *Social Forces* 87/2: 993–1014.

Drabek, Thomas E. 2010. *The Human Side of Disaster*. Boca Raton, FL: CRC Press.

Drabek, Thomas. 1986. *Human System Responses To Disaster: An Inventory of Sociological Findings*. NY: Springer-Verlag.

Dynes, Russell R. 1970. *Organized Behavior in Disaster*. Lexington, MA: Health Lexington Books.

Dynes, Russell R. 1994. "Community Emergency Planning: False Assumptions and Inappropriate Analogies." *International Journal of Mass Emergencies and Disasters* 12/2: 141–158.

Dynes, Russell R. 2003. "Finding Order in Disorder: Continuities in the 9-11 Response." *International Journal of Mass Emergencies and Disasters* 21/3: 9–23.

Edwards, Margie L. Kiter. 1998. "An Interdisciplinary Perspective on Disasters and Stress: The Promise of an Ecological Framework." *Sociological Forum* 13/1: 115–132.

Eguchi, R., C. Huyck, B. Adams, B. Mansouri, B. Houshmand, and M. Shinozuka. 2003. *Resilient Disaster Response: Using Remote Sensing Technologies for Post-Earthquake Damage Detection*. Buffalo, New York: Multidisciplinary Earthquake Engineering Research Center.

Fischer, Henry W. 2008. *Response to Disaster*, 3rd edition. Lanham, MD: University Presses of America.

Fritz, Charles E. 1961. "Disasters." Pp. 651–694 in *Contemporary Social Problems*, (Robert K. Merton and Robert A. Nisbet, eds.). Riverside, CA: University of California Press.

Fritz, Charles E. and J.H. Mathewson. 1957. *Convergence Behavior in Disasters: A Problem in Social Control*. Washington, D.C.: National Academy of Sciences, National Research Council.

Heath, Sebastian, Philip Kass, Alan Beck, and Larry Glickman. 2001. "Human and Pet-related Risk Factors for Household Evacuation Failure During a Natural Disaster." *American Journal of Epidemiology* 153/7: 659–665.

Homeland Security Advisory Council. 2009. *Homeland Security Advisory System, Task Force Report and Recommendations*. Washington, D.C.: Department of Homeland Security. Available at http://www.dhs.gov/xlibrary/assets/hsac_final_report_09_15_09.pdf, last accessed May 26, 2011.

Johnson, Norris. 1987. "Panic and the Breakdown of Social Order: Popular Myth, Social Theory, and Empirical Evidence." *Sociological Focus* 20/3: 171–183.

Johnson, Norris. 1988, "Fire in a Crowded Theater: a Descriptive Investigation of the Emergence of Panic." *International Journal of Mass Emergencies and Disasters* 6/1: 7–26.

Kendra, James M., and Tricia Wachtendorf. 2003. "Creativity in Emergency Response after the World Trade Center Attack." Pp. 121–146 *In Beyond September 11th: An Account of Post-Disaster Research*, (Jacquelyn L. Monday, ed.). Special Publication #39 Natural Hazards Research and Applications Information Center, University of Colorado: Boulder, CO.

Kendra, James M., Tricia Wachtendorf, and E.L. Quarantelli. 2003. "The Evacuation of Lower Manhattan by Water Transport on September 11: An Unplanned Success." *Joint Commission Journal on Quality and Safety* 29/6: 316–318.

Mileti, Dennis. 1999. *Disasters by Design*. Washington, D.C.: Joseph Henry Press.

National Governors Association. 1979. *Comprehensive Emergency Management*. Washington, D.C.: National Governors Association.

National Organization on Disability. 2005. *Special Needs Assessment of Katrina Evacuees*. Washington, D.C.: National Organization on Disability.

National Research Council, Committee on Public Responses to Alerts and Warnings on Mobile Devices: Current Knowledge and Research Gaps. 2010. *Public Response to Alerts and Warnings on Mobile Devices: Summary of a Workshop on Current Knowledge and Research Gaps*. Washington, D.C.: The National Academies Press.

National Science and Technology Council, Committee on Environment and Natural Resources. 2000. *Effective Disaster Warnings: Report by the Working Group on Natural Disaster Information Systems, Subcommittee on Natural Disaster Reduction*. Washington, D.C.: National Science and Technology Council.

Neal, David M. 1994. "Consequences of Excessive Donations in Disaster: The Case of Hurricane Andrew," *Disaster Management* 6/1: 23–28.

Neal, David M., 1995. "Crowds, Convergence, and Disasters," *Crowd Management* 2/1: 13–16.

Neal, David M., 2003. "Design Characteristics of Emergency Operating Centers," *Journal of Emergency Management* 1/2: 35–38.

Neal, David M., 2005. "Case Studies of Four Emergency Operating Centers," *Journal of Emergency Management* 3/1: 29–32.

Neal, David M. and Brenda D. Phillips. 1995. "Effective Emergency Management: reconsidering the bureaucratic approach." *Disasters* 19: 327–337.

Neal, David M., and Gary R. Webb. 2006. "Structural Barriers to Implementing the National Incident Management System," Pp. 263–282 in *Learning from Catastrophe: Quick Response Research in the Wake of Hurricane Katrina*, (Christine Bvec, ed.). Boulder, CO: Natural Hazards Center–University of Colorado.

Perry, Ronald W. Michael K. Lindell, and Marjorie R. Greene. 1981. *Evacuation Planning in Emergency Management*. Lexington, MA: Lexington Books.

Picou, J.S., B.K. Marshall, and Duane Gill. 2004. "Disaster, Litigation, and the Corrosive Community." *Social Forces* 82: 1497–1526.

Quarantelli, E.L. 1954. "The Nature and Conditions of Panic." *American Journal of Sociology* 60: 267–275.

Quarantelli, E.L. 1957. "The Behavior of Panic Participants." *Sociology and Social Research* 41: 187–194.

Quarantelli, E.L. 1960. "Images of Withdrawal Behavior in Disasters: Some Basic Misconceptions." *Social Problems* 8: 68–79.

Quarantelli, E.L. 2002. "The Sociology of Panic." Pp. 11020–23 in *International Encyclopedia of the Social and Behavioral Sciences*, (Paul B. Baltes and Neil Smelser, eds.). New York: Elsevier.

Quarantelli, E.L. and Russell R. Dynes. 1977. "Response to Social Crisis and Disaster." *Annual Review of Sociology* 3: 23–49.

Rodriguez, Havidán, Joseph Trainor, and E.L. Quarantelli. 2006. "Rising to the Challenges of a Catastrophe: The Emergent and Prosocial Behavior following Hurricane Katrina." *The ANNALS of the American Academy of Political and Social Science* 604: 82–101.

Sorensen, John. 2000. "Hazard Warning Systems: A Review of 20 Years of Progress." *Natural Hazards Review* 1: 119–125.

Sorensen, John H. and Barbara Vogt Sorensen. 2006. "Community Processes: Warning and Evacuation." Pp. 183–199 in *Handbook of Disaster Research*, (Havidan Rodriguez, Enrico L. Quarantelli, and Russell R. Dynes, eds.). New York: Springer.

The City of Oklahoma City. 1996. *Final Report: Alfred P. Murrah Federal Building Bpmbing, April 19, 1995*. Stillwater, OK: Fire Protection Publications.

Tierney, Kathleen J. 2003. "Disaster Beliefs and Institutional Interests: Recycling Disaster Myths in the Aftermath of 9-11." Pp. 33–51 in *Terrorism and Disaster*, (Lee Clarke, ed.). New York: Elsevier.

Tierney, Kathleen J. 2007. "From the Margins to the Mainstream? Disaster Research at the Crossroads." *Annual Review of Sociology* 33: 503–525.

Tierney, Kathleen J., Michael K. Lindell and Ronald W. Perry. 2001. *Facing the Unexpected.* Washington, D.C.: Joseph Henry Press.

United States Department of Justice. No date. *The ADA and Emergency Shelters.* Available at http://www.ada.gov/pcatoolkit/chap7shelterprog.pdf, last accessed January 25, 2011.

van Willigen, Marieke, Bob Edwards, Terri Edwards, and Shaun Hessee. 2002. "Riding out the Storm: The Experiences of the Physically Disabled during Hurricanes Bonnie, Dennis, and Floyd." *Natural Hazards Review* 3/3: 98–106.

Waugh, William. 2005. "The Disaster that Was Katrina." *Natural Hazards Observer.* Available at http://www.colorado.edu/hazards/o/archives/2005/nov05/nov05d1.html, last accessed January 25, 2011.

Webb, Gary R. and Francois-Regis Chevreau. 2006. "Planning to Improvise: The Importance of Creativity and Flexibility in Crisis Response." *International Journal of Emergency Management* 3: 66–72.

Wood, V. T., & Weisman, R. A. 2003. "A Hole in the Weather Warning System." *Bulletin of the American Meteorological Society,* 84/2: 187–194.

Wright, James, Peter Rossi, S.R. Wright and E. Weber-Burdin. 1979. *After the Clean-Up: Long-Range Effects of Natural Disasters.* Beverly Hills, CA: Sage.

Resources

- To learn more about the numerous voluntary organizations typically involved in the response phase and learn more about how you can contribute, visit the National Voluntary Organizations Active in Disaster website at www.nvoad.org

- To learn more about the impacts of disasters on different countries, visit the United Nations International Strategy for Disaster Reduction website at www.unisdr.org

- To learn more about training opportunities for first responders, visit the U.S. Department of Homeland Security website at www.dhs.gov/xfrstresp/

- To learn more about the challenges involved in responding to a catastrophic event like Hurricane Katrina, read about important lessons learned at http://georgewbush-whitehouse.archives.gov/reports/katrina-lessons-learned/

- To learn more about important response activities that can be undertaken during the first forty-eight hours after a disaster strikes, visit http://www.fema.gov/plan/ehp/response.shtm

Chapter **9**

Recovery

9.1 Chapter Objectives

Upon completing this chapter, readers should be able to:

1. Define, describe and understand recovery as a process that occurs in both short-term and long-term periods.
2. Base recovery processes on principles that promote a holistic and sustainable outcome for future events and populations likely to be affected.
3. Outline the key recovery challenges that are faced by those affected and those who seek to help.
4. Situate recovery planning as a community-based process that produces a consensus-based vision.
5. Encourage mitigation as a central element of recovery planning.
6. Foster an appreciation for the breadth of recovery planning elements that must be part of rebuilding a community.
7. Identify opportunities for both professional work and volunteer service in the area of disaster recovery.

9.2 Introduction

Most communities do not plan for the long-term challenges they will face after a disaster. Imagine what it might be like in your own community. Should a tornado, flood, earthquake, or hurricane of enough magnitude move through, you may be faced with responding at a personal level. Your challenges and those faced by your family would include at a minimum finding temporary housing and working to rebuild your home or find a rental unit. If the community where you live has low numbers of rentals and cost is an issue, you may have limited options for relocation. Should an event the scope of Hurricane Katrina impact your area, you may need to relocate as far away as another major city or even to another state. That means that your job would be compromised, undermining your ability to care for your household and family or even to continue your education.

Disasters do not always spare your other resources. You may have lost your car in the event. If you work at home, you may have lost computers, tools, and other items necessary for earning a living. Most people experience at least temporary displacement from their neighborhoods too, and then must move through a confusing, unfamiliar process without friends, neighbors, church, family, and significant others. Loss of social networks makes it even harder to regroup and move on to whatever the next phase holds.

For those of you interested in working in the field of emergency management, you are now very busy and your life has changed. If your home was spared, you are lucky because you can now concentrate on the challenges that face the broader community. First, you need to assess the damages so that insurance companies, relief organizations, and the state government can request assistance from outside if needed. As described in Chapter 8, this preliminary damage assessment (PDA) lays the foundation so that others can know what kind of resources to send. In the U.S., the PDA is the first step to securing federal assistance. In any nation, you will need to assess at a minimum the following:

- Numbers and types of houses damaged and extents of damage (minor to completely destroyed)
- Consideration of populations that may require additional assistance such as people living in nursing homes, assisted living facilities, state schools, and group homes
- Impacts on local utilities including power, telephone, cell towers, gas, water, and stormwater drainage
- Damage to critical infrastructure such as bridges, underpasses, railroads, subways, airports, waterways, and roads

- Impacts on local cultural and historical resources that represent a shared identity and heritage and may impact tourism and the local economy
- Hits taken by local businesses including home-based, locally owned, franchise, corporate, and other types of businesses

You will also need to coordinate with key members of your community's response and recovery team. Collaboration will be needed between at least these agencies and organizations:

- Public works to block off damaged streets and flooded areas and initiate coordination with waste removal services
- Waste removal to assess the potential of a local landfill to collect and take in debris appropriately including green waste, recyclable materials, and hazardous materials
- Public information to educate the public about recovery assistance, debris removal, and when and where they can initiate their own recovery, including ways to reach people speaking different languages, including sign language, people with disabilities, seniors who may be socially isolated, and people with low literacy levels
- Chambers of Commerce and local business associations
- Educators from pre-school through college and university levels
- Elected officials and those assigned to conduct short- and long-term recovery planning to rebuild the community
- Relief organizations, particularly those that bring in external resources and volunteers to work on rebuilding homes
- Local faith-based and community organizations that are likely to emerge as an Unmet Needs, Interfaith, or Long-Term Recovery Committee focused on the needs of low-income households
- Code officials tasked with designing stronger and safer structures by writing new codes
- Planners to redesign a more functional infrastructure resilient to additional damage
- Others interested in enhancing local quality of life such as parks and recreation, police and fire, environmental organizations and sports teams

Depending on the type of disaster and the scope of impact, recovery efforts can be addressed quickly or can take considerable time. Consider, for example, the thousands of people lingering in temporary trailers at the five-year mark after Hurricane Katrina in the U.S. The hurricane that occurred in 2005 still left local organizations working to rebuild both the private and public sectors along four states in 2010. The first question to consider with recovery is not how soon to start but how long it will take. Additional questions will task a recovery leader to determine who should be involved and where the resources will come from to build a stronger, more disaster-resilient community. The starting point, beyond hearing public officials say "we will recover," is what they mean by *recover*.

9.2.1 Defining Recovery

Quarantelli (1998) notes several ways to think about recovery. It means different things to different people and it is wise to keep that in mind when using the term. It is not unusual for a local official to go on television and proclaim that his or her community will rebuild. *Reconstruction* is not the only term that describes recovery. The rebuilding process needs to be thought through carefully as the post-disaster timeframe allows for rethinking *how* we rebuild. Reconstruction might serve as a chance to bring in greener materials allowing for more energy-efficient homes and businesses. The reconstruction period might also allow implementation of new designs that promote green space, improved storm water systems, and relocated utilities resistant to the next disaster. Reconstruction also could reduce the impacts of future disasters by incorporating storm-resistant hurricane shutters and roof clamps, safe rooms, elevations, and similar features. Reconstruction should be thought of as building back better. Integrating mitigation measures is a critical step (for more, see Chapter 10, Mitigation).

Restoration serves as another term that people use during the recovery period. Restoration or returning to the way things were may be appropriate in some cases. Restoration is appropriate for the historical and cultural elements of a community. An historic structure, for example, can re-use elements saved during debris removal to retain meaningful historic character. It is also possible to integrate mitigation features into restored buildings. By elevating an historic building above anticipated flood levels, it can retain its historic context and be made safe from future risks. Such steps safeguard our ancestry and the places that mean so much to us.

Rehabilitation is yet another term used during recovery: making things better, typically in a way that improves some element of a structure or a community. However, rehabilitation may result in demolition of low-income areas or changes that prevent original residents from returning. Some communities disallow trailer parks after a tornado but do not reintroduce affordable housing. After Hurricane Katrina, public outcry arose when the U.S. Housing and Urban Development in conjunction with the Housing Authority of New Orleans tore down public housing and reintroduced mixed income housing. The decision, according to protestors, resulted in fewer homes for those at lower income levels.

The *restitution* term carries a suggestion that some kind of legal action or compensation is expected. This is usually the case where an entity or agent is deemed to be at fault as a result of hazardous materials releases, failures of levee systems, or terrorist attacks. Assigning blame and securing compensation can take considerable time as shown after the attacks of September 11, 2001 and the levee failures in New Orleans after Hurricane Katrina.

Experts suggest that *recovery* is best thought of as a process involving a series of stages or steps. *Short-term recovery* would include the restoration of key utilities and infrastructure and placing people into temporary housing. *Long-term recovery* involves the community in tackling how, when, and where to rebuild, sets a timeline to do so, and organizes people, resources, and organizations in moving toward a consensus-based vision of normalcy. Typically, emergency managers are most involved in short-term recovery. Long- term recovery is more likely to be managed by elected officials, special task forces, and relief organizations. This is unfortunate because the expertise of emergency managers may not be tapped. It is up to those involved in the profession to remain well integrated into the various tasks of recovery which we turn to next.

9.3 Recovery Challenges

In this section we work through various challenges associated with recovery from a disaster. While each disaster is unique, certain common elements must be addressed for a sense of normalcy to return. Context also makes a difference with recovery. As you can read in Box 9.1 on the Haiti earthquake of January 2010, sometimes even meeting the most basic of human needs such as clean water can take considerable time and have great consequences.

9.3.1 Transitioning from Shelter into Housing

Displaced persons move through four phases of sheltering and housing (Quarantelli 1982) that transition them from emergency shelters they may create themselves into temporary shelters established by organizations that provide food, water, and cover from the elements. The third phase (temporary housing) and the fourth (permanent housing) will be discussed later in this chapter. Sometimes, people must find shelter in makeshift locations such as overpasses, their cars, or tents. Ideally, temporary shelters will be set up by experienced organizations. Internationally, the Sphere Project (2004) provides guidelines for establishing temporary shelter. Six standards are recommended:

- *Strategic Planning.* People should have the right to be near their homes, their economic livelihoods, and social networks where

BOX 9.1 HAITI EARTHQUAKE OF JANUARY 2010

In many disasters, particularly in developed nations, recovery follows a predictable pattern with organizations stepping in to provide relief, guide people through rebuilding, and help restore the infrastructure. The Haiti earthquake of January 12, 2010 (magnitude 7.0) damaged an already struggling nation dealing with excruciating poverty and significant health, economic, and political challenges. Although much attention has moved away from Haiti, the struggle to regain any sense of normalcy remains and will for some time.

In October 2010, an unusual outbreak occurred: cholera. This disease is caused by contracting a bacterial infection spread through contaminated food and water. In Haiti, the most likely source of the post-earthquake epidemic was water. The bacteria cause severe diarrhea and dehydration. An infant exposed to the bacteria can die within hours. Haiti's severely damaged health care sector has struggled to provide care. In response, the U.S.-based Centers for Disease Control issued this warning to relief organizations:

> The earthquake in January caused significant damage to buildings, roads, hospitals and clinics, and other key infrastructure. All forms of communication and basic services in Haiti remain extremely limited. Shortages of food, water, transportation, and adequate shelter are ongoing. Many medical facilities have been operating beyond maximum capacity, and the current sanitation situation poses serious health risks. The U.S. Embassy's ability to provide emergency consular services is limited, and the U.S. government has discontinued evacuation assistance. Persons who wish to help with relief efforts in Haiti need to be aware that, despite their good intentions, travel to Haiti will increase the burden on a country that is struggling to support its citizens in need. Living conditions for relief workers are difficult, and the availability of food supplies, clean drinking water, and adequate shelter is limited.

Humanitarian relief organizations have worked for years to provide basic services to Haiti, and the basic services were further compromised by the earthquake and subsequent health scares. One such effort, Living Waters for the World, provides low-cost water treatment plants. In concert with a sister effort, Solar Under the Sun (see Figure 12.4 in Chapter 12), the treatment plants use Haiti's large sun field to produce low-cost and sustainable solar energy. Through a faith-based effort of the Presbyterian Church, clean water is now produced in Guatemala, Honduras, Mexico, El Salvador, Dominican Republic, Kenya, Peru, Ecuador, Bolivia, Nicaragua, Belize, Ghana, Thailand, the U.S., and Venezuela.

In discussing recovery, it is essential to understand context and what one country may need differs from what another needs. Despite the severe gaps in economic development among nations, clean water means the difference between life and death everywhere and should never be taken for granted.

Sources: Centers for Disease Control, http://wwwnc.cdc.gov/travel/content/travel-health-warning/haiti-earthquake.aspx. Living Waters for the World, www.livingwatersfortheworld.org. Solar Under the Sun, www.solarunderthesun.org

possible. Collective settlements should be avoided. Locations providing shelter should ensure safety from future hazards.

- *Physical Planning.* Local practices should be used to create shelters, linking people to their families and neighbors. Safe services including water should be provided.
- *Covered Living Space.* People have the right to privacy and dignity within a living space. A minimum of 3.5 meters per person is recommended. Space should allow for local cultural practices and normal household activities including sleeping, washing, and dressing.
- *Design.* Living spaces should be appropriate for the local community, afford protection from the elements, and provide for their health and safety.
- *Construction.* Local building practices should be used for shelter and local people should be hired to construct the dwellings.
- *Environmental Impact.* Any negative impact on the physical environment should be minimized including the debris that humans accumulate in shared spaces; local materials should be used to construct living spaces.

In general, the second stage of shelter and housing is called temporary shelter with several types of public shelters usually available. General population shelters open to the public as needed. Typically, emergency managers assume that about 20% of the evacuating public will go to a shelter. Most shelters in the U.S. are opened and operated by trained staff and volunteers from the Red Cross. Many states support that effort with other NGOs and public agencies such as the public health service on an as-needed basis. Public shelters tend to host populations that lack resources to pay for hotels or social networks that provide beds. General population shelters are required to admit people with disabilities and service animals (FEMA 2010). Local animal care organizations may open pet shelters that ideally are co-located near the human population.

Most shelters open and close fairly quickly. Elongated stays can occur under some conditions such as catastrophic events or in areas where affordable, permanent housing is not available. Another factor that influences shelter stay is whether accessible housing becomes available, particularly for senior citizens and families that include individuals with disabilities. Another type is the *functional needs shelter* or medical shelter that opens for people in need of services beyond what a general shelter can provide such as residents evacuated from a nursing home, those who need advanced medical care, and patients with dementia who may need supervisory support or security. The functional needs shelter provides a highly specialized environment with well-trained health care personnel (Phillips et al. 2011).

Communities house residents in many different ways. You may live in a mobile home or perhaps rent an apartment. Maybe you own a house or live with your parents. If you are older, you may reside with your children or in an assisted living facility. Perhaps you have a disability and live in government-funded public housing. In some countries, people live in refugee camps, small villages of mud huts, or densely packed urban areas. And some people may have been homeless before a disaster occurred.

The first step in post-disaster recovery efforts involves finding safe and secure housing. Doing so can be harder than expected. In many developed nations, people assume they will find temporary housing (the third phase in moving from displacement to relocation) in rental apartments or houses while their homes are repaired. Countries such as the U.S. may provide eligible applicants with funding to rent units, travel trailers, or mobile homes (Figure 9.1). This strategy is used when housing suffers massive damage (for example, from Hurricane Katrina) and in areas that lack rental units and/or affordable housing. In countries where large numbers of people experience dislocation, the effort to provide housing can be overwhelmingly difficult and the results minimal (Figure 9.2). Ten months after the 2010 Haiti earthquake killed nearly 300,000 people, another 1.2 million remained in temporary settlements. Relief organizations responded with additional rolls of plastic sheeting, blankets, and water containers. An international engineering assessment determined that of 289,491 post-earthquake existing

FIGURE 9.1 Temporary trailers in the Lower Ninth Ward of New Orleans, about six months after Hurricane Katrina in 2005. (Photo by Brenda Phillips)

FIGURE 9.2   Temporary relief camp in Naggapattinam, India after the Indian Ocean tsunami of 2004. (Photo by Brenda Phillips)

structures, only 52% were habitable; 26% needed repairs to make them safe; and 21% were considered unsafe (USAID 2010).

Beyond temporary shelter, that in cases like Haiti may become extended temporary or even permanent shelter, four strategies can be used to reach the fourth phase: permanent housing (Comerio 1998). The *redevelopment model* involves national agencies in designing recovery plans. Agencies will work together to create systematic master plans. This type of planning is most common under a highly centralized government and in a context of extensive damage. In many countries where homeowners carry insurance, such a model is unlikely. The model also assumes government support of the population and sufficient resources to do so.

A second model is called *capital infusion*; outside aid is rendered through NGOs. The Haiti earthquake and Pakistan flooding of 2010 represent two examples. In both cases, most relief must come from the outside due to a lack of sufficient resources within the nations. Humanitarian standards, such as those described by the Sphere Project, should apply but may not always be met. It is often up to external organizations to provide relief often in situations where travel to a site is compromised and/or personal safety of relief workers is in doubt (see Box 9.1). Outside relief, while appreciated, is also not always culturally or environmentally appropriate. It is critical to provide donations that fit with local needs and relieve conditions without creating congestion and disposal issues.

A third model for permanent housing recovery is more typical in developed nations and is called the *limited intervention model*. Insurance is used to help people recover from their losses. In many nations, government assistance will be available as well in the form of resources, grants, expertise, loans, and personnel. Those with insurance and the means to survive a disaster are most likely to do so. Without government assistance and help from NGOs, some populations (see Section 9.4) are unlikely to recover quickly or at all (Peacock and Girard 2000). The last is the *market model*. In this scenario, affected people must survive on their own with limited support from others. To think through the impact of this model, consider how much insurance and money you or your family have available at this moment. Clearly, this model results in "winners and losers" determined on the basis of personal funds (Comerio 1998, p. 127). The ability to find permanent housing often depends on the impact of a disaster on ability to earn a livelihood.

9.3.2 Businesses

Preparedness is key to surviving disaster within the business community. Unfortunately, as discussed in Chapter 11, most business owners do very little to prepare (Webb, Tierney, and Dahlhamer 2000). Take a minute and think about places where you and family members work. What would happen if those businesses had to close due to a disaster? Downtime is the first consideration. Downtime is defined as the length of time that a business cannot provide its goods and services to the public. How long would the business have to be closed? Would the closure be due to a direct hit or an indirect impact such as loss of utilities? Restaurants, dry cleaners, coffee shops, and computer stores cannot operate without water. Employees cannot ring up sales and banks cannot offer services without power. Wages are lost and employees cannot regroup to handle their own damages. A closed business faces the prospect of never opening again. It is imperative that businesses reopen and that customer traffic return as soon as possible.

Displacement can also occur. FEMA (2001) estimates that one foot of flood water displaces a business for 134 days. Two feet of water require a business to relocate for 230 days; with three feet of water, a business must operate from a new location for at least a year. Most businesses have not developed contingency plans for such long-term displacement and thus face considerable risk.

Consider also the range of businesses that may need assistance. Small businesses face the highest risk of disaster impact, usually because they have less cash flow and fewer resources to use after a disaster. Smaller businesses are also more likely to be operated by women and minority groups, and a disaster creates a more significant employment loss that affects entire families. Small businesses that are home-based (home repairs, carpentry, cabinet making, consulting, child care, and sewing) are particularly at risk (Enarson 2001). Larger businesses have more employees to help with the recovery and may have alternative locations to provide infusions of goods, services, and funds (Webb et al. 2000).

Business recovery can be challenging, but there are some success stories. After the 1989 Loma Prieta earthquake in Santa Cruz, California, business owners and the city worked together to erect signs redirecting customers to open locations, erected tent pavilions to serve as temporary locations, and concentrated on rebuilding the downtown. Customers even turned out to help move merchandise to new locations. This community-focused effort resulted in a fairly strong recovery from the earthquake. External assistance may not be readily available for businesses. The U.S. Small Business Administration offers loans of up to $1.5 million for up to thirty years of repayment for those who qualify. Economic injury disaster loans may also be available.

After the Indian Ocean tsunami destroyed the vendors along a main street of Velankanni, India, the Oxfam NGO provided funds to rebuild and also provided support to fishing communities by offering new boats and teaching people new skills such as crab farming. Saltwater contamination on agricultural lands required further help for those now hungry and in need of resources to regrow crops. These livelihood interventions proved critical to the survival of local communities and businesses, particularly those managed by poor women (Oxfam 2008).

To summarize, business recovery means calculating downtime and displacement costs along with the costs of lost inventory and impacts on employees to determine the potential to recover. All types of businesses are critical to a community-s recovery—from home-based enterprises to major corporations. The businesses most likely to survive invest in appropriate advance preparedness and contingency planning (see Chapter 11). Those most likely to need support are small businesses, particularly those in developing nations and those operated by historically disadvantaged populations. Insurance and savings may not be sufficient to survive, and both governmental and NGO assistance may be needed. Without a means to earn a living, community members cannot recover.

9.3.3 Infrastructures and Lifelines

As noted in the section on businesses, the loss of utilities and infrastructure can disrupt businesses directly and indirectly. A study of Memphis, Tennessee found that businesses needed electricity the most followed by phone services, water, wastewater treatment, and natural gas (Tierney, Nigg, and Dahlamer 1996). The study revealed that the businesses most likely to close first from disaster-related utility disruptions were business and professional services, followed by manufacturing and construction, wholesale and retail firms, and then banks, insurance offices, and realtors. It is worth bearing in mind that the study covered indirect effects caused solely by utility disruption. A direct impact could cause more significant impacts. The 1994 Northridge, California earthquake, for example, resulted in an average loss of $156,273 to affected businesses (Tierney 1996).

FIGURE 9.3 Damaged beds from the Naggapattinam area hospital within India. Most of the hospital sustained major damage from the 2004 Indian Ocean tsunami and had to be rebuilt farther inland in a safer location. Rapidly responding staff and family members saved every patient exposed to the floodwaters. (Photo by Brenda Phillips)

Disasters produce social impacts, primarily the disruption to personal lives from managing hygiene to getting to and from work and school. A 1998 ice storm that affected Canada put four inches of ice on the ground. One in five Canadians lost power for up to three weeks. Senior citizens were a particular concern as they are more affected by heat, cold, and social isolation than younger residents. Canada sent out large numbers of military to find and support those affected, the largest peacetime deployment in the nation's history (Scanlon 1999). We need a functioning infrastructure including roads, ports, and bridges to travel about. We need utilities so we can shower, make food, and take care of the sick (Figure 9.3). Cell phones are commonplace in most countries as are social media that connect people and allow exchange of information in times of crisis.

Recovery from disaster requires an emphasis on several important concepts. One of the first is the importance of mitigating future risks (National Research Council 1994). To achieve mitigation, we must understand that many infrastructure systems are interconnected and that damage to one can result in a rolling effect on others, for example, when a power blackout leads to traffic signal outages, street congestion, and communication disruptions (Zimmerman 2003). Recovery must thus incorporate flexibility by integrating resilience, robustness, and adaptability (Zimmerman 2003), for example, by implementing alternatives such as wireless connectivity in addition to direct lines. Physical components and social dimensions of the infrastructure must be addressed. How people manage disasters, such as choosing to place sand bags to redirect flood waters away from a water treatment plant is key (Zimmerman 2003). The ultimate goal of an infrastructure-focused recovery is to build a more robust system with physical and social means to resist future disasters. Bridges can be rebuilt to be more flexible for earthquakes. Buildings can be made more blast-resistant for windborne debris and terrorist attacks. Levees can be strengthened to resist flooding and storm surges. Communications systems should have redundancies and flexibility for rerouting. Such mitigation can be done if the political will, public support, and financial means to do so are in place.

9.3.4 Psychological Impacts

As described in Chapter 8, many misconceptions concern the impacts of disasters on the human spirit. Media messages often lead us to assume that everyone impacted is immediately subject to post-traumatic stress disorder (PTSD). However, diagnosing such a condition takes a minimum of six months. Research also indicates that a minority of people may experience associated stress reactions such as flashbacks or painful recall. Disaster survivors experience higher levels of anxiety than the general public (Norris, Friedman, and Watson 2002; Norris et al. 2002), and it is wise to offer outreach in a variety of ways to those affected.

Those more likely to be affected seem to have common characteristics. One study after September 11, 2001 discovered that about 18% of children exposed to the trauma experienced stress reactions. However, only 27% of the children received counseling at parental request (Fairbrother et al. 2004). Middle-aged people get a lot of social support from friends and family but also serve as key caregivers for other survivors and that can increase stress (Norris, Friedman, and Watson 2002; Norris et al. 2002). Older survivors may actually react better than we expect, in part because they have a lifetime of coping skills from similar experiences to draw upon (Prince-Embury and Rooney 1988).

The magnitude of a disaster and extent of exposure also influence how we respond. Massive disasters that undermine response capabilities, render survivors open to the elements, and cause the deaths and injuries of loved ones impact our ability to manage stress. In areas where disasters force people to flee and people lose neighbors to deaths, injuries, and dislocations, the loss of social networks undermines abilities to cope. While most of the time people respond fairly well to crisis, in conditions of such magnitude it is important to know when it is necessary to intervene and offer psychological recovery programs.

What is key to psychological recovery from disaster is the set of social relationships that exists prior to a disaster. Working on those social ties to make them strong is critically important as is relying on them after a disaster. Social resources and relationships matter after a disaster and by connecting with those we love we can begin to regain a sense of support that reduces stress. Finding ways to bring people together to support each other, such as reuniting families, developing support groups, forming neighborhood work teams, and convening community-based recovery committees, can be helpful. The goal is to enable people to reconnect socially to help them psychologically.

Because many readers are considering careers in the emergency management field, it is important to understand that good mental health is something that we should all work toward so that we can handle stress and assist survivors. After the 1995 Oklahoma City bombing, for example, firefighters turned to their family and relatives as their most common strategy for addressing stress (North et al. 2002). Training and education for what to expect in a disaster helps as does experience. It is also good to process any disaster experience with a trained professional (Phillips et al. 2008; Jenkins 1998).

Programs for psychological recovery tend to be funded in an ad hoc manner and often through donations made to faith-based or voluntary organizations. The American Red Cross offers trained and credentialed mental health support. Church World Services outlines a code of conduct for disaster spiritual care and Lutheran Disaster Response trains and certifies chaplains. These organizations can be contacted for advice and support. Communities can also design their own programs to orient people toward psychological well-being. Community memorials are common after disaster, often at the one-month and one-year anniversaries (Eyre 2006). School programs can also be offered to children, an especially important step when their school or community is directly impacted. Involving mental health professionals in working with children is essential as is restoring normal elements of children's worlds (Figure 9.4). Encouraging people to take time off, pursue personal fitness, eat nutritionally, and minimize alcohol and drug use is usually advised by professionals as well. And , a central component of any program for psychological recovery other than processing the event is training people to handle future stresses including disasters.

9.3.5 Environmental Concerns

Disasters carry the potential to harm our environment via releases of hazardous materials and poor decisions about managing debris, rebuilding homes, and treating nature's resources. When considering the environment around us, it is important to think through rebuilding of communities.

FIGURE 9.4   A new playground in Plaquemines Parish, Louisiana after Hurricane Katrina. (Photo by Brenda Phillips)

Community recovery planning should consider impacts on animals, plant life, water quality, and the air (to name a few) along with the potential to rebuild in an environmentally friendly manner.

In recent years, attention has turned to the options available to rebuild in a "green" manner that draws from renewable resources, promotes energy efficiency, and integrates design into the environment. Recovery, when focused on sustainability, also offers a more promising future for generations ahead of ours (Mileti et al. 1995; Mileti 1999).

Consider, for example, what you can do with the debris after a disaster. It might surprise you to discover that you can reuse mud, sand, and dirt accumulated from floods and landslides. Properly managed, it can be used as topsoil or landfill cover. Shingles torn off by hurricanes can be reused for resurfacing asphalt roads. Metals torn from vehicles, billboards, and homes can be sorted and sold for scrap, producing a profit for an affected community. Flooded buildings can be stripped and salvaged and windows, cupboards, and other items can be resold or reused. Communities can also mulch tree limbs and other green matter, then use it in parks, schools, and other public locations. Creative thinking can minimize the amount of debris sent to landfills and reduce rebuilding costs (EPA 1995; FEMA 2007; Brickner 1994).

Public education about the environment is also important. Recovery leaders should inform the public of their responsibility to sort home debris properly and safely into recyclable, reusable, and hazardous piles. Officials need to follow careful guidelines for removal, disposal, and incineration of debris (FEMA 2007). Debris management must be carefully monitored so that the environment is not damaged further by hazardous materials that could leak into the ground and groundwater.

Some events are environmental disasters. In 2010, an accident occurred at BP's Deepwater Horizon Well. The explosion and resulting damage leaked extensive amounts of oil into the Gulf of Mexico. Commercial and recreational fishing had to be shut down and beaches closed for clean-up. The accident happened at the start of shrimping season and the onset of summer tourism, and the economic damage became significant. Agencies and organizations worked diligently to save wildlife, endangered wetlands, and fragile estuaries. As of this writing, the full impact of the oil, both economically and environmentally, is still being assessed including the deaths of baby dolphins in the spring of 2011. Studies underway by EPA and other researchers are investigating water quality, air quality affected by spilled and burned oil, chemical dispersants, sediments, and impacts on larvae to determine integration into the food chain and other effects. Continued research will be necessary to assess the long-term impact of the accident. In October 2010, President Barack Obama issued an executive order to establish the Gulf Coast Ecosystem Restoration Task Force to develop a strategy and performance indicators for ecosystem restoration. The order involved a minimum of eleven federal agencies, departments and offices, five states, and affected tribes in crafting a strategy due in 2011.

9.3.6 Historic and Cultural Resources

All communities have origins and histories. Artifacts representing that legacy connect people with each other, build a sense of personal and collective identity, and give people a strong desire to return home. By working to identify such historical and cultural resources and protect them before and after a disaster, an emergency management professional can help people retain their sense of ancestry and social connections and encourage them to rebuild their communities. A historic property is defined as "any prehistoric or historic district, site, building, structure, or object included in, or eligible for inclusion in, the National Register of Historic Places" (FEMA 2005). Cultural resources include the built environment, monuments, art and sculpture in museums and around our communities, and the ways of life that represent a shared cultural heritage.

Where do you live? What is important to you where you are located? If you are a student in a college or university program, are you wearing your school colors today? Perhaps a T-shirt or cap with the name or mascot? If so then you inherently understand why places are important to people. If you bleed orange, or scarlet and gray, or blue and gold, you probably connect to Oklahoma State University, The Ohio State University, or the University of Delaware (as do your authors).

Besides historical and cultural values, places offer economic importance. We travel to coastal areas to enjoy the beaches and oceans, go to capital cities to tour museums, and visit areas that feature the culture and history of First Nations/Native American people. Travel and tourism generate significant revenue for businesses and taxes that support local economies. Restoration of those locations allows people to pursue their livelihoods and retain the meanings of places in their hearts and minds.

The National Historic Preservation Act (NHPA) was amended in 2000 to require FEMA and other federal agencies to consider how any actions they take such as demolition, relocation, or rebuilding will affect the historic values of properties including tribal areas. A Heritage Emergency National Task Force of forty-one federal agencies and historic preservation organizations provide support (Quarantelli 2003). Each state or tribal area in the U.S. also has a historic preservation officer who can serve as a key resource for identifying historical and cultural heritage and offering strategies to maintain the integrity of properties or objects. Many communities have local historical associations that work to preserve locally meaningful places. Together, these groups and agencies serve as important resources for community recovery planning efforts.

9.4 Community-Based Recovery Planning

Communities must be involved in making decisions about recovery. How, where, and when homes, businesses, and infrastructures are rebuilt impact each of us. By participating, we bring ideas, insights, and support to the planning table. In this section, we look at reasons for involving the public in recovery and basic strategies for initiating recovery planning efforts.

When we involve people in activities such as recovery planning that impact our futures, we bring something else as well: *social capital*. Think of social capital as akin to money: a resource that develops when people engage in social interaction (Nakagawa and Shaw 2004; Uphoff 2000; Woolcock 2000). Several kinds of social capital can emerge. *Bonding* social capital arises from connections of people across similarities. After Hurricane Katrina, for example, the state of Mississippi held forums across the affected areas so that people with similar interests could view and comment on rebuilding options. Similarities may arise from long-held ancestral ties to an area, historic interests, or economic livelihoods. Coming together reveals those ties and helps people bond during the decision making process.

Bridging social capital accrues when people from different backgrounds come together. In southeastern India after the tsunami, economic interests comprised agricultural, fishing, crafts, business, and health concerns to name a few. When recovery planning efforts bring people together, they determine common concerns and act on those collectively, perhaps by rebuilding a commercial district. Working in concert often produces more ideas and a synergy that can sustain people despite seemingly different interests. People also produce *linking* social capital (Woolcock 2002). Linking is crucial in a community trying to recover. New partners will come to the table, such as city officials, NGOs, and the faith community. Without their linkages, people will struggle to return, especially those with low incomes or challenging medical conditions. Linking organizations represent crucial recovery resources; bringing them together to produce the desired social capital is an important step in launching recovery efforts.

Structural social capital reflects who we are in our communities. An architect knows how to build structures, often with disaster-resistant designs that reflect local historical and cultural character. Bankers and corporate executives know where donations and grants can be obtained. Participation by all levels of occupations should be considered. The person who picks up trash every day sees the impact of debris on the environment and where storm water drains are clogged. Mothers offer insights into what teenagers need, who may be at risk for domestic violence in a neighborhood after a disaster, and how to connect across a school system or set of recreational activities. In short, no one should be excluded from participating because of position in society. Rather, structural social capital results when we use all the knowledge embedded in our various family and community roles.

Finally, *cognitive* social capital is defined as the attitudes people bring to the planning table (Woolcock 2002). The attitudes may stem from cultural backgrounds, faith traditions, and psychological traits. Attitudes can spur or impede community planning. As one example, viewing recovery as an opportunity rather than as a daunting challenge opens the door to possibilities: mitigation, greening the community, serving low income families, harnessing solar and wind power, and more. The key point is to amass the energies and resources that people produce through social contact.

9.5 Basic Recovery Planning

The two types of recovery planning are (1) planning before an event and (2) planning afterward. Unfortunately, the kind that occurs afterward is most common. This is undesirable because this planning often occurs in the context of confusion, sadness, and very long work days. Although this text urges readers to conduct pre-recovery planning, the reality is that most will do so after an event.

FEMA (2005) concurs with the concept that social capital is key and recommends that local leaders drive the recovery process. Local people know their community best. While outsiders, including consultants, can serve as facilitators, the best practice is to involve those expecting to return to the community in key decisions. FEMA also recommends that specific projects be identified to provide a vision of what needs to be done and allow people to work collectively to make it happen. Mitigation efforts should also always be introduced into any reconstruction element to reduce future disaster impacts. The Ministry of Civil Defence and Emergency Management in New Zealand concurs with this general approach and empowers local civil defence emergency management groups (CDEMs) to work collectively. New Zealand emphasizes the notion of linking social capital by bringing a wide range of partners to the recovery planning table. For more about long-term recovery approaches in the U.S. and New Zealand, see Boxes 9.2 and 9.3.

Experts agree that recovery planning should involve the entire community (FEMA 2005; Norman 2004; Quarantelli 1997; Schwab et al. 1998). Key steps in that process include determining the extent of damages and possible ways to fund recovery projects. A recovery task force should be convened with a local leader at the helm. Initial efforts should involve a wide array of stakeholders to generate bridging social capital and build consensus around a vision for the rebuilt sectors. Planners should think through the impacts on future generations so that the community is sustainable and does not pass risks on to children and grandchildren. The goal should be to make the community more viable. A comprehensive plan should address key elements, link projects to funding, and generate a timeline. Project leaders should keep the public informed and actively engaged. Project elements should include several major factors as noted below.

Housing—What should homes look like after a disaster? A disaster should generate new codes that safeguard the public from future impacts. Rebuilding thus can become challenging as residents and building owners move through the process of securing permits and working toward the collective vision of a community recovery plan. This may take considerable time as many who must rebuild may have never experienced the process. In some communities, the public need for help and support at the local government level can be considerable. If outside organizations help rebuild, it will be necessary to inform and monitor their work to ensure compliance with new codes. Attention must also be paid to those likely to slip through the cracks of rebuilding; populations most likely to be at risk include low income families, single parents, seniors, and people with disabilities. Everyone should have a chance to come home again, but it may take concentrated linking social capital to make it happen (Figure 9.5 and Figure 9.6).

BOX 9.2 FEMA NATIONAL RECOVERY FRAMEWORK

In February 2010, FEMA released a draft National Recovery Framework for the U.S. with support from the Department of Homeland Security and the Department of Housing and Urban Development. Following its own recommended practices for planning, FEMA led outreach efforts to solicit input throughout the nation using in-person forums and online mechanisms. Known as the Long Term Recovery Working Group, the agencies launched the effort with a set of planning principles summarized here:

- *Individual and Family Empowerment.* Families are critical to planning a recovery process and should be consulted. They are the heart of a community and the reason for initiating a full and meaningful recovery effort.
- *Leadership and Local Primacy.* Local leaders bring expertise and insights to the table for planning a recovery. Intergovernmental partnerships between local and federal government should be fostered to serve the public good.
- *Preparation for Recovery.* Pre-planning for an event is ideal and should cross all sectors: government, individuals, families, businesses, and the volunteer sector.
- *Partnerships and Inclusiveness.* Everyone has value in a given community and should be heard from when disaster recovery efforts ensue. A wide range of perspectives generates a broader set of potential issues and solutions. In particular, historically underrepresented populations or those whose voices are not always heard—such as children—should be consulted.
- *Communications.* It is important to ensure that the entire public receives and understands recovery messages. People as stakeholders have the right to know what is planned that will affect them and their families.
- *Unity of Effort.* Recovery planning should convene people so that they can generate a shared vision of how recovery should proceed. Building consensus across stakeholder groups is paramount.
- *Timeliness and Flexibility.* Recovery should identify and meet needs as they are identified. Many needs may require careful assessment and identification so that people do not slip through the cracks. Efforts to provide recovery assistance in a step-wise process should occur.
- *Resilience and Sustainability.* Mitigate, mitigate, mitigate. Incorporate structural and non-structural elements to foster disaster resistance.

Source: FEMA. http://www.fema.gov/pdf/recoveryframework/omb_ndrf.pdf

BOX 9.3 NEW ZEALAND CIVIL DEFENCE EMERGENCY MANAGEMENT GROUPS

In 2004, the Ministry of Civil Defence and Emergency Management in New Zealand generated a holistic recovery framework for the entire nation. Building upon the concept of a civil defence emergency management (CDEM) group, the ministry provided guidance on who should work together as well as what they should focus on. CDEM groups came about from the CDEM Act of 2002 mandating their development. Groups should include local authorities as identified by their regional council boundaries. Government alone would not be responsible for emergency management tasks including recovery, however. Also included were police, fire, health, lifeline utilities, businesses, community groups, and volunteer organizations.

These groups were tasked to identify hazards, assess risks, and determine appropriate actions to take to be ready, reduce risks, respond to, and recover from disasters. Because the islands comprising New Zealand face risks from flooding, earthquakes, tsunamis, volcanoes, and even power crises, they had a significant challenge. The ministry recommended the all-hazards approach familiar to you now from Chapter 2 of this book and also recommended that technical expertise and information (research) be integrated into CDEM group planning. Although local governments ultimately bore responsibilities for initiating efforts, the ministry also advised that individual and community responsibility be made manifest by educating the public about area hazards and risks. Should an event occur, local groups should take the lead in recovery.

Four main areas serve as the organizing framework for the recovery efforts (Norman 2006). First, the social environment includes safety, health, and welfare. CDEM groups should attend to the well-being of those affected by making efforts to reduce risks. Should disaster occur, taking care of those injured including follow-up care should occur. Welfare includes a wide array of efforts, including psychological care to those affected along with basic provision of food, water, and shelter. Second, the built environment needs to be a focus. Within this sector, groups need to plan for residential dwellings, public buildings, lifeline utilities, and the commercial sector. Their efforts would tie into a third area of concern, economic environments. For this component, groups should concentrate on individual, business, infrastructure, and governmental elements. Individual attention would include concern over maintenance of personal wages and salaries needed for recovery purposes. The fourth area, the natural environment, also requires discussion within the CDEM group. The focus should include biodiversity and ecosystems, natural resources, amenity values, and waste and pollution issues. In short, New Zealand embraces an integrated, interconnected, and holistic recovery planning framework by activating partnerships among a wide array of local organizations and government.

Sources: Norman, Sarah. 2006. New Zealand's holistic framework for disaster recovery. *Australian Journal of Emergency Management,* 21: 16–20; Ministry of Civil Defence and Emergency Management. 2002. *Director's Guide to CDEM Groups*. Wellington.

FIGURE 9.5 A home rebuilt by Mennonite Disaster Service volunteers allows a family to return home after the 2005 U.S. Gulf Coast hurricanes. (Photo by Mennonite Disaster Service, with permission)

FIGURE 9.6 Homes remain to be rebuilt after the U.S. Gulf Coast hurricanes in the Holly Grove neighborhood of New Orleans, Louisiana. (Photo by Brenda Phillips)

Businesses—We must make business recovery a priority. In many cities, tax revenues from businesses support key social and governmental services. Business recovery task forces may spring from the broader community plan, and care should be taken to address the range of affected businesses. After the Indian Ocean tsunami, fishermen faced the loss of their habitat and destruction of the fishing fleets. Hurricane Katrina meant that those with home-based businesses needed micro-loans to re-secure key resources. The attacks of September 11, 2001 created significant losses by restaurants, hotels, ports, and the airline industry. By conducting an assessment of damages to all affected, a comprehensive effort can be drafted to return businesses to functional status. Damage to the infrastructure may mean that cities need to re-route traffic, re-establish parking areas, and publicize their business sectors so that customers return. Employees may need temporary support while businesses experience downtime and displacement but do not lose valued personnel. Cities may need to provide temporary business locations. Businesses may need to consider deliveries via alternative routes including Internet sites. Mitigation should always be a priority when rebuilding so that the local economy and services are not so disrupted again. Finally, the business sector can join the housing recovery in rebuilding green by using environmentally friendly building materials, paints, chemicals, low-energy lights, heating, cooling, and boiler systems (Smart Energy Design Assistance Center 2006).

Environmental Resources—Planning around environmental concerns should address several elements. A first step is to identify and consider how to handle environmentally sensitive areas and endangered or threatened wildlife. Some disasters such as hazardous materials releases may directly threaten local flora and fauna. Others may be impacted through human decisions. Safeguarding the environment should always be considered a key element for protecting an area—not an optional step. Planners should encourage the views of environmentally knowledgeable experts and advocates as they also bring social capital into the planning process. It may be necessary to prohibit construction on some lands or add elements that protect locations from run-off and other impacts during reconstruction. Re-introducing elements lost to a disaster can serve as a focal point for community involvement. For example tree plantings serve to absorb future storm water and promote energy efficiency when placed correctly around homes and businesses. Local climate should be considered, particularly in areas subject to extremes of heat and cold. In hotter areas, xeriscaping practices introduce drought-resistant native plants. Recovery also allows communities to address invasive plants that make disasters worse, such as eastern red cedars and eucalyptus trees that fuel wildfires. New technologies such as wind farming and solar power may be introduced. Continued monitoring of the environment should also be included in recovery planning so that disaster effects can be assessed over time. This applies to natural and human-made disasters such as hazardous materials events and terrorism. In the aftermath of September 11, 2001, long-term studies of airborne particulates have been crucial to understanding the effects on first responders (see Chapter 8).

Historic and Cultural Resources—Places are important to people, and their shared love for places will bring them to the planning table. Emphasizing the historic and cultural character of a location can thus generate a focus for recovery planning. Communities may view recovery as a time to emphasize their uniqueness and rebuild with more focused architectural designs. The colors of New Orleans, for example, spread across the homes of a new Musician's Village, and historic preservationists have worked to elevate classic architecture across the city. Downtown sectors may be rebuilt with a turn-of-the-century feel or designs reflective of their ethnic origins. Community recovery teams can encourage debris removal efforts to salvage historic bricks and facade elements so that the old look can be re-established. To imagine Paris without the Eiffel Tower, London without Buckingham Palace, Moscow without St. Basil's Cathedral, or Spain without its plazas is to understand how important places are economically, historically, and in terms of people's identity.

Infrastructure—The cost of infrastructure repairs can be significant. Repairs can be so costly that in many countries the infrastructure lags and requires considerable updating. Disasters afford opportunities for update work. Roads can be redesigned to improve traffic flow and manage storm water runoff better. Bridges can be rebuilt to new earthquake-resistant standards. Ports can benefit from new docks and traffic routing technologies. By involving community input, we can ensure a good fit between what people need and the quality of their lives from their perspectives.

Psychological Recovery—Communities usually fail to include means for social and psychological recovery in their plans. This is unfortunate because the bases for community planning are the well-being and spirit of residents. Even those most resilient to disasters face the enervating effects of daily struggles to rebuild. Moving past debris piles for months or years can be mentally draining. By introducing a means to build and maintain community spirit, the social capital leaders seek to harness and apply whatever can be continued. Most communities have cadres of social workers, faith leaders, and psychologists capable of suggesting ways to build programs for the public. The variety of local residents should be considered first. In some areas, public employees working on disasters have faced considerable turnover. Because they must deal with a frustrated and exhausted public, attention should be given to public employees through time off, debriefings, and clear support and recognition of their efforts. Other populations face psychological stress as well, and experts should be tapped to develop programs for children, seniors, historically disadvantaged groups, and others who may be at higher risk for disaster-related stress. Programs can represent a range of options, from public celebrations of re-opened businesses and homes to private reunions on the anniversary of the event and individual and group therapy. A community may also want to encourage people to just be together through picnics, housing fairs, and fitness and sporting events. Often, the best psychological support a community can give is a means to rebuild lost or disrupted social networks. Communities typically plan anniversary events and memorials to remember those lost and recognize movement forward (Figure 9.7).

FIGURE 9.7 Hurricane Katrina memorial near Pass Christian, Mississippi. (Photo by Brenda Phillips)

BOX 9.4 SUFFERING RECOVERY

Joselin Landry

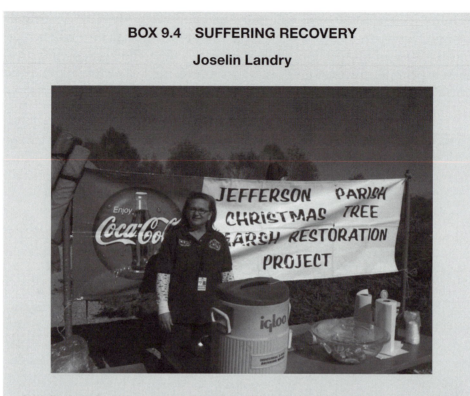

Joselin Landry earned a master's degree in environmental sociology from the University of New Orleans. While she worked as a graduate assistant at the Center for Hazards Assessment, Response and Technology (CHART), Hurricane Katrina hit the Gulf Coast. She has since worked in recovery as a specialist with public outreach, environmental, and communications responsibilities in Louisiana. For the 2008 Iowa floods and tornadoes, she assisted in long-term recovery planning. Her experiences have prompted her to join the Jefferson Parish Certified Emergency Response Team (CERT) to serve and protect her community.

As a resident of Louisiana, I am suffering recovery. In August of 2005, I evacuated for three weeks until electricity was restored in our neighborhood. I say I had no damage to my home, because so many I knew lost everything. Once home, I had nothing—no fuel, water, food, and almost nobody. I had to hunt for everything—lumber, groceries, medications, a doctor, mechanic, and even an operating library. I learned to stand in line, be patient, and do without things. I started going through my house, feeling a bit guilty about my good fortune, thinking of things I didn't use often and maybe didn't really need. I then realized good fortune doesn't mean I had to get rid of rarely used items. That's when I understood I was suffering recovery.

Then I got a phone call asking if I wanted to work in long-term recovery. Of course I wanted to be a part of the recovery. While working in long-term recovery I met some of the most dedicated, hard working, intelligent, and compassionate people who came to Louisiana to help us recover. Now, suffering recovery meant twelve-hour days, seven days a week, working on recovery issues. Recovery is very hard work.

I questioned my co-workers, "Where do we start when there is nothing here?" The answer: "We start where there is 'something,'" in neighborhoods where there was electricity, food, fuel, and people, and then work outward. That was a hard rule to follow because so many people after Hurricanes Katrina and Rita believed that *all* neighborhoods were where we should start. No matter how much or little loss you had, everyone suffered recovery. Louisiana's recovery was and is a whole-nation event.

Now, more than five years later, I still work long hours on recovery. My work involves ensuring regulations and statutes are sternly followed, creating mounds of paperwork, and paying attention to every dollar spent and how it is spent. We verify that applicants for assistance are 'eligible,' and confirm the eligibility of their facilities and their declared damages. Eligible applicants also pay close attention to regulations and statutes, create mounds of paperwork, and are determined to be eligible for and collect every dollar possible for their cash-poor governments, citizens, and beneficiaries.

On both sides of the coin (or the dollar) people suffer recovery: those experiencing recovery, those aiding the recovery, and those of us who ride on the fence line of experiencing the recovery by aiding it (me). Suffering recovery has encouraged me to be aware of hazards. Knowing about potential hazards (of any shape or form) makes us better prepared. Suffering recovery helped me understand how women, children, and the elderly are more vulnerable in any hazard event, and I try to bring this knowledge to others as I prepare my community and myself for future events.

As a student of emergency management, please join me in being prepared so others don't have to suffer recovery as we have.

Ultimately, we restore communities because people live and work in places that provide meaning to them. Our efforts to plan both before and after disaster should address the human element as well as the built elements (see Box 9.4).

9.6 Working and Volunteering in Recovery

There are always more than enough opportunities to work and volunteer during disaster recovery. One common route to disaster recovery work is to become involved in a cadre of disaster workers deployed when an event occurs. Disaster workers may serve in an area for a few weeks to a few years until recovery work begins to dwindle. Consider also these recent job announcements:

- *Infrastructure Manager.* Responsible for the effective, efficient performance of the Infrastructure Program within the Disaster Recovery

Unit of the State of Louisiana, U.S. http://www.coscda.org/jobs/
LAJob_0910.pdf

- *Environmental Technician, Oil Spill.* Environmental science and protection technicians, including health. Performs laboratory and field
tests to monitor the environment and investigate sources of pollution,
including those that affect health. Under direction of an environmental scientist or specialist, may collect samples of gases, soil, water, and
other materials for testing and take corrective actions as assigned.
[Louisiana Workforce Commission, listed October 29, 2010.]
- *Disaster Recovery Specialist.* Witt and Associates advertised for this
Baton Rouge, Louisiana, position in 2011, seeking an individual able
to work with clients in a consulting capacity. They required knowledge of FEMA, incident command, and expertise in public assistance and mitigation projects.

Volunteers are critical to recovery efforts. In fact, more volunteers are needed
and for far longer during recovery than in any other phase of disaster.
Despite this reality, most people want to help during response. What is most
helpful is to work through an experienced disaster organization, secure relevant training including safety issues, and enter affected areas only with the
approval of local authorities. Once there, volunteers pick up, clean up, muck
out, sort debris, move furniture, install roofs, tape, and mud sheetrock, paint,
and help people move back in. Many volunteer organizations exist around
the world. Perhaps one might be of interest to you (see Chapter 12 on NGOs).

- *Faith-Based Organizations.* Most denominations provide volunteer
opportunities through mission activities and experienced disaster-related groups within their churches, synagogues, or mosques.
Lutheran Disaster Response, Presbyterian Disaster Assistance, and
Mennonite Disaster Service all work on rebuilding projects for years.
Typically the faith-based volunteer works on homes of the least fortunate that suffer the most destruction. Without their assistance,
many people could not go home again.
- *Community Organizations.* A number of community-focused organizations also dive into volunteer activity when disaster occurs.
Habitat for Humanity may have local or state chapters in existence
or may set up a chapter specific to a disaster site. Local community
organizations may also recruit and commit volunteers to efforts in
their home locations or facilitate the influx of external volunteers.
- *Civic Organizations.* Perhaps you or a family member belongs to
a civic-minded organization such as the Lions Club, Rotary, or
Kiwanis. These organizations exist to serve the public, usually in a
specific capacity. By joining such an organization you can be ready
to join efforts to assist those affected by disasters.

BOX 9.5   RECOVERY IN JAPAN

As this book went to press, Japan's recovery from the combined earthquake, tsunami, nuclear reactor accidents, dam break and volcano eruption had yet to unfold. As you learned in Chapter 4, the "Na-Tech" Japan experienced likely caused a different kind of recovery to unfold. In this box, we look at the challenges that would be faced and some likely scenarios that should be in progress.

Debris Removal

Both response and recovery depend on disposing responsibly of all the debris generated by disaster. The 9.0 earthquake, fourth strongest in recorded history, caused massive building collapses. The rapidly following tsunami splintered those buildings, shoved cars into interiors, tore apart infrastructure, and pushed debris inland for six miles. As we quickly learned, multiple nuclear reactors experienced internal failure, emitting radiation across the surrounding area and ocean. Early efforts to remove debris meant pushing it aside so that search and rescue crews could find the living and recover the estimated 18,000 who perished. Further debris removal will need to be carefully monitored. In addition to the possibility of radiation contamination, disposal crews, homeowners and businesses will find hazardous materials (paint, pesticides, household chemicals) strewn throughout the massive debris field. Normally, we sort that debris into hazardous materials, then into matter that can be safely incinerated, recyclable green matter (such as trees and shrubs turned into mulch), re-usable dirt and mud (typically sifted and then used for landscaping or similar purposes), road materials and concrete that can be re-used as fill, and metals that can be pulled out with magnets and recycled such as cars, awnings, and even appliances. After the 1995 Kobe earthquake, for example, Japan put concrete into the ocean as a method of disposal, hoping to generate artificial reefs (Hayushi and Katsumi 1995). But this time, it is likely debris removal will take some time because of the "newness" of the Na-Tech combination, particularly the radiation exposure.

Homes and Families

As of late March, 2011, nearly a half million Japanese residents remained homeless with many staying in public shelters. It was unknown how many children had become orphans although the 2004 Indian Ocean tsunami experience suggests that well over 1,000 could now be without parents. Initial reports indicate higher mortality among the elderly and people with disabilities, indicating that many children have lost their grandparents and adults have lost their mother and father. Thousands of homes have disappeared or may be uninhabitable due to radiation. Challenges will include providing affordable housing for thousands who have lost their livelihoods along with their possessions and other recovery resources. Areas in and near the impacted zones are not likely to recover for some time, perhaps up to five years, if radiation exposure allows for rebuilding that soon. A variety of types of housing will need to be offered for single families, college students, seniors, and multi-generational families. Relocation into other cities is likely, so pursuing currently available housing will probably be attempted first and may require considerable support for those who need to learn new jobs to support their families. Exploration of the models proposed by Comerio elsewhere in this chapter will need to be thought through as insurance probably will not provide sufficient coverage for surviving households and businesses. Government support along with donations from nongovernmental organizations and volunteers will be needed. In contrast to Haiti, though, Japan's resources as a developed nation should spur their overall reconstruction with a caveat given to the nuclear plant issues yet unfolding as of this writing. As of March 21, 2011, a minimum of 126,000 buildings including homes and businesses had been destroyed (USAID 2011). These numbers are likely to increase once ground assessment has been conducted including damage to interiors.

Psychological Recovery

Based on what we know about psychological recovery, it is likely that some survivors will face challenging times ahead. Although people do fairly well in most disasters, several indicators suggest potential problems. First, we know that exposure serves as a key factor influencing the development of trauma. Many of those who survived did so with minutes to spare and watched as the tsunami destroyed their homes, neighborhoods, and communities. Such exposure to trauma increases the potential for the development of stress-related trauma, including post-traumatic stress disorder. Rates may also be higher among women, minority populations, and children although these groups also prove resilient in many cases. The supportive, community-oriented Japanese culture should help in this. Because children lack a frame of reference for trauma, they face difficulties if parents do not involve them in trauma counseling. Ways to aid children are based on age-groups from play therapy offered to the youngest survivors to individual and group counseling for older adolescents and teenagers. Even volunteer efforts, which may seem burdensome for survivors, can prove therapeutic. Elderly survivors may split into those who do well and those who experience increased trauma. What seems to predict that trauma for the elderly, as well as for others, is how separated people are from their social networks. Those who remain embedded in caring family and neighborhood relationships typically fare better. In this disaster, though, social networks have been torn apart, probably forever. After the Kobe earthquake, a nursing college sent students and faculty into the temporary housing units called *kasetu* set up for elderly survivors. There, they encountered isolated seniors with increased rates of alcohol and suicide. To prevent *kodokushi* (death alone and unnoticed) they moved residents into *kasetu* on the grounds of the College of Nursing. Priority went to families with members who were elderly, had disabilities, or who were single parents (Kako and Ikeda 2009). It is also true that senior citizens prove resilient with prior experience (prior disasters, family deaths, job losses) serving as a means to frame their recovery and support others.

Businesses

Initial reports suggest that Japan's economy, which depends on electronics, car production, agriculture, and seafood, has suffered a major hit. As the world's third largest economy, indicators yield a grim picture. The Nikkei index of the Tokyo Stock Exchange dropped sharply on the opening day after the disasters, causing alarm in other stock markets around the world. Though the Nikkei remained lower, levels slowly rebounded in the days following in other stock markets. The World Bank estimates that businesses overall will slow and then pick back up in mid 2011. They compared the consequences to the 1995 Kobe earthquake, when "Japan's trade slowed only for a few quarters; Japanese imports recovered fully within a year and exports rebounded to 85 percent of pre-quake levels." The World Bank added, "but this time around, disruption to production networks, especially in automotive and electronics industries, could continue to pose problems." As of March 21, 2011, rolling blackouts were in place across major parts of Japan. Such losses, while anticipated, do have an impact by introducing downtime to businesses outside of the impacted area.

Environment

Damage to the physical environment will probably fall lower in priorities than taking care of humans, but will nonetheless need to be investigated. Agricultural areas in Japan have been badly damaged in the northeast, including rice fields inundated by the tsunami. After the Indian Ocean tsunami, such sea water left salt residues on agricultural areas and rendered them unusable for some time. In addition, radiation levels have increased affecting potentially both food production and water supply. Though the sea appears calm, we have yet to ascertain what happened to the eco-system. After the 2004 tsunami, fishing villages suffered terribly in India. Boats, specific to a certain type of fishing, were destroyed. Fishing resources and the ports locals used were both lost. Tsunami wave action scoured the ocean floor, depleting vital nutrients and food chain sources. Typically abundant fish left the area, leaving people at a loss for commercial fishing and food for their families. Already it is clear that damage to fragile animal populations has occurred elsewhere. The Midway Atoll National Wildlife Refuge reported that albatross populations, in the midst of nesting season, lost close to 25% of their chicks. An additional 2,000 adult birds died in part because they do not fly. The area, home to other endangered species including the Hawaiian monk seal, the Hawaiian green turtle, and the Laysan duck will require additional assessments.

Infrastructure

Earthquakes and tsunamis can cause considerable damage to roads, highways, bridges, cellular towers, and other infrastructure that we rely upon. Aerial reconnaissance can already tell us of the physical damage visible to the eye, but structural damage inside the built environment must be assessed more closely—and will take some time to do so. As of March 21, 2011, at least 1,400 roads have been destroyed (USAID 2011). It can take years to rebuild these elements critical for ingress and egress to the damaged areas. Simply bringing in construction materials to launch rebuilding, let alone moving dump trucks of debris out of the area, may be stalled until arterial routes can be re-established.

Opportunity

Despite the pain that can be so easily seen in Japan, disasters also present opportunities. Given the extensive damage, it is likely that entirely new community developments will need to take place. Opportunities exist to rebuild in environmentally-friendly ways, using cleaner energies such as solar power. Community gardens can be created. Energy-efficient building designs, appliances and heating/cooling units can be installed which reduce energy dependency and household costs as well. Walkable, accessible communities can be put into place; buildings that feature universal design will make the built environment friendlier to people with disabilities and for those who experience physical challenges with the onset of aging. Certainly, mitigating risks from earthquakes, tsunamis and other disasters represent the most important single opportunity (for ideas, see Chapter 10). Local, prefecture-level and national Japanese governments now have the opportunity to create planned developments. In the decades following the magnitude 7.8 Tangshan, China earthquake of 1976 that killed 242,000 people, rebuilding efforts yielded long-term benefits. As one example, it was assumed that thousands of people with permanently disabling injuries would live for some time—and they did so, in 18 long-term care hospitals established to support them (Mitchell 2004). Leaders also reinvigorated the area economically with both existing and new initiatives. Today, Tangshan's population has rebounded to 1.7 million with "wide modern streets, attractive green spaces, a mixture of two, six and fifteen storey residential and commercial buildings, planned units developments, and reinvigorated industries; the urban area is cross-crossed by 180 miles of high-speed limited access highways; a new export-oriented economy has grown up; and the rebuilt metropolis ranks well up the list of China's top fifty most vibrant urban economies" (Mitchell 2004, p. 53).

References

CNN Wire Staff. 2011. "Tsunami Washes Away Feathered Victims West of Hawaii." Available at http://edition.cnn.com/2011/US/03/18/tsunami.birds.deaths/index.html, last accessed March 21, 2011.

Kako, Mayumi and Sugako Ikeda. 2009. "Volunteer Experiences in Community Housing during the Great Hanshin-Awaji Earthquake, Japan." *Nursing and Health Sciences* 11: 357-359.

Hayashi, Haruo, and T. Katsumi. 1996. "Generation and Management of Disaster Waste." *Soils and Foundations* pages 349-358.

Mitchell, Ken. 2004. "Reconceiving Recovery." Pp. 47-68 in *New Zealand Recovery Symposium*, edited by Sarah Norman. Wellington, New Zealand: Ministry of Civil Defence and Emergency Management.

U.S. Agency for International Development (USAID). 2011. Japan—earthquake and tsunami, Fact Sheet #10 (March 20, 2011). Available at http://www.usaid.gov/our_work/humanitarian_assistance/disaster_assistance/countries/Japan/template/fs/fy2011/japan_eqtsu_fs10_03-20-2011.pdf, last accessed March 21, 2011.

World Bank. 2011. "Impact of quake on Japan's growth likely to be 'temporary'; 'Limited impact' on strong regional economy, says World Bank East Asia and Pacific Economic Update." Available at www.worldbank.org.

Updated Information

Numbers and other information are likely to change as damage assessments reveal the extent of recovery needs. At present, good places to learn more include www.usaid.gov (U.S. Agency for International Development) and www.un.org (United Nations).

We will learn and read more about these volunteer organizations in Chapter 12. Until then, you are encouraged to search for more information on the types of organizations you would like to support. Once you have determined an appropriate organization, register with it, and seek out any training offered. Should a disaster occur where you live or where you would like to volunteer, go with an experienced organization that works hand-in-hand with locals. Do not be the spontaneous unaffiliated volunteer (SUV) who shows up, well-intentioned, but ultimately not as useful as a full team arriving months to years later and fully equipped to meet needs that others have forgotten.

9.7 Summary

Recovery is best conceptualized and approached as a process involving a series of stages and steps people and organizations move through. Recovery takes place in short- and long-term timeframes. Short-term term efforts address rapid restoration of critical lifelines and infrastructure; longer term efforts rebuild homes, businesses, and large-scale projects. To ensure an effective recovery, planners, workers, and volunteers should think holistically and address the entire community, not just one element (NHRAIC 2005). How we rebuild housing affects the environment and our abilities to get to work. By thinking through the interconnections of various dimensions of recovery, we foster higher quality of life for all.

An equally important element is mitigation. By incorporating disaster-resistant elements into rebuilt structures, we can reduce the effects of future disasters. It is certain that future generations will appreciate that effort as well. Regardless of where disaster strikes, it is crucial that locally affected populations must be involved in planning the recovery, preferably before the onset of a disaster. The reality is that most recovery planning takes place after an impact. To ensure that recovery occurs, an influx of workers and volunteers is often necessary. Participating in recovery with sensitivity for local customs, heritage, and environmental resources matters to those who have been harmed and results in better outcomes for survivors.

Discussion Questions

1. Why do terms matter? If an elected official says he or she plans to rehabilitate an area, how might residents respond? If homeowners begin to talk about restitution, what might ensue?

2. What are the practical implications of thinking about recovery as a process? How might an emphasis on steps and stages within a process influence recovery planning?

3. After reading Box 9.1 on the Haiti earthquake, describe your reaction to learning that people are still living in tented refuges made from plastic sheets. As you take a drink of water today, think about taking that sip for granted and the sense of privilege that divides nations and people.

4. If you were to lose your home to a disaster, what model of housing recovery would be most likely where you live? What would be your individual responsibilities under that model? Who might not be able to go home again based on that model?

5. Select an area of recovery that interests you, such as housing, environment, historic and cultural resources, or psychological recovery. What kinds of agencies, organizations, and advocates are available at the local, state, regional, or national level in your area? Would you need to reach out beyond national borders for support and assistance? What kinds of programs of the United Nations or NGOs might be of support?

6. Using the five different kinds of social capital, where would you try to find, nurture, and maintain the resources and richness that can

be generated by encouraging people to interact during the recovery period?

7. Review the elements of recovery planning mentioned here. Think how each element might be addressed in your own community based on a local hazard. What else should be included? Educational sectors? Health care? Sports and recreation?

8. Ask ten people in your community what they consider key to a good quality of life. What do they have now in place? What might be introduced after a disaster to enhance quality of life?

9. Does your community currently have a comprehensive development plan? Communities often rely on such plans after a disaster to generate recovery plans. What elements do you think could be used from a comprehensive development plan?

10. Which population groups in your community do you think would be most at risk after a disaster? How would you reach out to and involve them in a recovery planning effort?

11. What kind of career in the field of recovery interests you most and why?

References

Brickner, Robert. 1994. "How to Manage Disaster Debris." *C & D Debris Recycling*, Pp. 8–13.

Comerio, M. 1998. *Disaster Hits Home: New Policy for Urban Housing Recovery.* Berkeley: University of California Press.

Enarson, Elaine. 2001. "What Women Do: Gendered Labor in the Red River Valley Flood." *Environmental Hazards* 3: 1–18.

Environmental Protection Agency (EPA).1995. *Planning for Disaster Debris.* Washington, D.C.: U.S. Environmental Protection Agency.

Eyre, Anne. 2006. "Remembering: Community Commemoration after Disaster." Pp. 441–455 in *Handbook of Disaster Research*, (Havidán Rodríguez, Enrico L. Quarantelli, and Russell R. Dynes, eds.). New York: Springer.

Fairbrother, G., J. Stuber, S. Galea, B. Pfefferbaum, and A. R. Fleischman. 2004. "Unmet Need for Counseling Services by Children in New York City After the September 11th Attacks on the World Trade Center: Implications for Pediatricians." *Pediatrics* 113/5: 1367–1374.

Federal Emergency Management Agency. 2010. *Guidance on Planning for Integration of Functional Needs Support Services in General Population Shelters.* Washington, D.C.: FEMA.

Federal Emergency Management Agency. 2007. *FEMA 325.* Available at http://www.fema.gov/government/grant/pa/demagde.shtm, last accessed July 28, 2008.

Federal Emergency Management Agency. 2005. *Integrating Historic Property and Cultural Resource Considerations into Hazard Mitigation Planning.* Washington, D.C.: FEMA Publication 386-6.

Federal Emergency Management Agency. 2001. *Understanding Your Risks: Identifying Hazards and Estimating Losses, #386-2.* Washington, D.C.: FEMA.

Jenkins, Sharon. 1998. "Emergency Workers' Mass Shooting Incident Stress and Psychological Reactions." *International Journal of Mass Emergencies and Disasters* 16/2: 181–195.

Mileti, Dennis S., JoAnne Darlington, Eve Passerini, Betsy Forrest, and Mary Fran Myers. 1995. "Toward an Integration of Natural Hazards and Sustainability." *The Environmental Professional* 17/2: 117–126.

Mileti, Dennis. 1999. *Disasters by Design.* Washington, D.C.: Joseph Henry Press.

Nakagawa, Y., and R. Shaw. 2004. "Social Capital: A Missing Link to Disaster Recovery." *International Journal of Mass Emergencies and Disasters* 22/1: 5–34.

National Research Council. 1994. *Practical Lessons from the Loma Prieta Earthquake.* Washington, D.C., National AcademiesPress.

Natural Hazards Research and Applications Information Center (NHRAIC). 2005. *Holistic Disaster Recovery, revised.* Boulder, CO: NHRAIC/Public Entity Risk Institute.

Norman, Sarah. 2004. "Focus on Recovery: A Holistic Framework for Recovery." Pp. 31–46 in New *Zealand Recovery Symposium,* (S. Norman, ed.). New Zealand: Ministry of Civil Defence & Emergency Management.

Norris, F. H., M. J. Friedman, and P. J. Watson. 2002. "60,000 Disaster Victims Speak: Part II. Summary and Implications of the Disaster Mental Health Research." *Psychiatry* 65/3: 240–260.

Norris, F. H., M. J. Friedman, P. J. Watson, C. M. Byrne, E. Diaz, and K. Kaniasty. 2002. "60,000 Disaster Victims Speak: Part I. An Empirical Review of the Empirical Literature, 1981–2001." *Psychiatry* 65/3: 207–239.

North, C. S., L. Tivis, J. C. McMillen, B. Pfefferbaum, J. Cox, E. L. Spitznagel, K. Bunch, J. Schorr, and E. M. Smith. 2002. "Coping, Functioning, and Adjustment of Rescue Workers after the Oklahoma City Bombing." *Journal of Traumatic Stress* 15/3: 171–175.

Oxfam. 2008. Oxfam International Tsunami End of Program Report. Available at http://www.oxfam.org.uk/oxfam_in_action/emergencies/downloads/tsunami_four_year.pdf, last accessed October 26, 2010.

Peacock, Walter Gillis and Chris Girard. 2000. "Ethnic and Racial Inequalities in Hurricane Damage and Insurance Settlements." Pp. 171–190 in *Hurricane Andrew,* (W. Peacock, B. Morrow and H. Gladwin, eds.). Miami, FL: International Hurricane Center.

Phillips, Brenda D., Elizabeth Harris, Elizabeth A. Davis, Rebecca Hansen, Kelly Rouba, and Jessica Love. Forthcoming (2011). "Delivery of Behavioral Health Services in General and Functional Needs Shelters." In *Behavioral Health Response to Disasters,* (Martin Teasley, ed.). Boca Raton, FL: CRC Press.

Phillips, Brenda, Dave Neal, Tom Wikle, Aswin Subanthore, and Shireen Hyrapiet. 2008. "Mass Fatality Management after the Indian Ocean Tsunami." *Disaster Prevention and Management* 17/5: 681–697.

Prince-Embury, S., and J. F. Rooney. 1988. "Psychological Symptoms of Residents in the aftermath of the Three Mile Island Accident and Restart." *Journal of Social Psychology* 128/6: 779–790.

Quarantelli, E.L. 1982. *Sheltering and Housing after Major Community Disasters: Case Studies and General Observations.* Newark, DE: Disaster Research Center, University of Delaware.

Quarantelli, E.L. 1998. *The Disaster Recovery Process: What we Do and Do Not Know from Research.* Available at http://dspace.udel.edu:8080/dspace/handle/19716/309?mode=simple, last accessed January 28, 2011.

Quarantelli, E.L. 2003. *The Protection of Cultural Properties: the Neglected Social Science Perspective and Other Questions and Issues that ought to be Considered*. Newark, DE: University of Delaware, Disaster Research Center, Preliminary Paper #325.

Quarantelli, E.L. 1997. "Ten Criteria for Evaluating the Management of Community Disasters." *Disasters* 21/1: 39–56.

Scanlon, Joseph. 1999. "Emergent Groups in Established Frameworks: Ottawa Carleton's Response to the 1998 Ice Disaster." *Journal of Contingencies and Crisis Management* 7/1: 30–37.

Schwab, James., Ken. C. Topping, Charles. C. Eadie, R. E. Deyle, and R. A. Smith. 1998. *Planning for Post-disaster Recovery and Reconstruction*. Washington, D.C.: FEMA/ American Planning Association.

Smart Energy Design Assistance Center 2006. Fact Sheet 1. Available at www.sedac.org, last accessed January 28, 2011.

Sphere Project, The. 2004. *Minimum Standards in Shelter, Settlement and Non-Food Items*. Available at http://www.sphereproject.org/content/view/100/84/lang,English/, last accessed January 28, 2011.

Tierney, K. 1996. *Business Impacts of the Northridge Earthquake*. Newark, DE: University of Delaware Disaster Research Center.

Tierney, K., J. Nigg, and J. Dahlhamer. 1996. "The Impact of the 1993 Midwest Floods: business vulnerability and disruption in Des Moines." Pp. 214–233 in *Cities and Disaster: North American Studies in Emergency Management*, (Richard T. Sylves and William L. Waugh, eds.). Springfield, MA: Charles C. Thomas.

U.S. Agency for International Development. 2010. *Haiti Earthquake, Fact Sheet #3, Fiscal Year 2011*. Available at http://www.usaid.gov/our_work/humanitarian_assistance/ disaster_assistance/countries/haiti/template/fs_sr/fy2011/haiti_eq_fs03_10-15-2010.pdf, last accessed October 25, 2010.

Uphoff, N. 2000. "Understanding Social Capital: Learning from the Analysis and Experience of Participation." Pp. 215–250 in *Social Capital: A Multifaceted Perspective*, (P. D. a. I. Serageldon, ed.). Washington, D.C.: The World Bank.

Webb, G., K. Tierney, and J. Dahlhamer. 2000. "Businesses and Disasters: empirical patterns and unanswered questions." *Natural Hazards Review* 1/3: 83–90.

Woolcock, M. 2002. *Social Capital in Theory and Practice* 2000 [cited 2002]. Available from http://poverty.worldbank.org/library/view/12045/.

Zimmerman, Rae. 2003. "Public Infrastructure Service Flexibility for Response and Recovery in the Attacks at the World Trade Center, September 11, 2001." Pp. 241–267 in *Beyond September 11th: An Account of Post-Disaster Research*, (Jacquelyn L. Monday, ed.). Special Publication #39 Natural Hazards Research and Applications Information Center, University of Colorado: Boulder, CO.

Resources

- To view the Executive Order for Gulf Coast Restoration, visit http://www.whitehouse.gov/the-press-office/2010/10/05/executive-order-gulf-coast-ecosystem-restoration-task-force
- *Holistic Disaster Recovery*, available at www.colorado.edu/hazards/holistic_recovery
- National Disaster Housing Strategy (draft), http://www.fema.gov/good_guidance/download/10241

Chapter 10

Mitigation

10.1 Chapter Objectives

Upon completing this chapter, readers should be able to:

1. Understand the general ideas and purposes behind mitigation.
2. Know the types of structural mitigation actions that can be taken for various hazards.
3. Explain the advantages and disadvantages of structural mitigation.
4. List the different types of non-structural mitigation that can be undertaken to reduce hazard losses.
5. Discuss the advantages and disadvantages of non-structural mitigation.
6. Outline key steps that can be taken to conduct mitigation planning.
7. Identify job and volunteer opportunities in the field of mitigation.
8. Be sufficiently motivated to undertake mitigation steps in their own homes and workplaces.

10.2 Introduction

Mitigation means engaging in efforts that lessen the impact of disaster. Most of us see and even use aspects of mitigation during our everyday lives. For example, levees along rivers help prevent flooding. The use and enforcement of local codes help buildings withstand high winds or earthquakes. While mitigation is not the phase of disaster management that most people find exciting, it is the phase in the life cycle that can dramatically influence who lives and dies, which buildings survive, and the length and cost of recovery.

Most mitigation efforts can be placed into two different categories: structural mitigation and non-structural mitigation. Structural mitigation refers to physical changes to the built environment that lessen disaster impacts. Examples are building dams and levees to prevent flooding, hardening facilities to withstand the impact of a terrorist attack, and designing bridges to endure severe shaking. Non-structural mitigation efforts change human behavior about disasters. Examples of non-structural mitigation include public education programs focusing on tornado warnings, local land use planning that turns floodplains into parks rather than housing developments, and practicing good hygiene during cold and flu season. In this chapter, we learn about these examples and how communities engage in mitigation planning to reduce impacts. Much of this behind-the-scenes work pays off when disaster strikes and people are not harmed nor buildings destroyed.

Although always a part of the four phases of disaster, people often prefer to focus on issues of preparedness, response, or even recovery. However, mitigation efforts save lives and significantly reduce economic losses. Let's look at a few early examples in the U.S. In 1966, Presidential Executive Order 11296 required federal agencies to reduce floodplain development. Floodplains are areas where rivers and creeks may rise over their banks and inundate homes, businesses, and public facilities. By setting them aside or identifying means to reduce floodplain effects, people experience reduced risks. In the 1960s and 1970s, a variety of legislative acts addressed flood insurance, coastal management, and disaster relief as a means to reduce the costs of disasters (Godschalk et al. 1998). In 1980, FEMA created its first interagency hazard mitigation teams. As the 1980s progressed, FEMA partnered with various states on hazard mitigation projects, providing up to 50% of the costs.

In the 1990s, mitigation emerged as a key federal priority during the early years of the Clinton Administration. At that time, the U.S. government had a large debt and President Clinton made debt reduction a priority. He asked each cabinet member to find ways for reducing the deficit. James Lee Witt, the new director of FEMA, drew on his experience as a local disaster coordinator and state director of emergency management in Arkansas to make a recommendation to the president. Witt knew that mitigation efforts resulted in less money spent than the costs of a disaster response or recovery effort. Accordingly, Witt suggested that the federal government support local mitigation programs. Witt's efforts resulted in a number of related activities that gained support from most of the emergency management community.

Following the September 11, 2001 terrorist attacks, FEMA's focus changed back to preparedness and response issues. However, the mitigation imperative still exists within FEMA and provides important resources to communities attempting to minimize disasters including guidance for mitigation planning and funding hazard mitigation grants. We will look at these topics later in the chapter. First, we define and illustrate the two main kinds of mitigation initiatives: structural and non-structural measures.

10.3 Structural Mitigation

Structural mitigation centers on the built environment. Some structural mitigation measures prevent a hazard from rolling into a disaster. Examples include dams to hold back water, levees alongside waterways, hardening a facility by adding blast-resistant windows for tornadoes, and installing concrete barriers against intrusion. As seen in Figure 10.1, the Galveston (Texas) seawall stretches seven miles along the island shoreline. Reaching seventeen feet high, the wall affords some mitigation against storm surges. However, hurricanes, storm surges, and wind damage do not always respect such efforts as demonstrated when Hurricane Ike struck the area in 2008. But the event inspired additional mitigation efforts—a common result after a disaster. People and officials seem most motivated after a disaster occurs to prevent damage from happening again. Before a disaster, it can be very challenging to get the public excited about reduction of the effects. Those who pursue such efforts are often considered champions of uncelebrated causes (see Box 10.1; Meo, Ziebro, and Patton 2004).

FIGURE 10.1 Galveston Seawall built after the 1900 hurricane when nearly 8,000 residents died. (*Source:* FEMA News Photo/Bob McMillan.)

BOX 10.1   GILBERT F. WHITE, "FATHER OF FLOODPLAIN MANAGEMENT"

Gilbert White. (*Source:* University Communications, University of Colorado Boulder. With permission.)

Gilbert F. White, known worldwide as the "father of floodplain management," joined the University of Colorado (CU) Boulder faculty in 1970 as a professor of geography and director of the Institute of Behavioral Science where he remained active in academic work into his 90s. He founded CU's Natural Hazards Research and Applications Information Center, the nation's leading repository of knowledge on human behavior in disasters, in 1974. White's work in natural hazards changed the way people deal with nature and made the world safer to inhabit. "Floods are 'acts of God,' but flood losses are largely acts of man," he wrote in 1942 in his doctoral dissertation, which has since been called the most influential ever written by an American geographer.

Today planners tend to look at the landscape the way White did, considering a broad range of alternatives to cope with floods including land use planning, upstream watershed treatment, flood-proofing buildings, insurance, emergency evacuation, and dams and other structures.

White was born on November 26, 1911 in Hyde Park, Illinois and earned undergraduate and graduate degrees from the University of Chicago. He studied the Mississippi River Basin for the federal government as a graduate student in the late 1930s, when many planners followed a flood control policy based on the construction of dams. White questioned the impacts of such projects and suggested alternatives that protected people as well as floodplain ecosystems.

After leaving the federal government in the 1930s, White never again had to apply for a job, according to Robert E. Hinshaw, a former college president who wrote a biography of White. And he never again worked for the federal government although he could easily have held positions of global importance, according to Hinshaw.

"He has refused to let himself be drawn into a government position that would force him to use a more formal decision-making process" and his personal beliefs were behind that decision, said Hinshaw, who also chaired the CU Denver anthropology department from 1982 to 1984.

White chaired the American Friends Service Committee from 1963 to 1969 and his Quakerism is a vital part of his life, said Hinshaw, who also is a Quaker. White's leadership style is consistent with the Religious Society of Friends' traditional consensus-building process, he said. That leadership style was highly effective in White's efforts to deal with contentious water issues in the Middle East from 1996 to 1999, and also in leading a task force that led to the establishment of the National Flood Insurance Program. White made lasting contributions to the study of water systems in developing countries, global environmental change, international cooperation, nuclear winter, and geography education.

White served as the Gustavson Distinguished Professor Emeritus of Geography at CU Boulder and was a member of the National Academy of Sciences, the American Academy of Arts and Sciences, and the Russian Academy of Sciences. His numerous awards include the nation's highest scientific honor, the National Medal of Science, presented in 2000. Among White's numerous other honors are the National Geographic Society's highest award, the Hubbard Medal, the United Nations' Sasakawa International Environmental Prize, and the Association of American Geographers' Lifetime Achievement Award. He received an honorary doctorate from CU Boulder in May 2006.

"The world is a better place for having had Gilbert in its midst," said Jane Menken, director of the Institute of Behavioral Science and a distinguished professor of sociology. "Gilbert was that rare combination—a distinguished scientist and an outstanding humanitarian committed to translating scientific evidence into policy and programs to better people's lives. His was a life to celebrate."

"We will always remember Gilbert, not only as a man of science and humanity, but as the person who set IBS on its present course and whose leadership and friendship were always accompanied by wisdom and enlightenment," said Richard Jessor, a founder and former director of the Institute of Behavioral Science and a CU Boulder distinguished professor of behavioral science.

FEMA Director David Paulison and Federal Flood Insurance Administrator and FEMA Mitigation Director David Maurstad, concurred: "Mr. White was a pioneer in a field which protects people and their homes," said Director Paulison. "At a time when the mainstream thought was to build bigger and stronger flood control devices, Mr. White was investigating creative—and effective—methods that promoted safety, but not at the cost of damaging rivers and waterways. His legacy is a program that keeps people safe, protects the environment and makes smart investments in mitigation activities at all levels of government" (FEMA 2006, Release HQ-06-145).

More information about White is posted on the CU Boulder Natural Hazards Center's Web site (http://www.colorado.edu/hazards/gfw/). Additional news releases about White can be found at http://www.colorado.edu/news/tributes/white.

Source: Courtesy of University Communications, University of Colorado Boulder. With permission.

10.3.1 Planned Environment

The involvement of various offices in communities in mitigation-related work is therefore a good thing. Many communities, for example, require stormwater drainage planning, and you should be able to observe those efforts where you live. Nature always had plans for when and where rains will flow. From a systems theory perspective (see Chapter 2), people do not always respect what Mother Nature intended and build homes on beautiful coastlines, along recreational lakes and rivers, and on or near floodplains.

Stormwater drainage planning serves as an important step in designing a neighborhood or community. Water flows differently after a structure is built. To ensure that rainfall flows where it needs to go and is directed into drains that flow to waterways requires careful planning. Ideally, communities will respect areas of high rainfall that show propensities for flooding. However, flooding represents the top hazard in many nations including the U.S. and we have a long way to go to work with nature in this area.

Other examples of planned environments are physical structures such as dams and levees. The U.S. Army Corps of Engineers typically takes responsibility for creating major projects that increase safety from flooding. Across the nation, thousands of such structures—large, small, and even makeshift—exist. In many areas, local and state governments shoulder responsibility for dam and levee maintenance. Private citizens are accountable for structures on their lands. Dams and levees must be maintained over time to ensure safety and maintenance requires expertise and funding. In difficult economic times or in less affluent areas, this task may be difficult to impossible. Consequently, the state of our mitigation infrastructure requires attention. To illustrate, consider that the American Society of Civil Engineers (ASCE 2009) awarded D grades to our dams nationwide. ASCE defines high hazard dams as those with potential to cause considerable risk to life and property. Thousands of such locations exist across the U.S. according to the ASCE, and most of the responsibility for maintenance and repair lies at the state government level. ASCE estimates that billions of dollars annually are needed for repairs.

Hard choices are often required to put structural mitigation measures into place. The levee failure in New Orleans after Hurricane Katrina represents a measure that failed to protect, in large part because political and economic choices had to be made about how much could be spent on the levee protection system, where to place the structures, and how much to spend to maintain them. The pre-Katrina system provided protection from a Category 3 storm. Katrina pushed a Category 5 surge into the levee system even though winds had fallen to Category 3.

10.3.2 Elevations

Another example of a structural mitigation measure is an elevation (Figure 10.2). Raising homes and businesses above the level of a likely flood or hurricane-related storm surge may allow their occupants to return quickly after minimal damage from water. Without such a measure, they may face months to years away from homes and businesses before reconstruction occurs. Unfortunately, elevation levels are often determined (or recalculated) after an event when people have already sustained damage. By assessing flood levels, new codes can be put into place for rebuilt or newly built structures. Elevating them out of harm's way considerably reduces the economic impact even though relocation out of a flood-prone area is ideal. People have good reasons for staying where they live and work, as will be seen in an upcoming section. For them, elevation may serve as the single best option. The cost, though, may make elevation difficult to afford; without elevation residents will find it harder to return home.

By now, it should be clear that a structural mitigation such as elevation above flooded areas is a hazard-specific measure rather than all-hazards approach. As another example, consider the options for protecting people in tornado alley. Safe rooms, typically underground or in the interior of a structure, represent relatively affordable options for many people. For

FIGURE 10.2   Louisiana home elevated after Hurricane Rita. (*Source:* Courtesy of Mennonite Disaster Service. With permission.)

FIGURE 10.3   Tornado safe rooms require concrete walls and a special ceiling frame. (*Source:* FEMA News Photo/Kent Baxter.)

building an above-ground safe room, it is best to follow careful guidelines (see FEMA Publication 361; Figure 10.3) although going underground remains the best protection. For those unable to afford options, some communities are working with local, state, and federal funding to build congregate shelters (Figure 10.4).

FIGURE 10.4   Newcastle (Oklahoma) built a 7,200-foot facility with a FEMA grant. The structure provides congregate protection for 900 people. (*Source:* FEMA News Photo/Win Henderson.)

10.3.3 Building Codes

Many communities also enact building codes and require developers, builders, and homeowners to secure permits, undergo inspections, and comply with the codes. Such rules exist to increase public safety although builders and developers occasionally fight them because of the added cost of complying. In areas of hurricane threats, for example, hurricane clamps may be placed to decrease the potential for wind damage to or loss of a roof. When portions of a roof blow away, they become dangerous missiles that cause further damage. By installing relatively inexpensive clamps, we increase not only our own safety and recovery but that of others around us. Another option at the community level is to install utility lines underground to reduce damage from storms and ice although this step is not feasible in areas subject to flooding—the most common type of disaster in the U.S.

Despite the massive destruction and loss of life from flooding due to Katrina, it is evident that developing nations and impoverished areas fare far worse in comparable events. Following on the premise that disasters generate disproportionate and unequal effects, consider the earthquakes of 2010. The Haiti earthquake, measured as a 7.0 event was far less powerful than the 8.8 earthquake that rumbled through Chile. Approximately

800 people died in Chile while approximately 300,000 perished in Haiti. Considerable differences exist between the two nations; the main differ-ence is ability to afford and enforce mitigation. Population density in areas close to the quakes also made a difference. The Haiti earthquake struck a highly populated capitol city. Chile dedicated considerable resources and expertise to increasing infrastructure and building safety through careful design and strict building codes. Despite enduring one of the most powerful earthquakes ever recorded, Chile survived far better than Haiti. Questions remain about how nations such as Haiti will ever be able to enhance mitiga-tion for their population. Without external assistance it is likely that con-siderable risk will remain. An even more powerful question concerns where that help will come from. Failing to help nations like Haiti and even impov-erished areas in our own nation constitutes an inherent determination that some populations are expendable.

10.3.4 Retrofit

Obviously, many communities contain older structures that may not meet current building codes. In those cases, it may be possible to retrofit the dwellings, apartment buildings, or business locations. Retrofitting can vary from extensive overhauls involving highly engineered solutions to easily introduced, affordable, but not as powerful elements. Retrofitting may not be easy because of the need for installations within interior walls, floors, and ceilings; this is an expensive proposition.

An excellent example of a pre-disaster earthquake retrofit occurred at the University of California Berkeley. The university conducted a hazard assess-ment and loss estimation because of the very real probability of earthquake damage from the Hayward Fault (Comerio 2000). The assessment included examining soil maps, the potential for ground shaking, and the positions of various campus buildings. The team looked at how faculty and students used the buildings and when the peak numbers of occupants would be inside. They also considered occasional, rare, and very rare earthquake events. A rare event of a 7.0 magnitude (using the Richter scale then) would cause the university to disrupt normal schedules for two years. A very rare event of 7.5 magnitude would close the campus completely for a year, affecting 8,900 university and community jobs with associated losses of $680 million in personal income and $861 million in related sales. Staggering numbers and widespread potential losses!

Where would you start to mitigate such impacts? Berkeley determined that seventeen buildings represented about 75% of the university's exter-nally generated research funds. Because research funds keep universities economically sound and represent their missions, administrators deter-mined that a twenty-year timeline to retrofit buildings would be needed and set aside $1 billion for projects. The University of California Berkeley is not alone in facing threats. Hurricane Katrina prompted the Department of Homeland Security to provide $92 million for rebuilding the Southern University at New Orleans. FEMA allotted $26 million to the University of Southern Mississippi's Gulf Park campus. The choice is quite clear: pay now, or pay later. By paying pre-disaster mitigation costs, future and repetitive losses can be reduced.

10.3.5 Advantages of Structural Mitigation

The benefits of implementing structural mitigation measures should be obvious. In short, lives are saved. The costs of rebuilding homes, infrastructure, and buildings are lessened. People return home faster, commute to work, and continue to earn livelihoods. Insurance companies do not have to raise premiums to offset payments. The psychological impacts of injuries and grief from living in tents or temporary housing and trying to understand why an event even occurred diminish more quickly. Mitigation demonstrates resilience of the built environment, made possible through human choices, in a way that ensures returning to normal quickly.

Mitigation also means that we may be able to live where we want to, along those beautiful seashores and in pine-laden mountains. All areas where people live are subject to hazards and associated risks, making hazard adjustment through mitigation a smart thing to do. In areas of repetitive losses, structural mitigation measures are required or people will simply have to leave the area—which may actually be the best answer (see upcoming section on relocations).

Consider also, that structural mitigation measures have some side benefits. Have you enjoyed boating, fishing, or skiing on a lake created by a dam? Recreational opportunities abound in such locations and generate tourist income for the local economy too. Dams can also produce electricity. Large-scale hydroelectric dams provide enormous amounts of power for communities and smaller facilities can power specific industries. Such dams do not come without controversy, however, as some have been charged with causing damage to ecosystems, particularly riparian habitats with native flora and fauna. The advantages of structural mitigation are always offset by the disadvantages and hard choices must be made by those affected and those who serve the public.

10.3.6 Disadvantages of Structural Mitigation

Disadvantages accompany the clear benefits of mitigation. The most common critique concerns the high costs of structural mitigation. The costs to rebuild the New Orleans area levee system presently hover around $10 billion and are expected to exceed that amount. Even when the levees are considered fully rebuilt, they likely will not afford 100% protection from the same kind of storm as Katrina. Simply stated, decisions have to be made about levels of protection. Deciding that level initiates tension across communities and among those outside the area who fund projects through their tax dollars.

Choices to rebuild structural mitigation measures and at what level come with harsh realities that no single protection is perfect, even in an area as historic, culturally rich, and economically important as the major port city of New Orleans. Conversely, there will always be events whose effects exceed the designs of structural mitigation measures. Putting a levee into place for a 100-year flood event sounds good—until a 500-year event comes along. Making choices about mitigation means considering the risks faced and determining what is feasible. Few would want the task of leading such a daunting yet important effort.

Other consequences may result as well. People may place their faith in structural mitigation measures that could result in risking their lives. People stay in areas subject to flooding because levees or seawalls exist. Experienced homeowners and those unfamiliar with the area including tourists who do not know any better sometimes remain in areas at risk. Rather than evacuating before a massive tornado outbreak, homeowners huddle in hallways, believing the walls and roof will hold or that the twister will miss them. We also tend to put off mitigation measures because disasters are simply not forefront in our daily lives, and we assume we can get around to mitigation later. Box 10.2 presents guidance for what you can do now for hazard protection in your area.

10.3.7 Successful Structural Mitigation Efforts

Successful structural mitigation efforts reduce risks to lives, livelihoods, and structures but success may be hard to measure. Mitigation efforts put into place may take years or even decades to provide payoffs. The Nisqually earthquake of February 28, 2001 struck the Seattle, Washington area. The earthquake, measured at 6.8 magnitude on the Richter scale caused damage to twenty-two counties. About 40,000 people applied to the federal government for aid, and the government reported that 50% of property damage occurred when chimneys failed. Nonetheless, the earthquake stands as an example of how mitigation measures put into place years earlier paid off with less damage than anticipated. Realizing an earthquake could occur again and damage could be reduced even further, FEMA launched a mitigation hotline to provide information to homeowners on how to minimize future risks.

A non-profit organization called the Cascadia Region Earthquake Workgroup offered conferences and seminars for businesses. Among those responding to mitigate future risks were Starbucks and the Boeing

BOX 10.2 HOUSEHOLD CHECKLIST FOR MITIGATION ACTION

Personal responsibility for life safety and material possessions falls into your hands. To your best abilities possible, integrate these mitigation measures into your household:

1. Purchase insurance to offset losses even if you are a renter. Can you really afford to replace your car, furniture, computer, schoolbooks and clothing?
2. Know area hazards. What is the local history of those hazards?
3. Determine risk. What are the probabilities that you will face those hazards at some time? Low, medium or high? Contact your local emergency management agency for advice.
4. Develop a preparedness kit. See Chapter 6 for more detail on this.
5. Practice protective actions such as earthquake drills and fire escapes to deal with wildfires, tornadoes, and other disasters.
6. Place copies of valuable documents, photos, and medical histories in secure locations outside your home.
7. Initiate hazard-specific mitigation. A sampling of what you can find do is listed below.

Earthquake Mitigation

- Establish a preparedness kit specific to your needs that includes water, food, and medications for at least three days.
- Know how to shut off utilities in your home. Keep appropriate tools to do so on hand.
- Brace furniture with brackets to reduce the possibility it will fall over and injure someone.
- Relocate hanging plants, large pictures, and frames that can cause injuries.
- Install latches on cupboard doors to prevent contents from falling out.
- Secure breakable items, especially those on higher shelves.
- Support family members with disabilities in their mitigation measures to ensure their safety as well.

Flood Mitigation

- Elevate your home if feasible.
- Do not build, buy, or rent in or near a floodplain.
- Elevate the furnace, heater, air conditioner, generator, electrical outlets, and other valuable home elements that may easily be damaged in a flood.
- Seal basement walls.
- Look around your home. Based on local history of flooding events, what could be the highest possible height of flood waters in your home? What items below that line can you not bear to lose or

replace? Purchase insurance or move irreplaceable items to a safer location.

Wildfire Mitigation

- Establish a safe perimeter around your home. Maintain at least a three-foot space between the side of your home and landscaping. More space is even better. Tear down vines that can catch fire near your home or roof.
- Remove dead branches, leaves, shrubs, and other vegetation that can easily catch fire. Ensure that branches are at least fifteen feet away from chimneys.
- Keep your lawn no higher than two inches.
- Eliminate landscaping that is highly combustible. Check with area experts to determine which vegetation is a local fire concern.
- Keep firewood at least 100 feet away from your house.
- Stay alert for wildfire and no-burn ban messages. Wildfire conditions can cause unexpected ignitions that spread rapidly.
- Be prepared to evacuate when told to do so.
- Prepare family members, pets, and livestock for rapid evacuation.

These suggestions represent a distillation of advice from various sites. They should be considered minimum steps in the right direction. Additional research and action on your part is advised. Information can be found at the websites listed here and throughout the text. Many checklists and guidance brochures are available at www.fema.gov, www.ready.gov, www.redcross.org, and other reputable sites.

Corporation. Prior to the earthquake, most businesses engaged in general all-hazards mitigation, particularly non-structural efforts as described next. Post-earthquake, businesses increased some mitigation measures. They were more likely to do so if they took mitigation steps before the earthquake and remained worried after the event (Meszaros and Fiegener 2004).

Disasters prompt public attention and wise emergency managers use that time period to enhance mitigation efforts. After a series of tornadoes tore destructive paths across Oklahoma in 1999 and killed forty-four people, the federal and state governments launched initiatives to install interior or underground safe rooms. With grants available up to $2,000, homeowners moved quickly to build the safety features. Newly built homes with safe rooms sold rapidly. Funded through the federal Hazard Mitigation Grant Program, the result was one of the most successful intergovernmental mitigation partnerships in history. To this day, the state continues its efforts to encourage residents and builders to install tornado safe rooms (http://www.eeri.org/mitigation/files/resources-for-success/00089.pdf).

10.4 Non-Structural Mitigation

Non-structural mitigation also lessens disaster impacts. To define non-structural mitigation, think of actions people can take to reduce the impacts of area hazards. In most cases, changing behavior toward hazards can be less expensive and more effective than structural mitigation. One example of non-structural mitigation is to prevent building homes in a 100-year floodplain by setting aside that property for open space or parkland. When parkland floods, the water does not damage homes and residents suffer no deaths, injuries, or economic losses. Activities such as softball or soccer may be cancelled and may have to wait until the fields dry out. Non-structural mitigation thus involves making choices about how and where we build, how we manage land, and how we reduce potential losses via personal and collective actions. Although the line between structural and non-structural mitigation often blurs, it is important to note that both types of efforts play integral roles in risk reduction.

10.4.1 Land Use Planning

Land use planning is a future-oriented activity representing a proactive behavior rather than an action that results from a disaster impact (Godschalk, Kaiser, and Berke 1998). Land use planning typically involves two specific elements: location and design (Burby 1998). A first step is to limit building in hazardous locations. A second step determines the best design of a structure. For example, even if you disallow building in or near floodplains, homes may still be subjected to severe storms and high winds. A structure's ability to resist damage is critical.

While land use planning makes sense in terms of disaster risks, it has not always been supported by public officials and developers. A city council member may "get into a bind" trying to determine whom to support: city planners, developers wanting to invest in the community, or their constituents who may want to live in a desirable but hazardous location. In contrast, experts suggest that we think through the concept of creating sustainable communities "where people and property are kept out of the way of natural hazards, where the inherently mitigating qualities of natural environmental systems are maintained, and where development is designed to be resilient in the face of natural forces" (Godschalk et al. 1998b, p. 86). As we will see in an upcoming section on mitigation planning, creating a sustainable community with reduced risks from disasters requires not only assessment of risks alongside technical expertise but—importantly—community participation.

An imperative first step is to connect mitigation planning with land use planning. Often, the two efforts operate separately. Imagine, for example, a land use planning team designating an area for development when a mitigation planning team determines it should remain as open space to divert stormwater runoff. A related problem that disconnects the two is that mitigation planning often happens once with periodic (if ever) updates to the plan. Land use planning typically occurs in five- to ten-year cycles. The lack of overlap between them sometimes means that two very important partners are not always at the same table.

10.4.2 Building Codes and Enforcement

Earlier, we learned about the value of building codes that establish requirements for the built environment. Writing and enforcing the codes falls under the category of non-structural mitigation because those tasks require human involvement in making decisions and following through to ensure that builders and developers meet new code requirements. Code development and enforcement are usually conducted by city planning offices and code inspectors with influences from residents, builders, and city officials. City planners take on existing and new building construction, hoping to design a built environment that is culturally meaningful, environmentally sound, pleasing to residents, and acceptable visually.

Their work is certainly enjoyable as it allows for creativity as well as actions to serve the public. But their work can also be contentious as they try to find a common ground among what builders, developers, homeowners, and public officials think best, economical, and desirable. In recent years, for example, high pitched roofs have been popular, yet the pitch can determine whether a tornado takes the roof off or not. Flat or low pitched roofs face collapse from heavy snowfalls. Similarly, cedar shingle roofs were popular but represent significant threats during wildfires. Telling people they cannot make the choices they want to make or are considered aesthetically desirable can be challenging. Nonetheless, those who enforce codes clearly involve themselves in public safety.

Enforcing the codes serves as another example of the work in a public office. The degree to which the enforcement is maintained has been questionable in some areas. After Hurricane Andrew tore off roofs across southeast Florida in 1992, it was clear that codes did not account adequately for wind speeds (Ayscue 1996). To their chagrin, public officials watched as television crews filmed inside homes where nails clearly failed to attach the roofs to rafters—a problem inspectors should have caught during construction. Allegations of bribery and corruption abounded. Andrew claimed the lives of forty-one people and damaged 117,000 homes (90% within Dade County which includes the city of Miami; see Ayscue 1996). Stronger building codes (structural mitigation) coupled with code enforcement (non-structural mitigation) through inspections during construction could have made a difference.

After a disaster, people take greater interest in new codes as planners, engineers, and architects look for ways to mitigate future damages. Most communities take advantage of the moment to write new codes and enforcement typically increases. Additional challenges emerge as people want to rebuild and return home and may not be able to do so quickly. After an earthquake struck Santa Cruz, California in 1989, people who wanted to rebuild on nearby hillsides were denied permits because of a drought. Based on the earthquake and drought, it was unclear whether homes could be rebuilt safely on the hills. Similarly, some areas along the U.S. Gulf Coast have experienced slow rebuilding after the 2005 hurricanes. Costs to elevate homes, particularly in low-income areas, burdened families beyond their abilities to recover. Because many of these areas are home to indigenous populations who work in the fishing industries, real threats to their continued ability to remain in places with historic and economic value have emerged. New codes may displace others too. Some communities have chosen to disallow mobile home parks after a tornado due to widespread destruction. Although the effort to ensure safer housing is laudable, concern remains over the availability of affordable housing. Most students understand this conundrum: you want to live in a safe place but you still have to pay the rent. When decisions to build safer housing are made, it is also necessary to ensure that people do not lose their homes. The reality is that affordable housing may not be rebuilt.

10.4.3 Public Education

How frequently do you wash your hands every day? Such a simple act can significantly reduce your risk of catching a cold or the flu—and greatly diminishes your chances of spreading germs. Think about it. How many surfaces have you touched today? How many doorknobs and banisters? How many hands have you touched. How many people have you hugged? Have you exchanged money to buy coffee today? Each exchange transmits bacteria that can cause illness. Unless you have a week or two to spare during this academic term, maybe you should wash your hands and use an alcohol-based hand gel (see Box 10.3). And just so you are up to date, be aware that sneezing or coughing into your elbow is the recommended protocol rather than into your hands!

Many local and state governments launch hazard awareness events designed to catch your attention. Hopefully you have increased your awareness of personal hygiene needs by this point but how aware are you of exactly what to do and where to go should events warrant? Have you signed up for message services via your cellular devices or social media? How much attention do you pay when readiness messages come on television, through social media, or across your email? Communicating risk to the public and expecting

BOX 10.3   HOW DO YOU WASH YOUR HANDS?

When should you wash your hands?

- Before, during, and after preparing food
- Before eating food
- After using the toilet
- After changing diapers or cleaning up a child who has used the toilet
- Before and after caring for someone who is sick
- After blowing your nose, coughing, or sneezing
- After touching an animal or animal waste
- After touching garbage
- Before and after treating a cut or wound

What is the right way to wash your hands?

- Wet your hands with clean running water (warm or cold) and apply soap.
- Rub your hands together to make a lather and scrub them well; be sure to scrub the backs of your hands, between your fingers, and under your nails.
- Continue rubbing your hands for at least twenty seconds. Need a timer? Hum the "Happy Birthday" song from beginning to end twice.
- Rinse your hands well under running water.
- Dry your hands using a clean towel or air dry.

Washing hands with soap and water is the best way to reduce the number of germs they carry. If soap and water are not available, use an alcohol-based hand sanitizer that contains at least 60% alcohol. Alcohol-based hand sanitizers can quickly reduce the number of germs on hands in some situations, but they do not eliminate all types of germs. **Hand sanitizers are not effective when hands are visibly dirty.**

How should you use hand sanitizer?

- Apply the product to the palm of one hand.
- Rub your hands together.
- Rub the product over all surfaces of your hands and fingers until your hands are dry.

For more information on hand washing, visit CDC's Handwashing: Clean Hands Save Lives Website. You can also call 1-800-CDC-INFO or email cdcinfo@cdc.gov for answers to specific questions.

Source: Centers for Disease Control. http://www.cdc.gov/Features/HandWashing/ (a related video is available at the site).

them to take the recommended actions can be challenging. Because of the diversity within any community, sending messages can be time-consuming but ultimately rewarding. No one should die or be injured because he or she does not speak the local language or understand written communications.

The most effective way to transmit public education involves spreading accurate information through trusted networks. Using local organizations, faith-based locations, schools, and other facilities can increase the chance that people will pay attention because the information comes from places they frequent and from people they know. Placing information into the daily lives of people through the technologies they use and the places they visit also increases the chances of reaching the target populations. Design public education efforts to be transmitted through senior centers, for example, and ensure that messages are spread via television, radio, and Internet channels they prefer. Be aware that abilities to hear and interpret information vary greatly so public education efforts must reach a wide range of literacy levels and span languages present in a given community (Morrow 2010). It is not enough to give someone a brochure. By involving family, friends, neighbors, and others in sharing and reviewing brochure information you can increase understanding and retention. As the massive blizzard of February 2011 began its race eastward across thirty U.S. states, local emergency managers in Oklahoma used call-down lists to warn people to stay off the roads. Their plea stated that if people stayed home, first responders would be safe too. Appealing to people's altruistic nature to aid others can motivate them to heed public education messages.

10.4.4 Relocations

When repetitive losses continue to pile up, one option is to relocate permanently all affected residents and businesses. Relocations offer both advantages and disadvantages. Clearly, one advantage is that people no longer lose their homes or livelihoods to disaster. Another edge is that relocation reduces future costs for governments and insurance providers. Indirectly, we may all benefit because insurance rates do not increase. The disadvantages can be significant though. Would *you* like to move permanently away from neighbors and friends? The loss of social networks can be disruptive personally, especially after a disaster. Often, people's homes are tied to jobs such as farming and fishing locations. Places also represent cultural, environmental, and historical values. Where we grew up and choose to live often situates us in places that designate who we are and what we value. Giving up such places is not so easy.

Relocation may not be financially feasible either. Moving to a new location means that a family loses a significant economic investment. In cases of repetitive losses where people need assistance to relocate, government agencies may offer what is called a buyout. People who accept buyout assistance agree to take fair market value for their properties and move outside the hazardous area. The federal government offers up to 75% of the costs of a buyout with the remainder funded by state and local governments. The community makes a decision to offer a buyout program and then retains the properties for use as parklands or other open spaces.

Relocating businesses can be challenging too as funding may need to come from multiple sources. Public facilities that must be relocated can use government funding from multiple sources by applying to multiple agencies, but private firms must pay their own costs. The small community of Soldier's Grove, Wisconsin relocated. The cost of levees to reduce repetitive funding was estimated at $3.5 million in the 1970s and $10,000 annual maintenance fees were imposed. The costs were prohibitive for the town of 600 residents. The community approached government with a plan to relocate and began to do so in the late 1970s at a cost of $6 million. A flood in 2007 caused only minor damage in parks and campgrounds, saving businesses and homes (FEMA 2010c). Increasingly in the U.S., local governments must complete their mitigation planning to qualify for federal assistance. In locations where relocation is not feasible, other options can protect farmland, livestock, and family businesses (see Box 10.4). In short, efforts must be taken to move people, animals, and jobs out of harm's way.

10.4.5 Insurance

Do you have personal insurance for your car and home? Non-structural mitigation measures such as insurance provide a means to rebound from disasters. Carrying personal insurance, even if you are a renter, allows you to replace a computer, clothing, and furniture. Renter's insurance can be surprisingly inexpensive. While you may not want to pay even a small amount on a limited budget, contrasting your potential losses with the monthly premium may put this inexpensive mitigation measure into perspective.

You should take the time to visit with an insurance provider to determine your need for coverage including any limitations. Many insurance policies do not cover flooding or wind damage. To make up for this, the U.S. government offers the National Flood Insurance Program. Private insurance companies sell and service the policies that cost about $500 annually. The program insures homes up to $250,000 and covers contents up to $100,000. A number of conditions must be in place. For example, communities that offer the insurance must adopt and enforce ordinances that prohibit building on floodplains. You will also have to pay a deductible before your insurance

BOX 10.4   TO RELOCATE OR NOT TO RELOCATE?

Relocation: Medical Clinic Moved From Danger

North Dakota's historic 1997 Red River Valley flood nearly spelled doom for one small-town medical clinic. Inside the building, flood waters rose to six inches. A thick layer of mud covered the floor and mold had begun to grow. Despite efforts to clean and disinfect the building, the medical staff thought the health risk for patients was too high to treat them inside the building. Instead, the staff treated patients in their cars.

Floods are a regular occurrence in Drayton, a small city with a population of 900. It faces a flood threat practically every year. The clinic building, which also housed a local dentist, was at risk to flood again and again, even though it sat thirty-five feet above the normal river level. The river last reached the clinic's crawl space in the spring of 1999. It was the tenth recorded flood since 1980 alone.

To make matters worse, the riverbank had become increasingly unstable due to erosion from repetitive flooding. Because of this, there was not enough stability behind the clinic to build an emergency dike. Some thought it was only a matter of time before the weight of the building would cause the ground to collapse, sending the clinic tumbling toward the river. Residents and city officials felt something had to be done. The city's hospital closed in 1975, and the clinic was the only local medical facility available to residents. They knew they needed money to pay for a new building that was better protected from flooding. Through a public–private partnership, they received everything they asked for.

A financial package that included a grant from the U.S. Department of Housing and Urban Development Administration, proceeds from the National Flood Insurance Program, and donations from local organizations led to the purchase and remodeling of another building on the edge of town. Since July 1999, the clinic has been operating from a larger, newly remodeled facility about a half mile from the structure's original location on Main Street. Due to the recent disaster-resistant measures, the chances of the facility being damaged again are greatly reduced. It is also likely the clinic can remain open for patient care, even if flooding threatens other areas of the city.

Source: FEMA.

Not to Relocate, but to Still Protect

When flood impacts a farm community, there are many challenges and complications. Not only must residents get themselves out of harm's way, but they also must protect their livestock, secure farm equipment and supplies, and deal with many other issues. Jason Roetcisoender's family has owned their 120-acre farm in Duvall, Washington since the 1920s. Throughout that time, there have been numerous floods that have impacted their home and property. In a flood in 1975, while the farm was run by Jason's father, they lost thirty-two cows. In Duvall's flood-of-record in 1990, the family lost 120 animals to high water.

"After the flood in 1990, Washington State and King County approved emergency permitting for the installation of critter pads," said Mr. Roetcisoender. "The local farmers, including my father, went to them to try to find a solution to the flooding, and that was one of the remedies they came up with." A critter pad, or livestock flood sanctuary mound, is an area where approved fill material is used to raise the ground above the Base Flood Elevation (BFE). When flooding occurs, farmers move their livestock onto the pads to keep the animals out of the water's reach. Critter pads require special permitting and must be specifically designed to ensure they have a negligible impact on the floodplain. They also may not be built within the boundaries of a river's floodway. Since the Roetcisoenders completed their critter pad in 1991, they have had to use it on three occasions, including the November flood of 2006. In that incident, Mr. Roetcisoender was able to move over 300 head of cattle onto the pad and keep them safe. They also filled two of the family's trucks with feed and drove them up onto the pad to be safe and easily accessible.

In the nearby Town of Carnation, Michelle Blakely has a thirty-three-acre farm where she grows organic vegetables and fruits, and raises chickens, cows, pigs, and turkeys. When the Blakelys purchased the farm two years ago, a critter pad was already in place, built by the previous owner. According to Mrs. Blakely, the pad was part of the incentive to acquire the land. Unfortunately, in 2006, when the waters rose during the November flood, despite being above the BFE, the pad was not high enough. Upon returning to their home following a mandatory evacuation, the Blakelys found that all their chickens and turkeys were gone. The Blakelys suffered significant financial damage to their farm from the 2006 flood, a good portion of it in poultry losses. Not wanting to go through this again, they decided to raise the critter pad even higher. They purchased permitted fill, rented a bulldozer, and raised the pad almost three feet.

When the floodwaters came again in December of 2007, the Blakelys felt they were ready. Working fast, the Blakelys managed to relocate their birds from coops on different areas of their property to the elevated pad, even as rising waters surrounded them. If the chickens and turkeys had not been moved to the critter pad, they would have been lost. This time, the Blakelys managed to save almost 1,500 birds from floodwaters.

Sources: FEMA. 2010a. Medical Clinic Moved from Danger. http://www.fema.gov/mitigationbp/brief.do?mitssId=1565; FEMA. 2010b. Moo'ving on Up. http://www.fema.gov/mitigationbp/briefPdfReport.do?mitssId=5446

covers any losses. If appropriate insurance is in place, people who face the possibility of flooding can stay in homes likely to be close to where they earn their livelihoods. Moving out of harm's way is not always economically possible, so insurance can mitigate potential economic losses (for more information, visit www.floodsmart.gov).

10.4.6 Advantages of Non-Structural Mitigation

Advantages of non-structural mitigation include options that are less costly than structural measures. Educational programs can range from public talks to more expensive public awareness campaigns. By reaching out to those at risk, public officials empower individuals to take responsibility for their own safety. Outreach also links public officials to public behavior that can have a significant impact. In the case of pandemic planning, for example, educating the public to engage in healthy behaviors as simple as washing hands can stem a potential outbreak. Targeting those most likely to become ill such as seniors or expectant mothers can save lives.

While non-structural mitigation measures usually require some investment, such as for insurance, the payoffs can be enormous. You will be able to rebuild and replace furniture, clothing, and computers. Setting aside land for green space or parks serves the public good and enhances quality of life for all. Because structural elements are so costly to install and maintain, non-structural measures represent affordable options for many individuals and communities.

10.4.7 Disadvantages of Non-Structural Mitigation

If you are among the few who hear public advice about washing your hands and sneezing into your elbow, then disregard that information, you can understand the disadvantages of non-structural mitigation. People and businesses have to take responsibility for the mitigation information they receive and their failures to do so.

Another problem with non-structural mitigation may be that an individual may not be able to afford insurance. For low income families, insurance costs can be prohibitive. It is not unusual to discover the cheapest insurance fails to cover specific hazards like wind and flooding. Or certain aspects of reconstruction such as debris removal and installation of a concrete foundation slab are not covered. Smaller businesses also have trouble affording non-structural mitigation measures. Finally, those seeking adoption and support for non-structural mitigation projects have to secure public attention and commitment. Mitigation is often not on the public mind until well after a disaster strikes.

10.4.8 Successful Non-Structural Mitigation Projects

As noted earlier in this chapter, former FEMA Director James Lee Witt initiated several related projects to promote mitigation with an emphasis on non-structural techniques. One was named *Project Impact* that partnered government guidance with local stakeholder involvement. Designed as a grass-roots mitigation project, the steps included:

- Find and involve a range of community partners such as those in government and from community groups as well as business leaders and local citizens.
- Assess area hazards and the risks they may pose.
- Establish action steps that need to be taken in priority order and set aside or secure resources.
- Educate the public about the projects and their potential to offset future losses.

In a study of Project Impact for FEMA, researchers at the University of Delaware's Disaster Research Center examined seven pilot communities. Through in-person interviews, they assessed how the project handled risk and hazard assessments, mitigation efforts, partnerships, and public education activities (Wachtendorf et al. 2002). After three years of activity, they determined that the pilot communities pursued both structural and non-structural activities. To accomplish risk assessment, they conducted vulnerability analyses, inventoried resources, and assessed capabilities.

Partnerships also generated a wide range of public education efforts such as disaster fairs. Even costly structural mitigation efforts including retrofits were included in their initiatives. The communities also experienced success in recruiting business partnerships that represented half of the partners among the seven communities. Participation from local governments steadily increased throughout the three-year study period. The communities involved also faced uphill struggles to retain their partnerships when turnover occurred among key personnel and funding initiatives. Overall, Project Impact may have had its biggest impact by empowering local people to assess their risks and work together to reduce losses (Wachtendorf et al. 2002). As noted earlier, Project Impact disappeared after September 11, 2001 as the emergency management pendulum swung back from mitigation to response.

A more recent FEMA effort involved a number of institutions in its Disaster-Resistant Universities (DRU) initiative (FEMA 2003, see Box 10.5). As the example from the University of California Berkeley illustrated earlier, universities and colleges represent considerable economic investments and opportunities. They generate more than tuition dollars, as faculty and staff seek external funding for basic and applied research projects. Their grants fund research and pay for student assistants, laboratories, research centers, support staff, and even utilities, computers, library resources, and more. The money that universities expend for their work supports the broader community as people pay rent and mortgages, buy gas and groceries, and enjoy local recreational opportunities with their salaries.

BOX 10.5   BUILDING DISASTER-RESILIENT UNIVERSITIES

Monica Teets Farris

Monica Teets Farris is the acting director of the Center for Hazards Assessment, Response and Technology (CHART) at the University of New Orleans. She is a leader among those working on disaster reduction and resiliency in the university setting.

Dean of Liberal Arts, University of New Orleans. (*Source:* Photo courtesy of Monica Teets Farris. With permission.)

Anthony Russell, FEMA Region VI Director. (*Source:* Photo courtesy of Monica Teets Farris. With permission.)

Like all communities, university and college campuses are vulnerable to disasters. Over the past decades, university communities have been significantly impacted by both natural and man-made disasters. From hurricanes to acts of violence, students, faculty and staff, campus facilities, and research assets have been harmed. In August 2005, the campus of Dillard University in New Orleans, Louisiana was inundated with up to ten feet of flood waters due to Hurricane Katrina. On April 16, 2007, a Virginia Tech student shot twenty-one fellow students on campus resulting in the deadliest campus shooting in U.S. history.

Also like other communities, universities must do what they can to protect their citizens and critical assets. In the fall of 2000, FEMA launched a pilot program to assist institutions of higher learning in addressing vulnerabilities to natural disasters and mitigating the potential impacts. Similar to FEMA's Project Impact: Building Disaster Resistant Communities, the Disaster-Resistant University (DRU) program provided funds to enable universities to create mitigation programs that would include planning and project development.

In addition to providing funding, FEMA, with the assistance of six universities including Tulane University, University of Alaska Fairbanks, University of California Berkeley, University of Miami, University of North Carolina Wilmington, and University of Washington developed a program guidebook. *Building a Disaster-Resistant University* was published in August 2003 and is available on FEMA's website (http://www.fema.gov/institution/dru.shtm). This guidebook provides helpful information on the steps necessary to create a mitigation plan. These steps include the organization of resources, hazard identification and risk assessment, development of the planning document, and adoption and implementation of the plan.

Although the DRU project is no longer funded by FEMA, the concept remains. Universities and colleges may still apply for mitigation planning and project funds through FEMA's Hazard Mitigation Assistance grants. The University of New Orleans (UNO), supported by its Center for Hazards Assessment, Response and Technology (UNO-CHART), began its DRU program with a FEMA grant that funded the development of a hazard mitigation plan for its main campus. The plan, approved by FEMA in 2006, includes hazard profiles, a risk assessment, and a list of mitigation action items that include structural and non-structural projects (retrofits for wind and flood hazards, education and outreach. The goal of this planning effort is to reduce or eliminate potential impacts of natural and man-made hazards to which UNO is vulnerable. Moreover, this plan makes UNO eligible to apply for additional FEMA hazard mitigation funds. Since 2005, UNO has applied for and has been awarded additional FEMA funding to include satellite locations in its mitigation planning efforts and to begin scoping potential mitigation projects for its campuses. Most recently, FEMA, through the Louisiana Governor's Office of Homeland Security and Emergency Preparedness, awarded UNO a grant that allowed it to host a DRU workshop on its campus in February 2011. Over 100 people representing universities across the country attended.

In addition to funding, the DRU concept also endures through the continued development of a DRU community that shares information daily on the DRU listserv. Universities across the country and internationally rely on the listserv for information about all phases of emergency management including preparedness, response, recovery, and mitigation. The DRU listserv and archive, hosted and maintained by the University of Oregon Emergency Management Program, began in January 2005. Since then, university faculty, staff, and students have been able to share information on a variety of topics including planning, continuity of operations, mental health, pandemics, emergency communications equipment, and guidance on developing and implementing campus emergency exercises. The DRU Repository for housing documents shared by the DRU community is now hosted by the University of California Davis.

Disaster impacts on a university can be significant, causing disruption to student education, salaries of employees, and research projects that are conducted twenty-four hours, seven days a week in laboratories. Damage caused by earthquakes, hurricanes, flooding, and other events can result in enormous losses. Think also about the possible impacts of terrorism at a major sporting event or an explosion at a campus laboratory.

Mitigation measures to reduce the effects on universities and colleges start with a familiar series of steps. The first is organization by convening a planning group to work through the mitigation planning process. Second, that group should identify hazards and assess risks to structures and human life on their campus. A third step involves prioritizing areas for action with the understanding that (like Berkeley) not all desired actions are affordable. The final step leads to adopting and implementing mitigation measures.

Activities that may be familiar to you likely include text and email emergency messaging services (be sure your information is current for your system!). Less visible but equally important, your university probably has plans for evacuating people should a tornado approach during the football game or a bomb threat develop. Laboratories probably have installed shelving to prevent glass vials from shifting in an earthquake and trained staff on emergency procedures. Laboratories also install safety features such as eye protection and showers. Hopefully your campus has designated safe locations for inclement weather and clearly indicates them by visible signage and website content. Look around as you walk from class to class this week and see what you can spot.

10.5 Mitigation Planning

As noted throughout this chapter, mitigation takes a back seat to the other disaster phases. This is especially true in countries and locations that lack effective leadership, political will, and economic resources for mitigation. Several exceptions do exist. The U.S. Disaster Mitigation Act of 2000 (Public Law 106-390) set out new programs and requirements for mitigation work. The Hazard Mitigation Grant Program (HMGP) for example makes funding available in a post-disaster period. However, an HMGP grant requires that a community has a mitigation plan in place. The program thus rewards pre-disaster planning and promotes sustainability by empowering communities to identify their risks and prioritize solutions.

The mitigation plan approval process and allocation of HMGP funds also encourages local communities, states, and federal partners to cooperate and coordinate. By having a plan in place prior to disaster, people know what they can do afterward. They know the risky areas, have pre-identified solutions, and work together to design an effective, prioritized plan. Planning allows a community to take the time needed to think through the problems disasters present and be ready. Many solutions can be implemented before a disaster as well as afterward (FEMA #1, see Resources section).

After a disaster, a great deal of activity occurs to complete response actions and initiate recovery efforts. Recovery also offers a good time to raise mitigation concerns with residents and public officials. People can still see and are still dealing with the effects of an impact and are open to change.

10.5.1 First Steps in Mitigation Planning

Engaging in mitigation planning acknowledges that the public may not understand the importance of the actions. The public may not have a good memory if no 100-year flood event occurred in recent decades. Understandably, if a disaster falls outside collective memory, apathy may be the public response. Politicians may have other priorities besides mitigation as well, and feel they need to address economic, education, and other routine but pressing issues. The first step then is to inspire the public to become involved in and support mitigation planning. Public laws such as the Disaster Mitigation Act in the U.S. may inspire planning efforts. A community may work through an appointed committee with representatives from various sectors. Regardless of organizational details, mitigation planning must occur at the local level and reflect local hazards and risks.

Planning must involve an array of partners that represents all sectors: education (grade school through university levels), businesses of all sizes, utilities, recreational and tourist facilities, government, and residential sectors. Planners must consider and involve individuals in neighborhoods who are most vulnerable: women, racial and ethnic minorities, seniors living alone or in assisted living facilities, people with disabilities, and others at risk. Living in a trailer park should not keep you away from the planning table. Such homes are highly vulnerable to flooding and severe weather and thus their residents should participate in planning. No one should be excluded and efforts must be made to include people in meetings that are accessible and offer appropriate language and literacy levels (National Council on Disability 2009; Morrow 2010).

Planning should also reflect community culture. Perhaps your community has a history of appointing formal committees to accomplish public tasks. Or maybe you live in an area in which Native American residents rely on talking circles (Picou 2000). Honoring the local way of meeting and connecting leverages a community's existing social networks and knowledge bases and makes people feel more welcome at the planning table. By respecting what people value locally, we generate more interest in their participation in mitigation along with their personal, economic, and political support (see Box 10.6)

In California, three separate jurisdictions (the Berkeley Unified School District, the city of Berkeley, and the University of California Berkeley) worked together to reduce risk. The effort became possible through individuals who assumed the leadership and responsibility to make it happen (Chakos, Schulz, and Tobin 2002). As if earthquake threats were not enough, the area also suffered from a wildfire in the nearby urban area of Oakland, home to many who work in Berkeley. The three institutions created a task force and enacted special tax assessments to fund mitigation work. Berkeley also benefited from a community that believed truly in participatory democracy; people attend and join in actively when public debate emerges over various issues. With stakeholder involvement, Berkeley voted $390 million for mitigation projects. Beyond the public work approved, the community also worked to address risk in small businesses and residences by "developing appropriate seismic standards, finding affordable solutions, and providing new incentives for retrofit" although this effort has been challenging.

Why has Berkeley been so successful in tackling mitigation when other communities languish in that area? Political persistence paid off: "the impetus for change came from a handful of champions who tirelessly kept the issues in front of political leaders and the public, and who unashamedly lobbied at the local, state, and national level for information and resources" (Chakos et al. 2002, p. 64).

10.5.2 Hazard Mitigation Planning Process

FEMA provides an extensive set of mitigation planning resources (http://www.fema.gov/plan/mitplanning/index.shtm; see Resources section). The planning process involves several basic steps: (1) organize resources, (2) assess risks, (3) develop a mitigation plan, and (4) implement the plan. It sounds straightforward, but a plan can take time, even years to complete and require even more time to secure financial resources for implementation.

BOX 10.6   MITIGATION BEST PRACTICES

Ann Patton

Ann Patton of Tulsa, Oklahoma, specializes in disaster management, urban affairs, and grassroots partnership building. Mrs. Patton spearheaded the team that created Tulsa's award-winning flood hazard mitigation program that served as a national model for FEMA's Project Impact. FEMA awarded Mrs. Patton its top national public services award in 1998 and named Tulsa a national mentoring community in 2000. In 2004, the Oklahoma Floodplain Managers Association gave her its lifetime achievement award; Tulsa Partners gave her its J. D. Metcalfe Building Bridges Award for community service; and the City of Tulsa named an open-space floodplain park "Ann Patton Commons" in her honor. (***Source:*** Photo courtesy of Ann Patton. With permission.)

When a tornado wrecked a hundred homes in Cordell, Oklahoma, the Day Care Depot took a direct hit. The center windows blew in, and boards and debris blasted through walls and the roof. Inside, sixteen children and their caretakers were huddled securely in a reinforced concrete safe room built by a grandfather, Barney Donovan. Their neighborhood was splintered, but they all weathered the 2001 storm just fine.

Elsewhere, when the 6.8 Nisqually earthquake rocked Seattle that same year, thousands of homes were spared damage because their owners completed do-it-yourself earthquake retrofits. They learned how to brace and strengthen their homes in free Saturday morning seminars taught by a community volunteer, Roger Faris. On the other coast, when Hurricane Ike devastated Galveston in 2008, Paul Strizek's home was hardly touched, although his neighbor's house was swept away. Before the storm, Paul strengthened his house and raised it above the storm surge.

These success stories all testify to the power of *hazard mitigation*, an unfriendly but important term that covers actions taken before, during, or after a disaster to reduce or avert death, damages, disruptions, and other losses. An ounce of prevention really is worth a pound of cure. One study showed that every $1 spent on hazard mitigation produces at least $4 in benefits (Multi-Hazard Mitigation Council 2005). For that reason, many seasoned emergency managers work to create a community culture that values prevention and mitigation. But mitigation can offer challenges for managers, because— although the long-term value of prevention actions such as stronger building codes or floodplain buyouts often appear self-evident after disasters—they can be hard to sell in the short term.

Fortunately, emergency managers can learn from masters like Frank Reddish, the late Miami-Dade mitigation manager, who lured community leaders and volunteers into becoming mitigation missionaries. Frank created a mitigation planning committee whose work was so exciting that meeting attendance averaged 100 people. Over a decade, the committee completed hundreds of millions of dollars in mitigation projects, from major public works to shutters for seniors' homes. When Hurricane Wilma hit Miami in 2005, nothing that had been mitigated was damaged. Frank had two secret weapons: he never stopped preaching mitigation and his style was 100% collaborative because, "it's the only way to get things done."

Some other proven techniques for encouraging community mitigation include:

- Find one or more community champions for hazard mitigation, perhaps elected officials, TV weather people, or other influential citizens.
- Your champion may want to lead a local mitigation committee of both technical experts and interested citizens to offer public education, develop mitigation plans, and encourage mitigation actions.
- Develop a phased hazard mitigation plan based around your community's risks, heritage, and priorities.
- Arm the group with mitigation tips and inspirational success stories available from FEMA.gov, FLASH.org, IBHS.org, and other sites.
- Build collaborative partnerships with diverse groups, across the board of public, private, and nonprofit sectors. One key partner: the news media that hold the key to the most effective way to get out your message and whip up community buzz.

Without hazard mitigation, we are doomed to keep repeating the same disasters over and over again. Reducing disaster losses in the long haul depends first on understanding the risks and strengths peculiar to your own place and second mobilizing local talent in collaborative endeavors that can over time create communities that are safer, stronger, and better places to live.

Sources: Multi-Hazard Mitigation Council, 2005. Natural Hazard Mitigation Saves http://www.floods.org/PDF/MMC_Volume1_FindingsConclusionsRecommendations.pdf); Tulsans Know Tornadoes: Safe Rooms Take Tulsa by Storm (http://www.eeri.org/mitigation/files/resources-for-success/00089.pdf); Meo, Mark, Becky, Ziebro, and Ann Patton. 2004. Tulsa turnaround: from disaster to sustainability. *Natural Hazards Review,* 5: 1–9.

Step 1 involves a mitigation leader in assessing community support. First, identify the planning area such as the jurisdictional boundaries of your city or perhaps a specific neighborhood. Next, see whether the community is ready to begin the process and remove roadblocks to their participation and support. That means you will spend considerable time explaining the process and value of mitigation planning to the public and to community officials.

A public education effort may take the form of a series of media stories that cover past local disasters, describe their impacts, and map out risk areas. Efforts to convince public officials may focus on the long-term cost effectiveness of mitigation and stress that investment now pays dividends later .

As the efforts of James Lee Witt and FEMA demonstrated in the 1990s, mitigation usually requires a "powerful champion" to spearhead mitigation efforts (FEMA #1; Godschalk et al. 1998). Relentless leadership is essential to inspire effective partnerships, survive over the long haul, and encourage broad-based support (Godschalk et al. 1998). Good planners also work with other local agencies and tie mitigation into stormwater management, recreational planning, residential development, transportation design, capital improvement initiatives, and comprehensive planning.

Step 2 actively involves the mitigation planning team in assessing local hazards. Where can you find hazards information? Here is where the skills you learned in Chapter 3 on research methods pay off. Local memories provide a good start but may not be completely reliable. You can interview people who survived or remember disaster events and their impacts. People will remember an ice storm that cut off their power for three weeks and will be more likely to support underground utilities as a consequence. Newspapers and historical records also provide information about past events. Libraries, historical centers, museums, and archives all contain microfiche and vertical files of information about past disasters. Internet websites list severe weather and other disasters well back into previous centuries. What kind of information should you search for? Consider the locations where events occurred along with magnitude and frequency. The physical damages should be charted, and you should note where additional development has been placed vis-á-vis risky areas.

The human impact should be thoughtfully researched and presented too. Deaths and injuries are certainly important factors, as are the psychological and spiritual impacts. Losses of pets, livestock, and environmental resources matter as well. Disruptions to education, businesses, and health care should be noted. By amassing the information that affects a community in these relevant areas, you can build a strong case for mitigation projects. You now need to identify the locations exposed to risk. One way to do so is to conduct loss estimation. First, estimate losses to each location such as a school, hospital, or nursing home. Approximate how much damage a local disaster such as an EF3 tornado would inflict on a physical structure. Next, calculate the content losses inside each structure and the costs to replace them. A third element considers the loss of the structure and subsequent need to relocate a home or business temporarily or permanently. The combination of structure loss, content loss, and function loss compile into a total loss from a hazard event. Imagine an earthquake that severely damages or disrupts homes, schools, utilities, and businesses for weeks to months. The financial impacts alone are staggering (see Box 10.7 for an example of loss estimation).

After the data are accumulated and analyzed, present the information to the public to raise concern and support. And be creative. Attend worship services, speak to service organizations, distribute flyers, involve scout troops in delivering information door to door, distribute information at parent–teacher meetings, and invite neighborhood associations to hear your concerns (FEMA #2). Get people concerned and excited and keep in mind the considerable payoffs that may result.

Step 3 leads the community through mitigation planning (Burby 2001; Fordham 1998). Here you build upon the information you collected and the risks calculated and collectively determine appropriate actions. What are your community's goals and objectives? You may determine that the location of trailer parks along a river represents a considerable risk to those living in the area. Your goal is then to reduce impacts on their homes and lives. Options might include constructing a levee or relocating the trailer park to an area outside the floodplain. You may decide that the trailer park, if the owner is amenable, is a prime location for affordable elevated housing. Or, perhaps the schools in your communities are concerns due to severe weather. A key goal of your committee may be protecting future citizens by installing congregate safe rooms at each school, retrofitting the roofs with additional clamps, and adding blast-resistant doors and windows. Your committee then faces the biggest challenges: prioritizing the objectives into action steps and securing funding. These tasks may be the most daunting as you decide which locations and populations require the most immediate action (FEMA #3).

BOX 10.7 ESTIMATING YOUR POTENTIAL LOSSES

In its series of guidebook on mitigation, FEMA has offered a general formula to estimate losses. To do so, you must identify three key components: structure loss, content loss, and usage loss. Structure loss refers to building damage. If an F4 tornado takes out a house valued at $150,000 the total loss is $150,000. If only 50% of the house is damaged, the structural loss is $75,000.

Content loss refers to what you lose inside the home. FEMA estimates that if four feet of water entered a single-story home without a basement, about 43.5% of the contents would be lost. Stop for a minute and imagine what items in your home life are below four feet. Look around: carpets, furniture, televisions, electrical outlets, plumbing, bookcases, food, appliances, clothes, and shoes. Don't forget your pets either. Can you imagine the cost of replacing all of these items, especially if you do not have adequate insurance? The type of housing that you live in also matters. In contrast to a single-story home, a mobile home would suffer 90% content losses with four feet of water. Clearly, disproportionate outcomes affect people at different income levels.

Next, consider the usage losses. If you need to move, you may be lucky to rent a comparable unit and move quickly—if you are a renter. If you or your family own a home, you will probably need to rebuild in the same location for financial and occupational reasons. This means you will be displaced during the rebuilding. How much will it cost to house your family and for how long? You should assume that you will be out of your home for at least a month after most disasters. Displacement for those affected by the U.S. Gulf Coast storms and the Indian Ocean tsunami spanned years, not weeks or months. If you conduct a home-based business, you will also experience downtime as you struggle to replace the tools of your livelihood such as computers, carpentry or car repair tools, sewing machines, cooking utensils, or child care facilities that formerly generated income (for more on business recovery, see Chapter 11).

Finally, total your losses and consider how much you have available in savings and personal insurance. Does your insurance cover the local hazard? Those facing losses after Hurricane Katrina faced protracted legal battles when insurers refused to pay their claims. How long can you financially survive without a return on the financial investment you made by paying insurance premiums? Before you decide that insurance is not something to pursue, think about the full range of hazards that insurance does cover including fire and theft. Can you really survive without such coverage? Insurance usually reduces the risk of financial losses and sets many back on the road to recovery. As one of the main non-structural mitigation measures available to you, it would be wise to research what it covers, how much and under what circumstances vis-á-vis what you see as acceptable financial losses.

(**Source:** FEMA. 2001. Understanding Your Risks: Identifying Hazards and Estimating Losses. Report 386-4. Washington. FEMA mitigation resources can be viewed and downloaded at http://www.fema.gov/plan/prevent/bestpractices/index.shtm)

Physical and human vulnerabilities must be weighed when choosing action steps. This is the time when powerful voices may lobby for their own interests, and strong leadership will be required to stay on task to reduce risk for as many people as possible, particularly those least able to represent themselves.

In *Step 4,* your efforts result in an implementation strategy and timeline to reach the objectives. Continual efforts are required to secure funding because the project may fall from public view and interest after planning is complete. By continuing to present your mitigation efforts to the public as you did in earlier steps, you can keep the issue alive and remind people of progress. Each disaster in your community or in the area can be used as a visible reminder of the value of mitigation. While your mitigation work may seem unending and the payoff far in the future, the payoff will come someday. The lives you save may be those of your grandchildren (see Box 10.8).

BOX 10.8   HISTORIC PRESERVATION AND MITIGATION

Look around your home. What historic elements are present? Perhaps you have meaningful photographs or mementos. Maybe you have a family Bible dating back several generations. Perhaps you have a photograph of your grandparents on their 50th wedding anniversary. Tucked away inside a closet maybe you have your wedding dress or a baby's shoes. These treasures represent a connection to your past and tangible losses should a disaster strike. Consider, for example, that protestors seeking the downfall of the Egyptian government in 2011 formed a human chain around museums housing priceless antiquities. Across the embattled nation, citizens chose historic preservation in the midst of internal turmoil.

Maybe you live in a building with historic elements. Both historic district homes with high values and homes that may have fallen into disrepair but contain architectural elements important to a specific period are unique to a community. Look around your home, neighborhood, and community. Where are the places of historic meaning? To help you get started, visit http://www.nationalregisterofhistoricplaces.com/ to view a list of U.S. places on the Historical Register. Why have people worked to keep these locations intact? What do these places mean locally? Do they generate tourism revenue? Do they offer visitors a look at who lived here and why they chose this place?

Mitigation of historic treasures at a personal or collective level is important. For example, in Harper's Ferry, West Virginia, John Brown and others initiated a first resistance to the institution of slavery in the U.S. They died at the executioner's hands for their bold attempt but the place became famous nonetheless. Their legacy lives on through maintaining the site for educational and historic purposes. The famous anti-slavery orator Frederick Douglass and sociologist W.E.B. DuBois made Harper's Ferry a central place for making speeches and generating resistance, but the town experiences repetitive flooding. To save the site, several mitigation measures have been put into place (Noble 2001). Flood hatches and water-resistant doors have been installed. Site staff members have trained on which prioritized items to save first and the locations of pre-placed tools. As with recommendations earlier in this chapter, electronics and outlets were placed above the water line. John Brown's contribution to freedom of African Americans lives on through the dedication of those who participated in mitigation.

10.6 Working or Volunteering in Mitigation

Jobs in disaster mitigation open and close constantly and you should monitor websites that list employment opportunities. In 2011, FEMA announced that applicants could apply for a mitigation specialist position in Oakland, California. Salary ranged from $81,460 to $105,897. FEMA said, "When disaster strikes, America looks to FEMA. Now FEMA looks to you. Join our team and use your talent to support Americans in their times of greatest need. The Federal Emergency Management Agency (FEMA) prepares the nation for all hazards and manages federal response and recovery efforts following any national incident. We foster innovation, reward performance and creativity, and provide challenges on a routine basis with a well-skilled, knowledgeable, high performance workforce. You will serve in the Mitigation Division, Region 9, Federal Emergency Management Agency (FEMA), Department of Homeland Security (DHS) in Oakland, CA. In this position, you will serve as a program manager for implementation of the FEMA Hazard Mitigation Assistance grant programs and as liaison to state counterparts." The program manager was required to:

Provide technical assistance to states and sub-grantees.
Monitor the status and performance of HMA grants awarded to states.
Plan, coordinate, monitor, conduct, and complete environmental reviews.
Review, analyze, and provide input on guidance, policies, and procedures related to HMA programs.
Develop and present materials.
Serve in the Joint Field Office as the mitigation branch director.

Qualified applicants would need specialized experience in hazard mitigation programs, policies, and practices. That body of knowledge also requires understanding of environmental and historic preservation programs and the ability to work with a range of partners at all governmental levels including tribes. Ability to communicate effectively with an array of stakeholders would be essential, particularly in contexts that may become "contentious." Recent international listings in the area of mitigation include:

- Professional Assistant, Centre for Disaster Mitigation and Management, Anna University, Chennai, India, for "scientific research projects related to assessment of seismic risk of buildings in urban areas of Tamil Nadu State."
- Consultant, Disaster Mitigation and Management System, Mongolia, to "support implementation of the long-term strategy of Mongolia for disaster risk management to minimize vulnerability."

Multiple opportunities exist to volunteer in mitigation work because emergency managers need public involvement. Contact your emergency management agency to determine whether it is involved in such an effort and ask to become involved. If a plan has been passed, ask whether you can help implement it. If you are the emergency manager or mitigation leader, task area organizations with helping to retrofit the homes of seniors, conduct public education efforts, or raise funds to support objectives that reduce risk even further.

You may also want to launch a mitigation project through your fraternity, sorority, scout troop, sports team, or academic club. Certainly every community includes elderly residents and people with disabilities who face challenges implementing mitigation measures for their individual homes. Imagine, for example, organizing an effort to establish a wildfire perimeter around someone's home. Or, after reading this text, you may want to work with a homeowners' association to develop a public education project. Your actions may be as simple as conducting a personal hygiene (hand washing) demonstration at a local school or launching a tree-planting initiative to absorb stormwater runoff. You can make a difference.

10.7 Summary

Mitigation projects are undertaken to reduce the risks associated with hazards. Two main types of mitigation projects address the potential for harm to people, animals, and the built environment. Structural mitigation projects center on tangible projects such as dams, levees, safe rooms, and hurricane shelters to reduce damages disasters can generate. Non-structural mitigation projects are less tangible and include efforts to enforce building codes, purchases of insurance, public education, and mitigation planning. The planning measure involves stakeholders across the community in understanding hazards, estimating losses, and designing possible solutions.

Through discussion of the risks they face collectively, those engaged in mitigation planning come to understand where they need to leverage their resources. Both structural and non-structural mitigation projects result from the collective vision, although finding the economic and political will to enact sometimes expensive projects can be a challenge. One thing is certain: mitigation projects require a champion to launch and sustain efforts to reduce risks to the public. Because people tend to be more motivated to conduct mitigation work after a disaster, the champions of mitigation face a sustained battle to safeguard future generations. From a cost–benefit perspective, the results are certainly worthwhile.

Discussion Questions

1. What are the differences between structural and non-structural mitigation? Do any of the examples described in this chapter exist in your community, neighborhood, or home? Which ones can you find?

2. Who in your community would be a good "champion" for mitigation? What kind of leadership qualities should that person have?

3. Look at the library and internet sites for your community to identify disasters that struck in the past fifty years. What were they and where did they impact? How closely would you have been affected?

4. Look around your home. Inventory the contents and calculate the cost to replace all of them. Next, budget the amount you need to find an alternative place to live for six months while your home is rebuilt. Finally, if you are a homeowner, estimate the cost of rebuilding your home. Add the three factors together and compare the costs against your personal assets and insurance coverage. Do you have enough to recover?

5. Most communities need to plan for stormwater runoff. As you walk, bike, or drive around your community, what steps have been taken to handle runoff? How does water flow onto and away from properties? Is there a tree planting project to absorb stormwater naturally? Do the city code and/or development plan set aside floodplains and conserve wetlands? Does the development plan have an initiative to increase green space through increasing population density or other tradeoffs? Are there notices above stormwater drains that tell people not to allow chemicals and other runoff to enter area waters and ultimately affect drinking water? Does area development include the orange fences necessary to prevent silt and sediment from running off into and clogging stormwater drains? Is there a city effort to prevent flooding by keeping branches, leaves, and other debris out of streams, drains, and other areas where rain flows? Does the city offer incentives to developers to keep trees rather than bulldozing properties under construction?

References

American Society of Civil Engineers. 2009. *Report Card for America's Infrastructure.* Washington, D.C.: American Society of Civil Engineers.

Ayscue, Jon. 1996. "Hurricane Damage to Residential Structures: Risk and Mitigation." Working Paper #94 at http://www.colorado.edu/hazards/publications/wp/wp94/wp94.html, last accessed January 31, 2011.

Burby, Raymond J. 1998. "Natural Hazards and Land Use: An Introduction." Pp. 1–28 in *Cooperating with Nature,* (Raymond J. Burby, ed.). Washington, D.C.: Joseph Henry Press.

Chakos, Arrietta, Paula Schulz and L. Thomas Tobin. 2002. "Making it Work in Berkeley: Investing in Community Sustainability." *Natural Hazards Review* 3/2: 55–67.

Comerio, Mary. C. 2000. *The Economic Benefits of a Disaster-Resistant University.* Berkeley, CA: University of California Berkeley.

Federal Emergency Management Agency. 2001. "Business Increases Its Involvement in Earthquake Mitigation." Available at http://www.fema.gov/mitigationbp/bestPracticeDetailPDF.do?mitssId=2866, last accessed January 31, 2011.

Federal Emergency Management Agency. 2003. *Building a Disaster-Resistant University.* Washington, D.C.: FEMA Publication 443.

Fordham, Maureen. 1998. "Participatory Planning for Flood Mitigation: models and approaches." *Australian Journal of Emergency Management* 13/4: 27–34.

Godschalk, David, Timothy Beatley, Philip Berke, and Davis Brower. 1998. *Natural Hazard Mitigation: Recasting Disaster Policy and Planning.* Washington, D.C.: Island Press.

Godschalk, David, Edward J. Kaiser, and Philip R. Berke. 1998. "Integrating Hazard Mitigation and Local Land Use Planning." Pp. 85–118 in *Cooperating with Nature,* (Raymond J. Burby, ed.). Washington, D.C.: Joseph Henry Press.

Meo, Mark, Becky, Ziebro and Ann Patton. 2004. "Tulsa Turnaround: from Disaster to Sustainability." *Natural Hazards Review* 5/1: 1–9.

Morrow, Betty. 2010. "Language and Literacy." Pp. 243–256 in *Social Vulnerability to Disasters,* (Brenda D. Phillips, Deborah Thomas, Alice Fothergill, and Lynn Pike, eds.). Boca Raton, FL: CRC Press.

Meszaros, Jacqueline and Mark Fiegener. 2004. "Predicting Earthquake Preparation." Available at http://www.iitk.ac.in/nicee/wcee/article/13_571.pdf, last accessed January 31, 2011.

National Council on Disability. 2009. *Effective Emergency Management: Making Improvements for Communities and People with Disabilities.* Washington, D.C.: National Council on Disability.

Noble, B. J. 2001. "Lord willing n' the creek don't rise": Flood Sustainability at Harpers Ferry National Historical Park. *Cultural Resource Management* 24/ 8: 16–18.

Picou, J. S. 2000. "Talking Circles as Sociological Practice: Cultural Transformation of Chronic Disaster Impacts." *Sociological Practice* 2/2: 77–97.

Wachtendorf, Tricia, Rory Connell, and Kathleen Tierney, Kristy Kompanik. 2002. *Final Project Report #49 Disaster Resistant Communities Initiative: Assessment of the Pilot Phase-Year-3.* Newark, DE: University of Delaware, Disaster Research Center.

Resources

FEMA offers an extensive series of mitigation guidance publications available at www.fema.gov:

FEMA #386-1 Getting Started

FEMA #386-2 Understanding Your Risks

FEMA #386-3 Developing the Mitigation Plan

FEMA #386-4 Bringing the Plan to Life

FEMA #386-5 Using Cost Benefit Review in Mitigation Planning

FEMA #386-6 Integrating Historic and Cultural Resource Considerations into Natural Mitigation Planning

FEMA #386-7 Integrating Man-Made Hazards into Mitigation Planning

FEMA #386-8 Multi-Jurisdictional Mitigation Planning

FEMA #368-9 Using the Hazard Mitigation Plan to Prepare Successful Mitigation Projects

Chapter **11**

Public and Private Sector Partnerships

11.1 Chapter Objectives

Upon completing this chapter, readers should be able to:

1. Identify key actors and agencies in the public sector at the local, state, and federal levels.
2. Describe the roles and responsibilities of those public sector entities in the context of emergency management.
3. Discuss why it is important to consider the private sector in the context of disasters and emergency management, and describe the various kinds of impacts disasters have on businesses.
4. Explain why it is important for businesses to prepare for disasters, describe the kinds of activities they often undertake in responding to disasters, and discuss the relevance of the private sector to overall community recovery and mitigation.
5. Discuss the importance of public–private partnerships across all four phases of emergency management.

11.2 Introduction

Along with volunteer organizations, the public and private sectors play central roles in emergency management. In theory, all three sectors should work together to ensure effective preparedness, response, recovery, and mitigation. However, what we see in many cases is the phenomenon commonly known as "stove piping." In essence, people only talk to each other within their own segments of their own organizations. For example, people in a fire department may only talk about disaster issues to others within their department. Federal officials from one office in FEMA only talk to those directly reporting above and below them. Business disaster planners will communicate only within their companies and not share their plans with local or state disaster officials. Rather than flowing horizontally across departments and other organizations, information only goes up and down, as if it were in a stovepipe.

The issue of stove piping was highlighted following the September 11, 2001 terrorist attacks. Many federal agencies such as the FBI, CIA, National Security Agency, and others had important information about the planned attack. However, by not communicating with each other and sharing information, intelligence agencies were unable to "connect the dots" before the attacks (National Commission on Terrorist Attacks upon the United States 2004). Today, many aspects of public and private sector disaster management focus on sharing information before, during, and following disasters.

In this chapter, we describe the different tasks and responsibilities of governments and businesses to improve their overall emergency management capabilities. In the public sector, we look at the roles of local, state, and federal governments and also their relationships with each other. For the private sector, we discuss the impacts of disasters on businesses, preparedness strategies, response activities typically undertaken by the sector, the importance of businesses to overall community recovery, and the role of the private sector in mitigation. Finally, we emphasize the importance of the public and private sectors working together across all four phases of emergency management.

11.3 Public Sector

We all know that disasters are local. With this assumption, we will begin our discussion of the public sector by looking at the roles of local public officials—emergency managers and key decision makers such as city managers, mayors, and city council members. Other parts of local government, such as public works, parks and recreation, planning, fire, emergency medical services, and police also play key action roles. Next, we look at the role of state government including the governor, office(s) of emergency management and/or homeland security, and related state agencies. Then we review briefly the role of the federal government, focusing primarily on the duties and responsibilities of the president and congress along with FEMA's role in coordinating emergency management efforts at the federal, state, and local levels. Finally, we comment on how the private sector must also be a factor of an effective emergency management system.

11.3.1 Local Government

Because it probably affects our daily lives more than any other level of government, it is important for us to understand how local government works. In this section, we will identify various local governmental actors and agencies and describe their roles and activities in emergency management. As you read this section, you will notice that in addition to departments that have clearly delineated disaster-related responsibilities (police and fire), many others contribute to emergency management activities.

11.3.1.1 *Elected Officials and Emergency Management Offices*

In general, by law the highest elected local official carries the main decision making responsibilities for emergency management. For example, this may be the county judge or the head county commissioner in some states. For city governments, depending upon the type of structure, the highest elected official may be the mayor or the president of the city council. These elected officials have many different tasks to manage on a day-to-day basis and do not have time to run an emergency management department full-time on a daily basis. As a result, the elected official delegates these crucial emergency management tasks to a local emergency manager.

However, the office of emergency management can be located in any one of many different departments within a city or county government. Rare is the case where the local emergency manager reports directly to the elected official. Rather, we typically see the office of emergency management embedded within the fire or police department. These patterns developed historically when emergency management was not seen as a profession. The misperception that emergency management concerned only with responding to emergencies was a poor assumption; but because of it people with emergency response experience (police and firefighters) filled emergency management posts. A police officer or firefighter who held the title and performed the duties of an emergency manager reported to a police or fire chief. The chief reported to the city or county manager, who in turn reported to the elected official. As a result, the position of emergency manager was buried under local government bureaucracy.

As we will see, the problem of locating an emergency management function organizationally continues to plague state governments and FEMA. In addition, we also see this problem in the private sector, where business continuity planners are parts of information technology operations or fall under safety and security. In most cases, a layer or two of bureaucracy separates emergency managers and business continuity planners from key decision makers. Rare is the case where an emergency manager has direct access to a decision maker, even during a disaster (McEntire 2006; Edwards and Goodrich 2007).

11.3.1.2 Local Departments

Many if not all local government offices play key roles during a disaster. Sanitation departments work on debris removal and disposal. Utility workers ensure that power and gas lines are safe to use. Water and sewage departments make sure that water supplies are safe and sewage systems work properly. Workers from parks and recreation may be moved to other departments to help or their facilities may be used as staging sites or locations for coordinating outside volunteers. Budget and finance offices keep track of monies spent so that the city or county government can later be reimbursed by the federal government. In broader situations, mutual aid agreements come into effect and allow police and fire departments to cross jurisdictions to help other communities. In short, local departments become key players in a disaster and must be willing to work together for the response and recovery to be effective. This effectiveness is based upon good communications and relationships that can and should be built before disaster strikes.

11.3.2 State Government

State governments also play an important role in emergency management. Governors, for example, declare states of emergency after disasters strike—a crucial step in initiating subsequent response activities by the federal government. Some state agencies refer to themselves as offices of emergency management while others are known as offices of homeland security. In both cases, they play vital roles in promoting preparedness at the local level, assisting in response activities, and facilitating recovery. It is important, therefore, to have effective coordination of local governments and state agencies during normal times so they can work together smoothly when disaster strikes.

11.3.2.1 Role of Governor

Similar to the model of local government, the highest elected official of a state, the governor, is its lead emergency manager. He or she makes the key decisions related to emergency management. The state director of emergency management (see below) typically serves at the will of the governor and promotes his or her policies. Although a state director of emergency management can make recommendations, the ultimate decisions related to emergency management rest with the governor (Sylves 2008, p. 211).

A key role of a governor during a disaster is to make a formal request to the FEMA regional office to initiate a presidentially declared disaster. Another role is lobbying the president and congress for needed funding or changes in policy to assist states with disaster issues. Governors' interactions with FEMA regional offices before, during, and after disasters can also be important for obtaining a wide range of federal resources. Governors also control the national guard units in their states. Thus, when a crisis or disaster strikes, the governor has the power to direct the national guard to assist. The office of the governor becomes a key conduit for local and federal governments to work together to meet their goals. (Sylves 2008, pp. 95, 135–137). A governor must set a leadership example by his or her willingness to work with local and federal governments including the FEMA regional office, congress, and even the president. Importantly, the governor sets the tone for developing intergovernmental relationships and partnerships.

11.3.2.2 Emergency Management and Homeland Security Offices

In general, the state office of emergency management and/or homeland security handles the daily operations of emergency management. Similar to FEMA, these organizations are much more than response agencies. They provide training opportunities for local governments and help fund some initiatives for local emergency management offices. These state agencies also serve as important conduits for obtaining federal information and monies for local governments. The state offices assist local governments in gathering data for disaster declaration applications and provide the information to the regional FEMA office. In general, state offices promote effective and responsive emergency management. Similar to the situation with local emergency management offices, the state emergency management or homeland security office may be assigned to various organizational locations. Authorities to whom state directors in the U.S. report are listed below:

- Governor—12
- Adjutant general/military—18
- Homeland security—1
- Public safety—14
- State police—2
- Other—3

As you can see, only twelve of the fifty state emergency management directors report directly to governors. In most other cases, the state office of emergency management is part of a paramilitary organization such as the adjutant general/military, public safety, or state police (NEMA 2011). Thus, organizational roadblocks exist for most emergency management directors. In addition, the placement of emergency management within a paramilitary organization makes the "chain of command" an important concept. As a result, officials in state emergency management offices may be unintentionally stove piped. Information may be filtered as it moves up the chain of command to the governor and few if any formal mechanisms exist for information exchange with other state offices or organizations in the private sector. Furthermore, in most cases, a state director serves at the pleasure of the governor. A change of the governor may also mean a new state director of emergency management or homeland security.

The issue became more complicated after the September 11, 2001 terrorist attacks. As you recall from Chapter 1, the federal government created the Department of Homeland Security (DHS) in 2003. FEMA , formerly a lead agency reporting directly to the president, became part of DHS. Some states followed the same pattern. One state (Indiana) and one U.S. territory (Guam) followed this example by putting their offices of emergency management under their offices of homeland security (NEMA 2011). Other states created offices of homeland security in addition to keeping their offices of emergency management.

Oklahoma, where the authors of this textbook live, maintains two distinct offices. The director of the Department of Emergency Management reports directly to the governor, and the governor appoints the director. Key tasks of this office include assisting with emergency and disaster declarations, helping victims and communities obtain financial assistance following a disaster, and providing training opportunities for a wide range of hazards across all four phases of disaster (Oklahoma Department of Emergency Management 2011).

The Office of Homeland Security's main purpose is to protect Oklahoma from various types and forms of terrorist attacks. The office is under the Department of Public Safety and the director is appointed by the governor. The Oklahoma Office of Homeland Security also manages most of the state's grants for homeland security and emergency management. Since the office was established in 2004, it has managed over $100 million worth of grants related to terrorism and disasters (Oklahoma Office of Homeland Security 2011). In essence, most disaster (and of course homeland security) funding from the federal government is funneled through this office.

11.3.3 Accrediting State and Local Governments

The Emergency Management Accrediting Program (EMAP) focuses on improving state and local government (organizational) capabilities. During the National Emergency Management Association's (NEMA) annual meetings in 1997, the organization decided to create a set of standards for state and local governments. If state and local governments met these standards, they would become "accredited" organizations. Since NEMA's efforts are directed by the state emergency management directors, the effort carried a lot of weight. The criteria that government organizations must follow are known as emergency management standards. They were developed by state and local emergency managers and key emergency management organizations (NEMA, IAEMS, Department of Homeland Security) and consist of (NEMA 2011):

- Self assessment and documentation
- On-site assessment by a team of trained, independent assessors
- A committee for review and recommendation
- Accreditation decision by an independent commission

In all, sixty-three specific criteria must be met in order to obtain accreditation. Although too many to list here, examples of some of the general criteria include (EMAP 2010b):

- Specific emergency management office
- Budget and finance procedures
- Programs for such activities as hazard identification, risk assessment, and hazard mitigation
- Operational planning and incident management system
- Mutual aid
- Warning and communication
- Training and exercises
- Public education

11.3.4 Federal Government

When we think of the public sector response to disaster, we often think of the federal government. Historically, the first agency that came to people's minds was FEMA. Now, in light of the administrative changes described throughout this book, the first organization that comes to many peoples' minds is the Department of Homeland Security of which FEMA is now a part. As with the relationships of local and state governments, coordination of the federal government with other levels is imperative. To the extent that relationships can be forged and nurtured during normal times, interactions of the various levels of government are likely to be much smoother during and after a disaster.

11.3.4.1 Executive Branch

Generally, the president obtains his emergency powers through the Constitution. Article 2, Section 3 states that the president must ensure that laws of the nation are executed properly. Article 2 makes the president the commander in chief of the military, giving the president the power to use military resources. In addition, the Constitution allows the president at times of crisis to use the authority granted to the two other branches of government: legislative and judicial. Only twice have presidents used this power. Abraham Lincoln used it during the Civil War and Franklin Roosevelt used it during World War II. Although rarely used, the president may draw on this authority in time of a catastrophic event (Sylves 2008, p. 77).

The various cabinet level posts along with the president generally make up most of what we refer to as the "federal bureaucracy." Over the last fifty years, key cabinet level posts have stayed generally the same. In 2011, the current fifteen cabinet level posts include:

- Department of Agriculture
- Department of Commerce
- Department of Defense
- Department of Education
- Department of Energy
- Department of Health and Human Services
- Department of Homeland Security
- Department of Housing and Urban Development
- Department of the Interior
- Department of Justice
- Department of Labor
- Department of State
- Department of Transportation
- Department of the Treasury
- Department of Veterans Affairs

As previously noted, FEMA is currently under DHS. Beginning with President Clinton's administration in 1993, FEMA became a designated cabinet-level post. As a result, the FEMA director had direct access to the president and matters dealing with disasters often moved much more quickly and efficiently. However, with the formation of DHS in 2003, FEMA moved under DHS. Many in emergency management expressed concern about the move of FEMA and its perceived diminished importance and lack of direct communication with the president and others. These fears became reality during and following Hurricane Katrina in 2005 (Waugh 2005; 2006). The added layer of bureaucracy proved a major hindrance to the response effort.

The work done by the executive branch, coordinated by DHS and FEMA, lays the foundation for coordination among the various cabinet-level posts involved in disaster management. Coordination proceeds from the federal level down to the state and local governments. Documents, such as the National Response Framework and the CPG-101 disaster planning guide, are in part efforts by the federal government and DHS to promote communication and coordination among federal agencies dealing with disasters and between state and local governments.

For example, the CPG-101 document stresses that disaster planning should be local and must include stakeholders from the whole community. Thus, partnerships among public, private, and volunteer organizations are crucial if planning and response are to be effective. The document also stresses engagement of all sectors of a community, including the private sector (FEMA 2010b).

11.3.4.2 Congress

The role of congress is far more formal and much less hands-on than the role of the executive branch. Congress passes the budgets that allow the executive branch to operate and provides funding (grants, matching funds) to state and local governments for specific disaster projects and initiatives. Congress also provides funding for the President's Disaster Relief Fund. Although the president authorizes monies for disaster relief, congress must approve the funding. To date, congress has always approved the needed funding. Congress may also provide emergency supplements to bills related to disaster needs (Sylves, 2008, p. 95).

Sometimes the way we design and create organizations may stifle rather than enhance communications between departments of a bureaucracy and other organizations that may share the same goals. Throughout this chapter, we have discussed the roles and responsibilities of the local, state, and federal governments in the U.S. and described the difficulties of getting the various levels to work together. In some places, another level of government—transnational—must also be considered. The European Union (EU), for example, consists of more than two dozen countries throughout Europe. While each country has local, regional, and national governments, they also participate in the EU. Because of major flooding and heat waves in EU countries in recent years and large-scale disasters in other nations, the EU like the U.S. has changed its emergency management infrastructure. One of its key components, the Community Civil Protection Mechanism (CCPM) was established in 2001 (Wendling 2010). As shown in Box 11.1, a core unit within the CCPM is the Monitoring and Information Centre (MIC), whose job is to facilitate communication and coordination among multiple levels of government.

Finally, a constant tension often exists regarding how much the federal government can explicitly dictate specific local disaster policy to local governments. This issue of federalism runs constant throughout U.S. history and is part of emergency management policy. On the one hand, federal mandates can provide consistent standard approaches to disasters nationwide. On the other hand, communities and states have different cultures and ways of seeing the world, meaning how they approach a disaster issue may be different from the approach of another state. Such situations can both improve and impede disaster management across the four phases.

BOX 11.1 DISASTERS AND THE PUBLIC SECTOR IN THE EUROPEAN UNION

Monitoring and Information Centre (MIC): What is it?

The Monitoring and Information Centre (MIC), operated by the European Commission in Brussels, is the operational heart of the Community Mechanism for Civil Protection. It is available on a twenty-four/seven basis and is staffed by duty officers working on a shift basis. It gives countries access to the community civil protection platform. Any country affected by a major disaster—inside or outside the EU—can launch a request for assistance through the MIC.

Role

During emergencies the MIC plays three important roles:

1. **Communications hub**—Being at the centre of an emergency relief operation, the MIC acts as a focal point for the exchange of requests and offers of assistance. This helps in cutting down on the thirty participating states' administrative burden in liaising with the affected country. It provides a central forum for participating states to access and share information about the available resources and the assistance offered at any given point in time.
2. **Information provision**—The MIC disseminates information on civil protection preparedness and response to participating states as well as a wider audience of interested parties. As part of this role, the MIC disseminates early warning alerts (MIC Daily) on natural disasters and circulates the latest updates on ongoing emergencies and Mechanism interventions.
3. **Supports coordination**—The MIC facilitates the provision of European assistance through the Mechanism. This takes place at two levels: at headquarters level, by matching offers to needs, identifying gaps in aid and searching for solutions, and facilitating the pooling of common resources where possible; and on the site of the disaster through the appointment of EU field experts, when required.

Activation of Mechanism: MIC at Work

Inside EU

The Mechanism can be activated through the MIC by any participating state seeking prompt international assistance following a major disaster. A state usually calls on the Mechanism when the effects of the disaster cannot be matched by its own civil protection resources.

As soon as the MIC receives a request for assistance, the Centre immediately forwards it to its twenty-four-hour network of national contact points. These contact points represent the participating states' civil protection authorities. They assess their available resources and inform the MIC whether or not they are in a position to help. The MIC then matches the offers made to the needs and informs the requesting state of the type and quantity of available assistance from the Community.

Outside EU

As the use of the Mechanism is not restricted to interventions within the European Union, any third country affected by a disaster can also make an appeal for assistance through the MIC. Following a formal request for assistance from a third country, different procedures are applied for the activation of the Mechanism. In such cases, the Commission needs to consult the Presidency of the Council so as to determine the course of action it needs to take. For instance, if the emergency takes place in an area affected by conflict or civil unrest, the Council through the Presidency may declare it to fall under the so called *crisis management provisions* (Chapter V of the TEU). In this case the Council plays the lead role in coordinating the EU response. If it is not deemed a crisis management situation, the MIC follows its general operating rules.

Dispatching Assistance

Arrangements for the dispatch of the accepted assistance (delivery, transport, visa requirements, customs, etc.) are made directly between the offering and requesting states. If required, the MIC may play a facilitating role. Any intervention teams or assistance sent from the EU to a disaster area remain under the direction of the national authorities of the affected country, which has the right to ask European teams to stand down at any time. European teams are subject to local law and should operate in conformity with national rules and procedures governing their work.

To facilitate the technical co-ordination of European civil protection assistance a small team of experts can be dispatched on site by the MIC. This team will ensure effective liaison with local authorities and any other relevant actors so as to integrate European civil protection assistance into the overall relief effort and facilitate the work of European teams on the ground. Moreover, as they continue to monitor the emergency and assess its development, they can keep the MIC headquarters updated.

Coordination with Other Actors

Mechanism interventions in third countries, particularly in the developing world, are usually conducted in close collaboration with other actors, such as the UN Office for the Coordination of Humanitarian Affairs (OCHA), the Commission's Humanitarian Aid Department (ECHO), and the Red Cross when these are present on the ground.

Source: http://ec.europa.eu/echo/civil_protection/civil/prote/mic.htm

Thus some can claim that federalism in part created the poor response to Hurricane Katrina (Burby 2006; Menzel 2006; Sylves 2006).

11.4 Private Sector

For the most part, when we think about disasters and emergency management, we do not tend to think about businesses and the private sector. Rather, what comes to mind are police and fire departments, local emergency management agencies, FEMA, and other governmental and public sector agencies and actors such as those described in the previous section. Researchers have also largely ignored the private sector. As we have seen throughout this book, much of what we know about disasters and emergency management is based on studies of households, broader communities, and organizations, primarily those in the public sector.

11.4.1 Importance of Private Sector

In recent years, however, the situation has begun to change, and the private sector is attracting more attention. Three primary factors indicate it is important to consider the private sector in the context of disasters and emergency management. First, a major impetus for increased concern about the private sector is the growing awareness of the staggering financial costs of disasters.

Mileti (1999), in his widely cited book, reports disasters in the U.S. between 1975 and 1994 cost the nation an estimated $500 billion dollars in financial losses. More recently, Benson and Clay (2004) estimate that disasters worldwide during the 1990s produced average losses of $66 billion per year (in U.S. dollars). While it is certainly eye-opening to think about disaster financial losses over long periods and at the national and international levels of analysis, it is perhaps even more startling when we think about single disasters, such as the September 11, 2001 attacks and Hurricane Katrina, that produce economic impacts reaching tens of billions of dollars. Unfortunately, most projections are that these costs will continue to rise exponentially in the coming years as we are faced with more and worse disasters in the future.

Second, in addition to increasing our awareness of their financial impacts, recent disasters also highlighted the important role that the private sector plays in responding. For example, many key elements of the critical infrastructure in the U.S. and other countries including electricity, telecommunications, and transportation are owned and operated by private companies. When those systems sustain damage or fail during a disaster, the effectiveness of the overall response effort largely hinges on the ability of company workers to restore services quickly. As we emphasize throughout this chapter, with so much involvement by the private sector, the challenge of coordinating response activities is even more pronounced for emergency managers. Thus, to facilitate communication and coordination during the response period, it is important to reach out to businesses and include them in broader community preparedness initiatives before a disaster strikes.

Finally, we need to pay more attention to the private sector because of its integral role in stimulating overall community recovery from disaster. Local governments rely heavily on sales tax revenues to support their basic operations, provide essential services, and launch new community initiatives. When disasters strike, those funds can be dramatically impacted if numerous businesses are damaged and forced to close. In other words, not only do individual businesses suffer from disaster-induced interruptions and sales losses, but the broader community also suffers as a result of reduced sales tax income. The sooner local businesses resume normal operations, the sooner the community as a whole can follow the long path to recovery. Of course, as discussed in Chapter 9, recovery involves numerous key stakeholders, including individuals and households, community groups, and government agencies. We must also add businesses to that list.

It should be clear by now that the private sector is highly relevant to the study of disasters and the practice of emergency management. In the next section, we will describe the typical impacts of disasters on the private sector including physical damage to businesses, loss of electricity and other lifeline services, and others. We will also discuss the private sector in relation to the lifecycle of disasters and emergency management, highlighting the types of preparedness activities that best equip businesses to cope with disaster impacts, the typical activities of private sector companies during the response phase, factors that affect business recovery outcomes, and the role of the private sector in mitigation. Based on the importance of the private sector to all four phases, we conclude the chapter by discussing and emphasizing the need for greater cooperation and coordination between the public and private sectors in preparing for, responding to, recovering from, and mitigating future disasters.

11.4.2 Impacts of Disasters on Private Sector

As stated earlier, disasters can produce enormous financial impacts. In measuring the impacts, we often think about losses over an extended time or at very high levels of aggregation such as state, regional, or national economies (Webb, Tierney, and Dahlhamer 2000). Those kinds of measures are important and provide us useful information about the economic consequences but they sometimes overshadow and distort what happens at the level of individual businesses. In this section we get a better sense of direct, indirect, and remote impacts of disasters on businesses.

11.4.2.1 Direct Impacts

In addition to their broader financial impacts, disasters can directly affect individual businesses in a number of ways. Indeed, when we think about businesses and disasters, the direct impacts come immediately to mind (Figure 11.1). Direct disaster impacts on businesses include:

- Physical damage to the building housing the business
- Forced closure as a direct result of damage
- Loss of utility lifelines at the site, including electricity, water, sewage, and telecommunications.

In their study of disaster impacts on businesses and their long-term recovery from disasters, Webb, Tierney and Dahlhamer (2002) found that these kinds of impacts are fairly widespread. In South Florida, for example, fewer than 10% of business owners reported experiencing no physical damage to their facilities as a result of Hurricane Andrew in 1992. Among owners whose businesses were damaged, more than 75% indicated that the damage was disruptive or very disruptive to their operations. Indeed, most businesses were forced to close for at least some period and 35% were closed more than twenty-two days. In addition to physical damage to property, loss of utility lifelines (electricity, water and sewer, and telephone) can also force businesses to close after a disaster.

FIGURE 11.1   Squaw Creek near Ames, Iowa, flooded businesses and homes in August 2010. (*Source:* FEMA News Photo/Jace Anderson.)

Research suggests that the immediate disaster impacts felt by businesses can have significant longer term consequences. In particular, what happens in the immediate aftermath of a disaster can profoundly shape recovery outcomes for individual businesses and the community as a whole. At the individual business level, for example, those forced to close for longer periods are less likely to experience positive long-term recovery outcomes than those that closed for shorter periods and those that did not close (Webb et al. 2002). As stated previously, when businesses suffer losses, sales tax revenues also decline, negatively impacting broader community recovery efforts.

11.4.2.2 Indirect Impacts

In addition to physical damage, lifeline outages, and forced closure, businesses may also experience a range of indirect disaster impacts that occur off-site but negatively affect the ability of a business to operate. Typical indirect effects include (Webb et al. 2000):

- Inability of employees to go to work
- Inability of suppliers to deliver necessary items
- Declines in customers

The indirect effects on business operations can be significant, yet there is little individual business owners can do to prevent them. For example, workers may be unavailable because they must deal with their own disaster-induced problems at home. Similarly, supply chain disruptions may result from direct physical damage to a supplier's facility or blocked transportation routes that impede deliveries. Customers may also have to deal with damage to their own homes, may not be able to access heavily damaged business districts, or may shift spending priorities in the aftermath of a disaster, leading to gains for some businesses and losses for others.

As with physical damage, utility outages, and forced closure, indirect impacts experienced immediately after a disaster can also have much longer term consequences. Studies have shown that the more operational problems a business faces, like the ones described here, the less likely will be its positive recovery outcome over the long term (Webb et al. 2002). It is important, therefore, for owners to develop realistic business continuity plans to help them deal with the full range of direct and indirect disaster impacts they may face (see Chapter 7). As we will see in our discussion of private sector preparedness, continuity plans should consider employees, suppliers, nearby businesses, local government agencies, and others to maximize their effectiveness.

11.4.2.3 Remote Impacts

Disasters also sometimes produce remote impacts on businesses that are similar to but larger in scope and more difficult to predict and control than the indirect impacts described above. As discussed in Chapter 4, disasters are becoming increasingly complex in modern society. A driving force behind the growing complexity of crises and disasters is the increased interdependence of nations and the emergence and growth of a global economy. When a disaster strikes one part of the world, its impacts are often felt in many places at once. In other words, disasters are now capable of producing remote effects, many of which directly impact businesses in the private sector. As Quarantelli, Lagadec, and Boin (2006) point out, the effects of modern disasters multiply rapidly and are increasingly felt across geographical boundaries.

To illustrate the remote effects of disasters on the private sector, consider some recent examples in which an event in one place produced cascading effects across an entire region or even the entire world. In 2010, a volcanic eruption in Iceland had a major impact on air travel around the world. Passengers hoping to enter or leave major airports throughout Europe were stranded because of a massive cloud of volcanic ash. For days flights all around the world were cancelled, delayed, or rerouted, resulting in major disruptions and enormous financial losses. Similarly, in January, 2011, several severe winter storms and blizzards crippled airports in Chicago, Dallas, Atlanta, New York, Washington, D.C., and other major cities. As another example, consider the Deepwater Horizon spill in the Gulf of Mexico in 2010. It certainly dealt a major blow to the local communities along the Gulf Coast, but it also adversely impacted the supplies and prices of seafood and other commodities for the entire nation.

All these disasters produced economic impacts that transcended the local level and reverberated across large geographic regions. In thinking about disasters, therefore, business owners and emergency managers promoting higher levels of preparedness must consider a wide range of potential impacts. Direct impacts, including physical damage, utility outages, and forced closure are the most obvious ones, but there are other important impacts to consider. Indirect impacts, including worker unavailability, supply chain disruptions, customer declines, and the more remote effects described in this section must also be considered when preparing for disasters and developing effective business continuity plans.

11.4.3 Private Sector and the Life Cycle of Emergency Management

As we have seen, the private sector is a crucial component of emergency management. According to McEntire, Robinson, and Weber (2003, p. 453), "It is apparent that the private sector plays both vital and varied roles in emergency management. In fact, it is not an exaggeration to state that the contributions of businesses in mitigation, preparedness, response, and recovery activities have been woefully underestimated." They go on to say,

"The private sector interacts frequently with the public sector to fulfill necessary community disaster functions. Therefore, the lines between the public and private sectors appear to be blurring, disappearing, or perhaps even artificial." Given the vital role of the private sector in emergency management, we will discuss the roles of businesses in each of the four phases of the lifecycle of emergency management.

11.4.3.1 Preparedness

As we discussed in Chapter 6, businesses have done very little to prepare for the kinds of impacts described in the previous section. Chapter 6 reported that, for example, on surveys listing fifteen to twenty possible preparedness actions (storing a first aid kit, purchasing hazard-specific insurance, developing business continuity plans, having a building assessed by a structural engineer), business owners on average reported undertaking only about four items on the lists (Webb et al. 2000). Because of the wide range of impacts they will likely face from a disaster and the valuable contributions they can make to overall community response and recovery efforts, it is somewhat alarming to know that businesses are doing so little.

Of course, as we discussed in Chapter 6, it can be very difficult to persuade individuals, households, and, in particular, businesses, to take appropriate measures to ready themselves for events that present a low probability of occurrence even when the consequences from such events may be catastrophic. Business owners, particularly those who own small, local establishments, have bills to pay, payrolls to meet, and profits to protect, so it may be difficult to find room in their budgets to pay for engineering assessments, continuity plans, or higher insurance premiums.

As a result, research has shown that when they do undertake preparedness measures, businesses tend to implement activities that are simple, inexpensive, geared toward life safety, and site-specific (Webb et al. 2000). Site-specific preparedness measures are independent activities that require no coordination with other businesses or government agencies. Thus, the most common types of preparedness measures undertaken by businesses include obtaining first aid supplies, storing water, and talking to employees about disasters. While it is important to ensure the safety of business owners and employees, these activities do very little to prepare businesses for the kinds of impacts described above, particularly those originating off-site such as supply chain interruptions.

To adequately prepare for the diverse impacts of disasters, owners must develop comprehensive business continuity plans, possible relocation plans, and longer-term recovery plans (see Box 11.2). Unfortunately, however, very few engage in that kind of pro-active planning (Webb et al. 2000). Indeed, as Clarke (1999) points out, planning in the private sector often amounts to little more than the production of *fantasy documents*—symbolic plans produced

BOX 11.2   IMPORTANCE OF BUSINESS CONTINUITY PLANNING

Jodi Ouellette

Jodi Ouellette is a graduate of the University of North Texas with a bachelor of science in both emergency administration and planning and sociology. She has worked in the business continuity and disaster recovery field for ten years and currently holds the position of IT Business Continuity Planner at the corporate headquarters of a large Fortune 500 company in Plano, Texas. (Photo provided by Jodi Ouellette. With permission.)

Some say there is a fine line between disaster recovery and business continuity planning. Many companies will combine the two while others have a defined, obvious difference. I like to think of it as business continuity deals with the people while disaster recovery deals with the data. No matter how you look at it though, disaster recovery cannot exist without business continuity and vice versa.

According to the experts, business continuity is the "strategic and tactical capability of the organization to plan for and respond to incidents and business disruptions in order to continue business operations at an acceptable predefined level" (BS 25999-2:2007). Disaster recovery defines the resources, actions, tasks, and data required to manage the technology recovery effort. It provides for owners to define the maximum allowable outage (MAO) requirements for the "essential" applications. This definition is a component of a business continuity management program (*Disaster Recovery Journal,* http://www.drj.com/glossary/).

I currently work in the Information Technology Risk Management organization as a business continuity planner at the corporate headquarters of a large retail company. I have been writing disaster recovery and business continuity plans for a number of years and have seen many variations of how the organization addresses disasters in the business. Three business continuity planners work at corporate headquarters: A co-worker and I focus on the systems, applications, and hardware. The third planner focuses on the retail departments, processes, and facilities in addition to handling another responsibility—crisis management. In my role today, there is an obvious difference in the plans that are written. The business group has a set of business continuity plans (BCPs) and information technology (IT) has its own set of plans. Although the plans are all called BCPs, their contents are vastly different

I work in IT and must consider several factors before I can write a plan. First, I need to be sure I understand the business. What is the need? Will this plan be written for a new application? Perhaps a complete data center? Knowing and understanding the purpose of writing the plan is crucial. Next is the risk assessment—a detailed look at each hazard that could negatively affect critical functions or activities, after which I decide where the majority of the risk lies. The most serious threats are presented to the management, and they can either accept the risks or choose to mitigate them. After the risks are identified, I conduct a business impact analysis (BIA) that identifies the impacts the business would endure and determine as to the recovery time objective (RTO) and recovery point objective (RPO).

After the RTO and RPO are understood, the recovery strategy can be decided. Will the employees work from home? Go to an alternate location? Finally, I write the plan. I use a special database created specifically for disaster recovery and business continuity planning. It makes the writing easier, but part of my job is to also administer the software—add new users, train employees, fix the system as needed, etc.

Upon approval of the plan by the business continuity plan review board, it is time to exercise! Exercising is the one part of the BCP process where I can really get creative. I make sure all plans are exercised once a year. For these planned events, I like to mix it up a bit. Sometimes a tornado will take out an entire facility or an ice storm occurred, causing the roads to close and preventing employees from getting to work. Unfortunately, not all events are planned. I have had to activate BCPs for a number of reasons; my favorite was when a squirrel on a power line caused a power outage in one of our data rooms as well as the warehouse it controlled. Fortunately, my team was able to safely shut down all the systems in an orderly manner so that when power was restored, nothing crashed. Luckily we had exercised our plan two weeks earlier!

The final phase of business continuity planning is maintenance. Your plan is never complete. Each time a piece of software is updated, a new associate is hired, or a new department is formed, the plan must be updated. And each time, the plan gets better and better. Everyone knows these plans are needed and many consider the plans as insurance policies—necessary tools you hope you never have to use but if you ever do, you'll be glad that you have them.

to give the public, governmental regulators, and themselves the false impression that they are ready for disasters. Clarke focused his research on the oil industry and its lack of readiness for the *Exxon Valdez* spill in 1989, but the concept of fantasy documents applies broadly to all kinds of businesses.

While overall business preparedness is alarmingly low, specific factors influence readiness levels. These include *size, sector, property ownership*, and *previous disaster experience* (Webb et al. 2000). For the most part, larger businesses with more employees tend to be more prepared than their smaller counterparts. This is surprising because of the large number of small businesses and their importance to the functioning of the overall economy. Businesses in certain sectors of the economy, particularly those involved in finance, insurance, and real estate, tend to be more prepared than others, for example, the retail and service sectors. When a business property is owned rather than leased, the owners are also more likely to engage in disaster preparedness activities. Finally, as discussed in Chapter 6, previous disaster experience is often, though not always, associated with higher levels of preparedness.

Based on what we have discussed about the direct, indirect, and remote impacts of disasters, the following *preparedness principles* may assist in enhancing private sector readiness. First, business owners must think beyond simple life safety measures. Those are important, to be sure, but they are inadequate for dealing with other complex problems brought on by disasters. Second, business owners need to expand their activities beyond their own locations. It is very possible that a business can suffer disaster-induced interruptions even if its specific property sustained no damage. Suppliers can be impacted, transportation routes can be damaged, and customers may not be able to access the business property. Thus, business owners must also consider and prepare for a variety of off-site contingencies. Finally, businesses must coordinate their own preparedness activities with other businesses and with local governmental agencies. Fostering cooperation among businesses can be difficult because they are accustomed to competing with each other for customers. Institutions such as local chambers of commerce emphasize the shared interests of businesses and work to promote a collective well-being that can be used as a mechanism to promote increased preparedness.

11.4.3.2 Response

In Chapter 8, we discussed the response phase of disaster in great detail and focused on public sector organizations and the challenges they face. A primary emphasis of that discussion was the need for enhanced communication and coordination among the numerous and varied organizations that become involved in a disaster response effort. As we noted in that chapter, established organizations such as police and fire departments and emergency management agencies are not the only ones involved. Rather, various organizations including those that do not ordinarily have emergency-related responsibilities typically contribute to response efforts. Among these other contributing organizations are businesses from the private sector. Their involvement is often essential, but it also creates challenges for emergency managers involved in coordinating the overall response effort.

The role of the private sector during the response phase is diverse and varied (McEntire et al. 2003). For example, restaurant franchises, large-scale retailers, home improvement chains, heavy equipment rental stores, and many others often donate badly needed provisions, supplies, and services in the aftermaths of major disasters. Telecommunications and computer hardware and software companies often provide necessary equipment and technical expertise after disasters. Many other important response activities such as debris removal often rely heavily on paid subcontractors.

Many recent examples of major disasters involved pivotal roles played by the private sector during the response phase. After the 1995 bombing of the Murrah Federal Building in Oklahoma City, much of the media coverage focused on the heroic efforts of firefighters and emergency medical teams, but working alongside them at the scene were numerous representatives from the private sector. Workers from natural gas and electric companies in the state were there to shut down those services and ensure the safety of the site. Telecommunications companies set up mobile equipment to facilitate the use of cellular telephones, and contractors from major construction firms operated heavy equipment to lift and clear debris for rescue workers (Oklahoma City 1996).

Similarly, the response to the September 11, 2001 attacks at the World Trade Center also relied heavily on private utility and telecommunications companies, construction workers, and others to perform critical tasks such as debris removal, technical software support, mass fatality management, sanitation services, perimeter security and fencing, donations management, infrastructure repair, and others (McEntire et al. 2003). In Hurricane Katrina, the private sector was also heavily involved, particularly in debris removal. Because of its wide scope of impact, the hurricane produced enormous amounts of wreckage and debris (Mendonça and Hu 2006), and numerous private entities including waste management companies, landfill operators, and other contractors were involved (U.S. Government Accountability Office 2008).

As you can see, in virtually every recent major disaster in the U.S., the private sector was centrally involved in the response effort. Such widespread involvement magnifies some of the coordination and communication challenges we discussed in Chapter 8, and highlights the importance of promoting greater community-wide preparedness (Chapter 6).

While the private sector often provides necessary equipment, skills, and expertise that local governments may not have, we must also point out the potential for abuses with so much private sector involvement. It is possible, for example, for some companies to receive contracts that are perceived by others as unfair or biased; some companies may exploit a situation and overcharge for services provided. Thus, local officials, including emergency managers, must recognize the importance of the private sector to the overall response effort but also keep a close eye on potential abuses, always striving for integrity, fairness, transparency, and maximum effectiveness.

11.4.3.3 Recovery

As discussed in Chapter 9, the private sector also plays an important role in community recovery after a disaster. When businesses are able to get back online quickly, resume operations, and return to profitability, the entire community benefits from sales tax revenues that fund various services such as public safety, parks and recreation, public works, and others. As we have seen in this chapter and in Chapter 6, businesses do very little to prepare themselves for disasters and as a result often struggle to recover in both the short and long term. In this section, we will discuss business recovery from disasters, including factors that promote or impede business survival.

Two views surround the economic impacts of disasters (Webb et al. 2000). The first is the view that disasters have devastating impacts and drive many firms out of business altogether. The other view is that disaster impacts felt by local communities disappear and are absorbed by regional, state, and national economies (Wright et al. 1979). This macro-level view assumes that disasters do not have negative long-term economic impacts. In reality, the answer lies somewhere between these two extremes.

Perhaps the best way to think about the issue is to recognize that disasters produce winners and losers. On a broad level, most businesses recover from disasters—they at least return to their pre-disaster levels of functionality and profitability. However, some businesses have easier times getting to that point and may even come out ahead. Factors associated with positive recovery outcomes over the long term include size, sector, financial condition, and market scope (Webb et al. 2000; 2002).

Large businesses and those in good financial shape prior to a disaster typically fare better during recovery than their smaller and financially struggling counterparts. Also, businesses in certain sectors such as construction often experience dramatic increases in profits as the rebuilding process begins. Conversely, small retail stores often suffer severe declines, primarily because the sector tends to be crowded and highly competitive under normal conditions and even modest short-term declines in sales can have devastating effects. Finally, businesses whose primary markets extend beyond the local area, such as those with high Internet sales, tend to rebound more quickly because they are less dependent on local customers.

Interestingly, research has shown that two factors that we would expect to facilitate recovery among businesses (preparedness and the use of post-disaster financial aid) do not always produce the desired results. In other words, businesses with higher levels of preparedness and those that receive some form of financial aid are no more likely to report positive recovery outcomes than those that prepare less and do not use post-disaster aid. To explain the apparent ineffectiveness of business disaster prepared-ness, researchers have suggested that the efforts of business owners are mis-guided. As noted earlier in this chapter, owners are primarily interested in protecting themselves and their employees, which is obviously important, but they fail to prepare for the indirect and remote impacts discussed earlier. As for post-disaster financial aid such as low-interest loans from the Small Business Administration (SBA), it is possible that many business owners simply cannot afford to take on additional debt, even in the form of a loan with favorable terms. Consequently, rather than relying on these official sources of aid, many owners turn to personal savings and help from friends and family to get through a disaster (Webb et al. 2000).

An important implication of this discussion is that we need to pay more attention to businesses during the recovery process. Their survival and con-tinued profitability are central to the recovery of the broader community. However, close relationships between business recovery and community recovery are potential sources of conflict. After a major disaster, as recov-ery money begins flowing into the community from various sources, com-munity stakeholders may disagree on how best to use the funds. Some, for example, may promote the idea of economic development and want to use the money to help businesses; others may be more interested in providing support to families and households. Local officials including emergency managers must be sensitive to these kinds of potential conflicts and imple-ment a recovery process that takes multiple perspectives into account and develops sensible, fair, and effective solutions.

11.4.3.4 Mitigation

As with preparedness, response, and recovery, the private sector is also very important to the mitigation phase. Because of its innovation, entre-preneurship, and willingness to take chances, the private sector has greatly enhanced the quality of life in local communities and society at large. Businesses create jobs, perform critical services, and provide opportunities for leisure and recreation. However, business activity can also be risky, not only for the entrepreneur with money at stake, but for society as a whole when a disaster occurs.

Think, for example, about the Deepwater Horizon oil spill in the Gulf of Mexico. British Petroleum obviously saw the potential for huge profits by drilling far offshore in extraordinarily deep waters and decided the risk was acceptable. The company, of course, also had to convince governmental regulators and a skeptical public that the operation was safe and did so in part by using disaster plans to exaggerate its readiness to handle accidents. When the pipe burst, the company and the federal government were woefully unprepared, and the spill dragged on for months. As a result, catastrophic damage was inflicted on the environment and local communities, many of which depend heavily on tourism, fishing, and the petroleum industry suffered devastating social and economic impacts.

There are countless examples of businesses taking extraordinary risks in pursuit of short-term profits that later backfired and produced disasters. A key to the effective mitigation of natural and technological hazards, therefore, is for businesses and communities to pursue economic growth and development in sensible ways that avoid unreasonable risks and unnecessary harm. Individual businesses and larger industries are often reluctant, however, to embrace additional rules and regulations that they perceive as stifling and undermining their ability to compete in the global economy. Therefore, the challenge for local officials, emergency managers, the public, and the business community is to devise and implement strategies that satisfy the demand for growth and development while at the same time maximizing safety.

In his influential book, *Disasters by Design*, Mileti (1999) proposes a model of *sustainable hazards mitigation*. This is an approach that simultaneously allows continued economic success for businesses, maintains and protects safety and quality of life for residents, and preserves the surrounding natural environment. Some of the tools for achieving sustainable mitigation include:

- Land use planning and management
- Building codes and standards
- Insurance
- Prediction, forecast, and warning
- Engineering

All these elements are available, but their use shows substantial room for improvement. Local city councils and planning commissions, for example, continue to allow builders to develop flood-prone and other hazardous areas. Perhaps that situation will change with a fuller embracement of a sustainability framework. As building codes evolve, newly constructed buildings are safer, but many older buildings badly need retrofitting. There is clearly a role for engineering in terms of making our communities safer. As discussed in Chapter 6, we continue to develop ineffective warning systems that ignore what we know about how best to persuade people to take protective actions; that means room for improvement in this area. Finally, in places like Florida and California, hazard insurance is becoming extremely difficult if not impossible to afford. Clearly, there is a need for some kind of innovation or reform in the insurance industry.

Ultimately, the solutions to the problems we face in preparing for, responding to, recovering from, and mitigating disasters will require increased coordination and cooperation between the public and private sectors. In this section, we discussed the relevance and importance of the private sector to all four phases of disaster and emergency management. The remainder of this chapter discusses strategies for enhancing the relationships of the public and private sectors.

11.5 Enhancing Public and Private Sector Relationships

As shown in this chapter, both the public and private sectors face a number of barriers to effective communication. As shown in Box 11.3, one barrier is terminology. While individuals from different governmental organizations may speak the same technical language, they must often interface with business owners and consultants who are far less familiar with the acronyms commonly used by government officials. Over the past decade or so, various organizations have recognized the importance of breaking down these communication problems and devised means for these organizations and sectors to work together. Clearly, without cooperation, coordination, and communication, no activity conducted during the four phases of a disaster can be completed effectively.

As a result, Craig Fugate, the current FEMA director, made public–private relationships a key initiative. Director Fugate says, "There's no way government can solve the challenges of a disaster with a government-centric approach. It takes the whole team. And the private sector provides the bulk of the services every day in the community" (FEMA 2010a). Because of this reality, Director Fugate provided the needed personnel and resources to promote public and private partnerships at the local, state, and federal levels. FEMA also made specific grants available to help start public–private disaster planning initiatives. Key dimensions of developing the partnerships include (FEMA 2010a):

- Sharing situational awareness
- Identifying available response and recovery resources
- Memoranda of agreement or understanding
- Joint training and exercises
- Dedicated liaisons
- Established communication protocols
- Private sector representation within emergency operation centers (EOCs)
- Fully staffed business emergency operations centers

BOX 11.3 IMPORTANCE OF COORDINATION BETWEEN PUBLIC AND PRIVATE SECTORS

Scott Harris

Dr. Scott Harris counts experience spanning over twenty-eight years of environmental, health, and safety management in federal and state governments, consulting, industry, and university instruction. As a former federal on-scene coordinator for EPA Region 6 and a member of its emergency readiness team, he held DOD top secret and DOE Q security clearances and directed multi-agency planning, emergency response, and recovery activities for oil, chemical, biological and radiological releases, and exercises within a five-state region. Scott is an advisory member of the ASSE Healthcare Practice Specialty and a faculty member and course director at the NC OSHERC, part of the University of North Carolina at Chapel Hill Gillings School of Global Public Health. He earned a PhD in environmental science with a specialization in disaster and emergency management from Oklahoma State University and holds degrees in geology (BS) and public health (MPH) from Western Kentucky University. (Photo provided by Scott Harris. With permission.)

I've been doing emergency response work since the mid-1980s, usually without the luxury of adequate time and resources, and often without a bed, food, or sleep for days on end. I've worked eighteen to twenty-four hours per day for weeks at a time; I've been cursed at and called a "feeder at the public trough" by some and viewed as a "guardian angel" by others. Once,

I was even asked by a shy little girl in east Texas for my autograph. I have watched people die and been able to help save others, witnessed heroism and selflessness, and endured bone-crushing stupidity. The front line of this work moves incredibly fast and can be extremely unforgiving.

The incident management team (IMT) is a fixture in modern response work. EPA has the resources to maintain these teams, but private sector responsible parties (RPs) usually need response contractors to fill that need. In support of BP's response to the 2010 Deepwater Horizon oil release, for example, I was a planning specialist embedded with the U.S. Coast Guard in Sector Key West. We integrated the National Park Service and U.S. Fish and Wildlife Service into the planning process to develop site-specific tactical response plans for protection of the Dry Tortugas National Park, the Marquesas Islands, the Keys, and the southern Everglades. Our plans addressed a multitude of threatened and endangered species, refuges, marine sanctuaries, cultural artifacts, and sensitive ecosystems unique to the Keys and the inherent difficulties of oil spill response in these areas. The oil never reached the Keys, but well thought out plans are now in place and the resources committed to at least give them a fighting chance. Later in 2010, I served in Michigan as the RP planning section chief. The largest oil spill in the history of the Midwest complicated the response for both an EPA region and an RP with little experience in oil spills.

There may be hundreds, thousands, or even tens of thousands of response personnel involved, and the politics, power struggles, and economic and social impacts are huge. Everything depends on effective coordination. What the military calls "situational awareness" involves knowing what is going on around you and how it affects your operation. NIMS and ICS, by presidential directive, constitute the "common language" of all response activities in the U.S. The EPA speaks it very well and expects others to do the same, but RPs often fail in this area. My advice always: learn NIMS and ICS. Be able to run them, teach them, and live them. The concepts can be intimidating and seemingly filled with rigid structure and ritual, but fail to keep up and watch how fast you get marginalized on your own response.

The first casualty in battle is the plan and the simple fact is that when all else fails, the ability to improvise is key. You won't do that well without experience and vigilance. Demand it of yourself and others upon whom you rely.

While promoting these partnerships, FEMA does not assume that "one size fits all." Rather, it encourages state and local governments to work together to find what works best in their jurisdictions. Different local and state governments have taken different approaches to meet these objectives (FEMA 2010a). FEMA's most recent planning guide, CPG-101, also stresses and advocates the role of including the private sector in disaster planning. It states, "The private sector plays a critical role in any disaster, and it is important to ensure that they are active participants in the process, including involvement in jurisdictional training and exercise programs. An effective outreach program is critical in developing these partnerships" (FEMA 2010b, p. 53).

After the September 11, 2001 terrorist attacks, the state of Illinois started working with the private sector on infrastructure issues. This effort was called the Illinois Private Sector Alliance Project. Information sharing and the building of partnerships between the public and private sector drove this alliance; infrastructure protection was one of its key goals. Without a functioning infrastructure, both businesses and governments suffer. As the project report indicates, the private sector owns 85% of the infrastructure in the U.S. Another goal of the public–private partnership in Illinois was enhancing mutual aid and resources. As a result, the private sector will be represented in the state's emergency operations center during a disaster. All groups will participate and share information through a terrorism information center. The private sector would be included in disaster exercises held in the state. In addition, workshops, training, and websites would be implemented to enhance public–private relationships (FEMA 2010c).

The International Association of Emergency Managers (IAEMs) also strongly promotes the development of public–private relationships. A recent report from the perspective of a local emergency manager highlights basic steps in developing relationships. The recommendations focus on creating partnerships of local and regional businesses that can help provide key supplies to assist with disaster response and recovery. Stovall (2007, p. 4) recommends the following types of businesses to initiate relationships:

- Utilities
- Transportation companies
- Engineers and engineering companies
- Building inspectors
- Communications
- Debris monitoring and management
- Temporary housing manufacturers
- Construction companies
- Food, water, and ice retailers
- Hardware retailers
- Health care facilities
- Temporary staffing services
- Corporations
- Private security companies
- Private ambulance services
- General rental or supply outlets
- Restoration companies
- Warehouse spaces and temporary storage facilities

Emergency managers must also provide outreach to companies to assist them with their own disaster planning. Although large corporations employ disaster planners, many smaller companies do not have the resources or desire to spend money on disaster preparedness.

The U.S. Chamber of Commerce is also heeding the message that businesses must work with government to prepare for disasters. In a January 16, 2009 press release, Stephen Jordan stated, "Improving our emergency response strategies would prevent the loss of billions of dollars in future damages and business interruptions, which is typical of major disasters … Now is the time to advance 'Disaster 2.0' principles—focusing on readiness and resiliency, rebuilding communities to be more sustainable, and educating the different sectors on how to work together effectively" (U.S. Chamber of Commerce 2009).

Despite these efforts, emergency managers in government and business must be pro-active in making sure partnerships develop and work. Even today, top executives of companies may not see the full value of disaster planning (except for data back-ups), may be concerned about public sector encroachment on private sector businesses, and may focus on their companies' short-term rather than long-term existence. Developing partnerships among all sectors, and educating top executives on the importance of all aspects of disaster management must be a top priority now and in the future.

11.6 Working and Volunteering in Public and Private Sectors

There are numerous opportunities to volunteer or work in the public and private sectors. On the public side, of course, are opportunities at the local (city and county), state, and national levels. At the federal level, FEMA advertises for different types of positions including full-time, permanent employees, on-call response or recovery employees, and intermittent disaster assistance employees (http://www.fema.gov/about/career/index.shtm). At the local level, you may find opportunities for working, volunteering, or interning in several areas, particularly those involved in disasters and emergency management, including police and fire departments and dedicated emergency management agencies.

As we have seen in this chapter and others, other governmental agencies such as planning departments, community development agencies, and housing authorities perform disaster-related work including mitigation projects, applying for grant funding, mapping local hazards, and other functions. When you think about volunteering, seeking an internship, or applying for a job in the public sector, you should look beyond the most obvious places and consider working in one of the related areas. Below is a recent job announcement the authors came across. Notice how closely it relates to the issues discussed in this chapter, including the importance of coordination, communication, and business continuity planning.

> **Emergency Management Officer: Business Continuity**
> **(Human Relations Level 2)**
> **$55,584–$76,224 per annum.**
>
> **Alberta Municipal Affairs and Housing, Edmonton**. The Alberta Emergency Management Agency has an opening that will present challenges and opportunities in relation to business continuity planning for the public sector. The successful candidate will have the proven ability to successfully plan and implement business continuity planning projects while maintaining the ability to assist in the management of disruptions, emergencies and disasters of any type. Your primary responsibility will be assisting ministries in the development, validation and maintenance of their business continuity plans, as well as planning and conducting cross-government coordination and exercising of plans. You will also assist in business continuity training and awareness programs, and plan reviews.
>
> As a strongly motivated individual you will possess excellent multitasking skills allowing you to plan and implement business continuity planning projects while maintaining the ability to assist in the management of disruptions, emergencies and disasters of any type. Your strong presentation and communication skills will be a definite asset to you when leading and facilitating meetings. Your knowledge of or experience working with the Alberta Emergency Management framework, the Emergency Management Act, the Government Emergency Planning Regulation, Disaster Recovery Regulation, as well as Federal Acts and Legislation will be essential in ensuring success in the position.

In addition to the public sector, numerous opportunities exist for working or interning in the private sector. Boxes 11.2 and 11.3, for example, were written by former students of the authors who now work in the private sector. Jodi Ouellette does business continuity planning for a large retail company, and Scott Harris is a disaster response specialist employed by a consulting firm. In addition to this kind of planning and consulting work, emergency management training is useful in other areas of the private sector. Chemical companies and manufacturing plants require safety compliance officers, risk managers, and emergency response personnel.

For those seeking careers in the private sector, there are additional credentials beyond a college degree that you can earn. For example, the Disaster Recovery Institute International (DRII) developed levels of certification emergency managers in the private sector. The lowest to highest certification levels are:

- Associate Business Continuity Professional
- Certified Business Continuity Vendor
- Certified Functional Continuity Professional
- Certified Business Continuity Professional
- Master Business Continuity Professional

Each level generally represents a higher level of experience and further examination. For example, to obtain the Associate Business Continuity Professional level, one must pass an entry level exam and complete an application. The Master Business Continuity Professional level requires five years of experience in the field in at least seven core areas, passing a qualifying exam, completing the master case study exam, and completing an application and submitting references (https://www.drii.org/certification/certification_mbcp.php).

As you can see, there are numerous opportunities for working, volunteering, or doing internships in both the public and private sectors. Although we commonly think of emergency management as a responsibility of the public sector, we have shown that training in the field prepares you for a wide variety of job prospects including many in the private sector. As disasters continue to threaten our communities and their financial impacts continue to climb, it is very likely that those opportunities will expand.

11.7 Summary

In this chapter, we discussed the varied and diverse roles and responsibilities of both the public and private sectors across all four phases of emergency management: preparedness, response, recovery, and mitigation. While we often tend to think only about the public sector—governmental agencies—in relation to disasters, the private sector is becoming increasingly important to effective emergency management. As we have shown in this chapter, businesses suffer a variety of impacts when disasters strike, they perform many essential tasks during the response phase, and overall community recovery depends heavily on the ability of the local economy to rebound. Thus, to make our communities safer and more resilient in the future, the private sector must do a much better job preparing itself for disasters and enter into more effective partnerships with the public sector to mitigate future threats.

As we emphasized throughout this chapter, public–private partnerships have become cornerstones of modern emergency management. Yet, as we discussed, communication barriers at multiple levels threaten to undermine the effectiveness of those partnerships. Within the public sector, lack of communication and coordination at various levels of government are common. As difficult as it is to overcome those challenges, it is even harder in many cases to improve and enhance collaborations between the public and private sectors.

A major challenge for emergency managers of the future, therefore, is to devise more effective strategies for building collaborative relationships across multiple levels of government and between the public and private sectors.

Discussion Questions

1. What is "stove piping"? Why is it a problem, especially in relation to disasters and emergency management? What kinds of steps can organizations take to address the problem?

2. If a disaster strikes your community, what agencies and departments from the local government will be involved in the response effort? Do you think all of them are prepared? Are some more prepared than others? Why or why not?

3. What is the most effective way to persuade businesses to do more to prepare for disasters? Do we need more regulations or mandates to force them to do more? Are incentives such as tax breaks more effective? Research the topic and identify some examples of efforts to better prepare the private sector at the local, regional, or national level.

4. Think about a large-scale regional disaster, such as the Deepwater Horizon oil spill. How should we measure its economic impacts? What factors should be taken into consideration? Who should receive compensation for losses—those in the fishing industry, hotel owners, bars and restaurants? What would be a fair settlement price for all affected parties?

5. How do we best achieve an appropriate balance between the demand for economic growth in our communities and the need for safety and sustainability? Are some economic ventures too risky? Provide an example.

References

Benson, C. and E.J. Clay. 2004. *Understanding the Economic and Financial Impacts of Natural Disasters*. Washington, D.C.: The World Bank.

Burby, R. J. 2006. "Hurricane Katrina and the Paradoxes of Government Disaster Policy: Bringing about Wise Governmental Decisions for Hazardous Areas." *The ANNALS of the American Academy of Political and Social Science* 604: 171–191.

Clarke, L. *Mission Improbable: Using Fantasy Documents to Tame Disaster*. Chicago: University of Chicago Press, 1999.

Disaster Recovery Institute International (DRII). 2010. "Certification." Available at https://www.drii.org/certification/certification_mbcp.php, last accessed December 30, 2010.

Edwards, Frances L. and Daniel C. Goodrich. 2007. "Organizing for Emergency Management." Pp. 39–56 in *Emergency Management: Principles and Practice for Local Government*, 2nd edition, (William L. Waugh and Kathleen J. Tierney, eds.). Washington, D.C.: ICMA Press.

Emergency Management Accreditation Program (EMAP). 2010a. "EMAP History." Available at http://www.emaponline.org/index.php?option=com_content&view=article&id=52&Itemid=56, last accessed December 29, 2010.

Emergency Management Accreditation Program (EMAP). 2010b. *Emergency Management Standard.* Lexington, KY: Emergency Management Accreditation Program.

Federal Emergency Management Agency. 2010a. "Why Start a Public/Private Relationship," Available at http://www.fema.gov/privatesector/ppp_tools.shtm, last accessed February 2, 2011.

Federal Emergency Management Agency. 2010b. *Comprehensive Planning Guide 101.* Available at http://www.fema.gov/pdf/about/divisions/npd/CPG_101_V2.pdf, last accessed February 2, 2011.

Federal Emergency Management Agency. 2010c. "State Partnership – Illinois' Private Sector Alliance Project," Available at http://www.fema.gov/pdf/privatesector/illinois_partnership.pdf, last accessed February 2, 2011.

McEntire, David A. "Local Emergency Management Organizations." 2006. Pp. 168–182 in *Handbook of Disaster Research*, (Havidán Rogríguez, Enrico L. Quarantelli, and Russell R. Dynes, eds). New York: Springer.

McEntire, David A., Robie J. Robinson, and Richard T. Weber. 2003. "Business Responses to the World Trade Center Disaster: A Study of Corporate Roles, Functions, and Interaction with the Public Sector." Pp. 431–457 *In Beyond September 11th: An Account of Post-Disaster Research*, (J. Monday, ed.). Special Publication #39 Natural Hazards Research and Applications Information Center, University of Colorado: Boulder, CO.

Mendonça, David and Yao Hu. 2006. "Hurricane Katrina Debris Removal Operations: The Role of Communication and Computing Technologies." Pp. 283–304 in *Learning from Catastrophe: Quick Response Research in the Wake of Hurricane Katrina*, (Christine Bvec, ed.). Boulder, CO: Natural Hazards Center–University of Colorado.

Menzel, D. C. 2006. "The Katrina Aftermath: A Failure of Federalism or Leadership?" *Public Administration Review* 66/6: 808–812.

Mileti, Dennis. 1999. *Disasters by Design.* Washington, D.C.: Joseph Henry Press.

National Commission on Terrorist Attacks upon the United States. 2004. *The 9/11 Commission Report.* Washington, D.C.: Government Printing Office.

NEMA, 2011. *State Emergency Management Organizations.* Available at http://www.nemaweb.org/index.php?option=com_content&view=article&id=209&Itemid=377, last accessed February 1, 2011.

Oklahoma Department of Emergency Management 2011. Available at http://www.ok.gov/oem/, last accessed February 2, 2011.

Oklahoma Office of Homeland Security 2011. Available at http://www.ok.gov/homeland/, last accessed February 2, 2011.

Quarantelli, E.L., Patrick Lagadec, and Arjen Boin. 2006. "A Heuristic Approach to Future Disasters and Crises: New, Old, and In-Between Types." Pp. 16–41 *Handbook of Disaster Research*, (Havidan Rodriguez, E.L. Quarantelli, and Russell R. Dynes, eds.). New York: Springer.

Stovall, Shane, 2007. "Public-Private Partnerships in the 21st Century," Available at http://www.iaem.com/Committees/publicprivate/documents/PPPinthe21stCentury.pdf, last accessed March 2, 2011.

Sylves, R. T. 2006. "President Bush and Hurricane Katrina: a Presidential Leadership Study." *The ANNALS of the American Academy of Political and Social Science* 604/26: 26–56.

Sylves, Richard. 2008. *Disaster Policy & Politics: Emergency Management and Homeland Security*. Washington, D.C.: CQ Press.

The City of Oklahoma City. 1996. *Final Report: Alfred P. Murrah Federal Building Bombing, April 19, 1995*. Stillwater, OK: Fire Protection Publications.

U.S. Chamber of Commerce, 2009 (January 16). "Business Leaders Call for Change in Disater Response Strategies," Available at http://www.uschamber.com/press/releases/2009/january/business-leaders-call-change-disaster-response-strategies, last accessed March 2, 2011.

U.S. Government Accountability Office. 2008. *Hurricane Katrina: Continuing Debris Removal and Disposal Issues*. Washing, D.C.: U.S. Government Accountability Office.

Waugh, William. 2005. "The Disaster that Was Katrina." *Natural Hazards Observer*. Available at http://www.colorado.edu/hazards/o/archives/2005/nov05/nov05d1.html, last accessed January 25, 2011.

Waugh, William. 2006. "The Political Costs of Failure in the Katrina and Rita Disasters." *The ANNALS of the American Academy of Political and Social Science* 604/10: 10–25.

Webb, Gary R., Kathleen J. Tierney, and James M. Dahlhamer. 2000. "Businesses and Disasters: Empirical Patterns and Unanswered Questions." *Natural Hazards Review* 1/2: 83–90.

Webb, Gary.R., Kathleen J. Tierney, and JamesM. Dahlhamer. 2002. "Predicting Long-Term Business Recovery from Disaster: A Comparison of the Loma Prieta Earthquake and Hurricane Andrew." *Environmental Hazards* 4: 45–58.

Wendling, Cécile. 2010. "Explaining the Emergence of Different European Union Crisis and Emergency Management Structures." *Journal of Contingencies and Crisis Management* 18/2: 74–82.

Wright, James D. Peter H. Rossi, Sonia R. Wright, and Eleanor Weber-Burdin. 1979. *After the Clean-Up: Long-Range Effects of Natural Disasters*. Beverly Hills, CA: Sage.

Resources

- To learn more about the Stafford Act and the role of the federal government in responding to disasters, visit http://www.fema.gov/about/stafact.shtm
- The Comprehensive Preparedness Guide 101 (CPG-101) may be downloaded at www.fema.gov/pdf/about/divisions/npd/CPG_101_V2.pdf - 2010-12-09
- To obtain more information about the President's Cabinet and their related agencies (Section 11.3.4.1) see http://www.whitehouse.gov/administration/cabinet
- For a general understanding of the role of state governments in emergency response, see the National Emergency Management Association (NEMA) website at http://www.nemaweb.org/
- The International City/County Management Association (ICMA) website has extensive general information on the general role of local government. Key search words (e.g., emergency management,

disaster) allow you to obtain information related to emergency management and local government. http://www.nemaweb.org/

- Additional resources dealing with the private sector and disasters are available from the U.S. Small Business Administration (http://www.sba.gov/content/disaster-preparedness and http://www.sba.gov/content/disaster-assistance) and FEMA (http://www.ready.gov/business/index.html).

Chapter **12**

Non-Governmental Organizations

12.1 Chapter Objectives

Upon completing this chapter, readers should be able to:

1. List and define the range of non-governmental organizations active in disaster and humanitarian relief.
2. Discuss the roles and functions of non-governmental organizations working in a disaster context.
3. Identify career paths in non-governmental and international humanitarian relief work.
4. Understand the role that volunteers play in nonprofit and international humanitarian relief work.
5. Explain and enact effective practices for working cross culturally as a paid employee or a volunteer, particularly in contexts and geographic locations different from one's own culture.

12.2 Introduction

What happens when disasters overwhelm available resources, assets and personnel? Even where mutual aid agreements bring in other governmental or private resources, it may be necessary for non-governmental organizations (NGOs) to assist. In this chapter, we learn about the array of NGOs that provide assistance, usually through humanitarian service work. Worldwide, the majority of people affected by disasters could not recover from the devastating impacts caused by earthquakes, tsunamis, famine, and drought without the assistance of such NGOs. NGO efforts range from addressing unmet needs to serving as the primary response and recovery partners and may cover every aspect of a disaster from immediate response to long-term recovery. NGOs may provide basic needs such as food, water, shelter, and even medical care, business recovery assistance, job retraining, and rebuilding the infrastructure. NGOs, operating as partners with governments or as stand-alone organizations, represent critical resources that need to be organized and used effectively.

To learn about their role, this chapter starts with representative samples of domestic organizations and then moves to international contexts and examples. It would be a good idea to first review the typology of disaster organizations presented in Chapter 8 on Response. In that chapter, we learned about four types of organizations: expanding, established, extending, and emergent. Expanding organizations usually tap into volunteer bases to increase their capacity to respond.

For example, the Red Cross pays a small staff but deploys thousands of volunteers. Established organizations hold considerable disaster experience and can respond more rapidly and effectively such as when FEMA activates its National Response Framework. Extending organizations exist outside the disaster context but may offer resources such as heavy equipment to clear debris. Emergent groups and organizations appear usually after a disaster to draw attention to and act on unmet needs. In this chapter, we learn about the four types of NGOs. Astute readers will look for the four types as they read about the NGOs described to understand more deeply the nature of the organizations under discussion.

12.3 Nongovernmental Organizations

Governments rarely meet all the needs generated by disasters, particularly needs that tax organizational capacity, exceed available assets, and require additional personnel. Understandably, only so many people available can respond in a given area when disaster occurs and recovery can take months to years—even decades in some locations. Few disaster responses and recoveries take place without the assistance and support of people who work outside government and military organizations. The nongovernmental sector includes a wide array of organizations that may respond to a disaster from familiar ones like the Red Cross to some you may not know as well such as a disaster organization tied to faith communities.

This chapter walks you through the range of nongovernmental organizations so that you will understand their roles and functions in a disaster context. The chapter begins with familiar organizations active in the U.S. and many other nations, then transitions out to the broader international sector. The transition from the U.S. to the international community is important; it illustrates the importance of being able to move from a domestic context into a broader set of cultural, social, political, and economic circumstances.

12.4 Organizational Structures

As you learned in Chapter 8, four different types of organizations respond to disasters. In this chapter, we sort through NGOs a little differently so that you can see how they vary. We first look at large-scale organizations that subsume others to provide resources and support. Then we move on to traditional disaster organizations familiar to many readers. Finally, we cover faith-based, civic and community organizations that may entice your own volunteer efforts now or in the future. Watch closely for the terms learned in Chapter 8 as you move through this section: emerging, established, extending, and expanding organizations—and how they fit within NGO structures when responding to disasters.

12.4.1 Umbrella Organizations

An umbrella organization covers other organizations much like the spokes of an umbrella. Two types of umbrella-type coalitions appear to exist (Neal 1983). Indigenous (localized) coalitions emerge after a disaster following the emergence of local, grassroots groups. Exogenous (outside the community) coalitions form outside of a local disaster and try to contact local groups and organizations to address a particular problem such as a disaster. Indigenous coalitions appear to be primarily disaster-focused while exogenous coalitions have a broader agenda.

Existing organizations that operate under the umbrella may receive funding, guidance, personnel, and other resources to function. The United Way is one such umbrella organization (operating at the local level and maintaining national offices) that functions to collect and distribute funds to worthy organizations within a community.

In the disaster world, an entity like the U.S.-based National Voluntary Organizations Active in Disaster (NVOAD) connects member organizations interested in disaster service, develops guidance, facilitates communications and coordination, offers conferences and training, and links people across communities, states, and the entire nation. NVOAD currently lists nearly one hundred members on its website (www.nvoad.org) of which two-thirds come from the faith-based community.

Emergent organizations that appear after disasters may also serve as umbrella organizations. As described in Chapter 9 on Recovery, we learned

406   Introduction to Emergency Management

about long-term recovery committees. They connect different organizations to bring in volunteer labor, material supplies, and expertise. Local religious organizations may also create an interfaith committee among local religious denominations to facilitate exchange of information, identify unmet needs, and share resources.

Each of these umbrella organizations performs an ideal task: leveraging the social capital among them and distributing it equitably and efficiently. However, limited evidence to date suggests that sharing resources may not occur in an equitable fashion. In a study of twenty emergent citizen groups that involved over 200 interviews, the larger umbrella organization did help with raising money (Neal 1983). Indigenous coalitions were more successful in securing money and other resources than emergent groups arising from exogenous outreach efforts. Emergent citizen groups that operated under exogenous organizations tended to receive less money. Instead, their association resulted in benefits including coalition advice, pamphlets and other information, networking, and increased legitimacy. Such a trickle-down of resources results in maintenance of exogenous organizations.

Meanwhile, local emergent citizen groups may struggle to acquire funds. Lack of access to money, though, does not predict failure and local emergent citizen groups often experience success in their efforts to address local disaster situations (Neal 1983). It is likely that local networks, local influence, and focused efforts lead to their success.

In a study of Peruvian flooding created by El Niño rains (McEntire 1998), it became clear that communication, coordination, and inter-organizational contacts were critical to produce humanitarian relief. Umbrella organizations, particularly emergent ones, may struggle to generate these conditions. In Peru, key organizations did not coordinate well with the emergent umbrella organization, and problems developed between the umbrella and the responding government. Pre-disaster linkages help to create these conditions but a willingness to work cooperatively post-disaster is the key. To be an effective disaster organization operating as an umbrella for others requires sustained commitment in what can be trying circumstances. Dedicated attention to communication among the array of participating organizations is necessary (McEntire 1998).

Experience also matters with umbrella organizations because it brings in knowledge among established partners. In the U.S., NVOAD relationships have brought about tremendous benefits to damaged communities. After a massive tornado outbreak across Oklahoma in 1999, the Oklahoma Department of Emergency Management convened NVOAD partners from inside and outside the state less than forty-eight hours after the outbreak. At that meeting, people greeted each other by first names, shook hands, and set about identifying needs. Organizations present raised their hands to volunteer for various tasks from food and shelter to long-term rebuilding. The

Seventh Day Adventists offered to set up a donations coordination center. By the following day, a massive warehouse had opened in the state capitol to receive donations. It filled within twenty-four hours and the Adventists, supported by the local Housing and Urban Development office, began faxing inventory lists to the American Red Cross, Salvation Army, Goodwill stores, Baptist churches, and other partners to distribute food, clothing, diapers, appliances, and more. Their pre-existing relationships, coupled with knowing how to accomplish tasks within an umbrella structure, meant that within seventy-two hours of impact survivors received those donations.

Interestingly, Oklahoma NVOAD members had recently completed training which enabled them to step into a familiar role. Yet, considering that well over half of the organizations working under the Oklahoma NVOAD chapter came from other states, their abilities to quickly coordinate and meet needs was clearly due to training, coordination, communication, and inter-organizational relationships among people who knew and trusted each other. Their pre-disaster relationships based on experience and training made a critical difference to those suffering from housing loss, injuries, and unemployment during the worst days of their lives. The ability of Oklahoma groups to could tap into traditional, experienced disaster organizations resulted from their pre-disaster relationships. We turn to those traditional organizations next.

12.4.2 Traditional Disaster Organizations

Most nations host traditional disaster organizations within their boundaries although the organizations may vary by type, structure, and function. The Red Cross, for example, is one of the best known and widespread disaster-oriented organizations. In the U.S., the Red Cross functions to operate shelters, provide mass care (food), basic first aid, and psychological counseling after disasters. It uses donations to help survivors buy clothing, food, and basic furnishings.

After September 11, 2001, the Red Cross used funds to help with funeral expenses, medical bills, and trauma therapy. It worked with airlines to help survivors and family members return to the affected areas for the one-year memorial service. In the U.S., similar to many other nations, a national-level Red Cross also gathers donations, creates guidance and programming, and produces educational materials. State and local chapters develop capacities by using those materials to train and organize disaster action teams. By linking organizationally from the local through state and national levels, the Red Cross generates the ability to respond locally (local chapters vary in staff size, numbers of volunteers, and resources) with additional support from outside the affected area.

The Red Cross also links to international units and can collect funds to respond to areas in need, such as when the Canadian Red Cross gathered and responded to flooding in El Salvador after Tropical Storm Ida in 2010. Funds donated to Red Cross units worldwide went directly to aid survivors from the Haiti earthquake. Red Cross chapters also set up blood collection services to meet regular medical needs and those caused by massive tragedies. Other disaster services may involve Red Cross help too. In mid-December, 2010, for example, the Australian Red Cross sent aid workers to Christmas Island where a boat of asylum seekers from Iran and Iraq crashed on the rocks. Twenty-seven people died including eight children; forty-two survived and thirty sustained injuries. With established programs for refugees fleeing war, drought, famine, and other humanitarian disasters, the Australian Red Cross stands ready to assist with a variety of services including reconnecting survivors with families.

Another classic example of a traditional disaster organization is the Salvation Army. As a global organization, the Salvation Army combines a quasi-military framework with religious values. While it also ministers to people outside the context of disasters, its mobile food and beverage canteens are familiar sights to many picking up the pieces of their lives after disasters, and communities worldwide recognize the Salvation Army red kettles used to collect funds during the holidays. Originating in London, England in 1865, the organization sends staff and volunteers to deliver medical care, community development services (water, sanitation, literacy), and international humanitarian assistance. In 2010, the Salvation Army provided relief to Australia when twenty-two towns in Queensland went under water; delivered famine aid in Kenya, and helped Haitians struggling with a cholera outbreak after the Port-au-Prince earthquake (for more information, visit www.salvationarmy.org).

Traditional disaster organizations offer an established framework for delivering aid, knowing what is most needed, and providing personnel capable and trained to meet the needs. The Red Cross and Salvation Army are also expanding organizations through which trained, qualified, and often credentialed volunteers increase the reach of the organizations' missions and resources. As the most visible NGOs, they often receive significant donations. Because they are so visible, they also garner both acclaim and critique. What is critical to the success of a traditional expanding organization is organizational continuity—maintaining their organizational cultures and knowledge so critical to their previous success. These organizations, however, often experience difficult times when disasters fall off the public radar and donations thin. Despite their critical roles when disaster strikes, traditional organizations may experience some challenges ramping up to respond when they lack the resources to do so. Disasters usually generate funds that allow them to respond, in large part because they are so well known.

12.4.3 Faith-Based Disaster Organizations

Religion, as one of the major social institutions, provides a structure through people can organize to help (Durkheim 1912). Religion also functions to help people through major life events, and certainly a disaster counts as such an event. Faith can sustain people through trauma, even when sadness and grief feel overwhelming. Not surprisingly then, major faith traditions and many denominations have means to help those in need. Faith-based organizations (FBOs) appear similar to umbrella organizations. Some may have been around for a long time and have spun off or supported other disaster organizations. Others may stand alone. Some are well established with decades of experience and some emerged to address unmet needs after a disaster occurred. In this section, we will look at several examples of FBOs to illustrate what they do.

Minimal literature exists on how religious organizations operate in post-disaster contexts. Religious organizations generally foster meaningful participation and provide pre-existing structures and relationships through which to do so (Durkheim 1912). Religions deal with untoward events routinely. For example, faith traditions offer pre-existing norms and rituals for sudden bereavement, ranging from pastoral counseling to funeral services and compassionate meals. Nelson and Dynes (1976) verified that church attendance and devotionalism are associated with altruistic or helping behavior in a disaster context. FBOs tied specifically to disaster response provide a framework within which to provide meaningful service with a core of volunteers dedicated to help those in need.

Most commonly after disaster strikes, an overarching structure emerges to organize faith-based and related organizational efforts. In many communities beset by disaster, an umbrella-type interfaith organizational structure will emerge to work ecumenically. Ross (1980; see also Ross and Smith 1974) describes three different interfaith organization "sets" that evolve through three stages: crystallization or emergence, recognition or attempts to gain legitimacy, and institutionalization. Over time, organization sets decrease in size as the interfaith effort moves toward institutionalization.

The crystallization phase produces a higher level set of personnel to manage key tasks; by the third phase of institutionalization, middle- and lower-level personnel have been added. Finally, as time goes on, interfaith groups establish more formal interactions and communications (Ross 1980, p. 34). In summary, organizational efforts that were emergent (new people, new tasks, new division of labor) become more routine as time passes. Sutton also found that FBOs adapted their organizational structures, for example, dynamically adapting their volunteer bases to meet unique needs generated by September 11, 2001. Sutton adds, "Recognition of the work and leadership of congregations should lead to the inclusion of local faith-based organizations in community recovery plans" (Sutton 2003, p. 424).

Phillips and Jenkins (2010) provide a overview of the roles of FBOs in the Hurricane Katrina response that included an unusual range of activities: salvage work, debris removal, case management and related counseling, funding, donations management, volunteer labor and housing, reconstruction, transitions from shelter to temporary and permanent housing, advocacy efforts, satellite services for displaced congregations, child care, educational outreach, political activity, community organizing, facilitation of partnerships, and economic development. However, given the "outlier" or catastrophic nature of Hurricane Katrina (Quarantelli 2005), these findings may be atypical in that a broader range of faith-based help emerged across the affected areas. In general, though, we can usually count on the faith-based community to be involved in some capacity when disaster occurs.

One of the oldest and most experienced FBOs in Canada and the U.S. is Mennonite Disaster Service (MDS; www.mds.mennonite.net). Originating in 1950, this Christian organization seeks to be the "hands and feet" of Jesus in the world by reducing suffering experienced by people after disasters. Volunteers arrive soon after impact to clean up, muck out, clear debris, save family possessions, and shoulder the grief of those affected. Believing firmly in Galatians 6:2, they enter a community quietly to "fulfill the law of Christ and in so doing" bear the burden of traumatized families. After clean-up, MDS (Figure 12.1) may partner with other organizations to repair or rebuild the homes of low-income families, particularly senior citizens and people with disabilities. MDS participates actively with other organizations as members of the NVOAD mentioned earlier in this chapter to link into long-term recovery committees operating at the local level and leverage resources available through the umbrella organization.

MDS, which provides volunteer labor, may secure roofing materials from Lutheran Disaster Response, funds for wheelchair ramps from Catholic Charities, or case management assistance from the United Methodist Committee on Relief (UMCOR). By working together, these outside partners join collaboratively with locals to identify survivors and provide appropriate assistance. Their coordinated effort means that those most in need, often the people most likely to fall through the cracks of available assistance, have a chance to return home again. Without the help of faith-based organizations,

FIGURE 12.1   Mennonite Disaster Service volunteers working on a home in Grand Bayou, Louisiana. (*Source:* Brenda Phillips.)

many people would never have the ability to recover and would likely lose their possessions and funds that survived the disaster.

Church World Service (CWS) represents a broader global effort to assist in emergency situations. CWS also addresses food security, water purification, and refugee relief issues and also sends resources for disasters (www.churchworldservice.org) because it must:

- Stand on the side of the oppressed through advocacy with and for those most in need.
- Seek out unmet needs of all survivors—particularly people who were vulnerable and marginalized before the disaster.
- Provide a larger vision of life that includes emotional and spiritual care as well as physical rebuilding.
- Assist in long-term recovery of those in need.
- Restore and build community relationships.

Whether an FBO focuses on a single nation or becomes active worldwide, all FBOs typically operate from a belief system organized around core values: to relieve suffering as an act of faithful duty to underprivileged populations. To learn more, see the resource section at the end of this chapter.

12.4.4 Civic Organizations

Similar to faith-based organizations, most communities also host civic organizations. Rotary International, the Lions Club, the Moose, and the Elks usually organize around a particular service focus. Civic organizations usually do not focus on disaster concerns, but serve as extending organizations when disaster occurs. The Lions Club, for example, concentrates on vision issues. After Hurricane Katrina struck the U.S. Gulf Coast, they dispatched mobile vans so that optometrists could test vision and replace damaged or lost eyeglasses. Rotary International, which historically has concentrated on eradicating polio worldwide, has also provided disaster service. It currently concentrates its disaster efforts on fundraising, allowing established organizations to use the funds in appropriate ways.

After Hurricane Katrina, for example, the Rotary Club in Pass Christian, Mississippi, led by Dr. Frank Short, raised money to rebuild low-income homes. Dr. Short did so by contacting Rotary Clubs in all U.S. states and seven other nations. The Rotary Club in Naperville, Illinois led the way by funding several of the homes. Working in concert with the local long-term recovery committee, Rotary worked with MDS to launch the recovery. With Rotary dollars, local casework, and Mennonite volunteer labor, forty families returned home to Pass Christian (Figure 12.2).

Civic organizations present opportunities to those interested in raising money for disaster relief and recovery work. Such civic organizations offer established networks of people dedicated to public service. Their networks produce links to financial and social capital essential for NGOs. By educating these civic organizations on the most effective ways to help, emergency managers can direct critical resources toward acute needs.

12.4.5 Community Organizations

Community organizations differ from civic organizations in that they focus squarely on those in need locally before disaster strikes. In Santa Cruz, California, for example, a community organization served as advocate for pre-disaster homeless displaced from public shelters, tent cities, and doorways by the 1989 earthquake. After the 2008 earthquake in Sichuan, China, disability organizations expressed concern and provided support for those left out of mainstream assistance; cell phones played an important role in reconnecting people (Fu 2009). The Indian Ocean tsunami produced concern for orphaned children. Within India, community organizations opened orphanages, found relatives, and provided trauma care for the children. In Sri Lanka, concern arose over young females and adult women exposed to violence in massive refugee camps. With support from exogenous organizations, local relief organizations integrated protective elements into the camp settings to

FIGURE 12.2   Dr. Frank Short, a member of the Pass Christian Rotary Club, with Mennonite Disaster Service volunteers. (*Source:* Courtesy of Mennonite Disaster Service. With permission.)

reduce sexual exploitation, ensure modesty and female hygiene standards, and reduce the potential for harm (Rees, Pittaway, Bartolomei 2005).

Some community-oriented organizations operate regionally and even nationally but focus their efforts directly or indirectly on local needs. In Texas, Deaf Link of San Antonio provides twenty-four-hour, seven-day interpretation for shelters and general emergency preparedness information in American Sign Language videos and text (http://www.deaflink.com/ahas/shelter-link.php). In Louisiana, the Southern Mutual Help Association operates from New Iberia and funds disaster reconstruction work across the state. It generates funds, conducts casework, and works with faith-based and civic organizations providing volunteer labor (www.southernmutualhelp.org).

The Humane Society of the United States, with chapters at the state and local levels, has created guidance for pet care during disasters and provided grant funds as well. At state and local levels, humane societies develop pet evacuation plans, open public pet shelters, and coordinate to safeguard beloved non-human family members. In states like Alabama, the humane societies coordinate with and support the state response plan. The Alabama state plan organizes evacuation transportation and safe destinations for pets. Plaquemines Parish in Louisiana worked cooperatively with the local animal shelter to build a facility able to withstand a Category 5 hurricane. By combining NGO and community organization support with government planning, both Alabama and Texas will spur human evacuation and save human and animal lives.

Community organizations offer emergency managers an important connection to local residents. Staff and volunteers in community-focused organizations know and understand the local context. They know who is in need, which households may fall through the cracks, and the most effective ways to use incoming assistance. Community organizations also bring in expertise that emergency managers may lack. A local senior citizen center, for example, understands what seniors need and how to serve them. Senior centers offer experienced staff and volunteers capable of supporting the mobility, nutritional, and psychological needs of elderly residents. They understand the trauma of dislocation and the types of temporary housing necessary to provide adequate environments for senior citizens. Organizations focused on seniors also offer important networks such as contacts within public agencies that protect seniors from exploitation and fraud. Involving community organizations makes an emergency manager more effective in his or her job regardless of the phase—preparedness, mitigation, response, or recovery. To illustrate, in Florida and Alabama, the Senior Center/Safe Center program uses senior centers (with discernible blue roofs) as evacuation points, opens them as shelters, and then transitions the facilities into relief and recovery centers.

To summarize, it is critical that emergency managers integrate the wide array of locally knowledgeable NGOs into their toolboxes for responding when disaster occurs. To integrate further community organizations with emergency management agencies, the National Council on Disability (2009) made a series of recommendations specific to people with disabilities. The recommendations stand as best practices examples for any community:

- Integrate disability (and/or gender, aging, children, tribal, pet, environmental) organizations into umbrella organizations, particularly those that foster inter-organizational partnerships and relationships such as NVOAD.
- Integrate disability organizations into pre-disaster volunteer training.
- Integrate disability organizations into volunteer coordination centers and long-term recovery organizations.

- Actively seek out volunteers with disabilities to build a cadre of people ready to participate in disaster relief.
- Ensure that conferences, workshops, training opportunities are disability-friendly.
- Develop cross-training among emergency management and community disability organizations.

In summary, people work and/or volunteer in a wide variety of organizations when disaster occurs. Emergency managers must know and integrate these NGOs into their preparedness, planning, response, recovery, and mitigation activities. Those of you expecting to work outside the profession of emergency management should choose a type of organization that fits well with your professional and personal interests and stand ready to render appropriate assistance when disaster occurs. Selecting an experienced organization with an appropriate framework is especially important in an international context—our next topic.

12.5 International Humanitarian Relief

When people hurt, we certainly want to help. Providing help may be particularly challenging when we must cross national borders and cultures. In this section, we read first about how to work across cultures, examples of inappropriate relief efforts, and recommended procedures.

12.5.1 Working Cross-Culturally

Working effectively in another culture means you have to know the culture. Culture is defined as a design for living that influences how and where people live, work, and interact. Culture is based on language, considered by social scientists to be the foundation on which other cultural components rest. Language influences how we speak to each other and involves both words and the meanings behind them. Shared meanings result from common values over what we consider desirable and undesirable. Donating T-shirts and jeans may seem like a good idea. In reality, you would want to provide clothing appropriate to a climate and culture so that people feel, look, and interact with each other in comfortable ways that calm them and enable them to return to work. In this section, we consider the components of culture and how they influence our approaches to other cultures during a disaster.

Two central concepts derived from sociology represent divergent paths that an individual or their organization can take when working in another culture. These two concepts, ethnocentrism and cultural relativism, depict how people interact across contrasting cultures. Culture, defined as a design for living, influences values and beliefs that tell us what we like or do not like. Culturally based values characterize what is considered desirable or undesirable. Do you prefer tomato soup, for example, or perhaps menudo which is made from the stomach lining of a sheep or cattle? Is it appropriate for you to wear shorts and a tank top or does your culture consider it appropriate to cover yourself more modestly?

Culture also influences norms, defined as behavioral guidelines or rules for how to act (Sumner 1906). Norms include mores (pronounced more-ays) that represent critically important behaviors such as protection of infants from abuse. Folkways are types of norms and defined as behavioral guidelines that we follow because they are our customs. How we shake hands or make eye contact stem from our folkways. Do you squeeze someone's hand or do a fist bump? Do you look someone directly in the eye or just past their earlobe? Knowing these folkways enables you to succeed in another culture because they mean you understand and respect the ways of others. Not knowing these folkways or choosing not to respect them may cause people to think you are "just odd," and remain socially distant or result in complete ostracism. The ability to fit in makes it easier to do your work in another culture because it puts others at ease. But not everyone or every organization chooses to do so. Violating the mores can earn even harsher rebukes from banishment to imprisonment to a death penalty (Sumner 1906).

Ethnocentrism situates your response within your own cultural beliefs and values. When we behave from an ethnocentric frame of reference, we make judgments about other people's cultural values and norms. By turning up our noses at other people's cuisine, we offend them and implicitly tell them we do not value their culture or their hospitality. In many cultures, food is the way that people get to know us. If you don't like grasscutter, for example, you might want to re-think where you do volunteer or humanitarian work, or perhaps you could just learn to enjoy eating rats.

Ethnocentrism also influences the way that we understand and use time. In the U.S., people tend to cram as much as possible into a workweek or day of work. In many other nations, time is spent interacting with others and addressing priorities in a different way. In the past, people and organizations brought their ethnocentric assumptions about what they should do, where they should operate, and how they should deliver aid in disasters. This usually does not work. People who rush in with food they have cooked from their own cultural beliefs may cause significant gastrointestinal distress or discover that children may not even try to eat unfamiliar foods. Organizations that collect donated clothing may discover that survivors discard the used clothing because it is not appropriate for their culture or religious beliefs or suitable for the local climate or for the type of work required. After the Indian Ocean tsunami of 2004, people half a world away who donated boats were shocked to discover that those trying to recover in devastated fishing villages did not use the vessels. Why? Because the local fisher people needed specific kinds of boats, nets, and equipment to gather the local fish. If we truly want to help, we have to work from assumptions generated from local knowledge. Otherwise, good intentions may simply waste time and resources.

Working from a culturally relevant perspective requires that you do your homework to understand what will work for the specific disaster. The first step is researching the culture in which you will work or volunteer. Such an understanding emanates most effectively from local people, so if you are not yet in-country, find people who do understand the culture. You may find them in your own community, perhaps studying at a local university or within a community organization. Information on various cultures is often easily found on the Internet although care should be taken to consult a source that is as close to the local culture as possible. Check who created the document and be sure to take the time to find additional material. You will probably find widely conflicting information if you obtain information only from the Internet. Educate yourself as broadly as possible. It is also wise to take classes in both language and culture to enhance your ability to relate culturally. Language, as the foundation of culture, enables you to fit in better. In Spanish, for example, there are several ways to address people both formally and informally. Knowing which one to use is critical to your success when meeting and interacting in a Spanish-speaking region. People appreciate attempts to speak their language. Be aware though, that formal language classes may not teach local expressions so it is important to consider taking a language class locally. In Costa Rica, for example, you wouldn't just call people Costariqueños, you would call them "Ticos." And you would quickly learn that a common expression is "no te preocupes" which translates roughly to "no worries" in Australia or "chill" in the U.S.

12.5.2 Inappropriate Relief Efforts

When people are hurting and need the right things at the right time in the right place, we need to do the right thing. Although our hearts go out to those affected by disaster, we should stop first and think: what would be the most helpful? On what am I basing this assumption? After reading Chapter 8 on Response, you know that many times the wrong kinds of donations are gathered and sent to a disaster site, often causing unanticipated problems. Volunteers and staff must redirect their time to dealing with what can be overwhelming and often unnecessary items. Although well intentioned, donations of personal prescriptions and inappropriate clothing for a climate or culture can hinder response efforts. Think also about the challenges of receiving items at a damaged location. Earthquakes damage runways and roads. Flooding takes out bridges. Tsunamis destroy port facilities. Many disasters make it extremely difficult to transport relief items.

Experts concur that disaster relief may need to be coupled with development planning. Disasters are often intertwined with poverty, with some nations and populations faring far worse when hazards erupt into events. Development patterns such as rapid urbanization can increase risk by increasing population density in hazardous areas. Development that fails to consider disasters wastes resources (Anderson 1995; Fordham 2006). Effective development aids those most at risk from failed programs as well as disasters.

12.5.3 Appropriate Relief Efforts

After the 2010 Haiti earthquake, the U.S. Agency for International Development (USAID) issued this set of recommendations to guide humanitarian contributions (www.usaid.gov):

- A humanitarian organization with staff in the affected region should request the commodities being offered. The request must be very specific and the organization should approve the commodities after having reviewed all relevant technical specifications. The requesting organization should also have the capacity to distribute the commodities to the beneficiary population or be partnered with an organization in the region that does.

- The commodities offered should not be available for purchase in the affected region. Or if they are available locally, their procurement within the region should not be cost-prohibitive. The reason for this condition is that relief efforts should strive to support the regional economy through local procurement whenever possible, in order to promote sustainability and self-reliance. In addition, local procurement ensures cultural and environmental appropriateness.

- The commodities being offered must be useable and sustainable. The commodities should be adaptable to local technical and environmental conditions, such as voltage, dust, temperature, humidity, etc. When relevant, local language must be used (for example, computer operating systems, instruction manuals, and pharmaceutical labels should be in the local language). When necessary, appropriate technical training must be provided. The beneficiaries must be able to obtain associated supplies (for example, paper and toner cartridges for printers and copiers). Repair services for the commodities must be available locally.

These guidelines ensure that staff and volunteers in the damaged area will receive exactly what they need. More importantly, the influx of contributions will not undermine the locally struggling economy. The contributions will also be understandable as information will be written in language or symbols that are understood by all. After the Haiti earthquake, for example, starving residents threw away nutrition bars stamped with the current date. They assumed they had expired and feared they might be harmful. Inappropriate relief efforts run the risk of undermining the intended goal: to relieve suffering. It is critical that we are part of the solution, not part of miring humanitarian relief and extending suffering.

Typically, money is the best contribution. Money can be used locally to help the economy and buy exactly what is needed. When we donate funds to reputable organizations, they can transfer the money electronically and instantaneously. There is no need to secure transportation for money in the way transport is necessary if you collect clothing, furniture or building materials. After the Haiti earthquake, for example, several organizations and governments collaborated to set up 19,000 transitional temporary housing units. Funds donated to the Salvation Army and Rotary International, an FBO and civic organization partnership, sent boxes of critically needed items already organized and ready for shipment. By donating to trusted organizations that have experience in providing relief, we reduce the chances that our good intentions turn problematic. So unless you have a temporary housing unit in your closet that you can transport to Haiti, send money.

Longer term recovery efforts may allow you and relief organizations to expand beyond financial contributions. Should the above conditions be met, USAID recommends that material relief be managed based on these conditions (www.usaid.gov):

- The confirmed need of the beneficiaries for the commodities being offered: Specific characteristics, quality, and quantity should be clear and verified.
- The packaging and labeling requirements: Commodity contributions need to be packaged and labeled in specific ways in order for shipping, customs, storage, and distribution to proceed smoothly.
- The shipping arrangements, including funding: International shipping is very expensive and extremely complicated. A source of funding for the shipment must be identified before collections begin. A freight forwarder and consignee for the shipment must also be identified in advance.
- The humanitarian organization's local storage and distribution plan: The organization should have resources in the affected region ready to receive, offload, store, and eventually distribute the commodities to the beneficiaries.

Following on the earlier advice by Anderson (1995) and Fordham (2006), noted humanitarian Cuny (1983, see Box 12.1) said that disasters should

BOX 12.1   INTERNATIONAL HUMANITARIAN RELIEF WORK

Too many people die because the world does not care how relief work is done.

Fred Cuny

In 1983, Fred Cuny wrote, "The most basic issues in disasters are their impact on the poor and the links between poverty and vulnerability to a disaster … we must address the question of how to reduce poverty … if we hope to reduce suffering and to make a true contribution to recovery." As an international humanitarian deeply involved in disaster relief, Cuny understood disasters as the results of differential access to resources. Addressing that gap between people with resources and people without resources represented his life's work that took him to Guatemala, Bosnia, the Sudan, Somalia, Iraq, Ethiopia, Sri Lanka, Chechnya, and other places in need. Through establishing crucial partnerships, he supported refugees and disaster victims in need of food, clothing, shelter, water and safer, more humane conditions.

Cuny's philosophy centered on involving stakeholders in the process of helping themselves. Based on his international experience, from 1969 to 1995, he came to believe that certain factors influenced the success of any international relief program (Cuny 1983). First, the attitude that people bring into a relief situation matters. Those keen to help should not approach a stricken area in a paternalistic fashion as if the survivors needed a father figure to look after them. Rather, Cuny advocated helping victims to help themselves as a far more effective strategy. Second, how one relates to the affected community matters. Many outsiders perceive themselves as providers of relief. Conversely, outsiders should work in concert with local communities to identify goals and establish appropriate relief efforts. Local people know best what will work for them. Third, how decision making occurs matters. Cuny identified decision making as the critical element in determining success or failure of international humanitarian relief efforts. Certainly, providing relief offers charity, but from Cuny's perspective successful efforts are driven by a participatory process where decisions are made by locals supported by outsiders. Imagine the consequences of not doing so: when you leave an area where you have provided relief, the pre-disaster vulnerability remains. You have put a band-aid on and not addressed the cause of the injury.

Cuny concurred with Alan Barton (1970) that disasters lay bare the social problems of a society. Where do we start if providing aid is not the beginning, middle, and end of a relief effort? Cuny urged us to focus on poverty, development issues that undermine rather than build up, and the effects of rapid urbanization including housing prices and locations. Relief offered by outsiders typically centers on micro-level conditions at the individual or household level with tents, water, cots, blankets, and food as the primary solutions offered. Imagine a more macro-level approach that changes the life chances of people so that they and their children and their grandchildren have far better chances of surviving and thriving.

Cuny disappeared in Chechnya in 1995 and is presumed to have been murdered by Chechen rebels. Cuny earned many accolades for his work, but his standing legacy remains his approach to international humanitarian and disaster relief work.

address the conditions that undermine future resistance and thwart the development process. Cuny asked "Are you the kind of agency that counts the houses you built and measures your success by the number?" Outsiders who use an ethnocentric perspective also assume their technologies and solutions will solve the problem. Such a paternalistic approach simply does not work and "greater attention needs to be paid to non-Western knowledge and local environmental practices" (Bankoff 2004, p. 35).

Another common problem that undermines humanitarian aid and post-disaster programs comes from poor planning. One issue is poor conceptualization of projects—usually stemming from failure to involve local people. Ineffective programs also bring in outsiders to "fix" things rather than provide local training, jobs, and loans. Developing capacity must be done carefully and thoughtfully. Throwing money at people without a process and program in place will not be effective.

Cuny identified four common program models that operate in disaster relief situations. The "quick and dirty" program sends relief materials with minimal input from locals. The "firefighting" model puts out the fire but does not have a long-term impact on future events. The "development through disaster" model uses the post-disaster period to integrate development opportunities. Cuny calls the final option "planting the seed" because it offers disaster relief through a slower, development-focused process and is highly participatory.

12.5.4 International Standards for Humanitarian Relief

In 2003, the government of Sweden convened over a dozen nations and the European Commission to discuss appropriate humanitarian relief. The convention established a set of twenty-three principles to guide external donations (Figure 12.3). As basic guidelines, these nations affirmed the importance of sending appropriate aid as needed by beneficiaries. The principles confirm that donations should be sustainable and support long-term recovery and development. To be sustainable, donations must survive future impacts and be repaired or supported locally.

Starting points for local relief include damage and needs assessments conducted in-country with the guidance, input, and support of locals (PAHO

PRINCIPLES AND GOOD PRACTICE OF HUMANITARIAN DONORSHIP

Objectives and definition of humanitarian action

1. The objectives of humanitarian action are to save lives, alleviate suffering and maintain human dignity during and in the aftermath of man-made crises and natural disasters, as well as to prevent and strengthen preparedness for the occurrence of such situations.

2. Humanitarian action should be guided by the humanitarian principles *of humanity*, meaning the centrality of saving human lives and alleviating suffering wherever it is found; *impartiality*, meaning the implementation of actions solely on the basis of need, without discrimination between or within affected populations; *neutrality*, meaning that humanitarian action must not favour any side in an armed conflict or other dispute where such action is carried out; and *independence*, meaning the autonomy of humanitarian objectives from the political, economic, military or other objectives that any actor may hold with regard to areas where humanitarian action is being implemented.

3. Humanitarian action includes the protection of civilians and those no longer taking part in hostilities and the provision of food, water and sanitation, shelter, health services and other items of assistance, undertaken for the benefit of affected people and to facilitate the return to normal lives and livelihoods.

General principles

4. Respect and promote the implementation of international humanitarian law, refugee law, and human rights.

5. While reaffirming the primary responsibility of states for the victims of humanitarian emergencies within their own borders, strive to ensure flexible and timely funding, on the basis of the collective obligation of striving to meet humanitarian needs.

6. Allocate humanitarian funding in proportion to needs and on the basis of needs assessments.

7. Request implementing humanitarian organisations to ensure, to the greatest possible extent, adequate involvement of beneficiaries in the design, implementation, monitoring and evaluation of humanitarian response.

8. Strengthen the capacity of affected countries and local communities to prevent, prepare for, mitigate and respond to humanitarian crises, with the goal of ensuring that governments and local communities are better able to meet their responsibilities and coordinate effectively with humanitarian partners.

FIGURE 12.3 European Union's Principles and Good Practice of Humanitarian Donorship. With permission.

9. Provide humanitarian assistance in ways that are supportive of recovery and long-term development, striving to ensure support, where appropriate, to the maintenance and return of sustainable livelihoods and transitions from humanitarian relief to recovery and development activities.

10. Support and promote the central and unique role of the United Nations in providing leadership and coordination of international humanitarian action, the special role of the International Committee of the Red Cross, and the vital role of the United Nations, the International Red Cross and Red Crescent Movement and non-governmental organisations in implementing humanitarian action.

Good practices in donor financing, management and accountability

(a) Funding

11. Strive to ensure that funding of humanitarian action in new crises does not adversely affect the meeting of needs in ongoing crises.

12. Recognising the necessity of dynamic and flexible response to changing needs in humanitarian crises, strive to ensure predictability and flexibility in funding to United Nations agencies, funds and programmes and to other key humanitarian organisations

13. While stressing the importance of transparent and strategic priority-setting and financial planning by implementing organisations, explore the possibility of reducing, or enhancing the flexibility of, earmarking, and of introducing longer-term funding arrangements.

14. Contribute responsibly, and on the basis of burden-sharing, to United Nations Consolidated Inter-Agency Appeals and to International Red Cross and Red Crescent Movement appeals, and actively support the formulation of Common Humanitarian Action Plans (CHAP) as the primary instrument for strategic planning, prioritisation and coordination in complex emergencies.

(b) Promoting standards and enhancing implementation

15. Request that implementing humanitarian organisations fully adhere to good practice and are committed to promoting accountability, efficiency, and effectiveness in implementing humanitarian action.

16. Promote the use of Inter-Agency Standing Committee guidelines and principles on humanitarian activities, the Guiding Principles on Internal Displacement and the 1994 Code of Conduct for the International Red Cross and Red Crescent Movement and Non-Governmental Organisations (NGOs) in Disaster Relief.

FIGURE 12.3   Continued.

17. Maintain readiness to offer support to the implementation of humanitarian action, including the facilitation of safe humanitarian access.
18. Support mechanisms for contingency planning by humanitarian organisations, including, as appropriate, allocation of funding, to strengthen capacities for response.
19. Affirm the primary position of civilian organisations in implementing humanitarian action, particularly in areas affected by armed conflict. In situations where military capacity and assets are used to support the implementation of humanitarian action, ensure that such use is in conformity with international humanitarian law and humanitarian principles, and recognises the leading role of humanitarian organisations.
20. Support the implementation of the 1994 Guidelines on the Use of Military and Civil Defence Assets in Disaster Relief and the 2003 Guidelines on the Use of Military and Civil Defence Assets to Support United Nations Humanitarian Activities in Complex Emergencies.

(c) Learning and accountability

21. Support learning and accountability initiatives for the effective and efficient implementation of humanitarian action.
22. Encourage regular evaluations of international responses to humanitarian crises, including assessments of donor performance.
23. Ensure a high degree of accuracy, timeliness, and transparency in donor reporting on official humanitarian assistance spending, and encourage the development of standardised formats for such reporting.

Endorsed in Stockholm, 17 June 2003 by Germany, Australia, Belgium, Canada, the European Commission, Denmark, the United States, Finland, France, Ireland, Japan, Luxembourg, Norway, the Netherlands, the United Kingdom, Sweden, and Switzerland.

FIGURE 12.3 Continued.

2009). Donors should also be aware of the myths that surround international disasters and that relief efforts should take these into consideration. As one illustration, epidemics are often assumed to follow disasters when in reality they usually do not. Haste to cremate the dead out of such fear after an Indian earthquake in 2001 reduced fuel supplies needed to cook food for survivors. Realistic response must cover all needs in the context of what is likely to happen and not happen.

Donors providing international relief should also coordinate carefully not only with locals but with other donors to avoid duplication. Communication with locals leading the recovery efforts is critical and working through established or emergent channels to avoid duplication is necessary. Above all, do not over-react and assume you know what to send. Work with established systems that do not overwhelm local capacities to handle donations. Send what is needed at the right time to the right place to the right organization. As the Pan American Health Organization, an experienced disaster contributor, recommends: "Despite the tragic images which the media may show, it is necessary to form an overall view of the situation, waiting for the country's requests for aid, maintaining contact with the organizations in the field and relying on relevant, technical information are ways of becoming aware of the real needs of the population" (PAHO 2009, p. 25).

A faith-based initiative associated with two synods of the Presbyterian Church USA reflects these humanitarian relief guidelines. A synod is an organizational structure within a national faith-based framework. The Synod of Living Waters includes the states of Kentucky, Tennessee, Alabama, and Mississippi. Taking a cue from their synod name, church members created an organization called Living Waters for the World which has partnered with organizations in twenty-three other countries to deliver, install, and sustain basic water sanitation systems. In 2010, the Synod of the Sun (Oklahoma, Texas, Louisiana, and Arkansas) modeled the Living Waters for the World effort to create Solar Under the Sun which provides basic solar energy also in concert with local operating partners (see Resources section).

Mission teams first identify an area in need and raise funds to send an assessment team. Working with a local operating partner, they collectively find an appropriate place to build a solar-powered water treatment facility. The U.S.-based initiating partner then raises funds to buy parts, with as many items purchased in-country as possible. The U.S. partner then sends an installation team to teach local partners how to build, use, and maintain the water treatment plant and/or solar power facility. Over a period of nine years, the U.S. teams support local partners who eventually take over maintenance of the facility to sustain the joint effort. Water is life-saving. In locales where safe drinking water is not a guarantee, water can prevent children from dying from diarrhea—the leading cause of death for children under the age of three. Solar energy means that clinics can refrigerate medicines, power cell phones for emergencies, and children in orphanages can study at night. By following good principles for humanitarian relief, these organizations have built sustainable structures consonant with local needs.

Thirteen of the nineteen Living Waters for the World water treatment plants installed before the 2010 earthquake in Haiti survived the shaking, a promising result considering the massive devastation. Using parts salvaged from the damaged water treatment plants, a local operating partner built a new treatment plant to help survivors. Since the earthquake, Living Waters for the World and Solar Under the Sun have joined forces to convert existing or build new solar-powered water treatment plants in Haiti (Figure 12.4;

FIGURE 12.4 **Living Waters for the World and Solar Under the Sun collaborate with local operating partners to build and maintain solar-powered water treatment plants in Haiti. (*Source:* Courtesy of Solar Under the Sun. With permission.)**

http://www.solarunderthesun.org/ and http://livingwatersfortheworld.org). Their promising efforts suggest that principles for effective non-governmental and humanitarian relief can indeed work and even allow survival after one of the worst disasters in world history.

In reality, people will need immediate relief in many situations but it must be organized and distributed in ways that make sense locally. Longer term options will likely be needed as well, particularly in impoverished areas. Cuny recommends "integrated recovery programs" that respond holistically to people's needs and may involve housing, training and work, micro-loans, sustainable infrastructure, and more. As a result, Cuny (1983, p. 162) observed that a community "tends to recover more uniformly in a shorter, less turbulent recovery period." To understand the program elements that people need in their social, cultural, economic, and physical environments, experts recommend empowering community-based participation, our next topic.

12.5.5 Empowering Locals

As you can see from the above section, it is critical to work with local organizations, agencies and people to do the right thing when disaster occurs. We tend to assume, particularly in international situations, that people require extensive outside aid. While we certainly want to help those dealing with impoverished conditions that threaten response and recovery, we must do so in a

FIGURE 12.5   Voluntary organization members meet with government representatives after a tsunami affected American Samoa. (*Source:* Courtesy of Mennonite Disaster Service. With permission.)

manner that is effective. Media images suggest that we need to rush in with whatever we can gather. The truth is that in most situations local residents can provide useful guidance (Figure 12.5). They understand their own cultures, the local language, the important customs, and where the impacts are the most significant. After a cyclone, for example, road signs may be down and transportation arteries disrupted. We need local residents to navigate the area.

Local residents also understand how people interact, connect, and communicate. In many emergency shelters, cots are set up in rows. The first thing that families and friends usually do is rearrange the cots into areas that allow them to talk, monitor children, and feel secure. In temporary shelters like huts or tents, it is more difficult to move what is already set up, usually in sequential rows. People are generally assigned to the next available tent. This may seem expedient, but it can undermine important social networks and relationships that help people survive socially, psychologically, and even economically. People in some South American communities, for example, are accustomed to having homes surround a central courtyard where they visit, share food, and mind each other's children.

How should we best work with local residents? Whether in our own or in another country, we start by empowering people. Empowerment means that we ask people what they think is needed most, where it is needed, and what is the best way to get it there. Strategies for empowering people can include:

- Finding the leaders of pre-disaster organizations and convening a task force or long-term recovery committee.
- Allowing the leaders to elect a chairperson they know and trust.
- Paying the leaders for their time because they also may have been affected by the disaster.
- Enabling local leadership with technologies that enhance communication outside the community.
- Holding meetings in the local language.
- Honoring local customs such as how to structure a meeting, what type of organization works best, and how local leaders prefer to interact. A top-down structure may not be as effective as a collaborative, consensus-building model the locals can tell us about.
- Ensuring that people have voices at key planning, response and recovery meetings. This is particularly important for underrepresented groups within the affected area, particularly women, racial and ethnic minorities, the elderly, and people with disabilities.
- Turning off your personal microphone so that locals have a chance to speak or sign.

In *Working with Women at Risk*, Elaine Enarson et al. (2003), developed a workbook useful well beyond its emphasis on women. Available in a user-friendly format and written in both English and Spanish, the workbook walks a local working group through identifying local hazards. In an example of how important local knowledge is, they discovered that an electrical supply power surges constituted a hidden hazard in the Dominican Republic. In one tragic moment, a Dominican woman died from a power surge. Through a local effort designed to identify risks and provide solutions, the power surge issue came to the forefront because local women interviewed local women.

Empowering local residents means that local knowledge influences relief and recovery efforts. By reaching out to and honoring local residents, it is possible to identify exactly what is needed and avoid inappropriate contributions. Less time is wasted. More people are helped in a manner that is familiar to them and therefore more easily accepted. Empowering locals also makes your work or volunteering far more effective.

12.6 Working and Volunteering in a Non-Governmental Organization

You might consider two routes to gaining experience within a non-governmental organization active in disasters. The first is paid employment while the second comes through volunteer participation. Both routes generate insight about the non-governmental context and associated challenges while allowing you to derive considerable satisfaction in making a difference, often one person and one place at a time. Although the challenges of NGO work may be particularly frustrating—usually need overwhelms resources—seeing families lifted from poverty, able to feed their children, or move into a newly rebuilt, post-disaster structure makes all the hard work very worthwhile.

People who work in NGOs usually start at the bottom and work their way up. Education and experience matter because staff must truly understand the people and contexts in which they work. To be effective and move upward in a non-governmental career, you must pay your dues by learning how organizations function (or do not) and how you can effect success within them—sometimes in very challenging and difficult circumstances (see Box 12.2. Bob Counseller). You may also want to consider an internship first to learn whether international work is right for you. The Natural Hazards Project of the Organization of American States offers such opportunities and understandably requires fluency in another language (see Resources section). Similarly, organizations such as the Peace Corps provide entry points to learn about other cultures and how to work with local partners.

At this point, it should be clear that volunteering must be done in a manner that is sensitive to local cultures and fits in well with established organizations. However, the truth is that many people simply show up to volunteer assuming there is work to be done without regard for their ability to get into or move around a disaster site, without appropriate training, and without the ability to remain safe amid dangerous debris. As a result they interfere with ongoing response operations (Paton 1996). These kinds of people are known as SUVs or spontaneous unplanned volunteers (NVOAD n.d.). Although well-intentioned, they do not understand that volunteerism works most effectively through an organized structure and with appropriate training for the conditions.

It is best to plan your future volunteer efforts carefully. First, find an organization experienced in disaster relief with a reputation for following the principles discussed. Become affiliated by completing forms so that the organization knows where and how to contact you for help. Second, obtain appropriate training. Organizations with disaster missions usually offer training to their volunteers. The Red Cross, for example, offers specific kinds of training in shelter management, first aid, and psychological support. Other organizations may offer on-site training and supervision such as for debris removal and construction. While much volunteer effort may be unskilled, providing for the safety of the volunteers and the quality of the labor requires some management skill. Further, the response period when

BOX 12.2   WORKING INTERNATIONALLY IN EMERGENCY MANAGEMENT

Robert Counseller

Robert Counseller has post-conflict and development project management experience in eighteen countries across Africa, Asia, Central Asia, Europe, the Balkans, and the Russian Federation along with more than ten years of disaster-related study, research, and implementation experience in the U.S. and abroad. By stressing accountability to both donors and recipients, his multidisciplinary background targets strategic thinking and implementation for organizations working in development, disaster, and post-conflict environments.

I gravitated easily toward the concepts of emergency management. I readily embraced the FEMA model of planning, response, and recovery as it was taught at the University of North Texas in the 1980s. The concepts of mitigation felt almost intuitive to me. It all made sense. I understood that if people would undertake the planning, recognize what "phase" of a given disaster they were in, and then embrace mitigation as crucial, they could lessen their vulnerability and improve their lives.

What I couldn't see was being an emergency manager. I'm a field guy. I like to get out in the bush, visit project sites, and keep away from the office. I simply couldn't visualize myself sitting at a desk or going to meetings to convince a city or corporation that upgrading an alert system or improving off-site data storage was worthy of a line item in a new budget. I was lucky enough to be given "free range" on research paper topics as an undergrad and in the library I found a book that immediately changed my life. It continues to affect my thinking today.

The late Fred Cuny established Intertect and wrote *Disasters and Development* (Oxford Press, 1983). Reading that book, then meeting Cuny researching in his library in Dallas and later working with people from his Intertect staff out in the field, sent me on a journey that I'm on to this day.

The salient point Cuny argued in *Disasters and Development* was that the multi-billion dollar Third World aid and relief industry was very often doing more harm than good implementing disaster relief and "development" projects. In numerous cases, such projects only "developed" or perpetuated a population's vulnerability to catastrophe. Thirty years later, this is not necessarily a singular point of view. Even the most rudimentary research today would yield a number of similar and learned opinions. However, that does not mean that in design, implementation, and practice in the field, much has changed. In fact, it is my experience that the mistakes not only continue to be made, but they are amplified by the increased number of agencies and institutions currently involved with developing the Third World and responding to disasters both at home and abroad.

Cuny was killed while working in Chechnya in 1995. The international disaster community lost an icon of innovative thinking and implementation. Research has focused on the relationships between disaster and development in the Third World since then, but with Cuny gone, the research lost a focal point and its most innovative field implementer. Personally, I lost a mentor, but I kept the motivation to stay in the field and work on the issues.

Fundamental to my personal approach to working on these issues abroad is the FEMA planning model I was taught at UNT in the 1980s. Essentially, I view the processes and programs of "development" in the Third World as mitigation. From a "disaster management" view, programs that are meant to improve cropping methods for subsistence farmers , construct a village school, or establish a cold chain to deliver and preserve medicines and inoculations, for example, are all actions of mitigation—such programs can reduce a population's vulnerability.

Simply put, I am convinced that efforts of development anywhere in the world should be considered through the optics of disaster planning. Too many examples can be found at home and abroad where attempts at improving people's lives through "development" or relief have actually increased their vulnerability to catastrophe. I continue to find this fascinating and worthy of research and effort.

the disaster is fresh in their minds is when most people want to volunteer. In reality, the long-term recovery period is when most volunteers are needed. Be patient and know that if you volunteer it may be a year or more before you can join a volunteer site. Remember that it takes time to assess needs, set up projects, secure volunteer housing, and arrange to feed those helping hands. The wait will be worth it as not only will you be able to help when and

FIGURE 12.6 Faith-based volunteers working on a home damaged by Hurricane Ike in 2008. Photo courtesy of First Presbyterian Church, Stillwater, with permission.

where needed, but you will receive benefits as well. Volunteering makes us feel good about ourselves while enriching our understanding of the people we serve (Figure 12.6).

12.7 Summary

In this chapter, we learned that a variety of organizational structures exist to provide disaster relief. Umbrella organizations serve as hosts for other groups and often coordinate across organizations to share information and resources. A wide range of traditional disaster organizations exist as well. In a disaster situation, working or volunteering with an established, experienced, and reputable disaster organization is the best thing to do. You may want to rush in and donate what you can spare, but relief to those in need should emanate from what these experienced organizations recommend.

Your efforts to help those in need may move through several types of organizations. Many faiths offer organizations through which you can participate (Figure 12.6). Faith-based organizations provide needed relief, particularly with rebuilding during long recovery periods when most volunteers have lost interest. Civic organizations conduct fundraising events and may be able to extend their service focus to a local, post-disaster need.

Community organizations, while not usually disaster-oriented, often link disaster volunteers and organizations to those most in need of assistance. The most critical step to take is to understand what local people actually need and to support them in securing those resources. Empowering those who seem devastated may seem illogical when they are hurting but doing so can generate much-needed income, employment, and development. Overall, NGOs fill a crucial role in disasters especially if they do so in culturally sensitive ways that enrich rather than undermine future disaster resistance and development.

Discussion Questions

1. Describe the characteristics of disaster umbrella organizations. Under what conditions are they most effective?

2. Why is it useful for a faith-based organization to assist in a disaster-stricken community? If you wanted to volunteer for one, which one would you select and why? As a starting point, consider the FBOs listed as members (see their website links) at www.nvoad.org. Many FBOs now have facebook pages as well. Consider "liking" their page and watch what they do as you take this course.

3. Which civic organizations exist in your community? What is the focus of their service? What kinds of past projects have they under-taken? Consider contacting one or more of them and attending a meeting. Meet with the chapter president and ask about service work and whether the organization has been involved in disaster work. What was the experience like?

4. In your community, which population groups would you expect to have the greatest needs after a disaster? In many communities, they include low-income households, senior citizens, single parents, people with disabilities, children, and group homes. What community organizations operate locally or nearby that provide insight and experience into populations with the greatest needs? Consider contacting them and ask them if they have been involved in disaster work. Do they have disaster plans to continue their operations should the community be impacted by an event? What do they think they have to offer should a disaster occur? You might also think about contacting the local emergency management office to ask similar questions about how the office has (or has not) involved community organizations in disaster planning.

5. After reading the section on ethnocentrism and cultural relativism, list some of the values and norms considered desirable in your own

culture. If you were advising an outside organization arriving to help your community and culture, what would you suggest to help volunteers fit in and be as effective as possible?

6. Where would you like to work in a non-governmental organization? What appeals to you domestically and/or internationally? What advantages would international non-governmental work offer to you in terms of experience and future career paths?

7. Identify the top three non-governmental organizations you would like to volunteer for. What would you learn there? What could you contribute? Listen carefully to others as they describe their interests and motivations for such volunteer work. As a future emergency manager, how would you tap into that spirit of non-governmental work?

8. What kind of background do you have that would allow you to do volunteer work? What kind of work would you like to do? Where can you secure the required training? What kind of timeline do you need to be ready and trained before the next disaster?

References

Anderson, Mary B. 1995. "Vulnerability to Disaster and Sustainable Development: A General Framework for Assessing Vulnerability." Pp. 41–50 in *Disaster Prevention for Sustainable Development: Economic and Policy Issues,* (M. Munasinghe and C. Clarke, eds.). Washington, D.C.: The World Bank.

Anderson, Scott. 2000. *The Man Who Tried to Save the World: The Dangerous Life & Mysterious Disappearance of Fred Cuny.* NY: Random House.

Bankoff, Greg. 2004. "The Historical Geography of Disaster; Vulnerability and Local Knowledge." Pp. 25–36 in *Mapping Vulnerability: Disasters, Development and People,* (G. Bankoff, G. Frerks, and D. Hilhorst, eds.). Sterling, VA: Earthscan.

Barton, Allen. 1970. *Communities in Disaster.* NY: Doubleday.

Cuny, Frederick. 1983. *Disasters and Development.* Dallas, TX: Intertech Press.

Cuny, Frederick and Richard B. Hill. 1999. *Famine, Conflict and Response: A Basic Guide.* Kumarian Press.

Durkheim, E. 1912. *The Elementary Forms of Religious Life.* New York: Oxford University Press.

Enarson, Elaine, Lourdes Meyreles, Marta González, Betty Hearn Morrow, Audrey Mullings, and Judith Soares. 2003. *Working with Women at Risk: Practical Guidelines For Assessing Local Disaster Risk.* Miami, FL: International Hurricane Center, Florida International University. Available at http://www.ihrc.fiu.edu/lssr/workingwith-women.pdf, last accessed January 4, 2010.

Fordham, Maureen. 2006. "Disaster and Development Research and Practice: a necessary eclecticism?" Pp. 335–346 in *Handbook of Disaster Research,* (H. Rodriguez, E.L. Quarantelli, and R. Dynes, eds.). NY: Springer.

Fu, King Wa. 2009. "Media Use and Communications Needs of People with Disabilities During and After the Sichuan earthquake in China." Presented at the Wireless Emergency Technologies Conference, Atlanta, Georgia.

McEntire, David. 1998. "Towards a Theory of Coordination: Umbrella Organization and Disaster Relief in the 1997–98 Peruvian El Niño." Quick Response Report #105, Natural Hazards Research and Applications Information Center, Boulder, CO.

Mortenson, Greg and David Oliver Relin. 2006. *Three Cups of Tea: One Man's Mission to Promote Peace One School at a Time.* NY: Penguin Books

National Council on Disability. 2009. *Effective Emergency Management: Making Improvements for Communities and People with Disabilities.* Washington, D.C.: National Council on Disability.

National Voluntary Organizations Active in Disaster. No date. *Managing Spontaneous Volunteers in Times of Disaster: the synergy of structure and good intentions.* http://PointsofLight.org/Disaster, last accessed January 15, 2008.

Neal, David M. 1983. "Types and Functions of Community and Regional Social Movement Organizations with Grassroots Social Movement Organizations: A Look at Emergent Citizen Groups in Disaster." *Sociological Research Symposium Proceedings XIII.* Richmond, VA: Department of Sociology, Virginia Commonwealth University.

Nelson, L.D. and Dynes, R. 1976. "The Impact of Devotionalism and Attendance on Ordinary and Emergency Helping Behavior." *Journal for the Scientific Study of Religion* 15: 47–59.

Pan American Health Organization. 2009. *Be a Better Donor: Practical Recommendations for Humanitarian Aid.* Panama, PAHO/WHO. Available at http://new.paho.org/disasters/index.php?option=com_content&task=view&id=974&Itemid=1, last accessed January 4, 2011.

Paton, D. 1996. "Training Disaster Workers: promoting wellbeing and operational effectiveness." *Disaster Prevention and Management* 5/5: 11–18.

Phillips, Brenda D. and Pam Jenkins. 2009. "The Roles of Faith-based Organizations after Hurricane Katrina." Pp. 215–238 in *Meeting the Needs of Children, Families, and Communities Post-disaster: Lessons learned from Hurricane Katrina and Its Aftermath,* (Kilmer, R.P., Gil-Rivas, V., Tedeschi, R.G., & Calhoun, L.G, eds.). Washington, D.C.: American Psychological Association.

Quarantelli, E.L. 2005. "Catastrophes are Different From Disasters." Available at Social Science Research Council, Understanding Katrina page, available at http://understandingkatrina.ssrc.org/Quarantelli/, last accessed December 31, 2010.

Rees, Susan, Eileen Pittaway, and Linda Bartolomei. 2005. "Waves of Violence in Post-Tsunami Sri Lanka." *Australasian Journal of Disaster and Trauma Studies* 2, available at http://www.massey.ac.nz/~trauma/issues/2005-2/rees.htm, last accessed February 24, 2011.

Ross, Alexander. 1980. "The Emergence of Organizational Sets in Three Ecumenical Disaster Recovery Organizations." *Human Relations* 33: 23–29.

Ross, Alexander. & Smith, S. 1974. "The Emergence of an Organization and an Organization Set: a study of an interfaith disaster recovery group." Preliminary Paper #16, University of Delaware, Disaster Research Center.

Sumner, William. G. 1906. *Folkways.* New York: Ginn.

Sutton, Jeanette. 2003. "A Complex Organizational Adaptation to the World Trade Center Disaster: An Analysis of Faith-Based Organizations." Pp. 405–428 in *Beyond September 11th: An Account of Post-Disaster Research*, (Jacquelyn L. Monday, ed.). Special Publication #39 Natural Hazards Research and Applications Information Center, University of Colorado: Boulder, CO.

Thoits, P., L. Hewitt. 2001. "Volunteer Work and Well-being." *Journal of Health and Social Behavior* 42/2: 115–121.

Resources

- To learn more about Fred Cuny, visit http://www.pbs.org/wgbh/pages/frontline/shows/cuny/
- The International Rescue Committee page is located at http://www.rescue.org/
- The Pan American Health Organization offers extensive resources at its website, www.paho.org
- To learn more about the International Strategy for Disaster Reduction, go to http://unisdr.org/
- The Organization for American States hosts a Natural Hazards Project and supports the Hemispheric Eduplan in the educational sector. More can be found in both English and Spanish at http://www.oas.org/nhp/
- The Gender and Disaster Network provides extensive resources for those assisting people affected by gender stratification. www.gdnonline.org
- Information about disasters in Latin America and the Andes can be found at DisInventar, http://www.desinventar.org/ and its efforts are supported by many associated with La Red, a network of academics and practitioners. http://www.desenredando.org/index.html
- Church World Service offers a set of ten free webinar training sessions. To register and secure downloadable materials, visit http://www.cwserp.org/
- Living Waters for the World and Solar Under the Sun host websites and facebook pages. Start at www.solarunderthesun.org and www.livingwatersfortheworld.org

Chapter

The Next Generation of Emergency Managers

13.1 Chapter Objectives

Upon completing this chapter, readers should be able to:

1. Outline historical developments that have moved the profession of emergency management forward.
2. List continuing professional development opportunities that enhance the potential for professional advancement.
3. Identify various means to link research with practice to promote a scientifically informed profession of emergency management.
4. Critique available degree programs to find the best fit for your professional goals.

13.2 Introduction

In this chapter we encourage you to take on several tasks. First, we outline what is known about professional emergency managers and encourage you to consider the qualities needed for entry into the field. We also acknowledge the increasing diversity in the profession and move through what research suggests about underrepresented populations entering a field characterized historically by relatively homogeneous personnel. Routes to enhance your knowledge and professional development are then outlined. We start with how knowledge is transferred professionally in the field, with an emphasis on reading journals, attending professional conferences, finding a mentor, securing an internship, and obtaining appropriate training and certifications. The chapter concludes with a review of opportunities for continuing your education in the field and offers recommendations on how to find an appropriate degree program.

Throughout this chapter you will find examples of people working in various aspects of the field. Look at their contributions and perspectives as inspirations for what you might see yourself doing in the future. Take the time to look further into their agencies, businesses, and work settings as you ponder what the field of emergency management might offer you. Whether or not you select the field as your profession, remember that we all carry responsibility for staying alert to hazards, prepared for disasters, ready to respond when called upon, and involved in recovery and mitigation efforts. Emergency management begins with us.

13.3 Professional Emergency Managers

In 1987, Professor Thomas Drabek published what has since become a classic first look at the professional emergency manager. In his book, which was funded by the U.S. National Science Foundation, Drabek identified key structures and strategies that generated success for those interested in careers in the field. He cited coping strategies that enable emergency managers to succeed in environments that move quickly from routine paperwork to saving lives during a crisis. He also pointed out structures that enable success and explained how organizations are put together and managed effectively.

Embedded within both strategies and structures is an emphasis on relationships with the people that you will work with within and across your organization and areas of specialization. The process by which you will work within organizations and with others is considered equally relevant. As described in Chapter 7, planning is best accomplished as an effort that moves committed participants through a step-wise process. By working through the necessary steps, people generate working relationships that sustain them and their organizations through crises.

Drabek investigated the lives and jurisdictional contexts of twelve professional emergency managers. An additional fifty emergency managers were included through telephone interviews. Results indicated that effective directors regularly used five primary strategies. First, they supported their organizational partners by helping to increase their resource bases. Professionals did not simply look at their own needs; they worked with others to collectively secure necessary assets. Second, they secured support and assistance through establishing working committees. Third, they initiated joint ventures with other leaders in local agencies. Fourth, they brought in outside experts. Finally, they tackled controversial or threatening issues head-on as a means to manage conflict that would otherwise undermine their efforts. Through all the strategies that emergency managers use runs a collective thread that emphasizes the ability to work well with others and move a variety of partners toward successful initiatives.

In terms of structure and process, Drabek (1987) reported that effective emergency managers networked extremely well. They engaged in regular, sustained contacts with their jurisdiction and state officials. Rather than rely on informal relationships alone, they negotiated formal interagency agreements. They also collaborated with other agency heads to manage joint ventures to reach high level understanding of each other's capabilities and develop trust and confidence in their ability work together. Emergency managers interviewed by Drabek also reported that they developed memberships with other community organizations that enhanced their potential interactions and increased the frequency of their contacts with critical partners. In conclusion, Drabek indicated that several strategies served as the keys to success for professional emergency managers. These included working with others to coordinate rather than to control an agenda. Doing so requires sustained commitment to meeting and working with other agencies. Interagency efforts were best pursued through consensus building activities such as joint ventures. The result is a well established, professional network that leads to success.

The network alone though is not sufficient and Drabek found that emergency managers needed to continue their professional development—accordingly a focus of the rest of this chapter.

Networking should not be a difficult task for those involved in emergency management. For example, local civic groups (Lions Club, Rotary, Chamber of Commerce) need speakers for their breakfast or lunch programs. These events give emergency managers opportunities to promote key issues (e.g., tornado awareness during tornado awareness week). Before or after these meetings, the emergency coordinator can informally meet and talk with local civic and neighborhood leaders. Emergency coordinators should make an effort to meet for coffee with key government officials inside and outside their own political jurisdictions. In fact, one could argue that an emergency manager should spend at least half of his or her time outside the office developing and maintaining networks among the public at large and volunteer organizations.

Wilson (2001) analyzed the growth and development of emergency management as a profession. Generally, Wilson argues that emergency management is on the road to becoming a profession. Specifically, organizations such as the National Emergency Management Agency (NEMA) and the International Association of Emergency Managers (IAEMs) provide the basis for two key characteristics: accreditation of programs and certification of professionals. Accreditation ensures that specific institutions (e.g., a state agency) meet certain standards, for example, related to training and exercises conducted by state and local governments. Certification requires that individuals meet specific experience, training, and educational requirements. Chapter 5 covers the background and specifics of accreditation and certification. Not all states require accreditation. Furthermore, having a CEM is not yet a requirement for a job in emergency management. As such criteria develop and both individuals and programs garner these credentials, the expected results are increased salaries and greater respect for those who pursue careers in the field.

13.4 Diversifying the Field of Emergency Management

Few studies show how historically underrepresented populations have fared in the field of emergency management. Underrepresented populations, usually considered females, racial and ethnic minorities, and people with disabilities have yet to attract a major research investigation. In this section, we review what is known about the routes and experiences of women, racial and ethnic minorities, and people with disabilities into the emergency management profession. Encouraging a diverse workforce emerges as an important action to bring insights, expertise, and networks into the profession to link to those historically most vulnerable in a disaster context. Through a diversified workforce, we enhance our abilities to reach out to and connect with at-risk populations.

13.4.1 Women

Historically, the profession of emergency management has been male-dominated although that has been changing dramatically in the past two decades. One study conducted in California after the 1989 Loma Prieta earthquake looked at the experiences of women in the field of emergency management (Phillips 1990). Women who participated in the survey indicated that several factors prompted their success. One factor was having the credentials necessary to enter and participate—a condition that several deemed particularly relevant in a profession where most professionals were male. A second factor arose from experience in the field. Similar to what Drabek (1987) indicated, getting to know others and demonstrate competence mattered. Ten years after the Loma Prieta study, Wilson (1999) reported that little had changed to integrate women more fully into the field. Finally, in the 1990s during the Clinton administration, Kay Goss held the second-highest post at FEMA. Under the Obama Administration, Janet Napolitano became the highest-ranking woman in emergency management when she became secretary of the U.S. Department of Homeland Security.

Internationally, the expertise of women has been under-used in disaster situations despite the disproportionate impacts of such events on women and children (Noel 1998). Good examples stem from major international disasters in which the experiences of women, girls, and children were not sufficiently considered. Lessons learned from the 2004 Indian Ocean tsunami alerted people to the potential for human trafficking and child abuse among displaced populations. Integration of female-friendly perspectives can certainly enhance any emergency management activity. Experts have called for fuller integration of women into the practice of emergency management, with the assumption that their experiences and perspectives can generate insights conducive to improving disaster response and recovery (Enarson and Morrow 1998).

13.4.2 Racial and Ethnic Minorities

Little is known about the entry and career mobility of racial and ethnic minorities in the field of emergency management. Historically, patterns of occupational mobility tend to reflect patterns that initially benefit white women followed by racial and ethnic minorities largely as a reflection of affirmative action programs from the 1970s through the 1990s. What is clear is that disasters disproportionately affect people of color and that integration of a diverse workforce is deemed necessary to reflect the full range of cultures and backgrounds that influence how we prepare for, respond to, and recover from disasters.

Tribes and First Nations groups worldwide also struggled to become part of the emergency management picture even though their tribal lands and cultural resources sustain serious damage in disaster events. Along the U.S. Gulf Coast, for example, hurricanes, oil spills, and coastal erosion have decimated existing tribes by destroying homes, undermining abilities to engage in sustainable livelihoods, and scattering families to disparate areas. The U.S., like many other nations, respects federally recognized tribes as sovereign partners in emergency management planning and practice. Despite this recognition, dozens of tribes remain outside the planning perimeter because they have not yet secured legal status as federally recognized tribes. In those cases, outreach efforts by existing emergency management agencies must work with tribal leaders and relevant agencies to render appropriate assistance.

Understanding cultures that maintain particular ways of life requires insight that may not be part of the body of knowledge that an emergency manager has obtained. Consequently, finding ways to establish relationships and work with tribes in disaster-affected areas may take considerable time. Toward that end, FEMA launched efforts to work with federally recognized tribes as part of its Department of Homeland Security Consultation and Coordination Plan (FEMA 2010a). The plan includes making a concerted effort to engage in "regular and meaningful consultation and collaboration." As one strategy, FEMA invited three tribal representatives to serve on the National Preparedness Task Force and FEMA officials will collaborate with tribal leaders to plan response and recovery procedures prior to disaster.

13.4.3 People with Disabilities

Equal opportunity laws and the Americans with Disabilities Act targeted barriers that bar people with disabilities from being hired. Still, concern exists that such discrimination continues, particularly in the field of emergency management. Inabilities to meet needs associated with disability led to lawsuits and strong recommendations after people with disabilities were not included in evacuations, shelter accommodations (National Organization on Disability 2005), and accessible temporary housing after Hurricane Katrina (*Brou v. FEMA*).

As with the argument for gendered emergency management practice, we can assume that involving people with disabilities in every aspect of planning, preparedness, response, and recovery will improve outcomes for citizens with disabilities. Toward that end, FEMA launched efforts to hire regional disability coordinators at all ten regional offices in 2010 and 2011 with an eye toward changing emergency management practice.

13.5 Knowledge Transfer and Professional Development

In his book titled *Disasters by Design* (1999), Professor Dennis Mileti outlined findings from a survey on how professional emergency managers acquire knowledge (see also Fothergill 2000). Mileti found a disconnect between academics and practitioners. The world of academia requires that university faculty publish in scholarly journals but most emergency managers stayed away from such scientifically biased publications. Instead, they turned to conferences, trade journals, and social networks to gain insights into the practice aspects of their work.

This finding presents several concerns. First, why are emergency managers not reading scientific journals? In law, health care, veterinary practice, psychology, and other professions, practitioners must stay abreast of current findings. Not doing so imperils those they seek to help if critical information does not cross their desks. Emergency management, with its emphasis on life-saving activities, should merit the same attention. It is true, as you may well know, that many academic journals appear inaccessible because of scientific jargon that confuses rather than informs. Hopefully after reading this text, you will have found value in acquiring research skills that will enable you to read, understand, and use the considerable body of available disaster knowledge.

13.5.1 Bridging the Gap between Research and Practice

Well before the development of emergency management degree programs, Wohlwerth (1984) wrote in *Hazard Monthly* that a critical mass of research information "is not applied due to lack of community awareness and the lack of communication between scientists, the public, planners and policymakers." As a student in this course, it is up to you to bridge the gap between research and practice. Your own motivation will matter as much as the skills you need to understand and use disaster research. The value of education for making the connection is clear: your efforts will be based on empirical support that can improve policy and practice. Using research will strengthen planning, improve response, expedite recovery, and inspire mitigation to build more disaster-resilient communities.

Bridging the gap requires that you ask informed questions and search actively for good answers. How do you ask informed questions? Begin by thinking through the problem at hand, for example, what is the best strategy for conducting an evacuation? This type of question serves only as a starting point. After having read this book, you should clearly understand that many factors influence the methodology of evacuation. Who must be evacuated? What resources do they have for doing so—or what do they lack? How can emergency managers, community organizations, and officials make up for any evacuation deficits the public may experience and plan accordingly? What population groups exist and where are they located? How should I determine the locations of various populations and with which overlays? Transportation arteries? Community organizations with accessible vans? Pet shelters? All of the above?

To ask good questions and find relevant research, you will must know the lexicon—the vocabulary—of the field. This book serves as an introduction to commonly used concepts and practices but it is only the start of your learning journey. Terms change and definitions vary across the disciplines that influence the practice of emergency management. You need to work actively to understand those terms and their meanings. As explained in Chapter 9 the term "recovery" carries multiple connotations, depending on whether you are in construction, social work, or on a long-term recovery planning team. Knowing the lexicon means that you can fit into the work setting of your career and find the empirical information you need to do your job.

Reviewing studies in J-Stor, Google Scholar, and other database search engines requires you to think clearly and even creatively to find pertinent articles. Because the literature of the multidisciplinary field of emergency management is scattered across many journals, you will also have to understand variations in terms across the disciplines. Firefighters, for example, conceptualize recovery as retrieval of remains or items damaged in a fire. Psychologists view recovery as the result of an intentional, interactive process between therapist and patient. These very different conceptualizations will influence your search for information. You will also have to retain information from this course about concepts related to particular terms. For example, you may be able to find studies on protective action by searching for that term or you may need to look for shelter-in-place, evacuation, or duck-and-cover categories.

As you learned in Chapter 3 on research methods, a number of scientific journals can help answer your questions. By learning about those journals now and staying abreast of new developments, you can be ready to ask the right questions, find good answers, and even locate jurisdictions that have gone through similar experiences. Staying current can be as simple as having electronic tables of contents delivered to your inbox so that you can identify articles of interest. Memberships in research organizations also help you stay connected to researchers who produce that body of knowledge. Disaster researchers also use social media as tools to share research they and their colleagues produce.

Many readers will have picked up this textbook in an undergraduate class. Hopefully, this is just the first of several courses that you will take in the field. It is up to you to continue to hone your research skills by taking future classes in research methods using quantitative and qualitative procedures. Do not be afraid to take on these classes, as challenging as they may seem, because they will produce significant payoffs. And do not leave those skills behind when you graduate. Understanding how to read a research article is much like learning another language: if you don't use it, you lose it. Read journals regularly to maintain skills and keep you leading the field as an informed practitioner.

The Gender and Disaster Network (www.gdnonline.org) serves as one vehicle to help you stay informed on important topics. After the Indian Ocean tsunami, for example, researchers posted checklists and advice on how to establish shelters so that mothers could continue to nurse infants, modesty could be ensured to conform to related cultural and religious beliefs, and girls and women could be made safe from exploitation and violence. Their work reflects an effort made real through the life of dedicated practitioner Mary Fran Myers (see Box 13.1). Myers, an experienced floodplain manager, moved on to work as associate director of the Natural Hazards Research and Applications Information Center (www.colorado.edu/hazards). At the

BOX 13.1 BRIDGING RESEARCH AND PRACTICE: THE LIFE OF MARY FRAN MYERS

The Mary Fran Myers Award, established in 2002 by the Gender and Disaster Network, recognizes that vulnerability to disasters and mass emergencies is influenced by social, cultural, and economic structures that marginalize women and girls. Research-based practice that reduces loss of life, injuries, and property of women and girls can make a difference. The goal of the Gender and Disaster Network is to promote and encourage such an integration of research and practice.

Mary Fran Myers, co-director of the Natural Hazards Center at the University of Colorado at Boulder, received the first award in 2002. The Mary Fran Myers Award was so-named to recognize her sustained efforts to launch a worldwide network among disaster professionals for advancing women's careers and for promoting research on gender issues in disaster research in emergency management and higher education.

Mary Fran Myers served as co-director of the Natural Hazards Center for sixteen years until her untimely death in 2004. Reducing disaster losses, both nationally and internationally, was her life's work. During her tenure as co-director, Mary Fran was instrumental in maintaining the Natural Hazards Center's international reputation as a driving force in connecting hazards research and mitigation. Her work helped to bring about a fundamental change in national and international perspectives regarding hazards and helped institute new, more farsighted, and sustainable ways of dealing with extreme environmental events.

> Mary Fran was much more than her job title. She provided leadership, guidance, grace, and laughter, and established a standard of excellence that her colleagues both admired and strived to emulate. She was an innovator, a mentor, and a creative spirit who touched many lives and whose legacy has had a lasting impact on the global hazards community.
>
> For more information and a list of subsequent award winners, visit http://www.gdnonline.org/mfm_award.php. For a partial list of research that her life inspired, visit http://www.colorado.edu/hazards/research/qr/.
>
> *Source:* adapted from http://www.gdnonline.org/mfm_award.php, with permission.

center, she connected researchers and practitioners through conferences, writing opportunities, and grant funding. For her work, the Gender and Disaster Network established the Mary Fran Myers Award for those who connect research with practice in an effort to reduce suffering. The award alternates annually between developed and developing nations to reveal vulnerability, capacity, and progress. Seeking out those who work to bridge the gap between research and practice is worthwhile.

13.5.2 Collaborating with the Academic World

In 2003, the Disasters Roundtable of the National Academies (advisers to the nation on science, engineering, and medicine) convened both academics and practitioners to speak about the "Emergency Manager of the Future" (Hite 2003). After discussing desirable characteristics, participants summarized their recommendations. The future emergency manager is:

- Capable of identifying societal trends surrounding population dynamics, organizational configurations, the social and physical environments and evolving technology.
- Has a broad-based set of knowledge across the social and physical sciences including criminal justice, seismology, public administration, and community planning, to name a few.
- Uses an all-hazards approach for effective mitigation/prevention, preparedness, and response and recovery efforts.
- Builds collaborative relationships between researchers and practitioners.
- Integrates technology and research into the practice of emergency management.

Collaborating with the academic world will require efforts from both academics and practitioners—certainly a compelling reason for convening both groups to speak on the next generation of emergency managers in 2003. The focus on integrating technology alone deserves attention as it foretold the current emphasis on and concern with social media for educating and warning populations (see more on social media in Chapter 4).

By combining various sets of knowledge and abilities, the potential to leverage social capital to improve practice is considerable. As an example, concerns about at-risk populations in New Orleans surfaced well before the impact of Hurricane Katrina. Numerous social and physical scientists studied, presented on, and published accounts of those at risk. Just a few months before Katrina, University of New Orleans sociologist Shirley Laska foretold of the challenges the city would face should a major storm impact the area. A seventeen-foot storm surge would overflow and damage levees, leaving as many as 600,000 at risk because they had no means to evacuate (Laska 2004). Among the consequences of Hurricane Katrina only seven months after Laska's article were over 1,300 deaths that occurred because people could not evacuate. Using your knowledge of population dynamics, as suggested by the National Academies forum on future emergency managers as well as content learned in this book, you should by now realize those most at risk then were the elderly, low-income families, and people with disabilities along with caregivers for these populations who remained in the city. Most did not have cars to evacuate, and mandatory evacuation orders came the morning before the storm arrived. Dr. Laska, called to testify before the U.S. Congress, reported on the collective anguish of academics—referred to before the storm as doomsayers—whose advice was not heeded (see Box 13.2).

Since Katrina, academics and practitioners have collaborated on many levels to improve practice. One example comes from the efforts of EAD & Associates, LLC and Oklahoma State University (see Box 13.3). Together, this group of practitioners, faculty researchers, and graduate students collaborated to produce a volume for the National Council on Disability (NCD; 2009). Separate chapters address research findings and point out promising practices for preparedness, response, mitigation, and recovery. Among the items sent to the White House for action were federal, state, and local level recommendations. One federal level recommendation was the establishment of disability coordinator positions at all ten FEMA regional offices—positions that were consequently posted and filled. Representatives from the NCD also testified before Congress on the report. In 2009, Chairman John R. Vaughn based his comments on the NCD findings:

> Perhaps surprisingly, housing is one of the least examined areas of recovery research, despite its importance. Low-income housing tends to take a disproportionate "hit" during a disaster because it is likely to be older and less likely to comply with the standards of modern building codes; located in a floodplain or other hazardous area; and less structurally able to withstand an event (such as manufactured housing). Thus, seniors and people with disabilities at lower incomes presumably bear a higher risk of displacement from their homes.

BOX 13.2   DISASTER RESEARCHER
TESTIFIES BEFORE U.S. CONGRESS

Presented by Dr. Shirley Laska, Director, Center for Hazards Assessment, Research and Technology, University of New Orleans before the U.S. House of Representatives Science Committee Subcommittee on Research, November 10, 2005. Dr. Laska received the American Sociological Association's Public Understanding of Sociology Award for her work after Hurricane Katrina.

I was requested to give testimony to this committee for a few reasons—having disaster social science expertise, trying to apply the findings of social science research, being the director of a research center that was the victim of Hurricane Katrina, to name a few. More specifically, I was one of the scientists who predicted with unwavering accuracy that such an event as Katrina would happen and what the results would be when it did.

My predictions were a compilation of the research findings of many scientists, physical as well as social. And they too were speaking about what their findings told them. I was not a lone voice, but rather was among a chorus of scientists from both physical and social science disciplines who predicted that it would happen and what the consequences would be. The specialties of the other scientists included coastal geologists, coastal hydrologists who do hurricane impact modeling, geographers, demographers, stratification and community sociologists, coastal ecologists, civil engineers, political science policy specialists, and meteorologists. And the cases they made were not only in scientific journals but also in the popular media and applied professional publications such as *Scientific American*, *National Geographic*, *Natural History*, *Natural Hazards Observer*, *New York Times*, *Washington Post*, and *Los Angeles Times* and the prize-winning series in the *New Orleans Times Picayune*.

We also presented our conclusions at numerous professional gatherings. And when we did one could feel the audience inhale. A few would come up after the talk to tell us of their shock. Others would say we were exaggerating and dismiss us as "doomsayers." On occasion someone would follow up with an email, phone call and take steps to broadcast in their own professional or even personal world what we predicted was going to happen.

The last example of this before Katrina was a lengthy phone conference call a CHART colleague and I had with a NOAA official four days before Katrina hit. He had been horrified by the content of the abstract of my June Hart Senate Building presentation available on the American Meteorological Society website predicting Katrina in which I described the incredible challenges that the poor would experience evacuating the city.

Before the storm hit, he prepared a nationwide letter to the Catholic bishops. That was an important personal act but given the enormous data available, why didn't the existing research matter enough to prevent, or at least, reduce the devastation that has occurred? To put it differently, how could it be that the society at all levels was not organized or prepared "to hear"? The federal government has been the sponsor of most of the research that has been conducted by social scientists on environmental disasters. Because of its role it is the prime level of government to be leading an effort to expand the research and to facilitate its use; I encourage it to take stronger responsibility for using the findings to the betterment of society.

It is imperative that social science research be seen as an equal contributor to the physical sciences in asking the most pertinent research questions about environmental disasters, in formulating powerful research questions, and in receiving support to implement top quality research. But as that is accomplished we must find better ways for the organizations, the government agencies, the policy makers to value the findings and to address the obligations of their positions more responsibly (a finding of Bill Freudenburg's research on risk and "recreancy," *Social Forces*, 1993) and that concludes with recognition of the importance of using social science research findings.

Final thought. I was not participating in some abstract intellectual exercise during the last few years as I was drawing from my own and others' existing research to warn professional group after professional group of an impending Katrina. The result of those warnings not being heeded was the end of my community. And as our warnings were accurate, this doom assessment of the impact is not hyperbole. Recovery of coastal Louisiana from Hurricanes Katrina and Rita is in my opinion uncertain. We do not yet know if we have the family, organizational, and governmental resources, ability, and energy to accomplish it. And the cost to the society is astronomical. This is the outcome of scientists not being heard. And it doesn't get any more personal for a scientist than Katrina has been for me.

Source: Excerpted from http://science.house.gov/commdocs/hearings/research05/nov%2010/Laska.pdf

BOX 13.3   ACADEMICS AND PRACTITIONERS COLLABORATING FOR BEST PRACTICES

Elizabeth Davis, JD, EdM is the founder of EAD & Associates, LLC and the National Emergency Management Resource Center (NEMRC). With experience in emergency operations and a specialization in disabilities, she writes here on the value of research in combination with experience that is so necessary for emergency management practice.

The next generation of emergency managers will be a hybrid operating most adeptly somewhere between boots-on-the-ground practical experience-based knowledge and the academic ability to research and support policy decisions with the empirical data to uphold calculated decisions. As the old guard gives way to the newer professionals among us, it is precisely this balance of experience and learned knowledge we have found most valuable.

Using ourselves as an example, EAD & Associates, LLC is a boutique consultancy established by subject matter experts with the real-world field experience to focus on marginalized populations often left out of the initial paradigm. We work on the complex yet necessary issues pertaining to the spectrum of disability, age, medically managed issues, poverty impact, gender, language/culture, and other social factors that will impact or be impacted by disaster in unique ways. We use an empowerment model while working to achieve fully inclusive emergency management principles. That all said, within our ranks are JDs, MDs, PhDs, MSWs, RNs, and more master's degrees than can be listed. But the common thread tying us all together is that we are all trained emergency managers who have been in the trenches: ice storms, earthquakes, power outages, floods, tornado outbreaks, pandemics, terror attacks, transit strikes, airline crashes, and more.

It is the combination of experience and academic appreciation that enables us to find creative and appropriate solutions to complex issues facing our clients and ultimately those they serve. We find ourselves moving comfortably between assignments that can include reviewing administrative codes, drafting proposed legislation, reporting findings after months of research on a matter, testifying before Congress, designing field drills, testing plan components, or conducting direct community-based education. And of course, when called on we are packed and ready to go. The balance enables us to ponder solutions and possible resolutions when we have the luxury of time but, on the other hand, prepares us to make decisive on-the-spot decisions with confidence and conviction so that we can defend them later.

The new generation of emergency managers will need to either possess a well-balanced mix of knowledge (even if focused in a specialty area) or be able to recognize the value of partnering and bringing all parts of emergency management together. Having the academic- and research-based side to support planning decisions and funding allocations, especially in a politically and economically charged environment, is essential when it can also be tied to grounded applications and made operational.

And while considering the advantages of bringing different perspectives and skills to the table, it is worth considering the other players as well. Real world experience and academic strength are not just found in the traditional places either for that matter. A competent emergency manager will find partnership with the academic arena, the private sector, and the not-for-profit world as well. And a truly gifted emergency manager will know to look within the stakeholder groups themselves for insight, guidance, and solutions not experienced by everyone but that can be applied just the same during times of emergency. In considering this balance and how to achieve it, the new emergency manager will be working on shifting the current paradigm to one more focused on ensuring individuals and communities build resiliency into their basic toolsets so they can truly view each crisis as an opportunity to emerge on the other side farther ahead—rather than just relatively unscathed.

For more information, visit www.eadassociates.com and www.nemrc.net

NCD collaborated on multiple committees to influence national policies and procedures and ensure that people with disabilities would not be left in shelters awaiting temporary or permanent housing after disaster. Marcie Roth, FEMA's National Disability Coordinator announced in 2010 that FEMA's National Housing Framework recommended that states develop efforts inclusive of people with disabilities (FEMA 2010b). From research to practice, collaboration of academics and practitioners is finding ways to address gaps in emergency management practice.

13.5.3 Mechanisms to Transfer Knowledge and Stay Informed

Reading journals certainly represents an important way to bridge research and practice. Because experience also matters, other mechanisms to transfer knowledge and stay informed should be pursued as well. In this section, we look at some of those routes.

13.5.3.1 Mentoring

Relationships matter in this profession. By building strong and effective relationships, you lay a foundation to work well with others during crises. Perhaps the most important relationship that you can build comes from selecting a mentor—someone who guides, advises, and encourages you as you enter and move through the profession. A mentor can identify pitfalls and problems, offer solutions, and be there to listen to your questions. Mentors do not tell you what to do and how to do it. They are trusted individuals who can listen as well as advise. Your concerns are their concerns, and your professional development reflects their abilities to direct your path.

You would do well to choose wisely when selecting a mentor. While someone with political pull or connections may lure you and should be respected, you want a mentor who has your interests instead of his or her political career at heart. Choose someone with a career path similar to the one that you want who has good people skills and the time to spend with you. How do you find such a person? Attend conferences, join committees, serve on task forces, and get to know people. Your willingness to step up and serve will garner the attention of prospective mentors, open them up to serving in such a role. It will also build your résumé and networks at the same time. It is likely that a mentor will emerge over time as you begin to get to know people in the profession. Give it some time and choose wisely.

13.5.3.2 Internships

Emergency management graduates often moan about the wording in job announcements, particularly the requirements for experience. Understandably, a community would not want just anyone writing emergency plans and deciding when and how to issue warnings. While courses and degrees may separate yours from the pack of résumés on someone's desk, experience serves as an additional qualifier. How do you acquire experience? Throughout this text, we have mentioned opportunities for volunteer service. Another form of volunteerism, although sometimes paid, is the internship. An intern serves in an office of emergency management (or similar location) and supports the professional staff. Activities can range from administrative support to operational aspects, depending on the location and need. Increasingly, agencies offer internship opportunities for academic credit; some may offer salaries or transportation support (see Box 13.4).

Academic advisors may be able to secure internships for academic credit, so be sure to visit with your advisor if you are still in school. You may also be able to secure an internship on your own by contacting an emergency management agency. Many list internships, application deadlines, and requirements on their websites. Some internships may be very competitive but usually offer the best opportunities for learning in jurisdictions that present challenging issues. You may want to also seek out other opportunities and present yourself as an intern to a local business or agency that could benefit from your emergency management knowledge. If you secure an internship on your own and are still in college, be sure to ask for academic credit that will look good on a transcript and on your résumé.

13.5.3.3 Fellowships and Scholarships

A number of opportunities afford you the chance to gain additional experience and even funding during an academic career. The National Science Foundation in the U.S. has funded a number of Research Experiences for Undergraduates Sites (REUs) for groups of students and individual REUs for individual researchers. An REU site brings students in from across the nation to learn how to conduct research. Opportunities to apply are advertised widely at conferences, on websites, and through special announcements.

The National Science Foundation has funded students in engineering, meteorology, computer science, geography, and sociology among other disciplines—many of them focused on careers that generate research useful to the field of emergency management. The Disaster Research Center at the University of Delaware has an REU site for social science students interested in research careers (http://www.udel.edu/DRC/REU/REU.html). Prospective REU students compete to earn funded slots. They live at the university for the summer while they are instructed on how to conduct disaster research. Each student works with a mentor from his or her home institution to design and carry out a research project. Funding includes opportunities to travel to and present at professional conferences.

The Disaster Research Center has also partnered with other institutions that offer REUs, such as the University of Massachusetts Collaborative

BOX 13.4   RECENT INTERNSHIPS (DECEMBER 2010)

Organization of American States

"The OAS offers an unpaid Internship Program for a minimum three-month period starting in January, June, and September of each year. Interns at the Natural Hazards Project are directly involved in project work alongside project coordinators and the principal specialist. Both undergraduate and master's level students are eligible, as are participants in work–study programs. Students specifically interested in economic, engineering, environmental, geographical, meteorological, or political aspects of natural hazard mitigation are particularly encouraged to apply. Interested persons must apply through the OAS Student Intern Program, but we will also appreciate receiving by fax (202) 458-3560 a copy of your application. More information is available at: http://www.oas.org/EN/PINFO/HR/job.htm."

FEMA Higher Education Project

"The FEMA Emergency Management Institute (EMI) Higher Education Associates Program is designed to give students and faculty involved in emergency management college degree programs an opportunity to continue their education and/or research at EMI, located in Emmitsburg, Maryland about seventy-five miles northwest of Washington, D.C. The Associates Program is open to both students and faculty and entails an "intern-like" residence at the Emergency Management Institute, on the campus of the National Emergency Training Center to work on a pre-agreed upon project, projects, or research. Associates do not earn a salary nor will FEMA pay a per diem or other expenses. Associates will be responsible for meals and all other expenses while at EMI. FEMA will provide the associate with a private dormitory room for the stay and will reimburse the student associate for round-trip transportation expenses not to exceed the cost of a super-saver economy class airline ticket. EMI will not provide reimbursement for travel expenses for faculty associates. As the student is transitioning from junior to senior, a faculty member (preferably the candidate's advisor) should contact the EMI Higher Education Project Manager. After investigating the student's course background and career goals a suitable project will be chosen. The student, faculty member and project manager will negotiate the length of the stay, normally five–seven weeks. The student will be assigned a dorm room and a workstation with phone and computer. Projects will be submitted to the Higher Education Project Manager and an evaluation will be communicated to the student and the student's advisor. The student then will be granted credit hours by the student's school, as agreed upon in the negotiation phase."

Pan American Health Organization

PAHO is located in Washington, D.C. but has offices throughout North, Central, South America, and the Caribbean. To secure an internship, it is recommended that you be bilingual in Spanish, English, or Portuguese. To apply, visit www.paho.org and select the Employment, then Interns links. PAHO recommends becoming familiar with their structure and programs so that you can identify a unit that interests you. Your next step is to contact their area manager and describe what you have to offer to their program. Successful applicants will then be invited to submit a résumé describing their education, skills and languages.

National Academies Internships

The National Academies offers internship opportunities too. The Christine Mirzayan Science and Technology Policy Graduate Fellowship Program may be an option for you. The program is designed particularly for graduate students and post-doctoral scholars in "any social/behavioral science, medical/health discipline, physical or biological science, any field of engineering, law/business/public administration, or any relevant interdisciplinary field within the last five years." For more information, visit http://sites.nationalacademies.org/PGA/policyfellows/index.htm

Adaptive Sensing of the Atmosphere (CASA) project. While CASA focuses on wind engineering, it also involves social scientists to determine public response to improved radar-based warning systems. Since its inception in the early 2000s, CASA has engaged REU students as undergraduates and funded several through their doctorates (see Box 13.5).

The U.S. Department of Homeland Security has funded students as DHS-STEM scholarship recipients. Box 13.6 features DHS fellows, one an undergraduate student, the other a graduate student, who recently attended Oklahoma State University. DHS awards recipients complete tuition and fees along with monthly stipends to support their education toward a career in homeland security (including disaster management).

13.5.3.4 Training

Many organizations and jurisdictions offer continual training. Depending on local hazards, you may be able to take storm chaser classes to spot tornadoes or learn how to monitor and report flood conditions. National and international agencies may offer in-person and online training. In the U.S., for example, FEMA sponsors independent study courses that can be taken for certification. Their sequences include a Professional Development Series that is listed in many of their job announcements (http://training.fema.gov/IS/crslist.asp). FEMA also brings emergency managers to its campus in Emmittsburg, Maryland for more intensive workshops and classes (http://training.fema.gov/EMICourses/). States also set up training as well. Organizations like the Red Cross provide first aid, CPR, shelter manager, and disaster team training.

BOX 13.5 MAKING THINGS HAPPEN: NAVIGATING THROUGH GRADUATE SCHOOL AND STARTING A CAREER IN THE SOCIAL SCIENCES

Jenniffer M. Santos-Hernández
Oak Ridge National Laboratory

Navigating through graduate school is a difficult but not impossible process. As a student coming from a working class background, there were many questions for which I often lacked guidance at home. When I started college, I knew I was interested in sociology but I had no idea that I was going to pursue a research career focused on development, disasters, and emergency management. To navigate through the higher education system, I relied on professors, peers, student organizations, friends, and of course, the Internet.

As an undergraduate, I sought opportunities to apply what I was learning in the classroom and started getting involved in research. I always had questions and always believed that someone would help me to pursue my interests. I somehow convinced myself that the worst thing that could happen when I asked for an opportunity to do something was the possibility of getting a no for an answer. Therefore, asking many questions was how I learned more about opportunities for students and how to obtain them. Great places to start asking your questions in a relaxed environment are professional student organizations. As I got more involved with student organizations, I started meeting faculty in my program and started learning about internships, research projects, and other opportunities for students.

My mentor at the time highlighted the linkages between population issues and natural disasters and I became interested in understanding how people prepare for, cope with, respond to, and recover from disasters. More importantly, I became very interested on how disasters are not natural events, but social processes that are continuously 'in the making.' I talked to my professors about my interests and had the opportunity of working in the Center for Collaborative Adaptive Sensing of the Atmosphere (CASA), a National Science Foundation Research Center. My participation in research sealed my commitment to the social sciences and I decided to continue graduate studies in sociology.

I applied to several schools, including the University of Delaware (UD) because of its long-standing expertise in disaster studies. UD was also a partner of the CASA project. I was accepted into the graduate program in sociology and the CASA project provided me with not only the much needed funding to pursue a graduate education, but also with a space to develop as a researcher and scholar. As a graduate student at UD, I worked with leading researchers in the field at the Disaster Research Center—the oldest and one of the world's leading research centers in the area of disaster studies. With the mentorship I received from the faculty at the Disaster Research Center, I started exploring other projects, taking specialty courses in the areas that I was interested in, developing my own work, and advancing my research skills.

In addition to the opportunity to work for great mentors, my graduate program and the University of Delaware Office of Graduate Studies encourage and provide students with funding opportunities to be engaged in their field of study, to network, and to present their research at professional conferences. I became very active in the field and used those opportunities to conduct research, to attend professional meetings, to get involved in professional organizations, to share my work and learn from that of others, to learn about new books in my area of study, and ultimately to join a community of scientists who share a vocation for understanding social life, social change, and human behavior.

As I finish my PhD in sociology, I can say that all the hard work, all the days, nights and weekends spent trying to maintain a balance between coursework, research, extracurricular and personal responsibilities have allowed me to develop as a professional and as a human being. I was recently given the opportunity to be part of the Geographic Information Sciences and Technology (GIST) group at Oak Ridge National Laboratory. As a young researcher, it is certainly an honor and a great challenge to be called upon to contribute to the nation's scientific efforts. As with many other opportunities that I've had, I learned about the GIST group at a professional meeting, and by having the courage to ask questions and talk about my research I was given the opportunity to contribute to their research efforts. In simple words, in addition to your commitment, the key to navigating through the higher education system and starting your career is to always dare to ask your questions.

BOX 13.6 DEPARTMENT OF HOMELAND SECURITY FELLOWS PROGRAM

Jessica Fernandes-Flack   **Cody Bruce**

The DHS-STEM program (Department of Homeland Security—Science, Technology, Engineering, and Mathematics) educates and trains the next generation of homeland security professionals and researchers. Students in the program can come from the hard sciences, engineering, and the social sciences. The DHS-STEM program at Oklahoma State currently supports six undergraduate and graduate students obtaining degrees in sociology, fire and emergency management, political science, and engineering. In addition to their specific degrees, the program exposes the students to a multidiscipline approach to homeland security issues through specific classes, guest lectures, and field trips (including a paid trip to DHS in Washington, D.C.).

As an undergraduate at Oklahoma State University, **Jessica Fernandes-Flack** majored both in sociology and political science and minored in emergency management. Jessi has continued her graduate studies at Oklahoma State as a DHS-STEM award recipient and talks about the DHS program:

The DHS scholars program provided me with well-rounded knowledge about topics that are not typically addressed in undergraduate classes including terrorism and emergency management operations. The one-hour seminar gave students the freedom to explore topics that we were interested in and to discuss current events related to homeland security. The most interesting part of the program was the interdisciplinary approach that was taken to analyze DHS issues like terrorism and natural disasters.

Cody Bruce majored in political science with minors in emergency management and Middle Eastern studies at Oklahoma State University. At the time of this writing he is completing his first year with the DHS program in the fire and emergency management area and talks about his grant:

> The DHS Career Development Grant (CDG) that I received has been an invaluable enabler for my graduate education. This grant has not only provided me with the financial resources necessary to do well in graduate school, but has opened countless other doors. The grant has provided me with an opportunity to work with leaders in the field of emergency management in researching cutting-edge topics that will likely prove critical to the security of the United States at a later time. This grant has allowed me to network with leading scholars and professionals. The networking that I have been able to do has established connections with people who will undoubtedly be valuable resources in the future. Beyond this, I was able to attend the DHS Career Pathways Conference in Washington. This trip allowed me to see what other students were working on and what topics are pertinent to homeland security now and tomorrow.

Training is important for every professional to keep up to date on current trends in the field. For example, after NIMS became a foundation for disaster response, DHS, state emergency management offices and others offered NIMS training. Staying current is critically important to career development in emergency management.

13.5.3.5 Exercises and Drills

By passing courses you earn credentials that let you participate in disasters that occur and also in exercises and drills held locally. Most jurisdictions plan exercises or drills ranging from table-top walk-throughs of emergency operations plans to full-scale exercises during which people enact specific roles and decide what to do in certain scenarios. If you have training, are credentialed, and are connected to a local emergency management agency or organization, you can participate or may be allowed to observe drills and exercises. Take these opportunities to gain insight into how partners work together to address a threat event, the challenges they encounter, and the strategies they use to overcome them.

13.5.3.6 Conferences and Workshops

People build networks by working together, typically across organizations. Another way to build networks is to attend conferences and workshops in the field. A wide range of events occur worldwide so you will have many options from which you can select. Most states have emergency management organizations that host annual events and often co-host special workshops or training at regular intervals. By joining your state's emergency management organization, you will be able to attend and learn from these events.

A number of organizations also host annual conferences. Examples are the Natural Hazards Workshop offered through the University of Colorado at Boulder and the National Hurricane Conference. Other agencies also convene interested participants. The Office of the Federal Coordinator of Meteorology invites meteorologists, atmospheric scientists, and emergency managers to its annual Interdepartmental Hurricane Conference. Regional FEMA offices sponsor workshops on various topics as do FEMA, DHS, and other federal agencies tasked with emergency management roles.

Joining list.servs represents the best way to keep informed about upcoming conferences. The International Association of Emergency Managers (www.iaem.org), the Natural Hazards Center (www.colorado.edu/hazards), and others disseminate information routinely on conferences and workshops.

13.6 Degrees, Education, and Knowledge

Increasingly, emergency management jobs require at minimum a bachelor's degree. Finding the right program is important as considerable variations exist across colleges and universities. In this section, you will learn more about the development of higher education programs and how to select an undergraduate and graduate degree program. Just as described earlier in the mentoring section, choosing the right academic degree program is critically important. The knowledge base of the faculty along with the professional networks they offer and those that you will build among your peers can launch or expand your career in the field.

13.6.1 FEMA Higher Education Program

A major effort to enhance the professionalization of emergency management came through FEMA's Higher Education Program, focusing on the development of associate, bachelor's, and master's degrees in emergency management along with academic certificate programs. With the support of FEMA Director James Lee Witt, Associate Director Kay Goss, and FEMA's Emergency Management Institute Director John McKay, Wayne Blanchard organized the first FEMA Higher Education meeting in June, 1998. A key goal of this program was to establish emergency management programs in all fifty states. At the time, only one bachelor's program in emergency management existed at The University of North Texas along with a related bachelor's program at Thomas Edison University. About forty people, primarily representatives of universities thinking about starting a program, attended the meeting.

Today, over 400 people attend the annual meeting. Over 150 different types of emergency management programs exist, and most states have some type of emergency management program. In addition to the annual meeting leading to the exchange of ideas about what to teach and how to teach in emergency management, the program supports the development of numerous course syllabi and reading lists to assist with course development. Dr. Wayne Blanchard has assisted numerous university representatives with the substantive background to help develop their own college programs. Certainly, the FEMA Higher Education Program has played a key role in the emergence of emergency management degree programs and the continuing professionalization of the field. Describing the impact of the Higher Education Program in 2009, Blanchard (2011) made the following comments:

> In the 14 years since 1994 the EM Hi-Ed Program has helped foster growth in the higher education community to include more than 150 emergency management programs and expanded the reach of emergency management higher education into the practitioner community, approximately 10,000 students are enrolled in these programs and another 20,000 annually take courses within these programs. Our experience with Emergency Management Higher Education over the past decade leads to the following three general observations:
>
> * Approximately one dozen new programs appear annually with a current total exceeding 100.
> * Established programs become successful in attracting students.
> * Students who graduate attract employers and secure careers in the field.

13.6.2 What to look for in a Degree Program

Now that you have learned about the evolution of higher education programs, it is time to choose. In this section we look at undergraduate and graduate programs.

13.6.2.1 Undergraduate Programs

Undergraduate programs lead to bachelor's degrees. You are likely to have two options: an institution with a full major that grants a bachelor's degree in emergency management or a setting that offers a minor or concentration in the subject. A limited number of institutions currently offer degrees in emergency management. Based on your career interests, you may want to consider a fuller range of degree options including homeland security, public health, or international relief. While the majority of the degree programs are located in the U.S., it is becoming increasingly possible to secure related degrees in a number of countries (for a full, international list visit http://www.training.fema.gov/EMIWeb/edu/collegelist/internationaldrh/).

Many students select degree programs out of loyalty to a particular institution, family tradition, or cost, but other factors should be considered.

First, determine how long the program has been in existence. A number of programs have emerged in reaction to recent threats, particularly terrorism. New programs often struggle to acquire resources, particularly faculty knowledgeable in the degree area. Could this be the case with the institutions on your list? A good next step is to look at a program's website. Start by examining the credentials of faculty members listed there. First, do they have degrees appropriate to the field? Because emergency management as a discipline is relatively new, most faculty will hold degrees in the social sciences or related areas. Since it may be hard to determine their expertise, move on to look at their research interests that should reflect content similar to the chapter headings in this textbook. Interests alone, though, are not enough. Do faculty members publish in peer-reviewed scholarly journals on those topics (a list of journals appears in Box 3.2 in Chapter 3)? Listings of professional publications on a curriculum vitae (C.V.) indicate that a faculty member actively conducts research in the field and is recognized by his or her colleagues as an expert.

Next, look at the list of courses that the faculty members teach. Do they teach within their areas of expertise? Review the kinds of service work, consulting, and practical experience listed on their C.V.s. If they do not list such activities, contact them and ask. In many programs, a combination of research with practical application is highly desirable. What depth and breadth of knowledge and experience might the faculty offer in a class you would take?

The curriculum is important to consider too. Traditionally, emergency management degrees organize around the phases of disaster, but there may be deviations relevant to your interests. Hesston College in Kansas, for example, offers a disaster management degree centered on long-term recovery and special populations from a faith-based perspective. Take the time to look at a program's list of required and recommended courses. Can you obtain copies of the course syllabi and look at the readings and requirements? How will that content help you to acquire knowledge and prepare you for work in the area? Do the courses provide a broad range of knowledge that will give you a wide array of knowledge and offer career options? What about key areas standard in a discipline? Do the courses reflect time spent to teach you about the history of the field, the concepts and theories that drive understanding, and the methods needed to accumulate and critique information (Phillips 2005)?

Consider also the faculty of a program you are considering. Do members teach full-time in the program, part-time or just occasionally? Because of the limited number of institutions with full majors in emergency management, it is likely that you will need to consider another discipline with a minor or concentration in emergency management. The field is situated squarely in the knowledge base of the social sciences, so it is a good idea to consider a major in one of those disciplines (for a fuller description, refer back to Chapter 3).

Most students moving into emergency management with a social science focus usually choose sociology or geography. Depending on your interests, you may want to consider other disciplines. If you are interested in helping survivors, for example, psychology and social work represent possible choices. For those interested in public service, a degree in political science may suffice. Students anticipating a future in the private sector would be wise to take business, management, or hospitality degrees. Because the field is ever-broadening due to new and unanticipated threats, additional avenues may be appropriate. Criminal justice, forensics, and computer sciences allow you to map out a prospective career given terrorism and cybercrime threats to national security. Health career majors also give you options. Pandemic planning requires expertise in medical health care delivery systems along with emergency management background. You may even wish to specialize in areas that require knowledge tied to specific populations such as disability studies, Native Americans, or gerontology.

Even journalism majors may want to consider emergency management minors since much of their work stems from crisis occasions—traffic and aviation accidents, hazardous materials events, terrorism, epidemics, and major disasters to give a few examples. Do not rule out the physical sciences either. Preparing for and responding to hazardous materials events requires knowledge of chemicals and biological agents. By coupling a science major with emergency management, you may be able to broaden future career paths. Overall, to enhance your job prospects, you should consider another major or minor in a field noted above that reflects your interest in emergency management.

13.6.2.2 Graduate Programs

Similar concerns should drive your inquiries about a graduate degree, but far more intensely. The critical feature of any graduate program should be highly qualified faculty members who engage in research, know the profession, understand and contribute to informed practice, and have established records as good mentors. Their C.V.s should record steady and continued contributions to their claimed areas of expertise. Students who have graduated under their supervision should have secured employment and contribute to the field as professionals.

Several other issues also require assessment. Different types of graduate programs are available. At the master's level, you may be able to choose between a terminal or professional degree and a more traditional graduate degree. The first choice means completing your education with a master's in the field and moving into practice upon graduation. The program curriculum should reflect the practitioner orientation but should be squarely situated in an understanding of the empirical research, the relevant policies, and established practices. The more traditional master's degree moves a student through acquiring research skills tied to practical concerns. The goal is to enable the student to move into a doctorate-level program. Few doctoral level programs currently exist in the U.S. or in other nations. You may need to consider a discipline-specific degree with a specialization in disasters. To do so, you should have a strong background in the area with a degree naming that discipline (sociology, geography, psychology). Your credentials to enter a doctorate-level program should be exceptionally strong as such a program will tax your energies and capacities while simultaneously raising your level of knowledge to that of an expert researcher in the field.

A concern relevant to many students in the field stems from their personal situations. Many non-traditional or older students attempt to earn graduate degrees while working part- or full-time in the field. Doing so can be challenging as disasters do not respect academic schedules. However, non-traditional students often make up the majority of those matriculated in graduate programs and bring a valued sense of realism to the content and course discussion. Choosing to pursue a graduate degree can lead to a new career path, upward mobility within an existing employment situation, and personal satisfaction. Being a non-traditional student should never be a reason to not pursue such a degree. However, prospective students should look at an institution offering the degree and speak with faculty to ascertain their level of support for and understanding of non-traditional students. You will want to feel mentored and supported, so look for an institution's success in this area with non-traditional students.

Finally, an increasing number of institutions offer online courses or degrees. If you choose such a program, be sure to look at several aspects. First, how much experience do the faculty members have in offering distance courses? What do their students and alumni have to say about the courses and instructors? Have the faculty members published on distance education and are their views consistent with how you learn and with distance education pedagogy (Phillips 2004; Neal 2004)?

Second, how do those programs deliver content? Many programs use software platforms that deliver individual instruction via pre-established course assignments. How much interaction can you really have with such an arrangement? Education works most effectively when people can exchange views, ask questions, and actively question the assigned reading. Choose a platform that allows for you to participate in exchanges with professors and other students. Features that allow you to do so foster a collaborative learning environment that benefits *you*. Look for programs that use chat rooms, online video conferencing, video instruction, email, and social media. Assess the potential of a program to deliver the content and desired interactions by how rapidly and thoughtfully a professor responds to an email inquiry. Ask for an online videoconference to see how effectively the institution uses the technology and how well it communicates with you before you spend thousands of dollars in tuition. After all, you do want a really great job and career, right?

13.7 Where Will the Jobs Be?

At this point, you understand that disasters serve as agents of change. New policies and new practices result from events, particularly large disasters that challenge and strain organizational responses. Disasters drive job opportunities as well. When a nation activates its response and recovery plan, new people must often be brought in to conduct outreach, manage temporary housing, consult on mitigation and recovery planning, and handle other functions. These jobs may be temporary or, if a disaster is large enough, last for years or serve as routes into permanent positions. Organizations and businesses may also have unmet needs when disasters occur. A major oil spill along a coastline may prompt other companies to review their emergency response plans and hire new personnel.

As Quarantelli (1996; 2001) noted, we will see new, different, and bigger disasters. That means that the job potential in this field is—perhaps unfortunately—good. Just a few years ago, pandemic planning was not common. Today, nations must conduct such preparedness efforts domestically and with other nations. Air transportation makes an influenza outbreak halfway around the world only a flight of passengers away. Cyberwarfare represents a new security threat to military, corporate, and governmental targets—and career opportunities for those who seek to protect electronic assets, identities, and national security.

An observation reported in Chapter 1, that most nations are reactive rather than proactive with emergency management, may be very true with jobs as well. After the Loma Prieta earthquake struck the San Francisco and Santa Cruz areas of California in 1989, the American Red Cross—usually a relief operation—used donations to set up longer recovery programs. The terrorist attacks of September 11, 2001 prompted even more diverse kinds of programs, hiring professionals to assist with long-term counseling, physical and occupational therapy for survivors, and new job training. Because the attacks also damaged area infrastructure, specialists in re-establishing cellular service and tourism provided valuable consulting.

In the years since the attacks, cities assumed to represent future targets have brought on specialists in blast performance, hazardous materials, transportation routing, and evacuation planning. Extensive efforts have gone into educating the public about threats and how to handle them. Those efforts paid off in New York City in 2010 when a hot dog vendor noticed a bomb threat and notified police in time.

The Indian Ocean tsunami of 2004 brought dozens of NGOs into relief efforts. Child-oriented organizations stepped in to provide assistance. Nonprofits dedicated to reducing violence against women guided public shelters in providing safe accommodations. Corporations donated funds through NGOs to restore business sectors, educational facilities, and infrastructure. The tsunami affected thirteen nations and involved hundreds of people in new opportunities.

Hurricane Katrina generated attention on highly vulnerable populations such as senior citizens and people with disabilities. Expertise in gerontology and disability studies brought new faces to efforts addressing social vulnerability. The plights of pets and livestock prompted new work to link emergency management with animal care experts for planning protection, rescue, and medical care.

By staying abreast of emerging trends and concerns, you may position yourself well with the best set of knowledge, skills, and abilities (see Box 13.7 and Box 13.8). Today's future emergency manager should take courses across curricula to understand other cultures, geography, political conflicts, biology, and other languages. As the examples suggest in this section, people with degrees in education, psychology, chemistry, and veterinary medicine offer expertise in the field as well. Emergency management is clearly a profession that requires cross-disciplinary knowledge and an ability to work across and with other professions. The general education curriculum required at university levels is not there to fill seats and generate tuition. It is your ticket to the broad body of knowledge needed to meet current needs and anticipate future careers in emergency management.

Where are the projected job openings more specifically? A study published by the FEMA Higher Education Project suggests that significant changes are in store for emergency management and emergency services. Growth ranging from 12% to as much as 43% is predicted in some professions between 2002 and 2012 (see Figure 13.1). Wages look promising too although they will vary considerably based on specific types of work. Public sector and nonprofit jobs typically offer the lower salary range with corporate and private sector positions bringing higher annual incomes.

In late 2010, *U.S. News and World Report* published a list of the top fifty careers based on U.S. Labor Department statistics. Emergency management

BOX 13.7   A GLIMPSE INTO THE CRYSTAL BALL OF EMERGENCY MANAGEMENT

Shane Stovall

Shane Stovall graduated from the University of North Texas with a bachelor's degree in emergency administration and planning and has been designated a Certified Emergency Manager (CEM) by the International Association of Emergency Managers. He worked in the Charlotte County (Florida) Office of Emergency Management, then at General Physics Corporation's Homeland Security and Emergency Management Unit in Tampa, Florida. In October 2006, he became the director of the city of Plano's Department of Emergency Management and Homeland Security. Stovall currently serves as the chairman of the North Central Texas Regional Emergency Managers group. He also serves as co-chairman of the Public–Private Partnership Committee for the International Association of Emergency Managers, and chairs the Public–Private Partnership Committees for the Emergency Management Association of Texas and for the Dallas/Fort Worth Region.

As one looks into the future of emergency management, what is envisioned can be both exciting and very challenging. The opportunities that arise from new technologies and partnerships can assist emergency managers to be more effective and efficient in accomplishing their operational goals and objectives. The challenge for emergency managers will come from having to do more with less. With most organizations facing economic constraints, emergency managers are finding themselves with smaller staffs, fewer resources, and less time to meet the demands of an effective emergency management program. While these challenges will continue, they also present hidden opportunities to figure out new ways of conducting business. In one sense, this can be seen as healthy.

The emergency manager should not allow his or her organization to become stale with projects and program areas considered "safe" or "dealt with." The ever-changing faces of disasters and the different variables that come into play mean that emergency managers should never consider themselves to have completed their missions and have perfect organizations. Perfect organizations and programs do not exist. Let's take a look at some of the areas that may merit focus in the future.

Partnerships—As mentioned previously, there is no such thing as a perfect emergency management program. Every program has operational gaps or areas that can be improved upon (whether admitted or not). However, partnerships can be forged to help to fill some of these voids. Whether a public–private partnership or a partnership with a volunteer agency, partnership relationships can create win–win scenarios that can assist an emergency manager in improving his or her management program. These partnerships can be funded or non-funded. Most emergency managers are familiar with the use of outside services or products to handle a particular aspect of emergency management such as debris management. Such arrangements should be treated as partnerships, just like arrangements that may not be funded. Emergency managers will have to increasingly rely on these partnerships for their efforts to remain effective and efficient. If they fail to do so, they will risk mediocrity that may put their constituents (and jobs) at risk.

Technology—Emergency management relies on technological tools to achieve efficiency during mitigation, preparedness, response, and recovery efforts for their organizations. This trend will continue into the future. The challenge for emergency managers will be determining which tools best fit their organizations. No automated notification system, incident management software, social media tool, satellite phone, or piece software represents a silver bullet that serves all purposes for an emergency manager. The inundation of vendors demonstrating the latest and greatest technologies make it difficult to weed through all the devices to determine the best fit for an organization. Despite all the technology offered, the emergency manager will still have the challenge of figuring out what pieces of the technological puzzle can be used cost effectively to improve emergency and disaster operations.

came in fourth on that list, with a growth rate of 22% or 2,800 jobs between 2008 and 2018. Citing the attacks of September 11, 2001 along with continual natural disasters, the job market looks very promising for college graduates with bachelor's degrees in the field. In 2009, the median salary in the U.S. for emergency managers was $53,000 with a range from $28,370 to $90,340 (Grant 2010).

The field of emergency management also shares a history with the military. In China, for example, the army serves as the first responders moving into earthquake and flood zones. After the Indian Ocean tsunami, military units from many nations responded to assist with search and rescue, body retrieval, establishing relief camps, and feeding survivors. In the U.S., the military role has varied by event. While government carries the primary responsibility for response and recovery efforts, military units may step in

BOX 13.8 FUTURE OF EMERGENCY MANAGEMENT: A CANADIAN PERSPECTIVE

Michel C. Doré

Michel C. Doré, Ph.D. CEM earned a doctorate in sociology from the University of North Texas in 2000. He has extensive experience as an emergency responder. Most recently he was in charge of emergency response issues for the Province of Quebec, Canada. Currently he holds the title of the Assistant Deputy Minister of Health for the Federal Government of Canada, overseeing over 4,200 employees. He also represents the Health Department, serving on the Assistant Deputy Ministers Emergency Management Committee.

Our current professional environment presents an interesting paradox. Despite a growing collective understanding of the objective to improve our societal resiliency in response to a wide array of anticipated risks, the specialists in the field continue to diversify their perspectives and approaches. While this may enhance overall mobilisation and increase opportunities for various professionals to contribute to our collective endeavour, it also compounds our capacity to precisely define the field of emergency management and what distinguishes it from others.

Much has been achieved in Canada regarding the professionalization of the field. Universities and colleges offer undergraduate and graduate degree programs. Researchers and research institutions maintain research agendas to further advance our collective knowledge and develop an evidence-based approach to emergency management. Associations better support and promote the contributions of emergency managers. Public policies demonstrate strategic leadership and guidance to improve our collective societal resiliency such as the renewed Emergency Management Framework for Canada approved by federal, provincial, and territorial ministers responsible for emergency management that guides our Canadian efforts toward a disaster-free country (http://www.publicsafety.gc.ca/prg/em/_fl/emfrmwrk-en.pdf).

If academics continue to build bridges among and between disciplines, the policy makers and practitioners, through the current trend of issue management, continue to fragment the field. For example, beyond the traditional emergency management cluster, we now find among many others the risk and hazard specialists, the business continuity planners, the crisis managers, the contingency planners, and the homeland security specialists. Each group demonstrates a propensity to further subdivide their own field generating specific lexicons, methodologies, processes, training programs, and certifications.

The events of the last decade in Canada and abroad called for emergency managers to revisit their scope of practice and more so their planning assumptions. The global increase of terrorist attacks, extreme weather-related events (floods and hurricanes) associated with global warming, and the catastrophic seismic events (the Indian Ocean tsunami and the Haitian earthquake) force emergency managers to consolidate all existing assets and capabilities to build resiliency.

Canadian demography indicates a growing proportion of urban population on a small land footprint and a parallel declining proportion of rural population, resulting in a dispersed population on a large territory. This dispersion translates into diluted allocation of assets across the territory devoted to improve community safety while the urbanisation contributes to an increased vulnerability.

Developing resiliency requires the mobilisation of the local community and the support of regional and national governments and authorities. However, since many local communities have not yet directly suffered from a disaster or a catastrophe, they do not feel the need to mobilise. Even those who have been through a disaster will mobilise for a short while before residents and decision makers put the event behind, believing that such events never strike in the same place twice. In this context, it remains difficult to sustain not only emergency management programs and activities but more so the dedicated professional staffing required to achieve and sustain resiliency.

In order to improve our organisational effectiveness and professional achievement, it becomes necessary to consolidate efforts. Emergency managers occupy a strategic position to secure coherency and synergy among the various organisational activities and programs. For this to happen we need to manage our own professional paradox.

as needed. The army did so after Hurricane Andrew in 1992, by erecting massive tent cities in southeast Florida to house homeless survivors. The U.S. Coast Guard conducted rescue operations after Hurricane Katrina and coordinated response to the BP oil spill during the summer of 2010. Many nations lack sufficient military resources for response; Haiti serves as one example. The nation lacked military assets and police and firefighters suffered casualties in the massive earthquake that struck the capital city of Port-au-Prince. It is likely, though, that members of the military will play important disaster roles at some points in their careers. The war on terror serves as the most significant current example.

Growth in the private sector, usually categorized as business continuity or disaster recovery will also continue to grow. In some sectors such as the banking industry, federal and state laws require disaster planning and activities related to data backup. Fortune 500 companies all employ people involved with disaster planning. Major companies now realize the importance of hiring people who are knowledgeable about disasters to protect their bottom lines. Major businesses also recognize that disaster planning must integrate their workers' roles and families as part of an overall approach to disasters. Students with additional backgrounds in computers or safety and security will certainly have advantages for securing well-paying jobs in this area. The next generation of emergency managers appears to face a promising future.

13.8 Summary

The future is yours as the next generation of emergency managers. How will you move into it? Our hope for you is that you do so in a manner that ensures well-being for you and those around you, and we hope that you select a career dedicated to public safety. Whether you select a career in emergency management or not, we hope that the information contained here has been useful. From what you have learned, we hope that you go on to share information with your family, co-workers, and neighbors to improve the quality of the environment and help build sustainable and disaster-resilient communities. We hope that you volunteer for disaster situations with the proper training and credentials to do so. We hope that you make appropriate donations so that your good intentions benefit those in need. Most of all, we hope that you remain lifelong learners regarding disasters, remembering Quarantelli's admonition from Chapter 1: we will face new, emerging, and increasingly impactful disasters that we have not yet thought of or prepared for. That work is yours to do. Make it so.

Discussion Questions

1. Describe the perfect emergency manager. What kinds of experience, training, and education should that person have to work in your community?

2. How have education and the availability of degree programs advanced the profession of emergency management?

3. Which three strategies do you see as your next steps to take to move into the profession of emergency management?

4. What types of an additional major or minor area of study could enhance your job opportunities?

References

Blanchard, Wayne. 2011. "FEMA Emergency Management Higher Education Program Description: Background, Mission, Current Status and Future Planning." Emmitsburg, MD: FEMA, Department of Homeland Security.

Drabek, Thomas E. 1987. *The Professional Emergency Manager: Structures and Strategies for Success*. Boulder, CO: Institute of Behavioral Science.

Federal Emergency Management Agency 2010a. *Native American Policy*. Available at http://www.fema.gov/government/tribal/natamerpolcy.shtm, last accessed December 22, 2010.

Federal Emergency Management Agency. 2010b. *National Recovery Framework*. Available at http://www.fema.gov/pdf/recoveryframework/omb_ndrf.pdf, last accessed December 21, 2010.

Fothergill, Alice. 2000. "Knowledge Transfer Between Researchers and Practitioners." *Natural Hazards Review* 1/2: 91–98.

Grant, Alexis. 2010. "The 50 Best Careers of 2011." *U.S. News and World Report*, published online Dec 6, 2010. Available at http://money.usnews.com/money/careers/articles/2010/12/06/the-50-best-careers-of-2011.html?PageNr=1, last accessed December 21, 2010.

Hite, Monique C. 2003. *The Emergency Manager of the Future: Summary of a Workshop—June 13, 2003, Washington, D.C.* A Summary presented to the Disasters Roundtable, The National Academies. Washington, D.C.

Huseman, Kim and Monika Buchanan. 2005. "Emergency Management and Related Labor Market Data and Statistics, 2005." Available at http://www.training.fema.gov/EMIWeb/edu/jobmarket.asp, last accessed December 9, 2010.

International Emergency Management Association. 2007. *Principles of Emergency Management Supplement*. Available at http://www.iaem.com/publications/documents/PrinciplesofEmergencyManagement.pdf, last accessed March 4, 2011.

Mileti, Dennis D. 1999. *Disasters by Design*. Washington, D.C.: Joseph Henry Press.

National Council on Disability. 2009. *Effective Emergency Management: Making Improvements for Communities and People with Disabilities*. Washington, D.C.: National Council on Disability. Available at www.ncd.gov, last accessed December 21, 2010.

Neal, David M., 2004. "Teaching Introduction to Disaster Management: A Comparison of Classroom and Virtual Environments," *International Journal of Mass Emergencies and Disasters* 22/1: 103–116.

Noel, Gloria. 1998. "The Role of Women in Health-Related Aspects of Emergency Management: A Caribbean Perspective." Pp. 213–223 in *The Gendered Terrain of Disaster: Through Women's Eyes,* (Elaine Enarson and Betty Hearn Morrow, eds.). Westport, CT: Praeger.

Phillips, Brenda D. 2005. "Disasters as a Discipline: the status of emergency management education in the U.S." *International Journal of Mass Emergencies and Disasters*, 23/1: 85–110.

Phillips, Brenda D. 2004. "Using Online Tools to Foster Holistic, Participatory Recovery: an educational approach." Pp. 270–277 in *Proceedings of the Recovery Symposium*, New Zealand Ministry of Civil Defence and Emergency Management.

Phillips, Brenda D. 1990. "Gender as a Variable in Emergency Response." Pp. 84–90 in *The Loma Prieta Earthquake: Studies of Short-Term Impacts* (Robert Bolin, ed.). Boulder CO: University of Colorado Institute of Behavioral Science.

Quarantelli, E. L. 1996. "The Future is Not the Past Repeated: Projecting Disasters in the 21st Century from Current Trends." *Journal of Contingencies and Crisis Management* 4/4: 228–240.

Quarantelli, E. L. 2001. "Another Selective Look at Future Social Crises: Some Aspects of Which We Can already See in the Present." *Journal of Contingencies and Crisis Management* 9/4: 233–237.

Vaughn, John R. 2009. "Disaster Case Management: Developing a Comprehensive National Program Focused on Outcomes." Presented to the Ad Hoc Subcommittee on Disaster Recovery, Homeland Security and Governmental Affairs Committee, U.S. Senate, Washington, D.C. Available at http://www.ncd.gov/newsroom/testimony/2009/Senate_HSGAC_Disaster_Recovery_CaseManagement.htm, last accessed December 21, 2010.

Wilson, Jennifer. 1999. "Professionalization and Gender in Local Emergency Management." *International Journal of Mass Emergencies and Disasters* 17/1: 111–22.

Wilson, Jennifer L. 2001. *The State of Emergency Management 2000*. Doctoral Dissertation, Florida International University, Miami, FL.

Wohlwerth, Nancy. 1984. "Mitigation Research Seeking Demonstrations in Real World." *Hazard Monthly* 5/2: 8, 11,13.

Resources

- It is always wise to join professional associations to launch your career. Relevant associations include the International Association of Emergency Managers and the National Emergency Management Association. Visit their websites (www.iaem.com and www.nemaweb. org). Some associations offer student rates for memberships.

- Stay current in the field by browsing journals in the discipline through your library (see a list of journals in Chapter 3). Some maintain websites with open content such as the *International Journal of Mass Emergencies and Disasters* which also offers student subscription rates. www.ijmed.org

- The FEMA Higher Education Program website contains extensive resources for educators and students alike. You can find more content on academic programs at its website (http://www.training.fema.gov/ EMIweb/edu/collegelist/).

- The FEMA Higher Education Program and conference have driven many important issues regarding university degree programs and the profession. The FEMA Higher Education website has a wealth of information on many of the topics discussed in this chapter. Consult it if you have questions about college programs, the profession, and other related topics (http://www.training.fema.gov/emiweb/edu/).

Glossary

Agent-generic approach	Planning, preparing for, and responding to an event based on common characteristics across hazards.
Agent-specific approach	Planning, preparing for, and responding to an event based on a particular hazard such as terrorism.
Aggregate research	Examination of a cumulative body of data representing a larger population.
All-hazards approach	Planning, preparing for, and responding to an event based on a range of hazards as a measure of economy; assumes similarity of functions across hazards (e.g., communication, mass care).
Applied research	Study that produces a practical benefit; findings can be readily applied to a particular problem.
Archival research	Conducting studies using existing data such as EOC logs, organizational records or reports.
Basic research	Research activity that contributes to the body of knowledge and advances what we understand about a given area of inquiry.

Bonding social capital	Connecting people across similarities.
Bridging social capital	Connection of people from different backgrounds.
Building code	Set of regulations specifying how a structure must be constructed to resist local hazards.
Business continuity planning	Process that ensures an industry, corporation, or enterprise can function despite disaster; covers maintenance of computer records, relocation, re-opening, and other factors.
Catastrophe	Event that disrupts regional capacities to respond to those affected and requires resources outside the area for an extended time.
CBRN	Acronym for chemical, biological, radiological, and nuclear; describes materials or hazards.
Certification	Credential acquired after meeting training, experience, education, and other requirements.
Certified emergency manager (CEM)	Credential offered by the International Association of Emergency Managers based on a combination of experience, education, professional contributions, and other criteria as measured by examinations and supporting documentation.
Citizen Corps	Volunteer organizations that train and coordinate people to meet disaster, police, fire, and other community service needs.
Civic organization	Service organization with a specific mission that may extend its resources when disaster occurs.
Civil defense	Early name for emergency management focused on protection against nuclear attack in the U.S.
Code enforcement	Acting to ensure compliance with local building codes in an effort to save lives and reduce property damage.
Cognitive social capital	Attitudes that people bring to the planning table.
Command and control	Management approach by which a designated leader coordinates, issues commands, and attempts to centralize control of a scene or event.

Community-based planning	Involvement of all at-risk sectors of the public in preparing for a disaster impact, recovery, and mitigation.
Community organization	Social service or advocacy organization with expertise and networks that may be relevant when disaster strikes.
Comprehensive emergency management	The four phases of emergency management (preparedness, response, recovery, mitigation) based on an all-hazards approach.
Convergence behavior	Movement of people and resources to the scene of disaster even if not needed.
Corrosive communities	Relationships characterized by a lack of trust that undermines abilities to recover from a disaster.
CPG-101	Federal government guidance materials used for state and local response planning.
Credibility of research findings	A series of procedures such as peer team debriefing and outside review to increase confidence in the results of research.
Cross-sectional research	Research usually conducted via surveys to capture opinions at a point in time of a cross-section of a population.
Cultural relativism	Understanding a different way of life or culture from its perspective rather than yours.
Cultural resources	Built environment, monuments, art and sculpture in museums and around communities, and the ways of life that represent a shared cultural heritage.
Culture	Design for living that includes values, norms, language, symbols, and technology.
Cyberwarfare	Using computers and other technology for attacks and defenses.
Department of Homeland Security (DHS)	Federal agency created after the September 11, 2001 attacks; includes more than twenty federal agencies to coordinate U.S. security issues.
Disaster	Event that disrupts community functioning and requires resources beyond those used for routine emergencies (e.g., ambulances).
Disaster gypsy	Slang term for FEMA disaster reservist.

Disaster subculture	Set of beliefs held by people in a specific location regarding risks they face and procedures they should undertake (e.g., when to leave before a hurricane).
Disaster syndrome	Largely a myth that people respond to disasters by behaving in ways that are dependent on others; assumes people are incapable of responding adequately.
Displacement	Loss of residential or business premises.
Donations	Items given to disaster victims whether needed or not (money is best).
Downtime	Time during which a business cannot operate due to disaster disruption.
DRC	Disaster Research Center, now at the University of Delaware; the first center of its kind in the world, founded at The Ohio State University.
Dual disasters	Hurricane Hugo and the Loma Prieta earthquake both occurred in 1989 and spurred changes in federal disaster management in the U.S.
Elevation	Raising the first floor of a building above anticipated flooding levels.
Emergency	Event that can usually be handled by existing resources, particularly by first responders (fire, police, ambulance) but does not require activation of an EOC or disrupt the community.
Emergency assessment	Initial determination of scope of damage so that response can expand.
Emergency management accreditation program (EMAP)	Set of criteria by which an agency can be measured for its ability to be effective.
Emergency operations center	Fixed, mobile, or virtual site used by emergency managers to coordinate functional activities necessary to restore normal routines to a community.
Emergency shelter	Site such as a car or tent intended for short-term use by individuals after a disaster.
Emergency support function	Area around which agencies coordinate various activities under the National Response Framework.

Emergent norm theory	Sociological perspective describing how people respond and adapt to the dynamic conditions fostered by a disaster environment; evolution of new individual, group, and organizational behavioral guidelines.
Emerging organization	New entity arising from a disaster or hazard, usually in response to perceived unmet needs or concerns.
Empirical research	Careful study to generate data for analytical purposes.
Empowerment	Involving people, especially those at highest risk, to participate in all phases and activities of disasters.
Engineering	Knowledge used to influence the structure and integrity of the built environment.
Enhanced Fujita scale	Scale for measuring the intensities and impacts of tornadoes including wind speed and building damage.
Established organization	Organization in existence before a disaster with a mission dedicated to disaster functions.
Ethnocentrism	Assumption that your way of life and your culture are best or correct.
Evacuation	Leaving an area of risk as a means to save lives.
Exercise	Emergency management partners practice their roles vis-à-vis a potential disaster event.
Expanding organization	Entity that adds people and resources when disaster strikes, e.g., the Red Cross brings in volunteers to operate shelters.
Expedient hazard mitigation	Activities undertaken just prior to or shortly after the onset of a disaster (sandbagging in a flood or boarding windows in a hurricane) to protect lives and contain damage.
Extending organization	Entity that offers resources in a disaster such as a construction company loaning tools, equipment and personnel.
Faith-based organization	Organization tied to a specific religious denomination and offering volunteer assistance when disaster strikes.

Federal Emergency Management Agency (FEMA)	U.S. government agency tasked with preparedness, response, recovery, mitigation, and homeland security concerns at the national level.
Federal Response Plan	Original name for the U.S. national level plan for response to a catastrophic event; later renamed the National Response Framework.
FEMA Higher Education Project	Collection of faculty, practitioners, and experts who share resources and materials to further develop the range of academic degree programs.
Field research	Gathering data at a disaster site for inclusion in a formal study, e.g., interviewing shelter managers.
Flexibility	Demonstrated ability to adapt to changing, dynamic conditions that disasters often present.
Folkways	Routine norms that constitute socially accepted behavior such as sneezing into your elbow rather than into your hand (and then touching the doorknob on the way out of class).
Formal education	Securing a degree through an accredited institution.
Fujita scale	Original method of measuring tornadoes (see also Enhanced Fujita scale).
Functional need	Basic need that shelter providers and others must meet for people who need assistance with communication, transportation, medical care, and other basic needs to be able to maintain independence when disaster occurs.
Hazard	Natural, technological, or terrorist event such as an earthquake, chemical release, or explosion of improvised explosive device that could occur.
Hazard identification	Identifying the history, frequency, and location of specific hazards and how they may impact a given location.
Historic property	A prehistoric or historic district, site, building, structure, or object included in, or eligible for inclusion in, the National Register of Historic Places.
Incident command system (ICS)	Expanding organizational structure designed to manage basic needs for logistics, planning, operations, and other needs as they arise.

Incident management	Steps such as establishing an EOC, inter-agency and inter-governmental coordination, media communications and public information, documentation, and administrative and logistic support.
In-depth interviewing	Questioning and listening to a subject speak about his or her experiences on a given topic, using a set of open-ended interview questions.
Informant	Participant in a study who provides information about the organization in which he or she works—not just their own attitudes and behaviors.
Informational convergence	Social and mass media coverage of disasters.
Integrated emergency management	Activities coordinated across agencies.
Interoperability	Ability to exchange information during a crisis event through communications equipment or across organizations.
Knowledge transfer	Transmitting information from one area to another, particularly from the academic (social science, engineering, meteorology) communities to those in need of information (first responders, emergency managers) through journals, publications, conferences, workshops, consulting, training, volunteer work, and/or formal education.
Land use planning	Determining how land should be developed vis-á-vis local hazards.
LEMA	Local emergency management agency.
LEPC	Local emergency planning committee, originally intended to deal with chemical events.
Linking social capital	People from various organizations participate and connect planners to community resources.
Long-term recovery	Fully returning a community to its perceived sense of normalcy which may take days to years.
Longitudinal research	Studies that track changes over time such as the rates of recovery among different income groups or levels of support for funding a mitigation project.
Looting	Largely a myth of human behavior; people steal possessions of those affected by disasters.

Loss estimation	Series of steps for calculating the potential costs of displacement, downtime, content, and structural losses from a disaster.
Mass hysteria	Mythical behavior that assumes people fall apart irrationally when disaster occurs and that the feeling passes from person to person affecting a collection of individuals.
Material convergence	Arrival of donated items and other materials at the site of a disaster.
Material culture	Tangible items such as statues, paintings, historic buildings, and other elements that give people a sense of their collective identity.
Mentoring	Providing guidance and suggestions for someone new to a profession.
Mercalli scale	Calculation of the intensity and effects of earthquakes.
Mitigation	Activities that reduce or lessen the impact of a future disaster on the lives and property of a given location.
Mitigation planning	Process involving the community with experts to identify hazards and determine priority actions to reduce risks.
Mores	Significantly important standards that must be followed such as protecting women and children from violence and abuse in public shelters.
Mutual aid agreement	Pre-planned and written agreements across agencies and/or jurisdictions determining how assistance will be rendered during an emergency, disaster, or catastrophe.
Natech	Combination of a natural and technological disaster such as an earthquake rupturing petroleum vats.
National Incident Management System (NIMS)	Management structure behind the National Response Framework.
National Opinion Research Center (NORC)	Site of first disaster studies in the U.S.

National Response Framework	Current name of national plan to respond to a catastrophic event in the U.S.
Natural Hazards Center	Research center at the University of Colorado Boulder dedicated to generating studies with practical applications.
Natural sciences	Chemistry, biology and similar sciences that investigate the physical world.
Networking	Connecting with others in the profession to share information, build relationships, and support each other when disaster strikes.
NFPA 1600 Standard	Criteria embracing the four phases of disasters and recommending how disaster and emergency management and business continuity programs should function.
Non-governmental organization (NGO)	Agency or organization (often nonprofit) operating outside government circles that delivers varying kinds of assistance in a disaster.
Non-material culture	Intangible elements of culture including beliefs that influence how we behave in a disaster, such as delaying evacuation until we have gathered all members of our family.
Non-structural mitigation	Actions that build or foster resilience to disasters by reducing their effects such as enforcing building codes and purchasing insurance.
Norm	Behavioral guideline such as paying attention in class.
Observation	Research technique used to gather data by systematically recording what you see, such as how people communicate in an EOC.
Pandemic	Spread of a disease to large numbers of people and across national boundaries, threatening the lives and health of millions.
Panic	Largely a myth; the assumption that people will respond irrationally to disaster.
Participant observation	Technique to gather information for a study, such as working on a volunteer rebuilding site to understand voluntary organizations.

Participatory action research Study technique that empowers subjects to be active such as when local residents work with emergency managers and/or academics to investigate the potential impacts of mitigation projects.

Permanent housing Post-disaster stage that re-establishes a sense of normal routine; no further moves are required.

Personal convergence Arrival of people at a disaster when they should not necessarily be there.

Pet preparedness Ensuring that Fluffy gets on the bus to go to the shelter with Grandma along with their respective ready kits.

Planning A wide and appropriate range of partners develop strategies and procedures covering a range of disaster events and phases.

Preliminary damage assessment Determining disaster effects before submitting a request for external assistance or launching local recovery efforts.

Preparedness Set of activities that includes planning for disaster, conducting training and exercises, educating the public, and establishing settings (e.g., an EOC) for responding to a disaster.

Primary research An investigator collects his or her own data rather than using archival data or sources.

Project Impact FEMA initiative under the Clinton Administration to mitigate disasters through grassroots initiatives.

Protective action Movement designed to save your life by protecting against a specific hazard.

Public sheltering Providing the public with a location that allows protection from the elements before or after a disaster occurs.

Purposive sampling Selecting study participants because of their backgrounds, such as selecting emergency managers who have experience with chemical accidents.

Qualitative research Non-numerical data acquired via interviews, observations, archival data, visual data, or similar sources that allow an in-depth look at a specific topic.

Quantitative research Analysis of numerical data such as survey responses via a computer data analysis program.

Random sampling	Choosing people to survey or interview from a larger population in such a way that each person has the same chance of being selected.
Reconstruction	Rebuilding homes and businesses damaged by a disaster.
Recovery	Making decisions and taking steps to rebuild and return a community to a functioning status.
Rehabilitation	Improvement of a structure after a disaster so it is better than it was before the disaster.
Reliability	Consistency of a measurement in a research project.
Relocation	Buyout to offer fair market value to a home located in an area of repetitive losses so that the household moves to a safer location.
Representativeness of sample	Degree to which the people selected for a survey or interview reflect the larger population from which they were drawn.
Research	Investigation of a specified problem using established and accepted methods for collecting and analyzing the data.
Research ethics	Guidelines for treating participants in a research project.
Resilience	Ability to rebound from the impact of disaster.
Respondent	Person who participates in a research study.
Response	Activities organized to save lives, reduce property damage, and take initial steps to recover from a disaster.
Response-induced demand	Coordinating the mass of individuals and organizations involved in response including unsolicited or spontaneous help.
Restitution	Legal decision to award compensation based on damages in a disaster.
Restoration	Return of a disaster-damaged site to its original historic character.
Retrofit	Installing elements to an existing building to strengthen it to meet a local hazard such as bracing or fastening bookshelves against a wall in an earthquake area.

Richter scale	Scale for measuring earthquake magnitude (see also Mercalli scale).
Risk	Probability of that an event will occur at a given location and time.
Risk analysis	Calculating the potential for an impact and the associated losses based on findings of a hazard identification.
Risk assessment	Determining the probability that an event will occur at a given time and place and affect people who live there.
Risk perception	How people view the probabilities that something will happen to them.
Role abandonment	Myth that first responders, employees, and parents will leave their jobs or responsibilities when disaster strikes.
Safe room	Location that meets certain criteria to protect individuals and/or the public from severe weather.
Saffir-Simpson scale	System for measuring the strengths of hurricanes.
Scholarly journal	Publication containing peer-reviewed, scientific articles that reflect the highest standards of research after careful review for accuracy.
Secondary research	Using existing data such as archived survey results or census data.
Shelter in place	Staying where you are when disaster strikes.
Short term recovery	Efforts to put people, places, and property back to useful status so that long-term recovery can begin.
Snowball sampling	Selecting the next respondent to interview based on the recommendation of the present respondent; a type of referral to another person with expertise or insight.
Social capital	Ideas and energy that people produce by interacting with each other.
Social media	Tools such as Facebook and Twitter that allow people to interact and exchange information through computer technology on shared sites or platforms.
Social sciences	Sciences such as sociology, psychology, and geography that study human behavior.

Social vulnerability	Higher risk for injury, loss of life, and property damage faced by certain groups during a disaster.
Socio-political ecology theory	Perspective that views how people compete for resources in a process that determines winners and losers.
Space weather	Possible impacts on earth from space phenomena such as solar flares or geomagnetic storms.
Spatial tools for research	Geographic Information Systems (GIS) and Geographic Positioning System (GPS) that can be used to collect and/or analyze research data based on space, time, and location.
Stafford Act	Critical legislation that determines what the U.S. government can do in a disaster.
Structural mitigation	Changes that alter or strengthen the built environment to reduce the effects of disasters; examples are levees, blast-resistant glass, and safe rooms.
Structural social capital	Reflection of who we are and what status we hold.
Survey	Systematic accumulation of data by asking closed-end questions over the phone, online, or by mailed questionnaires.
Sustainability	Ability of an organization or community to survive over time.
SUV	Spontaneous, unsolicited volunteer.
Systems theory	Perspective focused on the interaction of the built, physical, and human environments.
Table-top exercise	Parties to disaster planning meet to discuss their roles in a specific disaster scenarios.
Temporary housing	Location that allows for re-establishment of basic household routines; not a permanent post-disaster location.
Temporary shelter	Site established to provide basic needs: food, water, and shelter.
Terrorism	Act designed to disrupt the structure and functioning of a community by inducing fear and distress; examples are violence, economic disruption, cyber attacks, and other means.
Therapeutic communities	Relationships that foster trust and healing and help people to move forward when disaster strikes.

Training	Short-term, focused learning opportunity.
Transferability	Potential for using research findings from one setting in another.
Umbrella organization	Organization that subsumes others under its structure to provide funding, guidance, and/or other resources.
Validity	Truth value of a research measure.
Visual method	Analyzing film or photographs to understand a research problem, for example how people set up, use, and rearrange a shelter.
VMAT	Veterinary Medical Assistance Team.
Warning	Notice to the public that an event is expected and they must act immediately to protect themselves.
Warning fatigue	Reduced willingness of people to take protective action after hearing a disaster warning because they do not perceive the threat as likely based on past warnings that were issued and negative impacts did not occur.
Watch	Conditions are right for an event to occur and you should remain alert to take action as recommended should a warning commence.

Index